Wissenschaftliche Untersuchungen
zum Neuen Testament · 2. Reihe

Herausgegeben von
Jörg Frey, Martin Hengel, Otfried Hofius

141

Odd Magne Bakke

"Concord and Peace"

A Rhetorical Analysis of the First Letter of Clement
with an Emphasis on the Language
of Unity and Sedition

Mohr Siebeck

ODD MAGNE BAKKE, born 1962; 1998 Doctor theologiae, University of Oslo; 1991–94 Research fellow, 1995–98 Lecturer in Church History, The School of Mission and Theology, The Faculty of Theology, Stavanger; since 1998 Associate Professor in Church History, The School of Mission and Theology, The Faculty of Theology, Stavanger.

Die Deutsche Bibliothek – CIP-Einheitsaufnahme

Bakke, Odd Magne:
"Concord and Peace" : a rhetorical analysis of the first letter of Clement
with an emphasis on the language of unity and sedition / Odd Magne Bakke. –
Tübingen: Mohr Siebeck, 2001
   (Wissenschaftliche Untersuchungen zum Neuen Testament: Reihe 2; 143)
   ISBN 3-16-147637-9

© 2001 J. C. B. Mohr (Paul Siebeck) Tübingen.

This book was typeset by Progressus Consultant KB in Karlstad (Sweden) using Minion MM and SymbolGreek typefaces, printed by Gulde-Druck in Tübingen on non-aging paper and bound by Buchbinderei Heinr. Koch in Tübingen.

Printed in Germany.

ISSN 0340-9570

For
KRISTIN

Acknowledgements

This book is a revised version of a dissertation accepted as a partial requirement for the degree of *doctor theologiae* by the University of Oslo in March 1998.

Many friends, colleagues, and mentors have contributed both to the original dissertation and to the product presented here, and I wish to thank them all for their help. In particular, I would like to mention Prof. David Hellholm at the University of Oslo, Norway, who supervised my dissertation and who continued to give generously of his time and advice during the revision of the manuscript. His wisdom, constructive criticism, personal support, and active interest have been invaluable during the years in which this book was being researched and written. I owe him a great debt of gratitude! I would also like to thank the other members of the New Testament Research Group at the Faculty of Theology, University of Oslo, for valuable criticism and feedback: Prof. Halvor Moxnes, Prof. Turid Karlsen Seim, and my fellow doctoral students Inger Marie Lindboe, Reidar Aasgaard, Jorunn Økland, and Tor Vegge. I have also received valuable advice and support from colleagues and friends at the School of Mission and Theology, Stavanger, Norway. I especially want to thank Prof. Torstein Jørgensen for his engagement in the project and for encouragement in time of difficulties, and Prof. Tor Hauken (now at the University of Bergen, Norway) for checking the Greek at an earlier stage; thanks are also due to the staff at the library of the School of Mission and Theology, most efficiently headed by the Rev. Arne B. Samulesen, for providing me with all the necessary literature.

Most of the work with this book was made possible through a generous research fellowship granted by the School of Mission and Theology for the period 1991-1994. Let me also express my sincere gratitude to Prof. Bruce C. Johanson of Walla Walla College (USA) for improving the English text, to Mr. Christer Hellholm of Progressus Consultant KB, Karlstad (Sweden) for technical assistance, for doing the typesetting of the final manuscript, including the composition of the indexes, as well as to the Research Council of Norway for a grant covering the printing of this book.

I am also in great debt to the editor of WUNT, Prof. Martin Hengel, for accepting the volume into this series.

Last, but definitely not least, I want to thank my wife Kristin for her loving support and encouragement despite the fact that she has had so often to compete with a rival named Clement. I dedicate this book to her.

Note on Texts, Citations and Abbreviations

The text of *1 Clement* used in this work is the one edited by J. A. Fischer. As a standard English translation we have chosen K. Lake's edition.

This investigation follows the following standards for abbreviations, citations, texts and translations:

Abbreviations of biblical, apocryphal, and early patristic writings follow those listed in the *Journal of Biblical Literature*'s "Instructions for Contributors" (Membership Directory and Handbook [1993], 386-388). Abbreviations of other patristic writings follow those listed in G. W. H. Lampe, *A Patristic Greek Lexicon*. Abbreviations of Philo and Josephus follow S. M. Schwertner, *Abkürzungsverzeichnis, Theologische Realenzyklopädie*.

References to classical texts follow the abbreviations listed in N. G. L. Hammond and H. H. Scullard, *Oxford Classical Dictionary*. Where texts and authors are not found in that list, the lists in H. G. Liddell and R. Scott, *A Greek-English Lexicon*, and in P. G. W. Glare, *Oxford Latin Dictionary* are used.

Classical texts are cited according to the text and translation of the Loeb Classical Library editions where available. The editions we have used regarding quotations from texts not included in Loeb Classical Library are indicated in the bibliography.

Abbreviations of periodicals and series follow those listed in S. M. Schwertner, *Abkürzungsverzeichnis, Theologische Realenzyklopädie*.

In this work there are notices such as "See chap(s). nn" and "See p(p). nn" that occur in footnotes. These notices always refer to chapter(s) and/or page(s) in the present volume.

Table of Contents

Acknowledgements... VII

Note on Texts, Citations and Abbreviations IX

Table of Contents... XI

1. Introduction 1
   1.1. First Clement – Some Introductory Remarks........................ 1
       1.1.1. Authorship.. 1
       1.1.2. Date.. 8
       1.1.3. Preliminary Remarks about the Background and
              Purpose of the Letter 11
   1.2. The Purpose of the Present Study................................ 13
   1.3. Methodological Considerations 16
       1.3.1. A Brief Overview of Different Approaches to
              Rhetorical Analyses 16
       1.3.2. The Rhetorical Approach Applied in the Present Investigation... 21
   1.4. The Relation between Rhetoric and Epistolography 26

2. First Clement as Deliberative Rhetoric 33
   2.1. The Hortatory and Dissuasive Aspect 34
       2.1.1. In Deliberative Rhetoric in General......................... 34
       2.1.2. In 1 Clement 35
   2.2. The Time Reference 36
       2.2.1. In Deliberative Rhetoric in General......................... 36
       2.2.2. In 1 Clement 37
   2.3. The Content of the Appeals 38
       2.3.1. The Appeals in the Theory of Deliberative Rhetoric............ 38
       2.3.2. The Appeals in Actual Deliberative Discourses and Letters...... 42
       2.3.3. Striving for the Common Good........................... 43

2.3.4. The Appeals in 1 Clement 45

    2.3.4.1.   Summary Appeals in 1 Clement..................... 53

2.4. The Use and Function of Examples 54

2.4.1. Examples in Deliberative Rhetoric in General 54

2.4.2. Examples in 1 Clement 57

2.5. Appropriate Subjects in Deliberative Rhetoric...................... 61

3. The Language of Unity and Sedition in 1 Clement 63

3.1. Introductory Remarks 63

3.2. Tools from the Theory of Semantic Fields......................... 65

3.3. Preliminary Remarks on ὁμόνοια, εἰρήνη and στάσις
    as Political Terms.. 72

    3.3.1. ὁμόνοια 72

    3.3.2. εἰρήνη 75

    3.3.3. στάσις... 79

3.4. εἰρήνη καὶ ὁμόνοια... 81

3.5. Political Terms and *topoi* Related to Concord in 1 Clement 1:1-3:4
    (*exordium* and *narratio*).. 84

    3.5.1. Political Terms in 1 Clement 3:2 84

        3.5.1.1. ἔρις καὶ στάσις 85

            3.5.1.1.1. στάσις 86

            3.5.1.1.2. ἔρις................................... 91

        3.5.1.2. ζῆλος καὶ φθόνος 93

        3.5.1.3. διωγμός καὶ ἀκαταστασία 97

        3.5.1.4. πόλεμος καὶ αἰχμαλωσία 98

        3.5.1.5. Summary of the Political Language 1 Clement 3:2 99

    3.5.2. Other Political Terms and *topoi* in 1 Clement 1-3 100

        3.5.2.1. συμφορά and περίπτωσις........................ 100

        3.5.2.2. μιαρός and ἀνόσιος Sedition, Alien to the
              Elect of God.................................... 105

        3.5.2.3. ἀπόνοια....................................... 107

        3.5.2.4. βέβαιος πίστις................................. 108

        3.5.2.5. σωφροσύνη 113

        3.5.2.6. ἀσφαλής...................................... 115

        3.5.2.7. ἐν τοῖς νομίμοις τοῦ θεοῦ ἐπορεύεσθε........... 117

3.5.2.8. ὑποτάσσω 119

3.5.2.9. Household Duties............................... 122

3.5.2.10. ἐταπεινοφρονεῖτε μηδὲν ἀλαζονευόμενοι......... 126

3.5.2.11. εἰρήνη βαθεῖα 136

3.5.2.12. ἀδελφότης..................................... 140

3.5.2.13. σχίσμα.. 143

3.5.2.14. τῇ παναρέτῳ καὶ σεβασμίῳ πολιτείᾳ
κεκοσμημένοι 145

3.5.2.15. δόξα 148

3.5.2.16. δικαιοσύνη καὶ εἰρήνη......................... 150

3.5.2.17. Summary of Other Political Terms and *topoi*
in 1 Clement 1-3................................. 154

3.6. Political Terms and *topoi* Related to Concord in 1 Clement 4:1-61:3
(*probatio*) 154

3.6.1. Political Terms and *topoi* Related to Concord
in 1 Clement 4:1-39:9 (θέσις /*quaestio infinita*) 155

3.6.1.1. Political Terms and *topoi* in 1 Clement 4:1-18:17 155

3.6.1.2. The Order of the Universe........................ 160

3.6.1.3. Political Terms and *topoi* in 1 Clement 23:1-36:6 167

3.6.1.4. The Army....................................... 174

3.6.1.5. σύγκρασίς τίς ἐστιν ἐν πᾶσιν 176

3.6.1.6. σῶμα, ἀλλὰ πάντα συνπνεῖ 179

3.6.2. Political Terms and *topoi* Related to Concord
in 1 Clement 40:1-61:2 (ὑπόθεσις /*quaestio finita*)............ 184

3.6.2.1. εὐτάκτως, τάξις, τάγμα 184

3.6.2.2. Political Terms and *topoi* in 1 Clement 46:1-48:6 188

3.6.2.3. ἀγάπη.. 191

3.6.2.4. Political Terms and *topoi* in 1 Clement 56:1-61:3 196

3.7. Political Terms and *topoi* Related to Concord
in 1 Clement 62:1-65:2 (*peroratio* and Epistolary Postscript) 198

3.8. Summary 201

4. Compositional Analysis of 1 Clement 205

4.1. Remarks Regarding the Approach 207
    4.1.1. *Dispositio* in Ancient Rhetoric 207
    4.1.2. Tools from the Status Theory of Ancient Rhetoric and
           Text-Linguistics. 210
    4.1.3. Limitations Regarding the Present Study .215
4.2. Compositional Analysis of 1 Clement 216
    4.2.1. Sub-Texts on Grade One 216
    4.2.2. Sub-Texts on Grade Two 218
    4.2.3. Sub-Texts on Grade Three. 232
    4.2.4. Sub-Texts on the Fourth and Following Grades. 235
           4.2.4.1.   Sub-Texts on the Fourth and Following Grades within
                      the *quaestio infinita* Section (4:1-39:9) 235
           4.2.4.2.   Sub-Texts on the Fourth and Following Grades within
                      the *quaestio finita* Section, 40:1-63:1 259
    4.2.5. Summary of the Compositional Analysis .277

5. The Social-Historical Situation 281

5.1. Introductory Remarks 281
5.2. A Brief Outline of the History of Research on
     the Nature of the Strife 283
5.3. 1 Clement 3:3 and the Social-Historical Situation 289
    5.3.1. A mere Rhetorical Cliché and Allusion to Isa 3:5? 290
    5.3.2. 1 Clement 3:3 in Its Graeco-Roman Context 292
           5.3.2.1.   Inequality as Cause for Sedition in the Ancient World. 299
5.4. Striving for Honour and Status. 302
    5.4.1. Patronage and the Role of Honour in Clement's
           Cultural Milieu 302
           5.4.1.1.   Patronage. 302
           5.4.1.2.   Honour 305
           5.4.1.3.   Honour as Cause of Strife and Sedition 310
    5.4.2. Patronage and Honour in 1 Clement. 311
5.5. Conclusion with regard to the Social-Historical Situation 316

6. General Summary and Conclusion 319

   6.1. The Main Characteristics of Deliberative Rhetoric in 1 Clement 320

   6.2. Terms and *topoi* Associated with the Topic of Concord 321

   6.3. The Compositional Analysis 322

   6.4. The Social-Historical Situation................................324

   6.5. The Result of the Present Investigation and the Question of
       Clement's Social Background 325

Appendix: The Function of References to Christ in Clement's
Argumentation for Concord 327

1. Introductory Remarks 327
2. Christology and Argumentation.....................................328

   2.1. *Exordium*, 1:1-2:8 328

   2.2. *Narratio*, 3:1-4 331

   2.3. *Probatio*, 4:1- 61:3 331

      2.3.1. *Quaestio infinita*, 4:1-39:9 331

      2.3.2. *Quaestio finita*, 40:1-61:3..............................337

   2.4. *Peroratio*, 62:1-64:1 340

   2.5. Summary 340

Bibliography 343

Index of Passages....................................369

Index of Authors 381

Index of Subjects 387

1. Introduction

1.1. First Clement – Some Introductory Remarks

The primary object for the present study is the so-called *First Letter of Clement*. The main aim is to identify its genre, function and composition. We shall attempt to demonstrate that a thorough analysis will lead to new insights with regard to some of the main questions in the research on *1 Clement*, i.e. the question of genre, the use and meaning of several terms and *topoi*, the composition of the letter, and the underlying cause of the conflict in the Corinthian Church from Clement's perspective. Before stating the purpose of the study in greater detail and discussing methodology, it is appropriate to make some general remarks about authorship, date, and the main purpose of the letter.

1.1.1. Authorship

The document known as *1 Clement* is one of the oldest extant Christian writings outside of the New Testament canon and is therefore one of our most significant sources with regard to the life and theology of Early Christianity. At a very early stage in the ancient tradition, this letter from the Roman Church to the Church in Corinth was attributed to a person named "Clement".[1] Although not much can be said with certainty about the identity of this person, ancient sources offer some information that can shed light on the issue. The name of Clement occurs in the so-called bishop lists, the first of which dates from the late second century. Irenaeus, as recorded in Eusebius' Church History, maintains that Clement was the third in the succession of Roman bishops after Peter, following Linus and Anacletus (or Cletus).[2] The same order is to be found in different lists from the fourth Century.[3] On the basis of the fact that we know that Irenaeus visited Rome and on the basis of the almost unanimous information given in the bishop lists it is a fair supposition that these men were significant leaders of the Roman Church at that time.

---

[1] Eusebius refers twice to the "epistle of Clement" which he wrote "in the name of the Church of the Romans" (*h.e.* 3.16.1; 3.38.1), and twice he designates the letter "the epistle of Clement to the Corinthians" without mentioning the entire Roman Church (*h.e.* 4.22.1; 4.23.11). The same author also refers to a letter of Dionysius of Corinth, Bishop of Corinth ca. 170 C.E. who speaks of the letter "formerly sent to us through Clement" (*h.e.* 4.23.11).

[2] Iren. *haer.* 3.3.3.

[3] For text references and a thorough discussion of the lists, see J. B. LIGHTFOOT, *The Apostolic Fathers I: Clement I* (1989, first printed 1889) 63f.; 201-345.

Nevertheless, this fact does not mean that we accept the concept of the office reflected in the lists, namely the implication that monarchical episcopacy was established at this point of time and that Clement was a bishop according to this understanding of the office. On the contrary, there is no indication in *1 Clement* that the monarchical episcopacy was established in Rome at the time of the composition of the letter.[4] Irenaeus' motive for presenting the so-called bishop lists seems to be obvious. At a time of increasing heresy, gnosticism in particular, the succession of bishops in Rome functioned as a guarantee of the unbroken transmission of the original faith proclaimed by Peter and Paul. The succession of bishops should demonstrate that heretical doctrine was a recent development. However, when Irenaeus and others give the impression that a monarchical episcopacy was established in the first century C.E. this is an anachronism. They project their own understanding of office back to the time of Clement.[5] This does not imply that the men who appear on the lists were not bishops and prominent leaders in the Church. They were indeed bishops. However, at that point of time one did not yet distinguish between bishops and presbyters. In other words, it seems more correct to call them presbyter-bishops. Since Irenaeus and others specifically mentioned these presbyter-bishops, it is likely that they were first among equals. In spite of the anachronistic character of the bishop lists, we have no reason to doubt that the actual persons were significant leaders of the Roman Church at the time stated in the lists. The literary tradition associated with Clement[6] in addition to *1 Clement* also indicates that Clement was a well-known and significant figure during his lifetime.[7] Therefore, in accord with the early tradition, there is no reason not to believe that this significant figure in the Roman Church was the author of the letter.

Many scholars are of the opinion that the man named Clement in *Hermas Vis.* 2.4.3 is identical with the author of *1 Clement*. According to this passage, which includes the

---

[4] The terms *presbyteros* and *episkopos* are used interchangeably in the epistle. J. B. Lightfoot, *The Apostolic Fathers I: Clement I* (1989, first printed 1889) rightly remarks that "the term 'bishop' is still a synonym for 'presbyter'" (69). D. A. Hagner designates Clement as a "'presbyter-bishop' …", not essentially different from other presbyter-bishops in the early Church", *The Use of the Old and New Testaments in Clement of Rome* (1973) 3. Cf. also H. E. Lona, *Der erste Clemensbrief* (1998) 446.

[5] So J. Lawson, *A Theological and Historical Introduction to the Apostolic Fathers* (1961) 27.

[6] The first of a large number of scriptures which came to be attributed to Clement at an early stage was *2 Clement* which is not really a letter, but a homily. For a recent commentary, see A. Lindemann, *Die Clemensbriefe* (1992) 184-261. Also connected with Clement are the legendary *Clementine Recognitions* and *Clementine Homilies* from the second or third century. Among other things, they deal with the history of Clement's family. A summary of this history is given by J. B. Lightfoot, *The Apostolic Fathers I: Clement I* (1989, first printed 1889) 14-16. Considering the legendary character of this story Lightfoot questions "whether its author ever intended it to be accepted as a narrative of facts" (*ibid.* 16). Further works written in the name of Clement are the two *Epistles of Virginity*, probably from the beginning of the third century, the *Apostolic Constitution* (fourth century) and five Latin letters that constituted a main part of the ninth century *False Decretals*. For further consideration of the literature associated with Clement, cf. J. B. Lightfoot, *Apostolic Fathers I: Clement I* (1989, first printed 1889) 100-103; 406-420; B. Altaner – A. Stuiber, *Patrologie* (1966) 47.

[7] Cf. D. A. Hagner, *The Use of the Old and New Testaments in Clement of Rome* (1973) 2f.; H. E. Lona, *Der erste Clemensbrief* (1998) 72.

earliest reference to a man named Clement belonging to the Roman Church, it is the duty of this man to send letters abroad. He apparently functions as a foreign correspondent or a church secretary.[8] Therefore it is likely, according to many scholars, that this person was the author of *1 Clement* as well.[9] The question of the composition and date of *Hermas* is complicated and extensively discussed in the research. It is reasonable to argue, however, that *Vis.* 2.4.3 belongs to a part of *Hermas* which was composed during the first decades of the 2nd century, that is to say between 100-120 C.E.[10] When one operates with the traditional date of *1 Clement*, i.e. 95-96 C.E., the chronology makes it somewhat difficult to agree with many scholars who argue that the Clement in *Hermas* and the author of *1 Clement* are one and the same person.[11] In this work we shall argue that one must operate within a broader frame of time when considering the date of the composition of *1 Clement*, namely 95-110 C.E.[12] If we are right, this implies that we can argue more plausibly with respect to chronology that the Clement mentioned in *Hermas* is the author of *1 Clement*.

We should note, however, that the letter itself, in contrast to many of the epistles in the NT, neither mentions an individual author nor refers to any individual authorities within the Church. The reverse is the case. The letter states that the author is "the Church of God which sojourns in Rome".[13] This collective aspect of the authorship is also reflected throughout the letter in the many first person plural forms. We should also note that this collective aspect of the authorship is reflected in early Christian tradition. In a letter which Dionysius, bishop of Corinth, sent to Rome around 170 E.C., he refers to it as the letter "sent to us through Clement".[14] Irenaeus similarly describes the sender of the letter as the whole Church when he says that "the Church in Rome despatched a most powerful letter to the Corinthians, exhorting them to peace".[15] Also,

---

[8] P. Lampe, *Die stadtrömischen Christen in den ersten beiden Jahrhunderten* (1989) depicts this person as a "Aussenminister" of the Church (336).

[9] So for example H. Lietzmann, "Zur altchristlichen Verfassungsgeschichte" (1914) *ZWTh* 55 (1914) 138; M. Dibelius, *Der Hirt des Hermas* (1923) 422; A. von Harnack, *Einführung in die alte Kirchengeschichte* (1929) 50; H. von Campenhausen, *Kirchliches Amt und geistliche Vollmacht in den ersten drei Jahrhunderten* (1963) 103; R. M. Grant, *The Apostolic Fathers. Vol. I. An Introduction* (1964) 39; P. Vielhauer, *Geschichte der urchristlichen Literatur* (1975) 539; K. Wengst, *Pax Romana and the Peace of Jesus Christ* (1987) 106; J. S. Jeffers, *Conflict at Rome* (1991) 32; G. Schneider, *Clemens von Rom* (1994) 16f. and partly N. Brox, *Der Hirt des Hermas* (1991) 107f.; C. Osiek, *Shepherd of Hermas* (1999) 18ff., 59.

[10] N. Brox, *Der Hirt des Hermas* (1991) 24. See further the discussion of "Komposition und Verfasserschafts-Problem" 25-33.

[11] Cf. P. Lampe, *Die stadtrömischen Christen in den ersten beiden Jahrhunderten* (1989) 172 n. 157: "Ihn [the author of 1 Clem.] mit dem Clemens von Herm Vis II 4,3 gleichzusetzen … ist verlockend, kollidiert aber ein wenig mit der wahrscheinlichsten Datierung des Hermasbuches (1. Hälfte bzw. gegen Mitte des 2. Jh.)", and similar H. E. Lona, *Der erste Clemensbrief* (1998) 66.

[12] See the present study pp. 8-11.

[13] *Praescript.*

[14] Eus. *h.e.* 4.23.11.

[15] Iren. *haer.* 3.3.3.

Clement of Alexandria refers to it in one passage as "the Epistle of the Romans to the Corinthians".[16]

When we speak of a collective aspect, we do not mean that the whole community participated in the composition of the letter. It is more likely that one individual composed the letter on behalf of the entire congregation. The unity in style and content also indicates that the letter is a product of a single author.[17] In other words, the collective aspect is not a contradiction of the opinion that Clement had the main responsibility for the content and the writing of the letter.

Concerning the identity, and the social and religious background of this significant figure in the Roman Church, it is difficult to say anything with certainty except that his acquaintance with and use of the Septuagint reflects a Hellenistic-Jewish tradition.[18] Eusebius maintains that the author of *1 Clement* was identical with the co-worker of Paul named Clement, as mentioned by Paul in Phil 4:3.[19] With respect to the chronology, it is possible that Clement as a young man, let us say at the age of twenty-five, had been a fellow-worker of Paul when the latter wrote to the Philippians in 61-62 C.E. Thirty years later the same person could have become a leader in the Roman Church. However, the remarks in *1 Clem.* 63:3 about the messengers, that they have "lived

---

[16]Clem. *str.* 5. 12. Cf. also Eus. *h.e.* 3.16.1; 3.38.1.

[17]A. STUIBER, "Clemens Romanus I", *RAC* 3 (1957) 192; K. WENGST, *Pax Romana and the Peace of Jesus Christ* (1987) 105f.

[18]For the use of the Septuagint in *1 Clement*, see G. BRUNNER, *Die theologische Mitte des ersten Klemensbriefs* (1972) 75-89; D. A. HAGNER, *The Use of the Old and New Testaments in Clement of Rome* (1973) 21-132; H. E. LONA, *Der erste Clemensbrief* (1998) 42-48. Lona concludes by stating that "Die Sprache von I Clem im allgemeinen, aber auch die massive Verwendung der griechischen Bibel deuten auf einen präzisen traditionellen Ort: das hellenistische Judentum" (58). Lona is of the opinion that both the vocabulary and certain aspects of the content of the letter show that Clement shares the same tradition as Philo. He emphasizes that elements in the letter that commonly have been regarded as Stoic are to be found in Hellenistic Judaism, particularly in works by Philo, and draws the conclusion that Clement's use of the alleged "Stoic" element is not a product of Clement's acquaintance with Stoicism, but must be explained by the fact that he draws heavily on Alexandrine Judaism. Lona states that the importance of Philo is not primarily connected with his authorship, "sondern um seine Rolle als Vertreter des alexandrinischen Judentums und somit auch als Zeuge des für die alte Christenheit – natürlich auch für 1 Clem – entscheidenden Versuches der Vermittlung zwischen dem überlieferten Glauben und der hellenistischen Kultur" (58-61, quotation 58). In my opinion there are some problems with Lona's argumentation. For if Philo functions as a "Zeuge", and thereby as an example for Clement in the attempt to communicate the Christian faith within a Hellenistic context, this does not exclude the possibility that Clement himself could have integrated Hellenistic elements independent of Hellenistic Judaism. Furthermore, in my opinion Lona draws too hasty a conclusion when he says that, since no Stoic elements are to be found in *1 Clement* which are not to be found in Alexandrine Jewish literature, this tradition is the source of the "Stoicism" in the letter. For what reason can one take it for granted that Clement so exclusively should have made use of a Hellenistic-Jewish tradition when one finds many striking parallels in Hellenistic sources regarding terminology, topics and motifs? In my opinion as I have stated above, though Clement clearly reflects a Hellenistic-Jewish tradition, it is significant to focus also upon Hellenistic sources in order to understand certain terms, *topoi*, the genre, the composition, and the general strategy of argumentation.

[19]Eus. *h.e.* 3.15.

among us without blame from youth to old age" seems to indicate that Clement had known them personally for more than thirty years and thus must have been a member of the Roman Church before the composition of Paul's letter to the Philippians. Another feature that indicates that the suggestion of Eusebius is quite improbable is the fact that Clement was a common name in the first and second centuries.[20] Likewise, the assertion of Tertullian that Clement was consecrated by Peter himself is not probable. On the other hand, the information given by Irenaeus that Clement "had seen the blessed apostles [Peter and Paul], and had been conversant with them"[21] is more likely to be historically correct. So, it is possible that Clement met Paul and Peter during their visits to Rome.[22]

The considerations above show that the evidence of early Christian literature offers little help regarding the background of Clement. Apart from the information given by Irenaeus that Clement met Paul and Peter in Rome, the literature offers no adequate information at all. Nothing is recorded about his religious and social background, except that he was a Christian at the time Paul and Peter visited Rome. Some scholars, however, have paid attention to other sources and other kinds of evidence that may connect Clement to the Roman aristocracy. One suggestion that would link Clement to the aristocratic elite is that the author of the letter may be identical with the consul Titius Flavius Clement, the cousin of Domitian. In 96 C.E., this consul was put to death, while his wife Domitilla was banished by the emperor. The sources mention different reasons for Domitian's treatment of his relatives. According to Dio Cassius the charge against them was "atheism (ἄθεος), a charge on which many others who drifted into Jewish ways were condemned".[23] Suetonius does not mention the charge, but gives what he considers to be the underlying motive for the action against Flavius Clement, i.e. a groundless suspicion of treason against Domitian. He does not mention Domitilla.[24] According to Eusebius, who does not record the death of Flavius Clement, Flavia Domitilla "was banished with many others to the island of Pontia as testimony to Christ".[25] This is not the place to consider in detail what light these passages throw on

---

[20]J. B. LIGHTFOOT, *Apostolic Fathers I: Clement I* (1989, first printed 1889) 22f.

[21]Iren. *haer.* 3.3.3.

[22]Cf. J. B. LIGHTFOOT, *Apostolic Fathers I: Clement I* (1989, first printed 1889) 73 n. 3, who maintains that the expression τοὺς ἀγαθοὺς ἀποστόλους in *1 Clem* 5:3 indicates that Clement met Paul and Peter, and D. A. HAGNER, *The Use of the Old and New Testaments in Clement of Rome* (1973) 3.

[23]Dio Cass. 67.14.1f.

[24]Suet. *Dom.* 15.1.

[25]Eus. *h.e.* 3.18.4. Eusebius points out that his source for this information is a pagan writer, a fact which corresponds with Eus. *Chron. Domitianus* 16, (Ed. R. HELM, *Die Chronik des Hieronymus* (1956) 192), where he says that the Roman author Bruttius (2nd or 3rd century) has recorded that a niece of the consul Flavius Clement, Flavia Domitilla, was banished to the island Pontia because of her Christian faith. For the discussion whether the actual sources record two different women with the same name or not, see P. LAMPE, *Die stadtrömischen Christen in den ersten beiden Jahrhunderten* (1989) 168. In our view, his suggestion that Bruttius is confusing Domitilla's connection with Flavius Clement seems plausible. It seems probable that Domitilla was not a niece of Flavius Clement, but his wife.

the religious status of these members of the Roman aristocracy.[26] So we will restrict ourselves to expressing our opinion that it is not likely that Flavius Clement was a Christian. If a person with the social rank of Flavius Clement were a Christian, we should expect that the sources would have mentioned this explicitly. He could, how-ever, have been a Jewish convert or a Jewish sympathiser,[27] but that is also uncertain.[28] Concerning Flavia Domitilla it is more likely that she had converted to Christianity or at least was a Christian sympathiser.[29] Since we are of the opinion that it is probable that Flavius Clement was not a Christian, it follows that the consul Clement and the leader in the Roman Church would be different persons.

This fact, however, does not exclude the possibility that the author of *1 Clement* was connected to the imperial house. J. B. Lightfoot maintained that Clement was "a man of Jewish descent, a freedman or the son of a freedman belonging to the household of Fla-vius Clement the emperor's cousin".[30] He based his opinion on the following: the sup-position that Flavius Clement and Domitilla were Christians; the similarity of names; the fact that at the time a large number of Jews were found among the slaves of the great houses; and Clement's acquaintance with the Greek Bible. Several scholars, while not rejecting this hypothesis, have rightly pointed out its lack of hard evidence.[31] J. S. Jeffers, however, has recently reinforced the view of a connection between *I Clement* and the imperial family of Flavius Clement and Flavia Domitilla. His arguments are largely based on archaeological evidence. Jeffers pays attention to inscriptions from the first century which demonstrate that Flavia Domitilla donated burial land to her dependants. Although none of the inscriptions reflect Christian use of the burial land, Jeffers argues that it is likely that Domitilla had also donated land to the Christian members of her household. The original users of the known catacombs of Domitilla were pagans,[32] but archaeological evidence shows that one part of them, the "Flavian" *hypogeum* was taken over by Christians (probably descendants of Domitilla) from the

---

[26]For a detailed discussion on this subject, see, e.g., J. B. LIGHTFOOT, *Apostolic Fathers I: Clement I* (1989, first printed 1889) 25-35; E. T. MERRILL "The Alleged Persecution by Domitian", *Essays in Early Christian History* (1924) 148-173; R. L. P. MILBURN, "The Persecution of Domitian", *CQ* 139 (1945) 154-164; P. LAMPE, *Die stadtrömischen Christen in den ersten beiden Jahrhunderten* (1989) 166-172; J. S. JEFFERS, *Conflict at Rome* (1991) 25-28.

[27]So J. S. JEFFERS, *Conflict at Rome* (1991) 27.

[28]R. L. P. MILBURN, "The Persecution of Domitian", *CQR* 139 (1945) 160.

[29]Regarding the religious status of Flavius Clement and his wife Domitilla we have basically adopted the conclusions reached in the sober investigation by P. Lampe.

[30]J. B. LIGHTFOOT, *Apostolic Fathers I: Clement I* (1989, first printed 1889) 61.

[31]A. VON HARNACK, *Einführung in die Alte Kirchengeschichte* (1929) 51; A. STUIBER, "Clemens Romanus I" *RAC* 3 (1957) 189; D. A. HAGNER, *The Use of the Old and the New Testaments in Clement of Rome* (1973) 4; J. S. JEFFERS, *Conflict at Rome* (1991) 33.

[32]J. S. JEFFERS underlines that the pagan character of the actual inscription should not lead one to draw any conclusion regarding the religious belief of the donator. They show only that Domitilla donated burial land to her dependents, *Conflict at Rome* (1991) 54.

early third century.[33] Furthermore, Jeffers attempts to demonstrate a connection between the warehouse beneath the San Clemente complex and the house church of Clement on first-century Flavian property. He argues that the warehouse was probably the site of this house church at one time.

> Later traditions, Jerome's comment being the most important, connect this site and probably the first-century warehouse with the author of *1 Clement*, a leader of the Christian congregations in Rome. No other explanation satisfactorily explains the strength with which early Christians connected this site with Clement. Although no Christian remains have been discovered on the first-century level of San Clemente, it is possible that the warehouse was used for Christian worship.[34]

Definitive evidence regarding both the religious status of Domitilla and Clement's affiliation with the Flavian household is still lacking.[35] On the other hand, Jeffers has substantiated the hypothesis that the author of *1 Clement* was an imperial freedman of the house of Flavius Clement and Domitilla. Although none of the available sources definitively confirm Jeffers' hypothesis, we find much of Jeffers' argumentation reasonable and plausible.

If this hypothesis is correct, we may also be able to say something about the social background of Clement. Usually an imperial slave boy went to school and learned the basics necessary for public service: Latin, Greek, and applied mathematics. After he had spent about ten years in the civil service, he would receive his freedom at around the age of thirty and could hold posts such as record officer, correspondent, accountant, or paymaster. In his forties he could move on to more responsible posts such as chief accountant, chief record officer, or chief corespondent. The freedmen's education and experience of the imperial bureaucracy gave them qualifications and abilities to exercise leadership in Rome's private associations.[36] In other words, if Clement was an imperial freedman – which is likely – he would have had an education that was better than average for a Greek-speaking resident in Rome. Also, it is highly probable that he would be familiar with rhetorical theory of the handbooks from his education and with rhetorical practice and letter writing from his work in the imperial bureaucracy. Besides the assumption that he had reached this level of education, as an imperial freedman, the letter itself reflects literary skills not common for a Greek-speaking resident in Rome.[37] Stephan Lösch even makes the assertion, based on a comparison of *1 Clement* with the *Letter of Claudius to the Alexandrians*, that Clement must have been

---

[33]J. S. Jeffers is conscious of the problem regarding the great intervening period: "The first Christians using this land would have to be at least the grandchildren of Domitilla's Christian dependents. But surely a story as dramatic as that of Domitilla, Clemens, and the Emperor Domitian would have survived several generations of family storytelling. The memory of a grant of burial land also would have been preserved from parent to child as part of the story" (*ibid.* 62).

[34]*Ibid.* 88.

[35]Cf. the review of D. J. BINGHAM, *Journal of Early Christian Studies* 1 (1993) 87 f.

[36]J. S. JEFFERS, *Conflict at Rome* (1991) 30.

one of the imperial slaves who composed official letters.[38] A. Stuiber maintains that Clement "besitzt rhetorische Bildung u. verwendet massvoll die Mittel der zeitgenössischen Kunstprosa",[39] W. Jaeger asserts that Clement's method of argumentation, i.e. proof by accumulated examples, is taken from current rhetorical practice and from rhetorical handbooks,[40] and J. A. Kleist holds that "Clement was doubtless an educated Roman and conversant with the requirements of good prose style".[41]

1.1.2. Date

We stated above that we have no reason to distrust the ancient tradition that ascribes the letter to Clement, a significant leader in the Church of Rome. According to the above-mentioned bishop lists Clement was a bishop during the last decade of the first century.[42] However, bearing in mind the anachronistic character of the lists, they tell us only that Clement was a significant bishop-presbyter at the time. Together with the men recorded in the so-called bishop lists and others, Clement may have been an influential leader of the congregation for a longer period than he functioned as the bishop of the Roman Church, according to the lists. This means that he may have written the letter either before or after the last decade of the first century.[43]

Clement's apology for not having written before has been a focal point, if not *the* focal point in the discussion relating to the date of the letter. The reason for the delay is that "sudden and repeated misfortunes (συμφορά) and calamities (περίπτωσις)" had befallen the Church in Rome (1:1). Since the fundamental work of J. B. Lightfoot, who interpreted συμφορά and περίπτωσις as referring to a persecution of the Roman Church under Domitian's reign (81-96 C.E.),[44] the majority of scholars have followed

---

[37]J. S. Jeffers remarks "that those who could write, such as Clement, must have been very unusual, even in the late first century" (*ibid.* 32). And K. WENGST, *Pax Romana and the Peace of Jesus Christ* (1987) is of the opinion that the author's "knowledge and his capacity for expressing himself in writing" indicate that he was a member of the higher social classes" (109).

[38]S. LÖSCH, "Der Brief des Clemens Romanus", *Studi dedicati alla memoria Paola Ubaldi* (1937) 181-186.

[39]A. STUIBER, "Clemens Romanus I", *RAC* 3 (1957) 195.

[40]W. JAEGER, *Early Christianity and Greek Paideia* (1965) 13; 113f. n. 3. Cf. also W. C. VAN UNNIK, "Studies over de zogenaamde eerste brief van Clemens", *Mededelingen* (1970) 31f. who asserts that Clement must have been familiar with the same rhetorical tradition of which Dio Chrysostom was the most famous exponent. This opinion is adopted by B. E. BOWE, *A Church in Crisis* (1988) 65.

[41]J. A. KLEIST, *The Epistles of St. Clement of Rome* (1946) 6.

[42]Eusebius, for instance, writes that Clement was bishop of Rome from the twelfth year of Domitian to the third year of Trajan, that is a period of nine years, 92-101 C.E. (*h.e.* 3.15; 3.34). On the chronology of the various bishop lists see J. B. LIGHTFOOT, *Apostolic Fathers I: Clement I* (1989, first printed 1889) 339-343.

[43]It seems that scholars who rightly point out that the monarchical episcopate was not yet established at the time when *1 Clement* was written, are not aware of this problem. D. A. HAGNER, for example, who although he calls Clement a "presbyter-bishop", maintains that external evidence, especially the bishop lists, indicates that the date of *1 Clement* is "almost certainly to be placed at 95 or 96 A.D.", *The Use of the Old and New Testaments in Clement of Rome* (1973) 4.

[44]J. B. LIGHTFOOT, *Apostolic Fathers I: Clement I* (1989, first pr. 1889) 58. See further 346-358.

his understanding. In combination with internal evidence such an interpretation led to what we may call the traditional view, i.e. that the letter must be dated to 93-96 C.E.[45]

For various reasons, however, there have been voices among scholars that have questioned the main assumption behind the traditional dating, maintaining that συμφορά and περίπτωσις refer instead to internal strife within the Roman Church.[46]

---

[45]E.g. A. von Harnack, "Der erste Klemensbrief", *Sitzungsberichte* (1909) 38-63 who even maintains that the date of the letter "zu dem Sichersten in der altchristlichen Literaturgeschichte gehört", 62; E. Molland, "Clemensbriefe", *RGG* 1 (1957) 1837; A. Stuiber, "Clemens Romanus I", *RAC* 3 (1957) 191; L. W. Barnard, "St. Clement of Rome and the Persecution of Domitian", *Studies in the Apostolic Fathers* (1966) 10-12; D. A. Hagner, *The Use of the Old and New Testaments in Clement of Rome* (1973) 4f; P. Vielhauer, *Geschichte der urchristlichen Literatur* (1975) 540; H. Köster, *Einführung in das Neue Testament* (1980) 727; A. Lindemann, *Die Clemensbriefe* (1992) 12. J. Fuellenbach rightly underlines the strong position of the traditional view in the research: "If there is any agreement among recent studies concerning the first epistle of Clement Romanus, it seems to be the date when the letter was written. Almost all scholars date the letter between 93 and 97 A.D", *Ecclesiastical Office and the Primacy of Rome* (1980) 1. However, other suggestions have also been put forward. For an earlier date, around 70 C. E. G. Edmundsen, *The Church in Rome in the First Century* (1913) 189ff.; A. E. W. Hooijberg, "A Different View of Clemens Romanus", *HeyJ* 16 (1975) 266-288; J. A. Robinson, *Redating the New Testament* (1976) 327-335; and for a later date, E. T. Merrill, "On 'Clement of Rome'", *Essays in Early Christian History* (1924) 217-241 argues for a date in the neighbourhood of 140 C. E. and C. Eggenberger, *Die Quellen der politischen Ethik des 1. Klemensbriefes* (1951) 182, for a date between 118-125 C.E. However, none of these alternative suggestions has been received with considerable favour among scholars. For a survey of the research until ca. 1970 regarding the question of date, see J. Fuellenbach, *Ecclesiastical Office and the Primacy of Rome* (1980) 1-3, and for a recent survey see H. E. Lona, *Der erste Clemensbrief* (1998) 75-78. On the basis of internal and external evidence Lona dates the letter to the second half of 90s.

[46]As far as we know, E. T. Merrill, "The Alleged Persecution by Domitian", *Essays in Early Christian History* (1924), was the first scholar who questioned the traditional view and asserted that Clement's language in the apology for delay indicates that nothing very terrible had shaken the Roman Church: "It sounds curiously like an apologetic introduction to a modern letter" (160). R. L. P. Milburn, "The Persecution of Domitian", *CQR* 139 (1945) 154-164, followed Merill and questioned the assumption that a persecution took place under Domitian at all. He concluded by maintaining that the Roman Church was prevented from writing earlier because it was suffering from the same problem that was now facing the Church at Corinth. L. W. Barnard, "St. Clement of Rome and the Persecution of Domitian", *Studies in the Apostolic Fathers* (1966) 5-18, opposes both Milburn's suggestion regarding domestic troubles as the reason for the delay and the suggestion that a persecution under Domitian had not taken place at all. Barnard argues, however, that a full scale persecution did not take place, but that the strategy of Domitian was to hit "persons of eminence whom he might suspect of undermining his authority" (8) and "he singled out individual Christians who were prominent members of the Church of Rome" (15). So also P. Keresztes, *Imperial Rome and the Christians* vol. I (1989) 96f. The suggestion that the language of delay in *1 Clement* refers to domestic affairs in the Roman Church has had a few advocates more recently. G. Brunner, *Die theologische Mitte des ersten Klemensbriefes* (1972), who builds upon K. Beyschlag, *Clemens Romanus und der Frükatholizismus* (1966), argues that since συμφορά "gehört 'traditionsgeschichlich' (im Sinne Beyschlags) in die Begriffsreihe Aufruhr, Verfolgung, Krieg, Gefangenschaft", it is likely that συμφορά in *1 Clement* refers to circumstances within the Roman Church, 102; further, in particular, L. L. Welborn, "On the Date of first Clement", *BR* 29 (1984) 35-54, and K. Erlemann, "Die Datierung des ersten Klemensbriefes", *NTS* 44 (1998) 591-607.

In our opinion, the latter view has not yet been sufficiently demonstrated.[47] We have, however, been able to identify a comparatively large number of passages that deal with the evil of internal strife where συμφορά is used to designate either the strife itself or the cause of the strife or the consequences of it.[48] We hope that our contribution will sufficiently demonstrate that the language of delay in *1 Clem.* 1:1 does not refer to persecution of the Church, but to internal strife and sedition.[49] Hence, the main assumption for the traditional date has to be rejected. This means that we must look for other evidence concerning the date of the letter.

Apart from the bishop lists the external evidence is rather scant. The most significant evidence is that presented to demonstrate a literary dependence between *1 Clement* and Polycarp's second letter to the Philippians.[50] Polycarp has on several occasions made use of *1 Clement*. It is a fair supposition that Pol. *Phil.* 13, the first letter of Polycarp, was written shortly after Ignatius had left Philippi on his way to Rome, while Pol. *Phil.* 1-12, 14, the second letter of Polycarp, was written about 140 C.E., and was possibly directed against Marcion.[51] In addition, when Ignatius recalls that "you taught others" in Ign. *Rom.* 3:1, this is perhaps an allusion to *1 Clement* and thus a possible item of external evidence.[52] In other words, the letter's *terminus ad quem* is 120-140 or perhaps 115-140 C.E.

In addition, as has been pointed out by scholars, there is internal evidence that sheds light upon the issue.[53] The references to the deaths of Peter and Paul and "a great

---

[47]This is also the case with regard to L. L. WELBORN, "On the Date of First Clement", *BR* 29 (1984) 35-54. We agree with his hypothesis that συμφορά and περίπτωσις refer to internal strife, and that these terms ought to be understood in the light of ancient texts that deal with the issue of unity and sedition. However, the number of passages Welborn has put forward are rather few, and some of them seem not to be adequate at all regarding his hypothesis.

[48]See the texts and discussion in chap. 3.5.2.1, pp. 100-105.

[49]Our opinion on this point is not a contradiction of the fact that a persecution directed against the leaders of the Roman Church probably took place under Domitian. However, we assert that the language of delay in *1 Clement* does not allude to this persecution, but to domestic affairs in the Roman Church.

[50]J. B. LIGHTFOOT, *The Apostolic Fathers I: Clement I* (1989, first printed 1889) 149-152; A. VON HARNACK, "Der erste Klemensbrief", *Sitzungsberichte* (1909) 40, followed by P. MIKAT, *Die Bedeutung der Begriffe Stasis und Aponoia für das Värstandnis des 1. Clemensbriefes* (1969) 10; P. VIELHAUER, *Geschichte der urchristlichen Literatur* (1975) 564; D. A. HAGNER, *The Use of the Old and New Testaments in Clement of Rome* (1973) 4; J. S. JEFFERS, *Conflict at Rome* (1991) 92 and most recently; J. B. BAUER, *Die Polykarpbriefe* (1995) 28-30.

[51]See for example R. M. GRANT, *The Apostolic Fathers. Vol. 1. An Introduction* (1964) 64f; M. SYNNES, "Polykarps Brev", *De Apostoliske fedre* (1984) 83f.; J. B. BAUER, *Die Polykarpbriefe* (1995) 18.

[52]So A. STUIBER, "Clemens Romanus I", *RAC* 3 (1957) 191; P. MIKAT, *Die Bedeutung der Begriffe Stasis und Aponoia für das Verständnis des 1. Clemensbriefes* (1969) 11; D. A. HAGNER, *The Use of the Old and New Testaments in Clement of Rome* (1973) 4.

[53]For internal evidence in general, see, e.g., J. B. LIGHTFOOT, *The Apostolic Fathers I: Clement I* (1989, first printed 1889) 348-358; A. VON HARNACK, "Der erste Klemensbrief", *Sitzungsberichte* (1909) 62f; D. A. HAGNER, *The Use of the Old and New Testaments in Clement of Rome* (1973) 4-6; J. S. JEFFERS, *Conflict at Rome* (1991) 91f.; A. LINDEMANN, *Die Clemensbriefe* (1992) 12; K. ERLEMANN, "Die Datierung des ersten Klemensbriefes", *NTS* 44 (1998) 605f.

multitude of the chosen" who were victims of jealousy and envy, probably allude to the Neronian persecution (64 C.E., *1 Clem.* 5-6). Clement says that these Christians lived "in the days nearest to us" and in "our own generation" (5:1). Such language gives the impression on the one hand that these events did not occur in the immediate past, but on the other hand that they did not occur so many years ago that the generation of Clement was no longer alive. Furthermore, the author refers to the Church in Corinth as ancient (ἀρχαία, 47:6). This expression might be a hyperbole rather than a description of the chronological age of the Church, but it seems more appropriate if used in the first decade of the second century, or later when the Corinthian Church was more than fifty years old, rather than at a much earlier date. Another indication of date is Clement's mention of the messengers who delivered the letter as men who have lived blamelessly "among us" (i.e. the Church) "from youth to old age" (63:3). Bearing in mind the fact that Christianity probably reached Rome at the end of the 40s or the early 50s, such a statement indicates that the letter could not have been written earlier than in the 90s. And lastly, in chaps. 42-44 Clement refers to apostolic succession. Here, clearly the time has come when the bishops appointed by the apostles are dead and the congregations themselves have appointed their successors (44:3-5). Thus, one has good reason to conclude that all this internal evidence suggests that the letter had been written during the first decade of the second century.[54] It is difficult, however, to operate with a safe and accurate date of the letter, if the main assumption for the traditional dating, i.e. that συμφορά and περίπτωσις refer to persecution of the Roman Church, is not valid.

1.1.3. Preliminary Remarks about the Background and Purpose of the Letter

The following summary of the occurrences in the Corinthian Church that prompted the Roman Church to send a letter does not pretend to describe the actual, historical situation, but will deal with Rome's perception of what happened. According to Clement the Christians in Corinth are in serious trouble because they are facing an "abominable and unholy sedition (στάσις), alien and foreign to the elect of God" (1:1), a sedition that caused the name of Church (1:1) as well as the name of God (47:7), to be blasphemed and many to stumble (46:9). Although στάσις is the principal term Clement uses to describe the problems, he also uses other words with negative connotations, some almost synonymous with στάσις. In contrast to the previous noble life that was marked by communal solidarity and care for each other (*1 Clem.* 1-2), the present situation is characterised by "jealousy and envy, strife and sedition, persecution and disorder, war and captivity" (ζῆλος καὶ φθόνος, καὶ ἔρις, καὶ στάσις, διωγμὸς καὶ ἀκαταστασία, πόλεμος καὶ αἰχμαλωσία, 3:2). He tries to convince the Corinthian Church by using well-known examples from history that the present state of affairs is connected with great evils, and concludes a list of examples by stating that "Jealousy

---

[54]Our argumentation is basically taken from the literature listed in note 45. However our discussion is not restricted by the assumption that the language of delay in 1:1 refers to a persecution. The discussion in the literature centres to a great extent around whether the internal evidence suggests that the assumed persecution alluded to is the persecution under Nero or Domitian.

(ζῆλος) and strife (ἔρις) have overthrown great cities, and rooted up mighty nations" (6:4). Likewise, the members of the Church, analogous to the inhabitants of a city, are in great danger (κίνδυνος, 14:2; 41:4),[55] for the ultimate consequence of ἔρις and ζῆλος is θάνατος (9:1).

Although there is no doubt that Clement views the present condition among the Christians in Corinth as very serious and dangerous, he is at first sight rather obscure about which concrete issues were at the root of the dispute. Not much information is given about the different factions, or about the reasons and motivations for the sedition in the Church.[56] However, the little information that is given is of interest. Clement states explicitly that some presbyters who have fulfilled their duty blamelessly have been removed from their ministry (44:6). The emphatic use of the noun "some" (ἔνιοι) indicates that not all of the presbyters were removed. Furthermore, although it seems that Clement holds the whole community as co-responsible for the present situation,[57] a smaller group is said to consist of the instigators (ἀρχηγός) of an abominable jealousy (ζῆλος, 14:1), and sedition (στάσις, 51:1). This group is said to have "laid the foundation of the sedition" (οἱ τὴν καταβολὴν τῆς στάσεως ποιήσαντες, 57:1). Hence, these members of the Church had the main responsibility for the trouble facing the community. When Clement first mentions the sedition, he describes these persons as "a few rash and self-willed persons" (ὀλίγα πρόσωπα προπετῆ καὶ αὐθάδη, 1:1), and in 47:6 he defines ὀλίγος as "one or two persons" (ἐν ἢ δύο πρόσωπα). Regarding the number of instigators, Clement may be right, but it is clear that other members of the congregation had associated themselves with them. This seems to be reflected in 44:6 where he blames the community as a whole for having removed some of the presbyters, and perhaps in 3:3 where Clement describes the "rebels" as the worthless (ἄτιμοι), those of no reputation (ἄδοξοι), the foolish (ἄφρονες) and the young (νέοι). If these characterizations designate different groups of members of the community, it indicates that more than "one or two persons" were involved.

If Clement is vague regarding the description of the different groups involved in the strife and the actual content of the conflict, he is quite clear when it comes to the overall purpose of the letter, i.e. he urges the Christians in Corinth to cease from strife and sedition and instead re-establish peace and harmony. In addition to the many exhortations throughout the letter, this is made very clear in the *peroratio*[58] where the author

---

[55]Cf. 59:1: "no little danger (κινδύνῳ οὐ μικρῷ)", and 47:7 without emphasising the level of κίνδυνος.

[56]This fact has been a constant challenge to scholars and is reflected in the many suggestions regarding the historical situation in the Corinthian Church as to which groups of people were involved and what the motive for the strife was. For a summary of different answers given by scholars, see K. BEYSCHLAG, *Clemens Romanus und der Frühkatholizismus* (1966) 1-47; J. FUELLENBACH, *Ecclesiastical Office and the Primacy of Rome* (1980) 4-7.

[57]Cf. the emphatic use of "each" (ἕκαστος) in 3:4. and J. FUELLENBACH, *Ecclesiastical Office and the Primacy of Rome* (1980) 4: "Apparently, the majority of the community had taken a silently tolerant attitude toward the removals".

[58]For the definition and function of the *peroratio* in *1 Clement*, see pp. 226-232.

describes the entire letter as an "entreaty for peace and concord" (κατὰ τὴν ἔντευξιν, ἢ ἐποιησάμεθα περὶ εἰρήνης καὶ ὁμονοίας, 63:2). What concrete actions Clement's appeal for peace and concord imply for the Corinthian Church are, however, not so evident, except for the reinstatement of the removed presbyters (54:2).

1.2. The Purpose of the Present Study

As indicated above, *1 Clement* is one of the most important sources for our understanding of the life and theology of Early Christianity. In fact, Clement has even been called the first "Doctor" of the Church.[59] Therefore, it is not surprising that this letter, about one and a half times as long as Paul's letter to the Romans, is one of the writings from the post-apostolic period that has been the object of greatest interest from scholars.[60] The focus of much research has been on the development of the ecclesiastical office: What kind of church organisation and church structure is reflected in the letter? Does the letter contain any claim for primacy? However, a lot of other issues have also been dealt with in detail, among which we mention the question of author, date, occasion, structure, literary form, sources and religious-historical background.

We find little need to give a general review of the history of the research, since good reviews have been provided by other scholars. In particular we shall point to the previously mentioned dissertation by J. Fuellenbach[61] who provides a review of every major study on *1 Clement* from A. von Harnack[62] to ca. 1975.[63] We shall, however, give a brief history of research on the nature of the strife as an introduction to the chapter dealing with the social-historical situation. For the other parts of the investigation our position on previous research that is relevant for the present study will be remarked on throughout the work, particularly in the notes.

The bibliography in John Fuellenbach's book demonstrates the immense number of published works that deal with different topics concerning *1 Clement*. However, only two scholars have attempted to interpret the letter in the light of the ancient rhetorical tradition: W. C. van Unnik and B. E. Bowe.[64] In his important article published in 1970, van Unnik demonstrated that the significant word pair εἰρήνη καὶ ὁμόνοια in *1 Clement* was a common formula in Greek speeches and writing that aimed at putting

---

[59] Cf. the heading of chap. 2 in J. B. LIGHTFOOT, *The Apostolic Fathers I: Clement I* (1989, first printed 1889) 14-102: "Clement the doctor".

[60]The Swedish scholar O. ANDRÉN's remark is still appropriate when he says that *1 Clement* "vidrörts av snart sagt alla forskare på den äldsta kyrkans område", *Rättfärdighet och frid* (1960) 10.

[61]*Ecclesiastical Office and the Primacy of Rome* (1980).

[62]*Einführung in die alte Kirchengeschichte* (1929).

[63]Besides the work of J. FUELLENBACH, extensive reviews of the research are given in K. BEYSCHLAG, *Clemens Romanus und der Frükatholizmus* (1966) 1-47; E. W. FISHER, *Soteriology in First Clement* (1974) 7-48; and partly J. W. WILSON, *The First Epistle of Clement* (1976) 6-25.

[64]W. C. VAN UNNIK, "Studies over de zogenaamde eerste brief van Clemens", *Mededelingen* (1970) 149-204; B. E. BOWE, *A Church in Crisis* (1988) 58-73.

an end to στάσις.[65] Furthermore, he argued that basic characteristics of deliberative rhetoric are reflected in *1 Clement*. Van Unnik draws the conclusion that it is fruitful to examine the letter, in particular the function of certain of its key terms, within the frame of deliberative rhetoric urging concord in civil affairs. In a part of her book, B. E. Bowe discusses the rhetorical genre of *1 Clement*. She mainly summarizes the findings of van Unnik, but by means of using much of the same comparative material as he does she succeeds in presenting a few more parallels between such material and *1 Clement*.[66] She thereby strengthens and confirms van Unnik's conclusion. These works are valuable contributions that enhance our understanding of the rhetoric of the letter. But their approach is limited, since they focus almost solely on the question of rhetorical genre and leave out other important aspects of the letter's rhetoric, e.g. the question of its rhetorical composition. In addition to casting light on the argumentative structure, this question is important to consider with a view to defining the rhetorical genre. Furthermore, in order to define the rhetorical genre as securely as possible one has to demonstrate that the main topic of the letter is appropriate to the actual genre. So, although the works of W. C. van Unnik and B. E. Bowe have shown that it is fruitful to consider Clement's rhetoric, and although they have given a preliminary argumentation in support of the thesis that *1 Clement* ought to be regarded as a piece of deliberative rhetoric urging concord, no one yet has provided an in-depth study of the letter from the point of view of its rhetoric. Therefore, in the present study, besides using a traditional exegetical (philological, literary and historical) approach, we will emphasize *rhetorical*

---

[65]After showing that the word pair εἰρήνη καὶ ὁμόνοια is fundamental in *1 Clement* and not an ad hoc formula (162, 176), W. C. van Unnik interprets εἰρήνη καὶ ὁμόνοια in the light of ὁμόνοια in Greek literature, and demonstrates convincingly that the word pair was a common formula in Greek speeches and writing that aimed to abolish στάσις in civil affairs. He refers to the following Greek texts: Dion Chrys *Or.* 39.2; 40.26 (The reference in the article to 40.36 is a misprint. The actual quotation is from 40.26), 41.6; Plut. *De garr.* 17; *De Alex. fort.* 1.9; *De superst.* 4; Lucian *Hermot.* 22; Dio Cass. 44.24.3; 44.25:3-4; Diod. Sic. 16.7.2; Dion. Hal. *Ant. Rom.* 7.60:2; Epict. *Diss.* 4. 5.35, and to the following Latin texts: Tac. *Hist.* 3.80.4; Suet *Otho* 8.1; Cic. *Fat.* 2; Sall *H.* 1.77.13. Further, van Unnik notes and emphasizes the significance of the fact that Clement refers to the letter as a συμβουλή (*1 Clem.* 58:2). He argues that the term is not an expression of general advice, but is a *terminus technicus* for advice given to an ἐκκλησία and which gave rise to deliberative rhetoric. To support his view, he has pointed out numerous passages from discourses that deal with ὁμόνοια where the orator designates his advice as a συμβουλή. He highlights the following texts: Aristid. *Or.* 24.7; Philostr *VS* 1.9.4; Isoc. *Or.3;* Dio. Chrys. *Or.* 38.1; Iambl. *VP* 9. 45. In addition, cf. the references in notes 92-99, pp. 183-185. Van Unnik has thus demonstrated that some of the stock terms in Clement belonged to the conventional political language that discussed concord and strife within different political bodies and has suggested that *1 Clement* ought to be read as deliberative rhetoric urging concord. The view that Clement's phrase εἰρήνη καὶ ὁμόνοια is standard political terminology is adopted by several scholars; see the literature references, n. 343.

[66]She holds that Clement's use of ἀλαζονεία, φιλονεικία, αὐθάδεια shows that he "adopts standard Hellenistic rhetoric against seditious people" and that Clement uses the terms κίνδυνος and σωτηρία in a similar way as Dio Chrysostom and Aristides in their discussions on concord. Furthermore, she argues that *1 Clement* has a parallel structure with Dio Chrys. *Or.* 38 and with Aristid. *Or.* 23 (*Or.* 42 according to the text edition used by her) B. E. Bowe, *A Church in Crisis* (1988) 63, 69, 72.

analysis. Thus, the study intends to demonstrate that by paying sufficient attention to the rhetoric of the letter we will enhance our understanding of the overall *genre, function* and *composition* of the letter.

To express it succinctly, the main thesis of this investigation includes the following points: (1) that Clement, in his response to what he considers to be a dangerous situation for the Corinthian Church, applies the primary features of deliberative rhetoric; (2) that throughout the letter he applies terms and *topoi* commonly used in discourses, letters and other types of literature that deal with the political problem of factionalism; and (3) that the sub-texts on different levels in one way or another have also been integrated into Clement's appeal for concord. Hence, *1 Clement* ought to be classified as deliberative rhetoric, or more precisely, *deliberative rhetoric urging concord.*[67]

To define the rhetorical genre of *1 Clement* could in itself be the only aim of a study like this. This would have been a useful and legitimate research project. The present investigation, however, has a broader purpose. The different steps that are necessary for demonstrating the rhetorical genre of the letter must also deal with several important issues in *1 Clement* research. We intend to show that the actual steps in the approach we have chosen will enable us to offer new suggestions regarding several significant issues under discussion:

1. On the basis of an investigation of the language of unity and sedition in *1 Clement* and on the basis of a compositional analysis of the entire letter we intend to demonstrate that topics related to concord form the basic theme of the letter.

2. Contrary to the commonly held view that it is not possible to find a dominant theme in the first main part of the letter at all,[68] and against the view that the dominant theme is order,[69] we will argue that a dominant, unifying theme is to be found in the first main part as well as in what follows it, and this theme is concord.

3. We aim to offer a new and fuller explanation of the macrostructure of the letter.

---

[67] This means that the present work intends to integrate other aspects and give a more extensive discussion of the question of genre than the studies given by W. C. van Unnik and B. E. Bowe. Although we shall argue in the present investigation that *1 Clement* ought to be regarded as deliberative rhetoric urging concord, this does not imply that we are of the opinion that the letter could not also reflect elements of other genres than the rhetorical genres. It appears that *1 Clement* contains features of the Hellenistic Jewish homily, see, e.g., H. THYEN, *Der Stil der jüdisch-hellenistischen Homilie* (1955), especially 16f. and 111; O. B. KNOCH, *Eigenart und Bedeutung der Eschatologie im theologischen Aufriss des ersten Clemensbriefes* (1964) 44; L. WILLS, "The Form of the Sermon in Hellenistic Judaism and Early Christianity", *HThR* 77 (1984) 283-285; O. SKARSAUNE, "The Development of Scriptural Interpretation in the Second and Third Centuries", *Hebrew Bible / Old Testament* (1996) 381-384. For an overview of different suggestions regarding the genre of *1 Clement*, see J. FUELLENBACH, *Ecclesiastical Office and the Primacy of Rome* (1980) 9-11. In the present investigation, however, we shall confine ourselves to focusing on the rhetorical genre of *1 Clement*.

[68] See the present investigation, p. 205.

[69] See the present investigation, p. 205 and n. 1235 on page 278.

4. Moreover, the present study intends to offer a new suggestion on what Clement considered to be the underlying reason for the removal of the presbyters. We will attempt to show that it was not, as commonly held, a conflict between spirit and office or any other of the suggestions put forward so far by other scholars, but primarily a conflict between people of different socio-economical status in which striving for honour appeared to be an important aspect.

5. We intend to enhance the understanding of several terms and *topoi* by interpreting them in the light of the semantic field of concord in antiquity.

6. And lastly, the conclusions to the different parts which constitute this study will attempt to shed light on Clement's social background.

1.3. Methodological Considerations

We stated above that we will place emphasis on a rhetorical analysis in our investigation. As far as we know, no one has carried out a comprehensive rhetorical analysis of a writing of the Apostolic Fathers.[70] Consequently, one cannot turn to works on the Apostolic Fathers for a discussion of methodology. With regard to the field of New Testament research, the reverse is the case. Since *1 Clement* and the other writings of the Apostolic Fathers are close to the time and the environment of the New Testament Scriptures, in particular the letters, it is more fruitful to pay attention to relevant rhetorical analysis as applied and to methodology as developed in this arena.

1.3.1. A Brief Overview of Different Approaches to Rhetorical Analyses

In spite of the fact that in the last 20-25 years a great number of rhetorical analyses of NT Scriptures have been produced, in particular on the Pauline letters,[71] there is no consensus among scholars about what rhetorical criticism is, and upon what resources that criticism draws.[72] At the risk of oversimplification, we may distinguish four main approaches to rhetorical criticism.

---

[70]The following works on the Apostolic Fathers employ different aspects of rhetorical analysis: W. C. VAN UNNIK, "Studies over de zogenaamde eerste brief van Clemens", *Mededelingen* (1970) 149-204; B. E. BOWE, *A Church in Crisis* (1988); D. L. SULLIVAN, "Establishing Orthodoxy", *The Journal of Communication and Religion* 15 (1992) 71-86; E. BAASLAND, "Der 2. Clemensbrief und frühchristliche Rhetorik", *ANRW* 2. 27.1 (1993) 78-157; O. M. BAKKE, "Ignatiusbrevas Retoriske Genre", *TTK* 66 (1995) 275-291. The article by E. Baasland is the only work that employs rhetorical criticism on a full scale. However, none of the listed works discuss the question of methodology to any great extent.

[71]See M. A. POWELL, *The Bible and Modern Literary Criticism* (1992); D. F. WATSON and A. J. HAUSER, *Rhetorical Critisism of the Bible* (1994) for comprehensive bibliographies.

1. The starting point for the revival of interest in rhetorical criticism among scholars in the Old Testament goes to a great extent back to J. Muilenburg's presidential address to the Society for Biblical Literature in 1968.[73] Here Muilenburg urged his audience to go beyond form criticism and its focus upon conventions, i.e. the typical, and to pay more attention to the unique and artistic features of texts, i.e. to patterns of words and motifs, to style, to rhetorical tropes or figures – that is the rhetoric of the text. A primary concern for Muilenberg was to point out devices that connected text units and helped to set the boundaries of text units. This means that for Muilenburg rhetorical criticism was primarily a matter of style. Though it is questioned whether it is appropriate to talk about a Muilenberg school,[74] some scholars have applied rhetorical criticism in terms of Muilenberg's understanding of the matter. This type of rhetorical criticism shares many features with literary criticism.[75]

2. Another school operates with models of rhetorical criticism that are indebted to antique Graeco-Roman rhetoric and applies this theory of argumentation especially to Paul's letters. In addition to focusing upon rhetorical tropes and figures, this branch of rhetorical criticism emphasizes *invention* and *arrangement of arguments* in a letter discourse. H. D. Betz was the first scholar who provided a rhetorical analysis of an entire writing in the New Testament in these terms. In his work on Galatians[76] he argued that the letter was composed with classical categories of invention, arrangement and style in mind and that these could be used as an interpretative tool. Although this pioneer work

[72]For historical reviews and the current situation in rhetorical criticism, see V. K. ROBBINS and J. H. PATTON, "Rhetoric and Biblical Criticism", *Quarterly Journal of Speech* 66 (1980) 327-337; W. WUELLNER, "Where is Rhetorical Criticism Taking us?", *CBQ* 49 (1987) 448-463; C. C. BLACK, "Rhetorical Questions", *Dialog* 29 (1990) 62-70; *idem*, "Rhetorical Criticism and Biblical Interpretation", *ET* 100 (1989) 252-258; *idem*, "Rhetorical Criticism and the New Testament", *Proceedings of the Eastern Great Lakes and Midwest Biblical Societies* 8 (1988) 77-92; J. LAMBRECHT, "Rhetorical Criticism and the New Testament", *Bijdr.* 50 (1989) 239-253; J. BOTHA, "On the Reinvention of Rhetoric", *Scriptura* 31 (1989) 14-31; B. FIORE, "Rhetoric and Rhetorical Critisicm", *Anchor Bible Dictionary* (1992) 5.715-19; D. STAMPS, "Rhetorical Criticism and the Rhetoric of New Testament Criticism", *JLT* 6 (1992) 268-279; D. F. WATSON, "Notes on History and Method", *Rhetorical Criticism* (1994) 101-125.
[73]J. MUILENBURG, "Form Criticism and Beyond", *JBL* 88 (1969) 1-18. For the impact of Muileberurg, see W. WUELLNER, "Where is Rhetorical Criticism Taking us?", *CBQ* 49 (1987) 451; A. J. HAUSER, "Notes on History and Method", *Rhetorical Criticism* (1994) 14-15; D. F. WATSON, "Notes on History and Method", *Rhetorical Criticism* (1994) 107.
[74]W. WUELLNER, "Where is Rhetorical Criticism Taking us?", *CBQ* 49 (1987) 451; A. J. HAUSER, "Notes on History and Method", *Rhetorical Criticism* (1994) 3 n. 1.
[75]W. WUELLNER, "Where is Rhetorical Criticism Taking us?", *CBQ* 49 (1987) 451f. in depicting the way rhetorical critisism is employed in the Muilenberg school concludes: "Reduced to concerns of style, with the artistry of textual disposition and textual structure, rhetorical criticism has become indistinguishable from literary criticism, as is evident in the works of two leading critics: L. ALONSO-SCHÖKEL [*The Inspired Word. Scripture in the Light of Language and Literature* .New York: Herder, 1965] and R. ALTER [*The Art of Biblical Narrative*. New York: Basic Books, 1981, *The Art of Biblical Poetry*. New York: Basic Books, 1985]".
[76]H. D. BETZ, *Galatians* (1979). His work on Galatians has been followed by a work on the Corinthian correspondence, *2 Corinthians 8 and 9* (1985).

has been criticised on several points, it marks a starting point for a new branch within New Testament research and has instigated many subsequent works.[77]

However, Betz did not provide a systematised discussion of methodology, since he was writing a commentary using ancient rhetoric as a methodological device. The first scholar to provide a methodology for rhetorical criticism of the gospels and epistles of the New Testament was G. A. Kennedy, a scholar in the classical field.[78] Kennedy's proposed methodology integrates Betz's method into a more comprehensive and systematic model. This methodology consists of five interrelated steps: (1) Definition of the rhetorical unit. (2) Definition of the rhetorical situation – that is a situation in which the persons, events and exigency invite utterance.[79] (3) Determination of the rhetorical problem or *stasis* and of the rhetorical genre. (4) Analysis of the invention, arrangement and style. (5) Evaluation of the rhetorical effectiveness of the rhetorical unit to meet the rhetorical exigency.

It seems that the methodology provided by G. A. Kennedy came at the right moment, since a vast number of works which employed Kennedy's methodology emerged in the following years.[80]

Rhetorical criticism in line with Kennedy's methodology and the way in which it is practised by Betz is an historical enterprise. It utilises a systematic and well-conceptualised discipline from the Graeco-Roman era, systematically presented in the ancient rhetorical handbooks, to analyse the New Testament. To employ rhetorical analysis of an ancient text is to attempt to interpret the text through a fundamental feature of Graeco-Roman culture.

Besides the above-mentioned scholars, who are perhaps the two scholars that have made the most influential contribution in the field of rhetorical analysis, we will focus on another scholar who has, in our opinion, provided an important contribution to questions of methodology, i.e. M. M. Mitchell. She is a disciple of Betz and has had the opportunity to consider the objections to the pioneering work of her supervisor and to further develop his methodology. In her convincing work on 1 Corinthians, she lists five mandates for rhetorical criticism of New Testament texts which are adhered to in her study:

---

[77]Cf. now M. M. MITCHELL, "Reading Rhetoric with Patristic Exegeses. John Chrysostom on Galatians", *Antiquity and Humanity* (2001) 333-355.

[78]G. A. KENNEDY, *New Testament Interpretation through Rhetorical Criticism* (1984) 33-38.

[79]G. A. Kennedy adopts L. Bitzer's definition of the rhetorical situation in L. F. BITZER, "The Rhetorical Situation", *Philosophy & Rhetoric* 1 (1968) 1-14.

[80]D. F. WATSON characterises this methodology as "extremely influential as a starting point for rhetorical analysis", "Notes on History and Method", *Rhetorical Criticism* (1994) 111. Watson himself was the first scholar who utilised Kennedy's methodology in a full scale rhetorical analysis of an entire New Testament book, *Invention, Arrangement, and Style: Rhetorical Criticism of Jude and 2 Peter* (1988).

A. Rhetorical criticism as employed here is an historical undertaking.

B. Actual speeches and letters from antiquity must be consulted along with the rhetorical handbooks throughout the investigation.

C. The designation of the rhetorical species of a text (as epideictic, deliberative, or forensic) cannot be begged in the analysis.

D. The appropriateness of rhetorical form or genre to content must be demonstrated.

E. The rhetorical unit to be examined should be a compositional unit, which can be further substantiated by successful rhetorical analysis.[81]

As will be clear in the discussion of the methodology applied in the present work, we are of the opinion that Mitchell's proposed steps for rhetorical criticism represent an advance on the methodology of her forerunners in the field.

3. The third main school finds an approach that depends solely on Graeco-Roman rhetoric to be too limited, and therefore maintains that it must be supplemented with *modern rhetorical theory*. Representatives taking this approach argue that Graeco-Roman rhetoric does not "address all theoretical, practical, philosophical questions posed by speech"[82] and consequently, a rhetorical analysis must, in addition to Graeco-Roman rhetoric, make use of different forms of modern rhetoric as well.[83]

Modern rhetoric represented by the works of W. J. Brandt, K. Burke, and Ch. Perelman and L. Olbrechts-Tyteca is often used as a theoretical foundation in this branch of rhetorical criticism.[84] In particular the "new rhetoric" of Perelman and Olbrecht-Tyteca has been influential. Here rhetoric is defined as a theory of argumentation and the authors stress the importance of the rhetorical situation for argumenta-

---

[81]M. M. MITCHELL, *Paul and the Rhetoric of Reconciliation* (1991) 6.

[82]D. F. WATSON, "Notes on History and Method", *Rhetorical Criticism* (1994) 113.

[83]We may quote C. J. CLASSEN, "St Paul's Epistles and Ancient Graeco-Roman Rhetoric", *Rhetoric and the New Testament* (1993) as illustrative of the opinion that rhetorical criticism should not draw on Greco-Roman rhetoric alone: "When one turns to the categories of rhetoric as tools for a more adequate and thorough appreciation of texts, their general structure and their details, one should not hesitate to use the most developed and sophisticated form, as it will offer more help than any other. For there is no good reason to assume that a text could and should be examined only according to categories known (or possibly known) to the author concerned. For rhetoric provides a system for the interpretation of all texts (as well as of oral utterances and even of other forms of communication), irrespectively of time and circumstances (except, of course, for the fact that some rules of rhetoric immediately concern the external circumstances)" (268); and further, "… there is no reason why one should restrict oneself to the rhetoric of the ancients in interpreting texts from antiquity, and not avail oneself of the discoveries and achievements of more recent times" (290).

Other scholars who advocate a similar opinion are, among others, J. BOTHA, "On the reinvention of Rhetoric", *Scriptura* 31 (1989) 14-31; L. THURÉN, *The Rhetorical Strategy of 1 Peter* (1990) 52-57; W. WUELLNER, "Rhetorical Criticism and its Theory in Culture-Critical Perspective", *Text and Interpretation* (1991) 171-185; S. M. POGOLOFF, *Logos and Sophia* (1992) 24-26.

[84]W. J. BRANDT, *The Rhetoric of Argumentation* (1970); K. BURKE, *The Rhetoric of Religion* (1970, first printed 1969); CH. PERELMAN and L. OLBRECHTS-TYTECA, *The New Rhetoric* (1971), originally published as *La Nouvelle Rhetorique: Traite de l'Argumentation* (Presses Universitaires de France, 1958).

tion and social history, and emphasize that all speech is rhetorical.[85] We should note that the authors never claim that their theory is solely built upon ancient rhetoric.[86] Though it draws upon classical sources as well, their theory depends to a great extent on more modern philosophical problems.[87]

A relatively large number of scholars combine modern rhetoric with other analytical tools. D. F. Watson lists the following: "literary criticism, text linguistics, semiotics, social description, stylistics, reader-response criticism, discourse analysis, and/or speech act theory".[88] Though these cross-disciplinary studies are difficult to categorise, we have chosen to integrate them in the present approach to rhetorical criticism.

4. Some scholars combine ancient rhetoric with various models of modern linguistics and literary criticism.[89] Though the approach taken varies to some extent, there appears to be a tendency in the works of these scholars for the tools of modern text linguistics to play a more important role than those of ancient rhetoric. The justification for integrating modern (text-)linguistics is to a certain extent due to its development from ancient rhetoric.[90]

---

[85]For a survey of the main features of Perelman and Olbrects-Tyteca's "new rhetoric", see B. L. MACK, *Rhetoric and the New Testament* (1990) 14-17.

[86]CH. PERELMAN and L. OLBRECHTS-TYTECA, *The New Rhetoric* (1971) 6: "It is clear, however, that our treatise on argumentation will, in certain respects, go far beyond the bounds of the ancient rhetoric and at the same time neglect certain aspects of the matter which drew the attention of the ancient masters of the art". The reason why the authors presented their work as a *new rhetoric* is that since logicians and modern philosophers of the 20th century have not been interested in rhetoric, "the present book is mostly related to the concerns of the Renaissance" (5).

[87]The first scholar to propose a rhetorical analysis based on "the new rhetoric", was W. WUELLNER in his article "Greek Rhetoric and Pauline Argumentation", *Early Christian Literature* (1979) 177-188. The first monograph-sized effort based on Perelman and Olbrechts-Tyteca's work was F. SIEGERT, *Argumentation bei Paulus gezeigt an Röm 9-11* (1985). For other studies, see for instance E. FIORENZA, "Rhetorical situation and Historical Reconstruction in 1 Corinthians", *NTS* 33 (1987) 386-403; N. ELLIOTT, *The Rhetoric Of Romans* (1990); and several articles in D. F. WATSON, ed. *Persuasive Artistry* (1991).

[88]D. F. WATSON, "Notes on History and Method", *Rhetorical Criticism* (1994) 115. For actual works, see the bibliography in D. F. WATSON and A. J. HAUSER, *Rhetorical Criticism* (1994) 163-205.

[89]E.g., the monograph-size studies by Scandinavian scholars like B. OLSSON, *Structure and Meaning in the Fourth Gospel* (1974); D. HELLHOLM, *Das Visionenbuch des Hermas als Apokalypse* (1980); B. WIKLANDER, *Prophecy as Literature* (1984); B. C. JOHANSON, *To All the Brethren* (1987); W. G. ÜBELACKER, *Der Hebräerbrief als Appell. I.* (1989); J. HOLMSTRAND, *Markers and Meaning in Paul* (1997).

See also W. WUELLNER, "Der Jakobsbrief im Licht der Rhetorik und Textpragmatik", *LingBibl* 43 (1978) 5-66.

[90]See especially H. KALVERKÄMPER, "Antike Rhetorik und Textlinguistik" (1983) 349-372; cf. further D. HELLHOLM, "Amplificatio in the Macro-Structure of Romans", *Rhetoric and the New Testament* (1993) 123.

1.3.2. The Rhetorical Approach Applied in the Present Investigation

In the present study we will confine ourselves to applying ancient rhetoric as a tool of analysis. Such an approach does not imply a general discredit to the use of modern rhetoric as an interpretative tool. The usefulness of combining ancient and modern rhetoric has been demonstrated in several works.[91] When, however, the main aim is to uncover what an ancient author wants to say and how the audience understood the message by paying attention to the overall genre, function, and composition of a discourse (or letter), it suffices to use ancient rhetoric. As we shall attempt to demonstrate in what follows, the systematised and well- conceptualised discipline of ancient rhetoric provides a good basis for our purpose.

An assumption inherent in the chosen approach is that the author of *1 Clement* was familiar with rhetoric, either through formal education or through interaction with oral and written expressions of ancient rhetoric. We have seen above that it is possible that Clement was an imperial freedman and that he had learned rhetoric in schools and from his work in the imperial bureaucracy. Even one of the strongest advocates of modern rhetoric, L. Thurén, admits that close identification of ancient techniques is meaningful if one "can reasonably assume that the authors had learnt those techniques by name at school".[92] But the restriction to ancient rhetoric does not depend on the imperial freedman hypothesis. Considering the essential role of rhetoric in Graeco-Roman culture in general, it is a fair supposition that a leader of the Roman Church at the beginning of the second century would at least have experienced different expressions of ancient rhetoric in the form of discourses or letters, and that he would therefore himself, whether consciously or not, make use of it in his own way of argumentation.[93]

---

[91] For example F. Siegert, *Argumentation bei Paulus gezeigt an Röm 9-11* (1985) and L. Thurén, *The Rhetorical Strategy of 1 Peter* (1990).

[92] L. Thurén "On Studying Ethical Argumentation and Persuasion", *Rhetoric and the New Testament* (1993) 470.

[93] Early in the first century C.E. rhetoric became the primary discipline in Roman higher education. Because of the significant role of rhetoric in society, rhetoric was considered to be "the crown and completion of any liberal education worthy of the name", H. I. Marrou, *A History of Education in Antiquity* (1956) 196, see also 194-205. On ancient education and the place therein of rhetoric, see further M. L. Clarke, *Higher Education in the Ancient World* (1971), especially 11-45; E. E. Bonner, *Education in Ancient Rome* (1977). However, the art of rhetoric was not exclusive to just the wealthy or the well educated. In the first century C.E. rhetors were found in all of the great cities in the Roman empire and the art of the rhetors was much admired by the common people. D. A. Liftin, *St. Paul's Theology of Proclamation* (1994), describes the role of rhetoric in society at that point of time with the following words: "Rhetoric played both a powerful and pervasive role in first century Greco-Roman society. It was a commodity of which the vast majority of the population were either producers or, much more likely, consumers, and not seldom avid consumers" (132). And further: "Moreover, this popularity of oratory was very broad-based. It seemed to permeate the entire Greco-Roman world, from the emperors to the man in the street … Dio was expressing the feelings of the multitude as much as his own when he spoke of 'the uncontrolled craving which possesses me for the spoken word.' [*Or.* 19.4] … As a result of its popularity oratory was ubiquitous in the Greco-Roman world of the first century … The truth is that rhetoric was not merely ubiquitous in the Greco-Roman culture; more than that, it was endemic, an inherent part of life" (124f.).

Lastly, as noted above, several scholars maintain on the basis of the style and language in *1 Clement* that the author was most probably an educated man familiar with rhetoric.

By restricting ourselves to employing Graeco-Roman rhetoric as a tool of analysis in the present study, it means that the rhetorical criticism employed here is an historical enterprise. Or, to use the words of D. F. Watson, this kind of rhetorical criticism "stands between ahistorical literary criticism and historical-criticism".[94] In other words, the present work stands, broadly speaking, in the tradition of G. A. Kennedy and H. D. Betz in spite of major differences in their approaches. If one chooses to confine oneself to ancient rhetoric as a tool of analysis, we are of the opinion that M. M. Mitchell's approach represents an improvement with respect to methodology. Consequently, this study will take its point of departure in her five rules for rhetorical analysis.[95] We must, however, add that Mitchell's proposed methodology lacks one element which should be included in a rhetorical analysis of an ancient text, namely that the appropriateness of rhetorical form or genre and content to the communication situation must be demonstrated.[96] In the present investigation we shall deal with the basic feature of the communication situation, i.e. the events in the Corinthian Church which prompted the Roman Church to intervene, in chapter five: *the Social-Historical Situation*. This chapter will discuss the basic elements of what rhetorical criticism commonly calls the "rhetorical situation". This is in line with the above-mentioned methodology proposed by G. A. Kennedy.

Although the present investigation will start with the tools of ancient rhetoric, this does not mean that we confine ourselves to ancient rhetoric as such. We find it useful to apply tools from modern text linguistics in some parts of the study. Due to the fact that the *dipsositio* of ancient rhetoric was basically one-dimensional, we find it necessary to go beyond ancient rhetoric in order to work out the argumentative structure of the letter in the compositional analysis.[97] In this task a text linguistic model applied in several works by D. Hellholm provides us with useful tools.[98] But we emphasize also that with respect to the compositional analysis the study starts with tools from ancient rhetoric

---

[94]D. F. WATSON, "Notes on History and Method", *Rhetorical Criticism* (1994) 110.

[95]In addition, since the basic topic in 1 Corinthians and *1 Clement* is the same, much of the material she has collected and her observations regarding 1 Corinthians is directly applicable to *1 Clement*. This will be particularly obvious in our presentation of deliberative rhetoric and the political background of some of the terms in *1 Clement*.

[96]The significance of the communication situation in rhetorical analysis is emphasized by D. HELLHOLM, "Enthymemic Argumentation in Paul", *Paul in His Hellenistic Context* (1995). He says that "it is imperative to realize that the most important characteristic of rhetorical argumentation is in fact the way in which the *communication situation* is put into focus" (126). In note 31 on the same page he maintains that "most urgent in rhetorical as well in linguistic interpretations of texts is 'die explizite Rückbindung einer Argumentation an Sprechsituationen/Dialogsituationen' as has been emphasized by Schecker" (M. SCHECKER, "Argumentationen als allokutionäre Sprechakte", *Theorie der Argumentation*, Ed. M. SCHECKER, TBL 76, Tübingen: Narr 1977, 75-138, quotation 81).

[97]See the discussion in chap. 4.1.2, pp. 210-213.

[98]See the present investigation, n. 1009 for literature references.

and employs these whenever they offer any help. It makes use of tools from modern text linguistics only when ancient rhetoric does not provide any rules for further text delimitation. Furthermore, we shall use features of the theory of semantic fields as a theoretical basis for our investigation of terms associated with concord in antiquity. This means that although with respect to methodology we have placed ourselves in the tradition of those scholars who regard rhetorical criticism as an historical enterprise, we find it useful and necessary to supplement their methodology with tools from modern text linguistics. However, the tools of modern text linguistics do not play such a fundamental role in the present investigation as they do in those works mentioned above which combine ancient rhetoric and text linguistics as analytical tools.

In this study *ancient rhetoric* includes both the theory of antique rhetoric described in the *rhetorical handbooks*, and *actual* composed speeches and letters. The ancient rhetorical handbooks are indeed important with regard to our knowledge of the ancient rhetorical tradition,[99] but we will avoid letting these handbooks be the sole source for our understanding of antique rhetoric. We will take into consideration the simple fact that, although the ancient rhetorical handbooks are *descriptive*, they must systematize and do so more than what is found in actual practice, because they are abstractions from a wide range of practice.[100] So, if a rhetorical analysis of an antique text, in our case *1 Clement*, should consult only the handbooks, there is a risk that one may over-systematize and overschematize, and force structures onto the letter which did not exist in actual contemporary rhetorical discourses or letters.[101] Therefore, we agree with those scholars who emphasize that rhetorical criticism must consult both the ancient

---

[99]The ancient handbooks are Aristotle, *The Art of Rhetoric*; [*Rhetorica ad Alexandrum*]; Cicero, *de Inventione*; [*Rhetorica ad Herennium*]; Quintilian, *Institutio Oratoria*.

We take it for granted that a scholar consults the books him or herself and does not rely solely on secondary literature about antique rhetoric. This is of course not to say that a scholar should not consult modern handbooks. Many of the compendia of ancient rhetoric are of great value and provide systematic outlines of rhetoric. The standard treatments are: R. VOLKMANN, *Die Rhetorik der Griechen und Römer in systematischer Übersicht* (1855); C. S. BALDWIN, *Ancient Rhetoric and Poetic* (1924; repr. 1959); H. LAUSBERG, *Handbuch der Literarischen Rhetorik* (1990, first printed 1960); G. A. KENNEDY, *The Art of Persuasion in Greece* (1963); idem, *The Art of Rhetoric in the Roman World* (1972); idem, *Classical Rhetoric and its Christian and Secular Tradition* (1980), and J. MARTIN, *Antike Rhetorik* (1974).

[100]See D. E. AUNE, *The New Testament in Its Literary Environment* (1987) 199; D. F. WATSON, "Notes on History and Method", *Rhetorical Criticism* (1994) 112: "Currently this approach [rhetorical criticism] almost exclusively depends upon rhetorical theory alone. Such restrictive reliance upon the rhetorical handbooks can lead to an imbalanced view of the New Testament documents. Ancient theory was descriptive, not prescriptive; an abstraction from previous rhetoric and its situations. However, the situations were to be the guide to rhetoric as need arose, not theory".

[101]The historical approach to rhetorical criticism has often been criticised for forcing structures onto a text and for employing rhetorical categories in a rigid way through eagerness to demonstrate that a text is influenced by ancient rhetoric. See, e.g., D. F. WATSON, "Notes on History and Method", *Rhetorical Criticism* (1994) 111.

handbooks as well as actual speeches and letters.[102] In addition, we must note the fact that the handbooks differ in opinion on many points.[103] This fact also indicates that the theory prescribed in the handbooks must be compared with actual speeches.

The handbooks themselves point out that the *dispositio* varies within the three main genres.[104] In particular we should pay attention to the statements that various parts of a speech may be omitted to suit a particular situation.[105] In other words, there is a large degree of freedom concerning the arrangement of a speech. In view of this, some may ask whether the question of rhetorical arrangement is relevant at all in a rhetorical analysis. We partly agree with the critical view implied in such a question, *if* – and we emphasize "if" – the analysis relies solely on the rhetorical handbooks.[106] However, if the analysis includes actual relevant speeches and letters as comparative literature, we are convinced that rhetorical arrangement is a vital element in a rhetorical analysis and may enhance our grasp of the letter. In the present investigation we intend to demonstrate that a comparison of *1 Clement* with other deliberative speeches will illuminate our understanding of the composition of the letter. We should not forget that, even if

---

[102]See, e.g., W. A. MEEKS' critique in his review of Betz, *"Galatians: A Commentary on Paul's letter to the Churches in Galatia* (1979)*", JBL* 100 (1981) 304-307 for "referring almost exclusively to rhetorical and epistolary *theory* rather than to specific examples of real apologies and real letters from antiquity. He does not offer us a single instance of the apologetic letter with which we can compere Galatians" (306, italics in original). Cf. further the comments in reviews of Betz's *Galatians* by P. W. MEYER and D. E. AUNE in *RStR* 7 (1981) 318-323 and 323-328 respectively. M. M. MITCHELL, *Paul and the Rhetoric of Reconciliation* (1991), states that "These handbooks present us with one type of evidence for what is *prescribed* for rhetorical discourse, and they put forth a far more regular, strict and almost mechanical view of rhetorical composition than actual speeches and letters embody. Using the handbooks alone in doing rhetorical analysis of ancient texts leads to a similarly mechanistic analysis, especially in regard to the arrangement of the argument" (8f.). Although we agree with Mitchell's warning against using the handbooks alone in doing rhetorical analysis, we cannot follow her when she states that the ancient rhetorical handbooks are prescriptive. They are based on practice and are therefore *descriptive* (cf. note 98 above). Perhaps rhetorical criticism is in a transition regarding this question. D. F. WATSON, *Invention, Arrangement, and Style* (1988), following the methodology proposed by G. A. Kennedy, used only ancient handbooks as analytical tools in doing rhetorical criticism. Although Watson says that this "methodology was shown to be workable and fruitful for exegesis" (D. F. WATSON, "Notes on History and Method", *Rhetorical Criticism* (1994) 111), it is interesting to note that the same author has emphasized that "It is imperative at this point in the debate that we shift from theory and handbooks to systematic analysis of the rhetoric of the extant literary epistles of ancient orators themselves" (*ibid*, 123, cf. also 112).

[103]F. SOLMSEN, "The Aristotelian Tradition in Ancient Rhetoric", AJP 62 (1941) 35-50.

[104]Eg Arist. *Rh.* 3.13.1-3; 3.14.12; [*Rh. Al.*] 29-37; Quint. *Inst.* 3.8.6-11; 4.2.4f.

[105]Arist. *Rh.* 3.14.8,12; Cic. *Inv. Rhet.* 1.21.30; Quint. *Inst.* 4.1.72.

[106]Cf. the warning of C. J. CLASSEN, "St Paul's Epistles and Ancient Graeco-Roman Rhetoric", *Rhetoric and the New Testament* (1993): "On *dispositio* rhetorical theory may be consulted, but extreme caution is called for, as has been pointed out. Perhaps the most useful aspect which practical oratory can illustrate is that the best orator disguises his knowledge of the theory, that he alters accepted patterns and adjusts them to the particular case and his special intention … Correspondingly, in trying to understand a particular composition, one should always look not primarily [misspelling in Classen] for what is in accordance with the rules or with general practice, but for the contrary" (289f.).

there is a large degree of freedom regarding arrangement according to the handbooks, there is in fact some advice that is based on practice.

According to the ancient rhetorical handbooks one of the main points under *invention* is the use of one of the three classical genres, i.e. forensic, deliberative and epideictic,[107] which suits the message.[108] In the present study we shall give a preliminary definition of the genre of *1 Clement* before the compositional analysis proceeds.[109]

The question of genre is taken seriously in this investigation. The first step in the process of defining the genre of *1 Clement* is to delineate the main characteristics of deliberative rhetoric, both as it is reflected in the rhetorical handbooks and in real speeches and letters, and to investigate to what extent these characteristics are to be found in the letter (chap. 2). If we succeed in identifying the main elements of deliberative rhetoric in *1 Clement*, the first and necessary criterion for classifying the letter as deliberative rhetoric is accomplished. However, even if the main elements of the deliberative genre are found throughout the letter, the question of whether that rhetorical genre is appropriate to the subject under discussion must still be addressed.[110] Therefore, as the second step in the process of defining the genre, we must inquire whether

---

[107]All handbooks operate with these three main genres, Arist. *Rh.* 1.3.3, 9; Cic. *Inv. Rhet.* 1.5.7; *Top.* 24.91; [*Rhet. Her.*] 1.2.2; Quint. *Inst.* 2.21.23; 3.3.14f.; 3.14.12-15. For futher details see the discussion in Arist. *Rh.* 1.4-10; [Rh.Al.] 1.1421b.7ff; Cic. *Inv. Rhet.* 2.4.12- 58,175; *De Or.* 2.81.333-85, 349; Quint. *Inst.*3.4. See further G. A. KENNEDY, *The Art of Rhetoric in the Roman World* (1972) 7-23; J. MARTIN, *Antike Rhetorik* (1974) 9f., 15-210.

[108]Concerning the relation of content and genre, see Arist. *Rh.* 1.4.7; 1.9.1; 1.10.1; [*Rh. Al.*] 1.1.1421b 1ff.; Cic. *Inv. Rhet.* 2.51.155-156. This is rooted in the different issues or ends which each rhetorical genre is appropriately concerned with. (See the discussion below in chap. 2.)

[109]Scholars differ in the way which they structure their rhetorical criticism. In his proposed methodology for rhetorical criticism H. D. BETZ, *Galatians* (1979); *idem, 2 Corinthians 8 and 9* (1985), works out the compositional analysis before he discusses function and genre. G. A. KENNEDY *New Testament Interpretation through Rhetorical Criticism* (1984) 36f., and M. M. MITCHELL, *Paul and the Rhetoric of Reconciliation* (1991), include the definition of genre prior to arrangement. See the discussion in the latter work, pp. 11f., n. 39. Mitchell is right when she holds that "To some degree this represents a difference not so much in the research methodology (where both are of course mutually interdependent) but in the structure of the scholarly argument which reports the results of that research". In spite of this, there are some substantial reasons for giving a (preliminary) definition of the genre prior to the composition analysis. This will, as noted by Mitchell, help us to minimise the danger of circular argumentation that always is a risk in any literary-critical analysis. Furthermore this is the most important point in our opinion, one must be careful in drawing definitive conclusions with respect to the question of genre on the basis of the rhetorical *dispositio*, because of the fact that there is a great deal of freedom regarding the arrangement of a discourse (see above, p. 23). If one succeeds, however, in finding parallels in the composition of actual speeches, one stands methodologically on safer ground in drawing inferences regarding genre. But even in such cases, it is preferable that a preliminary determination of the genre of the actual text should be made by an attempt to demonstrate that typical characteristics of a certain genre in fact occur.

[110]C. J. CLASSEN, "St. Paul's Epistles and Ancient Graeco-Roman Rhetoric", *Rhetoric and the New Testament* (1993) in commenting on the methodology provided by M. M. Mitchell asks why this should be necessary (291, n.78). If our point of departure is that rhetorical criticism is a historical undertaking, it seems self-evident that there must be consistency between genre and content. Both ancient rhetorical theory and practice show that each genre was appropriate to particular topics.

the same main theme that is dealt with in *1 Clement* is to be found in the lists of appropriate themes for deliberative rhetoric in the rhetorical handbooks and whether it is dealt with in extant deliberative speeches and letters. As pointed out in chapter 1.2, we will argue that topics associated with concord constitute the basic theme in the letter. In order to substantiate this thesis it is necessary for us first to go through the whole letter and to investigate the language of unity and of sedition (chap. 3). If we succeed in showing that throughout the letter we find terms and *topoi* associated with the concept of concord in actual deliberative discourses that urge concord and in other types of ancient literature that deal with concord, this would provide strong evidence in support of our thesis. Because of the length of the letter, this part of the study will constitute a large section of our investigation. However, it is only after we have worked out the compositional analysis that we can draw a definite conclusion regarding the main theme of the letter (chap. 4).[111] If this analysis makes it likely that the sub-texts on different levels function as integrated parts in Clement's appeal for concord, we shall have demonstrated with a high degree of certainty that concord is the basic theme. This means that the last criterion for the definition of the overall genre will be satisfied, i.e. that the main theme in *1 Clement* is of such a nature that it was appropriate for the author to employ the deliberative genre to communicate his message. This does not imply that features of the two other main genres would not be found as well, but they would have to be interpreted within the prevailing genre.[112]

1.4. The Relation between Rhetoric and Epistolography

Before we go further and attempt to apply the previously discussed method to *1 Clement*, one important question must be considered, namely the relationship between rhetorical theory and epistolography. In the methodological steps discussed above it is assumed that rhetorical theory and practice have influenced the author of *1 Clement*. The general relationship between Graeco-Roman rhetoric and epistolary genre is, however, a question under discussion.[113] This is not the place to enter into that discussion in detail, but some considerations are appropriate.

A feature that at first sight appears to indicate that Graeco-Roman rhetoric is *not* likely to have influenced letter writing in antiquity to any great degree is the fact that

---

[111]Here we differ from M. M. MITCHELL, *Paul and the Rhetoric of Reconciliation* (1991) 11f., n. 39. She is of the opinion that it is possible, and even necessary, to give "a complete demonstration" of the genre of a text before preceding with the compositional analysis. Mitchell underlines correctly that rhetorical criticism must demonstrate the compatibility between genre and content (*ibid.* 14). But the problem with Mitchell's position is the fact that to a great extent it is the composition analysis that reveals the content and the main topic of a text. Therefore, one is not able to demonstrate the compatibility between genre and content before one has worked out the compositional analysis. To be clear, this means that it is not possible to give a complete demonstration of the genre before the compositional analysis is undertaken.

[112]Ancient rhetorical handbooks also point out that features of the three genres are often employed in one and the same discourse. See Arist. *Rh.* 1.9.35; [*Rh. Al.*] 5.1427b 31ff.; Quint. *Inst.* 3.4.11; 3.4.16: "all three kinds rely on the mutual assistance of the other"; Cic. [*Rhet. Her.*] 3.8.15.

most rhetorical handbooks do not discuss the role of rhetoric applied to letters. Quintilian is the only classical theorist of rhetoric previous to or contemporary with *1 Clement* who makes a remark on letter writing at all. He does, however, very briefly comment on the style appropriate to the letter.[114] Also, Theon in his *Progymnasmata* mentions letter writing as one of the exercises in *prosopopoieia*, but he does not give any instruction in letter writing.[115] This does not mean that other rhetoricians were not familiar with the theory of letter writing. Cicero, for instance, reflects knowledge of epistolary theory in his writings and was probably familiar with manuals on letter writing.[116] If we take this fact into account, the silence of the rhetorical handbooks concerning the rhetoric of the letter is even more notable. The first extant rhetorical handbook that integrated epistolography with rhetorical theory was that of Julius Victor from the fourth century C.E. But his discussion is restricted to stylistic matters.[117]

This lack of interest in other elements of rhetorical theory (such as invention and arrangement) is characteristic of letter-writing manuals that mainly focus upon the classification of various types of letters and of styles appropriate to them.[118] Notwithstanding this, an interesting statement occurs at the beginning of the treatise *De Elocutione* which may indicate a link between rhetoric and epistolography.[119] Here the author makes reference to a statement attributed to Artemon, the editor of Aristotle's

---

[113]For an overview of the discussion, see, e.g., A. J. MALHERBE, *Ancient Epistolary Theorists* (1988), in particular 2-11; *idem*, "Hellenistic Moralists and the New Testament", *ANRW* 2.26.1 (1992) 267-333, in particular 283-285; *idem*, "Seneca on Paul as Letter Writer", *The Future of Early Christianity* (1991) 414-421; B. C. JOHANSON, *To All the Brethren* (1987) 42f.; F. W. HUGHES, *Early Christian Rhetoric and 2 Thessalonians* (1989) 24-30; L. THURÉN, *The Rhetorical Strategy of 1 Peter* (1990) 57-64; E. R. RICHARDS, *The Secretary in the Letters of Paul* (1991) 132-136; 140-144; C. J. CLASSEN, "Paulus und die antike Rhetorik", *ZNW* 82 (1991) 1-33; *idem*, "St Paul's Epistles and Ancient Graeco-Roman Rhetoric", *Rhetoric and the New Testament* (1993) 265-291; G. STRECKER, *Literaturgeschichte des Neuen Testaments* (1992) 86-95; D. DORMEYER, *Das Neue Testament im Rahmen der antiken Literaturgeschichte* (1993) 190-198; J. T. REED, "Using Ancient Rhetorical Categories", *Rhetoric and the New Testament* (1993) 292-324; W. G. MÜLLER, "Brief" *Historisches Wörterbuch der Rhetorik* II (1994) 60 - 76, in particular 62f. and 66-69; D. F. WATSON, "Notes on History and Method", *Rhetorical Criticism* (1994) 120-125; R. BRUCKER, *"Christushymnen" oder "epideiktische Passagen"?* (1997), in particular 253-79; M. M. MITCHELL, "Brief", *RGG* I (1998) 1757-1762, in particular 1759; H.-J. KLAUCK, *Die antike Briefliteratur und das Neue Testament* (1998).

[114]Quint. *Inst.* 9.4.19f.

[115]Theon, *Progymnasmata* 10.236 (Spengel 2.115.22).

[116]A. J. MALHERBE, *Ancient Epistolary Theorists* (1988) 2f.

[117]Julius Victor *Ars rhetorica*, 27 (*De Epistolis*), translated in A. J. MALHERBE, *Ancient Epistolary Theorists* (1988) 62-65.

[118]Pseudo-Demetrius, Τύποι Ἐπιστολικοί and Pseudo-Libanius, Ἐπιστολιμαῖοι Χαρακτῆρες in A. J. MALHERBE, *Ancient Epistolary Theorists* (1988) 30-41, 66-81.

[119] In the manuscript tradition *De Elocutione* is falsely attributed to Demetrius of Phalerum. The date of the treatise is still in dispute among scholars. Different suggestions vary from third century B.C.E. to the first century C.E. Cf. the discussion in A. J. MALHERBE, *Ancient Epistolary Theorists* (1988) 2. It is not necessary for the purposes of our study to make any decision on this question, since all suggestions operate with a date previous to or contemporary with the composition of *1 Clement*.

letters, concerning the definition of a letter. According to him "a letter ought to be written in the same manner as a dialogue", since the letter is regarded as one of the two sides of a dialogue.[120] Such a definition of a letter has obviously an oral element and may therefore indicate a connection between letter writing and rhetoric.

In addition, some statements that may link letters to discourse are to be found in actual letters. Cicero describes a letter as chatting,[121] and through the letter the author has a kind of talking with the recipient of the letter.[122] Seneca reveals the oral aspect of a letter when he writes that he prefers to view the letter as a conversation.[123] Although the references are rather few, they at least reflect a point of view that saw the letter as a "speech in the written medium".[124]

Despite the references mentioned above, which seem to link letter and speech together, the sources in general give the impression that rhetorical theory and epistolary theory, at least in the early stages, were not integrated.[125] Regarding the *Progymnasmata*, however, an explanation can be given of this circumstance. When discussing the reason why there is no section in the *Progymnasmata* containing instructions on letter writing, M. L. Stirewalt argues with respect to Theon:

> This omission can be accounted for at the elementary level by the fact that the Greek *Progymnasmata* were for pupils of the primary and slightly advanced levels beginning in Theon's book with declension. Introductory exercises were based on the simplest chreic form. The simple chreia was easily converted into a simple epistole. Devoid of common epistolary formulae the epistole retained the chreic nucleus, the saying (or action), and presented it as coming directly from a hero or mentor. Thus the pupil was introduced to the epistole at an elementary stage for basic, formal exercise according to the same instruction as those given for the chreia. Therefore no separate consideration of epistolai was necessary at this level.
>
> On the other hand at the higher level epistolai were associated with panegyric and protreptic exercises. Instruction and exercises included argumentation, prosopopoeia, narrative, history, and thus exceeded the purposes of the handbooks.[126]

---

[120]*De Elocutione* 223: ὅτι δεῖ ἐν τῷ τρόπῳ διάλογόν τε γράφειν καὶ ἐπιστολάς, A. J. MALHERBE, *Ancient Epistolary Theorists* (1988) 16f.

[121]Cic. *Att.* 8.14.1.

[122]Cic. *Att.* 8.14.1; 9.10.1; 12.53.

[123]Sen. *Ep.* 75.1. Cf. A. J. MALHERBE, "Hellenistic Moralists and The New Testament", *ANRW* 2.26.1 (1992) 285: "Seneca's letters also contain many references to his own circumstances and conduct. Their ability to convince proceeds from the authoritative person of Seneca the teacher, who is conscious of the truth of what he writes. He wishes his letters to be exactly what his conversation would be if he were with Lucilius. His letters are only a substitute ...".

[124]A. J. MALHERBE, *Ancient Epistolary Theorists* (1988) 12.

[125]S. K. STOWERS, *Letter Writing in Greco-Roman Antiquity* (1986) states that "Letter writing remained only on the fringes of formal rhetorical education throughout antiquity. It was never integrated into the rhetorical systems and thus does not appear in the standard handbooks" (34), and further "the letter-writing tradition was essentially independent of rhetoric" (52). A. J. MALHERBE, *Ancient Epistolary Theorists* (1988) 3, argues that "It is thus clear that letter writing was of interest to rhetoricians, but it appears only gradually to have attached itself to their rhetorical systems".

[126]M. L. STIREWALT, JR., *Studies in Ancient Greek Epistolography* (1993) 63.

While rhetorical theory distinguishes only between three species of discourse, the manuals on epistolography operate with many types of letters.[127] We should note that, although Demetrius sometimes discussed formal features and *topoi* connected with a particular type of letter, he classified letters mainly according to "typical situations and social contexts of letter writing. This meant classification according to typical purposes that letter writers hoped to accomplish".[128] This kind of classification implies that a large variety of types of letters could emerge to fit new social contexts, and these new types are not possible to classify either in terms of the three main genres of rhetoric or in the categories listed by the epistolary theorists.[129] It seems, however, that the theory itself assumes a link between certain types of speeches and letters. Epideictic rhetoric corresponds to letters of blame or praise, judicial rhetoric to accusatory or apologetic letters and deliberative rhetoric to letters of admonition or advice.[130] This fact does not, however, offer a decisive answer to the question of congruency between rhetorical theory and epistolography on these matters. Although there seems to be a certain correspondence in *function* between certain types of letters and the three rhetorical genres, this does not necessarily mean that the epistolography has adopted the rules of rhetorical theory on invention and arrangement.

Must we thus, on the basis of the paucity of discussion of epistolography in rhetorical theory, draw the conclusion that the system of rhetoric made an impact upon letter-writing to only a very limited degree? In our view this is too hasty an assumption. It is in fact possible that letter writing in practice reflected a high degree of influence from rhetorical conventions in spite of the fact that epistolography was not an integrated part of the rhetorical handbooks.[131] A possible influence can of course only be confirmed by an analysis of actual letters.[132] At this point we must be content with referring to

---

[127]Pseudo-Demetrius operates with 21 types of letter.

[128]S. K. STOWERS, *Letter Writing in Greco-Roman Antiquity* (1986) 23. Cf. also 54.

[129]D. E. AUNE, *The New Testament in Its Literary Environment* (1987) 203, warns against a rigid classification of the early Christian letters in terms of categories of the theory of rhetoric and epistolography because the majority of the letters are "multifunctional and have a 'mixed' character".

[130]Cf. A. J. MALHERBE, *Ancient Epistolary Theorists* (1988) 32-41 for these types of letters according to Demetrius; *idem*, "Hellenistic Moralists and the New Testament", *ANRW* 2.26.1 (1992), asserts that "The ancient handbooks which provided instruction in letter-writing came from the schools of rhetoric" (283); W. G. MÜLLER, "Brief", *Historisches Wörterbuch der Rhetorik* II (1994), maintains that "In der Antike entwickelte sich die Theorie und Praxis des Briefschreibens unter dem Einfluss der Rhetorik. Der B.[rief] wurde in Stil und Aufbau den Gesetzen der Rhetorik unterworfen" (62). Also S. K. STOWERS, who is of the opinion that systematic rules for letter writing were never developed as they were for discourses, admits that "the rules for certain types of speeches, however, were adapted for use in corresponding letter types", *Letter Writing in Greco-Roman Antiquity* (1986) 34.

[131]The relationship between theory about letters and the practise of letter writing as well as the relationship between epistolography and rhetoric are problems that still have not found their solutions in present research. Cf. M. M. MITCHELL, "Brief", *RGG* I (1998) 1759.

[132]Cf. D. DORMEYER, *Das Neue Testament im Rahmen der antiken Literaturgeschichte* (1993), who correctly states that the relationship between the rhetorical genres and letters "ist nur im Rahmen der gesamten antiken Briefliteratur zu beantworten" (190).

some works that indicate a strong connection between ancient letters and rhetorical conventions. Perhaps the most interesting is J. A. Goldstein's study of the letters of Demosthenes. After a rhetorical analysis of letters 1-4, he concludes by stating that "all four have been shown to be *demegoriae* which conform to fourth-century rhetorical practice".[133] In his discussion of fictitious letters M. L. Stirewalt emphasizes that the authors use rhetorical forms and that an author may intend to demonstrate his rhetorical ability.[134] Likewise many current works on the Pauline epistles have shown with varying degrees of success that Paul utilised the conventions of invention, arrangement and style.[135] These works indicate that there was a closer connection between rhetoric and actual letter writing than the theory reflects. D. E. Aune summarizes, "By the first century B.C., rhetoric had come to exert a strong influence on the composition of letters, particularly among the educated. Their letters functioned not only as means of communication but also as sophisticated instruments of persuasion and media for displaying literary skill".[136]

It is likely that many of Paul's letters and the writings of the apostolic fathers were supposed to be read in the churches.[137] Through a letter an author tried to persuade the audience of a certain attitude or action in a particular case. In other words, the letters that were read in Church had in many ways a similar function to discourses. Thus it is reasonable to term a letter a *sermo absentis ad absentem*[138] or with Seneca a substitute for a conversation.[139] If we take this into account, it is a fair supposition that the corpus of the letter reflects the rhetorical conventions prevailing in the author's environment.[140]

On the basis of this discussion, it is of interest to interpret *1 Clement* in the light of Graeco-Roman rhetorical tradition and to see to what extend such an approach will achieve a new understanding of the letter. Furthermore, a rhetorical analysis of *1 Clem-*

---

[133]J. A. GOLDSTEIN, *The letters of Demosthenes* (1968) 180.

[134]M. L. STIREWALT, JR., *Studies in Ancient Greek Epistolography* (1993) 15f. Stirewalt points to a study that shows rhetorical influence in two Pythagorean letters (ALFONS STÄDELE, *Die Briefe des Pythagoras und der Pythagoreer: Beiträge zur Klassischen Philologie*, 115 [Meisenheim: Verlag Anton Hain, 1980]) and to a work that argues that the letters of Bruto had their origin in rhetorical exercise (R. E. SMITH, "The Greek Letters of M. Junius Brutus", *CQ* 30 [1936] 201-203).

[135]See D. F. WATSON and A. J. HAUSER, *Rhetorical Criticism of the Bible* (1994) for a bibliography.

[136]D. E. AUNE, *The New Testament in Its Literary Environment* (1987) 160. See also W. SCHRAGE, *Der erste Brief an die Korinther* I (1991) 75.

[137]Cf. 1 Thess 5:27; Col 4:16; Rev 1:3; *1 Clem.* 47:1f; *Herm. Vis.* 2.5.3; Just. 1 *apol.* 67.

[138]H. PLETT, *Einführung in die rhetorische Textanalyse* (1975) 17; D. HELLHOLM, "Amplificatio in the Macro-Structure of Romans", *Rhetoric and the New Testament* (1993) 125. R. FUNK, *Language, Hermeneutic and Word of God* (1966) states that "the letter ... is an appropriate substitute for oral word – it is as near oral speech as possible – yet it provides a certain distance on the proclamation as event" (248). Cf. also W. G. MÜLLER, "Brief", *Historisches Wörterbuch der Rhetorik* II (1994) 62: "Vom Bewerbungsschreiben biz zum Liebesbrief und vom Leserbrief bis zum offenen politischen B.[rief] nimmt der B.[rief] oftmals den Charakter eines rhetorischen Plädoyers an".

[139]See n. 123 above.

[140]Cf. D. F. WATSON, "Notes on History and Method", *Rhetorical Criticism* (1994) 125.

ent will also function as a contribution to the ongoing discussion about the influence of rhetorical conventions on letter writing in antiquity.

2. First Clement as Deliberative Rhetoric

The aim of this chapter is to show that the basic features of deliberative rhetoric are to be found in *1 Clement*. If we succeed in this task the first and necessary criterion for defining it as γένος συμβολευτικόν will be fulfilled.[141] In order to do so an outline of the fundamental and characteristic elements of this rhetorical species will be given, and then an investigation as to what degree they are to be found in the epistle itself will be carried out.

As noted in chapter 1, ancient rhetoric operated with three main genres of rhetoric. The genre which the author finds appropriate in each individual case depends on the communication situation. Aristotle, for instance, states that "The kinds of Rhetoric are three in number, corresponding to the three kinds of hearers ... Therefore there are necessarily three kinds of rhetorical speeches, deliberative (συμβουλευτικόν), forensic (δικανικόν), and epideictic (ἐπιδεικτικόν)".[142]

It is not necessary to discuss the distinguishing features of each genre in detail, but it should suffice to give an overview. A diagram by D. Hellholm outlines the main features of the three "genres with regard to subject matter, teleological function, primary time aspect, main line of argumentation and genetic communication situation also referred to as 'model case' or – in terms of biblical scholarship – 'Sitz im Leben'". It offers such an overview in a way that is lucid and useful:[143]

---

[141]On deliberative rhetoric in general see, R. VOLKMANN, *Die Rhetorik der Griechen und Römer in systematischer Übersicht* (1855) 294-314; J. KLECK, *Symbuleutici qui dicitur sermonis historiam criticam per quattuor saecula continuatam* (1919); H. L. HUDSON-WILLIAMS, "Political Speeches in Athens", *CQ* 1 (1951) 68-73; G. A. KENNEDY, *The Art of Persuasion in Greece* (1963) 203-206; I. BECK, *Untersuchungen zur Theorie des Genos Symbuleutikon* (1970); J. MARTIN, *Antike Rhetorik* (1974) 167-176; H. LAUSBERG, *Handbuch der literarischen Rhetorik* (1990) 123-129.

[142]Arist. *Rh.* 1.3.1-3.

[143]D. HELLHOLM, "Enthymemic Argumentation in Paul" 13f. (a previous longer version of "Enthymemic Argumentation in Paul", *Paul in His Hellenistic Context* (1995) 119-179. Of primary sources Hellholm refers to Arist. *Rh.* I.3.3-6; Anaximen. *Rh.* 1.142b, and to the following modern studies: H. F. PLETT, *Einführung in die rhetorische Textanalyse* (1975) 15; H. HOMMEL, "Griechische Rhetorik und Beredsamkeit", in E. VOGT, ed., *Neues Handbuch der Literaturwissenschaft*. Band 2: *Griechische Literatur*, Wiesbaden: Athenaion, 1981, 367ff.; M. FUHRMANN, *Die antike Rhetorik* (1984) 81-83; H. LAUSBERG, *Handbuch der literarischen Rhetorik* (1990) 53-63, 86ff., 123ff., 129ff.; J. MARTIN, *Antike Rhetorik* (1974) 15ff., 167ff., 177ff.; R. BARTHES, "Die alte Rhetorik", in J. KOPPERSCHMIDT, ed., *Rhetorik*. Band 1: *Rhetorik als Texttheorie*, Darmstadt: Wissenschaftliche Buchgesellschaft, 1990, 68.

Genera causarum / Genera rhetorices / τρία γένη τῶν λόγων
Genus iudiciale / γένος δικανικόν

(A) Subject matter: Right or wrong
(B) Function (teleological):   Accusatory or defensive
                                             [= change of situation]
(C) Primary time aspect: The past
(D) Line of argumentation: Enthymemes (mainly)
(E) Communication situation   Oration of prosecutor or advocate in
    (genetic) – *res dubia* [= model case]: court (δικαστήριον)

Genus deliberativum / γένος συμβουλευτικόν

(A) Subject matter: Advantage or disadvantage
(B) Function (teleological):   Hortatory or admonitory/
                                             recommending or dissuasive
                                             [= change of situation)
(C) Primary time aspect: The future
(D) Lines of argumentation: Examples (mainly)
(E) Communication situation   Political oration, *e.g.* before the
    (genetic) – *res dubia* [= model case]: assembly of the citizens (ἐκκλησία /
                                             βουλευτήριον)

Genus demonstrativum / γένος ἐπιδεικτικόν

(A) Subject matter: Honor or dishonor
(B) Function: (teleological):   Praise or blame [= constancy/
                                             (change) of situation]
(C) Primary time aspect: The present
(D) Line of argumentation   Amplification (mainly)
(E) Communication situation   Oration before a festive or casual
    (genetic) – *res certa* / *res dubia*   gathering (πανήγυρις)
    [= model case]:

Since the present study will argue that it is appropriate to classify *1 Clement* as deliberative rhetoric, we shall outline in some detail below the characteristics of this type of
rhetoric before demonstrating that these are to be found in it.

2.1. The Hortatory and Dissuasive Aspect

2.1.1. In Deliberative Rhetoric in General

The main function of deliberative rhetoric is to advise an audience to take, or to dissuade it from taking, a particular course of action in the future:[144] "The deliberative
kind is either hortatory (προτροπή) or dissuasive (ἀποτροπή); for both those who
give advice in private and those who speak in the assembly invariably either exhort or

---

[144]Concerning the "Sitz im Leben" for deliberative rhetoric, see J. Martin, *Antike Rhetorik* (1974)
167.

dissuade" (Arist. *Rh.* 1.3.3). Anaximenes speaks of εἶδος προτρεπτικόν and εἶδος ἀποτρεπτικόν[145], the author of *Rhetorica ad Herennium* of *suasio* and *dissuasio*[146], and both Fortunatian[147] and Quintilian[148] of *suadere* and *dissuadere*.[149]

2.1.2. In 1 Clement

There is no doubt whatsoever that the intention of the author of *1 Clement* is to *advise* the Corinthian Christians to take, or *dissuade* them from taking, certain actions in the future. This is reflected in the abundant use of hortatory subjunctives, a grammatical form which occurs over seventy times in the letter. Furthermore, to make the alternatives clear for the audience, and in order to point out his advice and dissuasion in an obvious way, the author makes use of a two-part structure: on the one hand he advises a particular action or attitude, and on the other he dissuades from the opposite action or attitude. Even if the order may change, the two-part, exhortative pattern is an important feature of the author's strategy in persuading the audience. This protreptic/apotreptic pattern is repeated, as noted by B. E. Bowe, at several points throughout the letter:[150]

> Wherefore let us put aside (ἀπολίπωμεν) empty and vain cares, and let us come (ἔλθωμεν) to the glorious and venerable rule of our tradition ... (7:2).

> ... let us turn (ἐπιστέψωμεν) to his pity, and abandon (ἀπολιπόντες) the vain toil and strife and jealousy which leads to death (9:1).

> Let us, therefore, be humble-minded (ταπεινοφρονήσωμεν) brethren, putting aside (ἀποθέμενοι) all arrogance and conceit and foolishness and wrath ... (13:1).

> ... let us fear (φοβηθῶμεν) him, and leave off (ἀπολίπωμεν) from foul desires of evil deeds ... (28:1).

> ... let us do (ποιήσωμεν) all the deeds of sanctification, fleeing (φεύγοντες) from evil speaking ... and abominable pride (30:1).

> Let us then join ourselves (κολληθῶμεν) to those to whom is given grace from God; let us put on (ἐνδυσώμεθα) concord in meekness of spirit and continence, keeping ourselves far from (πόρρω ἑαυτοὺς ποιοῦντες) all gossip and evil speaking and be justified by deeds, not by words (30:3).

> But how shall this [sc. receiving a share of the promised gifts] be, beloved? ... if we seek (ἐκζητῶμεν) the things that are well-pleasing and acceptable to him; if we fulfil

---

[145]Anaximen. *Rh.* 1.1.1421b 9.

[146]Cic. [*Rhet. Her.*] 1.2.2.

[147]Fortunat. *Rh.* 1.1.17f.

[148]Quint. *Inst.* 3.4.15.

[149]J. MARTIN, *Antike Rhetorik* (1974): "Die beratende Rede kann nun nicht nur im positiven Sinne etwas anrarten oder empfehlen, sondern auch umgekehrt, von etwas abraten, etwas ablehnen oder vor etwas warnen" (167).

[150]B. E. BOWE, *A Church in Crisis* (1988) 67f. The following overview is taken from Bowe, with the addition of *1 Clem.* 7:2 and with a few minor alterations.

(ἐπιτελέσωμεν) ... and follow (ἀκολουθήσωμεν) the way of truth, casting (ἀπορρίψαντες) away from ourselves all iniquity ... (35:5).

Learn to be submissive (μάθετε ὑποτάσσεσθαι), putting aside (ἀποθέμενοι) the boastful and haughty self-confidence of your tongue ... (57:2).

It is therefore right that we should respect so many and so great examples, and bow (ὑποθεῖναι) the neck, and take up (ἀναπληρῶσαι) the position of obedience, so that ceasing from (ἡσυχάσαντες) vain sedition we may gain without any fault the goal set before us in truth (63:1).

This abundant use of hortatory subjunctives, including the protreptic/apotreptic pattern, is consistent with the author's characterisation of the letter as a συμβουλή.[151] Συμβουλή had become a *terminus technicus* for advice given to an ἐκκλησία and gave rise to one of the three main genres of Greek rhetoric. In addition, the author refers to the letter as an ἔντευξις περὶ εἰρήνης καὶ ὁμονοίας (63:2).[152] It does not seem to be accidental that the author used precisely these designations of the letter. As W. C. van Unnik has shown, the expression "peace and concord" is a typical combination in the συμβουλή given to *ekklesia* which urges its members to put an end to sedition and party strife.[153] This subject will be dealt with thoroughly in chapter 3.

2.2. The Time Reference

2.2.1. In Deliberative Rhetoric in General

If the main function of deliberative rhetoric is to advise an audience to take or to dissuade it from taking a particular action, the logical time reference is the future. It is impossible to give advice that affects the past. That the future time aspect is a key feature of deliberative rhetoric is also stated explicitly in the rhetorical handbooks. When Aristotle gives an outline of the main features of the three rhetorical genres, he points out that the future is the appropriate time for deliberative rhetoric, "for the speaker, whether he exhorts or dissuades, always advises about things to come" (Arist. *Rh.* 1.3.4).[154] The other species of rhetoric, the forensic and the epideictic, are characterised by a past and a present time frame respectively.[155] Also, Quintilian states explicitly

---

[151]"Receive our counsel (συμβουλή), and there shall be nothing for you to regret" (58:2).

[152]The expression "peace and concord" is not an *ad hoc* formulation, but occurs five times throughout the letter (20:10:11; 60:4; 63:2; 65:1).

[153]W. C. VAN UNNIK, "Studies over de zogenaamde eerste brief van Clemens", *Mededelingen* (1970) 181ff.

[154]Cf. also Arist. *Rh.* 1.6.1; 1.8.7. The fundamental time frame in the respective species of rhetoric is also reflected in the passage where Aristotle distinguishes between the species according to the role of the audience: "Now the hearer must necessarily be either a mere spectator or a judge, and a judge either of things past or of things to come. For instance, a member of the general assembly is a judge of things to come; the dicast, of things past; the mere spectator, of the ability of the speaker. Therefore there are necessarily three kinds of rhetorical speeches, deliberative, forensic, and epideictic" (*Rh.* 1.3.3).

[155]Arist. *Rh.* 1.3.4.

that deliberative rhetoric deals with the future: "we deliberate about the future" (*Inst.* 3.4). This, however, does not mean that the particular time reference connected with the different species of rhetoric is the only adequate time reference. Aristotle notes that deliberative rhetoric may contain elements of the present as well.[156] Quintilian goes on to maintain that even the past is appropriate within deliberative rhetoric: "The *deliberative* department of oratory (also called *advisory* department), while it deliberates about the future, also enquires about the past" (*Inst.* 3.8.9). So, even if the basic time frame is the future, it is also logical that the adviser partly takes his departure from a point in the past and in the present in order to get as good a base as possible for his advice or dissuasion. Sometimes a decision made in the *past* has to be revoked or changed in the *future*, e.g., as in Corinth.

2.2.2. In 1 Clement

If we turn our attention to *1 Clement*, it is not difficult to find future-directed statements. There are indeed so many of them that we may establish without hesitation that the future is the main time frame. Above we have noted the abundant use of the hortatory subjunctive, which occurs over seventy times. Each of these implies either advice or dissuasion concerning a particular course of action in the future. Let us just mention a few examples:

> Wherefore let us put aside (ἀπολίπωμεν) empty and vain cares, and let us come (ἔλθωμεν) to the glorious and venerable rule of our tradition … (7:2).

> …let us turn to (ἐπιστρέψωμεν) his pity, and abandon (ἀπολιπόντες) the vain toil and strife and jealousy which leads to death (9:1).

> …let us do (ποιήσωμεν) all the deeds of sanctification… (30:1).

> …let us put on (ἐνδυσώμεθα) concord… (30:3).

> …let us then beg (δεώμεθα) and pray (αἰτώμεθα) of his mercy that we may be found in love, without human partisanship… (50:2).

In addition to the hortatory subjunctive many imperative statements are to be found. Among them we mention that the author exhorts the Corinthian Christians that the whole body must be preserved (σωζέσθω) in Christ, that the Christian should be subject to his neighbour (38:1), that those who laid the foundation of the sedition shall submit to the presbyters and receive the correction of repentance (57:1).

The future time aspect is also evident when the author states that, if the Corinthian Church receives the counsel (συμβουλή), there will be no reason to regret it (58:2), and that the Christian Community in Corinth will be a source of joy and gladness, if they are obedient to the content of the letter (63:2). In both cases a particular course of action in the future is projected to have a certain effect upon the Corinthians and the Romans respectively.

---

[156] Arist. *Rh.* 1.6.1; 1.8.7.

However, even if the future is obviously the dominant time frame in *1 Clement*, there are elements of past and present time as well. The author takes his departure in the past and describes the previous life in the Corinthian Church marked by a "virtuous and honourable citizenship" (*1 Clem.* 1-2). Then still in the past, he goes on to speak of the change which took place within the church. In contrast to the previous communal life of love and concord, the negative behaviours of jealousy (ζῆλος) and envy (φθόνος), strife (ἔρις) and sedition (στάσις), persecution (διωγμός) and disorder (ἀκαταστασία), war (πόλεμος) and captivity (αἰχμαλωσία) had arisen (3:2). Since these evils were still dominating the Corinthian Church,[157] the author turns to the present time and maintains that "righteousness (δικαιοσύνη) and peace (εἰρήνη)" are absent, and "men walk neither in the ordinances of his [God's] commandments nor use their citizenship worthily of Christ" (3:4).

In addition to the past aspect already mentioned, many examples from the past are used as a means of persuading the audience to follow the proposed course of action. This fact, however, cannot be used to argue that *1 Clement* should be classified as forensic rhetoric. The abundant use of examples taken predominantly from the past indicates instead that the genre in question is deliberative.[158]

Of the three rhetorical species, only the deliberative fits *1 Clement* with respect to time frame. It is a letter from the Church in Rome which gives advice about behavioural changes in the life of the community. Therefore the future is the appropriate time frame. We should note that the occurrences of past and present time are in line with Quintilian's statement that the orator in deliberative rhetoric also enquires about the past and with Aristotle's statement that deliberative rhetoric also contains elements of present time.

2.3. The Content of the Appeals

2.3.1. The Appeals in the Theory of Deliberative Rhetoric

So far we have focused on two of the main features of deliberative rhetoric, the hortatory/ dissuasive aspect and the future time aspect. We have seen that both are characteristic of *1 Clement*. Now we shall turn more directly to the content of the advice and dissuasion given concerning the future. As Aristotle expresses it, we will investigate the "end" (τέλος)[159] of deliberative rhetoric.

As previously mentioned, deliberative rhetoric according to Aristotle may be distinguished from the two other species of rhetoric by its end (τέλος). The end of the forensic rhetoric is the just or unjust, the end of the epideictic speaker is the honourable or disgraceful, and "the end of the deliberative speaker is the expedient or harmful" (τῷ μὲν συμβουλεύοντι τὸ συμφέρον καὶ βλαβερόν).[160] The concrete action that is

---

[157]Cf. 46:9: "Your schism has turned aside many, has cast many into discouragement, many to doubt, all of us to grief; and your sedition (στάσις) continues".

[158]Cf. chap. 2.4.

[159]Arist. *Rh.* 1.3.5.

considered to be expedient or good in each particular case depends on the situation and the final aim of the person involved. Thus, the orator must take into consideration the audience's perception of what is expedient and if necessary attempt to redefine it.[161] The overall perspective is that which is good and expedient for the audience.

> *Similarly, the deliberative orator, although he often sacrifices everything else, will never admit that he is recommending what is inexpedient (ἀσύμφορος) or is dissuading from what is useful (ὠφέλιμος) … (Arist. Rh. 1.3.6).*

If one wishes to persuade an audience to a particular course of action in the future, the orator must attempt to prove that this action is expedient for the audience. If on the other hand one tries to dissuade an audience from a particular course of action, the orator must try to demonstrate that such an action would be harmful. This emphasis on the expedient is also to be found in Latin rhetorical handbooks where the term *utilitas* corresponds to the Greek τὸ συμφέρον. The author of *Rhetorica ad Herennium* maintains that the orator in deliberative discourse "will throughout his speech properly set up Advantage (*utilitas*) as his aim, so that the complete economy of his entire speech may be directed to it".[162] Cicero, for his part, refers to Aristotle's definition of the end as τὸ συμφέρον, but he juxtaposes the honourable with the expedient as the end of deliberative rhetoric.[163]

However, the appeal in deliberative rhetoric is not limited to advantage, as already indicated by the reference to Cicero above. Although the appeal to advantage is indeed an important element in the appeal of deliberative rhetoric – perhaps the most essential – the different handbooks operate with different lists of appeals. Even Aristotle, who emphasizes the appeal to τὸ συμφέρον, is unclear to some extent whether the appeal to advantage is the *only* appeal in deliberative rhetoric. When he discusses the elements that are involved in advantage, he tends to juxtapose συμφέρον with δίκαιον.[164] Other theorists extend the number of topics or appeals that belong to a deliberative argument.[165] According to Anaximenes the orator must convince the audience that the

---

[160]Arist. *Rh.* 1.3.5. See also G. A. KENNEDY, *The Art of Persuasion in Greece* (1963) 204; *idem, New Testament Interpretation through Rhetorical Criticism* (1984) 36f.

[161]"But since the aim before the deliberative orator is that which is expedient (τὸ συμφέρον), and men deliberate, not about the end, but about the means to the end, which are the things which are expedient in regard to our actions; and since, further, the expedient is good, we must first grasp the elementary notions of good and expedient in general" (Arist. *Rh.* 1.6.1). "Lastly and above all, each man thinks those things good which are the object of his special desire, as victory of the man who desires victory, honour of ambitious man, money of the avaricious, and so on in other instances. These are the material from which we must draw our arguments in reference to good and the expedient" (Arist. *Rh.* 1.6.30).

[162]Cic. [*Rhet. Her.*] 3.2.3.

[163]Cic. *Inv. Rhet.* 2.51.156 (*honestatem et utilitatem*). Cf. also Quint. *Inst.* 3.8.34; 3.8.42.

[164]Arist. *Rh.* 1.6.16: "Lastly, justice, since it is expedient in general for the common weal".

[165]There was no agreement among the rhetorical theorists about the name under which the appeals were placed. See the comments in M. M. MITCHELL, *Paul and the Rhetoric of Reconciliation* (1991) 27.

course of action concerning which he is going to advise or persuade is δίκαιον, νόμιμον, συμφέρον, καλόν, ἡδύ, ῥάδιον.[166] However, not all of these topics carry the same weight. The orator should, if possible, first show that the act is just, and secondly that it is expedient (*Rh.* 32.1439a).[167] Similar lists of appropriate appeals in deliberative rhetoric are to be found with minor variations throughout the rhetorical tradition. The rhetorical handbook attributed to Aristides recognizes the following topics for discussion: The just, the advantageous, the possible, the easy, the necessary, the safe, the good, the pious, the natural, the pleasant, and the opposite of these things (τὸ δίκαιον, τὸ συμφέρον, τὸ δυνατόν, τὸ ῥάδιον, τὸ ἀναγκαῖον, τὸ ἀκίν-δυνον, τὸ καλόν, τὸ εὐσεβές, τὸ ὅσιον, τὸ ἡδύ καὶ τὰ ἐναντία τούτοις).[168] According to the author of *Rhetorica ad Alexandrum* the common topics in deliberative speech are the "just, lawful, expedient, honourable, pleasant and easily practicable" (δίκαια ὄντα καὶ νόμιμα καὶ συμφέροντα καὶ καλὰ καὶ ἡδέα καὶ ῥάδια πραχθῆναι).[169] Here we should pay attention to the fact that ὁμόνοια is a subtopic of the advantageous.[170] In Hermogenes we actually find six different lists of τελικὰ κεφάλαια that are appropriate in deliberative rhetoric. They differ both in the number of topics (from four to six) and in the topics themselves. In any case, we should note that some topics occur in all and some in almost all of the lists. Here it is sufficient to note that τὸ συμφέρον and τὸ δυνατόν occur in all, and that τὸ δίκαιον and τὸ νόμιμον are to be found in all except one.[171]

In the Latin handbooks we also find discussions of the appeals in deliberative rhetoric. We have already mentioned that Cicero prefers to speak of honour (*honestas*) and advantage (*utilitas*), as opposed to Aristotle who confined himself to talking about advantage as the end.[172] The deliberative discourse is about "*quid honestum sit et quid utile*".[173] He goes on to define *honestas* as "anything that is sought wholly or partly for its own sake".[174] *Honestas* consists of four parts: wisdom, justice, courage and temper-

---

[166]Anaximen. *Rh.* 1.4.23-26.

[167]Anaximenes lives up to his recommendation in his own exemplary arguments, where he for the most part appeals to τὸ συμφέρον and τὸ δίκαιον, as I. BECK, *Untersuchungen zur Theorie des Genos Symbuleutikon* (1970) 158-161, notes.

[168]Aristid. *Rh.* 399.21-25 (Spengel 2.503).

[169]Arist. [*Rh. Al.*] 1.1.1421b 23-26.

[170]"Expedient (συμφέρω) for a state are such things as concord (ὁμόνοια) ..." (Arist. [*Rh. Al.*] 1.1.1422a 12f.). When the author gives examples of how to argue from analogy to the expedient, he again stresses this aspect: "As it is expedient (συμφέρω) for people in health to be on their guard against contracting disease, so also it is expedient for states enjoying a period of concord to take precautions against the rise of faction" (οὕτω καὶ ταῖς πόλεσιν ὁμονοούσαις συμφέρον ἐστὶ προσκοπεῖν μὴ στασιάσωσιν, 1.1422b.84-86). Cf. also 2.1424b.17-20 where he states that "one who wishes to advocate a law has to prove that it will be equal for the citizens, consistent with the other laws, and advantageous for the state, best of all as promoting concord (ὁμόνοια)".

[171]For text references and overview of the topics in the different lists, see J. MARTIN, *Antike Rhetorik* (1974) 173.

ance (*prudentiam, iustitiam, fortitudinem, temperantiam*).[175] *Utilitas* is defined as things which "attract us only [not] by their intrinsic worth but also by the advantage to be derived from them".[176] This class includes glory, rank, influence and friendship (*gloria, dignitas, amplitudo, amicitia*).[177] Cicero, however, may also describe advantage with the word pair "security and power" (*incolumitas et potentia*). Security is related to the maintenance of safety (*salus*), and "power is the possession of resources sufficient for preserving one's self and weakening another".[178]

For the anonymous author of *Rhetorica ad Herennium*, as also for Aristotle, advantage (*utilitas*) is the superior concept and the orator should set up advantage as his aim (*finis*) throughout the speech. However, he divides *utilitas* into two subdivisions: security and honour (*tutamen, honestas*). Security, as with Cicero, is connected with avoidance of a present or imminent danger. The honourable is divided into the right and the praiseworthy (*rectum, laudabile*). *Rectum* is divided into four subheadings: wisdom, justice, courage and temperance. *Laudabile* is connected by events which produce an honourable remembrance.[179]

Quintilian states very briefly that he does not restrict deliberative oratory to questions of expediency (*utilitas*), and that he prefers Cicero's view that deliberative rhetoric is first and foremost concerned with what is honourable (*hoc materiae genus dignitate maxime contineri putat*).[180]

This outline of the "end" of deliberative rhetoric shows that there was some discussion over the relative hierarchy of deliberative appeals. While we are aware of the different approaches and the lack of unanimity on certain points, it is beyond any doubt that certain appeals are intrinsic to deliberative rhetoric. The appeal to τὸ συμφέρον occurs in every list of appropriate topics in the Greek handbooks. Aristotle in particular emphasizes this aspect. In addition to τὸ συμφέρον, the topics of δίκαιον, νόμιμον and καλόν are very common. Also, in Latin handbooks *utilitas* is a dominating topic, along with *honestum*, and their subdivisions among which we should mention *iustitium*.

---

[172]Cic. *Inv. Rhet.* 2.51.156. Cicero reflects a discussion of which of these is to be regarded as superior. "For there is nobody … who does not think that moral worth (*dignitas*) is the highest object of ambition, but for the most part expediency (*utilitas*) wins the day when there is a covert fear lest if expediency be neglected worth will also have to be abandoned. But differences of opinion arise either on the question which of two alternatives is more expedient, or even supposing there is agreement about this, it is disputed whether the chief consideration should be integrity (*honestas*) or expediency (*utilitas*)" (*De Or.* 2.82.334-35).

[173]Cic. *Inv. Rhet.* 2.4.12.

[174]Cic. *Inv. Rhet.* 2.53.159.

[175]Cic. *Inv. Rhet.* 2.53.150-54.164.

[176]Cic. *Inv. Rhet.* 2.55.166.

[177]Cic. *Inv. Rhet.* 2.55.166.

[178]Cic. *Inv. Rhet.* 2.56.169.

[179]Cic. [*Rhet. Her.*] 3.2.3-4.8.

[180]Quint. *Inst.* 3.8.1.

2.3.2. The Appeals in Actual Deliberative Discourses and Letters

If we leave the *theory* of antique rhetoric for a while and turn our attention to rhetorical practice, we will see that the practice confirms the theory. The appeal to τὸ συμφέρον is abundant in deliberative rhetoric.[181] Among the many possible examples, we shall confine ourselves to giving some from Isocrates, Aelius Aristides and Dio Chrysostom.

In *Or. 8, On the Peace*, Isocrates argues that Athens must lay aside the ambitions of empire and instead recognise the right of each Hellenic state to be free and independent. Accordingly, he proposes that it should make peace "not only with the Chians, the Rhodians, the Byzantines and the Coas, but with all mankind" (*Or.* 8.16). Isocrates also argues that one must not find the terms of peace more expedient for the city (μᾶλλον τῇ πόλει συμφερούσας) than a peace in line with his proposal (*Or.* 8.16). Previously in the same discourse Isocrates states that what he is going to deal with is "advantageous to the state" (τῇ πόλει συμφέρον, *Or.* 8.10). Farther on he maintains that at the present time the citizens of Athens take a position which has the consequence that they are not gaining their true advantage (τοῦ συμφέροντος, *Or.* 8.28f.).[182]

In dealing with the benefit of concord (ὁμόνοια) for a city, Dio Chrysostom states that "when a city has concord, as many citizens as there are, so many are the eyes with which to see that city's interest" (συμφέρον, *Or.* 39.5). And in a passage reminding the Apameians about previous discourses addressed to them, he says that he has "made many speeches in behalf of concord (ὁμόνοια), believing that this was advantageous for the city" (συμφέρειν τῇ πόλει, *Or.* 40.16).[183] Aelius Aristides in one of his discourses on concord focuses upon the work of Solon in bringing the common people together with the rich, "so that they might dwell in harmony in their city, neither side being stronger than was expedient for all in common" (κοινῇ συμφέρει, *Or.* 24.14).[184]

Furthermore, many of the other topics prescribed in rhetorical theory occur as well. Isocrates exhorts the Greeks to *homonoia* because it is δίκαιον, συμφέρον, δυνατόν, ῥᾴδιον.[185] In *On the peace* he advises the Hellenes to make peace with all mankind on the basis of the covenants of peace they entered into with the king of Persia

---

[181]See the fine discussion with plentiful references in M. M. MITCHELL, *Paul and the Rhetoric of Reconciliation* (1991) 25-32.

[182]For other appeals to τὸ συφέρον by the same author, see for instance Isoc. *Or.* 4.18; 5.3, 10, 15, 25, 45, 72, 127; 6.4, 34, 37, 38, 74, 77; 7.62, 84; 31.62, 66, 70, 74.

[183]For other appeals to τὸ συμφέρον in discourses on concord see, Dio Chrys. *Or.* 31.32; 34.16; 38.49; 40.19; 48.6.

[184]Cf. also *Or.* 23.7, 32, 46, 65. For many other text references, both from the classical and Graeco-Roman period, to the frequent appeal to τὸ συμφέρον in deliberative rhetoric, see M. M. MITCHELL, *Paul and the Rhetoric of Reconciliation* (1991) 30-32. She concludes by stating that in rhetorical theory the appeal to advantage was considered to be the major feature of deliberative argumentation, a viewpoint which is confirmed in deliberative speeches and letters.

[185]Isoc. *Or.* 5.32-34, 35-38, 39-56, 57-67, 68-80; 6.35-36.

and with the Lacedaemonians by appealing to δίκαιον and to συμφέρον.[186] Moreover, he advises them to surrender their ambition concerning the dominion of the sea, because it "is neither just (δίκαιον) nor capable (δυνατόν) of being attained nor advantageous (συμφέρω) to ourselves".[187] In the *Areopagiticus*, after discussing the decline of politics in Athens, he goes on to point out that a future danger (κίνδυνος) will face the Athenians, if the earlier democracy is not re-established.[188] In the *Panegyricus* Isocrates makes an appeal to the audience in which he states that Athens' claim to leadership is just (δικαίως)[189] and noble (καλόν),[190] and that the campaign against Persia would be just (τὸ δίκαιον)[191] and expedient (συμφέρω).[192] This shows that a synthesis of argumentation of different appeals – advantage, justice, honour and possibility – is characteristic of Isocrates.[193]

2.3.3. Striving for the Common Good

Before we turn our attention to *1 Clement* again, we must deal with one more aspect of appeal to advantage, namely, for whom the proposed course of action is advantageous. The "Sitz im Leben" of political rhetoric was basically the political assembly, the *ecclesia*. Though the political system in antiquity was different from the political assembly in western democracies, there are some parallels. One was the politicians' task, idealistically speaking, of taking care of the overall interests of the whole country or the city state. The politicians and their advisers were not to seek their own individual interests, but the commonwealth's good. Therefore, it is not surprising that both theory and actual speeches reflect this ideal.

In Aristotle's discussion on different kinds of constitutions he uses the individual constitution's concern for "the common advantage" (τὸ κοινῇ συμφέρον) as a measure for classification (Arist. *Pol.* 3.4.7-3.5.4). The "constitutions that aim at the common advantage (τὸ κοινῇ συμφέρον) are in effect rightly framed in accordance with absolute justice" (3.4.7). Furthermore, he designates constitutions "with an eye to the

---

[186]"For we shall not find terms of peace more just and these nor more expedient for our city" (Isoc. *Or.* 8.16).

[187]Isoc. *Or.* 8.66. As pointed out by G. A. KENNEDY, "Focusing on Arguments in Greek Deliberative Oratory", *Transactions of the American Philological Association* 90 (1959) 132: "Isocrates refuses to admit that there can be a conflict between self-interest, justice and honor; and in recommending a course of action he gives equal weight to a variety of arguments". See Isoc. *Or.* 8.31-32 where Isocrates explicitly discusses the relationship between different appeals and denies that there may be a conflict between them.

[188]Isoc. *Or.* 7.16.

[189]Isoc. *Or.* 4.20.

[190]Isoc. *Or.* 4.23.

[191]Isoc. *Or.* 4.183.

[192]Isoc. *Or.* 4.184.

[193]Cf. G. A. KENNEDY, "Focusing on Arguments in Greek Deliberative Oratory", *Transactions of the American Philological Association* 90 (1959) 132f.: "However advantageous any course of action, in Isocrates' view it must coincide with justice and honour and be in accord with the traditions which had brought Athenians to their finest hours".

common interest" (τὸ κοινῇ συμφέρον) to be the right ones, while those adminis-
tered with an eye to the private interest of the rulers are described as deviations.[194] To
give another example, Philo says that, if he is going to act as a councillor (ἐάν τε
βουλεύω), he "will introduce such proposals (γνώμη) as are for the common good
(κοινωφελής), even if they be not agreeable. If I speak in the general assembly I will
leave all talk of flattery to others and resort only to such as is salutary and beneficial".[195]

A noticeable element in deliberative rhetoric urging concord is the appeal to seek
"the common good" which in practice means to put an end to factionalism and establish harmony instead. Dio Chrysostom's *Or.* 34 serves as a good example. In this discourse the present state of individualism and egoism in which people seek their own
welfare is contrasted with the desirable situation in which people have the common
good in view:

> For only by getting rid of the vices that excite and disturb men, the vices of envy, greed,
> contentiousness, the striving in each case to promote one's own welfare at the expense
> of both one's native land and the common weal (τὴν πατρίδα καὶ τὸ κοινῇ
> συμφέρον) – only so, I repeat, it is possible ever to breathe the breath of harmony in
> full strength and vigour and to unite upon a common policy (Or. 34.19).

Farther on in the same discourse, Dio Chrysostom emphasizes the harmful seditious
consequences for a city, if anyone should stand "aloof in sentiment from the common
interest" (τοῦ κοινῇ συμφέροντος, Or. 34.22).

A similar, but no less illustrative example of the appeal to the common good in a
deliberative argument urging the audience to cease from factionalism is to be found in
Demosthenes *Ep.* 1.

> First of all, men of Athens, it is necessary that you bring about harmony among your-
> selves for the common good of the State (ὁμόνοιαν εἰς τὸ κοινῇ συμφέρον τῇ
> πόλει) ... (Ep. 1.5).

A basic point that Demosthenes makes in this appeal is that, in a situation where factionalism threatens the State, the audience should turn away from individualism and
private interests and seek the common good instead.[196] Firstly, that factionalism in
antiquity was considered to be an outcome of the behaviour of individuals and groups
who placed their own interest above the common interest, and secondly, that the appeal
to the common good was a topos in deliberative rhetoric urging concord, are both well
attested.[197]

Furthermore, the orator may try to demonstrate that the proposed action will be
beneficial for everyone involved in a certain matter. Isocrates attempts to convince

---

[194]The expression τὸ κοινῇ συμφέρον occurs three more times in Arist. *Pol.* 3.4.7-3.5.4.
[195]Philo *Jos* 73.
[196]For other examples of the appeal to "the common advantage" in deliberative rhetoric on concord, see Dem. *Ep.* 1.5, 9, 10; Aristid. *Or.* 24.5; Dion. Hal. *Ant. Rom.* 6.85.1. Here we just note that
Clement uses the same strategy when he urges the Corinthians to cease from strife and sedition:
ζητεῖν τὸ κοινωφελὲς πᾶσιν, καὶ μὴ τὸ ἑαυτοῦ (48:6). Cf. also 1 Cor 10:33; *Barn.* 4.10.

Philip that to reconcile the Greek states is an act "which is expedient for our city and for you" (περί τε τῶν τῇ πόλει καὶ τῶν σοὶ συμφερόντων).[198] Also, he attempts to persuade the king of Sparta that the proposed course of action is "practicable and expedient for you, for your city, and for all the Hellenes at large" (δυνατὰ καὶ συμφέροντα καὶ σοὶ τῇ πόλει καὶ τοῖς ἄλλοις ἅπασιν).[199]

In some cases the adviser has to try to free himself from the suspicion that he is seeking his own interest. To illustrate this we may quote a passage from Demosthenes:

> For my own part, I have never yet chosen to court your favour by saying anything that I was not quite convinced was to your advantage; and today, keeping nothing back, I have given free utterance to my plain sentiments. Yes, certain as I am that it is to your interest to receive the best advice, I could have wished that I were equally certain that to offer such advice is also to the interest of the speaker; for then I should have felt much happier. But, as it is, in the uncertainty of what the result of my proposal may be for myself, yet in the conviction that it will be to your interest to adopt it, I have ventured to address you. Whatever shall be to the advantage of all, may that prevail![200]

To sum this up, the appeal aims at a communal advantage. The adviser presents advice with the interest of the common good in view, the common good of the *ecclesia*, the city, or the whole country. The task of the adviser is to think holistically, to serve the whole community and not the private interests of himself or particular groups of people.

2.3.4. The Appeals in 1 Clement

We find many appeals appropriate in deliberative argumentation in *1 Clement*. Although the word which seems to be the technical term for advantage, τὸ συμφέρον, does not occur, subtopics of this concept and the opposite are to be found. Also, as we are attempting to show, a fundamental element in Clement's argumentation is based on explicit and implicit appeals to what is expedient for the Church in Corinth.

An important element in Clement's argumentation is to clarify the consequences of strife and sedition, which are presented as very harmful and dangerous for the community in Corinth, as we shall see. Of interest in this connection is the ζῆλος / φθόνος complex in *1 Clem.* 3:2–6:4 which plays an important role in the letter. ζῆλος is introduced as the origin of death (δι᾽ οὗ καὶ »θάνατος εἰσῆλθεν εἰς τὸν κόσμον«, 3:4)

[197]See M. M. MITCHELL, *Paul and the Rhetoric of Reconciliation* (1991) 144f. for further text references. She summarizes: "Because factionalism is the problem of self-interest placed above the common interest, in deliberative speeches urging concord it is very common for orators to try to get the divided parties to forsake their individual interests and together strive for the common good" (144).

[198]Isoc. *Ep.* 3.1.

[199]Isoc. *Ep.* 9.19.

[200]Dem. *Or.* 4. 51. The same stress on the fact that he is not advising in his own interest is also striking in *Ep.* 1.10: "I do not think, however, that I have the right while satisfying my private resentments to hurt the public interest (τὸ κοινῇ συμφέρον), nor do I at all mix my private enmity with the general good (τὰ κοινῇ συμφερονία). On the contrary, the conduct I urge upon the rest of men I think I ought to be myself the first to practise". See also Isoc. *Ep.* 6.14.

in a quote from Wis 2:24. After having stated this, Clement gives fourteen examples of the way in which ζῆλος and φθόνος have disrupted the peace and harmony of human relationships and led to strife, discord and death. The author intends this to prove by means of examples taken from the Christian tradition. First he focuses upon examples taken from the Old Testament: the Cain and Abel story, Jacob's flight from Esau, the prosecution of Joseph, Moses' flight from Egypt, Aaron and Miriam lodged outside the camp, Dathan and Abiram who were brought alive into Hades, and the persecution of David. In two of these examples, Clement explicitly asserts that death is caused by ζῆλος (and φθόνος); the fratricide, and the death of Dathan and Abiram. Then Clement focuses his attention on some "noble examples" from his own generation. Before putting forward concrete examples, he states that "through jealousy (ζῆλος) and envy (φθόνος) the greatest and most righteous pillars of the Church were persecuted and contended unto death" (5:2). Peter and Paul are named among these pillars. In addition to them a great number of the chosen became victims of jealousy (ζῆλος). Clement concludes the list of examples by stating that ζῆλος καὶ ἔρις "have overthrown great cities, and rooted up mighty nations" (6:4).

It is worth noticing that in 6:4 Clement links ζῆλος with ἔρις, a term expressing strife and sedition. Also in other passages Clement links ζῆλος καὶ φθόνος with terms depicting discord (3:2; 5:5). The rhetorically formed statement in 3:2 provides a good example of the escalation of evil as it progresses from bad to worse: ἐκ τούτου ζῆλος καὶ φθόνος, ἔρις καὶ στάσις, διωγμὸς καὶ ἀκαταστασία, πόλεμος καὶ αἰχμαλωσία (3:2). One notices that the calamities are arranged in an escalating order of seriousness, and that each pair leads to the next and is thus the cause of the following calamity. This indicates that the basic nature of ζῆλος, φθόνος, and ἔρις is the same. In the end they will lead to war.

In 5:5 the word pair ζῆλος καὶ ἔρις is used to refer to the cause of the persecution of Paul, and in 6:4 the same pair is said to have effected the overthrow of great cities and the destruction of mighty nations. It is not clear whether Clement distinguishes between these concepts or not. However, it is plausible, as in 3:2, that ζῆλος generates ἔρις. In any case, these two concepts are closely connected.[201] The important point in this connection is to note that Clement expresses how dangerous the present state of affairs is for the Corinthian Christians by linking ζῆλος with ἔρις. The ultimate consequence of ἔρις is θάνατος, death. This is said explicitly in the exhortation in 9:1: "Let us turn to his pity, and abandon the vain toil and strife (ἔρις) and jealousy (ζῆλος) which leads to death (εἰς θάνατον)".

In order to demonstrate that the term θάνατος encompasses both physical death, i.e. the final destruction, and condemnation by God, we shall briefly examine some texts where the word θάνατος occurs. In 3:3, as mentioned earlier, Clement states that ζῆλος brought about that θάνατος εἰσῆλθεν εἰς τὸν κόσμον. Here Clement alludes

---

[201]Regarding the coupling of ζῆλος and φθόνος with ἔρις in Early Christian literature, see Rom 1:29; 13:13; 1 Cor 3:3; 2 Cor 12:20; Gal 5:20; Phil 1:15-17; 1 Tim 6:4. Cf. also E. W. Fisher, *Soteriology in First Clement* (1974) 78 -82.

to Wis 2:24 according to which God created human beings to be immortal, but the devil caused death to come into the world. It seems clear that only physical death is connoted by θάνατος since it is contrasted with the original immortality of human beings. Therefore, it appears that θάνατος in 3:4 refers to physical death. The first in the list of examples, i.e. the narrative about Cain and Abel, supports this view. The list is introduced by a quotation formula "for it is written" in which γάρ points back to the assertion in 3:4 and forward to the following quotation from Scripture that aims to prove this assertion. According to the author the narration about Cain and Abel demonstrates that "jealousy and envy wrought fratricide" (4:6). The death of Abel was a physical death.[202]

It is, however, a fair supposition that in 51:4 θάνατος encompasses the final destruction and condemnation by God, i.e. eternal death. Clement puts forward Korah and his flock as an example of men who hardened their hearts. They were condemned by God and "'went down into Hades alive' and 'death shall be their shepherd'" (51:4). ᾅδης is in classical, Jewish and Christian literature a designation of the underworld as a place of death, sometimes contrasted with heaven.[203]

This brief consideration of the term θάνατος suggests that it expresses more than just physical death. The main aspect is certainly the physical aspect, but one passage also seems to indicate that it encompasses eternal death and condemnation by God. Therefore, when Clement in his exhortation in 9:1 asserts that strife and jealousy lead to death, this functions as a strong warning of the consequences of the present state of affairs among the Corinthian Christians. Physical and eternal death, which is the ultimate consequence of strife and sedition, represents the greatest danger to the community.[204] So, in agreement with a fundamental feature in the argumentation of deliberative rhetoric Clement points out the harmful and dangerous consequence for the audience, if its members do not follow the proposed course of action.[205]

Yet, this is not all. In order to make clear how serious the situation is from Clement's point of view, he repeatedly and explicitly warns about the danger which the Corinthian community exposes itself to.[206] 14:2 is illustrative of this view:

For we shall incur no common harm (βλάβη), but great danger (κίνδυνος μέγας), if we rashly (ριψοκινδύνως) yield ourselves to the purpose of men who rush into strife and sedition, to estrange us from what is right.

With the question of genre in view, it is interesting to observe that the word for harmful (βλαβερός) is used in the same way as it is by Aristotle when he clarifies the end

---

[202]It appears that θάνατος also in 4:9; 5:2; 8:2; 9:3; 16:9, 10, 13; 55:1; 56:3; 56:9 merely means physical death.

[203]For text references, see W. BAUER, *A Greek- English Lexicon* (1979) 16f.

[204]Cf. B. E. BOWE, *A Church in Crisis* (1988) 29.

[205]Cf. Arist. *Rh.* 1.3.5, Cic. [*Rhet. Her.*] 3.3.4.

[206]Cf. B. E. BOWE, *A Church in Crisis* (1988) 29: "The repetition of κίνδυνος / κινδυνεύω in *1 Clement* underscores Rome's view that jealousy (ζῆλος), and its products strife and sedition (ἔρις καὶ στάσις) carry an ominous threat or danger".

(τέλος) of deliberative discourse. The only difference is that in 14:2 Clement uses a noun, while Aristotle uses an adjective.[207] Of course, this corresponding vocabulary may be accidental, but it is an interesting observation when the question of genre is considered. On the other hand, the most emphatic expression of the danger facing the Corinthians is expressed by the term κίνδυνος. Note the use both of κίνδυνος and ῥιψοκινδύνως in 14:2. This rhetorical device of paronomasia, where the same word stem recurs in proximity but expresses a dissimilar meaning, intensifies the threat of danger.[208] The danger connected to strife and sedition is not insignificant in Clement's view; on the contrary, the level of danger is regarded as great (κίνδυνος μέγας).

Clement also emphasizes the level of danger elsewhere in the letter. The more knowledge about the will of God the Christians have been entrusted with, the greater the risk they incur (μᾶλλον κινδύνῳ, 41:4). Also, 59:1 is very elucidating concerning the warning of danger where the author states that, if the Corinthian Church does not take note of what God has spoken to them through the letter, "they will entangle themselves in transgression and no little danger" (κινδύνῳ οὐ μικρῷ).

The term κίνδυνος is also to be found in 47:7, in this case without emphasizing the level of danger. The crisis facing the Corinthian Church has not only lead to blasphemy of the Lord, but it has created danger (κίνδυνος) for the Christians themselves.

In these references it seems plausible that, although the term κίνδυνος includes a reference to the destructive effects of the present strife and sedition for the church as a political body, it refers primarily to eternal destruction and condemnation.[209] Such an interpretation of the danger facing the Church in Corinth corresponds with the interpretation that θάνατος, as the ultimate consequence of ζῆλος and ἔρις, also implies eternal death. In any case, the discussion above should have been sufficient to demonstrate that the author, consistent with rhetorical theory and practice, warns the audience of the danger of not following the proposed course of behaviour.

However, Clement does not simply clarify the consequence of the present strife and sedition. He also points out the opposite, that which is expedient and safe for the community in Corinth. Σωτηρία is contrasted to θάνατος and κίνδυνος as the ultimate advantage.[210]

The goal of the Christians in Corinth is that they shall be saved. In the *exordium* Clement praises the Corinthians for their exemplary community life in the past.[211] Among other things, they are praised for the solidarity that existed among "the broth-

---

[207] Arist. *Rh.* 1.3.5.

[208] Cf. B. E. Bowe, *A Church in Crisis* (1988) 29.

[209] R. Knopf, *Die Zwei Clemensbriefe* (1920) 65, 124; O. B. Knoch, *Eigenart und Bedeutung der Eschatologie im theologischen Aufriss des ersten Clemensbriefes* (1964) 191; B. E. Bowe, *A Church in Crisis* (1988) 30; A. Lindemann, *Die Clemensbriefe* (1992) 56, 165; H. E. Lona, *Der erste Clemensbrief* (1998) 512.

[210] The verb σῴζω and the noun σωτηρία occur throughout the letter, and are obviously keywords, σῴζω: 2:4; 7:6; 11:1; 12:1; 16:16; 21:8; 37:5; 38:1; 58:2; 59:3; 59:4, and σωτηρία: 7:4, 7; 18:14; 39:9; 45:1.

[211] For the definition and function of the *exordium* in *1 Clement*, see pp. 218-223.

ers". In this context we limit ourselves to noting the motivation for the previous good relations among the members of the Church, namely "that the number of his [God's] elect should be saved (εἰς τὸ σώζεσθαι) with mercy and compassion" (2:4). In the list of examples where Clement shows that God has given a place for repentance in all generations, both Noah's and Jonah's preaching of repentance are mentioned. The result of the people's repentance was salvation, even for the people of Nineveh, though they were aliens to God (7:6f.). Clement explicitly points out that the aim of repentance is salvation (σωτηρία), and the "advantage" of Lot's hospitality and piety was salvation out of Sodom (Λὼτ ἐσώθη ἐκ Σοδόμων, 11:1). Likewise, the harlot Rahab was saved because of her faith and hospitality (12:1). Clement's appeal to his audience to seek salvation is expressed explicitly in the exhortation in 38:1: "Let, therefore, our whole body be preserved (σωζέσθω οὖν ἡμῶν ὅλον τὸ σῶμα) in Christ Jesus".

The exhortation at the end of the *probatio* is illuminating for the author's view concerning salvation as the ultimate goal and advantage for these Christians.[212] The Roman Church exhorts them to receive its advice (συμβουλή). If they do, the Christians in Corinth will not regret it because they "shall be enrolled and chosen in the number of those who are saved through Jesus Christ" (ἔσται εἰς τὸν ἀριθμὸν τῶν σωζομένων διὰ Ἰησοῦ Χριστοῦ, 58:2). In the present critical situation coloured by "great danger" and "death", the Roman Church clarifies the conditions for and the regimen of how to achieve the ultimate advantage, salvation.

The occurrence of the contrasting pair σωτηρία and great κίνδυνος in *1 Clement* is particularly striking against the background of the author of *Rhetorica ad Herennium's* and Cicero's definition of *utilitas*. As already noted, security (*inculumitas, tutam*) is considered to be one of the subheadings of *utilitas*. This security is connected to the maintenance of safety (*salus*). In particular we should pay attention to remarks contained in *ad Herennius* that security "is to provide some plan or other for ensuring the avoidance of a present or imminent danger".[213] The warning in *1 Clement* against the present state of affairs in order to avoid κίνδυνος fits hand in glove with this definition.

To avoid "the present or imminent danger" facing the Christian community in Corinth is, of course, advantageous for the community. Therefore, Clement may describe the admonition he has put forward in the letter as "good and beyond measure helpful (ὠφέλιμος) for it unites us to the will of God" (56:2).

Note also that the word ὠφέλιμος occurs at the beginning of the *peroratio* where the author states that he has written sufficiently about things which befit worship "and are most helpful (ὠφελιμωτάτων) for a virtuous life to those who wish to guide their steps in piety and righteousness" (62:1). The appeal to what is useful in this important passage thus reveals a basic feature in Clement's strategy of argumentation.[214]

---

[212]For the definition and function of the *probatio* in *1 Clement*, see pp. 232-277.

[213]Cic. [*Rhet. Her.*] 3.2.3.

[214]The *peroratio* is the conclusion of a discourse and functions as a recapitulation of the main points of the *probatio*. For the definition and function of *peroratio* in *1 Clement*, see pp. 226-232.

So far, we have demonstrated that Clement explicitly warns of a danger connected with the present conditions in the Corinthian Church. In doing so he appeals both explicitly and implicitly to the advantage and the usefulness of the course of action proposed in the letter. We have not dealt, however, with a common question in deliberative rhetoric, namely the one or ones for whom the action is considered to be advantageous and useful. Nor we are in the dark regarding this question. The author openly states the basic sphere of advantage. After he has referred to the shameful report of the revolt against the presbyters (στασιάζειν πρὸς τοὺς πρεσβυτέρους) which has reached the Roman Church (47:6), and after having maintained that the present situation creates danger (κίνδυνος) for them, Clement urges the Corinthian Christians to put an end to the strife and to beseech the Master to restore the holy and seemly practice of love for the brethren (φιλαδελφία, 48:1). He continues by stating that this implies that each and everyone should seek "the common good of all and not his own benefit" (ζητεῖν τὸ κοινωφελὲς πᾶσιν, καὶ μὴ τὸ ἑαυτοῦ, 48:6). In other words, to seek τὸ κοινωφελές is the answer to the crisis in the Corinthian Church. In the author's view, it seems that the present situation is conditioned by the opposite, i.e. the individual is seeking his own advantage. This is not explicitly expressed, but the emphatic use of the noun ἕκαστος in 3:4[215] and the statement that each one is lead by the lusts of his wicked heart (3:4) indicates that the Church in Corinth is marked by individualism and egoism and that they therefore seek the best for themselves exclusively. Clement counters this individualism and egoism by defining the basic sphere of advantage for these Christians, not as individuals, but as an entire Church. He attempts to redefine their conception of what is advantageous. The true advantages are not connected to the individual's own wishes and ambitions, but are served only when those of the entire ἐκκλησία are served. Clement's appeal to seek the common good is reflected throughout the letter by his insistence upon the communal identity of the Corinthians: Christians are described as ἀδελφότης,[216] πόλις,[217] οἱ ἐκλεκτοὶ τοῦ Θεοῦ,[218] σῶμα,[219] ποίμνιον τοῦ Χριστοῦ,[220] as fellow athletes[221], as soldiers[222], and as a household.[223]

---

[215] Each one (ἕκαστος) deserts the fear of God ... and each one (ἕκαστος) walks ... according to the lusts of his wicked heart".

[216] *1 Clem.* 2:4.

[217]Clement praises Corinth for having displayed in the past "virtuous and honourable citizenship" (τῇ παναρέτῳ καὶ σεβασμίῳ πολιτείᾳ κεκοσμημένοι, 2:8); and then upbraids the community in the present day for not "using their citizenship (πολιτεύομαι) worthily of Christ" (3:4); a summary statement in 6:1 describes "the elect" as people who lived holy lives (ὁσίως πολιτευσαμένοις); the Christians should be citizens (πολιτευόμενοι) worthy of God (21:1); he talks about "the conduct of those who live without regrets as citizens (οἱ πολιτευόμενοι) in the city (πολιτεία) of God (54:4). All these passages either imply or express explicitly that the Church is viewed as a πόλις. Regarding Clement's use of political language, cf. chap. 3 in the present investigation.

[218]ἐκλεκτός: 1:1; 2:4; 6:1; 46:3, 4, 8; 49:5; 52:2; 58:2; 59:2, ἐκλέγομαι: 43:4; 50:7; 59:3, 64:1.

[219]Our own σῶμα (37:5); τὰ μέλη τοῦ Χριστοῦ (46:7).

[220]*1 Clem.* 16:1; 44:3; 54:2; 57:2.

[221]The ἀγών motif: 2:4; 7:1; 35:4.

[222]*1 Clem.* 37.

All these ecclesiological images and metaphors presuppose a communal and corporate aspect of the Church.[224] The exhortation to seek the common good is therefore well prepared and is in fact an expression of this communal identity of the Church. Clement's strategy is to redefine the Corinthians' goal from one of self-interest to one of community interest in order to persuade them to seek the common good.

After finishing this exhortation, Clement introduces a hymn of love, which is most likely influenced by 1 Corinthians.[225] Clement's hymn, however, is to a great extent expanded and coloured by the situation in Corinth and by the purpose of his letter. We have in mind primarily the passage where Clement relates love and schism, sedition and concord to each other: negatively expressed by "Love admits no schism (σχίσμα), love makes no sedition (στασιάζω)", and then positively uttered in "love does all things in concord" (ὁμόνοια, 49:5). This connection between love and communal harmony is also reflected in the admonition to "beg and pray of his mercy that we may be found in love, without human partisanship (δίχα προσκλίσεως ἀνθρωπίνης), free from blame" (50:2). The proper way to achieve the goal of the common good by the Christian behaviour is obviously to live in love.

The connection between love and the common good, and what practical conclusions Clement draws from it concerning the dangerous situation in the Corinthian Church is well illustrated in chapter 54. Here, the author says that those among the Corinthians who are noble, compassionate and filled with love will leave the community voluntarily, if they recognise that they were the cause of "sedition and strife and divisions" (54:2). In other words, love leads the individual Christian to put aside his individual aims and ambitions and instead behave in accordance with what is advantageous for the entire Church. This focus upon the common good, that people should act in self-sacrifice with the common good for the entire community, is also the basic theme in the examples in *1 Clem.* 55.

The foregoing observations demonstrate that in concert with deliberative rhetoric Clement warns of the great danger that the continuing state of affairs will bring and emphasizes the usefulness and advantage of his proposed course of action in order to persuade the audience. Furthermore, in a manner consistent with deliberative rhetoric, the author indicates both explicitly and implicitly for whom the proposed action will be useful and advantageous, namely the entire Church. As the ideal of the true politician was to put forward τὰς κοινωφελεῖς γνώμας,[226] Clement gives advice concerning a particular course of action to the κοινωφελής. In doing so he employs a *topos* of deliberative rhetoric that urges concord.[227]

---

[223] *1 Clem.* 1:3; 21:6-8.

[224] B. E. Bowe, *A Church in Crisis*, (1988) 77-105 emphasizes this aspect of Clement's ecclesiology. Cf. also E. W. Fisher, *Soteriology in First Clement* (1974) who convincingly has demonstrated the essentially corporate understanding of salvation in *1 Clement*.

[225] See the present study pp. 191-195.

[226] Philo *VitMos* 2.9; *SpecLeg* 4.170.

[227] See above pp. 43-45.

In the examination of deliberative rhetoric above it has been demonstrated that in addition to setting forth advantage and usefulness and their opposites, the rhetor used other appeals in order to persuade his audience to adopt his proposed course of action. Among the most common were τὸ δίκαιον, τὸ νόμιμον, τὸ καλόν. As just noted, a fundamental strategy of Clement in his efforts to establish peace and concord in the Corinthian Church is to warn the Corinthians that the present state of affairs is dangerous – in contrast with his proposed action, which is advantageous. Like most deliberative speakers, Clement also employs other appeals from the arsenal of appeals at hand in deliberative rhetoric. A prevalent appeal is τὸ δίκαιον.[228] Attempting to convince the Corinthians to turn away from "those who in pride and unruliness are the instigators of an abominable jealousy", he says that it is δίκαιον and ὅσιον to obey God rather than them (14:1). In a similar context, he says that it is δίκαιον not to desert God's will (21:4). In this context also, following the will of God is contrasted with following the will of the instigators of the strife and sedition. In addition, by employing the Lord himself as an example, Clement appeals explicitly to the need to "work the work of righteousness" (ἔργον δικαιοσύνης, 33:8).

We observe, furthermore, that Clement maintains that the present state of affairs in the Corinthian Church is marked by ἀνόμιμον. In contrast with the previous golden time when everybody "walked in the laws of God",[229] at the present time no one walks according to the law of God's commandments.[230] This emphasis on the fact that the Corinthians' position is against the law of God functions as an implicit appeal to behave according to τὸ νόμικον. A more explicit appeal is made in 37:1 where Clement admonishes the Corinthians to serve as in an army following God's commands. The importance of behaving in accordance with God's commandments is also obvious in that salvation in Jesus Christ is connected to obedience to these commandments.[231]

Another important appeal in *1 Clement* is τὸ καλόν. After describing the negative and serious consequences of jealousy and strife, the author exhorts the Corinthians to turn to the glorious and venerable rule of tradition and see what is good (καλός) in the sight of the Creator.[232] By means of a quotation from Isaiah, which basically aims to

---

[228]That the appeal to the just plays an important role is reflected in the frequent use of words with the word stem δικαιο-. Cf. G. BRUNNER, *Die theologische Mitte des ersten Klemensbriefs* (1972) 64, who says that the word stem δικαιο- occurs 4,7 times per 1000 words. By way of comparison the word stem occurs 1,7 times per 1000 words in the New Testament.

[229]*1 Clem.* 1:3.

[230]μηδὲ ἐν τοῖς νομίμοις τῶν προσταγμάτων αὐτοῦ πορεύεσθαι, *1 Clem.* 3:4.

[231]In these two passages the noun πρόσταγμα is used. It is not likely that Clement distinguishes qualitatively between πρόσταγμα and νόμος; both are expressions of the will of God and thus the ultimate *lex* for a Christian Church.

[232]*1 Clem* 7:2. The expression "to do τὰ καλά before him" is to be found three more times: once in 21:1, "Take heed, beloved, lest his many good works towards us become a judgment on us, if we do not good (τὰ καλά) and virtuous deeds before him in concord," and twice in the rather long prayer in which Clement among other things prays that God will guide their steps "to do the things which are τὰ καλά and pleasing before" God (60:2), and that the rulers must behave according to that which is "good and pleasing" (61:2).

show that repentance has been possible in every time and in every generation, the Corinthians are encouraged to cease from their wickedness and learn to do good (καλός) instead (8:4). Also, Clement describes the admonition to submit to the will of God, which involves ceasing from sedition and strife and submitting to the legitimate presbyters, as "good (καλός) and beyond measure helpful" (56:2). Furthermore, the term καλός appears twice in a comparative construction (46:8, 51:3).

It should also be noted that *1 Clement* makes an appeal to the glory and the reputation of the Corinthians. As a consequence of the present strife, the venerable (σεμνός) and famous (περιβόητος) name of the Church in Corinth, a name worthy of all men's love, has been greatly reviled (μεγάλως βλασφημηθῆαι, 1:1). Likewise, their reputed love for the brethren (τὸ σεμνὸς τῆς περιβοήτου φιλαδελφίας) has diminished (47:5). Therefore, Clement admonishes them to beseech God that he may restore the honourable (σεμνός) love of brethren (48:1).

Clement frequently describes individuals who set examples to be imitated as famous and noble. In other words, they have an honourable remembrance. Peter and Paul are characterised as noble examples (τὰ γενναῖα ὑποδείγματα),[233] and Paul has "gained the noble fame (κλέος) of his life".[234] Besides these, the author exhorts the Corinthians to imitate other Biblical persons whose qualities are praised.[235]

We may ask why the author of *1 Clement* emphasizes the fame and the venerable character of those individuals who set an example and why he makes references to the nobility and the fame of the Corinthian church. With respect to the former we believe that the main purpose is to amplify *ethos* and thereby increase their authority as good examples to follow. Also, it appears to be implied that the Christians in Corinth will gain some of the same fame and good reputation as these individuals, if they behave in accordance with the example they set. As to the latter, that Clement consciously plays upon the audience's desire for fame and good reputation seems to be rather obvious, if we take into consideration the explicit reference to σεμνός (1:1; 48:1), περιβόητος (1:1) and κλέος (5:6; 54:3). However, most noteworthy in this regard is the fact that the appeal to glory and good remembrance is an appropriate appeal in deliberative rhetoric, as we have seen above.[236]

2.3.4.1. Summary Appeals in 1 Clement

The investigation of τελικὰ κεφάλαια has demonstrated that Clement, as prescribed in ancient rhetorical handbooks and reflected in actual deliberative speeches and letters, employs standard appeals in deliberative rhetoric in order to persuade the Corinthian Christians to re-establish concord. Although the *terminus technicus* for the basic appeal, τὸ συμφέρον, does not occur, the negative appeal to βλαβερός, and in particular to κίνδυνος, is prevalent. Furthermore, the emphasis on the facts that the present

---

[233] *1 Clem.* 5:1.
[234] *1 Clem.* 5:6.
[235] Elijah, Elisha, Ezekeil, Abraham, David, *1 Clem.* 17-19.
[236] See Cic. *Inv. Rhet.* 2.55; [*Rhet. Her.*] 3.2.3; 3.4.7-8.

course of action leads to death and that the proposed course of action leads to salvation functions as a strong implicit appeal to the advantageous. In addition, he makes appeals to τὸ δίκαιον, τὸ νόμιμον, τὸ καλόν and to glory and good remembrance. In other words, the nature of the appeals which Clement employs in his argumentation is another indication that the species of rhetoric he employs is deliberative.

2.4. The Use and Function of Examples

2.4.1. Examples in Deliberative Rhetoric in General

So far we have discussed the time reference, the hortatory and dissuasive aspect, and the appeals in deliberative rhetoric. We shall now turn to the characteristic forms of proof (πίστις) in this type of rhetoric. Aristotle distinguishes between two fundamental forms of proof: example (παράδειγμα) and enthymeme (ἐνθύμημα).[237] There is general agreement in the whole rhetorical tradition that "examples are most suitable for deliberative speakers, for it is by examination of the past that we divine and judge the future".[238] However, this does not mean that proof by examples cannot be applied in forensic rhetoric as well.[239] But it should be underscored that in deliberative rhetoric, in contrast to forensic rhetoric, examples constitute a basic element of the argumentation. This means that it is not sufficient simply to identify and count examples, and to draw a conclusion regarding genre from this observation.[240] The decisive factor is how the examples function in the argumentation.[241] One main reason why examples may be an

---

[237]Arist. Rh. 2.20.1. Cf. J. MARTIN, Antike Rhetorik (1974) 102: "Die πίστεις teilt Aristoteles ein in solche, die durch Induktion (ἐπαγωγή) gebildet werden und in solche, die durch Syllogismus oder auch scheinbaren Syllogismus gebildet werden. Der Syllogismus der Rhetorik ist das ἐνθύμημα, die Induktion das παράδειγμα". However, Aristotle asserts that argumentation using enthymemes is met with greater approval (Arist. Rh. 1.2.10f.). But if the orator does not have any enthymemes, Aristotle advises him to "employ examples as demonstrative proofs (ἀπόδειξις), for conviction (πίστις) is produced by these" (Rh. 2.20.9).

[238]Arist. Rh. 1.9.40. Cf. also 3.17.5; Cic. [Rhet. Her.] 3.5.9; Quint. Inst. 3.8.36; and further R. VOLKMANN, Die Rhetorik der Griechen und Römer in systematischer Ubersicht (1885) 298; G. A. KENNEDY, The Art of Persuasion in Greece (1963) 204; idem, New Testament Interpretation (1984) 36. There is some discussion and minor differences concerning the designation and categorisation. Aristotle distinguishes between two types of παράδειγμα: things that actually happened (πράγματα προγεγενημένα) and stories that one invents (τὸ αὐτὸν ποειεῖν), which he further divides into comparison (παραβολή) and fable (λόγος) (Rh. 2.20.2). Arist. [Rh. Al.] mentions only historical examples (παράδειγμα) (8.1429a 21-29). Cicero places exemplum in a subcategory under comparison (Inv. Rhet. 1.30.49), but in Topica he places exemplum in a subcategory of similitudo (10.44). Quintilian's classification agrees with Aristotle's, for he says that παράδειγμα / exemplum consists of παράδειγμα / exemplum (= historical example) and παραβολή / similtudo (Inst. 5.11.1-2).

[239]B. J. PRICE, Παράδειγμα and Exemplum in Ancient Rhetorical Theory (1975) 101.

[240]A. LUMPE, "Exemplum", RAC 6 (1966) 1230-39, has shown in this overview of classical theory and the use of examples in ancient literature that examples occur in many types of literature.

efficient tool in an argumentation is simply expressed by the universal truth that people choose to do "all things that those whom they admire deliberately choose to do".[242]

If we ask what kind of examples the theorists find appropriate, we will see that all agree that examples from the past should be applied.[243] However, some of the theorists emphasized the value of "examples that are akin to the case and those that are nearest in time or place to our hearers".[244] The examples could be historical or invented,[245] and

---

[241]This is correctly emphasized by M. M. Mitchell, *Paul and the Rhetoric of Reconciliation* (1991) 40, n. 94. Cf. also Arist. *Rh.* 20.20.9 (quoted above). In this passage Aristotle also stresses that, if deductive proofs are not possible, the orator must use not only one example, but a series of examples. However, among the theorists there was some discussion about the function of the examples. Arist. [*Rh. Al.*], who gives only a small amount of information concerning the use of examples, seems basically to agree with Aristotle. The author asserts that examples "should be employed on occasions when your statement of the case is unconvincing (ἄπιστος) and you desire to illustrate it, if it cannot be proved by the argument from probability, in order that your audience may be more ready to believe your statement …" (8.1429a 22ff.). Cic. [*Rhet. Her.*] on the other hand, stresses, in disagreement with those who say examples correspond to testimony, that examples should never function as proofs but merely as illustrations; "First and foremost, examples are set forth, not to confirm or bear witness, but to clarify (*Primum omnium, exempla ponuntur nec confirmandi neque testificandi causa, sed demonstrandi*) … The difference between testimony and example is this: by example we clarify the nature of our statement, while by testimony we establish its truth" (4.3.5). B. J. Price, Παράδειγμα *and Exemplum in Ancient Rhetorical Theory* (1975) has, however, observed a discrepancy between theory and practice. In Cic. [*Rhet. Her.*] 2.19.29 examples are used to strengthen the proof by argument from analogy rather than merely to adorn it (90). Cicero actually says very little about the function of examples. However, it is obvious that examples are designed to persuade the audience by affecting their emotions according to B. J. Price, Παράδειγμα *and Exemplum in Ancient Rhetorical Theory* (1975) 127. Also, Cicero's *practice* shows that he found the examples to be a very effective tool for argumentation, so M. R. Cosby, *The Rhetorical Composition and Function of Hebrews 11* (1988) 102. Quint. holds that examples are a kind of proof and that they may serve to convince the audience of a proposed action (*Inst.* 5.11.1).

[242]Arist. *Rh.* 1.6.29.

[243]E.g. Arist. *Rh.* 1.9.40; 3.17.5; [*Rh. Al.*] 8.1429a.21; Cic. *Inv. Rhet.* 1.30.49; Quint. *Inst.* 5.11.1-2. For "theoretical" statements in real speeches and letters cf. Andoc. 3.2: "one must use the past as a guide to the future, gentlemen"; 3.32: "The examples (παράδειγμα) furnished by our past mistakes are enough to prevent men of sense from repeating them"; Aristid. *Or.*23.41: "You could prove this by the example of past events"; *Or.* 24:23: "there is this benefit to be gained from the past, the application of well known examples (παράδειγμα) to the present".

[244]Arist. [*Rh.Al.*] 32.1439a 1-3. According to this author, *exempla* persuasively recount well-known events from *recent* history to illustrate the validity of a case. And further, Cic. [*Rhet. Her.*] asserts, in polemic against the Greek rhetorical tradition that "we need not yield to antiquity in everything" (4.2.4). Cf. also B. J. Price, Παράδειγμα *and Exemplum in Ancient Rhetorical Theory* (1975) 27. The discussion of past contra present examples is reflected in actual speeches and letters themselves among which we mention some examples: "… but I appeal to you and yours, using as examples not aliens, but members of your own family" (Isoc. *Or.* 9.77); "For since you have no need to follow alien examples but have before you one from your own house …" (Isoc. *Or.* 5.113) and "… for you need not go abroad for examples to teach you how to win success" (Dem. *Or.* 3.23). For other examples and for examples in letters, see R. Volkmann, *Die Rhetorik der Griechen und Römer in systematischer Übersicht* (1885) 236, and M. M. Mitchell, *Paul and the Rhetoric of Reconciliation* (1991) 40.

could be either positive, i.e. an example to follow, or negative, i.e. a cautionary example.[246] It is not surprising that orators often presented examples of people who were
admired and highly respected by the audience and urged the audience to act as they
did.[247]

The very essence in deliberative proof by examples is that the examples function as
an implicit, and in many cases even as an explicit, appeal to the audience to imitate the
positive and to avoid the negative. If we turn to actual discourses and letters, we will see
that the practice confirms the theory prescribed in the ancient handbooks.[248] First we
shall pay attention to some examples from Isocrates. As is common in deliberative rhetoric, the orator recommends the audience to imitate the *forefathers*.

> *We know, moreover, that those who became the founders of this city entered the
> Peloponnesus with but a small army and yet made themselves masters of many pow-
> erful states. It were fitting, then, to imitate (μιμήσασθαι) our forefathers and, by
> retracing our steps, now that we have stumbled in our course, try to win back the
> honours and the dominions which were formerly ours (Or. 6.82).*

In another passage he argues that the Athenians should return to the state of democracy of the past by appealing to them to imitate their forefathers:

> *Now I have come before you and spoken this discourse, believing that if we will only
> imitate (μιμέομαι) our ancestors we shall both deliver ourselves from our present ills
> and become the saviours, not of Athens alone, but of all the Hellenes; but it is for you
> to weigh all that I have said and cast your votes according to your judgement of what is
> best for Athens (συμφέρειν τῇ πόλει, Or. 7.84).*

In *On the Peace* he first refutes the claim of the opponents to imitate the examples put
forward by them, and then he makes an appeal to the audience to follow the good
examples put forward by himself:

---

[245]See n. 238 above; A. LUMPE, "Exemplum", *RAC* 6 (1966) 1230f.; J. MARTIN, *Antike Rhetorik*
(1974) 119-121; B. J. PRICE, *Παράδειγμα and Exemplum in Ancient Rhetorical Theory* (1975) 27-39.
For further literature, see M. M. MITCHELL, *Paul and the Rhetoric of Reconciliation* (1991) 41, n. 101.

[246]Arist. [*Rh. Al.*] 1429a. 21f. describes the negative examples as παραδείγματα ἐναντίαι. M. M.
MITCHELL, *Paul and the Rhetoric of Reconciliation* (1991) states that "in deliberative speeches, both
positive and negative παραδείγματα are used" (40f., n. 98). She makes reference to K. JOST, *Das Beispiel und Vorbild der Vorfahren bei den attischen Rednern und Geschichtschreibern bis Demosthenes*
(1936) 19.32 on "warnende Beispiele" who quotes Dem. *Or.* 6.19; 19.232, 263; 23.107, 116; Andoc.
3.32.

[247]For more text references, see M. M. MITCHELL, *Paul and the Rhetoric of Reconciliation* (1991)
41.

[248]For the appeal to imitation as an integral part of arguing by παράδειγμα in Isocratres and
Demosthens, see K. JOST, *Das Beispiel und der Vorfahren bei den attischen Rednern und Geschicht-
schreibern bis Demosthenes* (1936) 149-153, 159-161, 226-231. Cf. also M. M. MITCHELL, *Paul and the
Rhetoric of Reconciliation* (1991) 42-46, who takes the text examples from Jost.

> *For we have been depraved for a long time by men whose only ability is to cheat and delude – men who have held the people in such contempt that whenever they wish to bring about a state of war with any city, these very men who are paid for what they say have the audacity to tell us that we should follow the example of our ancestors (ὡς χρὴ τοὺς προγόνους μιμεῖσθαι) … Now I should be glad if they would inform me what ancestors they would have us imitate (Or. 8.36f.).*

Furthermore, in the same discourse, after having mentioned different people not worthy of imitation, he concludes by saying that "we must emulate and imitate (μιμήσασθαι) the position held by kings of Lacedaemon" (Or. 8.143).

Proof by means of example, in many cases followed by an explicit appeal to imitate the actual examples given, is abundant in deliberative texts throughout the rhetorical tradition and is to be found in discourses approximately contemporary with *1 Clement*. Dio Chrysostom, for instance, presented Rome as an example for the citizens of Apameia to follow: "In emulation (μιμούμενος) of that city [Rome] it is fitting that you should show yourselves gentle and magnanimous toward men who are close to you" (Or. 41.10). And Aelius Aristides, when counselling the Rhodians to cease from faction and establish concord, exhorts them to "imitate the form and fashion of a household" (Or. 24.32).[249]

2.4.2. Examples in 1 Clement

Just from a quick glance through *1 Clement*, the reader will recognise the abundant use of examples. In line with both the theory and practice of deliberative rhetoric, the author employs proof by example. This is particularly clear from the frequent lists of examples given. We do not intend to examine these lists thoroughly in this connection, but rather to identify them and make some preliminary comments with respect to the question of genre.[250]

In 3:4 the author states that ζῆλος caused death to enter the world. In order to prove this assertion, Clement presents several examples taken from the Old Testament of the terrible consequences of ζῆλος καὶ φθόνος.[251] Among other things, jealousy and envy led to fratricide, persecution and slavery. But Clement does not stop with examples from "the old time", he continues with ὑπόδειγμα from "the days nearest to us" (5:1). He is thinking of Peter and Paul who became victims of jealousy and envy

---

[249]For further text references, see M. M. MITCHELL, *Paul and Rhetoric of Reconciliation* (1991) 44, note 112. As an illustration of proof by example and the call to imitation in deliberative letters Mitchell quotes Pl. *Ep.* 7, where he exhorts the friends of Dion to imitate their dead leader: "I counsel (συμβουλεύω) you, his friends, to imitate (μιμεῖσθαι) Dion in his devotion to his fatherland and in his temperate mode of life" (7.336C), and Isoc. *Ep.* 2.5, where he counsels Philip by letter: "I think that you would profitably (συμφέρω) imitate (μιμεῖσθαι) the fashion in which our city-states conduct the business of warfare".

[250] We will deal more thoroughly with the argumentative function of the examples in chap. 4.

[251]Clement mentions the Cain-Abel story, the Jacob-Esau story, the persecution of Joseph, Moses' flight from Pharaoh, Aaron and Miram who were lodged outside the camp, Dathan and Abiram, and the persecution of David (4:1-13).

and because of these vices "were persecuted and contended unto death" (5:2). Besides these "pillars of the Church", many of the chosen endured many indignities and tortures caused by ζῆλος (6:1). He concludes the list of examples by stating that ζῆλος καὶ ἔρις "have overthrown great cities, and rooted up mighty nations" (6:4). In this way he confirms the assertion that ζῆλος caused death to enter the world. Concerning the list of examples we observe that in line with the theory and practice of deliberative rhetoric Clement uses respected and admired examples of the forefathers and also that he employs well-known examples from recent history as proofs.[252] After having demonstrated that the Master has given occasion for repentance to all generations by means of examples taken from the Old Testament, Clement exhorts the Corinthians to obey God's will and cease from strife and jealousy which leads to death (9:1).[253] The challenge to "fix our gaze" on those who perfectly served him, introduces a list consisting of examples taken from the Old Testament (9:2). The call to pay attention to these examples from the past functions as an appeal to imitate them. The examples aim to concretely demonstrate the blessings that follow from obedience to God's will. In contrast with the present state of affairs, which is marked by a failure to obey God's will, and which leads to death, the examples demonstrate that obedience leads to blessing and salvation.[254] Thus the list of examples functions as proof of the advantage to the Corinthian Church of following the exhortation given in 9:1.

In *1 Clem.* 16:1 a list begins by giving examples of the humility (ταπεινοφροσύνη) shown by many noble men of the Christian tradition. The author emphasizes that Christ came not in pride and arrogance but in humility (16:2). He concludes chapter 16 by paying attention to Christ's example (ὑπογραμμός) and poses the rhetorical question "for if the Lord was thus humble-minded, what shall we do ...?" (16:17). We note that the author explicitly states that Christ is given to them as an example. It is, of course, not surprising that the founder of Christianity is presented as an example to imitate. Nevertheless, in the light of the use and function of examples in deliberative rhetoric, it is interesting to note that Clement emphasizes this particular aspect of Christ. In line with deliberative rhetoric the author goes on to call on the audience to "be imitators" (μιμηταὶ γενώμεθα) of some noble examples (17:1). He calls on the Corinthian Church to imitate the following humble-minded "ancestors": Elijah, Elisha, Esekiel, Abraham, Job and David (*1 Clem.* 17-18). The list of examples serves to underscore the greatness of humility, and thus is a proof of the necessity to follow the exhortation to be humble-mined as presented previously in the letter (13:1).

In 45:3 Clement asserts that nowhere in the Holy Scriptures can it be found "that the righteous have been cast out by holy men". On the contrary, the righteous were per-

---

[252]Cf. above nn. 244f.

[253]Clement put forward just two examples of the possibility of repentance: Those who obeyed, Noah and Jonah, were saved.

[254]Enoch was found righteous in obedience, and was translated, and death did not befall him (9:3); through Noah the Master saved the living creatures; Abraham was regarded as righteous and a son was given to him in his old age (10:6f.); Lot was saved from Sodom (11:1); the harlot Rahab was saved (12:1).

secuted by the wicked. As proof Clement refers to Daniel who was cast to the lions and
to Ananias, Azarias and Misael who were shut up in the fiery furnace (45:6-7). They
endured the calamities, however, and "were enrolled by God in his memorial for ever
and ever" (45:8). Against this background Clement exhorts the Christians in Corinth
to be imitators of such examples: "We also, brethren, must therefore cleave to such
examples" (ὑποδείγμασιν κολληθῆναι, 46:1).

In addition to the above, lists that take examples from the Old Testament and Early
Christian tradition are to be found in 31:2-4, 45:4-8, 51:3-5, 52:2-53:5, and 55:2-6.

Additionally, we should note that explicit calls to follow examples occur at two
other points in the letter. In 33:8 the Lord himself is used as a model of good works and
Clement exhorts his audience to "follow his will without delay". Furthermore, in the
peroratio[255] examples of the fathers previously presented in the letter are described as
great examples that the Corinthians Christians should follow (62:2-63:1).[256]

So far we may say that, in view of the use of lists of examples and the explicit call to
imitate the forefathers, proof by example plays an important role in *1 Clement*. However, Clement does not use the common Greek term used for examples, i.e.
παράδειγμα found in either the rhetorical handbooks or in actual deliberative
speeches, but ὑπόδειγμα, as we have seen.[257] It is noteworthy that in the New Testament, in Early Christian literature and in Hellenistic Judaism the term ὑπόδειγμα is
the term normally used for "example".[258] This fact indicates that Clement has become
influenced by Hellenistic Judaism and Early Christian traditions regarding this form of
argumentation. Furthermore, two other observations appear at first sight to point in
the same direction. First, it is obvious that the bulk of the content of the lists of examples is taken from the Old Testament. Clement goes into detail to some extent by mentioning names and giving information about concrete events.[259] The picture is quite
different when the author draws on examples (ὑπόδειγμα) from the gentiles (55:1).
Here he does not mention names or connect the examples to concrete historical epi-
sodes, but is brief and general in his references.[260] Secondly, lists of examples were to be
found in the Old Testament, in Hellenistic Judaism and in the Christian tradition prior
to Clement.[261]

That a Christian author uses examples from the Holy Scriptures and designates
them with the term commonly used in the Christian tradition is not at all surprising. It
is exactly what we should expect. A Christian has obtained a new citizenship and also

---

[255]For the definition and function of the *peroratio* in *1 Clement*, see pp. 226-232.

[256]"It is therefore right that we should respect so many and so great examples (ὑποδείγμασιν),
and bow the neck, and take up the position of obedience" (63:1).

[257]5:1 (2x); 6:1; 46:1; 55:1; 63:1.

[258]E.g., John 13:15; Heb 4:11; Jas 5:10; 2 Pet. 2:6; 2 Macc 6:28, 31; Sir 44:16.

[259]E.g., *1 Clem.* 4-7; 9-12; 17f.

[260]However, the example of the Phoenix, which functions as proof of a resurrection in the future,
is given in more detail (*1 Clem.* 25).

[261]E.g., Ezek 20; 1 Macc 2:51-60; 3 Macc 2:3-8; 6:2-8; 4 Macc 16:15-23; 18:9-19; Sir 44-50; Heb. 11.
For more references, see A. LUMPE, "Exemplum", *RAC* (1966) 1240f.

new "ancestors". It is therefore almost self-evident that the author should turn to these respected and admired "ancestors" (πατήρ)[262] to find appropriate examples as proof in his argumentation.[263] Nor it is surprising that Clement has learned from and has become inspired by Early Christian authors with good rhetorical skills, e.g., the author of Hebrews.[264] Therefore, one may not exclude the possibility that to a great extent Clement could have learned how to apply the predominantly biblical examples in his argumentation also from the Graeco-Roman rhetorical tradition, in so far as the lists of examples function exactly as prescribed in the ancient handbooks and are practised in actual deliberative speeches.[265]

So far, we have dealt with lists of examples consisting of historical examples from the Old Testament and the Early Christian tradition. In addition, Clement makes use of many invented examples. He employs the metaphor of the body (σῶμα)[266] and the analogy of an army[267] to prove the necessity of a mutual subjection and the advantage of a certain mixture of the great and the small. In *1 Clem.* 20 the peace and harmony of the universe is presented as an example to the Christians in Corinth. In 1:3 the author describes the previous good conditions in the Corinthian Church in terms of a household.[268] This praise of previous conditions functions as an example of how the state of being should have been in the Church. Concerning the question of genre it is significant that these invented examples are common in Greek political thought and deliberative rhetoric when an orator appeals to his audience to cease from factionalism and to pursue concord.[269] As will be demonstrated at a later point in this study, although

---

[262]*1 Clem.* 62:2.

[263]Regarding the attic orators it is argued that they "chose their historical examples carefully and in so doing took into consideration the audience's knowledge of history and opinions towards events and persons held by it", I. WORTHINGTON, *A Historical Commentary on Dinarchus* (1992) 19. Similar to this practise Clement's choice of examples takes into consideration the Corinthians' knowledge of the biblical history and their attitude towards the actual examples.

[264]Cf. P. LAMPE, *Die stadtrömischen Christen in den ersten beiden Jahrhunderten* (1989) 181, and M. R. COSBY, *The Rhetorical Composition and Function of Hebrews 11* (1988) 19, who maintains that Clement has "copied the technique of Hebrews 11".

[265]W. JAEGER, *Early Christianity and Greek Paideia* (1961) 13 describes Clement as the second Demosthens because of the similarity between them in applying examples. For the relationship between the literary methodological strategy in a text and the concrete content, see E. PLÜMACHER, *Lukas als hellenistischer Schriftsteller* (1972) 50f.: "Diese Methode, durch bewußte, an einem bestimmten literarischen Vorbild orientierte Stilisierung des zur Darstellung kommenden im Leser Assoziationen an eben dieses Vorbild hervorzurufen hat nicht erst Lukas entwickelt. Sie kennzeichnet vielmehr eine ganze Epoche hellenistischer Literatur … *Dabei beschränkt sich der Vergleich selbstverständlich auf die Methode des Hervorrufens von literarischen Assoziationen und bezieht sich natürlich nicht auf den Gegenstand dieser Assoziationen"* (italics mine).

[266]Our own σῶμα (37:5), the Christians as τὰ μέλη τοῦ Χριστοῦ (46:7).

[267]*1 Clem.* 37:1-4.

[268]Cf. also *1 Clem.* 21:6-8.

[269]The body (Dio Chrys. *Or.* 34.18, 20; 38:11-12; 39.5; 41:9; Aristid. *Or.* 23.31; 24:16), an army (Aristid. *Or.* 23.34), the universe (Dio Chrys. *Or.* 38.11; 40:35-39; 48.14-15; Aristid. *Or.* 23.76-77; 24.42), a household (Dio Chrys. *Or.* 38.15; Aristid. *Or.* 24.7-8, 32-34). These invented examples will be dealt with in chap. 3.

Clement modifies and uses the examples in a Christian framework, the fact that he *uses* such examples indicates that the author is familiar with the current rhetorical tradition.

Furthermore, Clement employs the change of day and night and the myth of the Phoenix as examples in order to demonstrate that a resurrection will take place in the future.[270] Also, like Paul Clement employs a personification of ἀγάπη which is followed by an application to the Corinthian Church as an example.

2.5. Appropriate Subjects in Deliberative Rhetoric

So far we have seen that the hallmarks of deliberative rhetoric are to be found in *1 Clement*: the hortatory and dissuasive aspect, the future used as the basic time reference, a standard set of appeals and proof by examples. These facts indicate that *1 Clement* is deliberative rhetoric. However, in order to offer a definitive determination of the rhetorical genre of the letter, we must demonstrate according to the previously discussed methodology that the main theme of *1 Clement* is appropriate to deliberative rhetoric.

Ancient rhetorical handbooks operate with particular topics appropriate for each of the three main genres. Deliberative rhetoric deals with public affairs of common interest for the city.[271] Aristotle, for instance, states that:

> The most important subjects about which all men deliberate (βουλεύονται) and deliberative orators (οἱ συμβουλεύοντες) harangue, are five in number, to wit: ways and means, war and peace, the defence of the country, imports and exports, legislation (Rh.1.4.7).[272]

Similar lists which confirm that such topics were common and appropriate in deliberative rhetoric are to be found in handbooks both prior to and later than Aristotle. Anaximenes, the author of *Rhetorica ad Alexandrum*, enlarge the number of topics, but the resemblance is apparent.[273] That such political topics were appropriate in deliberative rhetoric down to the Graeco-Roman period is attested by Cicero,[274] Quintilian[275] and Dio Chrysostom[276]. Concerning the present study it is interesting to note that the topics of *war* and *peace* (πόλεμος καὶ εἰρήνη) occur in every list.[277]

---

[270]*1 Clem.* 24:2-25:5.

[271]In general, see R. VOLKMANN, *Die Rhetorik der Griechen und Römer in systematischer Übersicht* (1885) 294; J. MARTIN, *Antike Rhetorik* (1974) 168f.

[272]περί τε πόρων, καὶ πολέμου καὶ εἰρήνης, ἔτι δὲ περὶ φυλακῆς τῆς χώρας, καὶ τῶν εἰσαγομένων καὶ ἐξαγομένων, καὶ περὶ νομοθεσίας (1.4.7).

[273]Anaximenes operates with seven topics (*Rh.* 2.2.1423a 22ff.; 2.3.1423a 30-1425b 35 according to J. MARTIN, *Antike Rhetorik* [1974] 168f.): religious ritual, legislation, the form of the constitution, alliances and treaties with other states, war (πόλεμος), peace (εἰρήνη) and finance.

[274]According to J. MARTIN, *Antike Rhetorik* (1974) 169 Cicero in *De Or.* 2.82.83 has Arist. *Rh.* 1.4.7 in view, "wenn er als Inhalt einer beratenden Rede, die *utilitas* als ihr Ziel betrachtet, angibt: *commoda pacis, opum, potentiae, vaectigalium, praesidi militum, ceterarum, quarum fructum utilitate metimur, itemque incommoda contrariorum*".

The rhetorical handbooks and the theoretical statements in actual speeches are confirmed in a vast number of extant discourses.[278] There is no doubt that war and peace are common topics in the rhetoric of the assembly, i.e. in deliberative rhetoric. Furthermore, we should note that another fundamental topic in deliberative rhetoric looms in connection with these topics, i.e. the topic of ὁμόνοια, concord, either within the city-state or between city-states that naturally belonged to the same area and thus constituted a body of cities.[279] The value of concord, the opposite of schism and strife, could not be overestimated in antiquity.[280] It is significant that a certain type of deliberative rhetoric emerged, i.e. συμβουλευτικὸς λόγος περὶ ὁμονοίας.[281] The basic function of such rhetoric was to persuade the audience to cease from factionalism (στάσις) and seek concord (ὁμόνοια).[282] Deliberations on factionalism and concord were thus common and appropriate subjects of deliberative discourses, both in speeches and in letters.

In the next chapter we shall argue that throughout the letter we find terms and *topoi* associated with the concept of concord. This approach requires us to go through the whole letter and focus upon the language of unity and sedition in *1 Clement*. Success in this task will provide a strong indicator that the topic of concord is the main theme of the letter. It would also show that the dominant theme was common in deliberative rhetoric.

---

[275]Quintilian states that for Cicero deliberative rhetoric deals chiefly with political subjects, as is consistent with the Greek rhetorical tradition. Also, when he continues and discusses the adviser's necessary level of knowledge, he states that the adviser has to be familiar with the following topics of deliberative rhetoric: peace, war, troops, public works and revenue (*Ideoque suasuris de pace, copiis, bello, operibus, vectigalibus, Inst.* 3.8.14).

[276]Dio Chrysostom asserts that a person who deliberates (βουλεύω) about public matters must have knowledge because "these matters are sometimes of the greatest importance, such as concord and friendship of families and states, peace and war, colonisation and the organisation of colonies, the treatment of children and of wives" (καὶ τούτων ἐνίοτε τῶν μεγίστων ὄντων, περὶ ὁμονοίας καὶ φιλίας οἰκιῶν καὶ πόλεων καὶ περὶ εἰρήνης καὶ πολέμου καὶ περὶ κατοικισμοῦ καὶ περὶ κατοικίσεως, περί τε παίδων καὶ περὶ γυναικῶν, *Or.* 26.8).

[277]Cf. *1 Clem.* 3:2 where war and captivity, among other things, are contrasted with the previous situation which had been marked by "a profound and rich peace" (2:2). In this investigation we will try to demonstrate that Clement's use of these and other political terms must be interpreted in the light of political rhetoric.

[278]E.g., Isoc. *Or.* 4-18; Dio Chrys. *Or.* 31; 34; 38-41; Aristid. *Or.* 23-24. In some passages πόλεμος and εἰρήνη occur together (Isoc. *Or.* 8.2, 12 ; Aristid. *Or.* 24.19).

[279]That this topic was appropriate in deliberative speeches is, as we have seen, maintained in the theory of rhetoric as well (Arist. [*Rh. Al.*] 1.1422a.10-15; 1.1422b.30-35), and in Dio Chrysostom's theoretical statement regarding important topics for those deliberating about public matters (*Or.* 26.8).

[280]The history and the use of this term will be dealt with in chap. 3.

[281]Thrasym. *Περὶ πολιτείας*; Antipho Soph. *Περὶ ὁμονοίας*; Isoc. *Or.* 4; *Ep.*3; 9; Pl. *Ep.* 7; Ps-SALL. *Ep.* 2; Dio Chrys. *Or.* 38-41; Aristid. *Or.* 23-24; (Herodes Atticus) *Περὶ πολιτείας*. Cf. the discussion in M. M. MITCHELL, *Paul and the Rhetoric of Reconciliation* (1991) 63, n. 207.

[282]For text references where στάσις functions as a counter term to ὁμόνοια, see the present investigation, pp. 86-91.

3. The Language of Unity and Sedition in 1 Clement

3.1. Introductory Remarks

In line with the previous discussion of methodology, the next step in the process of determining the rhetorical genre of *1 Clement* is to demonstrate that the main topic of the letter is of such a nature that it is appropriate to the use of deliberative rhetoric to communicate the author's message. Thus, by an investigation of the content and the language of Clement's argumentation, this chapter aims to show that political terms and *topoi* are to be found throughout the whole letter. More precisely, we intend to show that much of the argumentation is based on a series of *topoi* commonly used in extant discourses and letters that urged their audiences or readers to cease from sedition and establish concord in a political body. We will also show that throughout the letter we find terms associated with the concept of concord.[283] If this task is successful, we shall have established that topics related to concord constitute the main theme of the letter. This will advance our argument further that *1 Clement* ought to be classified as deliberative rhetoric on concord (συμβουλευτικὸς λόγος περὶ ὁμονοίας) and that the exhortation to ὁμόνοια determines the argumentation and the basic content of the letter.[284] However, we cannot state definitively what the main topic of the letter is before we have carried out a compositional analysis.

---

[283]The Greek term *topos* (Latin *locus*) literally means 'place' and refers to either a 'theme' or an 'argument'. Aristotle distinguished between *konoi topoi* (general topics) which could be used in any kind of rhetoric (*Rh.* 2.18-19), and *idioi topoi* (particular topics) "peculiar to each class of things" (*Rh.* 1.2.22). For particular topics in deliberative rhetoric, see the present investigation, chap. 2.5. From what we have said above it follows that in this investigation the latter type of *topos* is meant: we shall focus upon *topoi* specific to deliberative rhetoric urging concord. Furthermore, in line with Aristotle and other ancient rhetoricians, the term *topos* in the present study refers both to a 'theme' and an 'argument'. For a discussion of meanings of *topos*, see A. J. MALHERBE, *Moral Exhortation* (1986) 144f.; D. E. AUNE, *The New Testament in Its Literary Environment* (1987) 172-174; Ø. ANDERSEN, *I Retorikkens Hage* (1995) 154-160.

[284]W. C. VAN UNNIK, "Studies over de zogenaamde eerste brief van Clemens", *Mededelingen* (1970), serves as a good starting point for further research. As mentioned above, pp. 13f., van Unnik has given evidence in support of the fact that some of the stock terms in *1 Clement* belonged to the conventional political language that discussed concord and strife within different political bodies and has suggested that the letter ought to be read as deliberative rhetoric urging concord. However, van Unnik deals with only a few terms in *1 Clement*, in particular εἰρήνη, ὁμόνοια and συμβουλή, and does not deal with other terms and *topoi* in the letter associated with the concept of ὁμόνοια. Therefore, in building upon van Unnik's work, we intend to discuss a greater number of terms and *topoi* and to demonstrate that they are associated with the concept of ὁμόνοια.

Besides extant discourses and letters that urge concord, it is fruitful to also consult other types of literature, e.g., historical works. This is because a lot of literature deals with political issues and therefore contains political vocabulary that may throw new light upon certain terms in *1 Clement*. Here it is necessary to emphasize that we do not intend to deal in general with political terms and *topoi* used in the letter, but that we are confining ourselves to those terms and *topoi* which in one way or another are related to the concept of concord. The reason for taking our departure in the concept of concord is that the frequent use of the term ὁμόνοια together with its antonym στάσις, as well as their occurrences in important passages in the letter, indicate that these terms are the principal ones expressing concord and sedition respectively.[285]

In this investigation we define 'political' in a rather wide sense, as belonging to a body of citizens. A household, an assembly, a religious club or a city, etc., may be designated as political bodies. This means that ἡ ἐκκλησία τοῦ θεοῦ[286] in Corinth may be viewed as a political body, a body with its own structure and membership, and that the problem facing the church in Corinth may be described in political terms.

Of course, this does not mean that the author interprets the ultimate cause of the conflict from a political perspective. We shall, however, in the present investigation and particularly in this chapter, stress the political nature and background of some important terms and *topoi* associated with concord in antiquity which Clement utilises to settle the conflict at Corinth. With such a point of departure it follows that we shall deliberately take a somewhat one-sided approach in our discussion of the language of unity and sedition in *1 Clement*. Although Clement draws heavily upon the Septuagint, and to a lesser degree the New Testament, in his argumentation, and although it appears that he is influenced a great deal by Hellenistic Judaism, we shall consider the use of the actual terms in these contexts only to a limited degree. We shall not discuss different meanings of a term in detail, and we shall not discuss in any depth its use in different religious contexts either previous to or contemporary with the composition of *1 Clement*. We confine ourselves instead to focusing on the way in which the actual terms used are related to the concept of concord. Some may find such an approach too narrow and too one-sided and may rightly argue that it will exclude important aspects and connotations of the terms under consideration. However, in so far as ὁμόνοια and στάσις appear to be the principal terms expressing unity and sedition respectively, and in so far as these terms emerged and had a long history in the Greek world before the composition of *1 Clement*, it is important to consider the language of Clement in the context of his wider cultural milieu and attempt to see to what extend he reflects conventional terms and *topoi* associated with the ideal of concord. Although the use of a certain term or expression, for instance the important term δικαιοσύνη, certainly was influenced by the language of the LXX, it is at the same time also possible that Clement used the term because it belonged to the cluster of terms that was related to concord. By having chosen this limited approach, we hope to enhance our understanding of several

---

[285]See the present investigation chaps. 3.3.1 and 3.3.3.

[286]*1 Clem. praescr.*

terms in *1 Clement* and to discover why Clement found these terms appropriate when dealing with the topic of 'concord'.

3.2. Tools from the Theory of Semantic Fields

As just mentioned, we shall attempt to demonstrate in this chapter that throughout the letter Clement employs many conventional terms and *topoi* linked to the concept of ὁμόνοια. In order to do so we have to compare the language of *1 Clement* with other literature from antiquity dealing with concord. Such an approach, in which we take the term ὁμόνοια as our point of departure and try to identify terms and conceptions commonly connected with it, means that among other things we should consider the semantic field (or in German the Wortfeld) of the term 'concord'.

The expressions *semantic field* and *Wortfeld* are technical terms for a theory that has emerged in the field of linguistics. More accurately it may be described as a branch of structural semantics, a branch which has attracted much attention from linguistic scholars since the fundamental work by J. Trier in 1931.[287] Since we do not intend a full-scale application of this theory in the present investigation, it is not necessary to give it a detailed explanation. It suffices to focus upon a few basic points and some terms which are relevant to this study.

Although the work of J. Trier was significant for the advancing discussion and development of the theory, we need to focus at this point on some of the more fundamental ideas of Ferdinand de Saussure (1857-1913) "on whose theories practically the whole modern science of language, traditional linguistics as well as structuralism, is based".[288] It is possible to group his main thoughts under four headings: (1) the distinction between synchronic and diachronic approaches to language study, (2) the structural approach to language, (3) the connection between structuralism and conventionality, (4) the contrast between language system, i.e. *langue*, and the actual use of language, i.e. *parole*.[289]

It is the second heading in particular, i.e. the structural approach, which is fundamental for the further development of the theory of semantic fields. De Saussure regarded language as a system where the interrelated units obtain their value or meaning through their relationship to the whole. He says that "language is a system of interdependent terms (*les termes sont solidaires*) in which the value (*la valeur*) of each term results solely from the simultaneous presence of others". And further, "Within the same language, all words used to express related ideas limit each other reciprocally ... The

---

[287]For the early history of the theory, see H. GECKELER, *Strukturelle Semantik und Wortfeldtheorie* (1971) 86-114. Geckeler designates Trier as "den eigentlichen Begründer der Feldlehre" (102). See also L. VASSILYEV, "The Theory of Semantic Fields", *Linguistics* 137 (1974) 79-93.

[288]K. BALDINGER, *Semantic Theory* (1980) 3.

[289]For an outline of these headings, see A. C. THISELTON, "Semantics and New Testament Interpretation", *New Testament Interpretation* (1977) 79-89, and similarly J. LYONS, *Semantics 1* (1977), who gives an outline of "The Saussurean dichotomies" (238-250).

value (*la valeur*) of just any term is accordingly determined by its environment".[290] To summarize, a word or any other linguistic sign has no sense or meaning in isolation from others words or linguistic signs; words derive their meanings from the relationship of equivalence and contrast which hold among them.[291]

When de Saussure talked about the relationship of a linguistic unit to the rest of the system, he distinguished between *syntagmatic* and *associative* relationships. The *syntagmatic* is a *linear* relationship, where a linguistic unit is chained together with other words or units at the same level. "The syntagmatic relations which a unit contracts are those which it contracts by virtue of its combination (in a syntagm, or construction) with other units at the same level".[292] It is, however, with regard to the theory and significance of the associative or the *paradigmatic* relation (the common term applied by linguists after de Saussure) that de Saussure offers the most important contribution to the field of linguistics.[293] This term does not refer to the relationship between words or linguistic units found in an actual utterance, but to the relationship between a given item and any word or linguistic unit which might have been chosen in its place. Or, to use the words of J. Lyons, "The paradigmatic relations contracted by units are those which hold between a particular unit in a given syntagm and other units which are substitutable for it in the syntagm".[294] For example, in the utterance 'the old woman' the noun 'woman' is paradigmatically related to 'lady', 'female', 'man', 'cat', etc.[295]

De Saussure's view of the importance of regarding a linguistic unit in relation to its place in the system of language has become a basic point in modern structural linguistics. Lyons, for example, says that "the defining characteristic of modern, 'structural' linguistics" is the conviction that "linguistic units have no validity independently of their paradigmatic and syntagmatic relations with other units".[296]

---

[290]Cited from A. C. Thiselton, "Semantics and New Testament Interpretation", *New Testament Interpretation* (1977) 82.

[291]*Ibid.* 82. K. Baldinger, *Semantic Theory* (1980) 4, comments upon the new insight of de Saussure: "The elements of language are not lacking in mutual relationships with neighbouring elements, but rather, they all form a connecting network, so that change in one element may involve change in another element, on each level of language, from sound ... continuing on through morphology and syntax up to the lexicon".

[292]J. Lyons, *Semantics 1* (1977) 240. Let us take the expression 'the green house' as an example. In this statement the lexeme 'green' is syntagmatically related with the definite article 'the' and the noun 'house'. Furthermore, on a different level, the letters h-o-u-s-e are syntagmatically related in English, but not the letters o-s-h-u-e.

[293]J. Lyons, *Language and Linguistics* (1981): "It was one of Saussure's major achievements ... to have made clear, at the turn of the century, the interdependence of syntagmatic and substitutional relations" (96).

[294]J. Lyons, *Semantics 1* (1977) 241.

[295]For further discussion with examples, see e.g. J. Lyons, *Introduction to Theoretical Linguistics* (1969) 70-81; P. Cotterell & M. Turner, *Linguistics & Biblical Interpretation* (1989) 156-159.

[296]J. Lyons, *Introduction to Theoretical Linguistics* (1969) 74f. See also *idem, Language, Meaning and Context* (1981) 58, 75.

The 'father' of the Wortfeldtheorie adopted de Saussure's view of language as a system and built upon it in his works.[297] A primary concept of Trier was that on the synchronic level language might be structured in *Wortfelder* "die nebeneinander oder in hierarchischen Verhältnissen zueinander stehen können". Furthermore, each individual semantic field, for its part, forms a structured whole consisting of different linguistic units which are interrelated with each other.[298] Consequently, a basic point for Trier was that a word has sense only as a part of a larger whole, i.e. it obtains meaning only within a field.[299] An important question then is what constitutes a Wortfeld or in what way the linguistic units are interrelated. The following statement of Trier is illuminating:

> Die Geltung eines Wortes wird erst erkannt, wenn man sie gegen die Geltung der benachbarten und opponierenden Worte [*sic*] abgrenzt. Nur als Teil des Ganzen hat es Sinn; denn nur im Feld gibt es Bedeuten.[300]

This statement implies that Trier considers the semantic relationship of similarity of meaning and of opposition of meaning as constitutive in establishing a semantic field. Accordingly, A. C. Thiselton summarizes the task of a semanticist as Trier considered it:

> ... to set up lexical systems or sub-systems (Wortfelder) in terms of semantic relations of sameness or *similarity* of meaning (synonymy); of opposition or *incompatibility* of meaning (antonymy or complementarity); and of a special kind of *inclusiveness* of meaning (hyponymy) as where one word expresses a class ('furniture') to which the items belong ('chair', 'table').[301]

Since the work of Trier, the theory of semantic fields has been much discussed among scholars, and different definitions have been provided which attempt to define more precisely a semantic field and to develop a more accurate terminology. Here, we must restrict ourselves to noting E. Coseriu's definition:

---

[297] H. GECKELER, *Strukturelle Semantik und Wortfeldtheorie* (1971) 101f.

[298] J. TRIER, *Der deutsche Wortschatz* (1931) 1: "Das Wortfeld ist zeichenhaft zugeordnet einem mehr oder weniger geschlossenen Begriffskomplex, dessen innere Aufteilung sich im gegliederten Gefüge des Zeichenfeldes darstellt, in ihm für die Angehörigen einer Sprachgemeinschaft gegeben ist ... Die das Wortfeld, den Wortmantel, die Wortdecke mosaikartig zusammensetzenden Einzelworte legen – im Sinne ihrer Zahl und Lagerung – Grenzen in den Begriffsblock hinein und teilen ihn auf".

[299] *Ibid.* 2: "Die Worte [*sic*] im Feld stehen in gegenseitiger Abhängigkeit voneinander. Vom Gefüge des Ganzen her empfängt das Einzelwort seine inhaltliche begriffliche Bestimmtheit".

[300] *Ibid.* 6. In "Das sprachliche Feld", *Neue Jahrbücher für Wissenschaft und Jugendbildung* 10 (1934) 430, Trier offers the following definition of a Wortfeld: "Felder sind die zwischen den Einzelworten und dem Wortschatzganzen lebendigen sprachlichen Wirklichkeiten, die als Teilganze mit dem Wort das Merkmal gemeinsam haben, dass sie sich ergliedern, mit dem Wortschatz hingegen, dass sie sich ausgliedern".

[301] A. C. THISELTON, "Semantics and New Testament Interpretation", *New Testament Interpretation* (1977) 90.

Ein *Wortfeld* ist in struktureller Hinsicht ein lexikalisches Paradigma, das durch die Aufteilung eines lexikalischen Inhaltskontinuums unter verschiedene in der Sprache als Wörter gegebene Einheiten entsteht, die durch einfache inhaltsunterscheidende Züge in umittelbarer Opposition zueinander stehen.[302]

This definition is not incompatible with Trier's view. Both emphasize the need to consider the paradigmatic structure of a linguistic unit in terms of similarity and opposition in order to grasp the meaning of a term, since in the system of language an individual word receives its meaning only from the others. Both stress that the semantic study of a word must take its departure first of all from related meanings of words, and should not be based on different meanings of isolated words.[303]

Insofar as a semantic field is established, among other things, by semantic relations of sameness or similarity of meaning and of opposition or incompatibility between different linguistics units, the terms *synonymy* and *antonymy* are of great importance.[304] Although we can not enter into the scholarly discussion about synonymy and antonymy in detail, some comments are in order.

In order to call two words synonyms certain criteria must be fulfilled. Some linguistic scholars hold that the conditions for real or absolute synonyms are (1) interchangeability in all contexts, and (2) identity in both cognitive and emotive import.[305] According to H. Geckeler the great majority of linguistic scholars agree that no words fulfil these criteria and are of the opinion "dass im System der Sprache keine bedeutungsgleichen Wörter existieren". Therefore, it has been common practice to apply the

---

[302]E. Coseriu, "Lexikalische Solidaritäten", *Strukturelle Bedeutungslehre* (1978) 241. Adopted by H. Geckeler, *Strukturelle Semantik und Wortfeldtheorie* (1971) 244. See also E. Coseriu, "Die lexematischen Structuren", *Strukturelle Bedeutungslehre* (1978) 261. Cf. the similar definition of J. Lyons, *Semantics 1* (1977) 268: "Lexemes and other units that are semantically related, whether paradigmatically or syntagmatically, within a given language-system can be said to belong to, or to be members of, the same (semantic) field; and a field whose members are lexemes is a lexical field. A lexical field is therefore a paradigmatically and syntagmatically structured subset of the vocabulary".

[303]Cf. the criticism directed against some of the contributors to *TDNT* for having been too one-sidedly interested in the different meanings of single words and for not having dealt with the semantic relations between words, expressed first of all by J. Barr, *The Semantics of Biblical Language* (1961). For an outline of J. Barr's thought, see K. A. Tångberg, "Linguistics and Theology", *BiTr* 24 (1973) 301-310; P. Cotterell and M. Turner, *Linguistics and Biblical Interpretation* (1989) 109-123. When discussing the contribution of structural semantics to the lexicography of biblical languages, E. A. Nida, "Implications of Contemporary Linguistics for Biblical Scholarship", *JBL* 91 (1972) 85, asserts among other things that "In the first place, critical studies of meaning must be based primarily upon the analysis of related meanings of different words, not upon the different meanings of single words ... There are, of course, some very important reasons for this approach by domains, but most important is the fact that related meanings of different words are much closer in semantic space than are different meanings of the same word".

[304]"Synonymie und Antonymie lassen sich als inhaltliche Verhältnisse innerhalb des Wortfeldes darstellen", H. Geckeler, *Strukturelle Semantik und Wortfeldtheorie* (1971) 233f.

[305]So S. Ullmann, *Grundzüge der Semantik* (1967) 102; H. Geckeler, *Strukturelle Semantik und Wortfeldtheorie* (1971) 236. For the distinction between "cognitive" and "emotive" meaning, cf. J. Lyons, *Introduction to Theoretical Linguistics* (1969) 448-450.

term synonym not to "bedeutungsgleiche" but to "bedeutungsähnliche" words.[306] Other, more detailed, definitions of the term synonymy have been provided.[307] It appears, however, that in spite of the rather sophisticated terminology used, these add little or nothing to the broader definition just mentioned.[308] In the present work, when we apply the term synonym, it is used in line with this broader understanding of the term, e.g. the term synonym designates words not with identical but with a similar meaning.

Similarly, many different definitions of the term antonym or *opposition* (as preferred by some scholars) are offered.[309] C. K. Ogden, for instance, operates with nearly twenty distinctive types of semantic opposition.[310] H. Geckeler offers a simpler definition and distinguishes between three types of antonyms.

> Ein Antonym ist ein Wort, das zu einem anderen im kontradiktorischen (*gerade: krumm*), konträren (*kommen:gehen*) oder korrelativen (*Bruder: Schwester*) Gegensatz steht.[311]

Although this definition seems reasonable, in our use of the term *antonym* we will not distinguish between the three types. We will apply the term in a rather broad way, i.e. 'antonym' will be used to cover all kinds of incompatibility of sense.[312]

---

[306]H. GECKELER, *Strukturelle Semantik und Wortfeldtheorie* (1971) 235.

[307]J. LYONS, *Introduction to Theoretical Linguistics* (1969) 448, for instance, differentiates between (1) complete and total synonymy, (2) complete, but not total, (3) incomplete, but total and (4) incomplete, and not total. Regarding the first category we note that Lyons admits that beyond any doubt there are very few such synonyms in language.

[308]Cf. H. GECKELER, *Strukturelle Semantik und Wortfeldtheorie* (1971) 236f.: "Aber auch diese Linguisten [S. Ullmann, J. Lyons, O. Duchacek] können als Beispiele für 'pure synonyms', bzw. 'complete and total synonyms', bzw. 'synonymes parfaits absolus' höchstens auf den terminologischen Wortschatz verweisen".

[309]Already Aristotle offered relatively comprehensive and still valuable considerations and definitions of different forms of oppositions or antonymy, see W. RAIBLE, "Von der Allgegenwart des Gegensinns (und einiger anderer Relationen)", *ZRP* 97 (1981) 2-4; *idem*, "Zur Einleitung", *Zur Semantik des Französischen* (1983) 18.

[310]A. C. THISELTON, "Semantics and New Testament Interpretation", *New Testament Interpretation* (1977) 90. Also J. Lyon prefers the expression "oppositeness of meaning" instead of *antonymy* as a headterm as much as he distinguishes between three types of "oppositeness of meaning" of which the term *antonymy* depicts one of them. For the other two he uses the terms *complementary* and *converseness*, see J. LYONS, *Introduction to Theoretical Linguistics* (1969) 460-470. This usage was adopted by A. C. THISELTON, "Semantics and New Testament Interpretation", *New Testament Interpretation* (1977) 90 -92.

[311]H. GECKELER, *Strukturelle Semantik und Wortfeldtheorie* (1971) 238.

[312]J. LYONS, *Language and Linguistics* (1981) 154, calls such a use the broader interpretation of the term. Similarly W. RAIBLE, "Zur Einleitung", *Zur Semantik des Französischen* (1983,) who defines the broad meaning of 'antonymy' "als Oberbegriff für die Gegensatzrelation" (19). This is adopted by D. HELLHOLM, "Die argumentative Funktion von Römer 7.1-6", *NTS* 43 (1997) 392.

As noted above, one of the semantic relations within a semantic field is described as *inclusiveness* of meaning or *hyponymy.* [313] This paradigmatic relation "is the relation which holds between a more specific, or subordinate, lexeme and a more general, or superordinate, lexeme, as exemplified by such pairs as 'cow': 'animal', 'rose': 'flower'". [314] 'Cow' is a hyponym of 'animal' and 'rose' is a hyponym of 'flower'. More particular different kinds of roses would be hyponyms of 'rose'. In other words, such an approach to language makes it possible to arrange terms in a taxonomy or to talk about a hierarchy of language. In the literature colour systems are often referred to as providing an example:[315]

colour				
red	orange	yellow	green	blue
tangerine	gold	chartreuse		aqua

Here the term 'colour' is the superordinate word or the 'archilexeme', the technical term which is preferred by some scholars.[316] The terms lower down in the hierarchy, the hyponyms of colour, give meaning to and fill the archilexeme 'colour' with content. Although overlap is not allowed in a real taxonomy, the concept of taxonomy may also be used in a somewhat imprecise way. In the latter meaning we may say that the chart above is taxonomic.[317] According to A. Lehrer one finds, except in a relatively few domains, "structures that are hierarchically arranged but with some overlap".[318]

As noted above, in the present chapter we intend to demonstrate that throughout the letter Clement applies many *topoi* and terms associated with concord. This means that we hold that topics related to concord constitute the cardinal theme in *1 Clement*. Therefore it is possible to view ὁμόνοια (and εἰρήνη, see on the right below) as an archilexeme, and other terms which express unity, e.g. ἀγάπη, σωφροσύνη, δικαιοσύνη, τάξις, as hyponyms of this word in the letter. As will be shown below, these terms, among many others, are related to concord and give meaning to that concept. One should note, however, that in the case of the five occurrences of the phrase εἰρήνη καὶ ὁμόνοια (or in the opposite order), which Clement has adopted from the

---

[313]A. LEHRER, *Semantic Fields and Lexical Structure* (1974) holds this as "one of the most basic and important notions in structural semantics" (23).

[314]J. LYONS, *Semantics* 1 (1977) 291.

[315]E.g., A. LEHRER, *Semantic Fields and Lexical Structure* (1974) 24.

[316]Cf. H. GECKELER, *Strukturelle Semantik und Wortfeldtheorie* (1971) 245 who states that "Das *Archilexem* entspricht inhaltlich der Gesamtbedeutung eines Wortfeldes; es stellt als gemeinsamer Nenner die inhaltliche Grundlage für alle Feldglieder dar".

[317]A. LEHRER, *Semantic Fields and Lexical Structure* (1974) 24.

[318]*Ibid.* 24.

rhetorical tradition reflected in political discourse περὶ ὁμονοίας,[319] the terms
εἰρήνη and ὁμόνοια are used interchangeably and function as a hendiadys.[320] For
this reason, to include the term εἰρήνη as a part of the archilexeme for the above-mentioned terms appears to be correct. The relation between the archilexeme and some of
its hyponyms in *1 Clement* may thus be presented in the following taxonomy:

```
- - - - - - - - - - - - - - - - - - - - - εἰρήνη καὶ ὁμόνοια - - - - - - - - - - - - - - - - - - - - - - - -
     ἀγάπη        |      σωφροσύνη      |      δικαιοσύνη      |        τάχις
- - - - - - - - - - - - - - - - - - - - - - - - - - - - - - - - - - - - - - - - - - - - - - - - - - - - - -
```

As will be argued further on, the antonym of ὁμόνοια (καὶ εἰρήνη) in *1 Clement* is
στάσις. In the present chapter we shall attempt to show, among other things, that
Clement applies many terms and *topoi* which are associated with στάσις in antiquity,
and which therefore belong to the semantic field of ὁμόνοια. For instance, the terms
ἔρις, ζῆλος, φθόνος, ἀκαταστασία, and σχίσμα give meaning to the concept of
στάσις and could therefore be described as hyponyms. In many cases, however, it is
difficult to determine whether it is preferable to regard certain of the mentioned terms
as hyponyms or as synonyms when we operate with the above-mentioned broad definition of synonymy. This means that in the negative semantic field of ὁμόνοια we hold
that στάσις is the archlexeme with associated hyponyms which give meaning and content to it. Consequently we might present a taxonomy corresponding to that of
ὁμόνοια.

```
- - - - - - - - - - - - - - - - - - - - - - - - - - στάσις - - - - - - - - - - - - - - - - - - - - - - - - - -
    ἔρις      |      ζῆλος      |      φθόνος      |      ἀκαταστασία      |      σχίσμα
- - - - - - - - - - - - - - - - - - - - - - - - - - - - - - - - - - - - - - - - - - - - - - - - - - - - - - -
```

As previously mentioned, we are not going to apply the theory of semantic fields to its
fullest extent, but shall restrict ourselves to an application of the basic insights of this
theory in the present chapter. This will be accomplished by paying attention to the
semantic field of ὁμόνοια in an attempt to demonstrate that many terms and *topoi* in *1
Clement* must be understood in the light of their syntagmatic and paradigmatic relations to this term. We shall attempt to show that Clement reflects conventional language
of the ancient world in contexts where the topic of concord was treated in political bodies.[321] In order to show this, it is not necessary to consider whether an actual term
functions as a synonym or hyponym of ὁμόνοια and στάσις respectively. It will suffice
to demonstrate that it belongs to the semantic field of ὁμόνοια.

---

[319]For the use of this phrase εἰρήνη καὶ ὁμόνοια in political rhetoric urging concord in other literature in antiquity that deals with concord in a political body and in *1 Clement*, see chap. 3.4.

[320]For a definition of the concept hendiadyoin, see P. VON MÖLLENDORFF, "Hendiadyoin", *Historisches Wörterbuch der Rhetorik* 3, 1344-50, especially 1347.

We must emphasize here the need to distinguish between the semantic field of concord in *1 Clement* and the semantic field of concord in the entire literature of antiquity that deals with this topic. It follows from what we have just said that we shall focus primarily upon terms and *topoi* in *1 Clement* which show that Clement applies traditional language and *topoi*. A consequence of this approach is that certain terms that seem to be linked to the semantic field of concord in *1 Clement*, but do not appear to reflect conventional use, will not be dealt with. For example, this is the case with the term φιλοξενία. Clement appears to associate this virtue with concord. However, because we have not found a similar association in other literature from antiquity dealing with unity in a political body, this term will be treated as outside the scope of this study. Nevertheless, our approach will cover the majority of terms, including the most important ones that belong to the semantic field of concord in *1 Clement*.

3.3. Preliminary Remarks on ὁμόνοια, εἰρήνη and στάσις as Political Terms

3.3.1. ὁμόνοια

The term ὁμόνοια occurs 14 times[322] in *1 Clement*. It is the principal term for expressing the ideal state of unity that should have characterised the Corinthian Church. As previously mentioned, the author designates the whole letter as an appeal (ἔντευχις) for ὁμόνοια καὶ εἰρήνη (63:2).[323] Here he explicitly states the purpose of the letter, i.e. to urge the Corinthian Church to seek ὁμόνοια καὶ εἰρήνη. In line with this purpose, he presents the ὁμόνοια καὶ εἰρήνη of the universe as an example for the Christians in Corinth to follow (20:1-21:1). He then goes on to make several other references to it. He exhorts them to put on ὁμόνοια in meekness of spirit and continence (30:3), and to gather together with ὁμόνοια in conscience (34:7). Those who "perform the commandments of God in concord" are called blessed (50:5). Then he prays to the Lord that he should "give concord and peace to us and to all that dwell on the earth" (60:4). Finally, at the end of the letter, he exhorts the Corinthian Church to send back the Roman messengers quickly, in order that they may report the peace and concord which the Roman Church prays for and desires (65:1). This appeal for concord and peace is also reflected throughout the letter by the many admonitions to cease from the present strife and sedition.

---

[321]Cf. K. BERGER, *Exegese des Neuen Testaments* (1977), who says that "Semantische Felder sind mehr oder weniger konventionelle Wortverbindungen … Es handelt sich in der Tat um Sprachkonventionen, die je mehrmals auftreten müssen, um als solche erkannt zu werden. Nur auf der Basis der Konventionen sind dann individuelle, neue Wortverbindungen überhaupt erst feststellbar. Semantische Felder sind demnach regelmässig wiederkehrende Wortverbindungen" (138).

[322]*1 Clem.* 9:4; 11:2; 20:3,10, 11; 21:1; 30:3; 34:7; 49:5; 50:5; 60:4; 61:1; 63:2; 65:1. In addition the verb ὁμονοέω occurs one time (62:2).

[323]Cf. also 65:1 where the author asks to send back quickly the messengers from the Roman Church "in order that they may report the sooner the peace and concord which we pray for and desire".

How characteristic the term ὁμόνοια is in the letter becomes clear when we compare it with the frequency of the term in both anterior and contemporary Christian literature. It is quite striking that the word group does not occur at all in the NT. A possible explanation of this absence could be the infrequent occurrences of the term in LXX, eleven times altogether.[324] Among the other Apostolic Fathers the term occurs seven times in the letters of Ignatius[325] and twice in Hermas.[326] Both the high frequency of the term in *1 Clement* compared to contemporary Jewish and Christian literature and the important role it plays in the letter attests that ὁμόνοια is a stock term in *1 Clement*. Or more precisely, ὁμόνοια, in conjunction with the terms and conceptions associated with it, is *the cardinal* term.

As already indicated, the background of the term is not to be found in Jewish or Christian tradition, but occurs frequently in the Hellenistic world.[327] In this area the word group ὁμόνοια/ὁμονοέω had a relatively long history before the composition of *1 Clement*. The word group appeared at a very significant moment in Greek history, i.e. at the end of the Peloponnesian war.[328] At that time different *poleis* were facing factions and internal strife and the term expressed the challenge to establish ὁμόνοια in order to save the very *polis* itself.[329] That ὁμόνοια was regarded as of fundamental impor-

---

[324]Ὁμονοέω: Lev 20:5; Esth 4:17; Dan 2:43, ὁμόνοια: Pss 54:14; 82:5; Wis 10:5; 18:9; Sir 25:1; 4 Macc 3:21; 13:23, 25, according to E. Hatch and H. A. Redpath, *A Concordance to the Septuagient*, vol. II (1954) 993. After having outlined the occurrences and the use of ὁμόνοια/ὁμονοέω in the Jewish literature, G. Brunner, *Die theologische Mitte des ersten Klemensbriefes* (1972), correctly concludes by stating that "Sowohl die späte Zeit wie die Bedeutungen weisen auf hellenistische Herkunft des Begriffes hin, so dass man zur Aufhellung der Bedeutung der Wortgeschichte nachspüren und dafür ein längeres Verweilen im ausserbiblischen Bereich in Kauf nehmen muss" (135).

[325]Ignat. *Eph.* 4:1, 2; 13:1; *Magn.* 6:1; *Trall.* 12:2; *Phld* insc; 11:2.

[326]*Herm. Man.* 8:9; *Sim.* 9.15.2.

[327]For studies on the concept ὁμόνοια in the Graeco-Roman world, see H. Kramer, *Qvid valeat ὁμόνοια in Litteris Graecis* (1915); E. Skard, *Zwei religiös-politische Begriffe* (1932); J. de Romilly, "Vocabulaire et propagande ou les premiers emplois du mot ὁμόνοια", Melanges de Linguistique (1972) 199-209; A. Moulakis, *Homonoia* (1973); A. R. R. Sheppard, "Homonoia in The Greek Cities of The Roman Empire", *AncSoc* 15-17 (1984-86) 229-252; K. Thraede, "Homonoia (Eintracht)", *RAC* 16 (1994) 176-290.

[328]H. Kramer, *Qvid valeat ὁμόνοια in Litteris Graecis* (1915) 13; E. Skard, *Zwei religiös-politische Begriffe* (1932) 67; J. de Romilly, "Vocabulaire et propagande ou les premiers emplois du mot ὁμόνοια", Melanges de Linguistique (1972) 199-201; A. Moulakis, *Homonoia* (1973) 19-23; K. Thraede, "Homonoia (Eintracht)", *RAC* 16 (1994) 176-180.

[329]H. Kramer, *Qvid valeat ὁμόνοια in Litteris Graecis* (1915), summarizes the use of the term at this time by stating that "ex omnibus locis quos attulimus statuendum esse mihi videtur voci ὁμόνοια inde a temporibus quibus res publica Atheniensium certaminibus factionum valde perturbata est i.e. a fine belli Peloponnesiaci a scriptoribus vel oratoribus Atticis certam vim attributam esse: pacem et concordiam factionum, quae antea inter se vehementissime persequebantur" (27). Kramer's summary is based on a discussion of the following texts, pp. 16-26; Democr. frg. 249 D; 250 D; 255D; Archyt. frg. 3:9ff; Xen. *Mem.* 3.5.14-16; 4.4.16; 4.6.14; *Hell.* 2. 4.38; Thuc. 8.75; 93.3; Thrasym; Arist. *Ath. Pol.*39.6; 40.2f; Andoc. *De myst.* 73; 76; 106; 108; 109; Lys. *Or.* 2.18, 43, 63, 65; 25.20-23, 27, 30; Isoc. *Or* 18.44, 68. See also R. Höistad, *Cynic Hero and Cynic King* (1948) 108; A. Fuks, *The Ancestral Constitution* (1975) 102-106.

tance for a city is well attested throughout the Graeco-Roman period as well. According to Plutarch, for instance, the quest for ὁμόνοια and avoidance of sedition was the basic aim of local politics and were seen as the only way to save the city from destruction.[330] Likewise in the view of Dio Chrysostom, the establishment and maintenance of ὁμόνοια is a precondition for making good use of other advantages of city life.[331] This aspect is also emphasized by Aelius Aristides who states that those cities that maintain ὁμόνοια are the best to live in, in contrast to cities that are driven by στάσις, which is "a terrible, disruptive thing, and like consumption".[332] In short, it was a common thought that ὁμόνοια was the greatest value of a city.[333] The fundamental importance of ὁμόνοια was not limited to domestic affairs within a single city. It was also an essential political virtue in the relationships between cities that belonged to the same area,[334] and it was even seen as an expression of the ideal relationship between all Greeks, the ideal of a Pan-Hellenic concord.[335] However, the ideal of ὁμόνοια was not merely a political virtue that belonged to the domain of politicians. It was a universally recognised ideal and value that ought to penetrate the whole of society and was discussed in a variety of literary genres.[336] Accordingly, the ideal of ὁμόνοια was also applied to smaller political and social units, not only to the different relationships within the family or the household in general,[337] but also to particular members of the household, i.e.

---

[330]Plut. *Mor.* 814 F-815 B; 824 A-C.

[331]Dio Chrys. Or. 39.7.

[332]Arist. *Or* 23.31. See also *Or.* 24.12ff.

[333]See K. THRAEDE, "Homonoia (Eintracht)", *RAC* 16 (1994) 182, 185, 189 with text references.

[334]Dio Chrysostom, for instances, argues for the benefit of concord and advises the audience to establish concord between Prusa and Apamea, between Nicomedia and Nicaea, the leading cities of Bithynia, and between Tarsus and its neighbours Aegae, Adana and Mallus (*Or.* 40; 41; 38; 33; 34). See further the discussion including a great number of references to texts in K. THRAEDE, "Homonoia (Eintracht)", *RAC* 16 (1994) 195-197.

[335]The ideal of Pan-Hellenic concord emerged at a point of time marked by endless strife between the city states and was seen as an impetus to mobilise against the national enemies, Persia and Macedonia, Lys. *Or.* 33.6; Isoc. *Or.* 4.85, 104ff; Dem. *Or.* 9.38-39; 26.11. See further A. MOULAKIS, *Homonoia* (1973) 54-59; A. R. R. SHEPPARD, "Homonoia in The Greek Cities of The Roman Empire", *AncSoc* 15-17 (1984-86) 229; K. THRAEDE, "Homonoia (Eintracht)", *RAC* 16 (1994) 191-194. It was first of all Aristides who developed and adapted this ideal to fit a new political framework of loyalty to the Empire. He argued that the decline of the Greeks and all the Greek cities had been caused by factions setting themselves against each other and by a general state of disharmony. But at the present time when all were united under one emperor and one common law it was madness not to cease from strife and sedition and instead establish concord (*Or.* 24.31ff.). He presented the concord that, according to him, existed between the brother emperors, Marcius Aurelius and Lucius Verus as an example to follow for those belonging to the Empire (*Or.* 23.78-79). Cf. C. A. BEHR, *P. Aelius Aristides. The Complete Works.* vol. 2 (1981) 368 n. 82.

[336]Dio Chrys. *Or.* 38.10: "Well then, concord (ὁμόνοια) has been lauded by all men always in both speech and writing. Not only are the works of poets and philosophers alike full of its praises, but also all who have published their histories to provide a pattern (παράδειγμα) for practical application have shown concord to be the greatest of human blessings … ."

[337]*POxy.* 3057.15; Pl. *Alc.* 1.126.E-F; Plut. *Mor.* 144B-C; 511C; Dio. Chrys. *Or.* 38.15; Aristid. *Or.* 24.7-8, 32.

spouses,[338] and brothers.[339] An example has also been found in which the ideal of ὁμόνοια is applied to an association.[340] The high estimation of ὁμόνοια is illustrated by the fact that during the 4th century B.C.E. in Greek and Roman religion ὁμόνοια or *Concordia* became personified and worshipped as a goddess. The goddess ὁμόνοια represented concord within the city-state and was a symbol of the unity of all the Greeks,[341] so much so that an image of the goddess was often placed on coins.[342]

This brief survey of the use of ὁμόνοια should suffice to indicate its basic use during the Graeco-Roman era before and at the time when *1 Clement* was written. It was held that ὁμόνοια should be manifested in different political bodies from the macro-level of Pan-Hellenism to the micro-level of the household, and that the term designated a state of being free from sedition and fraction.

So far we have not dealt with the many conceptions and notions associated with the concept of ὁμόνοια. In the course of the present chapter, our attempt to identify political terms and *topoi* in *1 Clement* will need to focus on some aspects of the concept of concord in greater detail in those cases where they can illuminate the content of the letter. The preceding survey of the term already indicates that ὁμόνοια had a long history in the Greek arena as a political virtue that should permeate the relations between the members of different kinds of social units or political bodies. This means, as some scholars have rightly pointed out, that it is necessary to pay attention to the political character of the term in reading *1 Clement*.[343]

3.3.2. *εἰρήνη*

The term εἰρήνη occurs 21 times in *1 Clement*. In five instances the term constitutes a part of the word pair εἰρήνη καὶ ὁμόνοια (or ὁμόνοια καὶ εἰρήνη). As noted above, Clement makes use of this word pair in the significant statement which summarizes the purpose of the letter as an appeal for εἰρήνη καὶ ὁμόνοια (63:2). For both this reason and because the terms are used interchangeably elsewhere in the letter, we have stated that the terms εἰρήνη and ὁμόνοια function as a hendiadys in *1 Clement* when they are coupled with the conjunction καί. In the *exordium* the term εἰρήνη is

---

[338]Lycurg. frg. 11-12.3.2; Men. frg. 584. See further K. THRAEDE, "Homonoia (Eintracht)", *RAC* 16 (1994) 203 for discussion and other references.

[339]Men. frg. 262. For more evidence and discussion of the use of concord in such a context, see H. KRAMER, *Qvid valeat ὁμόνοια in Litteris Graecis* (1915) 45-49. Cf. also his summary regarding contexts in which the ideal of ὁμόνοια occurred: "iam vidimus tres significationes principales voci ὁμόνοια attribui: concordiam civilem, concordiam omnium Graecorum, concordiam familiarem" (49).

[340]This is pointed out by M. M. MITCHELL, *Paul and the Rhetoric of Reconciliation* (1991) 64 n. 210, who noticed that ὁμόνοια is applied to two associations of bakers, *SEG* 33 (1983) 1165.

[341]See H. KRAMER, *Qvid valeat ὁμόνοια in Litteris Graecis* (1915) 49-51; E. SKARD, *Zwei religiös-politische Begriffe* (1932), 69, 102-105; K. THRAEDE, "Homonoia (Eintracht)", *RAC* 16 (1994) 205-211 and the texts cited in these works.

[342]H. KRAMER, *Qvid valeat ὁμόνοια in Litteris Graecis* (1915) 49-51; H. J. ROSE, "Homonoia", *OCD* (1982) 526.

used twice to express the proper state of the Corinthian Church.[344] To begin with, the author praises the nature of the community's life in the past before the στάσις arose by saying, among other things, that it was characterised by εἰρήνη βαθεῖα, "a profound peace" (2:2). Then turning to the present the author complains that "righteousness and peace" (δικαιοσύνη καὶ εἰρήνη) are now far removed (3:4). In these passages the term εἰρήνη denotes a state of peace within the Church as opposed to a state of στάσις. Later in the letter the term εἰρήνη also expresses the ideal community life of the past (19:2a). As an example to be followed by the Christians, in 19:2-20:11 Clement presents the peace and concord so typical of how the different elements of the universe relate and co-operate. This is expressed in 19:2 and 20:1,9, and specifically together with ὁμόνοια in 20:10f. Furthermore, in the prayer at the end of the *probatio*[345] Clement prays that God may grant εἰρήνη (ὁμόνοια) to Christians and to all who live on earth (60:4). He prays for εἰρήνη (ὁμόνοια) on behalf of rulers (61:1), and "that they may administer with piety in εἰρήνη and gentleness the power given to them" by God (61:2). Then in the *peroratio* Clement gives a summary of the letter by listing the main topics which have been dealt with.[346] Among other things, he says that the Corinthians have been reminded to please God almighty by living in concord in love and εἰρήνη (62:2). At the very end Clement prays that God may bless each individual by giving them εἰρήνη together with other virtues (64:1). Lastly, after using a meta-communicative clause[347] to describe the whole letter as an appeal for εἰρήνη καὶ ὁμόνοια (63:2), he exhorts the Corinthians to send the messengers back to the Romans quickly in εἰρήνη, so that they may give their reports about the re-establishment of εἰρήνη καὶ ὁμόνοια in the Church (65:1).[348] Though the author uses the term εἰρήνη with different connotations, it is clear that it primarily depicts a state of peace that should permeate the Christian community. This is also the case in the use of the verb εἰρηνεύω which occurs five times. In 54:2 εἰρηνεύω is contrasted with στάσις, ἔρις,

---

[343]L. SANDERS, *L`Hellénisme de Saint Clément de Rome et le Paulinisme* (1943) 126-130; W. JAEGER, *Early Christianity and Greek Paideia* (1961) 13f.; P. MIKAT, *Die Bedeutung der Begrieffe Stasis and Aponoia für das Verständnis des 1. Clemensbriefes* (1969) 28; W. C. VAN UNNIK, "Studies over de zogenaamde eerste brief van Clemens", *Mededelingen* (1970); *idem*, "Tifer Friede", *VC* 24 (1970) 261-279; G. BRUNNER, *Die theologische Mitte des ersten Klemensbriefes* (1972) 134-138; K. WENGST, *Pax Romana and the Peace of Jesus Christ* (1987) 105-118; B. E. BOWE, *A Church in Crisis* (1988) 64-67; K. THRAEDE, "Homonoia (Eintracht)", *RAC* 16 (1994) 244f. H. E. LONA, *Der erste Clemensbrief* (1998) 621, admits: "Es lässt sich nicht bestreiten, dass die ganze Einstellung in 1 Clem vom Ideal des Friedens und der Eintracht bestimmt ist. Man kann sogar einen Schritt weiter gehen und festhalten, dass dieses Ideal auch einem weit verbreiteten politischen Ideal entsprach". On the basis of this statement, it is quite surprising that Lona in his extensive and in many ways impressing study only to a very limited degree attempts to show how this ideal has made an impact on Clement's vocabularly, and how it is reflected in his argumentation.

[344]For the definition of the *exordium* in *1 Clement*, see pp. 218-223.

[345]For the definition of the *probatio* in *1 Clement*, see pp. 232-277.

[346]For the definition of the *peroratio* in *1 Clement*, see pp. 226-232.

[347]For the definition and function of a meta-communicative clause, see 213f.

[348]The other occurrences of the term εἰρήνη are found in *pre*, 15:1; 16:5 (LXX quotation); 22:5 (LXX quotation); 60:3.

and σχίσμα. Those who practise love will leave the Church voluntarily, if they are causing sedition and strife, in order that the flock of Christ may "have peace (εἰρηνεύω)
with the presbyters set over it". Then in 63:4 Clement emphasizes that the reason for
intervening in the Corinthians' affairs is their "speedy attainment of peace" (εἰρηνεύω).[349]

The term εἰρήνη is used very frequently in the LXX in a wide range of contexts.[350]
It is always used to translate the Hebrew *shalom*: "the sense of the root is 'be well, complete, safe and sound' and *shalom* expresses 'the state of a being who lacks nothing and
has no fear of being troubled in its quietude; it is euphoria with security. Nothing better
can be desired for oneself and others'".[351] Thus εἰρήνη depicts well-being in general
and is opposed to evil and danger in every possible form.[352] It is often used to express
the good which comes from God, i.e. salvation and victory.[353] A basic idea is that peace
is a gift of God. God gives aid or well-being to the people who trust and love him.[354]

In general, the Synoptic Gospels reflect the Old Testament meaning of εἰρήνη, but
here the concept is applied to Jesus, the Messiah who offers salvation.[355] An important
aspect of Paul's use of εἰρήνη is that he transforms the Jewish concept into an internal,
spiritual peace given to the Christian on the basis of the work of Christ.[356] There are
also a few examples of the use of the term in the sense of civil and political peace, i.e. the
unity that follows a previous period of hostility within a group,[357] and the brotherly
harmony within the Christian communities.[358]

In secular Greek the basic meaning of the term εἰρήνη differs from the common
Jewish and Christian use. Here it usually "designates a political and social phenomenon, first of all the state of a nation that is not in war".[359] Thus it designates a state or
period of peace and is used as an antonym for πόλεμος.[360] It is, however, not restricted
to the absence of war. The fact that εἰρήνη and φιλία are almost always linked in treaties of alliance and of peace indicates that εἰρήνη implies an arrangement for the future

---

[349]The others occurrences of the verb εἰρηνεύω are found in 15:1 ("let us cleave to those whose
peacefulness is based on pity") and twice in the quotation of Job 5:17-26 in 56:6-15.

[350]For the use and the meaning of the concept εἰρήνη in secular Greek, the LXX and the New Testament, and the use of *shalom* in the Hebrew Bible, see W. FOERSTER, G. VON RAD, "εἰρήνη, εἰρηνεύω
κτλ.", *TDNT* 2, 400-420; E. DINKLER, "Friede", *RAC* 8 (1972) 434-505; C. SPICQ, "εἰρηνεύω, εἰρήνη
κτλ", *Theological Lexicon of the New Testament* 1, 424-438.

[351]C. SPICQ, *Theological Lexicon of the New Testament* 1, 427.

[352]Cf. for example Gen 15:15; 26:9; Judg 6:23; 18:5; Dan 3:98; 1 Sam 10:4; 20:42; 2 Sam 15:27;
18:29; Ps 34:27; 33:14; 121:8; Prov 3:17 and the comments in W. FOERSTER, G. VON RAD, "εἰρήνη,
εἰρηνεύω κτλ.", *TDNT* 2, 407.

[353]Cf. for example Lev 26:3-6; Isa 26:3; 32:17f; 45:7; Jer. 16:5; Ps 29:11; 85:8-14.

[354]Ps 41:9; Job 5:23; Sir 47:13:16, and the comments in C. SPICQ, *Theological Lexicon of the New
Testament* 1, 428-29.

[355]Cf. Luke 1:79; 2:14; 19:38.

[356]Cf. for example Rom 5:1f.; 15:13; 1 Cor 7:15 and E. DINKLER, "Friede", *RAC* 8 (1972) 463.

[357]Acta 7:26; 24:2. In 7:26 Stephen recalls Moses who intervened between and united two quarrelling Hebrews (Ex. 2:13f.). C. SPICQ, *Theological Lexicon of the New Testament* 1, remarks with respect
to this passage that "This is the classic secular sense of peace: the cessation of hostilities" (431).

[358]Gal 5:22; Eph. 4:3.

that provides an "opportunity for all sorts of happiness and prosperity".[361] Thus εἰρήνη is the state of peace which is a precondition for other blessings for both land and people.

With respect to the present study, it is interesting to note that εἰρήνη is linked with ὁμόνοια in political rhetoric and other discourse that deal with the topic of concord in different political bodies. I shall refer to and discuss a great number of such texts later in this study.[362] Therefore, I shall confine myself here to the comment that these terms express the happiness and well-being of the actual political body, most often a city or several cities that belong to the same area. Furthermore, in many cases it is difficult to make any distinction between the meanings of the terms. A careful appraisal, however, would indicate a tendency that ὁμόνοια describes internal relations more frequently, while εἰρήνη refers to external relations. This is significant for our analysis, since it means that εἰρήνη was used to depict an ideal state of unity or concord within different social units in opposition to sedition and civil strife.[363]

This brief survey of the use of the term εἰρήνη in Judaism, the New Testament, and the secular Greek tradition, should suffice to indicate that Clement was heavily influenced by the last mentioned tradition. In accord with the secular Greek tradition, the term εἰρήνη depicts a social phenomenon in *1 Clement*; it designates a state of peace and unity among the Corinthians as opposed to a state of sedition and strife. This is the case at least in 2:2, 3:4, 19:2, 60:4, 62:2, 63:2, and 65:1. The simple fact that Clement reflects the well-known formula εἰρήνη καὶ ὁμόνοια in Hellenistic literature that deals with the topic of unity among people of the same political unit is a strong indication that he uses εἰρήνη mainly in its Greek political sense.[364] Nevertheless, this is not to deny that he appears to have also been influenced by certain aspects of the Jewish conception of εἰρήνη, i.e. that the peace appears to be a gift given by God (2:2; 60:1; 64:1),[365] and that the wish for the Roman messengers to return in peace may reflect the use of the term to express a general sense of well-being (64:1). Regarding the latter, however, it is possible that the peace of the messengers is directly related to how the Corinthian Church would respond to the letter, i.e. that the messengers' experience of

---

[359]C. Spicq, *Theological Lexicon of the New Testament* 1, 424; W. Foerster, G. von Rad, "εἰρήνη, εἰρηνεύω κτλ.", TDNT 2, 401; R. Bloch, "Eirene" *Der neue Pauly* 3, 921. This is not to say that we do not find quite a few occurrences of a political use of εἰρήνη in the LXX where it is used as an antonym of war. See, for example, 1 Kgs 2:5; 5:26; Deut 20:10; 1 Sam 7:14. However, this is not the common use of the term in the LXX.

[360]See for example Isoc. *Paneg.* 4.172; *I. Gonn.* 2:1; 7:5; 9:6; 10:4; 11:9; Diod. Sic. 3.64.7; Dio Chrys. *Or.* 38:15.

[361]C. Spicq, *Theological Lexicon of the New Testament* 1, 425.

[362]See chaps. 3.4 and 3.5.2.11, and partly 3.5.1.1.1.

[363]Cf. C. Spicq, *Theological Lexicon of the New Testament* 1, 425: "If peace is the situation of a nation that is not at war, it also defines the public order, relations between citizens, and social peace, as opposed to discord, trouble, and sedition".

[364]For other scholars who argue that Clement reflects the Greek political use of the term εἰρήνη, see the literature listed above, n. 343.

[365]Cf. H. E. Lona, *Der erste Clemensbrief* (1998) 128.

peace would depend on the extent to which the Corinthians paid attention to the message of the letter and re-established peace and concord.[366] In spite of these apparently Jewish aspects in the use of the term, it seems as suggested above and as we will argue farther on in this study, that Clement primarily reflects a Greek political concept of peace.

3.3.3. στάσις

Though Clement makes use of a number of terms when he describes the communal behaviour among the Christians in Corinth, the στάσις/στασιάζω lexical alternatives seem to provide the principal term. We are led to this assertion because Clement employs this expression at the beginning of the *exordium* where he clarifies the occasion for writing and thus indicates the main subject of the letter.[367] The occasion for writing is the dispute about certain matters among the Christians in Corinth, which the author designates as an "abominable and unholy sedition" (μιαρᾶς καὶ ἀνοσίου στάσεως, 1:1). That στάσις is the principal term is also reflected by the fact that στάσις/στασιάζω are the most frequent words that refer to sedition. The noun στάσις which occurs nine times and the verb στασιάζω which occurs seven times are to be found throughout the letter.[368] Sometimes the author uses the term στάσις by itself to describe the occurrences in the Corinthian Church. In addition to the passage just cited from 1:1, this is the case in 57:1 where the author exhorts those "who laid the foundation of the sedition" (ἡ καταβολὴ τῆς στάσεως) to submit to the presbyters, and in 63:1 where Clement urges the Corinthian Church to cease from vain sedition (μάταιος στάσις). However, στάσις is often linked with other terms that also refer to sedition. Besides 3:2, ἔρις and στάσις are used in conjunction with one another in 14:2[369] and 54:2[370] (also with σχίσμα), and in 2:6[371] and 46:9[372] στάσις is used in conjunction with σχίσμα. On the basis of the fact that the author, as just noted above, makes use of the term στάσις when he introduces the main topic of the letter (1:1), and that he characterises the whole letter as an appeal for ὁμόνοια καὶ εἰρήνη (63:2), it seems to be obvious that στάσις and ὁμόνοια (καὶ εἰρήνη) are used as antonyms in the letter.[373]

---

[366]Ibid. 638.

[367]For the definition and the function of the *exordium* in *1 Clement*, see pp. 218-223.

[368]The noun; *1 Clem.* 1:1; 2:6; 3:2; 14:2; 46:9; 51:1; 54:2; 57:1; 63:1, the verb; 4:12; 43:2; 46:7; 47:6; 49:5; 51:3; 55:1. H. E. Lona, *Der erste Clemensbrief* (1998) correctly states that "Mit στάσις wird der Vorgang in Korinth zusammengefasst" (140).

[369]"For we shall incur no common harm, but great danger, if we rashly yield ourselves to the purposes of men who rush into strife (ἔρις) and sedition (στάσις), to estrange us from what is right".

[370]"Let him cry:- 'If sedition (στάσις) and strife (ἔρις) and divisions (σχίσματα) have arisen on my account, I will depart …'".

[371]"All sedition (στάσις) and all schism (σχίσμα) was abominable to you".

[372]"Your schism (σχίσμα) has turned aside many … and your sedition (στάσις) continues".

[373]Cf. K. Thraede, "Homonoia (Eintracht)", *RAC* 16 (1994) 243: "Dass στάσις … ausdrücklich den Gegensatz bildet [to *homonoia*] … unterstreicht folgerichtig den 'weltlichen' Zuschnitt von H[omonoia]", and H. E. Lona, *Der erste Clemensbrief* (1998) 527.

In the LXX the term στάσις is found 22 times. However, it is worth noticing that it is only in Prov 17:14 that it designates discord within a political body.[374] In the NT στάσις is used seven times and commonly designates "uproar" and "strife" in different kinds of political bodies.[375] It is worth observing, however, that στάσις in the NT never depicts sedition or strife within a Christian Community. As for the Apostolic Fathers apart from *1 Clement*, the term στάσις does not occur at all. In other words, in the LXX, the NT, and in the other Apostolic Fathers the term στάσις depicting strife in a political body occurs eight times altogether, while the word group στάσις/στασιάζω with a political meaning is found 16 times in *1 Clement*. This fact both reflects the significance of the term in *1 Clement* and indicates that we must focus predominantly on traditions other than the Jewish or Christian ones in order to ascertain the meaning and use of this term.[376]

On the basis of the fact that στάσις functions as an antonym for ὁμόνοια in *1 Clement*, and in view of the foregoing overview of the history and application of ὁμόνοια, it is not surprising that the formative background of the concept of στάσις emerged in the Hellenistic arena. The concept of στάσις has a relatively long history in Greek political thought.[377] It was employed in a socio-political context and became frequently used in the literature from the fifth century B.C.E. That point of time marked the beginning of a very turbulent period in Greek history characterised by internal fighting and internal war between different states.[378] In the literature that deals with these occurrences the term στάσις commonly designates civil war or internal strife between the states.[379] However, both in this period and later, the term had a broad range of meaning. It could designate the group of people itself involved in a con-

---

[374]For an overview of the use of στάσις in LXX, see G. Delling, "στάσις", *TDNT* 7. 570.

[375]Mark 15:7; Luke 23:19, 25: revolt against the Romans or strife among the Jews; Acts 15:2: conflict in opinion between Paul and Barnabas and Jews regarding the circumcision; Acts 19:40: disturbance among the people of Ephesus; Acts 23:7: a theological conflict between the Pharisees and the Sadducees; Acts 24:5: Paul is accused of fomenting strife among the Jews all over the world.

[376]It is possible that Clement's use of στάσις is influenced by the LXX and Hellenistic Judaism in general. However, we can not follow H. E. Lona, *Der erste Clemensbrief* (1998) 140, when he states, after having referred to certain passages in the LXX and in Josephus, that "Der Sprachgebrauch in I Clem ist von der LXX beeinflusst und allgemein vom hellenistischen Judentum" without paying attention to neither the long history of the term στάσις in Greek political thought or to the use of the term as an antonym for ὁμόνοια in a political context. Lona's approach is too narrow to grasp the background of and the use of this important term in *1 Clement*.

[377]For the term in general, see H.-J. Gehrke, *Stasis* (1985); A. Lintott, *Violence, Civil Strife and Revolution in the Classical City* (1982); M. I. Finley, *Politics in Ancient World* (1983) 105-121; L. L. Welborn, "On the Discord in Corinth", *JBL* 106 (1987) 85-111.

[378]That the concept of στάσις emerged in a political context and that one must pay attention to this fact in interpreting *1 Clement* has been recognised by numerous scholars. See for example P. Mikat, *Die Bedeutung der Begriffe Stasis und Aponoia für des Verständnis des I. Clemensbriefes* (1969); W. C. van Unnik, "Studies over de zogenaamde eerste brief van Clemens", *Mededelingen* (1970); J. W. Wilson, *The First Epistle of Clement* (1976) 39ff; B. E. Bowe, *A Church in Crisis* (1988) 65-67; G. Delling, "στάσις", *TDNT* 7. 568.

flict,[380] a "party formed for seditious purposes"[381] and "faction, sedition and discord".[382] To sum up:

> All levels of intensity were embraced by the splendid Greek portmanteau-word *stasis*. When employed in a social-political context, *stasis* had a broad range of meanings, from political grouping or rivalry through faction (in its pejorative sense) to open civil war. That correctly reflected the political realities. Ancient moralists and theorists, who where hostile to the realities, understandably clung to the pejorative overtones of the word and identified *stasis* as the central malady of their society.[383]

As noted above, in antiquity ὁμόνοια was a universally recognised ideal and value considered to be of fundamental importance for different political bodies, especially the city state. On the other hand, στάσις was regarded as the greatest threat to and malady of a political body. As we shall demonstrate later on, ὁμόνοια and στάσις were used as antonyms when one dealt with the issue of unity and sedition;[384] in fact they were technical terms for unity and sedition respectively.

3.4. εἰρήνη καὶ ὁμόνοια

The author links ὁμόνοια and εἰρήνη five times in the letter by means of the conjunction καί. When he describes the harmony of the universe he says, among other things, that "the smallest of animals meet together ἐν ὁμονοίᾳ καὶ εἰρήνῃ" (20:10), and that the Creator and Master ordered the different elements of the universe to be in εἰρήνη καὶ ὁμονοίᾳ (20:11). Clement prays to God that he should give ὁμόνοιαν καὶ

---

[379]H.-J. GEHRKE, *Stasis* (1985) 7. Regarding the distinction between στάσις and πόλεμος cf. G. DELLING, "στάσις", *TDNT* 7, 569: "Hostility between those who belong together is στάσις, while hostility between enemies is πόλεμος, Plat. Resp., V. 470b; hence hostility between Hellenes is to be called στάσις, 470c d>II, 401, 23 and 28".

[380]H.-J. GEHRKE, *Stasis* (1985) 7 n. 29, refers to Aesch. *Cho.* 458.114; *Eum.* 311; *Ag.* 1117; *Supp.* 12 (Danaos as στασίαρχὸς); Phld. 1.5.34f.; Antid. frg. 2,1 K.

[381]H. G. LIDDELL - R. SCOTT, *A Greek - English Lexicon* (1973) 1634, with references.

[382]*Ibid.* 1634, with references.

[383]M. I. FINLEY, *Politics in the Ancient World* (1983) 105. When στάσις is used in a social-political context to mean "political group or a party", we must not associate this meaning with the modern sense of the term: a party with fixed memberships, ideologies and structures. A "party" in antiquity did not have as rigid and formal structure as modern parties. So different subgroups with special interests belonging to an overall community could be described as parties. In modern language we would in many cases talk about groups. P. J. J. VANDERBROECK, *Popular Leadership and Collective Behavior* (1987) 26, summarizes: "The general picture of the Roman Republic in modern historiography holds that political parties, in the sense of an organized group of individuals whose concerted action is independent of the issue, did not exist. For certain political problems, ad hoc coalitions were formed between families and their supporters or between politicians and an interest group. They were factions who at every political discussion had a different composition". See also M. M. MITCHELL, *Paul and the Rhetoric of Reconciliation* (1991) 71.

[384]See pp. 86-91.

εἰρήνην (60:4). In the meta-communicative clause[385] in 63:2 he characterises the whole letter (ἡ ἐπιστολή) as an entreaty περὶ εἰρήνης καὶ ὁμονοίας. At the very end of the letter he asks the Corinthians to send the messengers back quickly in order "that they may report the sooner the εἰρήνην καὶ ὁμόνοιαν" which the Roman Christians pray for and desire (65:1).

One notes that these terms do not occur in the same order. In three occurrences of the word pair, the term εἰρήνην comes first, while in the two other occurrences the term ὁμόνοια is put first. This fact indicates that the terms are used interchangeably. Clement's change of word order is especially striking in the two occurrences of the word pair in 20:10f. After having first presented the smallest animals as examples of the ideal ὁμονοία καὶ εἰρήνη in 20:10, he changes the order to εἰρήνη καὶ ὁμονοία in the summary statement in 20:11, where he describes the relationship between the different elements of the universe. It is not possible to distinguish between the two terms. The word pair appears to constitute a single concept in *1 Clement*, and it is therefore appropriate to view the terms ὁμόνοια and εἰρήνη as a *hendiadys*.[386] There is, however, a statement that might imply that in general ὁμόνοια is the superordinate word or the archilexeme in the letter. In the *recapitulatio* Clement says, among other things, in 62:2 that the letter has reminded the Corinthians "to live in concord, bearing no malice, in love and peace" (ὁμονοοῦντας ἀμνησικάκως ἐν ἀγάπῃ καὶ εἰρήνῃ).[387] Here the expression ἐν ἀγάπῃ καὶ εἰρήνῃ qualifies the nature of the community life expressed by the verb ὁμονοέω. The term εἰρήνη gives meaning to and is a further determination of the verbal clause. This is significant because it is a part of the *recapitulatio*, and might therefore hint at the relationship between the terms ὁμόνοια and εἰρήνη in the letter in general. But this is only a hint, and for the reasons mentioned above, it seems to be safer to conclude that when the terms ὁμόνοια and εἰρήνη are linked with the conjunction καί, they function as a hendiadys.

W. C. van Unnik has demonstrated that the linking of these terms is not a product of Clement's creativity, but reflects common language that deals with the issue of unity within a social or political body.[388] It would be superfluous to reiterate van Unnik's observations in detail. Nevertheless, because ὁμόνοια and the word pair εἰρήνη καὶ ὁμόνοια are stock terms in *1 Clement* and thus are a natural starting point in identifying political language, we will present some texts to show how conventional Clement's language is on this point.[389]

Let us start with Dio Chrysostom. In *Or.* 49.6 he remarks that the Italian Greeks learned and benefited from their familiarity with Pythagorean philosophy. This is manifested in the way they handled their domestic affairs, i.e. with the greatest concord and peace (μετὰ πλείστης ὁμονοίας καὶ εἰρήνης πολιτευσαμένους). Furthermore, when he tries to persuade the Nicaens to cease from civil strife, he argues that "it

[385]For the definition and function of a meta-communicative clause, see p. 213f.
[386]So also B. E. Bowe, *A Church in Crisis* (1988) 65.
[387]For the definition and function of *recapitulatio* in ancient rhetoric, see pp. 226f.
[388]See the present study, pp. 13f.

is fitting that those whose city was founded by gods should maintain peace and concord (εἰρήνη καὶ ὁμόνοια) and friendship toward one another" (*Or.* 39.2).

Perhaps the most illuminating passage cited by W. C. van Unnik is the discourse where Dio advises his home city Prusa to be reconciled with Apameia. Here he takes as his departure the common appeal in deliberative rhetoric to what is profitable for the audience. He argues that peace is better than war and friendship is better than enmity.

> For peace and concord (εἰρήνη καὶ ὁμόνοια) have never damaged all those who have employed them, whereas it would be surprising if enmity (ἔχθρα) and contentiousness (φιλονικία) were not very deadly, very mighty evils. Moreover, while concord (ὁμόνοια) is a word of good omen, and to make trial of it is most excellent and profitable for all, strife (στάσις) and discord (διαφορά) are forbidding and unpleasant words even to utter, and much more are their deeds and more forbidding. For the fact is, strife (στάσις) and discord (διαφορά) involving saying and hearing said many things one might wish to avoid, and doing and experiencing them too (Or. 40.26).

In each of these passages from Dio εἰρήνη καὶ ὁμόνοια refers to the internal relationship between the inhabitants of a city or between cities that belong to the same area, and is contrasted with στάσις as is made explicit in *Or.* 40.26.

If we turn our attention to Plutarch we will see that he applies the word pair in a similar way. Plutarch says that the symbolic action of Heracleitus, after he was asked to express some opinions about concord, demonstrates that "to be satisfied with whatever they happen upon and not to want expensive things is to keep cities in peace and concord" (εἰρήνη καὶ ὁμόνοια, *Mor.* 511 C). According to the same author Otho states: "For I do not see how my victory can be of so great advantage to the Romans as my offering up my life to secure peace and concord" (εἰρήνη καὶ ὁμόνοια, *Otho* 15.6). And finally, in *De fortuna Alexandri* Plutarch remarks about Alexander as a philosopher, namely that the purpose of his expedition was not to win for himself luxury and immoderate living, "but to win for all men concord and peace (εἰρήνη καὶ ὁμόνοια) and community of interests" (*Mor.* 330 E).

These examples should sufficiently demonstrate that Clement's appeal to εἰρήνη καὶ ὁμόνοια throughout the letter reflects a well-known formula in Hellenistic literature which discusses the issue of unity among people who naturally belong to the same political unit. The fact that the word pair does not occur at all (as far as I know) in Jewish texts shows that there can be no doubt that this stock phrase is adopted from the

---

[389]In addition to the texts highlighted by van Unnik (see n. 65) we have succeeded in finding a relatively large number of texts where the word pair εἰρήνη καὶ ὁμόνοια, or the inverse order ὁμόνοια καὶ εἰρήνη, is used to describe the relationship between members of a political body: Dem. *De Cor.* 167; Diod. Sic. 3.64.7; 16.60.3; Plut. *Caes.* 23.4; *Oth.*15.6; Dio Chrys. *Or.* 1.6; 38.14; Dio Cass. 53.5.1. For other references where the terms εἰρήνη and ὁμόνοια are not linked with καί, but occur in the same context expressing the unity within a political body, cf. Diod. Sic. 11.87.5; 22.8.5; Plut. *Ages.* 33.2.7; *Caes.* 12.1.8; *Oth.* 13.3; *Mor.* 824.c.5; Dio Cass. 41.15.4; 48.31.2; 53.5.4. K. Thraede, "Homonoia (Eintracht)", *RAC* 16 (1994) 178, notes that ὁμόνοια "schon seit dem 4. Jh. vC., hauptsächlich bei Philosophen, in Verbindung z B. mit εἰρήνη oder φιλία antreffen".

Hellenistic tradition.[390] In this tradition the word pair expresses in particular, as is emphasized by W. C. van Unnik, the happiness and well-being of the actual political body.[391] The word pair εἰρήνη καὶ ὁμόνοια becomes almost a single concept, requiring a singular verb.[392] However, to the degree that it is possible to make a distinction between the terms, ὁμόνοια seems to be used more frequently to designate the internal relations within the state, whereas εἰρήνη refers more to its external relations.[393] But one cannot use this distinction as a basis for any conclusions regarding the affairs in the Corinthian Church and conclude, for example, that the use of εἰρήνη indicates that the sedition relates to relationships with other Churches. It is likely that Clement used the word pair εἰρήνη καὶ ὁμόνοια because it was a common phrase that was used without any distinction between the terms when one dealt with unity and sedition in a political body.

3.5. Political Terms and topoi Related to Concord in 1 Clement 1:1-3:4 (exordium and narratio)[394]

3.5.1. Political Terms in 1 Clement 3:2

Clement's description of the state of affairs in the Corinthian Church in 3:2 serves as a good point of departure for identifying political language that is associated with the question of *homonoia*. This rhetorically composed statement contains many terms that explicitly refer to factionalism or the cause of factionalism among the Christians at Corinth. In contrast to the previous noble time, when "all sedition and all schism was abominable" to them,[395] the present time is marked by ζῆλος καὶ φθόνος, ἔρις καὶ στάσις, διωγμὸς καὶ ἀκαταστασία, πόλεμος καὶ αἰχμαλωσία (3:2). The first four of these terms play a fundamental role in the letter. Above we have noted that στάις is the principal term in *1 Clement* for describing sedition, and that it functions as an antonym for ὁμόνοια (and εἰρήνη).[396]

---

[390]This means that although εἰρήνη is a very important term in the LXX and in Judaism in general, Clement's use of the term εἰρήνη must primarily be understood in the light of its political use within the Hellenistic tradition. After commenting on the striking coupling of εἰρήνη and ὁμόνοια, E. DINKLER, "Friede", *RAC* 8 (1972), states that "Es bricht hier eine Terminologie durch, die den F.[riede] humanisiert u.[nd] teilweise politisch idealisiert" (467). It is interesting that even H. E. LONA, *Der erste Clemensbrief* (1998), who throughout his study argues that Clement's vocabulary and conceptions are rooted in Hellenistic Judaism, must admit that the significant ideal of εἰρήνη καὶ ὁμόνοια in the letter "einem weit verbreiteten politischen Ideal entsprach" (621).

[391]W. C. van UNNIK, "Studies over de zogenaamde eerste brief van Clemens", *Mededelingen* (1970) 32f.

[392]*Ibid.* (1970) 29 points to the above cited passage in Dio Chrys. 40.26. B. E. BOWE, *A Church in Crisis* (1988) 65, refers in addition to the similar passages in Dio Chrys. *Or.* 39.2; 49.6.

[393]W. C. van UNNIK, "Studies over de zogenaamde eerste brief van Clemens", *Mededelingen* (1970) 32.

[394]The disposition of the subsequent investigation of terms and *topoi* related to concord in *1 Clement* will follow the macro-structure of the letter as it is pointed out in chap. 4.

[395]*1 Clem.* 2:6.

Clement applies the term ἔρις many times throughout the letter, often linked with other terms that refer to discord: with στάσις in 3:2, 14:2, 54:2[397]; with ζῆλος in 5:5,[398] 6:4,[399] and 9:1[400]; and with διχοστασία, σχίσμα and πόλεμος in 46:5[401]. In addition to these passages the term is found in 44:1[402] (with no conjunction combining it with other terms that refer to sedition), and also in a list of vices in 35:5.

In addition to the above-mentioned occurrences of the term ζῆλος in conjunction with ἔρις this important term is also found in many other passages. In a number of these passages ζῆλος is linked to φθόνος and functions as a single concept designating either the subject, the cause, or the effect of an action (3:2; 4:7; 4:13; 5:2). However, it may also have the same function without a linking word (3:4; 4:8, 9, 10, 11, 12, 13; 6:1, 2, 3; 14:1; 39:7; 43:2; 45:4; 63:2). ζῆλος and φθόνος are vices and thus they do not designate domestic concord. However, as will be demonstrated below, these terms belonged to the cluster of terms in antiquity that were often used in discussions on domestic discord. That ζῆλος and φθόνος refer to internal strife in *1 Clement* seems to be obvious from, e.g., the connection of ζῆλος with ἔρις in 6:4 where the word pair functions as a single subject requiring a single verb. Here the author concludes a list of examples of the terrible effects of ζῆλος and φθόνος with the statement that ζῆλος and ἔρις have destroyed many cities. Although ζῆλος and ἔρις in 6:4 form one single subject, the terms ought not to be considered as synonyms. Instead it is reasonable to suppose that ζῆλος generates ἔρις.[403]

This brief survey shows that Clement uses a cluster of terms related to discord and strife when he describes the communal behaviour in the Corinthian Church he wants to change. He links different terms in a way that does not make it easy to distinguish their meaning. This at least is the case with the terms ἔρις, στάσις and σχίσμα. Hence these terms ought to be viewed as synonyms.

3.5.1.1. *ἔρις καὶ στάσις*

In spite of the fact that we argue that στάσις is the principal term in *1 Clement* depicting sedition in the Corinthian Church, we choose to treat the term ἔρις under the same heading. The reason for this is that in *1 Clem.* 3:2 these terms occur as a word pair coupled with καί. Since στάσις is the principal term, we shall deal with it first.

---

[396]See pp. 79-81.

[397]Quoted in n. 370.

[398]"Through jealousy and strife (διὰ ζῆλον καὶ ἔριν) Paul showed the way to the prize of endurance".

[399]"Jealousy and strife (ζῆλος καὶ ἔρις) have overthrown great cities, and rooted up mighty nations".

[400]"... and abandon the vain toil and strife (ἔρις) and jealousy (ζῆλος) which leads to death".

[401]"Why are there strife (ἔρις) and passion and divisions (διχοστασία) and schisms (σχίσμα) and war (πόλεμος) among you?"

[402]"Our Apostles also knew through our Lord Jesus Christ that there would be strife (ἔρις) for the title of bishop".

[403]Cf. the present study, p. 46.

3.5.1.1.1. στάσις

The political background for στάσις has been sketched above. However, some additional remarks on this term are appropriate. In particular we shall pay attention to passages where στάσις functions as an antonym for ὁμόνοια in order to demonstrate how conventional Clement's employment of this term is. That these terms were used as antonyms is the case not only in regard to literature belonging to a limited period in Hellenistic times, but is well testified down to the Graeco-Roman period as well. Here we must content ourselves with focusing upon a few examples from authors in the centuries nearest to *1 Clement*.[404] First some evidence from a few historians. Diodorus Siculus reports a myth about the third Dionysius according to which one of Dionysius' great deeds was as follows:

> ... he composed the quarrels between the nations and cities and created concord (ὁμόνοια) and deep peace (πολλή εἰρήνη) where there had existed civil strife (στάσις) and wars (πόλεμος, 3.64.7).

In addition, after the inhabitants of the Italian city Thuri had been divided into factions (ἐστασίαζον πρὸς ἀλλήλους),[405] they now, being free from civil discord (τῆς στάσεως ἀπολυθέν), "returned to the state of harmony which they had previously enjoyed" (εἰς τὴν προυπάρχουσαν ὁμόνοιαν ἀποκατέστη).[406] That the same author uses the terms στάσις and ὁμόνοια to depict the relationship between members of a smaller political body as well is clear when he praises the strategic skills of Hannibal. These skills according to Diodorus were manifested by the fact that he never at any time experienced faction (στάσις) among his troops, but on the contrary he succeeded in maintaining "concord (ὁμόνοια) and harmony (συμφωνία)".[407]

Furthermore, Dionysius Halicarnassensis praises the state of affairs in Rome under the rule of Numa because civil dissension (στάσις) did not break the concord (ὁμόνοια) of the city.[408] An illustrative example, both concerning how one considered στάσις in general and how στάσις and ὁμόνοια were used as antonyms, occurs in a speech of Decius to the senate.[409] By referring to a previously sanctioned law he defends the right of the plebeians to appeal to the people when oppressed by the patricians. First he argues what a terrible thing discord is:

> For, come now, if anyone should ask you what you regard as the greatest of the evils that befall states and the cause of the swiftest destruction, would you not say it is discord (διχοστασία)? I, at least, think you would (Ant. Rom. 7.42.1).

---

[404]Regarding the 5th-3th Century B.C.E., see, e.g., Isoc. *Or.* 3. 41.1-4; 12.258f; 18.44, 68; Xen. *Mem.* 4.6.14; *Lys. Or.* 2. 63.7f; 18.17-18; Arist. *Eth. Nic.* 8.1.4; 9.6.2; Polyb. *Hist.* 6.46.7.f. In addition see, H.-J. GEHRKE, *Stasis* (1985) 357 n. 11.

[405]Diod. Sic. 12.35.1.

[406]Diod. Sic. 12.35.3.

[407]Diod. Sic. 29.19.1. In addition to the above cited passages, see also 7.12.2; 7.12.4; 36.7.2.

[408]Dion. Hal. *Ant. Rom.*2.76.3.

[409]Dion. Hal. *Ant. Rom.*7.40-46.

Then he continues to argue that if the plebeians are deprived of their liberty, which in fact happened according to Decius, and if they are deprived of justice (δίκη) and law (νόμος), it would lead to the greatest evils for the commonwealth mentioned above. He rhetorically asks the following:

> For who is there among you so stupid … as not to know that if the people are allowed to render judgment in causes in which the law gives them the authority, we shall live in harmony (ὁμόνοια), whereas, if you decide to the contrary and deprive us of our liberty … you will drive us again into sedition (στασιάζειν) and civil war (πολεμεῖν)? For if justice and law are banished from a state, sedition (στάσις) and war (πόλεμος) are wont to enter there (Ant. Rom. 7.42.2f.).⁴¹⁰

In addition to the passages cited above where the antonyms στάσις and ὁμόνοια are applied to internal conditions in a city, Dionysius uses these terms to depict internal relations in smaller political units as well, i.e. the army⁴¹¹ and the consuls⁴¹².

According to Dio Cassius in a speech delivered to the senate, Caesar regarded it as a sign of his strength that no one at home was engaged in sedition (στασιάζων) and the conditions in Rome were marked by the fact that all were at peace (εἰρηνούντων) and were harmonious (ὁμονοούντων).⁴¹³ However, conspiracy against Caesar "brought upon the Romans seditions (στάσις) and civil wars once more after a state of harmony (ὁμόνοια)" and the conspirators threw Rome into disorder (ἐστασίασαν).⁴¹⁴ In this critical situation Cicero challenged the people and told them that it was up to them to choose "either harmony (ὁμόνοια) and with it liberty, or seditions (στάσις) and civil wars" (πόλεμος ἐμφύλιος),⁴¹⁵ and he urged them to return to the "old-time state of peace (εἰρήνη) and friendship (φιλία) and harmony" (ὁμόνοια).⁴¹⁶ In his argumentation he reminded them of how former citizens had often quarrelled, but when they were reconciled they lived their lives in peace and harmony (ἐν εἰρήνῃ καὶ ὁμονοίᾳ). ⁴¹⁷

When we now turn to the most important literature in relation to our investigation, i.e. deliberative letters and discourses on *homonoia*, it becomes even more clear how pervasive the terms ὁμόνοια and στάσις were and how closely they were related to the

---

⁴¹⁰The senator Appius responded to Decius' discourse and summarized a basic point in this discourse when he said that Decius pointed "out how excellent a thing harmony is (ἀγαθόν μὲν ὁμόνοια) and how terrible a thing sedition (στάσις), and that, if we cultivate the populace, we shall live together in harmony "(ἐν ὁμονοίᾳ, Dion. Hal. *Ant. Rom.*7. 53.1).

⁴¹¹Dion. Hal. *Ant. Rom.* 9.5.5.

⁴¹²Dion. Hal. *Ant Rom.* 8.75.4. For other passages of the same author where στάσις and ὁμόνοια function as opposite concepts, see *Ant.Rom* 6.35.2; 6.41.2; 7.53.1; 10.30.5; 10.33.2.

⁴¹³Dio Cass. 53.8.2.

⁴¹⁴Dio Cass. 44.1.2-2.1.

⁴¹⁵Dio Cass. 44.24.2.

⁴¹⁶Dio Cass. 44. 24.3f.

⁴¹⁷Dio Cass. 44. 25.3f. For other references, see, e.g., Plut. *Cat. Ma.* 21.4; *Pomp.* 47. 3; *Alex.* 9.6; Joseph. *Ant* 14.58; *Ap* 2.294; *Bell* 1.460; 4.132f; 5.72; 5.441; 6.216; App. *BCiv.* 1. pr.6; 4.3.14; Ath. *Deipn.* 12.74.37f; Philostr. *VA* 4.8 (2x); 5.41; *VS* 1.493.

issue of the internal relations in a political body. In Dio Chrysostom's discourse to the Nicomedians on concord with the Nicaeans he makes it clear at the beginning what he is going to deal with. First he intends to speak about concord (ὁμόνοια) in general, "and then over against that to set off strife (στάσις) and hatred in contradistinction to friendship".[418] He praises ὁμόνοια because it preserved all the greatest things, while through its opposite, στάσις, everything is destroyed:

> ... we are not all sensitive to concord (ὁμόνοια), but, on the contrary, there are those
> who actually love its opposite, strife (στάσις), of which wars and battles constitute
> departments and subsidiary activities ... (Or. 38.11).

Dio reiterates explicitly that ὁμόνοια and στάσις are counter terms when he subsequently contrasts wars, factions, and diseases (πόλεμοι καὶ στάσεις καὶ νόσοι) with peace, concord, and health (εἰρήνη καὶ ὁμόνοια καὶ ὑγεία).[419] Furthermore, when he argues that reconciliation between Nicomedia and Nicea will be profitable for the two cities he asserts the following:

> ... that the strife (στάσις) still going on has not been profitable for you down to the
> present moment, that so many blessings will be yours as a result of concord (τὰ ἀγαθὰ
> ἐκ τῆς ὁμονοίας), and that so many evils now are yours because of enmity – all this
> has been treated by me at sufficient length (Or. 38.48).

Likewise, when he urges the Niceans to cease from civil strife, he applies ὁμόνοια and στάσις as antonyms. He says that, since the city Nikomedia was founded by a god, it is suitable that the inhabitants should maintain "peace and concord and friendship toward one another" (εἰρήνη καὶ ὁμόνοια καὶ φιλία πρὸς αὐτούς),[420] and he points out that the gods take careful notice of men who live in concord (ὁμονοοῦσιν). However, where men are torn by civil strife (στασιάζοντες) they do not even hear each other.[421] In addition, στάσις is dangerous for the city, but a city in concord (πόλει ὁμονοούσῃ) will experience all things that are useful.[422] When Dio tries to persuade his home city Prusa to live in concord with the neighbouring city Apameia, he argues that on the one hand "peace and concord" (εἰρήνη καὶ ὁμόνοια) have never damaged those who have experienced them and that concord is a word of good omen. On the other hand "strife and discord (στάσις καὶ διαφορά) are forbidding and unpleasant words even to utter".[423]

We find similar utterances in discourses of Aelius Aristides. In a situation where the leading cities in Asia struggled for the first position in rank, Aelius argues that "friend-

---

[418]Dio Chrys. Or. 38.8.

[419]Dio Chrys. Or. 38.15.

[420]Dio Chrys. Or. 39.2.

[421]Dio Chrys. Or. 39.4.

[422]Dio Chrys. Or. 39.6f.

[423]Dio Chys. Or. 40.26. Cf. 48.16f: "And civil strife (στάσις) does not deserve even to be named among us, and let no man mention it". Concerning στάσις and ὁμόνοια as counter terms, see also Or. 40.35-37; 48.14f.

ship and concord" are a source of great good[424] for both the nation, the leading cities and the individuals, while faction is the cause of the most extreme evils.[425] He also applies the counter terms ὁμόνοια and στάσις to the internal relations within a single city. He asks the audience if they believe that they will be more loved by the gods if the city is in a state of faction than if they govern the city with good order and concord.[426] Likewise, the terms are applied to smaller units. He says that in every government there is no more serious threat to the existing conditions than faction. On the other hand, all men agree that concord is a fair thing and a means of safety.[427]

We do not at all claim to have presented an exhaustive coverage of passages where ὁμόνοια and στάσις occur as antonyms. This is not necessary with regard to our task. However, the examples we have collected should serve our purpose to adequately demonstrate that the terms were commonly used when one dealt with the question of unity and discord within different political units. These same terms occur in different types of literature, but are especially prevalent in Dio Chrysostoms' and Aelius Aristides' discourses on concord. We have not dealt with the reasons for στάσις, nor have we considered the question of how concord was established in the different cases. Our primary intention has been simply to show that στάσις belonged to the political vocabulary that dealt with the question of unity and strife within social units, and that στάσις and ὁμόνοια function as antonyms in these contexts. Nor have we discussed in detail the meaning of the term στάσις in the different passages we have focused upon. Nevertheless, it seems obvious that the term has the following range of meanings: faction, strife, civil discord, civil strife, sedition.[428] Some of the passages referred to above also demonstrate that στάσις was regarded as a great malady for society. Discord (διχοστασία) is "the greatest of the evils that befall states and the cause of the swiftest destruction"[429] and faction is "the cause of the most extreme evils".[430]

---

[424]Cf. Aristid. *Or.* 34.4: "but no one has ever disputed the fact that concord is the greatest good for cities". For the high estimate of concord, see also *Or.* 34.7, 26, 45.

[425]Aristid. *Or.* 23.53. Aristides emphasizes many times how great an evil faction is, cf. *Or.* 23.31, 40, 48, 54f, 57; 24.26, 30, 32.

[426]Aristid. *Or.* 24.47.

[427]Aristid. *Or.* 24.4. Also in Isocrates' *Panegyricus* we find an example of a similar use of the counter terms στάσις and ὁμόνοια. Here he exhorts the Greeks to live in concord in order to wage war against Persia. According to Isocrates a war against the barbarians is a means to be liberated from the poverty that afflicts their lives at the present time, and that "plunges the whole world into war and strife (εἰς πολέμους καὶ στάσεις) – then surely we shall enjoy a spirit of concord" (ὁμονοήσομεν, Isoc. *Or.* 4.174). This is the only passage in this discourse where στάσις and ὁμόνοια are explicitly contrasted with each other. Notwithstanding this, Isocrates uses the term at other times when he describes past and present conditions among the Greeks; and when we keep in mind the occasion of the discourse, it is likely that the term στάσις is contrasted with ὁμόνοια in these passages as well. Isocrates blames the barbarians, among other things, for the civil strife (στάσεις) they caused among the Greeks (*Or.* 4.114). The past has been filled with every form of horror, according to Isocrates, and he is thinking of wars (πόλεμοι) and factions (στάσεις) among themselves that have led to the fact that some people are being put to death contrary to law (*Or.* 4.167f.).

This means that when Clement chooses to depict the occurrences in the Corinthian Church with the term στάσις it is probably by no means fortuitous. It is, on the contrary, likely that Clement deliberately uses this particular term as the principal one to apply to the trouble facing the Church at Corinth. Clement's use of it both reveals his indebtedness to political vocabulary and demonstrates his awareness of using appropriate language to handle the issue.[431] Furthermore, and this is probably the most important reason for Clement to use just this particular term as the principal term for the happenings in the Corinthian Church, i.e. στάσις was connected in antiquity with very negative connotations and was viewed as the greatest evil to society. When Clement refers to the conflict as στάσις, it is therefore not a neutral designation of the situation in the Corinthian Church, but shows how serious and dangerous the situation was in the eyes of the author. By using it to describe the conflict in the congregation Clement gives the impression that he considers the present situation as a serious social threat to the life of the Church as a community. Just as στάσις is regarded as the greatest evil to society in that it has caused the greatest disasters, the στάσις in the Corinthian Church involves the greatest danger for the community. So when Clement explicitly states that the community will incur a great danger (κίνδυνος), if its members follow

---

[428]M. I. FINLEY, *Politics in the Ancient World* (1983) 105, asserts that *stasis* in a political context had a broad range of meaning from political grouping or rivalry through faction to open civil war. And he states further that "Nor, as we have seen, can we give a statistical picture of *stasis*. But we can say that *stasis* was a permanent threat, appearing in the record, when it does, as a political or constitutional conflict; not only between oligarchy and democracy but also between factions within either camp" (111).

[429]Dion. Hal. *Ant. Rom.* 7.42.1.

[430]Aristid. *Or.* 23.53.

[431]We note that Paul does not apply the term στάσις in 1 Corinthians when he discusses the strife in the congregation. Instead he prefers a group of other terms (σχίσμα, ἔρις, διχοστασία, φιλόνεικος, αἵρεσις, ἀκαταστασία). The fact that Paul does not use the most common term for sedition and domestic discord is striking. The suggestion of M. M. MITCHELL, *Paul and the Rhetoric of Reconciliation* (1991) 76f., n. 66, that indicates that Paul has deliberately avoided the term στάσις by pointing to rhetorical parallels is not convincing. When Dio Chrysostom in *Or.* 48.16f. maintains that "civil strife (στάσις) does not deserve even to be named among us, and let no man mention it", this ought rather to be understood as an emphasis of the fact that στάσις must not occur at all, that one must avoid behaving in a manner that gives cause for στάσις. The simple fact that Dio Chrysostom himself uses the term στάσις in many of his discourses also indicates that Mitchell is wrong at this point. That Paul does not use at least one of the *technical terms* ὁμόνοια and στάσις is in fact the most serious objection against the otherwise well-attested thesis of Mitchell that in 1 Corinthians Paul employs traditional deliberative rhetoric urging ὁμόνοια. However, the most interesting point regarding the present investigation is that in spite of the fact that the *technical terms* ὁμόνοια and στάσις do not occur in 1 Corinthians where Paul deals with sedition and strife at that point of time, Clement employs these stock terms in deliberative rhetoric urging concord. We may ask why. It is of course not possible to give a decisive answer to this question, but, in our opinion, the most reasonable answer is that Clement had better knowledge of this rhetorical tradition than Paul, and judged that these stock terms were appropriate for the subject under discussion. In addition, Clement may also have employed these terms because of their rhetorical force.

the purposes of men who rush into strife (ἔρις) and sedition (στάσις),[432] he reflects a common *topos* from the political arena.

Another question is whether the members of the Church at Corinth themselves would have described the occurrences that took place with such a strong term as στάσις. We cannot presume that they would. However, if Clement had succeeded in getting the congregation in Corinth to agree with his definition of the communal behaviour as στάσις, he would have made an important advance towards achieving the purpose of the letter. The members of the Church would probably have immediately got negative associations with the term στάσις. But if the readers of the letter, contrary to all expectations, did not recall the evils connected with στάσις, Clement's emphasis on the dangerous and evil consequences of στάσις would have reminded them of it.[433]

3.5.1.1.2. ἔρις

As mentioned above, Clement sometimes links στάσις with ἔρις when he depicts the occurrences that took place in the Corinthian Church. This coupling with στάσις, as well as the frequency of the term ἔρις, indicates that it is a fundamental term in the letter.[434] The present situation in the Corinthian Church is conditioned by ἔρις,[435] a situation that is dangerous for the community because ἔρις is the cause of death and destruction.[436]

The general meaning of the term ἔρις is "strife, quarrel, contention".[437] However, the term has a more specific meaning in a political context where it often designates domestic discord. As noted by L. L. Welborn, it expresses more than discussion and disagreement in general, but is much stronger.

> Ἔρις is hot dispute, the emotional flame that ignites whenever rivalry becomes intolerable. It invariably appears in accounts of ancient political life the moment the pressure of circumstances, that is, the approach of an enemy or the election of mutually hostile consuls, draws the citizens into confused knots.[438]

Welborn cites Plutarch's description of the situation at Rome when Caesar had crossed the Rubicon as an example of the use of the term in such a context. The people were divided concerning their attitude to Caesar – some supported him and some were

---

[432] *1 Clem.* 14:2.

[433] For example *1 Clem.* 14:2; 46:9.

[434] It occurs nine times. For text references see p. 85. This term occurs also in other ECL to describe strife and discord among member of the Church (1 Cor 1:11; 3:3; Titus 3:9; Phil 1:15; Ign. *Eph.* 8:1) and in a list of vices (Rom 1:29; 13:13; 2 Cor 12:20; Gal 5:20; 1 Tim 6:4). However, in none of these writings is the term employed nearly as frequently as in *1 Clement*. Although it is possible that Clement took over this term from Paul's letters, in particular 1 Corinthians, it seems more likely, when we compare the frequency of this term with other ECL, that Clement had other models.

[435] *1 Clem.* 3:2; 46:5.

[436] *1 Clem.* 6:4; 9:1; 14:2.

[437] H. G. LIDDELL and R. SCOTT, *A Greek-English Lexicon* (1973) 689 with references.

[438] L. L. WELBORN, "On the Discord in Corinth", *JBL* (1987) 87.

frightened. It is understandable in a conflict like this, where the future of the whole city was in question, that the conflict became emotional and that it culminated in violent disturbances throughout the city. Plutarch describes this emotional conflict as ἔρις.[439]

Another illustrative use of the term ἔρις by the same author occurs when he discusses the duty of the statesman. The statesman must act to "instil concord and friendship (ὁμόνοιαν ἐμποιεῖν καὶ φιλίαν) in those who dwell together with him and to remove strifes (ἔριδα), discords, and all enmity".[440] Here Plutarch explicitly contrasts ἔρις with ὁμόνοια. We should also note that Plutarch employs ἔρις and στάσις as synonyms. Immediately prior to the passage cited, he emphasizes the peacemaking role of a statesman in a similar way. The greatest and most noble function of a statesman is to prevent "factional discord (στασιάζω)".[441] In other words, when Plutarch defines the vital task of a statesman as being to prevent internal strife by using the term ἔρις in one place and στασιάζω in another, it shows that he uses these terms interchangeably.

If we turn to Dio Chrysostom, we will also find that according to him ἔρις belongs to the political vocabulary that describes domestic concord. At the end of the discourse that urges the Nicaeans to cease from civil strife and establish concord, like a father who prays for his children, he prays to the gods on behalf of Nicea. He prays that the gods (Homonoia among them) may implant unity in Nicea and "that they may cast out strife and contentiousness and jealousy" (στάσιν δὲ καὶ ἔριδα καὶ φιλονικίαν ἐκβαλεῖν).[442] The cluster of terms the orator uses to describe the present conditions function as antonyms to the terms designating the ideal of unity, namely a passion for love, singleness of purpose, a unity of wish and thought (ἔρωτα καὶ μίαν γνώμην καὶ ταῦτα βούλεσθαι καὶ φρονεῖν).[443] Also, in a speech to the Council of Apameia urging the audience to be reconciled with Prusia, he argues that friendship and concord (ὁμόνοια) are most expedient for both sides. However, he knows "how difficult it is to eradicate strife (ἔρις) from human beings".[444] These passages from two of the discourses on concord suffice to demonstrate that in Dio Chrysostom ἔρις is a part of the political vocabulary that designates discord and strife, and that it is used as an antonym to concord and its synonymous terms.

Furthermore, at the beginning of the discourse Περὶ ὁμονοίας ταῖς πόλεσιν Aelius Aristides states explicitly that the topic he is going to deal with is concord toward one another, "a very noble and proper topic for discussion".[445] In this connection we

---

[439]Plut. *Caes.* 33.3. In addition, Wellborn points to Thuc. 6.35; 2.21; App. *BCiv.* 2.2.6; 3.86.357; Joseph. *Ant* 14.470.

[440]Plut. *Mor.* 824 D. When Plutarch emphasizes this duty, he is simply following up what he has stated above regarding the greatest blessings which States can enjoy: "peace, liberty, plenty, abundance of men, and concord" (824 C).

[441]Plut. *Mor.* 824 C-D.

[442]Dio Chrys. *Or.* 39.8.

[443]Dio Chrys. *Or.* 39.8.

[444]Dio Chrys. *Or.* 41.8f. For other passages from the same author where ἔρις is contrasted to ὁμόνοια, see Dio Chrys. *Or.* 48.6; *Or.* 77/78.39.

should note that later in the discourse he employs the term ἔρις to describe the factional activities of the cities that competed for first place,[446] that he explicitly contrasts ἔρις and φιλονεικία (contention) with *homonoia*,[447] and that ἔρις and στάσις function as almost synonymous terms.[448]

These examples adequately demonstrate that ἔρις was commonly applied to denote political discord,[449] and that it functioned as a synonym of στάσις and thus an antonym for ὁμόνοια. In other words, ἔρις belonged to the semantic field of ὁμόνοια. The fact that the term is linked with and functions as a synonym to στάσις also shows the strong connotations associated with ἔρις.[450] In short, when Clement chooses to describe the strife and discord in the Corinthian Church as ἔρις, it is probably no accident. Rather, it is likely that he deliberately uses this common political term in his argument for concord.

3.5.1.2. ζῆλος καὶ φθόνος

We noted above that the terms ζῆλος καὶ φθόνος play an important role in *1 Clement*, particularly in chapters 4-6 where the author describes the evil effects of these vices. The basic meaning of ζῆλος is jealousy, but it could be given either a positive meaning, i.e. "eager rivalry, emulation",[451] "zeal, ardor",[452] or a negative meaning, i.e. "jealousy, envy".[453] In this connection the manner in which Aristotle distinguishes between ζῆλος and φθόνος is interesting:

> Emulation therefore is virtuous and characteristic of virtuous men, whereas envy is base and characteristic of base men (ἐπιεικές ἐστιν ὁ ζῆλος καὶ ἐπιεικῶν τὸ δὲ φθονεῖν φαῦλον καὶ φαύλων); for the one, owing to emulation, fits himself to obtain such goods, while the object of the other, owing to envy, is to prevent his neighbour possessing them (Arist. Rh. 2.11.1).

According to Aristotle ζῆλος is a feeling of pain (λύπη) caused by someone possessing something *we* do not have, but which is possible to achieve by emulation. In other

---

[445] Aristid. *Or.* 23.2f.

[446] Aristid. *Or.* 23.12.

[447] Aristid. *Or.* 23.28f.

[448] Aristid. *Or.* 23.40; 23.57-58.

[449] For further text references, see H. G. LIDDELL and R. SCOTT, *A Greek-English Lexicon* (1973) 689, and the passages pointed out by M. M. MITCHELL, *Paul and Rhetoric of Reconciliation* (1991) 81.

[450] In addition to the texts cited and referred to from D. Chrysostom and A. Aristides, we may point to passages from historical works that demonstrate the seriousness of ἔρις. ἔρις and στάις are used interchangeably in Dion. Hal. *Ant. Rom.* 1.87 (together with φιλονεικία); App. *BCiv.* 3.12.86; Joseph. *Bell* 4.128-132 (together with ταραχή, πόλεμος ἐμφύλιος, φιλόνεικος). Cf. also Ps.-Phoc. *Sent.* 74-75, that compares ἔρις with cancer. We may also note that Ἔρις is personified as the Greek counter goddess of Ὁμόνοια, the goddess of Discord, H. G. LIDDELL and R. SCOTT, *A Greek-English Lexicon* (1973) 689.

[451] H. G. LIDDELL and R. SCOTT, *A Greek-English Lexicon* (1973) 755, with references.

[452] W. BAUER, *A Greek-English Lexicon* (1979) 337, with references.

[453] *Ibid.* 337, with references.

words, ζῆλος is rooted in a genuine desire to possess something others possess, not *because* they have it, but because we do not have it and want it. Hence ζῆλος may be a virtue. φθόνος is also called a feeling of pain (λύπη), but it is not an expression of genuine desire to achieve the actual benefit. Rather, it is generated by the fact that *others* have it.[454] This means that φθόνος is always a vice.[455]

However, in spite of these theoretical distinctions, many authors use ζῆλος and φθόνος interchangeably to depict vices.[456] So when Clement employs ζῆλος and φθόνος as synonymous terms,[457] it is not unique to this author, but reflects a traditional usage. We may add that we do not find these terms combined in the New Testament. Thus it is not likely that any New Testament writings functioned as a model for Clement in his linking of them. What we should pay special attention to concerning the task in this chapter is that these vices were associated in antiquity with behaviour which disturbed the community and thus were the root of strife and war.[458] Plutarch, for instance, characterises ζῆλος and φθόνος (together with φιλονεικία) as "emotions most productive of enmity (ἔχθρα)",[459] and it is "of no slight importance to resist the spirit of contentiousness and jealousy (ζηλοτυπία) among brothers when it first creeps in over trivial matters", because it could develop into war.[460] Referring to *Lysias* 2.48 L. L. Welborn characterises ζῆλος as "the gnawing, unquiet root of civil strife – the real psychological cause of war".[461] That social strife and wars are attributed to φθόνος

---

[454]Arist. *Rh.* 2.11.1.

[455]Cf. E. MILOBENSKI, *Der Neid in der Griechischen Philosophie* (1964) 69f.: "Der ζῆλος ist in seiner Intention also positiv. Nicht so der Phthonos. In ihm ist nämlich, sofern man ihn seinem Wesen nach betrachtet, dieses den ζῆλος auszeichnende Moment des Habenwollens zurückgedrängt, mithin auch die Unlust über den eigenen Mangel ... Im Phthonos '(ergeht) die Intention unmittelbar auf fremden Schmerz ... nicht auf eigene Lust, wie immer Lust die objective Folge der Befriedigung des Strebens sein mag', im Zelos dagegen ergeht die Intention auf eigene Lust, nie, auch nicht mittelbar, auf fremden Schmerz". For a more thorough description of Aristotle's concept of φθόνος, see *ibid.* 59 - 96. Cf. also L. T. JOHNSON, "James 3:13-4:10 and the *Topos* ΠΕΡΙ ΦΘΟΝΟΥ", *NT* 25 (1983) 335. Johnson notes that Plutarch operates with a different sort of distinction between μῖσος and φθόνος. μῖσος (hate) always tends toward the harming of others, but φθόνος needs not. The reference to Plut. *Mor.* 536F, that Johnson cites, however, is not good. A main point in this passage is the similarity between hatred and envy. As antonyms of goodwill Plutrach says he considers "hatred and envy to be the same". But later on Plutarch distinguishes between μῖσος and φθόνος in the way Johnson proposes. See, e.g., *Mor.* 538D-F.

[456]E.g., Plut. *Mor.* 86 C; 91 B; 485 E; Pl. *Phlb.* 47 E; 50 B; *Symp.* 213 D; *Leg.* 679C; Democr. frg. 191; Lys. *Or.* 2.48; Hdn. 3.2.8; 1 Macc 8:16.

[457]The terms are connected with καί in *1 Clem* 3:2; 4:7; 5:2 and are used interchangeably in chaps. 4-6.

[458]H. E. LONA, *Der erste Clemensbrief* (1998), must admit that Clement's use of ζῆλος goes beyond the Christian and Hellenistic Jewish tradition. But, according to Lona, there is not much to gain in turning to the Greek literature (139). The following discussion intends to show how fruitful it is to read Clement's use of ζῆλος (and φθόνος) exactly in the light of this tradition.

[459]Plut. *Mor.* 86 C, cf. also 91 B.

[460]Plut. *Mor.* 488 A.

[461]L. L. WELBORN, "On the Discord in Corinth", *JBL* 106 (1987) 87.

is explicitly stated by Demokrit: "φθόνος γὰρ στάσις ἀρχὴν ἀπεργάζεται".[462] Furthermore, Herodian diagnoses the cause of civil strife and factional politics (στάσις καὶ διάφορος γνώμη) that broke out in Bithynia when the news of Severus' victory spread as not being "partisanship for or against one of the warring emperors so much as jealousy and inner-city rivalry" and envy and destruction of their compatriots (ὡς ζήλω καὶ ἔριδι τῇ πρὸς ἀλλήλας φθόνω τε καὶ καθαιρέσει).[463]

Because of the nature of φθόνος and its effects upon a political body it is not surprising to find passages that contrast φθόνος and ὁμόνοια.[464] After an exhortation not to be envious, the *Sentences of Pseudo-Phocylides* presented the heavenly beings as models of harmony. The stars and the moon are all ἄφθονοι, and the relationship between them is characterised by concord (ὁμόνοια). In support of this the author concludes: "For if there were strife (ἔρις) among the blessed ones, heaven would not stand firm". [465] We should note that the terms φθόνος, ἔρις and ὁμόνοια all occur in this passage, and that the first two are interrelated and function as antonyms of ὁμόνοια. Furthermore, in his oration περὶ φθόνου Dio Chrysostom describes the qualities of the ideal philosopher in contrasting terms. First he presents some qualities that should not characterise a true philosopher, i.e. "arousing strife or greed or contentions and jealousies and base desires for gain" (οὐ στάσιν ἐγείρων οὐδὲ πλεονεξίαν οὐδὲ ἔριδας καὶ φθόνους καὶ αἰσχρὰ κέρδη). Then in contrast he presents positive qualities that should distinguish him, i.e. "reminding men of sobriety and righteousness and promoting concord" (σωφροσύνης δὲ ὑπομιμνήσκων καὶ δικαιοσύνης καὶ ὁμόνοιαν αὔξων).[466] Regarding this passage we also note that φθόνος (linked with other political terms commonly related to strife and discord) is contrasted with ὁμόνοια.

That φθόνος (and ζῆλος), to use the words of Plutarch, involves "emotions most productive of enmity", and that it may lead to ἔρις and στάσις, implies that death is the ultimate consequence of φθόνος. This is even stated explicitly by Plato. Plato

---

[462]Democr. frg. 245. Regarding Demokrit's concept of φθόνος E. Milobenski, *Der Neid in der Griechischen Philosophie* (1964) emphasizes "seine Gefährlichkeit für das Gemeinschfsleben. Der Phthonos ist der Anfang des Bürgerkrieges" (3). On φθόνος as a cause of στάσις, cf. also D. Loenen, *Stasis* (1953) 16.

[463]Hdn. 3.2.7f. Instead of φθόνω τε καὶ καθαιρέσει, C. R. Whittaker (LCL) prefers φθορᾷ τε καὶ καθαιρέσει, probably because of a presumed parallel between the more abstract cause of the actions expressed by the word pair ζῆλος and ἔρις and the concrete consequence expressed by the word pair φθορά and καθαίρεσις. However, since no support of Whittaker's reading is found in the codices and the reading of the codices makes good sense, we prefer not to change the text witnesses.

[464]L. T. Johnson, "James 3:13-4:10 and the *Topos* ΠΕΡΙ ΦΘΟΝΟΥ", *NT* 25 (1983) 336: "That φθόνος opposes friendship is obvious, and since friendship involves a certain harmony (ὁμόνοια) between people, it follows that envy should destroy ὁμόνοια".

[465]Ps.-Phoc. *Sent.* 70-75. Cf. also E. Milobenski, *Der Neid in der Griechischen Philosophie* (1964) 7; L. T. Johnson, "James 3:13-4:10 and the *Topos* ΠΕΡΙ ΦΘΟΝΟΥ", *NT* 25 (1983) 336.

[466]Dio Chrys. *Or.* 77/78.39.

includes φθόνος among the passions (ἐπιθυμίαι) that can lead to murder.[467] He also discusses the punishment for murder caused by φθόνος and is of the opinion that such an act requires capital punishment.[468]

This should suffice to demonstrate that the terms φθόνος and ζῆλος are appropriate when one deals with the topic of internal strife and discord, and that the terms belong to the semantic field of ὁμόνοια. These vices were considered to be the cause of ἔρις and στάσις, and could also lead to death. Hence, when Clement connects φθόνος and ζῆλος with ἔρις[469] and στάσις[470] and attempts to demonstrate by means of historical examples that death is the ultimate result of these vices,[471] he reflects commonplaces of his cultural environment.

---

[467]Pl. *Leg.* 870 C-D. Cf. also L. T. JOHNSON, "James 3:13-4:10 and the *Topos* ΠΕΡΙ ΦΘΟΝΟΥ", *NT* 25 (1983) 336.

[468]Pl. *Leg.* 869 E. For a more detailed discussion on this aspect of Plato's conception of φθόνος cf. E. MILOBENSKI, *Der Neid in der Griechischen Philosophie* (1964) 41-47. In particular we should note Milobenski's emphasis on the political aspect of φθόνος: "Aber schwerwiegender ist abermals die 'politische' Konsequenz: dass nämlich letzten Endes die ganze Gemeinschaft durch das Tun und Treiben eines neidischen und missgünstigen Individuums in Mitleidenschaft gezogen und möglicherweise sogar der eigentliche Zweck des Staates und der Gesetze die sittliche Förderung der Bürger untergraben wird" (44).

[469]*1 Clem* 3:2; 5:5; 6:4; 9:1. The coupling of ζῆλος and φθόνος with ἔρις is also found in the New Testament and LXX. The conjunction of ζῆλος and ἔρις usually occurs in lists of vices: Rom 13:13; 2 Cor 12:20; Gal 5:20. In 1 Cor 3:1-3 Paul asserts that one of the causes of the internal strife in the Corinthian Church was that the Christians still behaved like fleshly men, since there was ζῆλος and ἔρις among them. Regarding the three last passages W. BAUER, *A Greek-English Lexicon*, remarks that "ζῆλος seems to be coordinate with ἔρις in the sense of 'rivalry' or 'party-attachment'" (337). That factionalism is a human failing was a *topos* in antiquity, M. M. MITCHELL, *Paul and the Rhetoric of Reconciliation* (1991) 82. In Sir 40:4 and 40:9 the terms are found together in catalogues of woes. The combination of φθόνος with ἔρις occurs in the catalogues of vices in Rom 1:29 and in 1 Tim 6:4. In Phil 1:15-17 the terms characterise those who preach Christ in the spirit of partisanship. E. W. FISHER, *Soteriology in First Clement* (1974), is of the opinion that "1 Clement need have looked no further than [1] Cor. 3:3 for its diagnosis of the situation at Corinth in which ζῆλος and ἔρις are identified as the central cause of the deterioration of the Corinthian Church" (80). Fisher may be right, but the following facts do not support his case: a) the ζῆλος – φθόνος concept plays a more significant role in *1 Clement* than in the letters of Paul, b) the conception of ζῆλος – φθόνος in antiquity was connected with strife and factionalism, and c) we find many other terms in *1 Clement* derived from ancient politics. All these features may suggest that it is not primarily Paul who is the model for the use of these terms, but rather that Clement employs commonplaces of his cultural environment. This is not to deny that Paul's use of the actual terms might have influenced Clement.

[470]*1 Clem.* 3:2; 4:12; 14:1f.; 43:2. We should note that the conjunction of ζῆλος and στάσις does not occur at all in the New Testament. This fact also indicates that Clement used different models than Paul regarding the ζῆλος – φθόνος conception.

[471]That ζῆλος and φθόνος may cause death is explicitly stated in 4:7: "You see, brethren, – jealousy and envy (ζῆλος and φθόνος) wrought fratricide"; in 5:2: "Through jealousy and envy (διὰ ζῆλον καὶ φθόνον) the greatest and most righteous pillars of the Church were persecuted and contended unto death"; and in 9:1 he maintains that ζῆλος and ἔρις lead to death. In addition, cf. 3:4; 4:12; 6:1, 4.

3.5.1.3. διωγμός καὶ ἀκαταστασία

The third word pair in 3:3 describing the situation in the Corinthian Church is διωγμός (persecution) καὶ ἀκαταστασία (instability, anarchy, confusion).[472] διωγμός occurs only in this passage in *1 Clement*, but the verb διώκω (persecute) occurs a number of times. It expresses the evil action to which prominent members of the people of God have been exposed as caused by φθόνος and ζῆλος.[473] We have not been able to find texts that explicitly link διωγμός with φθόνος and ζῆλος. However, from what we have just stated above about the nature of φθόνος and ζῆλος – that these vices are associated with *stasis* and war – it is understandable why Clement finds this term appropriate. In a chaotic situation characterised by *stasis* and war, it is likely that persecution took place against of one of the factions involved. If we pay attention to the record of the historians of antiquity, we will see that the term διωγμός was often used when they recounted that one of the parties in a war was persecuted.[474]

The term ἀκαταστασία occurs three times in the letter.[475] It is morphologically related to στάσις and, as just mentioned, means "instability, anarchy, confusion".[476] Also, ἀκαταστασία belonged to the cluster of terms in antiquity that referred to factionalism and civil strife. For instance, Polybius reports on the chaotic and turbulent situation that emerged when the hired armies of Carthage claimed their stipulated wages and the commander in-chief told them that it was not possible to meet their claims. He notes that this answer "produced at once a spirit of dissension and sedition" (διαφορά καὶ στάσις)[477] and states:

> Gesco [*a previous general in Sicily*] *saw how complete was the disorganization* (ἀκαταστασία) *and disturbance* (ταραχή), *but valuing more than anything the interest of his country and foreseeing that if these troops became utterly deaf to all considerations of humanity, Carthage would evidently be in the gravest danger* (κινδυνεύω) ...[478]

---

[472]H. G. Liddell - R. Scott, *A Greek-English Lexicon* (1973) 48.

[473]*1 Clem.* 4:9, 13; 5:2. Cf. also 45:4.

[474]E.g. Diod. Sic. 2.6.3; 4.48.5; 13.9.6; 16.68.3; Polyb. *Hist.* 1.34.9; 3.45.3; 5.86.1; 11.17.4; Dion. Hal. *Ant. Rom.* 3.25.3; 3.26.3; 11.33.4.

[475]*1 Clem.* 3:2; 14:1; 43:6.

[476] C.f. also A. Oepke, "ἀκαταστασία *TDNT* 3, 446.

[477]Polyb. *Hist.* 1.67.2.

[478]Polyb. *Hist.* 1.70.1. For other references by the same author, see 14.9.6 and 32.5.5 where ἀκαταστασία is paired with ταραχή as in the passages cited above. In Dion. Hal. *Ant. Rom.* 6.31.1 ἀκαταστασία and διχοστασία (sedition) are used interchangeably. Cf. also Nic. Dam. 90 frgs. 130; 110. The second century astrologer Vettius Valens applies "the term ten times in lists of misfortunes meted out by the various planets and stars, often accompanied by other terms of social and political upheaval: στάσις (190.33; 191.25; 230.34), ταραχή (190.33; 191.25 [misprint for 191.29]), ἔχθρα (191.3,26; 193.14; 197.4), and ζηλοτυπία (191.25)", thus M. M. Mitchell, *Paul and the Rhetoric of Reconciliation* (1991) 173 n. 656. Mitchell also pays attention to the cognate verb καταστασιάζω, to "overpower by forming a counter-party", in the passive; "to be factiously opposed or overpowered", by referring to H. G. Liddell - R. Scott, *A Greek-English Lexicon* (1973) 913. She thereby demonstrates the political context of the verb (173 n. 657).

The use of ἀκαταστασία in connection with political rivalry is also found in the New Testament. In 1 Cor 14:33 ἀκαταστασία is used as the opposite of εἰρήνη (peace), in 2 Cor 12:20 Paul links ἀκαταστασία with ἔρις and ζῆλος, and the Epistle of James associates ἀκαταστασία with ζῆλος and ἐριθεία (3:16).[479]

This means that, when Clement describes the situation at the Corinthian Church as ἀκαταστασία and says that the instigators of the sedition acted in ἀκαταστασία, he uses conventional language related to the issue of political upheaval and demonstrates once again his ability to choose appropriate language.

3.5.1.4. πόλεμος καὶ αἰχμαλωσία

The last word pair in 3:2 characterises the Corinthian situation in terms of πόλεμος καὶ αἰχμαλωσία (war and captivity). Clement also uses the word πόλεμος together with other terms related to the situation at Corinth in 46:5 where he asks, "Why are there strife and passion and divisions and schisms and war among you?" (ἱνατί ἔρεις καὶ θυμοὶ καὶ διχοστασίαι καὶ σχίσματα πόλεμός τε ἐν ὑμῖν;). It has been noted that πόλεμος καὶ αἰχμαλωσία (war and captivity) may not express the real historical situation at the Corinthian Church at all. We agree with the view that the terms are figurative and are an expression of Clement's hyperbolic style.[480] However, what should be emphasized in this connection is that the rhetorical force of these terms in all likelihood is not the only reason for Clement's use of them. As we have seen above the topic of war was found in all the lists of appropriate topics in deliberative rhetoric, a fact that is confirmed by a number of extant discourses as well.[481] Therefore, the introduction of the topic "war" ought also to be understood in the light of the fact that it was a part of the traditional topic of deliberative rhetoric.[482] Furthermore, since faction was regarded as "the cause of the most extreme evils" in the ancient world, it is equally to be expected that πόλεμος would be connected with the evils of strife and sedition. Dio Chrysostom, for instance, states of Diogenes that he kept himself clear of "rivalries (φιλονεικία), wars (πόλεμος), and factions (στάσις)".[483] According to the same author in a discussion on possible future allies, Tyndareus argued that one should not "leave any cause for war (πόλεμος) and dissension (στάσις) among the Greeks".[484] Also, in one of his discourses on concord, he says many love the opposite of concord – they love "strife (στάσις) of which wars (πόλεμος) and battles (μάχη) constitute departments and subsidiary activities". He goes on to say that such an attitude is contrary to the general view that wars, factions, diseases (πόλεμοι καὶ στάσεις καὶ

---

[479]Regarding 1 Cor 14:33 M. M. MITCHELL concludes: "this key term (ἀκαταστασία) clearly refers not to some general undefined unruliness, but to the specific manifestation of Corinthian partisanship and divisiveness in the worship of the community" (*Paul and the Rhetoric of Reconciliation* (1991) 173).

[480]So R. KNOPF, *Die zwei Clemensbriefe* (1920) 48; B. E. BOWE, *"A Church in Crisis"* (1988) 27, 61.

[481]See p. 61.

[482]So also B. E. BOWE, *"A Church in Crisis"* (1988) 61.

[483]Dio Chrys. *Or.* 6.31.

[484]Dio Chrys. *Or.* 11.53.

νόσοι) are regarded as evils.[485] The connection between strife and war cannot be made more explicit than by Aelius Aristides: "Actually, where there is faction, there is also war against ourselves; but where there is proper war, the danger is both simple and easier".[486] Clement's use of the term αἰχμαλωσία is understandable when we take account of the fact that in many cases war led to captivity for some of the people involved.[487] This means that when Clement describes the condition in the Corinthian Church as πόλεμος καὶ αἰχμαλωσία, he uses a common topic in deliberative rhetoric and makes use of conventional language connected with the issue of strife and sedition.[488]

3.5.1.5. Summary of the Political Language 1 Clement 3:2

We have attempted above to demonstrate that all the terms Clement uses in 3:2 to depict the situation in the Corinthian Church belong to conventional political language that dealt with the cause of sedition, the sedition itself, or the consequence of sedition. Some of the terms were especially common in deliberative rhetoric urging ὁμόνοια. Later in the present work it will be argued that *1 Clem.* 3:2 is a part of the *narratio* section.[489] In other words, when Clement gives a report of the occurrences that have taken place in the Corinthian Church, he employs terms that belonged in a general way to the semantic field of concord. This observation is significant with respect to what the author considered to be the main subject in the letter, i.e. concord among Christians.

---

[485]Dio Chrys. *Or.* 38.11, 13.

[486]Aristid. *Or.* 23.55. Cf. B. E. BOWE, *A Church in Crisis* (1988) 61.

[487]For the use of the nouns αἰχμαλωσία and αἰχμαλωτός or the verb αἰχμαλωτίζω in such a context, cf., e.g., Polyb. *Hist.* 1.80.4; 1.83.8; Dion. Hal. *Ant. Rom.* 1.34.2; 3.66.1, and several references listed by H. G. LIDDELL and R. SCOTT, *A Greek-English Lexicon* (1973) 45.

[488]Contra K. BEYSCHLAG, *Clemens Romanus und der Frühkatholizismus* (1966) 143, who argues that the expression πόλεμος καὶ αἰχμαλωσία in "c. 3.2 einer älteren – und dann sicher apologetischen – Überlieferung folgt, in welcher ursprünglich vom Ungehorsam (bzw. Unglauben) Israels und seiner Bestrafung durch 'Krieg und Gefangenschaft' die Rede war", more precisely it is "vor allem an die babylonische Gefangenschaft gedacht" (141). Our main objection to Beyschlag's line of argumentation in general is that the literature he uses as comparative literature for *1 Clement* is to a great extent more recent than *1 Clement*. Regarding the expression πόλεμος καὶ αἰχμαλωσία Beyschlag's conclusion is based to a great extent on a comparison with *Clem. recogn* 1.37.1. In spite of the error connected with such a methodology, it seems likely that the fundamental topic in Israel's history – that apostasy from God leads to captivity – has influenced Clement in his choice of expression. His allusion to Deut 32:15 in 3:1 may point in this direction. The context of Deut 32:15 deals specifically with the cardinal sin of Israel, i.e. apostasy from God. However, the evidence we have put forward above from Greek literature makes it more likely that the way Clement expresses himself is rooted primarily in political language connected with the topic of unity and strife.

[489]See chap. 4, pp. 224-226.

3.5.2. Other Political Terms and topoi in 1 Clement 1-3

In the following we intend to focus upon other terms and *topoi* not discussed in chapter 3.5.1, but which are associated with the ideal of ὁμόνοια. We shall begin at 1:1 and move sequentially through the chapters.

3.5.2.1. συμφορά and περίπτωσις

After the prescript the author continues with an apology for not having written before.[490] He says that the Church at Rome had not paid attention to the occurrences in the Corinthian Church because it had itself been exposed to "sudden and repeated misfortunes (συμφορά) and calamities" (περίπτωσις, 1:1).[491] As mentioned in the introductory chapter, since the fundamental work by J. B. Lightfoot on the Apostolic Fathers, συμφορά and περίπτωσις have traditionally been interpreted as an allusion to the persecution of the Roman Church under Domitian's reign (81-96). We noted also that some scholars have questioned the traditional view, maintaining instead that συμφορά and περίπτωσις refer to internal strife and sedition in the Roman Church. The most significant exposition of the latter view is an article by L. L. Welborn where he succeeded in identifying some passages where συμφορά and περίπτωσις constitute a part of the political vocabulary regarding internal strife.[492] Welborn's article is a good starting point, especially on the political background of the term συμφορά.[493]

Concerning συμφορά the most illuminating examples that Welborn presents are found in Diodorus Siculus. This author links στάσις and συμφορά. After the inhabitants on the island Euboea fell into strife among themselves (ἐστασίασαν πρὸ ἀλλήλους) and the island was devastated, they were "admonished by the disasters (ταῖς συμφοραῖς), the parties came to an agreement (εἰς ὁμόνοιαν) and made peace (εἰρήνην) with one another".[494] Here συμφορά designates either the internal strife itself or the consequences of the strife. It is also interesting to note that in this passage συμφορά occurs in a context where ὁμόνοια and εἰρήνη are antonyms of στάσις.

---

[490]We cannot follow L. L. WELBORN, "On the Date of First Clement", *BR* 29 (1984) when he argues that it was "customary for one who gave advice on concord to excuse his delay by reference to personal or domestic hindrances" (46). As far as we can see, neither Dio Chrys. *Or.* 40.1 nor Aristid. *Or.* 24.1, each of whom Welborn uses as evidence, contains any excuse for not having intervened at an earlier point of time.

[491]A,C¹ and S read περιπτώσεις while H reads περιστάσεις. Beside the fact that H in general represents a linguistic improvement of A, the support of C¹ and S is so strong that we follow A and read περιπτώσεις. For the relationship between A and H with regard to text criticism, see, e.g., J. A. FISCHER, *Die Apostolischen Väter* (1966) 21; G. SCHNEIDER, *Clemens von Rom* (1994) 60.

[492]L. L. WELBORN, "On the Date of First Clement", *BR* 29 (1984) 35-54. Regarding the A, C¹ and S' reading περιπτώσεις Welborn has not found any texts or inscriptions where this term occurs in connection with internal strife. However, if one follows H and reads περιστάσεις, Welborn has demonstrated that this term is found in inscriptions that deal with internal strife. He refers to *OGI* 335.15 (second century B.C); Ditt., *Syll* 685.137 (139 B.C.); *OGI* 339.17 (133 B.C.); Ditt., *Syll* 730.20; Ditt., *Syll.* 708.7 (100 B.C.); *OGI* 194.3, 47f.

The number of adequate texts, however, that Welborn has referred to is quite limited. In our opinion, we are in need of more instances to confirm his thesis and to help settle the question. Therefore, in the following we will present some of the passages we have been able to identify where συμφορά occurs in political contexts that discuss internal strife.

Isocrates clearly includes στάσις among the συμφοραί that used to strike the Greek *polis*. Among other things, the Spartans are praised for their concord among themselves (τῆς πρὸς ἀλλήλους ὁμονοίας). The strongest proof of this concord, according to Isocrates, is that the Spartans, in contrast with other Hellenic states, have not "been involved in the misadventures (συμφορά) which are wont to happen to states, … in the city of the Spartans no one can show an instance of civil faction (στάσις)".[495]

In addition to the passage of Diodorus Siculus cited by Welborn, there are two other passages from the same author that throw light on the political background of συμφορά. Because he wanted to seduce a girl, a Roman lawmaker wrongly claimed before the magistrate that the girl was his slave. After the magistrate had listened to the charge, he handed the girl over to the lawgiver as his slave. Her father, however, enlisted the sympathy of soldiers of the army because of the injustice that his daughter had suffered. This episode gave raise to internal strife. Diodorus Siculus writes:

> Since a great spirit of contention (φιλοτιμία) now threatened the state, the most respectable citizens, foreseeing the greatness of the danger (τὸ μέγεθος τοῦ κινδύνου), acted as ambassadors between both parties to reach an agreement and begged them with great earnestness to cease from the civil discord (στάσις) and not plunge their fatherland into such serious distress (μεγάλαι συμφοραί, 12.25.1f.).

In addition to our main point in this connection, i.e. that Diodorus obviously characterises the consequences of internal strife with the term συμφορά, we should pay attention to the fact that he describes the present situation as involving a great danger

---

[493]Before Welborn pays attention to the political background of συμφορά and περίπτωσις, he considers the meaning of these terms. With reference to Liddell and Scott he maintains that συμφορά in Attic Greek often means nothing more than "event" or "circumstance", and that περίπτωσις has a similar neutral meaning: "experience" or "accident". This fact leads him to conclude that "there is no linguistic justification for interpreting the words *symforai kai periptoseis* (or *peristaseis*) as an allusion to persecution. Later chapters show that the author can speak plainly of *diogmos* and *thlipsis*" (39). He therefore opposes a "strong" translation of these terms as "misfortunes and calamities", K. Lake, *The Apostolic Fathers 1* (1977) 9; "Unbilden und Missgeschicken", A. von HARNACK, *Einführung in die alte Kirchengeschichte* (1929) 12; "Heimsuchungen und Drangsale", J. A. FISCHER, *Die Apostolischen Väter 1* (1966) 24. However, we should note that Welborn does not mention that according to H. G. LIDDELL and R. SCOTT, *A Greek-English Lexicon* (1973) 1688, συμφορά also may have the "strong" meaning "misfortune". Concerning συμφορά Welborn points to the following texts: Thuc. 2. 59.2; 61.3-4, 4 Macc 3:21; Diod. Sic. 16.7.2; Joseph. *Bell* 5.32. However, not all these passages are as convincing on this point as Welborn maintains. In the two references to Thucydides συμφορά is not linked to internal strife, but is a result of external war.

[494]Diod. Sic. 16.7.2.

[495]Isoc. *Or.* 12.258f.

(κίνδυνος) for the inhabitants of the *polis*. He uses precisely the same language that Clement uses to describe the consequences of the present strife and sedition for the Corinthian Church.[496] In other words, in this passage from Diodorus συμφορά is used together with other conventional terms which were used when internal strife was discussed in antiquity.

In addition, Diodorus writes about the serious civil strife (μεγάλη στάσις) that took place in Corcyra.[497] According to him, there had never been greater quarrelling (ἔρις) and contentiousness (φιλονεικία) in any other state. This strife led to bloodshed, with fifteen hundred of the leading citizens being killed (Diod. Sic. 13.48.2). However, the most important thing to note in this connection is that he describes the accidents that took place with the term συμφορά (Diod. Sic. 13.48.3). It is not clear whether συμφορά refers to the civil strife itself or to the bloodshed caused by the strife. Perhaps we should not draw so great a distinction between cause and effect, since each depends on the other. It seems reasonable to suggest that συμφορά refers both to the internal strife itself and to what it caused.

In his speech *To the Rhodians: Concerning Concord* Aelius Aristides uses the term συμφορά twice. First he compares his reaction toward the misfortune (συμφορά) of an earthquake and then his reaction toward the report that the Rhodians "distrust one another, have taken sides, and are involved in disturbances".[498] In the first case Aristides accommodated himself toward the ambassadors who reported the happenings, but in the second case he did not know whether he should believe or disbelieve the report. What we wish to stress in this connection is that he estimates the second situation to be much more terrible. Although the term συμφορά is not applied explicitly to sedition itself or to the result of discord, the term is used implicitly to describe the seriousness of the situation. If the earthquake had involved συμφορά, how much worse was the strife and discord among the Rhodians!

The second time Aristides uses συμφορά it is linked more directly to the internal strife facing the Rhodes. The orator argues that the change of status of the Greeks and all the Greek cities is not caused by military intervention by enemies but by factions against each other and by a state of general disharmony. Previously, when Greek affairs were in a state of dissension, Aristides could understand why the Rhodians were involved in strife, but now there is no reason for such behaviour. So he warns them:

> ... *the misfortune (συμφορά) is even greater if in such times as these when there is no fear or danger and it is possible to enjoy as much felicity as one wishes, you shall intentionally abandon, as it were, the portion of the public fund that has fallen to you (Or. 24.30).*

---

[496]"For we shall incur no common harm, but great danger (μᾶλλον κίνδυνος), if we rashly yield ourselves to the purposes of men who rush into strife and sedition" (*1 Clem.* 14:2. See also 41:4; 47:7; 59:1).

[497]Diod. Sic. 13.48.

[498]Aristid. *Or.* 24.3.

In this passage συμφορά obviously refers to the consequence of στάσις of which the "nature is ever to deprive people of their existing advantages".[499]

Philo links *stasis* with συμφορά. According to Philo desire for money or glory or pleasure is the source of internal faction (στάσις). The important point in this connection is that the factions have led to the result that "land and sea are filled with ever-fresh calamities (συμφορά) wrought by battles on sea and campaigns on land".[500]

A connection between στάσις and συμφορά is found in comparatively many passages by Josephus as well. For instance, he uses the term συμφορά to describe the situation of the Israelites when the Kingdom had ended and the ten tribes had to emigrate from Judaea. According to him, the beginning of this misfortune was the στάσις against Roboamos.[501] At the beginning of *The Jewish War* Josephus writes that he cannot refuse to give his personal sympathies scope to bewail his country's misfortunes (ταῖς τῆς πατρίδος συμφοραῖς), because "it owed its ruin to civil strife" (στάσις)".[502] Farther on, Herod is said to have faced incurable misfortunes (ἀνήκεστος συμφορά), "for the dissension (στάσις) in the palace was like a civil war".[503] In all these passages the author employs the term συμφορά when he describes the dangerous consequences of στάσις for different political bodies.[504]

It is time to conclude this brief survey of the use of the term συμφορά in texts that discuss the issue of internal strife and discord in different political bodies. As we have seen, the term occurs both in discussions of strife and sedition between different πόλεις that naturally belonged to the same political body of Greek city-states and in discussions of strife and sedition within a certain πόλις, within a people, or within a household. In this political context συμφορά may refer to the strife and discord itself, or to the evil consequences of the strife, or to both. These examples should suffice to demonstrate that συμφορά belonged to the conventional language used when strife and concord within a political body were discussed. This fact indicates that when Clement refers to the συμφορά facing the Roman Church in his apology for not having turned to the affairs in the Corinthian Church at an earlier point of time, it is plausible that he alludes to internal strife. Just as συμφορά in the above-mentioned texts refers to στάσις, or the dangerous consequences of στάσις for a political body, in *1 Clement* συμφορά refers to serious problems within the Roman Church caused by internal strife. It is against this background that we advocate a "strong" rendering of the term and read "misfortunes", and not because the term alludes to a persecution of the Church.[505]

---

[499] Aristid. *Or.* 24.30.

[500] Philo *Decal* 152f.

[501] Joseph. *Ant* 9.281f.

[502] Joseph. *Bell* 1.10f.

[503] Joseph. *Ant* 16.188f.

[504] In addition to the above-mentioned passages from Josephus, we may point to the following passages by the same author where the connection between συμφορά and στάσις is reflected: *Bell* 1.27; 2.411; 6.1; 6.207f. However, the connection is not so obvious as in the passages cited in the main text.

That Clement uses the term συμφορά to allude to internal strife seems to be confirmed later in the letter. We have 7:1 particularly in mind where the author discloses the reason for writing. He says that the letter is not only written to admonish the Christians in Corinth, but also that they may remind themselves (ἑαυτοὺς ὑπομιμνήσκοντες). The interesting point in this connection, however, is the reason for the need to include the Roman Church in the admonition as well, i.e. that they are in the same arena (σκάμμα) and that the same struggle (ἀγών) is before them. As the context makes clear, the author has just concluded the list of examples of the grim consequences of ζῆλος καὶ ἔρις by stating that "they have overthrown great cities, and rooted up mighty nations" (*1 Clem.* 6:4). This would seem to suggest that σκάμμα is not the pit of the Roman coliseum, but the moral arena where the Christian athlete strives. Likewise, the ἀγών is not the struggle against wild beasts, but against the power of ζῆλος καὶ ἔρις.[506] In other words, the author gives the readers the impression that the Roman Church has to struggle with the same problems as they have themselves. The abundant use of the hortatory subjunctive in first person plural by which the author includes himself in the admonition shapes the same impression and is consistent with the statement in 7:1.[507]

It is therefore reasonable to infer that the term συμφορά refers to internal strife and sedition. Regarding the term that is linked with συμφορά, i.e. περίπτωσις, we have not been able to demonstrate a similar connection with internal strife. In fact, we have not been able to identify a single passage where the word περίπτωσις occurs in such a

---

[505]Contra L. L. WELBORN "On the Date of First Clement", *BR* 29 (1984) 35-54. In spite of his overall thesis being correct, i.e. that συμφορά must be interpreted in the light of discussions on internal strife, he advocates the more colorlessness "event" or "circumstance". In addition to the references to H. G. LIDDELL and R. SCOTT, *A Greek-English Lexicon* (1978) 1688, J. H. MOULTON and G. MILLIGAN, *The Vocabulary of the Greek Testament* (Grand Rapids: Eerdmans, 1980) 598, he adduces Aesch. *Eum.*1020; Soph. *OT* 33; *Trach.* 1145; Eur. *Ion* 536; Herod. 7.49; 1.32; Thuc. 1.140.1; *Socr. Ep.28*; Aesch. *Pers.* 445; Dio Chrys. 29.19; 34.28 and others as evidence (38f.). On the basis of Welborn's main thesis it is puzzling to us that he, when discussing the rendering of the term, he lets the use of the term in these passages serve as references, and not the passages where συμφορά is used in connection with internal strife. If he had pointed out, as we have, a greater number of passages where συμφορά occurs in such a political context, he would probably have seen that a stronger rendering is to be preferred and that such a rendering does not need to imply support for the traditional view that interprets συμφορά as an allusion to persecution.

[506]Cf. L. L. WELBORN "On the Date of First Clement", *BR* 29 (1984) 47, who also refers to Dibelius.

[507]Another issue is whether or not the Roman Church was *in fact* facing the same problem with internal strife and faction as the Corinthian Christians were according to Clement. It is possible that the author consciously wanted to create the impression that the Roman Church was facing the same problems as the Church in Corinth so that it should not appear to be lording it over the brethren in Corinth. However, with the aim of this chapter in view, it is not necessary to take up a position regarding this question. We limit ourselves to pointing out *how* the author recounted the case and how the audience most likely would have perceived it.

context.[508] In general this word has the colourless meaning of "experience".[509] However, it may also have the stronger meaning of "misfortune".[510] This fact opens up the possibility that περίπτωσις may refer to internal strife which in the view of Clement indeed leads to "misfortune". Additionally, it is possible to view the word pair συμφορά and περίπτωσις as a hendiadys. If this is correct, it supports both the strong rendering and the view that περίπτωσις alludes to internal strife.

3.5.2.2. μιαρός and ἀνόσιος Sedition, Alien to the Elect of God

After his apology for not having written before, Clement refers to the questions disputed among the Corinthians and mentions explicitly that a στάσις has struck the Church. He depicts this στάσις as μιαρός and ἀνόσιος (abominable and unholy) and as "alien and foreign to the elect of God" (1:1). He takes the Corinthian Christians' status as the people of God as a point of departure and argues that this status is inconsistent with the present situation in the Corinthian Church. Because God has elected them and they live in "the city of God"[511] sedition ought not to occur. This line of argument is remarkably like the one Dio Chrysostom utilises when he advises the Niceans to cease from civil strife:

> But it is fitting that those whose city was founded by gods should maintain peace and concord and friendship (εἰρήνη καὶ ὁμόνοια καὶ φιλία) toward one another (Or. 39.2).

What Dio Chrysostom asserts here positively is almost the same as what Clement has expressed in a negative way, namely that people belonging to a divinely founded city ought to maintain "peace and concord". In other words, strife and sedition is inconsistent with the will of Nicaea's founders. Likewise, in his discourse on concord to the Rhodians Aristides also connects the issue of concord with their relationships to the gods. First he asks rhetorically if the audience believe that they are more loved by the gods if they "are in a state of faction (στασιάζοντες) and unrest and hate one another" than when they govern their "city with good order (εὐνομία) and concord (ὁμόνοια)".[512] And so he continues:

---

[508] As mentioned above L. L. WELBORN, "On the Date of First Clement", *BR* 29 (1984), has pointed out several inscriptions where the reading of Η περιστάσεις occurs in association with strife and sedition in a political body; see n. 492 above. A problem with the in many ways illuminating article by Welborn is that he neither discusses nor distinguishes between the different readings at this point. It appears that he prefers the reading of H. We have argued above that the reading of A is preferable. Therefore we do not find the findings of Welborn concerning περιστάσεις relevant regarding the present study.

[509] H. G. LIDDELL and R. SCOTT, *A Greek-English Lexicon* (1973) 1384f.

[510] W. BAUER, *Greek-English Lexicon* (1979) 650.

[511] Cf. *1 Clem.* 54:4 where the author explicitly uses the metaphor πολιτεία τοῦ Θεοῦ for the Christians.

[512] Aristid. *Or.* 24.47.

> Well! If you are beloved by the gods, do you think that you should be involved in fac-
> tion and unrest (στασιάζειν καὶ ταράττεσθαι) and live to suit the curses of your
> enemies or rather on the contrary act in accordance with the prayers of men of moder-
> ation ...? Since faction is both foreign to you and hateful to the gods (στάσις ὑμῶν
> ἀλλότριον καὶ θεοῖς ἐχθρόν), and concord (ὁμόνοια) appears to be the only
> means of safety, it is surely proper to accept the result as you would the calculation of a
> sum (Or. 24.48).

A basic element in Aristides' line of argumentation is that domestic discord is not con-
gruent with their status as beloved of the gods because the gods hate faction.[513] A consequence of this axiom is that, just as Clement regarded στάσις as foreign (ἀλλότριος)
to the elect of God, Aristides regarded faction as foreign (ἀλλότριος) to the beloved of
the gods, in this case the Rhodians. It appears therefore that his appeal, in which he
refers to the audience's relationship with the gods or the God, was a *topos* in deliberative
rhetoric urging concord.[514]

As noted above, Clement describes the στάσις by using the adjectives μιαρός and
ἀνόσιος. The latter in particular and its positive counterpart are important terms that
occur throughout the letter.[515] Clement is probably to some degree influenced by the
use of the term ὅσιος in the LXX where it also occurs frequently.[516] However, in this
connection we should underscore the political connotations of the term. In the religion
of the Greek *polis* the main point was to show the gods fidelity due to their role as
founders of the city and in this type of political religion ὅσιος is "technische Bedeu-

---

[513]That concord was connected with the gods is well attested in Graeco-Roman literature. The
concordant constitution of Lycurcus is regarded as being of divine origin (Polyb. *Hist.* 6.48.2). In one
of his discourses on concord Dio Chrysostom contrasts the divine origin of concord with the human
origin of factionalism: "However, the only respect in which we fall short of the blessedness of the gods
and of their indestructible permanence is this – that we are not all sensitive to concord (ὁμόνοια), but,
on the contrary, there are those who actually love its opposite, strife" (στάσις, *Or.* 38.11). Thus it is the
divine heavenly bodies that offer the best examples of concordant behaviour: "Do you not see in the
heavens as a whole and in the divine and blessed things that dwell therein an order (τάξις) and concord (ὁμόνοια) and self-control (σωφροσύνη) which is eternal [?] ... these things ... are wont to be
preserved as a result of their mutual friendship and concord (φιλία καὶ ὁμόνοια) for ever, not only
the more powerful and greater but also those reputed to be the weaker" (*Or.* 40.35f.). In contrast with
the divine origin of concord, factionalism is a human failing; in addition to Dio Chrys. *Or.* 38.11, cf.
Thuch. 3.82.2; Dion. Hal. *Ant. Rom.* 6. 66.1; 8.52.1 and the discussion on this "well-attested *topos* in
Greco-Roman literature" and Paul's employing of it in *1 Cor* in M. M. Mitchell, *Paul and the Rhetoric
of Reconciliation* (1991) 82.

[514]This of course does not mean that Clement's argumentation on this point is rooted in Hellenistic religion and the common sense of the Greek-Roman world. But Clement seems to make use of a
topos that he transfers and adjusts to a Christian context.

[515]ἀνόσιος, *1 Clem.* 1:1; 6:2; 45:4, ὅσιος, *1 Clem.* 2:3; 14:1; 45:3, 7; 56:16; 58:1, ὁσιότης, *1 Clem.*
29:1; 32:4; 48:4; 60:2. By comparison it occurs ten times in the whole NT, see A. Schmoller, *Handkonkordanz* (1982) 369.

[516]For the use of the term in the LXX, see F. Hauck, "ὅσιος κτλ.", *TDNT* 5, 490f.

tung verschaffte. Es war ein politisches Wort".[517] The term had a wide range of meanings, but it was often used in connection with obedience to the law of the gods.[518] At the same time, it also had a wider meaning and could depict actions that were in accordance with natural law and ancient customs.[519] However, in antiquity one generally did not distinguish between a religious and a secular sphere with respect to obedience to the law of the *polis*. A. A. T. Ehrhardt summarizes what it was for men in antiquity:

> [Es war] … die gerechte Verfassung und Verwaltung der Polis ein entscheidender Teil ihres Gottesdienstes. Gute Ordnung wurde gerade auf diese Weise zur religiösen Pflicht; die Revolution wurde zum Sakrileg. Die Polis war von einem geistigen Prinzip beherrscht, das von den Göttern stammte. Durch die Anstrengungen ihrer Bürger, sie in Harmonie mit dem göttlichen Willen zu bringen, wurde sie heilig.[520]

So when Clement describes the sedition as ἀνόσιος he is consistent with this political use of the word.[521] As discussed above, he regarded sedition as inconsistent with the Corinthians' status as the people of God and thus as a transgression of his laws.[522] That it is appropriate to depict sedition as ἀνόσιος is confirmed by the fact that, according to Dio Cassius, Agrippa refers to this evil as στάσις ἀνόσιος as well.[523]

3.5.2.3. ἀπόνοια

After Clement has described the sedition as μιαρός and ἀνόσιος he goes on to describe the present state of affairs as ἀπόνοια (1:1). This term occurs once more in the letter where it is also connected with the present state of discord. In 46:7 he finishes a series of rhetorical questions, each of which contains a number of political terms related to domestic discord, by asking why the present situation has reached such an ἀπόνοια that the Christians at Corinth forget that they are members of each other. The basic meaning of this term is "loss of all sense", "madness",[524] but in some passages the term depicts a particular kind of madness, i.e. the madness connected with sedition and political upheaval.[525] This fact may indicate that ἀπόνοια belonged to the cluster of terms associated with the topic of internal strife. Thus it is another example of appropriate language.[526]

---

[517] A. A. T. EHRHARDT, *Politische Metaphysik von Solon bis Augustin* vol. 1 (1959) 60. For a discussion of this political term, see 53-69.

[518] F. HAUCK, "ὅσιος κτλ.", *TDNT* 5, 489.

[519] *Ibid.* 490 with text references.

[520] A. A. T. ERHARDT, *Politische Metaphysik von Solon bis Augustin* vol. 1 (1959) 69.

[521] *Idem. Politische Metaphysik von Solon bis Augustin* vol. II (1959) 55, where he says that of the many political expressions in *1 Clement* "gehört vor allem ὅσιος, das ein Lieblingswort des Klemens ist".

[522] A connection between the present state of sedition in the Corinthian Church and behaviour contrary to the commandments of God is made explicit in *1 Clem.* 3:4.

[523] Dio Cass. 52.15.5.

[524] H. G. LIDDELL and R. SCOTT, *A Greek-English Lexicon* (1973) 211.

3.5.2.4. βέβαιος πίστις

Clement moves on to praise the noble life of the Christians at Corinth previous to the present strife and sedition. As he begins his praise he focuses on their excellent and steadfast faith (βέβαιος πίστις, 2:2). It is not fruitful or necessary in view of the scope of this investigation to discuss the different meanings and applications of the term πίστις in Early Christianity in general or to discuss Clement's use of the term in detail.[527] We will confine ourselves to saying that is seems reasonable to assert that in

---

[525]This was first recognised by P. MIKAT, *Die Bedeutung der Begriffe Stasis und Aponoia* (1969) 24f., who points to the following texts (besides the one reference, Antig. Nic. *Apud Hephaestionem Astrologum*. 2:18, given in H. G. LIDDELL and R. SCOTT, *A Greek-English Lexicon*, 211), Eus. *h.e.* 4. 2:1f; 4. 6:1ff; Philo *Abr* 213; *SpecLeg* 1.79; 4.222; *Som* 2.277; 2.290; *Decal* 59. He also points out that the corresponding Latin terms *amentia, dementia, insania* and *vesani* were associated with *superstitio*. Concerning the Greek texts the connection between στάσις and ἀπόνοια is made most explicit in the passages from Eus. *h.e.* where the author describes the Barkochba rebellion as στάσις and the attitude of the rebellious as ἀπόνοια. However, a problem regarding these passages, which Mikat uses as the main support for his theses, is that they are dated more than 200 years later than *1 Clement*. In none of the other Greeks texts adduced by Mikat is ἀπόνοια linked with στάσις. Closest to στάσις is the use in Philo *Abr* 213; *SpecLeg* 4:222 where ἀπόνοια is linked respectively with quarrelling and political opposition. In addition to the texts above referred to by Mikat, cf. Joseph. *Bell* 5.34; 5.424, and the discussion in H. E. LONA, *Der erste Clemensbrief* (1998) 118. Lona correctly notes that "Die Begrifflichkeit, zu der als entgegengesetzes Ideal die Eintracht (ὁμόνοια) gehört, ist aus dem politischen Leben übernommen" (118).

[526]Although P. MIKAT, *Die Bedeutung der Begriffe Stasis und Aponoia* (1969), has correctly pointed out the political connotations of the term ἀπόνοια, and even though we agree with him when he asserts that when Clement describes the effect of ζῆλος with the terms στάσις and ἀπόνοια it was "gewiss kein Zufall literarischer Topologie" (22), we cannot follow his conclusion and overall thesis. Mikat argues that the political authorities could have considered the events in the Corinthian Church as a revolt. If they had done so, that would have justified an intervention against the Church as an assembly which disturbs political order and stability. Mikat points to literature and texts that demonstrate that such a step by the imperial powers was a common means of re-establishing political order and stability (23f.). Thus the στάσις and ἀπόνοια are not only a danger to the communal life within the Church itself, but the "great danger" facing the Corinthian Church (*1 Clem*. 14:2; 47:4; 59:1) refers to persecution and intervention from imperial powers; also adopted by J. S. JEFFERS, *Conflict at Rome* (1991) 96. Furthermore, Mikat argues that Clement's reference to συμφορά and περίπτώσις in *1 Clem*. 1:1, "das heisst auf die Verfolgung in Rom hin", connects "die 'grosse Gefahr' durch stasis und aponoia" with war and persecution of the Church (26). Considering the latter, we have attempted to demonstrate that συμφορά and περίπτώσις do not allude to persecution, but to internal discord within the Roman Church. If we are correct, Mikat's argumentation relies partly on a false supposition and is therefore weakened. Regarding the term στάσις we have demonstrated that it is a term commonly applied in discussions on concord. Furthermore, Clement makes no explicit references to an intervention by the imperial power if the sedition should continue. It is reasonable to assume that he would have done so if that was what the "great danger" consisted of. Finally, at least in some passages, κίνδυνος refers obviously to the eschatological danger; see 2.3.3. For an outline and criticism of Mikat's view, see A. W. ZIEGLER, "Politische Aspekte im Ersten Klemensbrief", *FKTh* 2 (1986) 67-74; *idem*, "Die Frage nach einer politischen Absicht des Ersten Klemensbriefes", *ANRW* 2.27.1 (1993) 55-62.

[527]For the application of the term in Early Christianity, see W. BAUER, *A Greek English Lexicon* (1979) 622ff.

the majority of the occurrences of the term in *1 Clement* it is used primarily to express a Christian virtue.[528] Faith is foremost faithfulness and obedience to the will of God. Clement's use of Abraham as an example of faith and obedience in *1 Clem*. 10 is illustrative. Abraham "was found faithful (πιστός) in his obedience (ὑπήκοος) to the words of God" (10:1). In obedience (δι᾽ ὑπακοῆς) he left his country and his family; he believed (ἐπίστευσεν) God (10:6); "because of his faith and hospitality (διὰ πίστιν καὶ φιλοξενίαν) a son was given him in his old age" whom Abraham in his obedience (δι᾽ ὑπακοῆς) offered as a sacrifice to God (10:7).[529] Later in the letter Clement again uses Abraham as an example and asks if he did not became blessed "because he wrought righteousness and truth through faith" (δικαιοσύνην καὶ ἀλήθειαν διὰ πίστεως ποιήσας, 31:2). Although an author obviously might use the same term with different connotations in different contexts, it is likely that it is the aspect of faithfulness and obedience to the will of God that is significant when Clement praises the Corinthians for their steadfast faith in 1:2. The subsequent context seems to confirm this view. After Clement has praised the past noble life of the Corinthian Christians by means of three rhetorical questions in 1:2, he gives his reasons for doing so in 1:3, introducing them with the causal conjunction γάρ. The second point Clement mentions is that they "walked in the laws of God". In other words, they were faithful and obedient to the will of God.[530] In the light of the fact that elsewhere in the letter Clement emphasizes that to live according to the will of God will secure concord in the Church, it is reasonable to maintain that the term πίστις in 1:2 is also associated with concord.[531] Their steadfast faith contributed to concord in the communal life.

Furthermore, of interest in this connection is the fact that a political use of the term πίστις may lead to the same conclusion. It is not fruitful to list the many meanings of πίστις in the Greek world, but we should note that it "always implies confidence, which is expressed in human relationships as fidelity, trust, assurance, oath, proof, guarantee".[532] Of particular interest are the occurrences of πίστις in historical works dealing with military conflicts or civic disorder. Sometimes it is reported that the parties involved made an oath or other assurances of good faith (πίστις) when they sealed political alliances and treaties. Herodotus, for instance, writes that after the Athenians and their allies had defeated the Persians "the Samians bound themselves by pledge

---

[528]πίστις occurs together with other virtues, e.g., in 3:4 (δικαιοσύνη, εἰρήνη, φόβος); 5:6-7 (δικαιοσύνη); 12:8-13:1 (δικαιοσύνη, ἐπιείκεια, μακροθυμία, ταπεινοφρονοῦντες); 35:2 (δικαιοσύνη, ἀλήθεια, παρρησία, πεποίθησις, ἐγκράτεια, ἁγιασμός); 62:2 (ἀγάπη, ἐγκράτεια, σωφροσύνη, ὑπομονή, δικαιοσύνη, ἀλήθεια, μακροθυμία, ὁμονοοῦντες, ἀγάπη, εἰρήνη, ἐπιείκεια, ταπεινοφρονοῦντες); 64:1 (φόβος, εἰρήνη, ὑπομονή, μακροθυμία, ἐγκράτεια, ἁγνεία, σωφροσύνη).

[529]O. ANDRÉN, *Rättfärdighet och Frid* (1960) 93, correctly notes that "det troliga är att πίστις här innebär Abrahams trohet och lydnad. Denne räknas honom till rättfärdighet, liksom lydnaden visar att han är πιστός". Cf. aslo H. E. LONA, *Der erste Clemensbrief* (1998) 517.

[530]Although the conjunction γάρ points back to everything mentioned in 3:2, and thus not only to the steadfast faith, it includes this aspect as well.

[531]See, e.g., the present investigation, p. 163.

[532]C. SPICQ, "πίστις", *Theological Lexicon of the New Testament* 3, 110.

(πίστις) and oath (ὅρκιον) to alliance with the Greeks". [533] Also, the Athenians decided to make an alliance (τὸ συμμαχικόν) with the Samians, Chians, Lesbians, and the islanders who have fought with them, "and [they] bound them by pledge and oaths to remain faithful and not desert their allies" (πίστι τε καταλαβόντες καὶ ὁρκίοισι ἐμμενέειν τε καὶ μὴ ἀποστήσεσθαι).[534] Further, Xenophon uses the expression "having concluded a treaty" (πίστεις πεποιημένος) when he reports on an agreement between different parts (*Hell.* 1.3.4).[535] Dionysius Halicarnassensis gives a report of the Volscian ambassadors who were sent to Rome in an attempt to get back the lands which the Romans had taken from them. They said that their complaints against the Romans would cease and "that for the future they should be friends (φίλος) and allies (συμμάχος) …. Also, they declared that it would be a sure pledge of friendship (πιστὸν αὐτοῖς τῆς φιλίας) if they received back the lands and the cities".[536] Also in Plato πίστις is associated with friendship, i.e. πίστις sometimes denotes a pledge of loving friendship (*Phaed.* 256 C-D). Furthermore, Dio Cassius reports that the Assassins urged the Romans to live in harmony (ὁμόνοια) with them, "binding themselves by the strongest oaths that they would faithfully (πιστούμενοι) carry out that promise" (44.34.3f.).

These examples show that πίστις could designate assurance, a pledge or an agreement in a political context. More accurately, when different parties in times of war made allies, the πίστις was meant to guarantee loyalty toward other parties in a way which would be mutually beneficial in the future for the parts involved. Thus πίστις forms a basis for co-operation and for friendly relations. This implies that it was considered to be significant both for the concord and for the well-being of the members of a political body in general. An illustration regarding the latter is a decree of Delphi from 125 B.C.E. which says that Athens has taught the Greeks that "the greatest good for humans consists in relations of mutual good faith".[537]

That πίστις is associated with concord seems to be substantiated by the fact that we have found passages where πίστις is explicitly linked with ὁμόνοια. This is the case when Diodorus Siculus reports a change in a chaotic situation in Egypt. After a period of two years without any head of government, which led the masses to get involved in tumults and killing one another, the twelve most important leaders formed a league. Diodorus says that, after entering into "agreements setting forth their mutual goodwill (ὁμόνοια) and loyalty (πίστις), they proclaimed themselves kings".[538] In *The Panath-*

---

[533]Hdt. 9.92.

[534]Hdt. 9.106.

[535]For other references to a similar use of πίστις, see, e.g., Hdt. 3.74; Thuch. 4.51; 5.45.2; Joseph. *Bell* 2.21; 3.31; 3.334; 3.345; 3.391. For the use of the term πίστις in Josephus, see further D. M. HAY, "*Pistis* as 'Ground for Faith' in Hellenized Judaism and Paul", *JBL* 108 (1989) 461-476. With respect to Josephus, Hay comments that πίστις often expresses "a pledge not to injure another party, especially in wartime" (469).

[536]Dion. Hal. *Ant. Rom.* 8.9.3.

[537]C. SPICQ, "πίστις", *Theological Lexicon of the New Testament* 3, 115 n. 14.

[538]Diod. Sic. 1.66.1f.

enaic Oration Aelius Aristides among other things applauds the Athenians for their concern over public affairs in time of war and in times of need in the past:

> They contended on behalf of their common country and for common prizes, and it was not prescribed for one party to run the risks and another to rule in the event of success. Therefore concord and trust in one another (ὁμόνοια μὲν καὶ πίστις ἀλλήλων) flourished throughout the city. If ever there was dissension (διασταῖεν), mutual recognition came easily (Or. 1.393).

Lastly, but no less important is the observation that the word pair ὁμόνοια καὶ πίστις is also found in one of Aristides discourses on concord. He refers to the Rhodians' forefathers as examples to imitate. In contradiction to the Rhodians' at the present time who by their "divisiveness have made many cities out of one", their ancestors who were formerly divided into three parts managed to live together and settled in one city. Of interest to our study is the fact that when Aristides explains why the forefathers managed to live in such a way, he asserts that it was because of their mutual concord and trust (ὑπὲρ τῆς πρὸς ἀλλήλους ὁμονοίας καὶ πίστεως).[539]

These extracts from D. Siculus and A. Aristides indicate that πίστις was associated with ὁμόνοια. However, it is difficult to define the semantic relationship between the terms in a more accurate way. Regarding the syntactic relationship we note that the terms are linked with καί and thus function as a single concept within the sentence. This demonstrates how closely these terms were linked when one dealt with unity in a political body. The pairing of ὁμόνοια and πίστις could lead us to view these terms as synonyms. However, it would also be reasonable to view πίστις as a hyponym of ὁμόνοια.[540] If so, πίστις gives content and meaning to ὁμόνοια. The fact that in all three of the passages referred to above ὁμόνοια is placed first in the word pair may point in this direction. In any case, it seems to be beyond any doubt that πίστις belongs to the semantic field of ὁμόνοια.

On the basis of this political use of πίστις, it is reasonable to assume that the term carries similar political connotations when Clement applauds the Corinthians for their steadfast πίστις in the past. Their mutual confidence contributed to a community life in agreement and concord.

The fact that Clement qualifies the past πίστις of the Corinthians with the adjective βέβαιος is probably no accident and appears to strengthen the point of view that πίστις carries political connotations in 1:1. Although the term βέβαιος or the verb βεβαιόω has obviously been used as a juridical term in contracts, it is interesting in this connection to note that it was also applied as a political term qualifying the nature of allies or peace treaties.[541]

For example, in the above-mentioned story about the Volscian ambassadors who were sent to Rome in order to make peace with the Romans, they said that a precondition for peace and φιλότης βέβαιος was that they should get back their cities and

---

[539] Aristid. *Or.* 24.49.
[540] For the definition of the term "hyponym", see chap. 3.2 pp. 70f.

lands from the Romans.[542] Further, it is interesting to note that βέβαιος or its derivatives are linked with the term concord. According to Diodorus Siculus the oracle of Delphi uttered that "there is no advantage to men to be brave, if they are at odds among themselves, or to be wholly of one mind (ὁμονοεῖν βεβαίως), if they are cowards" (7.12.4). Dio Chrysostom asks regarding a concord achieved in anger and only four days old: "Nay, who could regard as safe (ἀσφαλής) and sure (βέβαιος) that sort of concord (ὁμόνοια)?"[543] Further on in the same discourse in a situation where the audience's "own harmony is not assured" (βέβαιος ὁμονοέω) he advises that they should take careful and well-considered judgment.[544] Furthermore, he compares the situation of civil war at Athens with an earthquake and asks whether or not everything is unsettled, nothing stable (βέβαιος, Or. 48.13.)

On the basis of the political use of βέβαιος, and in particular its connection with ὁμόνοια in the texts just mentioned, it is probably no accident that Clement uses this term when he describes the nature of their πίστις in the past. We do not, in fact, need to pay attention to the political use of βέβαιος and its linking with ὁμόνοια in ancient literature to argue that βέβαιος in *1 Clem* 1:2 carries political connotations. Farther on in the letter, Clement himself uses this term in a way which obviously reflects a political usage. In 47:6 he blames the Corinthian Church for the present situation and says that it is extremely shameful "that on account of one or two persons the steadfast and ancient church of the Corinthians (τὴν βεβαιοτάτην καὶ ἀρχαίαν Κορινθίων ἐκκλησίαν) is being disloyal (στασιάζω) to the presbyters". Here the expression the "steadfast and ancient (τὴν βεβαιότης καὶ ἀρχαῖος) church" refers to a past without sedition and strife. It refers to a community life marked by concord and mutual love,[545] i.e. to the situation described in 1:2-2:8.[546] In other words, Clement reflects the conventional political use of the term βέβαιος.

---

[541]The political aspect of the term is demonstrated by M. M. MITCHELL, *Paul and the Rhetoric of Reconciliation* (1991) 105-107, with text references. For a juridical application of the term Mitchell points to G. A. DEISSMANN, *Bible Studies*. Trans. A. Grieve (Edinburgh: T & T Clark, 1901) 104-109. We find Mitchell's suggestion of why βέβαιος and cognates were applied to political bodies reasonable when she holds that this application "may be ultimately rooted in the image of the political unit as a building which is stable, strong and immovable, but which, when affected by στάσις, may totter or fall" (106f.). H. E. LONA, *Der erste Clemensbrief* (1998) 121, correctly notes that in Hellenistic Judaism the term βέβαιος expresses the quality of the faith, but he does not at all consider the political use of the term.

[542]Dion. Hal. *Ant. Rom.* 8.9.3. For the phrase φίλος βέβαιος by the same author see, e.g., 8.29.1. For other references, see M. M. MITCHELL, *Paul and the Rheotoric of Reconciliation* (1991) 106, n. 248.

[543]Dio Chrys. *Or.* 34.17.

[544]Dio Chrys. *Or.* 34.27.

[545]*1 Clem.* 47:5.

[546]Clement knows and refers explicitly to the strife Paul dealt with in 1 Corinthians. However, it seems that he deliberately attempts to underestimate the seriousness of this strife by saying that the Corinthians "were partisans of Apostles of high reputation" (47:4). Thus he might draw a picture of the community life of the Corinthian Church as he does in 1:2-2:8 in order to contrast the idealized past with the present situation.

Above we have seen that πίστις was associated with concord in a political body and belonged to the semantic field of concord. This fact in itself makes it reasonable to assert that πίστις carries political connotations in *1 Clem.* 1:2 and we might possibly view the paradigmatic relation of πίστις to concord as a hyponym. In addition, we have also seen that the adjective Clement uses to qualify the previous πίστις of the Corinthian Church, i.e. βέβαιος, was commonly used to describe the nature of concord in a social unit. This fact strengthens our suggestion that πίστις carries a political meaning in *1 Clem.* 1:2. Although Clement's use of the term πίστις reflects the conventional use of the term in the LXX expressing a relationship between God and his people, at the same time it is likely that the political use outlined above influenced his use of it.

3.5.2.5. σωφροσύνη

In his enumeration of praiseworthy features which made the Corinthian Church "venerable and famous, and worthy" of all men's love (1:1), Clement focuses upon the σώφρων εὐσέβεια (1:2). The σώφρων aspect of their previous community life is also emphasized in 1:3 where the Corinthians are praised because they taught the women to manage their households with all discretion (πάνυ σωφρονούσας). That the concept of σωφροσύνη plays an important role in the letter is obvious from what is said at the beginning of the *peroratio*[547] where the author gives a summary of the letter. Here σωφροσύνη is said to be one of the topics which Clement has covered in every aspect.[548]

For our purpose it is neither necessary nor possible to discuss the development of or the different meanings of this important virtue of the Greeks in detail.[549] Commonly σωφροσύνη expressed "moderation in sensual desires, self-control, temperance".[550] In classical Greek σωφροσύνη occurs primarily in the context of the public realm.[551] In the democratic *polis* it functioned as a restriction of the individualism and self-assertion of warrior *arete* and thus became an essential political virtue.[552] Since the virtue of σωφροσύνη functioned as a limitation on an individual's desire to further his own interests and wishes, it served the common interest of the community. By way of

---

[547]For the *peroratio* in *1 Clement*, see the present investigation, pp. 226-232.

[548]περὶ γὰρ πίστεως καὶ μετανοίας καὶ γνησίας ἀγάπης καὶ ἐγκρατείας καὶ σωφροσύνης καὶ ὑπομονῆς πάντα τόπον ἐψηλαφήσαμεν (*1 Clem.* 62:2).

[549]For a comprehensive study, see H. NORTH, *Sophrosyne* (1966).

[550]H. G. LIDDELL and R. SCOTT, *A Greek-English Lexicon* (1973) 1751.

[551]H. NORTH, *Sophrosyne* (1966) 1-257. She summarizes: "At the deepest level, sophrosyne is related to the Greek tendency to interpret all kinds of experience – whether moral, political, aesthetic, physical, or metaphysical – in terms of harmony and proportion. At a level more susceptible to historical analysis, it is an expression of the self-knowledge and self-control that the Greek *polis* demanded of its citizens, to curb and counterbalance their individualism and self-assertion" (258).

[552]K. J. TORJESEN, *When Women were Priests* (1993) 116, goes so far as to say that σωφροσύνη was "the principal form of arete associated with the city-state" and that "the transformation of σωφροσύνη into a political virtue was complete by the fourth century B.C.E".

comparison, ὁμόνοια was considered to be an advantage not only for the individuals in a political body, but for the entire community, and thus served the common interest. From these commonalities it is fair to infer that σωφροσύνη was connected with the ideal of concord. If one turns to Greek texts one will see that this supposition is confirmed, i.e. that σωφροσύνη furthers behaviour that leads to concord.

After H. North observes that "The topic of sophrosyne as a political virtue is expanded by Isocrates" for use in the context of political moderation and restraint in international affairs,[553] she goes on to note the connection between concord and *sophrosyne* in the *Panegyricus*. In this political discourse where Isocrates offers his "counsels (συμβουλεύω) on the war against the barbarians and on concord (ὁμόνοια)" among the Greeks,[554] he advocates that Athens must again lead the Greeks against the barbarians. In his argumentation he idealizes the ancestors for their exemplary behaviour. An essential feature of this behaviour was the practice of σωφροσύνη. North provides an important connection when she points out that, according to Isocrates, the practice of "sophrosyne towards the allies was linked with *homonoia*".[555]

An even closer link between σωφροσύνη and ὁμόνοια is expressed by Plato in his *Republic*. Among other things he says that σωφροσύνη "bears more likeness to a kind of concord (συμφωνία) and harmony (ἁρμονία) than the other virtues [*sophia* and *andreia*] did" (4.430 D-E).[556] Taking the conflicting elements in the state as his departure, Plato goes on to discuss the relations between these virtues. Unlike ἀνδρεία and σοφία, which are possessed by different groups of the citizens, σωφροσύνη should reside in all citizens. In this connection we note that when the rulers and the ruled agree on who should rule, according to Plato the city possesses σωφροσύνη in the sense of concord.

> ... we should be quite right in affirming this unanimity (ὁμόνοια) to be soberness (σωφροσύνη), the concord (συμφωνία) of the naturally superior and inferior as to which ought to rule both in the state and the individual (Resp. 4.432 A).

In other words, this definition of σωφροσύνη shows that Plato holds that this virtue should be manifested in ὁμόνοια and συμφωνία in the state.[557]

Though North argues that σωφροσύνη in the Hellenistic period became associated more with the individual's exercise of self-control, in particular with regard to the area of desire and appetite, we have found illustrative examples of the political use of

---

[553]H. NORTH, *Sophrosyne* (1966) 143.

[554]Isoc. *Or.* 4.3.

[555]H. NORTH, *Sophrosyne* (1966) 144. She refers to Isoc. *Or.* 4.3, 104, 173. She further notes that σωφροσύνη in this discourse "means considerate treatment of allied states" (144).

[556]See also Pl. *Resp.* 4. 431 E.

[557]M. SCHOFIELD, *The Stoic Idea of the City* (1991), points out that in Pl. *Resp.* 4 "ὁμόνοια is identified with σωφροσύνη, i.e. with one of the cardinal excellences the ideal state must exemplify, and where indeed the class system central to Plato's theory is so devised as to create the optimal conditions for the emergence of ὁμόνοια" (46). Cf. also the discussion in H. NORTH, *Sophrosyne* (1966) 172f.; J.-P. VERNANT, *The Origins of Greek Thought* (1982) 96.

the virtue in this period as well. In the following we confine ourselves to examples that reflect a connection between σωφροσύνη and concord.

Dionysius Halicarnassensis says that Romulus understood that a good government must promote "moderation and justice (σωφροσύνην τε καὶ δικαιοσύνην), as a result of which the citizens, being less disposed to injure one another, are more harmonious (ὁμονοοῦσι)".[558] That σωφροσύνη is a precondition for concord can hardly be expressed more explicitly than in the words of Dio Cassius when he says that "it is impossible for the people, unless moderation prevails (σωφρονεῖν), to be harmonious (ὁμονοέω)".[559] The close connection between σωφροσύνη and ὁμόνοια is also reflected in a political discourse of Dio Chrysostom where he urges the audience to show themselves "temperate (σωφρόνως) and well-behaved in assembly" and to adorn "themselves with mutual friendship and concord (ὁμόνοια)".[560] Furthermore, when Plutarch deals with the merits of Lycurgus he, among other things, reports how Lycurcus considered how to secure the happiness of an entire city. The precondition for achieving this happiness, according to Lycurgus, was "the prevalence of virtue and concord (ὁμονοίας) within its own borders". On the basis of this principle, Plutarch says that all the arrangements and adjustments of Lycurgus were directed towards making "his people free-minded, self-sufficing, and moderate (σωφρονοῦντες) in all their ways".[561] Thus the virtue of σωφροσύνη is obviously included in qualities which generate concord.

These few examples should suffice to prove our point, namely that the political virtue σωφροσύνη was closely linked with the concept of concord in a political body.[562] If the individual members of a social unit failed to restrain their own feelings and needs and to behave in a temperate manner, the solidarity among the members and consequently their concord would be in danger. The importance of σωφροσύνη for establishing or maintaining concord clarifies and to a great degree explains why Clement emphasizes this virtue in his appeal for concord in the Corinthian Church. To put it differently, Clement probably deliberately uses a political *topos* related to discussions on concord in a social unit. This means that when Clement praises the Christians at Corinth for their previous σωφροσύνη he implicitly praises them for their concord as well.

3.5.2.6. ἀσφαλής

Clement continues by praising the Corinthians for their hospitality (φιλοξενία)[563] in the past and their previous τελείαν καὶ ἀσφαλῆ γνῶσιν (1:2). In this connection we wish to focus on the term ἀσφαλής which literally means "immovable, steadfast" and

---

[558]Dion. Hal. *Ant. Rom.* 2.18.1.
[559]Dio Cass. 44.2.4.
[560]Dio Chrys. *Or.* 48.2.
[561]Plut. *Lyc.* 31.1.
[562]For other texts which reflect the connection between σωφροσύνη and concord, see, e.g., Dion. Hal. *Ant. Rom.* 2.74.1; *Dem.* 3; Dio Chrys. *Or.* 1.6; 32.37; Aristid. *Or.* 24.48; 24.54.

figuratively means "safe, secure".[564] The fact that we have succeeded in identifying a number of Greek texts where ἀσφαλής and cognates refer to a particular kind of safety and security, i.e. the safety and security connected with concord, is an important outcome of our task in the present chapter. Dio Chysostom, for instance, explicitly links ἀσφαλής with ὁμόνοια when he asks, "Who could regard as safe and sure (ἀσφαλῆ καὶ βέβαιον) that sort of concord, a concord achieved in anger and of no more than three or four days standing?"[565] Likewise when he presents the heavens and the divine beings that dwell therein as an example of concord, he asks the audience if they do not see "the stable (ἀσφαλής), righteous, everlasting concord of the elements".[566] We observe that in both these passages Dio uses the term ἀσφαλής to describe the right and perfect form of concord. It is therefore not surprising that this term is also found in passages that deal with the evil of sedition and the re-establishment of concord. Dionysius Halicarnassensis, for instance, writes that in a situation of sedition (στάσις) the consuls "considered by what means the commotion and sedition (στασιάζον) might speedily and safely (σὺν τῷ ἀσφαλεῖ) be removed".[567]

Admittedly, we have not been able to identify so many connections between ἀσφαλής and ὁμόνοια that we could rightly call ἀσφαλής a technical term. However, in our opinion we have presented sufficient material to make it likely that ἀσφαλής belonged to the cluster of relevant political terms relating to the issue of concord. On the basis of this suggestion it is a fair supposition that the political aspect of the term ἀσφαλής is also reflected in *1 Clement*. If this is correct, it follows that a feature of the ἀσφαλής γνῶσις, which characterised the previous life of the Corinthian Church, was that no strife and sedition occurred. This means that Clement's praise of the previous ἀσφαλής γνῶσις involves an allusion to knowledge that was manifested in a communal life free from internal discord.[568]

---

[563]The term φιλοξενία occurs relative frequently in *1 Clement*. In addition to its use in 1:2 it is found in 10:7; 11:1; 12:1, where it describes desirable behaviour of people in the Old Testament who are presented as examples for the Corinthians, and also in 35:5 as a part of a catalogue of virtues. The fact that Clement included the practice of φιλοξενία among the praiseworthy characteristics of the life of the Corinthian Church in the past appears to imply that he considered that φιλοξενία contributed to concord and peace. This would imply that Clement considered that the practice of φιλοξενία contributed to a community life characterised by concord. The suggestion of H. O. MAIER, *The Social Setting of the Ministry as Reflected in the Writings of Hermas, Clement and Ignatius* (1991), that Clement's stress upon φιλοξενία must be understood in the light of the general social setting of the Church gathered in wealthier people's homes seems to be reasonable (93). For further discussion on φιλοξενία in *1 Clement*, see H. CHADWICK, "Justification by Faith and Hospitality", *StPatr* 4.2 (1961) 281-285.

[564]H. G. LIDDELL and R. SCOTT, *A Greek-English Lexicon* (1973) 266; W. Bauer, *A Greek English Lexicon* (1979) 119.

[565]Dio Chrys. *Or.* 34.17.

[566]Dio Chrys. *Or.* 40.35.

[567]Dion. Hal. *Ant. Rom.* 9.44.1.

3.5.2.7. ἐν τοῖς νομίμοις τοῦ θεοῦ ἐπορεύεσθε

After completing the series of rhetorical questions that ended with the praise of the previous τέλειαν καὶ ἀσφαλῆ γνῶσιν of the Corinthian Church, Clement goes on to give the reason for this praise and thus to describe how the τέλειαν καὶ ἀσφαλῆ γνῶσιν was made manifest. First, he states what was probably the most essential aspect, i.e. that they "did all things without respect of persons (ἀπροσωπολήμπτως) and walked in the laws of God" (ἐν τοῖς νομίμοις τοῦ θεοῦ ἐπορεύεσθε, 1:3). He emphasizes that obedience to the laws of God was a basic feature in the previous noble life of the community when he ends his praise by saying that "the commandments and ordinances of the Lord were 'written on the tables of your heart'" (2:8).[569] At the present, however, the situation is the reverse. Now men do not walk "in the ordinances of his commandments (τὰ προστάγματα καὶ τὰ δικαιώματα τοῦ κυρίου) ..., but each goes according to the lusts of his wicked heart" (3:4). That the troubles in the Corinthian Church are rooted in disobedience to the laws of God is reflected throughout the whole letter. At the end of the *probatio*,[570] for instance, Clement states that everyone who has "performed the decrees and commandments (δικαιώματα καὶ προστάγματα) given by God shall be enrolled and chosen in the number of those who are saved through Jesus Christ" (58:2).[571] It is not surprising that a Christian leader should diagnose the cause of a problem in a Christian community as transgression of the will of God as expressed in his law and commandments, and that the solution to the problem is to return to his will and walk in his laws.

However, in view of our task in this chapter, it is interesting to note, firstly, that with only one exception[572] the terms Clement uses for law and commandments, i.e. δικαίωμα, νόμιμος, πρόσταγμα, are taken from "der Verwaltungssprache".[573] Sec-

---

[568]In *1 Clem.* 1:3, introduced with the causal conjunction γάρ, Clement gives the cause for his praise of the previous conditions at the Corinthian Church. He does not explicitly mention concord, but 1:3 contains terms and *topoi* related to the ideal of concord. There is no allusion or indication either in 1:3 or in the other parts of the letter to suggest that τέλειαν καὶ ἀσφαλῆ γνῶσιν should refer to any kind of gnosticism. So also, e.g., A. LINDEMANN, *Die Clemensbriefe* (1992) 28, H. E. LONA, *Der erste Clemensbrief* (1998) 122.

[569]Cf. Prov 7:3; 22:20.

[570]For the definition of the *probatio*-section in *1 Clement*, see the present study, pp. 232-277.

[571]For other explicit references to the commandment of God, see 37:1; 50:5 (πρόσταγμα). In addition to these explicit references and his emphasis on the significance of the need to obey the law of God, Clement makes abundant use of citation of, and allusion to the LXX in his argumentation. Many references to the LXX are introduced by the introductory formula γράφει or a similar expression. In one way we may say that the whole LXX is an expression of the will of God and thus functions as the law of God. For Clement's use of the Old Testament, cf. J. KLEVINGHAUS, *Die theologische Stellung der Apostolischen Väter zur alttestamentlichen Offenbarung* (1948) 45-77; D. A. HAGNER, *The Use of the Old and New Testaments in Clement of Rome* (1973) 21-132, O. SKARSAUNE, "The Development of Scriptural Interpretation in the Second and Third Centuries", *Hebrew Bible / Old Testament* vol. 1 (1996) 381-384.

[572]*1 Clem.* 13:3 is the only place where the biblical term ἐντολή is found.

[573]Cf. A. A. T. EHRHARDT, *Politische Metaphysik von Solon bis Augustin* vol 2 (1959) 56.

ondly, and more importantly there, is the fact that in antiquity behaviour in accordance
with the law was closely associated with the ideal of concord. An excerpt from Xenophon's *Memorabilia* is illuminating both with regard to this association and with regard
to the value of concord in general:

> And again, agreement (ὁμόνοια) is deemed the greatest blessing for cities: their sen-
> ates and their best men constantly exhort the citizens to agree (ὁμονοέω), and every-
> where in Greece there is a law that the citizens shall promise under oath to agree, …
> that they may obey the laws (τοῖς νόμοις πείθωνται). For those cities whose citizens
> abide by them prove strongest and enjoy most happiness; but without agreement
> (ὁμόνοια) no city can be made a good city, no house can be made a prosperous house
> (Mem. 4.4.16).[574]

Furthermore, Plutarch also reflects the close connection between obedience to the law
and concord. When he reports the noble works of Cleisthenes who destroyed the tyranny of the Peisistratidae, Plutarch writes that he "instituted laws (νόμους ἔθετο), and
established a constitution (πολιτεία) best attempered for the promotion of harmony
(ὁμόνοια) and safety (σωτηρία)".[575] Plutarch applauds Cleisthenes because he established law and a constitution as a means of advancing concord and safety. That the law
serves to establish and maintain concord is also implied when Plutarch deals with the
lyric poet Thales. According to Plutarch Thales hid himself behind the art of poetry, for
in fact he "did the work of one of the mightiest lawgivers". In this connection the reason
Plutarch gives for such a characterisation of the poet is significant, i.e. that "his odes
were so many exhortations to obedience (εὐπείθεια) and harmony (ὁμόνοια)".[576]
In other words, when Plutarch compares the poet Thales with the lawmakers, he
focuses upon the fact that both he and they exhorted people to live in obedience and
harmony. We get the unequivocal impression that a predominant task for a lawgiver, if
not the main task, is to produce laws which aim to secure obedience and harmony.

Another passage which is illustrative of the connection between law and concord is
a political discourse of Decius addressed to the senate. He describes the effect of a law,
which permits the plebeians to appeal to the people in cases where they felt oppressed
by the patricians, as the best means of preserving the harmony of the commonwealth
(τήν τε πόλιν ἐν ὁμονοίᾳ διεφυλάξατε).[577] Farther on in the discourse he explicitly states that law (and justice) is a prerequisite for concord in a city:

> … if the people are allowed to render judgment in causes in which the law gives them
> the authority, we shall live in harmony (ὁμονοίᾳ πολιτευσόμεθα) … For if justice

---

[574]K. Thraede, "Homonoia (Eintracht)", *RAC* 16 (1994) 184f., discusses the connection between
concord and obedience to the established law made by Xenophon. He rightly notes that Xenophon
links concord with εὐνομία and comments that it "bedeutet daher in erster Linie Gehorsam gegen
bestehende Gesetze" (185).
[575]Plut. *Per.* 3.1f.
[576]Plut. *Lyc.* 4.1.
[577]Dion. Hal. *Ant. Rom.* 7.41.1.

*and law (δίκη καὶ νόμος) are banished from a state, sedition (στάσις) and war
(πόλεμος) are wont to enter there.*[578]

It is consistent with this connection between law and concord that advice to follow the
established laws is commonly applied by philosophers and statesmen as a means of
putting an end to sedition and establishing concord.[579] In the discourse περὶ
πολιτείας, attributed to Herodes Atticus by some, the author advises the citizens to
cease from sedition by living "according to law" (κατὰ νόμον) instead of destroying
one another "lawlessly" (παρανόμος).[580] It is also obvious at the end of the discourse
that the speaker holds the opinion that living according to law leads to concord. Here
he contrasts his own advice with that of his opponents who dare to advise the citizens
"to have neither commonwealth, nor law, nor judgment" (μήτε πολιτείαν εἶναι
μήτε νόμον μήτε δίκας). This is the opposite of what the author advocates.[581] Furthermore, Aristotle goes on to speak about the stability of constitutions after he has
dealt with the causes for στάσις. Among other things he recommends that care should
"be taken to prevent men from committing any other breach of the law ... for transgression of the law (παρανομία) creeps in unnoticed".[582] Finally, in his "counsel" to
Dion's friends Plato urges them to renounce sedition and warns them that it will continue until they constitute common laws by which all can abide.[583]

In our opinion, the texts we have collected should demonstrate sufficiently that it
was a common belief in antiquity that to live according to the established law of a society was necessary in order to establish and preserve concord. Therefore we believe it is
reasonable to assert that Clement's approach is in accordance with this *topos* in view of
the following: (1) his emphasis on precisely the aspect of obedience to God's law in his
praise of past conditions, (2) his denunciation of present conditions in the Corinthian
Church, and (3) the role of God's law in the letter in general. In other words, just as obedience to law of a *polis* in antiquity is essential to achieve concord among its citizens, it
is also vital for citizens of the *polis* of God to walk in the laws of God in order to establish and maintain concord.

3.5.2.8. ὑποτάσσω

After Clement has stated that the Corinthians walked in the laws of God in the past, he
goes on to depict how this behaviour was manifested in their community life (1:3-

---

[578]Dion. Hal. *Ant. Rom.* 7.42.2f. For other references regarding the connection between observing
the law and concord, see, e.g., Dion. Hal. *Ant. Rom.* 2.74.1; 9. 45.1; 10.54.7; Dio Chrys. *Or.* 13.19;
36.31f.

[579]This is also rightly noted by L. L. WELBORN, "A Conciliatory Principle in 1 Cor. 4.6", *NT* 29
(1987) 341, who refers to texts of Herodes Atticus, Aristotle, Ps.-Plato cited below.

[580][Herodes Atticus] Περὶ πολιτείας 17-18, 29.

[581][Herodes Atticus] Περὶ πολιτείας 36f.

[582]Arist. *Pol.* 5.7.1.

[583]Ps.-Pl. *Ep.* 7. 336 D-337 B.

2:8).[584] First he mentions obedience to their rulers (ὑποτασσόμενοι τοῖς ἡγου-
μένοις ὑμῶν, 1:3).[585] The aspect of obedience or submission is found throughout the
letter and plays an important role in it.[586] Besides 1:3 the verb ὑποτάσσω expresses
submission to the political leaders in 61:1. In 57:1 Clement uses the verb ὑποτάσσω to
express the right attitude toward the leaders of the Church, he exhorts the instigators of
the sedition to submit to the presbyters. He also uses this verb to express mutual submission among the Christians. A feature of the Corinthian Church's noble past life was
that they were "yielding subjection rather than demanding it" (ὑποτασσόμενοι
μᾶλλον ἢ ὑποτάσσοντες, 2:1).[587] And further, the term depicts the movement of
heavens according to the will of God (20:1) and the Christians' submission to the will
of God (34:5).

There is no doubt that Clement exhorts his audience in many ways to submit to
existing structures, and that the exhortations, if followed, function therefore as a con-
servative element that maintains the status quo of the Corinthian Church.[588] We
should note, however, that the overall function of submission in *1 Clement* is to establish and preserve concord. The submission to the political leaders in 61:1 occurs in a
prayer for "peace and concord" (60:4). The exhortation to submit to the legitimate

---

[584]We note that this passage both begins and ends with praise of the Corinthian Church for their
past obedience of God's law. Thus these statements of obedience to law function as a frame for the content of this passage.

[585]ἡγουμένοι does not mean Church leaders, but political leaders as always in *1 Clement* (5:7;
32:2; 37:2, 3; 51:5; 60:4). So also A. LINDEMANN, *Die Clemensbriefe* (1992) 28. Contra B. E. BOWE, *A
Church in Crisis* (1988) 97.

[586]According to word statistics in G. BRUNNER, *Die Theologische Mitte des Ersten Klemensbriefs*
(1972) 64, the stem -ταγ- occurs 3.8 times for every one thousand words in *1 Clement* compared with
0.7 and 1.6 times in the whole New Testament and in the letters of Paul respectively. More exactly the
root ταγ- occurs forty-two times in *1 Clement*, according to B. E. Bowe, *A Church in Crisis* (1988) 107,
with text references. In this connection we shall consider only the verb ὑποτάσσω and its derivatives
ὑποταγή and ὑποτεταγμένως. However, we will note that we agree with Bowe when in opposition to
H. F. von Campenhausen (who is of the opinion that the idea of order in *1 Clement* is an autonomous
principle and the ultimate norm of the spiritual life) she writes that "it must be remembered that the
occasion of the letter (widespread strife and dissension in Corinth), and in particular Rome's view of
the dire consequences inherent in such a situation, influences the letter's paraenesis at every point. In
view of the crisis in Corinth, order becomes for Clement a means for preserving the very existence of
the church" (108).

[587]Cf. also 37:5 where Clement uses the different parts of body as an example of the necessity for a
common subjection (ὑποταγή), and 38:1 where he continues to exhort the Corinthian Christians to be
subject to their neighbours. Likewise, the author exhorts them to learn to be submissive (μάθετε
ὑποτάσσεσθαι) in 57:2. We should note, however, that the mutual subjection prescribed in *1 Clement*
does not involve equality among the members of the Church, but it is preferable to talk about mutuality within an established social order: 2:1 follows a household code; in 37:5 and 38:1 the mutual subjection is found in a context of an established order of rank and status; and the exhortation in 57:2
follows the exhortation to submit to the presbyters. This point is also noted by B. E. BOWE, *A Church in
Crisis* (1988) 110.

[588]Submission is to the legitimate civil leadership (1:3; 61:1), to the established leadership of the
Church (57:1), and to conventional rules for the household (1:3; 21:6).

leadership is explicitly addressed to the instigators of the sedition (57:1), which indicates that submission to the legitimate leadership is a means of removing the sedition. Likewise the exhortation to submit to the will of God (34:5) is a means of establishing peace and concord as long as this is consistent with the will of God. Such a submission is manifested in the peace and harmony of the universe, which is presented as an example for the members of the Christian community to follow (19:2-21:1). Also, the exhortation to submit to the conventional rules of the household is a means of avoiding the "jealousy which estranged wives from husbands" (6:3).[589]

Clement is by no means the only ancient writer that connects submission or obedience with concord. Even if the exact term ὑποτάσσω does not occur, the meaning of the term is reflected by Dio Chrysostom in *Or.* 36. In this discourse he presents a theory of the ideal city. Among other things he asserts that if the leaders of the city are men of prudence and wisdom (φρόνιμοι καὶ σοφοί) and the people obey them, in the manner of a choir and its conductor, the community is really a city. In the comparison of the leaders and the people of a city to a choir and its conductor the aspect of submission is clear:

> *Perhaps, then, someone might inquire whether, when the rulers and leaders of a community are men of prudence and wisdom, and it is in accordance with their judgement that the rest are governed, lawfully and sanely, such a community may be called sane and law-abiding and really a city because of those who govern it; just as a chorus might possibly be termed musical provided its leader were musical and provided further that the other members followed his lead and uttered no sound contrary to the melody that he set – or only slight sounds and indistinctly uttered (Or. 36.21).*

The image of the conductor and the chorus implies that submission to the leaders leads to concord among citizens. Farther on in the same discourse, Dio expresses this more explicitly when he says what the term "city" should be applied to:

> *… to an organization that is governed (κεκοσμημένος) by the sanest and noblest form of kingship, to one that is actually under royal governance in accordance with law, in complete friendship and concord (πάσης φιλίας καὶ ὁμονοίας, Or. 36.31-32).*

In other places Dio links concord to obedience to speakers who have correct ideas. When one praises human beings, Dio says, "it should be for their good discipline (εὐταξία), gentleness, concord (ὁμόνοια), civic order, for heeding those who give good counsel" (*Or.* 32.37). Those who give good counsel are probably established leaders whom Dio calls "good men" in another discourse. He says that the blessing of the city is dependent upon, among other things, people being obedient to them

---

[589]For a further discussion of the function of submission and the wider concept of order in *1 Clement*, see B. E. Bowe, *A Church in Crisis* (1988) 107-112. In particular note her correct emphasis that submission and order in *1 Clement* are "an indispensable means for preserving harmony in the community", and "the need for order and submission are, therefore, in dialectic with exhortations to concord and peace" (109, 112).

(πείθεσθαι[590] τοῖς ἀγαθοῖς ἀνδράσι, *Or.* 44.10). The continuation seems to imply that obedience to those leaders involves paying attention to pure Greek culture and education (παιδεύω) of the children, so the city may be truly Hellenic "free from turmoil, and stable ... refraining from discord and confusion and conflict with one another so far as possible" (*Or.* 44.10). In other words, it appears that established leaders are bearers of true Greek culture and a primary ideal of this culture is that there should be no sedition in the city.[591]

This indicates that when Clement exhorts the Church at Corinth to obey the established leadership he applies a *topos* connected with concord, i.e. to submit to or to obey the leaders of a political body secures the great value of concord. Furthermore, just as Dio describes the established leaders as true bearers of Greek culture, Clement also depicts the legal leaders at Corinth as bearers of true Christian values. They stand in the apostolic succession and have "ministered to the flock of Christ without blame, humbly, peaceably, and disinterestedly, and for many years have received a universally favourable testimony" (44:3).

The aspect of submission is also present when Dio Chrysostom appeals to concord by pointing to the order and harmonious unity of the cosmos: "For the sake of this harmonious unity, the stronger or larger planets freely 'submit' to weaker or smaller ones".[592] That the opposite of ὑποτάσσω to the existing leadership, i.e. the claim for power and the quest for new rulers often leading to discord, is well testified in ancient literature.[593]

On this basis it seems reasonable to assert that Clement's focus on submission must be viewed and understood as a means of achieving concord, and also that at this point he reflects conventional ideas associated with concord.

3.5.2.9. Household Duties

When Clement continues to depict how adherence to God's law was manifested in the Corinthian Church, he uses language associated with the so-called codes of 'household

---

[590]πείθω in middle and passive voice means "obey"; for text references see H. G. Liddell and R. Scott, *A Greek-English Lexicon* (1973) 1353.

[591]Cf. A. R. R. Sheppard, *"Homonoia* in the Greek Cities of the Roman Empire", *AncSoc* 15-17 (1984-1986) 251: "In these passages of Dio [Dio Chrys. *Or.* 44. 10f., 48.8], good order is presented in terms of obedience to established leaders and conformity to moral and cultural norms handed down by that leadership".

[592]M. M. Mitchell, *Paul and the Rhetoric of Reconciliation* (1991) 132, n. 405, who cites Dio Chrys. *Or* 40. 35f. and refers to Aristid. *Or.* 27.35; Philo *Jos.* 145; *Cong.* 133; *Spec. Leg.* 2.141 where the same idea is reflected. Mitchell asserts that ὁμόνοια resulting "from submission is a *topos* in ancient literature" and uses the passages listed above as a justification (and additionally M.Ant. 5.30 and to *ECL*; Ign. *Eph.* 2:2; *1 Clem.* 20:1; 37:1-5; 57:1-2), 179 n. 694.

[593]E.g., in *Eth. Nic.*9.6.2 Aristotle says, "When each of two persons wishes himself to rule, like the rivals in the *Phoenissae*, there is discord (στασιάζειν)". Cf. also Dio Chrys. *Or.* 11.130.

duties'.[594] In 1:3 he praises the Corinthians for paying honour to the aged and for enjoining "temperate and seemly thoughts" on the young (νέοις τε ... νοεῖν ἐπετρέπετε), for instructing the women "that they should do all things with a blameless and seemly and pure conscience (γυναιξίν τε ... ἐπιτελεῖν παρηγγέλλετε), yielding a dutiful affection to their husbands", and for teaching the women "to remain in the rule of obedience (ἔν τε τῷ κανόνι τῆς ὑποταγῆς) and to manage their households with seemliness (τὸν οἶκον σεμνῶς οἰκουργεῖν)". In 21:6-8 these elements of 'household duties' reappear in the form of an exhortation.[595] We note that in both passages three groups of persons are referred to in the same order: the aged (πρεσβύτερος) in 1:3, 21:6; the young (νέος) in 1:3, 21:6; and women, wives (γυνή) in 1:3, 21:6. The code in 21:6-8 adds a reference to children (τέκνον) at the end of the list.[596]

It is probably no accident that Clement pays attention to the relationships between different groups in the household in his praise of the past and in his appeal for concord. That each group should behave according to the conventional rules of behaviour seems in fact to be a *topos* related to the issue of concord. When Plato discusses the features that contribute to making the city good, he emphasizes "the principle embodied in child, woman, slave, free, artisan, ruler and ruled, that each performed his one task as one man and was not a versatile busybody".[597] In the view of Plato, it is important that each group acts according to the assigned function of the group and does not attempt to act as if he or she were a member of a different class. According to the rule of reason some rule and some are ruled.[598] In this connection one should note in particular that the rule of reason, manifested in the proper relationships between the members of the

---

[594]It is beyond the scope of this investigation to deal with the impact of the Greek and Roman household codes of duties in Early Christianity. That the community life of the Early Christians to some degree was influenced by these codes seems to be unquestionable. For some important recent studies on the subject, cf. J. E. CROUCH, *The Origin and Intention of the Colossian Haustafel* (1972); D. L. BALCH, *Let Wives Be Submissive* (1981); J. H. ELLIOT, *A Home for the Homeless* (1981); D. C. VERNER, *The Household of God* (1981); L. HARTMAN, "Some Unorthodox Thoughts on the 'Household-Code Form'", *The Social World of Formative Christianity and Judaism* (1988) 219-232. For additional literature, see the bibliographies in the works just cited.

[595]J. A. FISCHER, *Die Apostolichen Väter* (1966) 55 n. 132: "Die Verse 6-8 stellen eine 'Haus- und Gemeindetafel' dar (vgl. schon Klem 1,3), die Pflichten innerhalb der christlichen Familie und der christlichen Gemeinschaft aufzählt. Haus – und Gemeindetafelen finden sich bei Paulus (Eph 5,22-6,9; Kol 3,18-4,1; 1 Tim 2,8-3,13; 5,1-6,2; Tit 1,7ff; 2,1-10) und in 1 Petr 2,12 bis 3,7".

[596]This means that we do not include the first group mentioned in 1:3 and 21:6-8, i.e. the rulers (ἡγέομαι), in the codes of household duties. The reason for this should be obvious, since a household code is limited to regulating relationships and keeping order among groups belonging to the household.

[597]Pl. *Resp.* 4.433 C-D, cf. also A.

[598]D. L. BALCH, *Let Wives Be Submissive* (1981) 24 comments: "It is clear from [Pl. *Resp.*] IV 431C that the place of 'children and women and slaves' is one of submission; they are to be ruled just as the 'appetites' in a man must be ruled by 'reason'. Plato thinks that the rulers must be older and the ruled younger [Resp.] (III 412C)".

household, generates "friendship and concord [Pl. *Resp.*](442D) instead of faction in both city and individual [Pl. *Resp.*] (IV 441C-445B)".[599]

We have not found other passages that explicitly state that behaviour consistent with the household code creates concord. However, this is not so important in view of the fact that a relatively large number of passages reflect the idea that concord was viewed as an integral aspect of the household. Perhaps the most famous passage is found in Xenophon. He records that "everywhere in Greece there is a law that the citizens shall promise under oath to agree (ὁμονοήσειν)". Subsequent to this he gives the basis for this law, i.e. that the well-being of the *polis* as well of the house depends on a state of harmony.[600] This latter point is significant for our purposes here.

The cited passages mirror the common view that ὁμόνοια was a vital virtue connected to the household. This view is also reflected by Isocrates. He maintains that a sign of good kings is that "they must try to preserve harmony (ὁμόνοια), not only in the states over which they hold dominion, but also in their own households (τοὺς οἴκους τοὺς ἰδίους) and in their places of abode".[601]

If a man gives advice about concord, but at the same time is not able to maintain concord at home, the state of affairs at home diminishes his authority. Plutarch relates how Philip inquired about harmony among the Greeks. But because he lacked harmony at home, he received the following reply from Demaratus of Corinth:

> *A glorious thing for you, Philip, to be inquiring about the concord (ὁμοφροσύνη) of Athenians and Peloponnesians, while you let your own household (οἰκία) be full of all this quarrelling (στάσις) and dissension (διχόνοια)![602]*

Similarly, the orator Gorgias delivered a discourse to the Greeks at Olympia about concord (λόγον περὶ Ὁμονοίας), to which Melanthius responded:

> *'This fellow is giving us advice about concord (συμβουλεύει περὶ ὁμονοίας), and yet in his own household he has not prevailed upon himself, his wife and maidservant, three persons only, to live in concord (ὁμονοεῖν)'... A man therefore ought to have his household well harmonized who is going to harmonize State, Forum and friends (Plut. Mor. 144 B-C).*

One may say that the main point in these passages is that, if a man should give advice about concord with authority, he must have demonstrated that he manages to achieve concord in the political body where he has most influence, namely at home. At the same time the passages also presuppose that concord should reign between the members of the household.

---

[599]D. L. BALCH, *Let Wives Be Submissive* (1981) 24.

[600]Xen. *Mem.* 4.4.16.

[601]Isoc. *Or.* 3.41.

[602]Plut. *Mor.* 70 C. The same story is also recorded in *Mor.* 179 C. After Demaratus responded to Philip by stating that "much right have you to talk about the harmony (ὁμονοίας) of the Greeks when the dearest of your own household feel so towards you !" This version concludes with the remark that Philip "ceased from his anger and became reconciled (διηλλάγη) with them".

Lastly, but no less important, we should pay attention to the fact that Dio Chrysostom and Aelius Aristides in their discourses about discord both emphasize the need for concord in the household and mirror the common view that this concord depends on conventional behaviour in line with the household codes.

The latter reminds the audience of the opinion of Homer. Homer characterised the wisest Greeks as being those who prayed for Nausicaa that the gods would give her a husband and a home, and that they would both live in concord. Aristides continues by quoting this "common adviser and patron of the Greeks": "For there is nothing greater and better than this, than when husband and wife maintain their house with concordant thoughts".[603] Aristides goes on to compare the necessity for concord in a household to that of a city and argues the following:

> … if concordant thought is the single means of safety for the individual home, cities must be much more disposed in this way … If, therefore, that adviser thought that it was now opportune to pray for concord, even for those who where going to set up housekeeping, indeed it is the duty of those who have lived in a city from antiquity … (Or. 24.8).

Concord as an essential aspect of a household is also emphasized later in the speech when in his call for concord Aristides exhorts the Rhodians to "imitate the form and fashion of a household".[604] In what follows he reveals why the household is such a good model, i.e. because there is an order that regulates the common life in the house. The fathers rule the sons and the master the slaves. According to Aristides this order is a natural law truly declared by the gods.[605] In other words, according to the household code it is appropriate behaviour that generates concord. It is the single guarantee of safety.

Dio Chrysostom places greater emphasis on the harmony between man and wife, though he also pays attention to the relationship between different groups in the household:

> Again, take our households (οἰκία) – although their safety depends not only on the like-mindedness (ὁμοφροσύνη) of master and mistress but also on the obedience of the servants, yet both the bickering of master and mistress and the wickedness of the servants have wrecked many households … the good marriage, what else is it save concord (ὁμόνοια) between man and wife? And the bad marriage, what is it save their discord (διχόνοια)? Moreover, what benefit are children to parents, when through folly they begin to rebel (στασιάζειν) against them?[606]

[603] Aristid. *Or.* 24.7.

[604] Aristid. *Or.* 24.32.

[605] Aristid. *Or.* 24.33-35.

[606] Dio Chrys. *Or.* 38.15. In *Or.* 26.8 the same author includes "concord and friendship of families" (ὁμονοίας καὶ φιλίας οἰκιῶν) in a list of things which are of the greatest importance. Additionally, in one of his discourses on ὁμόνοια he says that peace is better than war and friendship is more profitable than enmity both for the families (οἴκοις) and the cities (*Or.* 40.26). Considering the relationship between man and woman, a similar expression to that just cited from *Or.* 38.15f. occurs in Musonius *Or.* 13B: "Without harmony (ὁμόνοια) of mind and character between husband and wife, what marriage can be good, what partnership advantageous?"

Lastly, Plutarch, who seems to reflect the general view on the relationship between husband and wife, summarizes his basic attitude as follows: "every activity in a virtuous household is carried on by both parties in agreement (ὁμονοούντων), but discloses the husband's leadership and preferences".[607]

The passages we have cited should suffice to indicate the following: firstly, that it was considered to be of great importance to establish and preserve concord in the household; and secondly that a presupposition for concord was that different groups of people belonging to the household should behave in line with conventional rules of conduct. Awareness that concord was associated with proper behaviour in the household facilitates the recognition of why Clement praised the Corinthian Christians for their previous behaviour, which had been in line with conventional rules for the household. Such behaviour established and maintained concord. Likewise, his exhortation to several groups of the household to behave in a certain way must be read in the light of the effect the advised behaviour had in creating and preserving concord (21:6-8). Considerations on proper behaviour in the household belonged to the semantic field of ὁμόνοια.

3.5.2.10. ἐταπεινοφρονεῖτε μηδὲν ἀλαζονευόμενοι

In the continuation of his praise of the past exemplary communal life of the Corinthian Church, Clement draws attention to the fact that they "were all humble-minded and in no wise arrogant" (ἐταπεινοφρονεῖτε μηδὲν ἀλαζονευόμενοι, 2:1). Here Clement introduces two topics which play important roles in the letter. The ταπεινο-word group is especially prevalent throughout the letter[608] and is presented as a means of solving the present crisis in the Church.[609] Clement explicitly exhorts the Corinthians to practise the virtue of humility of which Christ and men from the Old Testament were the greatest examples.[610] When he recapitulates the content of the letter, he says, among other things, that he has reminded them that they are bound to please God in concord and peace just as "our fathers, whose examples we quoted, were well-pleasing in their humility (ταπεινοφρονοῦντες) towards God, the Father and the Creator, and towards all men" (62:2). Another illuminating example of the significance of this virtue

---

[607]Plut. *Mor.* 139 D. For further discussion on Plutarch's view on the relationship between man and wife, cf. D. C. VERNER, *The Household of God* (1983) 68. For other references to the topic of concord in the household or between different classes in the household, cf. Arist. *Pol.* 1.2.20-22; Lycurg. frg. 11-12.3; Men. frg. 262; 584; Apollod. Car. frg. 10 (C. Austin, ed., *Comicorum Graecorum fragmenta in papyris reperta*. Berlin: Gruyter, 1973, 4).

[608]ταπεινοφροσύνη 6 times (*1 Clem.* 21:8; 30:8; 31:4; 44:3; 56:1; 58:2), ταπεινοφρονέω 12 times (*1 Clem.* 2:1; 13:1, 3; 16:1, 2, 17; 17:2; 19:1; 30:3; 38:2; 48:6; 62:2) and ταπεινός 4 times (*1 Clem.* 30:2; 55:6; 59:3, 4).

[609]For the significance of this word in *1 Clement*, see K. J. LIANG, *Het Begrip Deemoed in 1. Clemens* (1951); O. B. KNOCH, *Eigenart und Bedeutung der Eschatologie im theologischen Aufriss des ersten Clemensbriefes* (1964) 386-396; G. BRUNNER, *Die theologische Mitte des ersten Klemensbriefes* (1972) 128-134; B. E. BOWE, *A Church in Crisis* (1988) 112-121.

[610]Cf. 13:1-19:1 for instance, where the topic of humility is the basic one. For explicit exhortations to humility, see 13:1; 21:8; 30:3.

in re-establishing concord is found in 48:6. After Clement has dealt explicitly with the situation in the Corinthian Church, he concludes his exhortation to cease the sedition by saying that the more a man "seems to be great, the more he ought to be humble-minded (ταπεινοφρονεῖν), and to seek the common good of all and not his own benefit". In addition to the fact that he holds that the attitude of humility will create concord, we note that he defines humility as seeking "the common good" in contrast to seeking one's own benefit. Here Clement might be influenced by Phil 2:3f. where Paul draws a connection between humility and the common good.[611] However, we should also pay attention to the fact that in antiquity it was common to depict those who were involved in sedition as seeking their own interest and benefit instead of the common good.[612] Furthermore, Clement explicitly links ταπεινοφροσύνη and concord in 30:3 when he exhorts the Corinthians to put on concord (ὁμόνοια) by being humbled (ταπεινοφρονοῦντες) and self-controlled (ἐγκρατευόμενοι).[613] From these few remarks about his use of the term humility it should be clear that it plays an important role in gaining concord.[614] He prescribes the virtue of humility as medicine for the present state of sedition. This means both that ταπεινοφροσύνη belongs to the semantic field of concord in *1 Clement* and that it is a positive and highly valued virtue.

That the ταπεινο-word group carries positive connotations in *1 Clement* seems to suggest that the author stands predominantly in a Jewish-Christian tradition when he uses this word group. In addition to the negative connotations where, e.g., ταπεινός could mean "oppressed", "held down" by foreign and political military powers or "small", "base" in worth compared with others,[615] it also had a clearly positive meaning. It could mean "humble, modest" and ταπεινόω, "to humble oneself".[616] In the LXX the expression ταπεινώσατε τὰς ψυχὰς ὑμῶν occurs many times and means "to humble one's soul", "to fast". The main point with fasting "is not just the observance in which self-humbling finds visible expression but more particularly the subjection of the mind to God's will and judgment".[617] A similar connection between humility and obedience to the will of God is also found in *1 Clement*.[618] A significant aspect of the use of the ταπεινο-word group in the LXX is that God has taken sides with the humble-minded and will on the one hand humble the proud and arrogant and on the other

---

[611]So B. E. Bowe, *A Church in Crisis* (1988) 115: "This Pauline text (Phil 2:3-4) seems surely to have influenced the meaning and the choice of ταπεινοφροσύνη in *1 Clement*, with Paul's particular emphasis of putting the common good before ones own".

[612]See the present study pp., 43-45.

[613]The two participles express how to realise concord, cf. A. Lindemann, *Die Clemensbriefe* (1992) 96.

[614]O. B. Knoch, *Eigenart und Bedeutung der Eschatologie im theologischen Aufriss des ersten Clemensbriefes* (1964), argues that for Clement humility makes up the absolute basis for Church unity (392). B. E. Bowe, *A Church in Crisis* (1988) asserts that ταπεινοφροσύνη is the chief among the virtues Clement prescribes to resolve the crisis in the Church (112).

[615]W. Grundmann, "ταπεινός κτλ.", *TDNT* 8, 9 with references.

[616]*Ibid.* 6f., with references.

[617]*Ibid.* 7, with references.

[618]Cf. for instance *1 Clem.* 13:3; 14:3; 56:1.

exalt the lowly.[619] A positive sense of humility is also reflected in the Qumran *Manual of Discipline*. The Qumran Sect used "the lowly" as a term to define themselves and express their willingness to observe the Law.[620] Of particular interest is the fact that it linked humility with unity in the community: "For all shall be in a single Community of truth, of proper meekness, of compassionate love and upright purpose, towards each other in the holy council, associates of an everlasting society".[621]

The New Testament takes up and further develops the positive attitude of humility. For instance it is emphasized that in line with his promise (1) God will humble the proud and exalt the humble,[622] (2) that he will exalt the one who makes himself the servant of others,[623] but abase those who exalt themselves above others,[624] and (3) that the ταπεινός is the one who submits to his will.[625] Further, Paul contrasts the virtue of ταπεινοφροσύνη with ἐριθεία and κενοδοξία when he exhorts the Philppians to "leave no room for selfish ambition (ἐριθεία) and vanity (κενοδοξία), but humbly (ταπεινοφροσύνη) reckon others better than yourselves" (Phil 2:3). [626] The proper attitude of ταπεινοφροσύνη implies that one should serve others and should have no desire to be great or to have public esteem.[627] Or, to use B. J. Malina's summary of the biblical meaning of humility: "This value directs persons to stay within their inherited social status … Humble persons do not threaten or challenge another's right, nor do they claim more for themselves than has been duly allotted them in life".[628] In view of the use of ταπεινοφροσύνη in *1 Clement* it is interesting to note that the context of Phil 2:3 shows that Paul links ταπεινοφροσύνη with unity in the Church. In 2:2 he admonishes his readers to think the same thing (τὸ αὐτὸ φρονῆτε) [629]and to have the

---

[619]See, e.g., Pss 17:28; 33:18f; Prov 3:34; Isa 2:11, and the discussion in W. GRUNDMANN, "ταπεινός κτλ.", *TDNT* 8, 8-10.

[620]*Ibid.* 12.

[621]1QS 2:24-25. Cf. also 1QS 5:3f. and hereto B. E. BOWE, *A Church in Crisis* (1988) 113.

[622]Matt 23:12; Luke 14:11; 18:14.

[623]Luke 22:25-27; Mark 9:35; 10:42-44.

[624]Luke 14:11.

[625]Jas 4:10; 1 Pet 5:5f.

[626]In antiquity ἐριθεία and κενοδοξία were regarded as an underlying cause of strife in a political body. Regarding ἐριθεία, see Arist. *Pol.* 5.2.3. In Dio Chrys. *Or.* 38.29f. κενοδοξία expresses inappropriate ambitions to be called first, i.e. to claim a position and status which is not consistent with reality. See further chap. 5.4.1.3 for the view, common in antiquity, that seeking after glory often leads to strife.

[627]S. REHRL, *Das Problem der Demut in der profan-griechischen Literatur im Vergleich zu Septuaginta und Neuem Testament* (1961) in commenting upon Phil. 2:3 states that "niemand solle sichselbst wichtig nehmen in Dingen, die Ehre und Geltung und Stellung betreffen, wohl aber auf die Geltung des anderen bedacht sein" (182), and B. E. BOWE, *A Church in Crisis* (1988), quotes K. Thiemes who argues that ταπεινοφροσύνη is essentially "'the readiness for a lower position, lesser regard, the absence of any desire to be great or distinguished, to have external honor or public esteem or a name, to mean something, to play a role'" (114).

[628]B. J. MALINA, "Humility", *Biblical Social Values and Their Meaning* (1993) 107.

same love for each other. The basic subject in Phil 2:1-4 is the need for unity in the Church,[630] and ταπεινοφροσύνη is a virtue which generates such unity.

Scholars have noted the fact that the ταπεινο-word group carries positive connotations in the Jewish-Christian tradition to such a great extent that this represents a striking difference from classical and Hellenistic usage.[631] In the latter, the ταπεινο-word group has a clearly negative meaning in the majority of occurrences. It could designate an "insignificant", "weak", "poor" condition of man, city, or fatherland.[632] Furthermore, and this represents the clearest difference from Jewish-Christian use, ταπεινός meant "lowly", "servile", "without honor" with regard to the spiritual and moral state. It was often linked with ἀνελεύθερος, δουλικός, ἄδοξος, ἀγενής, [633] and could even express a physical or moral defect.[634] Such negative connotations indicate that Clement, in applying the ταπεινο-word group is not influenced by this tradition, but that he stands in a Jewish-Christian tradition.[635] The strongest advocate of such a point of view is K. J. Liang who goes so far as to argue that Clement's use of the term ταπεινός indicates that "it would be a fiction to contend that Clement is under intensive influence of the Stoa" in general. One of his main arguments is that the "classics … do not know the favorable meaning of ταπεινός" which implies that ταπεινός is not seen as a virtue.[636] Although this is correct regarding the majority of the occurrences of the ταπεινο-word group, we should note that one may in fact point to occurrences where ταπεινός has a positive meaning. These are often linked with other terms expressing highly estimated values in antiquity.[637]

Let us first present a passage from Demosthenes' oration *Against Meidias*:

---

[629]For this and similar expressions denoting unity in a political body, see, e.g., Polyb. *Hist.* 5.104.1; Dio Chrys. *Or.* 4.135; 34.20; Aristid. *Or.* 23.31, 42; Dion. Hal. *Ant. Rom.* 4.20.4; 7.59.7; 7.15.1, and further M. M. MITCHELL, *Paul and the Rhetoric of Reconciliation* (1991) 68f.

[630]Cf. D. A. BLACK, "Paul and Christian Unity", *JETS* 28 (1985) 299-308, when discussing the relationship between 1:27-30 and 2:1-4 asserts: "Unity of action in the face of opposition must rest on unity of intention and heart. This principle is expounded in 2:1-4 and then illustrated in 2:5-11" (305).

[631]W. GRUNDMANN, "ταπεινός κτλ." *TDNT* 8, 11f; B. E. BOWE, *A Church in Crisis* (1988) 113. Cf. the title of the work which as far as we know is the most detailed study of the use of the ταπεινο-word group in Greek, Jewish and Christian tradition; S. REHRL, *Das Problem der Demut in der profan-grie-chischen Literatur im Vergleich zu Septuaginta und Neuen Testament* (1961).

[632]For text references, see *ibid.* (1961) 27; W. GRUNDMANN, "ταπεινός κτλ.", *TDNT*, 8, 1.

[633]ἀνελεύθερος: Xen. *Mem.* 3.10.5; *Cyr.* 3.3.24 (opp. ἐλεύθερος); δουλικός: Pl. *Leg.* 6.774 C (δουλεία ταπεινὴ καὶ ἀνελεύθερος); ἄδοξος: Plut. *Mor.* 64 E; 69 C; Epict. *Diss.* I.4.25; ἀγενής: Arist. *Eth. Nic.* 4.3.26; Lucian *Cal.* 23; Plut. *Mor.* 66 D; 91 D; *Aem.* 9.1; *Demetr.* 30.4; *Cic.* 10. 4.

[634]E.g., Thuc. 2.61.28; Arist. *Pol.* 8.2.1f; *Eth. Nic.* 4.3.29-33; Polyb. *Hist.* 14.1.13. Further, see S. Rehrl, *Das Problem der Demut in der profan-griechischen Literatur im Vergleich zu Septuaginta und Neuem Testament* (1961) 27-31.

[635]E.g., K. J. LIANG, *Het Begrip Deemoed in 1 Clemens* (1951), who in the summary states that "it has become clear to us that ταπεινός as the virtue of humility in the LXX and in the later Jewish writings is of much the same sense as the word used by Clement" (136).

[636]*Ibid.* 136.

[637]This is pointed out by S. REHRL, *Das Problem der Demut in der profan-griechischen Literatur im Vergleich zu Septuaginta und Neuem Testament* (1961), e.g., 32f. and 38-41.

> *If in his past life he was so brutal (ἀσελγής) and violent (βίαιος) because it was*
> *impossible for him to be humble (ταπεινός γενέσθαι), it would be right to abate*
> *some of your anger as a concession to his natural temper and to the destiny that made*
> *him the man he is; but if he knows how to behave discreetly (μέτριος) when he likes,*
> *but has deliberately chosen the opposite line of conduct, it is surely obvious that, if he*
> *slips through your fingers now, he will once more prove himself the man you know so*
> *well (Or. 21.186).*

Here it is obvious that ταπεινός γενέσθαι carries positive connotations and that it includes among other things behaving μετρίως. μετρίως means "moderately", "within due limits" and expressed the acceptance of limits set by God and society.[638]

Furthermore, Isocrates also connects ταπεινῶς with μετρίως in *Or.* 12.20: "For I thought that it was so well known that I was waging war against the false pretenders to wisdom and that I had spoken so moderately (μετρίως), nay so modestly (ταπεινῶς), about". And in *Or.* 3.56 where he speaks on behalf of Nicocles ταπεινός expresses obedience and is linked with the ideal of preserving the royal law: "You should be self-effacing (ταπεινός) in your attitude toward my authority, abiding by our customs and preserving the royal laws". The obedience, i.e. to be ταπεινός, of subjects to governments is a precondition for safety not only for rulers, but for citizens as well. In other words, in this passage to be ταπεινός is viewed as a virtue.[639]

ταπεινός also carries positive connotations in Xen. *Ages.* 11.10f. where the author describes the virtues of Agesilaos:

> *To moderation (σωφρονεῖν) in times of prosperity he added confidence in the midst*
> *of danger.*
>   *His urbanity found its habitual expression not in jokes but in his manner; and*
> *when on his dignity (μεγαλόφρων), he was never arrogant (ὕβρις), but always rea-*
> *sonable (γνώμη); at least, if he showed his contempt for the haughty (ὑπεραύχων), he*
> *was humbler than the average man (τῶν μετρίων ταπεινότερος).*

When the author here describes the modesty of Agesilaos he on the one hand associates ταπεινός with the virtues σωφρονεῖν, γνώμη, μέτριος, and on the other hand contrasts it with ὑπεραυχέω and ὕβρις.[640]

---

[638]H. G. LIDDELL and R, SCOTT, *A Greek-English Lexicon* (1973) 1122; P. MARSHALL, *Enmity in Corinth* (1987) 191. S. REHRL, *Das Problem der Demut in der profan-griechischen Literatur im Vergleich zu Septuaginta und Neuem Testament* (1961), says in his dicussion of Dem *Or.* 21.186 that "ταπεινὸς γενέσθαι bedeutet hier klar: 'massvoll werden', eben das Gegenteil von dem, was Demosthenes 'aus-gelassen', 'frech', 'übermütigen, gewalttätigen' nennt. So verstehen wir also unter dem ταπεινός einen Menschen, der sein 'eigens Mass' kennt, der nicht über den dem Menschen durch die menschliche Ordnung gesteckten Rahmen hinausgreift: das Gegenteil des 'frechen, übermütigen, gewalttätigen', also ordungsfeindlichen Menschen" (33).

[639]Cf. *Ibid.* (1961), comments on this passage: "Dieser freiwillig geleistete Gehorsam ist hier auch klar als Tugend gekennzeichnet" (38). For similar use of ταπεινός Rehrl refers to Xen. *Hier.* 5.4; Diod. Sic. 2.7.5.24; Plut. *Mor.* 60 F.

In view of this there is no reason for asserting that ταπεινός could not be considered as a virtue among the Greeks.[641] Admittedly, we have not observed any example of ταπεινός used as a virtue in contexts where one dealt with the question of unity and sedition in a political body. It is, however, interesting to note that ταπεινός is both associated with virtues (σώφρων, μέτριος) which were related to unity in antiquity and contrasted with vices (ὕβρις, ὑπερήφανος) which were related to sedition.[642] In spite of that fact, it is not reasonable to assume that Clement was primarily inspired by this Greek use of ταπεινός. He was, as we noted above, rooted first of all in a Jewish-Christian tradition with respect to this term. On the other hand we should not be so quick, as several scholars have been,[643] to exclude the possibility that this Greek use could to a certain extent have had an impact on Clement. At least, the connection between ταπεινός and virtues and vices associated with the topic of unity and sedition in social units, indicates that Clement's exhortations to be ταπεινός as a means of achieving concord would sound appropriate in Greek ears which were familiar with the positive use of ταπεινός.

As indicated above, the theme of ἀλαζονεία expressed by the noun – or the verb ἀλαζονεύομαι – plays an important role in the letter. The noun covers the meaning "false pretension, imposture, boastfulness"[644] and "arrogance", and the verb means "boast, be boastful".[645] The ἀλαζών is one who is "'ascribing to himself either more and better things than he has, or even what he does not possess at all'".[646]

In addition to 2:1, there are two other instances where Clement uses the term ἀλαζονεύομαι or its noun or adjective derivatives as antonyms for ταπεινοφρονέω

---

[640]Also Plato contrasts ταπεινός with ὕβρις and associates it with σώφρων and μέτριος (Pl. *Leg.* 4.716 A-E). Cf. the discussion of this passage in S. REHRL, *Das Problem der Demut in der profan-grie-chischen Literatur im Vergleich zu Septuaginta und Neuem Testament* (1961) 40-44. Among other things Rehrl says that ταπεινός contrasts with "ὑβριστῆς, zu jenem Hochmütigen, der sich eben an Gott und seiner Gerechtigkeit versündigt … Aus ihr [εὐσέβεια] erwächst dem Menschen die Kraft zu, σώφρων und μέτριος zu sein. Das schönste Moment dieser beiden ist aber das ταπεινός. Es bezeichnet den ehrfürchtig gehorchenden, sich restlos unterwerfenden Mann der Tugens, den vor Gott Demütigen" (43). Passages where ταπεινός are contrasted with ὑπερήφανος and other terms expressing arrogance and haughtiness are found as well, see *ibid.* 45-54.

[641]Cf. C. SPICQ, "ταπεινός κτλ.", *Theological Lexicon of the New Testament* 3, 370: "*tapeinosis* was also considered a virtue even by pagans, namely, the virtue of modesty or moderation, associated with *praütes, hesychia, metriotes, kosmiotes*, and even *sophrosyne*; the opposite of *hybris, authadeia*, and *hyperephania*. S. Rehrl has provided abundant evidence of this".

[642]Regarding σώφρων, see chap. 3.5.2.5. μέτριος was often associated with σωφροσύνη expressing the ideal of moderation, measure in all things. In addition to the actual texts just quoted above, see, e.g., Plut. *Mor.* 150 D; 441 A; 989 B; *Ages.* 14.1; Joseph. *Bell* 2.208 and P. MARSHALL, *Enmity in Corinth* (1987) 191. Regarding ὕβρις and ὑπερήφανος, see the present study, pp. 168-169.

[643]K. J. LIANG, *Het Begrip Deemoed in 1 Clemens* (1951) 136; B. E. BOWE, *A Church in Crisis* (1988) 112-114.

[644]H. G. LIDDELL and R. SCOTT, *A Greek-English Lexicon* (1973) 59.

[645]W. BAUER, *A Greek-English Lexicon* (1979) 34.

[646]G. DELLING, art "ἀλαζών, ἀλαζονεία", *TDNT* 1, 226.

or its noun or adjective derivatives. He exhorts the Christians to put aside all arrogance (πᾶσαν ἀλαζονείαν) and to be humble-minded (ταπεινοφρονήσω) instead (13:1). Then as the ultimate example of humility he presents the fact that in spite of his power Christ did not come "with the pomp of pride or of arrogance ... but was humble-minded" (16:2). It is the leaders of the sedition in particular who are described as arrogant and boastful. They are "in pride and unruliness" (ἐν ἀλαζονείᾳ καὶ ἀκαταστασίᾳ) the instigators of an abominable jealousy (14:1), and they "boast in the pride of their words" (ἐγκαυχωμένοις ἐν ἀλαζονείᾳ τοῦ λόγου αὐτῶν, 21:5). It is, however, the entire Church that is addressed by Clement's exhortations to put aside ἀλαζονεία.[647] The foregoing texts establish three things: (1) that ἀλαζονεία and ταπεινοφρονέω are contrasted with each other; (2) that it is the leaders of the sedition in particular who are described as arrogant; and (3) that ἀλαζονεία is linked with other terms which are connected with sedition in a political body (14:1). These three facts indicate that to be arrogant or to boast was regarded as amounting to seditious behaviour within the Church.

When Clement deals with the topic of ἀλαζονεία his language obviously reflects a Hellenistic Jewish tradition.[648] However, the connection made between boasting and sedition appears to mirror conventional thoughts in Greek literature. When Dio Chrysostom in *Or.* 1 pictures Tyranny's throne, he says that it is ornamented with arrogance (ἀλαζονεία, 1.79), and attended by, amongst other things, insolence (ὕβρις) and sedition (στάσις, 1.82).

Clement makes a close connection between arrogance and self-praise (21:5). The theme of self-praise was a topic discussed in the ancient world.[649] From at least 100 B.C.E. conventions relating to self-praise existed.[650] Plutarch discusses circumstances in which self-praise may be an efficient means for a speaker or a statesman to achieve his ends,[651] but in general this activity was regarded as detestable. If the motive of ones' self-praise was to cause disgrace to another and to secure glory for oneself, Plutarch depicts such a person as odious and vulgar.[652] Further, Dionysius Halicarnassenis characterised self-praise as "the most vulgar and most invidious of tasks".[653] Instead of self-praise one should rather be praised by others.[654] This point of view is also explic-

---

[647] 13:1; 35:5; 57:2.

[648] H. E. Lona, *Der erste Clemensbrief* (1998) 212f.

[649] For relevant literature cf. E. A. Judge, "Paul's Boasting in Relation to Contemporary Professional Practice", *ABR* 16 (1968) 37-50; H. D. Betz, "De laude ipsius", *Plutarch's Ehtical Writings* (1978) 367-393; *idem, Der Apostel Paulus und die sokratische Tradition* (1972) 75-79; C. Forbes, "Comparison, Self-Praise and Irony", *NTS* 32 (1986) 8-10.

[650] C. Forbes, "Comparison, Self-Praise and Irony", *NTS* 32 (1986) 8. Plutarch deals explicitly with this topic in *On Praising Oneself Inoffensively* (*Mor.* 539-547). Self-praise is also a basic theme in Dio Chrys. *Or.* 57, see, e.g., 57.3-6.

[651] Plut. *Mor.* 539 E-545.

[652] Plut. *Mor.* 547 A. Cf. also 547 D where he says that "no other kind of talk is so odious or offensive" as self-praise.

[653] C. Forbes, "Comparison, Self-Praise and Irony", *NTS* 32 (1986) 8.

[654] Plut. *Mor.* 539 D. Cf. also Quint. *Inst.* 11.1.22.

itly expressed by Clement in two connections: (1) when he exhorts the Corinthian Christians to be praised by God instead of by themselves, for "God hates those who praise themselves"; and (2) when he states that testimony to their good deeds should be given by others.[655]

As mentioned above, Plutarch regarded glory-seeking as a motive for self-praise.[656] It is not unlikely in the view of Clement that this was the case at the Corinthian Church as well.[657] Therefore it is interesting to note that Aristotle draws a connection between seeking glory and honour and στάσις:

> *It is clear also what is the power of honour (τιμή) and how it can cause party faction (στάσις); for men form factions (στασιάζειν) both when they are themselves dishonoured (ἀτιμαζόμενοι) and when they see others honored (τιμώμενοι) …*[658]

In other words, the connection between glory-seeking and party faction, may also suggest, at least indirectly, that boasting or arrogance was associated with the evil of sedition in a political body. Also, we should note that Plutarch links self-praise with other terms which are related in *1 Clement* to the issue of unity and sedition, i.e. φθόνος[659] and ζηλοτυπία[660]/ ζῆλος[661].

Another aspect we should pay attention to is that according to Clement, as mentioned above, the founders of the sedition boasted in the pride of their words (λόγος αὐτῶν). It is not fruitful to list the wide range of common meanings of the term λόγος. Let us simply mention that it may designate "word" in general; in other words, the everyday meaning of λόγος as, "speech", "the subject under discussion, matter, thing".[662] We should note, however, that *logos* was commonly used as a technical term for a "speech" and that it was used in particular to mean a "speech, delivered in the court, assembly, etc".[663] That is to say, it is the product of rhetoric. If *1 Clement* reflects the latter meaning of λόγος, then the leaders of the sedition may be seen as boasting of their eloquence and probably using this cleverness in the controversy. In our view, there are some good reasons for taking the view that λόγος ought to be understood as an allusion to rhetoric. Firstly, the long rhetorical tradition in the Graeco-Roman world, which also played a powerful and pervasive role at the time of the composition of *1*

---

[655] *1 Clem.* 30:6. Cf. also *Rom* 2:29; *1 Cor* 4:5. For Paul's use of this *topos* in his combating of factionalism in the Corinthian Church at that point of time, see M. M. MITCHELL, *Paul and the Rhetoric of Reconciliation* (1991) 91-93.

[656] Cf. also Plut. *Mor.* 540 A; 541 A; 546 C.

[657] See chap. 5 for the view that striving for honour was an essential feature in the strife.

[658] Arist. *Pol.* 5.2.4. A connection between seeking glory and sedition is further reflected in *Pol.* 2.4.7 where Aristotle states that "civil strife (στασιάζειν) is caused not only by inequality of property, but also by inequality of honours (τιμή)".

[659] Plut. *Mor.* 540 B, D; 544 B.

[660] Envy and jealousy may cause self-praise, Plut. *Mor.* 540 B.

[661] Plut. *Mor.* 545 D.

[662] W. BAUER, *A Greek English Lexicon* (1979) 477.

[663] H. G. LIDDELL and R. SCOTT, *A Greek-English Lexicon* (1973) 1058 for references and other meanings of the term λόγος.

Clement, had created a love and passion for λόγος (and σοφία).[664] Accordingly, to be a rhetor or to have the gift of beautiful and artistic speech was associated with great honour.[665] In view of this it is understandable that people were tempted to boast of their rhetorical ability. Secondly, farther on in the letter in a context where Clement urges the Corinthians to cease from the present state of sedition, he also makes references to λόγος. As a means of achieving concord he exhorts them to "be wise in the discernment of arguments" (σοφός ἐν διακρίσει λόγων, 48:5). This vital task for decision-making by the Christians at Corinth is remarkably similar to the task of an audience according to Aristotle. At the beginning of *Rhetorica* 2 he states that "the object of Rhetoric is judgement" (κρίσις, 2.1.2). This point is stressed later in the same book when he asserts:

> *Now the employment of persuasive speeches is directed towards a judgement (πρὸς κρίσιν); for when a thing is known and judged, there is no longer any need of argument. And there is judgement, whether a speaker addresses himself to a single individual and makes use of his speech to exhort or dissuade, as those do who give advice or try to persuade, for this single individual is equally a judge, since, speaking generally, he who has to be persuaded is a judge ... and similarly in epideictic speeches, for the speech is put together with reference to the spectator as if he were a judge.[666]*

We are inclined to think that it is no accident that Clement reflects both the terminology and the concepts of the task of the audience as these are outlined in the rhetorical tradition.[667] Because the opponents argue for their view by means of rhetoric, Clement exhorts the audience, the Corinthian Church, to distinguish between the arguments, and to make wise judgments. This implies that Clement views rhetoric as a seditious element.

---

[664]See the fine outline of the historical development of ancient rhetoric in D. A. Liftin, *St. Paul's Theology of Proclamation* (1994) 21-134, and in particular his emphasis on the fact that this fundamental feature of Graeco-Roman culture, an element which also was pervasive in Corinth in the first century, led to a situation where "the love of λόγος and σοφία came easily to them [the youth] as part of an inherited culture, a παιδεία as old as Isocrates" (146).

[665]Isocrates, e.g., writes that "those who are skilled in speech are not only men of power in their own cities but are also held in honour in other states" (*Or.* 4.49). Further, Quintilian says that the Roman people have always held the orator in highest honour (*summa dignitas, Inst.* 2.16.8), and regarding eloquence it would not have been "difficult to produce either ancient or recent examples to show that there is no other source from which men have reaped such a harvest of wealth, honour, friendship and glory, both present and to come" (*Inst.* 12.11.29). That eloquence was connected with honour is emphasized by R. MacMullen, *Enemies of the Roman Order* (1966) 15, who states the following regarding the fundamental role of eloquence for upper class persons: "The one art in which cultivated people commonly expressed their cultivation, from the fifth century B.C. to the fifth A.D. [is one] we no longer practise nor value, and tend to ignore. That was *eloquentia*. For a thousand years it remained at the heart of classical civilization, placing its heroes upon embassies, rostrums, richly endowed chairs, and the platforms of special theaters; at last, as statues, upon pedestals in the Roman forum itself".

[666]Arist. *Rh.* 2.18.1. Also Quintilian stresses that the audience is always the orator's judge, *Inst. Or.* 10.1.18-19; 12.10.73. Cf. D. A. Liftin, *St. Paul's Theology of Proclamation* (1994) 84, 105.

In view of this it is worth noting that ancient authors indicate that rhetoric may be the cause of or a feature contributing to civil strife.[668] When dealing with the evil of στάσις which arose throughout the Hellenic world, Thucydides emphasizes the part that the misuse of language played in corrupting the moral vocabulary: "The ordinary acceptation of words in their relation to things was changed as men thought fit. Reckless audacity came to be regarded as courageous loyalty to party, prudent hesitation as specious cowardice, moderation as a cloak for unmanly weakness" (3.82.4). As a weapon in the struggle for power the party leaders on each side adopted "fair-sounding names" and the opponents proffered "fair words" which thus violated their "oaths of reconcilement" (3.82.7f.). Also, as a means of preventing στάσις, Aristotle counsels that one must not put faith in sophisticated arguments "strung together for the sake of tricking the multitude" (*Pol.* 5.7.2).[669]

Additionally, there is an important element in the Hellenistic culture which seems to be relevant in this connection, namely the contests in rhetoric. Competitions in rhetoric were a common, integrated part of the culture and thus reflected the competitive spirit of the Hellenistic milieu in general. The aim of the participants was not restricted to just winning an actual competition. It was considered to be of equal importance to obtain allegiance.[670] In as much as it was a basic aim for the individual rhetor to acquire followers, it is not surprising, if a group of followers became strong enough, that different parties and divisions could emerge. This is confirmed by Seneca the Elder who describes the followers of the two rival rhetoricians Apollodorus and Theodorus in Rome in the first century B.C.E. as *secta*.[671] The same author also reports that the declaimers, i.e. primarily the teachers of rhetoric, were criticised for aiming to win

---

[667] For the opinion that the phrase σοφία λόγου in *1 Cor* 1:17 refers to rhetoric – with the implication that people with rhetorical skills were to be found in the Corinthian Church at that point of time – see H. D. BETZ, "The Problem of Rhetoric and Theology according to the Apostle Paul", *L'apôtre Paul* (1986) 34-39; S. M. POGOLOFF, *Logos and Sophia* (1992) 99-127; D. A. LIFTIN, *St. Paul's Theology of Proclamation* (1994), 181-209.

[668] Cf. L. L. WELBORN, "On the Discord in Corinth", *JBL* 106 (1987) 102: "In their reflections upon civil strife, ancient authors show themselves aware of the dominant role of rhetoric". See further S. M. POGOLOFF, *Logos and Sophia* (1992) 173ff. We are indebted to these scholars for the passages we are going to present.

[669] These passages indicate a connection between rhetoric and στάσις. Regarding the other references presented by Welborn we are of the opinion that they are not at all so relevant as he maintains. The point in Thrasymachus *Peri politeias* seems to be that those involved in party strife do not understand each other, and not that rhetoric causes στάσις. Likewise, the stress in Ps.-Sallust, *Ad Caesarem Senem* 9.3; 10.6; 11.1, is not upon the connection rhetoric-στάσις, but on the fact that the author points out that the rhetorical skills of the leaders of faction threaten to overthrow the true wisdom.

[670] Cf. S. M. POGOLOFF, *Logos and Sophia* (1992): "This competitive nature was always part of classical rhetoric, in which speakers contested not just *what* word but *whose* word would prevail. ... Such contests of speech (ἀγῶνα λόγων) and wisdom were the business of all speakers throughout antiquity" (173f.). Regarding the occurrences of such contests Pogloff points to following texts: Eur. *Antiop.* frg. 189; Ar. *Ran.* 875-884; Pl. *Prt.* 335A; Diod. Sic. 20.2.1; Isoc. *Or.* 13.14; Plut. *Mor.* 153F-154 A.

[671] Sen. *Controv.* 10 pr. 15.

approval for themselves rather for the case. They bitterly competed to win admiration and to avoid ridicule.[672]

In the second century the divisive force of rhetoric became even more visible. The professors, i.e. the rhetors, now became instigators and leaders in cultural contests between rival groups or cities. G. W. Bowersock writes:

> A polemical literature came into being in the form of tracts by warring sophists, denouncing each other with wit and erudition ... Rivalry for pre-eminence among the greater cities of Asia Minor was a common thing in this age, as even a cursory reading of Dio Chrysostom will show. Empty titles and imagined superiority meant much to the local citizenry ... Sophists were cause for boasting, as were buildings, canals, or coinage ... At Rome, observed Philostratus, consulars and sons of consulars applauded one sophist and then the other, starting a 'rivalry such as kindles the keenest envy and makes malice even in the hearts of wise men'.[673]

Clement's warning against people who boasted of their words (ἐγκαυχωμένοις ἐν ἀλαζονείᾳ τοῦ λόγου αὐτῶν (21:5), must therefore, we believe, be interpreted in the light of the fact that rhetoric or sophisticated speech was considered to be a divisive force in society. He reflects a common experience in antiquity, i.e. that the use of eloquence could lead to strife and discord in a political body.

3.5.2.11. εἰρήνη βαθεῖα

After Clement has praised the Corinthian Christians because of their humility and the fact that they were in no way arrogant, he draws attention to their piety in the continuation of his praise of their previous communal life. They paid attention to the words of Christ and did not forget his sufferings. Thus (οὕτως) all of them received a "profound and rich peace" (εἰρήνη βαθεῖα καὶ λιπαρά) and the Holy Spirit was poured out in abundance on all of them (2:2). In other words, Clement describes this ideal condition of the previous communal life as εἰρήνη βαθεῖα καὶ λιπαρά.

We have seen above that peace was commonly linked with concord in texts which discussed the issue of internal unity and sedition.[674] In some cases it is even difficult to distinguish between the terms. For this reason it is likely that the expression εἰρήνη βαθεῖα καὶ λιπαρά is also associated with the concept of concord. We have not found any texts which link λιπαρός and εἰρήνη in a similar way to that found in 1 Clement. However, as some scholars have already pointed out, the phrase εἰρήνη βαθεῖα is

---

[672]See Sen. Controv. 9 pr. 1, and S. M. POGOLOFF, Logos and Sophia (1992) 176, for further details of Seneca's description of the atmosphere around the declamations and how attracted people were by the rhetors.

[673] G. W. BOWERSOCK, Greek Sophists in the Roman Empire (1969) 89-91, see further the whole chap. "Professional Quarrels", 89-100.

[674]See chap. 3.4.

found in relatively many ancient texts.[675] Let us focus upon some of the texts pointed out by W. C. van Unnik.[676]

When Dionysius Halicarnassensis gives an account of the consulship of Aulus Sempronius Atratinus and Marcus Minucius, he states that during this time no action occurred of either a military or an administrative nature worthy of mention. This means there were no foreign wars and an injunction decreed by the senate succeeded in calming "disturbances (νεωτερισμός) raised in the city by the poor" (*Ant. Rom.* 6.1.1). In other words, during this time neither a war nor discord took place. For this reason, Dionysisus says that "these consuls [Aulus Sempronius Atratinus, Marcus Minucius], then, had the opportunity, as I said, of enjoying a profound peace" (εἰρήνη ... βαθεῖα, *Ant. Rom.* 6.1.4). This means that the expression "profound peace" serves as a designation for a situation both free from *external* war and *internal* revolt.

Philo speaks about the priest Phineas (Num. 25:7-8) and says the following:

---

[675]J. B. Lightfoot, *The Apostolic Fathers I: Clement II* (1989, first pr. 1890) 17, pointed out the following Jewish and Christian texts: 4 Macc 3:20; Hegesipp. in Eus. *h.e.* 3.32; Athenag. *supplicatio* 1; *Lit. Bas.* p. 165 (Neale); Eus. *v.C.* 2.61. However, Lightfoot does not discuss how these texts may enhance our understanding of *1 Clement* or reflect upon the fact that all except one of these texts are more recent than *1 Clement*. The first scholar to provide a detailed investigation of the expression εἰρήνη βαθεῖα was K. Beyschlag, *Clemens Romanus und der Frühkatholizismus* (1966) 149-165. Beyschlag explores 4 Macc 3:20; 18:4; Athenag. *Presbeia* 1-2; Eus. *h.e.* 3. 32:6 (Hegesipp); 5.16:18f (Anonymus antimont.); Cypr. *Ep.* 75:10; Lactanz *De mortibus persecutorum.* 3; Or. *Exhortatio ad martyrium* 31; Philo *Somn.* 2.147, 229. However, the expression εἰρήνη βαθεῖα does not occur in three of these texts; 4 Macc 18:4; Eus *h.e.* 5.16, 18f (εἰρήνη διάμονος); Cypr. *Ep.* 75:10 (*post longam ... pacem*) and Lactanz *De mortibus persecutorum.* 3:5 (*longa pax*). Beysclag's approach is a combination of source criticism and tradition history. He aims to identify the source for the major themes in the first six chapters of *1 Clement*. He argues that the theme εἰρήνη βαθεῖα which is used as a counter concept to πόλεμος and στάσις is primarily an eschatological theme found in late Jewish and Early Christian Apologetic. Beyschlag also attempts to demonstrate a connection of the phrase εἰρήνη βαθεῖα with bloody persecution. He is of course aware that Clement has adapted the alleged martyr tradition to the situation at Corinth when he describes the revolt against the elders in the "martyr language" (see 135-166, especially 165f.). We will, however, question the methodology of Beyschlag. One problem is that almost all of the comparative texts are more recent, in some cases much more recent, than *1 Clement*. So also J. W. Wilson, *The First Epistle of Clement* (1976) 25. Furthermore, and this is our most fundamental objection to the work of Beyschlag, he uses only a few texts, all Christian and Jewish, as parallels and thus excludes, whether consciously or not, many other ancient texts. The importance of this fact was noted and demonstrated by W. C. van Unnik, "'Tiefer Friede' (1. Klemens 2,2)", *VigChr* 24 (1970) 261-279, in particular 264. In this article van Unnik pays attention to all ancient texts he was aware of in which the phrase occurs.

[676]Van Unnik discusses the following texts: Dion. Hal. *Ant. Rom.* 6.1.4; Philo *LegGai* 90; *Post* 184; *Som* 2.147; 2.229; *Ebr* 97; 4 Macc 3.20-21; Sen. *Ag.* 596 (*pax alta*); Luc. *Bellum Ciuile* 1. 249 (*pax alta*); Joseph. *Ant* 7.12, 3, 305; Eus. *h.e.* 3; 32:6; Lucian *Alex.* 25; *Tox.* 36; Athenag. *Supplicatio* 1; Hdn. *Ab excessu divi Marci* 4.10.1; 7.9,5; Or. *Jo.* 6. 1.5; *Eis martyrion* 31; Eus. *v.C.* 2.61.2-4; Chrys. *hom. in Mt.* 19.9; Synes. *Ep.* 29; *Lit. Bas.* (F. E. Brightman, *Liturgies Eastern and Western*, Oxford 1896, vol. 1, p. 407), *Orac. Sib.* 12. 85ff; 11.237.

*He delights in the maintenance of a well-ordered (εὐνομία) state under good laws
(εὐστάθεια), in the abolishing of wars (πόλεμος) and factions (στάσις) ... [It]
appears that states would have done rightly if before bringing against one another
arms and engines of war ... they had prevailed on their citizens one by one to put an
end to the disorder (στάσιν καταλῦσαι) which abounds within himself, and which is
so great and unceasing. For, to be honest, this is the original of all wars (Post 184f.).*

He goes on to say that, if disorder is abolished "the human race will attain to the experience and enjoyment of profound peace (βαθεῖα εἰρήνη), taught by the law of nature,
namely virtue, to honor God and to be occupied with his service, for this is the source
of long life and happiness" (*Post* 185). Here Philo deals with the happiness and well-
being of the State and asserts that these qualities depend on service to God because this
is a means of being fred from emotions which lead to στάσις. What is most important
in this connection is that Philo describes this well-being of the state, i.e. freedom from
both internal revolt and war, as βαθεῖα εἰρήνη.[677]

The unknown author of 4 Maccabees begins his section about the power of self-
control with a historic introduction:

*When our fathers were enjoying profound peace (βαθεῖα εἰρήνη) through their
observance of the Law (διὰ τὴν εὐνομίαν) and were faring so well ... certain men
took repressive measures against the communal harmony (νεωτερίσαντες ὁμόνοιαν) and implicated us in various disasters (συμφορά, 3:20f.).*

In this passage it is obvious that βαθεῖα εἰρήνη is connected to the ideals of the Greek
city, i.e. εὐνομία and ὁμόνοια, and depicts a time free from revolt.[678] Indeed, we may
even say that βαθεῖα εἰρήνη is not just connected with ὁμόνοια, but that these
expressions function as synonyms.[679]

Finally we present two passages of Herodianus which W. C. van Unnik was apparently not aware of, i.e. 4.14.6 and 8.2.4.

After a plot the prefect Macrinus obtained the principate and immediately faced an
urgent situation. Artabanus was going to attack Rome to punish the Romans and take
his revenge for men who had been killed while there was a peace treaty in force.[680] In
this situation Macrinus directed a speech to his troops and said the following:

---

[677]Cf. Philo *LegGai* 90; *Som* 2.147; 2.229; *Ebr* 97, for further references where "profound peace" is
contrasted with war and revolt. In the three last-mentioned references the expression is to some extent
individualized as much as it refers to the inner condition of the soul. However, in *Som* 2.147 the ideal
of profound inner peace of the individual is the model for the cities. Cf. the discussion of the texts in
W. C. VAN UNNIK, "'Tiefer Friede' (1. Klemens 2,2)", *VigChr* 24 (1970) 265-268.

[678]νεωτερίζω was a common word for revolutionary activities, cf. H. G. LIDDELL and R. SCOTT,
A Greek-English Lexicon (1973) 1172.

[679]W. C. VAN UNNIK, "'Tiefer Friede' (1. Klemens 2,2)", *VigChr* 24 (1970) 268, comments on the
relationship between these terms by concluding that "εἰρήνη βαθεῖα ist hier der Wohlstand des Staates und ist fast identisch mit ὁμόνοια".

[680]Hdn. 4.14.1.

> *As you can see, the barbarian is attacking with his entire eastern forces, believing that he has a just cause for his hostility because of our aggression and violation of a treaty in stirring up a war (πόλεμος) in a time of complete peace (ἐν εἰρήνῃ βαθείᾳ, 4.14.6).*

Here, to live in εἰρήνη βαθεῖα is clearly contrasted with war. It is, however, more difficult to say for certain if the phrase also refers to a situation free from revolt and internal strife. If the peace treaty brought about a situation where there was peace in the entire Roman empire without any inter-regional revolts (which is a possibility), the phrase εἰρήνη βαθεῖα would also depict a situation of concord. In any case, εἰρήνη βαθεῖα is a political phrase describing the well-being of a political body, i.e. the Roman empire.

Herodian records what happened in the Italian city Aquileia at the time of Maximinus' attack. Many citizens who lived in little towns and surrounding villages escaped and sought refuge in Aquileia because of its size and defensive wall. The interesting point for our purposes is Herodian's explanation of why a large section of the old wall had fallen into ruins.

> *… after the extension of the Roman empire, the cities of Italy did not need walls or weapons any more, and in place of war enjoyed complete peace (ἀντὶ πολέμων εἰρήνην βαθεῖαν) and a share of Roman citizenship (8.2.4).*

Here also the author explicitly contrasts "war" with "complete peace". Furthermore, it is likely that the phrase "complete peace" refers to internal peace as well. Previously the different Italian cities had been at variance with each other, but now when they are united under the Roman rule they live in harmony with each other, and walls are not needed.

On the basis of the texts discussed above it seems that the phrase εἰρήνη βαθεῖα belonged to the cluster of terms commonly applied in discussions on unity and sedition in political bodies.[681] More precisely, the expression designates the well-being of a city or a people in as much as the people are neither involved in *external* war nor *internal* στάσις. In other words, it refers to a time dominated by ὁμόνοια.[682] Because the phrase εἰρήνη βαθεῖα occurs in similar contexts in *1 Clement*, it is probable that Clement deliberately makes use of this political language connected with the ideal of concord.[683]

---

[681]So also W. C. van Unnik, "'Tiefer Friede' (1. Klemens 2,2)", *VigChr* 24 (1970) 261-279; *idem*, "Noch einmal 'Tiefer Friede'", *VigChr* 26 (1972) 24-28.

[682]Cf. the conclusion of W. C. van Unnik, "'Tiefer Friede' (1. Klemens 2,2)", *VigChr* 24 (1970) 277: "Überschaut man dieses Material, dann ergibt sich, dass, wo ein deutlicher Kontext vorliegt, der Ausdruck 'tiefer Friede' immer mit der Lage eines Staates verbunden ist und aussagt, dass dieser Staat sich in einem überaus glücklichen Zustand befindet, weder behelligt von auswärtigen Feinden noch von Revolutionen im Innern, sich also in vollständiger Harmonie befindet".

3.5.2.12. ἀδελφότης

Clement also describes the previous community life of the Corinthian Church in terms that indicate that the Christians always had the ultimate interest of the whole brotherhood in mind. In 2:4 he states that they always "strove on behalf of the whole brotherhood (ἀδελφότης) that the number of his elect should be saved (σῴζω)". First we note the simple fact that the term ἀδελφότης used by Clement is seldom used as a designation of a Christian community.[684] However, this designation is obviously related to the common practice among Christians of naming each other ἀδελφοί, a practice which we find many examples of in *1 Clement* as well.[685] It is also related to the practice of referring to the Christian community as a φιλαδελφία – a term which occurs twice in the letter. According to Clement, a consequence of the present strife and sedition is that their "famous love for the brethren (φιλαδελφία)" has diminished (47:5), and consequently the author urges the Corinthians to put an end to these evils in order to restore the holy and seemly practice of φιλαδελφία (48:1).

The topic of "brotherly love" seems to have been commonly discussed in the so-called 'popular morality'. In spite of this, Plutarch's *De Fraterno Amore* (*Mor.* 478-492) is the only extant treatise that offers a systematic presentation of what antiquity associated with this concept.[686] However, as pointed out by H. D. Betz, there are reasons for presuming that in this essay, which is based on a combination of the family ethic and

---

[683]It is difficult, however, to establish whether Clement adopted the phrase εἰρήνη βαθεῖα from Hellenistic Judaism or from the profane Greek city ideal. So also P. LAMPE, *Die stadtrömischen Christen in den ersten beiden Jahrhunderten* (1989) 177. On the one hand, the fact that the majority of the occurrences of the expression εἰρήνη βαθεῖα predating *1 Clement* are to be found in the Hellenistic-Jewish sources indicates that Clement is influenced by this tradition, so H. E. LONA, *Der erste Clemensbrief* (1998) 128f. On the other hand, the following points may indicate that Clement has adopted the phrase from the Greek city ideal: (1) The phrase occurs in at least one extant Hellenistic source from the 1st century B.C.E. and in a number of passages from Greek pagan authors in the 2nd century C.E. in contexts which reflect the ideal of Greek *polis*; (2) the expression εἰρήνη βαθεῖα is linked with terms and conceptions that were commonly used when one dealt with the subject of concord in the Greek *polis* or other political bodies in literature which is earlier than he above texts from Hellenistic Judaism; and (3) Clement frequently uses other terms and concepts related to the Greek city ideal. The two alternatives, however, are not mutually exclusive. It is possible that he was acquainted with the use of the phrase in both Hellenistic Judaism and in the Greek tradition. The most important observation to be noted in this connection is the fact that in both traditions the phrase εἰρήνη βαθεῖα expressed concord in a political body and thus belonged to the semantic field of ὁμόνοια. From this conclusion it follows that we oppose K. Beyschlag's opinion that the expression reflects a Jewish and Early Christian Apologetic, cf. n. 675.

[684]The only occurrences of this term in the NT are in 1 Pet 2:17 and 5:9. Among the other Apostolic Fathers it does not occur at all.

[685]*1 Clem*.4:7; 13:1; 14:1; 33:1; 37:1; 38:3; 41:1; 45:1; 45:6; 46:1; 52:1; 62:1. C.f. H. VON SODEN, "ἀδελφός κτλ.", *TDNT* 1, 144-146.

[686]For an introduction to *De Fraterno Amore*, see H. D. BETZ, "De Fraterno Amore" *Plutarch's Ethical Writings and Early Christian Literature* (1978) 231-234; R. AASGAARD, '*My Beloved Brothers and Sisters!*' (1998) 105-118.

friendship, Plutarch reflects commonly held views in antiquity.[687] It is beyond the scope of the present investigation to discuss in detail the concept of φιλαδελφία in antiquity or the relations between brothers in general.[688] In line with the task of this chapter, we shall focus upon only a single aspect connected with φιλαδελφία, namely that of concord.

It is obvious that the value of concord is fundamental in *De Fraterno Amore* in that this theme is touched upon throughout the treatise.[689] It is even reasonable to say that the main aim of the different pieces of practical advice given by Plutarch is to secure co-operation and harmony between brothers.[690] This is reflected at the beginning of the *probatio*[691] where Plutarch presents the human body as a paradigm for brotherly love and says that nature (φύσις) has divided the body into different members "for mutual preservation and assistance [and] not for variance and strife" (σωτηρίας ἕνεκα καὶ συμπράξεως κοινῆς οὐ διαφορᾶς καὶ μάχης).[692] Although the one body is a combination of moist and dry, hot and cold, the different elements work together in bodily harmony. He goes on to develop his paradigma further with an excursus on human hands and the way they co-operate. Similarly, like the two hands of a man, two brothers coming from one seed and one source must cooperate (συνεργέω) and always remain in goodwill (εὔνοια), harmony (συμφωνία) and concord (ὁμόνοια, 478 E-F). Plutarch expresses the opposite relationship, which corrupts and destroys, with the terms greediness (πλεονεξία) and strife (στάσις). Further on in the treatise, when he gives advice concerning brothers who divide their deceased father's property, he says that for some this process is "the beginning of implacable enmity (ἔχθρα) and strife (διαφορά), but for others the beginning of friendship (φιλία) and concord (ὁμόνοια)".[693] Also, in 484 B the ideal relationship between brothers is described as "concord and peace" (ὁμόνοια καὶ εἰρήνη). This ideal relationship between brothers corresponds with the expression "not mine" whereas "mine" expresses the opposite

---

[687]H. D. Betz, "De Fraterno Amore", *Plutarch's Ethical Writings and Early Christian Literature* (1978) 231f.: "We can assume that the family ethics upon which his essay is based was widely shared in antiquity, including, to an extent, Judaism and primitive Christianity. Plutarch spells out what most other writers simply presuppose as commonly shared morality of life experience" (232).

[688]For detailed studies, cf. K. O. Sandnes, *A New Family* (1994), and R. Aasgaard, '*My Beloved Brothers and Sisters!*' (1998) and the bibliographies in these works.

[689]E.g. Plut. *Mor.* 479 A-B; 483 D; 484 B; 490 F.

[690]See, e.g., the relatively long discussion in Plut. *Mor.* 483 C- 484 D on how brothers ought to divide their dead fathers' property in a way that does not create enmity and strife. Cf. also K. O. Sandnes, *A New Family* (1994) 120.

[691]For an outline of the composition of *De Fraterno Amore*, see H. D. Betz, "De Fraterno Amore", *Plutarch's Ethical Writings and Early Christian Literature* (1978) 234-236.

[692]Plut. *Mor.* 478 D. K. O. Sandnes, *A New Family* (1994), emphasizes the important role the human body plays as a paradigm of the relationship between brothers. He says that the body metaphor functions as a "philosophical and pedagogical expression of his advice to brothers and friends" (120). For his discussion of the two most important texts in this connection, 478 D-479 B and 485 B-486 A, and texts of other authors where the body metaphor occurs in the same connection, cf. 120 -130.

[693]Plut. *Mor.* 483 D.

relationship. In other words, Plutarch describes the proper relationship between brothers as concord and peace, which depends on an attitude of sharing as opposed to egoism.

A reason why Plutarch emphasizes the aspect of concord in his discussion of the proper relations between brothers is that concord secures well-being in family life:

> ... so through the concord (ὁμοφροσύνη) of brothers both family and household are sound and flourish, and friends and intimates, like an harmonious choir (ἐμμελὴς χορός), neither do nor say, nor think, anything discordant (ἐναντίος) ... (*Mor.* 479 A).

Although Plutarch's discussion is the only extant one that preserves an extended development of the ideal of concord among brothers, other authors also reflect this ideal. In one of his discourses on concord Dio Chrysostom mentions a number of social entities in order to demonstrate the necessity of concord. Among them the term ἀδελφότης occurs. He asks, "What is fraternity (ἀδελφότης) save concord of brothers (ἀδελφῶν ὁμόνοια)?"[694] Admittedly, the most common terms for unity among brothers do not occur in the fragments of Hierocles dealing with fraternal love, but the concept is implied in the way he depicts the proper relationship between them. Similar to Plutarch, Hierocles uses the body as a metaphor for this ideal relationship. Just as the different members of the body must co-operate and assist each other in order to perform their proper office, this is even more true for brothers. When Hierocles describes the relationship between brothers he uses such terms as συλλαμβάνω (assist), συνεργάζομαι (co-operate), and σύμπραξις (mutual work).[695] This aspect of mutuality and co-operation must necessarily both require and strengthen harmony between brothers.

On the basis of the texts we have discussed it is reasonable to say that the aspect of concord was fundamental in discussions on brotherly love in antiquity. In particular, we may note that in the most detailed discussion of the topic in the only extant source, i.e. Plutarch's *De Fraterno Amore*, the need for concord is emphasized. The ideal of concord is in focus to such an extent that we may ask whether the concern for harmony between brothers is not the main purpose of the treatise. In any case, it was a *topos* in the ancient world that when brothers lived in a proper relationship, this would lead to concord. This fact may explain why Clement depicts the church at Corinth as a brotherhood in his praise of their previous life of community. They had the benefit of the whole brotherhood in view, i.e. salvation, and they were sincere and innocent (2:4f.) –

---

[694]Dio Chrys. *Or.* 38.15. Regarding other examples of the necessity for concord Dio mentions a ship (*Or.* 38.14), a household, a chariot, a good marriage and a friendship.

[695]"Brothers are more naturally adapted to assist each other, than are the parts of the body. For the eyes, indeed, being present with each other, see what is before them, and one hand cooperates with the other which is present; but the mutual works of brothers are, in a certain respect, much more multifarious" (Stob. *Flor.* 4.27.20). For further discussion, see K. O. SANDNES, *A New Family* (1994) 122f.

attitudes which imply that their relationships were characterised by concord. Similarly in 47:5 and 48:1, when Clement links cessation of sedition with the restoration of the Corinthians' φιλαδελφία, this must be understood in the light of the fact that concord was considered to be a precondition for true φιλαδελφία in antiquity.[696]

3.5.2.13. σχίσμα

Clement applauds the previous communal life because the Corinthian Christians "were sincere and innocent, and bore no malice to one another" and that "all sedition (στάσις) and all schism (σχίσμα) was abominable" to them (2:5f.). We have already dealt with στάσις[697] and shall now focus on the term σχίσμα. At first glance it comes as a surprise that Clement should describe the past in such a way. He was familiar with 1 Corinthians where Paul utilised the term σχίσμα to designate the conflict in the Corinthian Church at that point of time. With this in view, how could he say that there was no σχίσμα in the past? One suggestion is that Clement did not consider the conflict Paul dealt with in 1 Corinthians to be so serious that it was worth mentioning. At least he may have regarded the previous conflict as entailing less guilt on the part of the Corinthian Church because they "were partisans of Apostles of high reputation, and of men approved by them" (*1 Clem.* 47:4). However, a more plausible suggestion is that Clement deliberately exaggerated the ideal picture of the past in order to enforce the rhetorical strength of his argument.

Clement applies the term σχίσμα later in the letter as well. Contrary to the noble past, σχίσμα has now "turned aside many, has cast many to discouragement, many to doubt, all of us to grief (46:9). In his panegyric on love he states that "love admits no schism" (σχίσμα, 49:5). The continuation demonstrates that σχίσμα functions as a synonym to στάσις and that these terms are antonyms of ὁμόνοια: "love makes no sedition (στάσις), love does all things in concord" (ὁμόνοια, 49:5).[698]

In profane Greek the neuter noun σχίσμα occurs rarely and designates literally things that are "split", "rift", or "rent". Also, it is primarily applied "in connection with divisions in parts of the body or the parts of plants".[699] An example of a pre-Christian metaphorical use of σχίσμα where the term designates a "rift" or a division in a political body can, however, be found. In *PLond* 2710.13 the leader of the brotherhood of Zeus Hypsistos forbids religious factions which are called σχίσμα.[700] As far as we know, this is the only pre-Christian use of the term referring to divisions or a rent within the social fabric of a community. Therefore, it may seem quite surprising that we

---

[696]In addition, B. E. Bowe, *A Church in Crisis* (1988) 88, points out that "the image of the Christian assembly as ἀδελφότης stands also behind the examples of jealousy which Clement recounts in 4.1-5.7, all of which specify the animosity among and between 'brothers'".

[697]See chap. 3.5.1.1.1 for the discussion of στάσις as a political term.

[698]The term occurs also in 54:2.

[699]C. Maurer, "σχίζω, σχίσμα", *TDNT* 7, 959-64, quotation 963 with references. Cf. also W. Bauer, *A Greek-English Lexicon* (1979) 797.

find in the New Testament[701] and Early Christian Literature[702] relatively frequent occurrences of the noun σχίσμα with such a meaning. However, if we pay attention to the verb from which the noun is derived, i.e. σχίζω, we will see that this is not so surprising. Although it is also the literal use which is most common in the case of σχίζω,[703] the verb is also found in a comparatively large number of passages where it is used metaphorically to describe divisions of persons with different views. There are two passages from Diodorus Siculus that provide illuminating examples. He gives an account of a war that broke out in Sicily between the Syracusans and Acragantini.

> The cities of Sicily were divided (σχιζομένων δὲ τῶν Σικελικῶν πόλεων), some of them taking the field with the Acragantini and others with the Syracusans (Diod. Sic. 12.8.4).

Further, in connection with the civil strife at Megara, Diodorus relates that people took different sides:

> When the betrayal became known throughout the city and while the multitude were divided according to party (καὶ τοῦ πλήθους σχιζομένου κατὰ τὴν αἵρεσιν), some being in favour of fighting on the side of the Athenians and others aiding the Lacedaemonians.[704]

M. M. Mitchell argues that the metaphorical use of σχίζω to refer to broken or split communities must be understood from the fact that the term's most frequent literal use refers to "divisions of parts of the body and other natural phenomena". Since the body-metaphor is commonly used as an image of a political organism, "the transference of σχίζειν and later its noun σχίσμα is easily accomplished".[705] Furthermore, she cites a

---

[700]According to M. M. MITCHELL, *Paul and the Rhetoric of Reconciliation* (1991) 72. Mitchell rightly notes that the astrological text, *Catalogus Codicum Astrologorum Graecorum* 11.2 (ed. Lambertin, Brussels, 1898, 122.24, and referred to by W. BAUER, *A Greek-English Lexicon* (1979) 797, and L. L. WELBORN, "On the Discord in Corinth", *JBL* 106 (1987) 87 n. 9), in which σχίσματα is linked with πόλεμοι, φόνοι, μάχαι and ἀλαζονείαι μεγάλαι in a list of misfortunes caused by the god Ares, is from the twelfth-century C.E., and thus cannot be taken as evidence for a pre-Christian and Early Christian use of the term. In addition, Welborn's reference to Hdt. 7.219 as an example of a metaphorical use of the *noun* σχίσμα is not adequate, because it is a past form of the *verb* σχίζω that occurs in this text.

[701]John 7:43; 9:16; 10:19; 1 Cor 1:10; 11:18; 12:25. With the literal meaning 'a rift in a garment', Matt 9.16; Mark 2:21.

[702]In addition to *1 Clement*; *Did.* 4:3 (οὐ ποιήσεις σχίσματα); *Barn.* 19:12 (οὐ ποιήσεις σχίσμα, εἰρηνεύσεις δὲ μαχομένους συναγαγών); *Herm. Sim.* 8.9.4 (σχίσματα ἐν ἑαυτοῖς ἐποίησαν); Just. *dial* 35 (ἔσονται σχίσματα καὶ αἱρέσεις).

[703]C. MAURER, "σχίζω, σχίσμα", *TDNT* 7, 959 with references; H. G. LIDDELL and R. SCOTT, *A Greek-English Lexicon* (1973) 1746.

[704]Diod. Sic. 12.66.2. This text is also cited by L. L. WELBORN, "On the Discord in Corinth", *JBL* 106 (1987) 86. For further references, see Diod. Sic. 16.29.1; Xen. *Symp.* 4.59; Hdt. 7.219; 8.34; Dion. Hal. *Ant. Rom.* 7.59.8; Plut. *Mor.* 481. C and Lucian *Asin* 450 which M. M. MITCHELL, *Paul and the Rhetoric of Reconciliation* (1991) 72, cites as "a clear example". In the New Testament the verb σχίζω refers to division in a political body in Acts 14:4 and 23:7 and in the Apostolic Fathers in Ign. *Phld* 3:3.

[705]M. M. MITCHELL, *Paul and the Rhetoric of Reconciliation* (1991) 73.

passage from Plutarch as evidence for the connection between the body metaphor and the verb σχίζω. In his discussion about enmity between brothers he states the following:

> ... *for just as things which have been joined together, even if the glue becomes loose, may be fastened together again and become united, yet if a body (σῶμα) which has grown together is broken or split (σχισθείς), it is difficult to find means of welding or joining it; so friendships knitted together through long familiarity, even though the friends part company, can be easily resumed again, but when brothers have once broken the bonds of Nature, they cannot readily come together ... (Mor. 481 C).*

It is interesting to note that we find a similar connection between the body-metaphor and the *noun* σχίσμα linked with other terms that designate discord in *1 Clement* as well. Clement asks rhetorically why there are strife (ἔρις), passion (θυμός), divisions (διχοστασία), schisms (σχίσμα), and (πόλεμος) among them. Then he goes on to ask why we raise up strife (στασιάζω) against our own body (σῶμα).[706] Together with other terms derived from ancient politics σχίσμα is used to express the idea that there is a split in the body which is a metaphor for the community, the Corinthian Church.[707] As we have attempted to demonstrate above, the term σχίσμα, and in particular the verb σχίζω from which it is derived, is an adequate term to use to depict social or political division.[708] As such, it belongs to the semantic field of ὁμόνοια as one of its antonyms.

3.5.2.14. τῇ παναρέτῳ καὶ σεβασμίῳ πολιτείᾳ κεκοσμημένοι

As an expression of the noble life of the Corinthian Christians in the past Clement goes on to say that they were adorned (κεκοσμημένοι) by a "virtuous and honourable citizenship" (τῇ παναρέτῳ καὶ σεβασμίῳ πολιτείᾳ, 2:8). Here he draws a picture of the Corinthian Christians as ideal citizens. This means that according to him the Corinthian Christians as citizens in the *polis* of God lived in a way which served the interest and the well-being of this city, i.e. the Church. We have already previously observed in this study that Clement frequently uses terms and *topoi* associated with concord in a city state and transforms them in a Christian context.[709] This means that he uses the metaphor of a *polis* as a model for the Church, so we can speak of Clement's 'polis-ecclesiology'.[710] Furthermore, we have seen that the question of concord was of vital significance and was a precondition for a city's well-being.[711] Therefore it is fair to assume that when Clement applauds the Christians at Corinth for their "virtues and honourable citizenship" of the past, he is alluding to the previous concord within the Church.

---

[706] *1 Clem.* 46:5-7.

[707] A. Lindemann, *Die Clemensbriefe* (1992) 137: "τὸ σῶμα τὸ ἴδιον ist die konkrete einzelne Gemeinde".

[708] So also L. L. Welborn, "On the Discord in Corinth", *JBL* 106 (1987) 86f.; M. M. Mitchell, *Paul and the Rhetoric of Reconciliation* (1991) 73.

[709] See, e.g., chaps. 3.3.1; 3.3.2; 3.3.3; 3.4; 3.5.1.1.1; 3.5.2.7.

The fact that Clement uses the verb κοσμέω to describe the citizenship of the Corinthian Christians, appears to confirm, or at least makes it likely, that our suggestion that the expression "virtues and honourable citizenship" is alluding to a state of affairs marked by concord. Above, it has been translated as "adorn". This was a common meaning of the term.[712] κοσμέω thus expresses the idea that the previous state of affairs was an adornment of the Church. We should, however, note that the term κοσμέω does not signify that something is adorned in general, but rather that the adornment is connected with a high degree of good order.[713] Something is viewed as an ornament because it is in good order.[714] Thus it is not surprising that κόσμιος was commonly linked with σωφροσύνη. Plutarch, for instance, talks about the "decorous conduct and modest behaviour of the young" (τῶν παίδων εὐκοσμίας καὶ σωφροσύνης),[715] and says that "a husband who loves what is good and honourable makes a wife discreet (σώφρων) and well-behaved (κόσμιος)".[716] He asks whether or not that man's ways are marked by either justice "or equality, or self-control, or decorum" (σωφροσύνη οὐδὲ κοσμιότης).[717] This link between κοσμέω and σωφροσύνη served "always to emphasize conformity to the rules of decency and modesty ... The Greeks have such a sense of beauty that they see the virtues, or perfect deportment, as a sort of ornament that enchants the eyes and stirs admiration".[718]

In view of this it is reasonable to argue that the aspect of order is present in Clement's use of the verb κοσμέω in 2:8 as well. When he praises the Corinthian Christians for their adornment he is thinking of their previous good order. That this aspect of order as a significant feature of κοσμέω is present is also consistent with Clement's

---

[710]So also B. E. Bowe, *A Church in Crisis* (1988), who concludes the discussion of *1 Clement's* "Rhetorical Genre" by stating among other things that "Clement views the church, analogously, as a πολιτεία or πόλις; the dangers of strife and discord, therefore, are as severe as they had proved to be for cities in the past" (73). K. Wengst, *Pax Romana and the Peace of Jesus Christ* (1987) 115, argues that Clement's positive attitude to Roman rule determines his picture of the Christian community and explains the political aspect of Clement's ecclesiology.

[711]See, e.g., pp. 73-75.

[712]H. G. Liddell - R. Scott, *A Greek-English Lexicon* (1973) 984, with many references.

[713]For the meaning "order" see H. G. Liddell – R. Scott, *A Greek-English Lexicon* (1973) 984 with references.

[714]C. Spicq, "κοσμέω, κόσμιος", *Theological Lexicon of the New Testament* 2, 330: "The denominative verb *kosmeo* – formed from *kosmos*, meaning 'order, good order,' then 'adornment' (Strabo 3.4.17), 'ornament' (SB 8381, 1; 8550,3)0 ... – always retains the fundamental meaning 'to put in order'".

[715]Plut. *Mor.* 11 D.

[716]Plut. *Mor.* 140 C.

[717]Plut. Mor. 97 C. For other references, both literary and inscriptions, see C. Spicq, "κοσμέω, κόσμιος", Theological Lexicon of the New Testament 2, 332. Spicq states that "The connection between *kosmios, sōphrōn (sōphrosynē)*, and *aidōs* is so constant in the Hellenistic period that it must be considered a literary topos from Xenophon on" (332).

[718]*Ibid.* 332f.

emphasis upon the need for good order to establish and maintain concord, which appears elsewhere in the letter.[719]

Additionally, we have succeeded in finding passages which explicitly link κοσμέω or κόσμιος with concord. For example, in connection with a conflict between the senate and the plebeians which could develop into civil war, Dionysius Halicarnassensis reports that a representative of the latter, after having listening to a political discourse of Minucius, "thought it to his interest that the commonwealth should become harmonious (ὁμονοῆσαι) and recover its ancient good order (κόσμος)".[720] In an urgent situation when facing attacks from external enemies Gaius Claudius argued in a discourse addressed to the Senate that the most efficient way to defend themselves was to put an end to internal strife and disorder. Only by being conscious of the fact that all men, both rulers and the ruled, basically have common interests, only then are men willing to undergo the necessary hardships in order to defend the *polis*. Therefore Claudius advised his audience to "give leave to everyone who so desires to speak in favour of harmony and good order" (ὑπὲρ ὁμονοίας δὲ καὶ κόσμου) among the citizens.[721] We also find that Dio Chrysostom makes a similar, clear connection between κόσμος and concord. In *Or.* 32.37 he presents qualities which he finds worthy of praise: "For when we praise human beings, it should be for their good discipline, gentleness, concord (ὁμόνοια), civic order (κόσμος πολιτείας)". Admittedly, in these passages κόσμιος or κόσμος[722] are not primarily used with the meaning "ornament", although it probably also carries this connotation. Notwithstanding this, they are examples of usage in association with concord and thus of belonging to the semantic field of concord.

Two passages from Aelius Aristides are of particular interest in as much as, besides linking harmony and κόσμος, he also uses these terms to depict the ideal city. In one of his discourses on concord he advises the audience not to think that factions are profitable in government and in their associations with one another, but that concord (ἁρμονία) is the highest good. He goes on to say, "This is the true adornment of cities (οὗτος ὁ τῶν πόλεων κόσμος ἀληθινός), this is their greatest protection, this is their greatest glory" (*Or.* 23.75f.). In an another discourse that advises concord Aristides says:

> For just as we praise the harmony (ἁρμονία) in the latter [a construction] and the fact that each element preserves its proper relationship, so it is also fitting to think that a well lived life takes place whenever harmony and order (ἁρμονία καὶ τάξις) prevail throughout. This adornment is truly proper to cities (οὗτος ὁ τῶν πόλεων ὡς ἀληθῶς κόσμος οἰκεῖος). This preserves both individual man and city (*Or.* 27.41).

---

[719]See our discussion on εὐτάκτως, τάξις, τάγμα in chap. 3.6.2.1. In our opinion, B. E. Bowe, *A Church in Crisis* (1988), is too vague when she says, without referring to any texts or secondary literature, that "here [*1 Clem.* 2.8] κοσμέω could also carry the connotation of the 'ordered' life in contrast to the present state of disorder in Corinth" (86 n. 41).

[720]Dion. Hal. *Ant. Rom.* 7.33.1f.

[721]Dion. Hal. *Ant. Rom.* 11.8.3.

[722]κοσμέω is formed from κόσμος, C. Spicq, "κοσμέω, κόσμιος", *Theological Lexicon of the New Testament* 2, 330.

These statements of Aristides where harmony and good order are described as the "true" and "proper" adornment of cities appear to be illuminating both with regard to Clement's choice of terms and the basic meaning of the expression "you were adorned by your virtuous and honourable citizenship" (2:8). Firstly, Aristides shows that it was appropriate to use κοσμέω or κόσμος in order to depict the ideal political condition within a city. Secondly, the passages of Aristides explicitly link the true and proper adornment of cities with a state of concord and good order. Thus it is most likely that when Clement says that the Christians at Corinth were adorned by their virtuous and honourable citizenship he is alluding to the previous state of concord and good order of the Church. This means that our observations concerning the use of κοσμέω in a political context, in particular its link with the idea that concord expresses the ideal condition of a city seem to confirm or at least make likely our understanding of the expression παναρέτῳ καὶ σεβασμίῳ πολιτείᾳ. Such a citizenship implies that one has the common good of the city in view, and that a vital feature of the well-being of a city is that concord and order should prevail. Or, in the words of Aristides, the true adornment of cities, harmony and order (ἁρμονία καὶ τάξις) "preserves (σῴζω) both individual man and city".

In the final part of his applause of the previous life of the Corinthian Church Clement states that they did all in the fear of God, and notes again that they behaved in a manner consistent with the commandments and ordinances of the Lord. We have seen above that according to him the noble past of the Corinthian Church is rooted in obedience to God's law. We have seen in addition – and that is more important in this connection – that in antiquity adherence to the law of society was perceived to be both a precondition to and a means of creating concord. So when Clement ends his praise of the life of the Corinthian Christians in the past by focusing on their obedience to the law of God, i.e. by saying that "the commandments and ordinances of the Lord were 'written on the tables of your heart'" (2:8), he reflects the *topos* that citizens of a *polis* must follow the law in order to secure concord.[723]

3.5.2.15. δόξα

After Clement has drawn a picture of the Corinthian Church as a community characterised by a life lived according to the commandments of God and manifested in communal solidarity and in concord, he goes on from 3:1 to describe the present state of

---

[723]The expression "written on the tablets of your heart" is probably a quotation or an allusion to Prov 7:3 and 22:20 where the need to follow the commandments of the Lord is emphasized. Clement probably uses this biblical expression in order to give authority to what he writes and to remind the Christians of the need to follow the Word of God. However, there is little in the actual contexts of these verses in Proverbs which seems to be analogous with the present situation in the Corinthian Church. This fact indicates that we should not go primarily to the Old Testament background in attempting to discover why Clement focuses here on the Corinthian Christians' adherence to the commandments of the Lord in the past. It is more fruitful to explain Clement's appeal for adherence to law in the light of his broader cultural milieu where, as we have seen, adherence to law was viewed as a precondition for concord. See our discussion in chap. 3.5.2.7.

affairs. In 3:1 he does not, however, state what actually took place. Instead he applies a passage from Deut 32:15a to the situation in the Corinthian Church "'My Beloved ate and drank, and he was enlarged and waxed fat and kicked'" (3:1). From this (ἐκ τούτου) "arose jealousy and envy, strife and sedition, persecution and disorder, war and captivity" (3:2).[724] The context of the passage quoted from Deuteronomy is Moses' closing discourse, i.e. Deut 27-32. At the end of this discourse Moses says that on basis of his experience with the Israelites' disobedience he knows that after his death they also will turn aside from the way of God (Deut 31:24-29). The passage Clement quotes goes on to say how "he [Jacob = Israel] forsook the God that made him, and departed from God the Saviour" (32:15b). In other words, the context of his quotation from Deut 32 seems to imply that just as the behaviour of the people of God in the Old Testament was apostasy from God, so the present behaviour of the Corinthian Church is apostasy – they have "departed from God the Saviour".[725] In spite of the fact that the use of the passage from Deut 32:15 made it obvious to readers (if they were familiar with the context in Deuteronomy) that Clement regarded the consequence of the actions of the Corinthian Church to be analogous to that of the Israelites in that both implied apostasy from God, we cannot see that this statement offers any information concerning what actually happened.

However, it seems that Clement sees a connection between the "glory and enlargement" (δόξα καὶ πλατυσμός)[726] of the Corinthian Church and their 'fall' expressed by the words of Deut 32:15. Thus, in view of the task of this chapter it is interesting to note that striving for glory and the wish to be great, often two sides of the same coin, caused strife and sedition in antiquity. To a great extent this is connected with the fact that the Mediterranean world was an 'honour-shame' culture. In such a culture honour was a pivotal value and much behaviour was directed toward increasing one's honour. Here we shall refrain from presenting evidence for the role of honour in the Mediterranean world in general and its connection with strife in a political body in particular, since we shall return to this subject in chapter 5, *The Social-Historical Situation*.[727] However, we will already indicate at this point that on the basis of the important role of honour in Clement's cultural milieu and in particular the connection between striving for honour and sedition it seems to be reasonable to assert that he thought striving for honour was involved in the trouble facing the Corinthian Church.

Clement's depiction in 3:3 of what took place points in the same direction. Here he lists four opposing groups of people who rose up against each other: οἱ ἄτιμοι ἐπὶ τοὺς ἐντίμους, οἱ ἄδοξοι ἐπὶ τοὺς ἐνδόξους, οἱ ἄφρονες ἐπὶ τοὺς φρονίμους, οἱ νέοι ἐπὶ τοὺς πρεσβυτέρους. We will deal at some length with the importance of

---

[724] For the association of these terms with concord, see chap. 3.5.1.

[725] Cf. the discussion in A. DAVIDS, "Irrtum und Häresie", *Kairos* 15 (1973) 168.

[726] For the meaning of πλατυσμός see W. BAUER, *A Greek-English Lexicon* (1979) 667; H. G. LIDDELL and R. SCOTT, *A Greek-English Lexicon* (1973) 1414. Here it refers to the "enlargement" of the Church, i.e. that the Corinthian Church has grown.

[727] See chaps. 5.4.1.2 and 5.4.1.3.

this statement and what it indicates with regard to the social-historical situation at some length in a later chapter of this work.[728] Here we confine ourselves to arguing that all the terms Clement uses to describe the different groups of people, except the fourth, were commonly used as socio-economic terms expressing status and honour. This fact indicates that according to him an essential aspect of the conflict was related to the issue of status and honour. Thus he depicts the strife at the Corinthian Church mainly as between different socio-economic classes.

3.5.2.16. δικαιοσύνη καὶ εἰρήνη

Clement describes one of the consequences of the upheaval to be that "δικαιοσύνη καὶ εἰρήνη (righteousness and peace) are far removed" (3:4). We have already dealt with the term εἰρήνη and attempted to demonstrate its political background where it was often applied in connection with discussions of unity and sedition in a political body. Here we shall focus upon the other term, δικαιοσύνη. It is a frequent term in *1 Clement* and occurs throughout the letter in different contexts.[729] As important as it is in Early Christian literature, it is beyond the scope of this chapter to discuss in detail the meaning and application of this term in *1 Clement*. Nonetheless, we mention that we agree with the opinion that Clement reflects a Jewish use of the term δικαιοσύνη in as much as this term in Clement depicts the right Christian way of living – to live according to the will of God. Just as δίκαιος usually refers the to pious man in the LXX, Clement uses this designation to describe the true Christian.[730]

However, the virtue of δικαιοσύνη was also a political virtue of great significance for life in the *polis*. Before we give some examples of this, we will simply note that Clement links the two terms δικαιοσύνη and εἰρήνη with the conjunction καί. This simple fact in itself suggests that the term δικαιοσύνη (like εἰρήνη) carries political connotations. Additionally, it indicates that δικαιοσύνη belongs to the semantic field of ὁμόνοια.

As in the LXX, the concept of δικαιοσύνη in the Graeco-Roman world was related to the observance of law. In as much as the law in the Classical and Hellenistic world was perceived to have a religious, political, and ethical magnitude it is not sur-

---

[728]See chap. 5.3, in particular 5.3.2.

[729]Paul taught δικαιοσύνη (5:7); Abraham was blessed because he wrought δικαιοσύνη and truth through faith (31:2); with God as an example the author exhorts the Corinthians to work ἔργον δικαιοσύνης (33:8); splendour in righteousness is one of God's gifts (35:2); those who walk through the gates of Jesus, in which is righteousness, in holiness and righteousness accomplishing all things without disorder are blessed (48:4); the Corinthians must please God with holiness in righteousness (62:2); LXX-citations (here we include all the categories which D. A. Hagner, *The Use of the Old and New Testaments in Clement of Rome* (1973) terms as citations, cf. Appendix I, 351f.) 10:6; 13:1; 18:15; 42:5; 48:2.

[730]O. Andrén, *Rättfärdighet och Frid* (1960) 54-97. For an overview of the Old Testament and LXX use, see, e.g., G. Schrenk, "δίκη, δίκαιος κτλ.", *TDNT* 2, 174-225. Regarding the LXX Schrenk says that "the δίκαιος is the man who fulfils his duties towards God and the theocratic society, meeting God's claim in this relationship" (185), and "δικαιοσύνη is the observance of the will of God which is well-pleasing to Him" (196).

prising that the virtue of δικαιοσύνη was of greatest significance.[731] Basically we may say that δικαιοσύνη was used in both a narrow and a broad sense. The narrow sense is strictly juristic with δικαιοσύνη depicting the observance of the law of the state. When a man lives in conformity with the law of a city he shows the virtue of δικαιοσύνη. Aristotle could define δικαιοσύνη as "a virtue which assigns to each man his due in conformity with the law" and conversely injustice is defined as claiming "what belongs to others, in opposition to the law". [732] At the time when the Greeks developed written law as the criterion for right and wrong the virtue of δικαιοσύνη replaced that of courage as the fundamental virtue under which all other virtues were subsumed.[733] As for the broad sense of δικαιοσύνη, Aristotle, e.g., cites a proverb of Theognis which says that, "In Justice (δικαιοσύνη) is all Virtue (ἀρετή) found in sum".[734] Further on he says that justice "is not a part of Virtue, but the whole of Virtue".[735] Both the broad meaning of this virtue and its importance for community life becomes clear when Aristotle defines δίκαιος as something which "produces and preserves the happiness (εὐδαιμονία), or the component parts of the happiness, of the political community".[736] This means that δικαιοσύνη includes all political and mortal virtues which serve to establish and maintain the well-being of the city. Of the virtues that were linked with or were an integrated part of δικαιοσύνη, these, i.e. ὁσιότης, εὐσέβεια, and σωφροσύνη were among the most important.[737]

Against the background of this fundamental role of δικαιοσύνη in the *polis* it is a fair supposition that to some extent it influenced Clement's use of it in his 'polis-ecclesiology'. It is, at least, not difficult to point out similarities. The reason why δικαιοσύνη is not found in the Corinthian Church during the period under discussion is the strife and sedition that still existed. A characteristic of this situation is, among other things, that members of the Church do not live in conformity with the law of God. Just as citizens of a Greek *polis* lack the virtue of δικαιοσύνη when they do not observe the law of the city, the citizens of the *polis* of God lack this virtue when they do not observe the law of God. Just as the happiness of a Greek city depended on the virtue of δικαιοσύνη,

---

[731] G. Schrenk, "δίκη, δίκαιος κτλ.", *TDNT* 2, 178.

[732] Arist. *Rh.* 1.9.7. Cf. also G. Schrenk, "δίκη, δίκαιος κτλ.", *TDNT* 2, 192f; W. Jaeger, *Paideia* vol. I (1945) 107.

[733] W. Jaeger, *Paideia* vol. I (1945) 105: "The new dikaosyne was a more objective quality; but it became arete *par excellence* as soon as the Greeks believed that they had found, in written law, a reliable criterion for right and wrong. After *nomos* – that is, current legal usage – was codified, the general idea of righteousness acquired a palpable content. It consisted in obedience to the laws of the state, just as Christian 'virtue' consisted in obedience to the commands of God".

[734] Arist. *Eth. Nic.* 5.1.15. W. Jaeger, *Paideia* vol. I (1945) 106, depicts these words of Theognis as "one of the most famous poetic utterances of the sixth century ... often quoted by later philosophers".

[735] Arist. *Eth. Nic.* 5.1.19.

[736] Arist. *Eth. Nic.* 5.1.13.

[737] See, e.g., Pl. *Euthphr.* 12 C-E; *Prt.* 330b; *Grg.* 507b, d; 508a-b; *Resp.* I.331a; Epict. *Diss.* 3.26.32; Polyb. *Hist.* 22.10.8f; Xen. *Mem.* 4.8.11.

the well-being of the Church likewise depended on this virtue.[738] Additionally, it is interesting to note that other important virtues connected with δικαιοσύνη in antiquity are found in *1 Clement* as well, i.e. ὁσιότης,[739] εὐσέβεια (1:2), σωφροσύνη (62:2; 64:1).

However, for the purposes of the present investigation the most important aspect of the political virtue of δικαιοσύνη in antiquity was its connection to ὁμόνοια. That these virtues were related to each other is not surprising when we bear in mind that in antiquity to live according to the established law of a society was perceived to be a precondition for the creation and maintenance of concord.[740] Of the passages in which we have been able to identify a connection between δικαιοσύνη and concord, a passage of Plato is among the most explicit. In a dialogue with Socrates after Thrasymachus agreed with Socrates that no city, army, bandits, thieves or any other group could accomplish anything if they wronged one another (ἀδικοῖεν ἀλλήλους), Socrates says:

> For factions (στάσις) Thrasymachus, are the outcome of injustice (ἀδικία), and hatreds and internecine conflicts, but justice brings oneness of mind and love (ἡ δὲ δικαιοσύνη ὁμόνοιαν καὶ φιλίαν, Pl. Resp. 1.351 D).

Similarly, in *Cleitophon* Socrates asserts that the peculiar effect of justice (δικαιοσύνης ἔργον) was to produce friendship in States. Socrates goes on to define, among other things, by defining real and true friendship as concord (ὁμόνοια). In other words, this means that ὁμόνοια is the effect of δικαιοσύνη (Pl. *Cleitophon* 409 D-E).

Similar, clear connections between δικαιοσύνη and ὁμόνοια are also found in Dionysius Halicarnassensis. When he records the effects of Numa's regulations concerning religious worship (2.74.1), he says, among other things, that they created "a passion for justice (δικαιοσύνης) which preserves the harmony of the State" (ἐν ὁμονοίᾳ τὴν πόλιν). This passage reflects the view that the virtue of δικαιοσύνη is fundamental in order to maintain concord in a city. The same author offers one more illustrative example when he deals with the political discourse of Decius' addresse to

---

[738]It has been noted by, e.g., O. ANDRÉN, *Rättfärdighet och Frid* (1960) 54 and D. A. HAGNER, *The Use of the Old and New Testaments in Clement of Rome* (1973) 352, that *1 Clem.* 3:4 is probably an allusion to Isa 59:14, ἡ δικαιοσύνη μακρὰν ἀφέστηκεν. In this passage the prophet lists the things that are no longer to be found in Israel: κρίσις, σωτηρία, δικαιοσύνη, ἀλήθεια. Andrén suggests that Clement's addition of εἰρήνη is influenced by the LXX where the expression δικαιοσύνη καὶ εἰρήνη describes a state of health among the people of God (54). Similarly H. E. LONA, *Der erste Clemensbrief* (1998) 143. Andrén and Lona may be correct in saying that Clement found this expression appropriate because of its occurrence and use in the LXX, but we shall argue that paying attention to the political background of these terms enhances our understanding of their meaning in *1 Clement* and of why Clement used them.

[739]ὁσιότης is linked with δικαιοσύνη in *1 Clem.* 48:4, and the noun ὅσιος is linked with δίκαιος in 14:1.

[740]See the present investigation pp., 117-119.

the senate. In this discourse Decius says that, if one expels justice (δίκη) and law (νόμος) from a state, it will lead to sedition (στάσις) and war (πόλεμος).[741]

The evidence from these passages indicates not only that δικαιοσύνη was a fundamental virtue of the *polis* in general, but that in particular it was significant, or even a precondition, for the concord of a *polis*. Thus, in our view it is adequate to call the connection of δικαιοσύνη – ὁμόνοια a *topos*. We hold, therefore, that Clement's use of the term δικαιοσύνη in 3:4 must be considered with this *topos* in view. In other words, when Clement blames the Corinthians because δικαιοσύνη is far removed, he not only uses the term δικαιοσύνη because it was a fundamental virtue of a *polis* with the well-being of the *polis* in general depending on it, but also because this virtue was necessary to preserve concord. When the Church at Corinth lacks δικαιοσύνη, this implies that the communion lacks concord as well. Finally, the connection between δικαιοσύνη and concord may also explain why Clement links this term with εἰρήνη; both are in fact related to the political question of concord.

The passage which follows shows that Clement sees that the absence of "peace and justice" is associated with loss of fear of God and with disobedience to God's commandment (3:4). As noted above, it is natural that as a Christian leader he is of the opinion that divisions among the Corinthians have their genesis in such behaviour. It is more important in this connection to note, however, that when he again focuses upon obedience to the law of God he uses a *topos* related to concord.[742]

Clement proceeds by blaming the Corinthian Christians for not using their citizenship in a manner worthy of Christ (3:4). Previously we have seen that a proper use of citizenship implies that the individual citizen has the common good in view and contributes to the harmony of his city.[743] Instead, however, each Corinthian "goes according to the lusts of his wicked heart" (3:4). This means that instead of living according to the will of God and worthily of Christ, the members of the Corinthian Church follow their own will and thus do not have the common good in view. They have replaced concern for the community as a whole with their own individual goals and wishes. Such egoistic behaviour is one of the characteristics of people involved in sedition.[744]

At the end of his condemnation of the present situation, Clement characterises the present behaviour of the Christians in Corinth by saying that they have assumed the attitude of unrighteous and ungodly ζῆλος. ζῆλος not only underlies the present state of affairs in the Corinthian Church, but is also regarded as an ultimate cause of death coming into the world (3:4).[745] This second occurrence of the term ζῆλος in *1 Clement* serves to point back to 3:2 and also forward to introduce the bulk of examples that

---

[741]Dion. Hal. *Ant. Rom.* 7.42.2. For other references, although not so illustrative as those mentioned above, see Din. *Against Philocles* 19; Dion. Hal. *Ant. Rom.* 2.75.4; Dio Chrys. *Or.* 34.45; *Or.* 77/78.39.

[742]See the present investigation pp., 117-119.

[743]See chap. 3.5.2.14.

[744]See chap. 2.3.3.

[745]An allusion to Wis 2:24.

function to demonstrate the evil consequences of ζῆλος (4:1ff.).[746] These examples constitute the beginning of the *probatio*,[747] i.e. main body of the letter. But before we enter into this section and progress through the whole letter it is appropriate to summarize the political terms and *topoi* in *1 Clem*. 1-3.

3.5.2.17. Summary of Other Political Terms and topoi in 1 Clement 1-3

We have seen above that in the first three chapters of the letter, i.e. in the *exordium* and the *narratio*, Clement applies many political terms and *topoi* that in antiquity belonged to the semantic field of ὁμόνοια. Besides the terms στάσις, ἔρις, ζῆλος, φθόνος, διωγμός, ἀκαταστασία, πόλεμος, and αἰχμαλωσία in 3:2, we have attempted to demonstrate that this is the case for the following terms or their derivatives: συμφορά, ἀπόνοια, πίστις, σωφροσύνη, ἀσφαλῆς, ὑποτάσσω, ταπεινοφρονέω, ἀλαζονεία, εἰρήνη βαθεῖα, ἀδελφότης, σχίσμα, κοσμέω, δόξα, δικαιοσύνη. We have also seen that *1 Clement* reflects the view that proper relations, as regulated by conventional rules, between different groups of the household promote concord. Furthermore, we have attempted to show that Clement uses the following *topoi*: (1) strife and sedition is a contradiction of the status of being beloved by God; and (2) to follow the established law of a society is a precondition for concord. The fact that so many terms and *topoi* associated with concord are found in the *exordium* and in the *narratio* is an important observation regarding the main topic of the letter. In these parts of a discourse an author typically indicates the fundamental theme and the main issue or subject he is going to deal with.[748]

3.6. Political Terms and topoi Related to Concord in 1 Clement 4:1-61:3 (probatio)

We have devoted a considerable amount of space to discussing political terms and *topoi* associated with the topic of concord in *1 Clem*. 1-3. Our discussion of these three chapters is in fact much longer than the following discussion on political terms and *topoi* in the rest of the letter. At first sight, this would seem to indicate an imbalance in our investigation, when we devote more space to these three chapters than to the other sixty-two. The explanation for this imbalance, if there is such, is actually quite simple. In the first three chapters Clement introduces the majority of such terms and *topoi* – in many cases in order to return to them later in the letter. Since we have chosen, with only a few exceptions, to discuss actual terms and *topoi* the first time they occur, our discussion of *1 Clem*. 1-3 would inevitably take up the most space. Furthermore, much of the content of chapters 3-64 consists of LXX quotations which are accurate in varying degrees.[749] These passages do not contain so many political terms and *topoi* as when Clement applies the LXX quotations to the Christians and uses his own wording in his

---

[746]For ζῆλος as a political term belonging to the semantic field of concord, see our discussion in 3.5.1.2.

[747]For delimitation of the letter, see chap. 4.

[748]See chap. 4.2.2 pp. 218-226.

[749]For a table of LXX quotations, see G. Schneider, *Clemens von Rom* (1994) 21.

argumentation. This fact also leads to the "imbalance" referred to above. These proce-
dures and circumstances, however, do not mean that political terms and *topoi* are not
found throughout the letter. On the contrary, as we go through the whole letter, in what
follows we intend to demonstrate that political language associated with concord
occurs throughout it.

3.6.1. Political Terms and topoi Related to Concord in 1 Clement 4:1-39:9 (θέσις /quaes-tio infinita)

3.6.1.1. Political Terms and topoi in 1 Clement 4:1-18:17

In 3:4 Clement holds that there is a connection between the present situation in the
Corinthian Church and the fact that its members are marked by ζῆλος. The consequence of ζῆλος is grave in as much as it caused death to enter into the world. As mentioned above, the return to the topic of ζῆλος in 3:2 functions as an introduction to a
series of historical examples taken from the Old Testament and the Christian tradition.
These examples were aimed at demonstrating the evil consequences of ζῆλος. ζῆλος
and φθόνος had caused fratricide.[750] ζῆλος had caused Jacob to run away from Esau,
Joseph to be persecuted nearly to death, Moses to be forced to flee from Pharaoh, and
Aaron and Miriam to be lodged outside the camp. It had brought Dathan and Abiram
down alive into Hades because of their rebellion against Moses. Also, because of ζῆλος
David had been persecuted by Saul.[751] Then Clement moves on to examples from the
Corinthians "own generation". "Through ζῆλος and φθόνος the greatest and most
righteous pillars of the Church were persecuted and contended unto death" (5:2). Here
he is specifically thinking of Peter and Paul (5:3-7). In addition, Clement reminds them
of the "great multitude" of Christian martyrs who were the victims of ζῆλος. It had also
caused women to be persecuted as Danaids and Dirces, and it had estranged wives
from their husbands. ζῆλος had not only caused death and destruction for individuals
and the people of God, but ζῆλος together with ἔρις had overthrown great cities and
uprooted great nations as well (6:4). In chapters 4-6 the term ζῆλος occurs as frequently as fourteen times, linked twice with φθόνος and twice with ἔρις. This means
that these chapters also contain many political terms related to the topic of concord.[752]

Now that Clement has presented the dangerous and destructive results of ζῆλος (as
well as φθόνος and ἔρις) he focuses in chapters 7-9 upon the possibility of repentance.
In the many exhortations in chapters 7-9 the author uses the first person plural subjunctive and thus includes the Roman Church as well as an addressee of the exhortations. According to Clement this is appropriate because the Roman Christians were
facing similar problems. He says that they fight "in the same arena and the same strug-

---

[750]The Cain and Abel story, *1 Clem.* 4:1-7.

[751]*1 Clem.* 8-13. In the Old Testament these stories are mentioned in Gen 27:41ff.; 37, Exod 2:14;
Num 12; 16; 1 Sam 18ff.

[752]For φθόνος and ἔρις as political terms belonging to the semantic field of concord, see the
present work, chaps. 3.5.1.2 and 3.5.1.1.2 respectively.

gle is before" them (7:1).[753] He exhorts the Corinthians to cease from "empty (κενός) and vain (μάταιος)" thoughts and to follow "the glorious and venerable rule" of the Christian tradition instead,[754] and to do "what is good and pleasing and acceptable in the sight of our Maker" (7:2-3). In other words, in a manner consistent with his description in *1 Clem.* 1-3 of the present state of affairs, Clement admonishes the Corinthians to behave according to the will of God. As we have pointed out, this is a means of securing concord among the Christians.[755]

After admonishing the readers to concentrate on the work of Christ who "brought the grace of repentance (μετάνοια) to all the world" (7:4), Clement goes on to present examples from the biblical tradition and passages from the Bible which serve to demonstrate that repentance has been possible in all generations (7:5-8:4).[756] In 8:5 he concludes that God desires all his beloved to participate in repentance. On the basis of the conclusion in 8:5 he goes further with a threefold admonition to obey the will of God:

let us obey (ὑπακούω) his excellent and glorious will;
let us fall before him as suppliants of his mercy and goodness;
let us turn to his pity, and abandon the vain toil and strife (ἔρις) and jealousy (ζῆλος) which leads to death (9:1).

We note that the nearest Clement comes to an explicit statement of what it means concretely to obey the will of God is when he says that it means to cease from strife (ἔρις) and jealousy (ζῆλος). As we have seen previously in this work, ζῆλος and the strife and sedition it causes is the seminal problem of the Corinthian Church. In line with this, it is natural that Clement focuses on precisely this feature in his admonition to obey the will of God.

In order to show the blessing, or advantage, of obeying the will of God, or in the negative, the danger of not doing so, Clement presents a series of examples in 9:2-10:7 taken from the Old Testament. First Enoch was "found righteous in obedience ... and

[753]We have argued previously that this statement alludes to strife and discord within the Roman Church (see pp. 104f.) In addition to the fact that it is likely that the actual situation in the Roman Church promoted Clement to use the first person plural subjunctive, he might also have chosen this inclusive language because he did not want to give the impression that the Roman Church pretends to lord it over the Corinthian Church. Further, both the remarks that the Romans and the Corinthians struggle in the same arena and the inclusive language are a means of creating solidarity and identification between the sender and the receiver of the letter. In other words, this is a way to create a positive *ethos* for the author and functions thus as a rhetorical strategy in the overall purpose of the letter. For argumentation through *ethos* and the strength of ethical appeal, see Arist. *Rh.* 1.2.3-4. And regarding identification of the author with the audience as a powerful means of creating positive *ethos*, see J. W. MARSHALL, "Paul's Ethical Appeal in Philippians", *Rhetoric and the New Testament* (1993) 358-360.

[754]When Clement describes their thoughts in such a way it implies that their present thoughts are of no benefit to them. Appeal to advantage is a hallmark of deliberative rhetoric (see chap. 2.3.1.).

[755]See chap. 3.5.2.7, and further p. 163.

[756]Clement pays attention to people's attitude to the message of Noah and Jonah. See D. A. HAGNER, *The Use of the Old and New Testaments in Clement of Rome* (1973) 69-72, for a discussion on what sources Clement uses in 8:3.

death did not befall him". Then, when Clement turns to Noah he does not use the term ὑπακοή but πιστός: "Noah was found faithful (πιστός) in his service". To be πιστός, however, in the service of God is nearly the same as it is to be obedient to the will of God.[757] Clement goes on to say that through Noah's faithful service God saved those who entered in concord into the Ark. In addition to the advantage connected with Noah's faithful service for mankind, we note that he emphasizes that the living creatures that entered the Ark ἐν ὁμονοίᾳ were saved. This would suggest that their safety was connected with their concord. Although he does not apply the term 'concord' explicitly to the Corinthian Church when it first occurs in the letter, the concord of the living creatures functions implicitly as an example to imitate.[758] However, the main point for Clement in 9:4 is to present Noah as an example of faithfulness.

Clement continues by discussing the greatest example of obedience and faithfulness in the Old Testament, namely Abraham (*1 Clem.* 10). He introduces Abraham by saying that he "was found faithful in his obedience to the words of God". In obedience he left his country and his fathers' house after God had told him to do so (10:1f.).[759] He also says that because of Abraham's "faith and hospitality" God gave him a son whom Abraham offered as a sacrifice as an expression of his obedience (δι᾽ ὑπακοῆς) to God (10:7).

In the following examples Clement emphasizes other characteristics besides explicit obedience to God, i.e. hospitality, piety and faith. He presents the example of Lot who because of his "hospitality (φιλοξενία) and piety (εὐσέβεια) was saved out of Sodom" (*1 Clem.* 11:1).[760] This demonstrates, according to Clement, that God does not forsake those who trust in him. On the other hand, Lot's wife who became a pillar of salt serves as a warning to those who are double-minded and have doubts concerning the power of God (11:2). Furthermore, because of her "faith and hospitality" (διὰ πίστιν καὶ φιλοξενίαν) Rahab, the harlot, was saved when the Israelites entered into Jerico (*1 Clem.* 12).[761] As we have just noted, although Clement's main focus is not upon the obedience manifested in these examples, this aspect is at least intimated. In the examples, hospitality, piety, and faith all imply an attitude of respect and obedience to the will of God as it is expressed through his messengers or his servants. Also, as previously observed, to live in obedience to God's will secures concord in a Christian Community.[762]

In 13:1-19:1 Clement again turns to the topic of humility. Previously in this study we have seen that this is an important topic in the letter, and that Clement sees the vir-

---

[757]Elsewhere in the present work we have argued that πιστός is linked to obedience to the will of God, cf. chap. 3.5.2.4.

[758]For concord as a political term, see chaps. 3.3.1 and 3.4.

[759]In 10:3-6 Clement quotes Gen 12:1-3; 13:14-16; 15:5f. Cf. D. A. HAGNER, *The Use of the Old and New Testaments in Clement of Rome* (1973) 351.

[760]Cf. Gen 19:1-29. For Lot's hospitality, see vv. 1-3.

[761]Regarding the hospitality of Rahab toward the Israelites, see Josh 2.

[762]Cf. e.g. chap. 3.5.2.7.

tue of humility as a means of achieving concord among Christians.[763] The manner in which Clement introduces this topic in 13:1, i.e. the first person plural subjunctive with οὖν, shows that he intends to make a connection between the exhortation to humility and what precedes it. In Clement's view, humility is an adequate response to the biblical examples of obedience and faith. Obedience to God leads to humility.

When Clement exhorts the Christians in 13:1 to be humble-minded, he also says that this means "putting aside all arrogance (ἀλαζονεία) and conceit and foolishness and wrath". Also, he quotes Jer 9:23-24 which exhorts man not to boast of himself. It is probably not an accident that Clement connects precisely these things with humility, since to be arrogant and to boast was commonly connected with divisiveness in antiquity.[764] After he has presented various *logia* from the Sermon on the Mount,[765] he continues by exhorting the Corinthians to walk in obedience to Jesus' holy words and to be humble-minded (*1 Clem.* 13:3). This shows how closely Clement linked obedience with humility.

Clement has used a great deal of space demonstrating the need for an attitude of obedience and humility. Now in 14:1 he indicates what this entails in practical terms. He applies the principle of obedience and humility to the strife and sedition disturbing the Corinthian Church. To obey God means that they turn from "those who in pride (ἐν ἀλαζονείᾳ) and unruliness (ἀκαταστασία) are the instigators of an abominable jealousy" (ζῆλος, 14:1).[766] In other words, to obey God implies that one should avoid people who cause sedition so as to prevent oneself from becoming involved. Expressed positively, obedience to God must be manifested in behaviour that promotes concord. Clement argues that this is both "right (δίκαιος) and holy" (ὅσιος, 14:1). Previously in this investigation we have seen that appeals to the "right" and the "holy" were common in deliberative rhetoric.[767] However, Clement does not restrict himself to arguing that avoidance of the instigators is a consequence of humility and obedience to God, or to appealing to what is right and holy. He makes use of a convention of deliberative rhetoric in his appeal regarding the great danger connected with the present state of affairs:[768] "For we shall incur no common harm (βλάβη), but great danger (κίνδυνος μέγας), if we rashly yield ourselves to the purposes of men who rush into strife (ἔρις) and sedition" (στάσις, 14:2).[769] Besides the fact that warning of danger was fundamental in deliberative rhetoric in general, we have also seen that strife and sedition in

---

[763]See our discussion 3.5.2.10 pp. 126-131.

[764]See our discussion 3.5.2.10 pp. 131-136.

[765]Matt 5:7; 6:14f; 7:1f; 7:12; Mark 4:24b; 11:25b. Cf. the discussion in D. A. HAGNER, *The Use of The Old and New Testaments in Clement of Rome* (1973) 135-151.

[766]Regarding the connection of pride (ἀλαζονεία) and unruliness (ἀκαταστασία) with strife in a political body, see chaps. 3.5.2.10 and 3.5.1.3 respectively.

[767]See chaps. 2.3.1 and 2.3.2.

[768]See chaps. 2.3.1 and 2.3.2.

[769]Concerning ἔρις and στάσις as political terms belonging to the semantic field of ὁμόνοια, see chaps. 3.5.1.1.2 and 3.5.1.1.1 respectively.

particular were often connected with danger to those involved.[770] Furthermore, it is interesting to note that there is a higher frequency of political language in the argumentation that Clement expresses in his own words than in the 'biblical' language of the scriptural examples, quotations and allusions from which he draws conclusions and makes applications to the Christian community. This fact gives us an indication of Clement's perception of what had been occurring among the Corinthian Christians.

After Clement has referred to the great danger connected with the present strife and sedition, he exhorts the Christians to be kind to one another. In order to demonstrate the need for such an attitude he again quotes Scripture, introduced by the formula γέγραπται γάρ (14:4). The passages he quotes say, among other things, that "the kind shall inhabit the land" but those who transgress the law of God shall be destroyed, and that "there is a remnant for a peaceable man" (ἀνθρώπῳ εἰρηνικῷ, 14:4-5).[771] From the last quotation Clement goes on to infer that one must unite with those "whose peacefulness (εἰρηνεύω) is based on piety" and not with those who hypocritically wish for peace" (εἰρήνη, 15:1). The rest of this chapter consists of quotations from Scripture which deal with the nature of hypocricy.[772] The exhortation to follow those whose peacefulness is based on piety and not those who hypocritically wish for peace refers to strife and sedition among Christians. Previously in this investigation we have seen that εἰρήνη belonged to the semantic field of concord and was commonly used in deliberative rhetoric urging concord.[773] Clement's exhortation in 15:1 implies that the instigators of the sedition also said they wanted peace, but this was not based on piety. In his view the consequence of their action was strife and sedition – the opposite of what they said they would promote.

In 16:1 Clement again turns to the topic of ταπεινοφροσύνη. The use of γάρ to introduce this topic shows that he makes a connection between what he has just stated in chapter 15 and this topic. When we dealt with *1 Clem.* 1-3, we saw that in the noble past when a "profound peace" prevailed in the Church the Corinthian Christians practised the virtue of ταπεινοφροσύνη, and that Clement elsewhere links ταπεινοφροσύνη and concord.[774] This indicates that he makes a connection between living in peace based on piety and ταπεινοφροσύνη. However, when he says, "For Christ is of those who are humble-minded (ταπεινοφρονούντων), not of those who exalt themselves (ἐπαιρόμενος) over His flock", γάρ explicitly points back to the "poor" and the "needy" mentioned in 15:6, whom the Lord will place in safety.[775] Those who exalt

---

[770]See chap. 3.5.1.1.1.

[771]He quotes Prov 2:21f; Ps. 36:35-38. Cf. D. A. HAGNER, *The Use of the Old and New Testaments in Clement of Rome* (1973) 60, 351.

[772]He quotes Isa 29:13; Ps.11:4-6; 30:19; 61:5f; 77:36f, cf. D. A. HAGNER, *The Use of the Old and New Testaments in Clement of Rome* (1973) 351f.

[773]See chap. 3.4.

[774]See chap. 3.5.2.10, pp. 126-131.

[775]Cf. A. LINDEMANN, *Die Clemensbriefe* (1992) 60.

themselves are the instigators of strife and sedition.[776] From 16:2 on he develops and emphasizes the ταπεινοφροσύνη of Jesus. In spite of his power Jesus Christ came not in pride (ἀλαζονεία) or arrogance (ὑπερηφανία), but was humble-minded (16:2).[777] As proof of this he quotes the rather long passages from Isa 53:1-12 and from Ps 22:6-8 (*1 Clem.* 16:3-16). In 16:17 he explicitly states why he focuses upon the ταπεινοφροσύνη of Jesus, i.e. because Jesus is the great example (ὑπογραμμός) of this virtue for Christians to follow.

After Clement has presented the greatest example of ταπεινοφροσύνη, he moves on to mention examples from the Old Testament. Firstly, he exhorts his readers to be imitators (μιμητής) of the prophets Elijah, Elisha and Ezekiel, and then mentions Abraham, Job, Moses, and David (17:1-18:17). He does not state directly that all these men possess ταπεινοφροσύνη, but the quotations from the Scripture which make up most of these chapters are meant to demonstrate that the men used as examples did not exalt themselves but expressed an attitude of ταπεινοφροσύνη.[778] That this is Clement's intended purpose with these quotations is also evident from 19:1 where he says that the humility and subordination of so many great men through their obedience have improved generations both in the past and at the present time. He obviously intends to say that the ταπεινοφροσύνη of these men has functioned as an example to imitate and in that way contributed to make others better. However, the summary statement in 19:1 not only points back to 17:1-18:7, but also functions as a summarizing conclusion of a larger section, 13:1-18:7, in which ταπεινοφροσύνη has been the basic topic.[779] Additionally we note that 17:1 expresses a close connection between ταπεινοφροσύνη and obedience.

3.6.1.2. The Order of the Universe

In 19:2-21:8 Clement uses a common *topos* of deliberative rhetoric that urges concord. Here he exhorts the audience to contemplate the peace and benefits given by God the Creator. More precisely he notes that the good order of the universe is something which is consistent with the will of God. The different parts of the universe co-operate and accomplish their duties in peace and harmony, submitting to the command of God. In the following quotation of chapter 20 the words with significance for the concept of concord are given in bold, and the words reflecting the view that the order of peace and harmony is based on the will of God are underlined:

---

[776]See *1 Clem* 21:5; 39:1 where the verb ἐπαίρω expresses behaviour connected with strife and sedition.

[777]Regarding the connection between ἀλαζονεία and sedition, see our discussion, pp. 131-136. Also the vices of ὑπερηφανία are connected with divisiveness; see 30:1 and in particular 57:2.

[778]Clement quotes Gen 18:27; Job 1:1;14:4f; Num 12:7; Exod 3:11; 4:10; Pss 50:3-19; 88:21. Cf. D. A. HAGNER, *The Use of the Old and New Testaments in Clement of Rome* (1973) 351f.

[779]So also A. LINDEMANN, *Die Clemensbriefe* (1992) 67.

1. The heavens moving at his appointment are <u>subject to him</u> in **peace**; *2. day and night follow the course <u>allotted by him</u> without hindering each other. 3. Sun and moon and the companies of the stars roll on, <u>according to his direction</u>, in* **harmony**, *in their appointed courses, and swerve not from them at all. 4. The earth teems <u>according to his will</u> at its proper seasons, and puts forth food in all abundance for men and beasts and all the living things that are on it,* **with no dissension**, *and changing none of <u>his decrees</u>. 5. The unsearchable places of the abysses and the unfathomable realms of the lower world are controlled <u>by the same ordinances</u>. 6. The hollow of the boundless sea is gathered <u>by his working</u> into its allotted places, and does not pass the barriers placed around it, but does even as <u>he enjoined on it</u>; 7. <u>for he said</u> "Thus far shalt thou come, and thy waves shall be broken within thee." 8. The ocean, which men cannot pass, and the worlds beyond it, <u>are ruled by the same injunctions of the Master</u>. 9. The seasons of spring, summer, autumn, and winter give place to another in* **peace**. *10. The stations of the winds fulfil their service without hindrance at the proper time. The everlasting springs, created for enjoyment and health, supply sustenance for the life of man without fail; and the smallest of animals meet together in* **concord and peace**. *11. <u>All these things the great Creator and Master of the universe ordains</u> to be in* **peace and concord**, *and to all things does he do good, and more especially to us who have fled for refuge to his mercies through our Lord Jesus Christ, 12. to whom be the glory and the majesty for ever and ever, Amen.*

This is one of the passages of *1 Clement* that has received a great deal of attention from scholars, partly because of its suggested liturgical origin, but primarily because of its alleged Stoic influence.[780] The foremost advocates of Stoic influence, particularly R. Knopf, L. Sanders, and C. Eggenberger, have gathered a number of passages from ancient authors influenced by Stoicism which serve as comparative material.[781] The collected texts demonstrate that the perception of the cosmos as an ordered unit where the different parts co-operate and exist in concord was common in Stoicism. Hence, it is not difficult to point out similarities with *1 Clem.* 20, concerning both single words

---

[780]To mention some of the most importance contributions: P. DREWS, "Untersuchungen über die sogen. clementinische Liturgie im VIII Buch der apostolischen Konstitutionen", *Studien zur Geschichte des Gottesdienstes* (1906) 12-21; R. KNOPF, *Die zwei Clemensbriefe* (1920) 74-83; G. BARDY, "Expressions stoiciennes dans la Ia Clementis", *RSR* 12 (1922) 73-85; H. FUCHS, *Augustin und der antike Friedensgedanke* (1926) 98-101; L. SANDERS, *L'hellénisme de Saint Clément de Rome et le Paulinisme* (1943) 109-129; C. EGGENBERGER, *Die Quellen der politischen Ethik des 1. Klemensbriefes* (1951) 79-104; W. ELTESTER, "Schöpfungsoffenbarung und natürliche Theologie im frühen Christentum", *NTS* 3 (1956/57) 93-114; O. ANDRÉN, *Rättfärdighet och Frid* (1960) 130-137; W. JAEGER, *Early Christianity and Greek Paideia* (1961) 14f.; A. HALL, "I Clement as a Document of Transition", *CDios* 81 (1968) 682-692; W. C. VAN UNNIK, "Is I Clement 20 Purely Stoic?", *Sparsa Collecta* 3 (1983) 52-58 (First published in *VigChr* 4 [1950]) 181-189); J. W. WILSON, *The First Epistle of Clement* (1976) 69-75; A. LINDEMANN, *Die Clemensbriefe* (1992) 76f; H. E. LONA, *Der erste Clemensbrief* (1998) 249-274.

[781]These texts include passages from Cic.; Arist. [*Mund.*]; Dio Chrys.; Hermetica and Aët. K. THRAEDE, "Homonoia (Eintracht)", *RAC* 16 (1994), notes that "Die Deutung des Kosmos als harmonische Einheit … einerlei ob sie in der Idee vom Universum als Polis … oder als Haus … wurzelt … so oder so ist die kosmologische H.[omonoia] frühestens seit dem 3. Jh. vC. in antikes Bildungsgut eingegangen" (199).

and expressions as well as content.[782] In particular Clement's stress upon the concord and peace of the universe expressed by the words in bold in the quotation above seems to reflect Stoic thought.[783] However, more recently scholars have rightly paid attention to the fact that we find similar thought regarding the good order of the universe in the Palestinian Jewish tradition[784] and in Hellenistic Judaism.[785] Furthermore, the stress Clement lays upon the belief that the order of the cosmos in peace and harmony ultimately is a result of the will of the Old Testament God – expressed in the terms underlined in the quotation – indicates, according to the same scholars, that the Stoic language and the conceptions of the universe to a great extent are subordinated to Christian ideas. Therefore, it has been argued that Clement's main purpose with this passage is not to demonstrate the order of the universe in itself, but to demonstrate that nature is subject to the will of God from which peace and order proceed.[786] We should note, however, that as far as we know, no Jewish texts explicitly use the terms "peace and concord" to describe the relationship between the different features of the universe. This indicates that at least this important thought in *1 Clem.* 20 is derived from the Greek arena.

Rather then enter into this discussion in detail, it is more important for the purposes of the present investigation to focus upon the *function* of *1 Clem.* 20 within the Epistle. Those scholars who emphasize the Jewish and Old Testament background of

---

[782]For detailed comparison of *1 Clem.* 20 with ancient texts influenced by Stoicism, see R. KNOPF, *Die zwei Clemensbriefe* (1920) 74-83; L. SANDERS, *L'hellénisme de Saint Clément de Rome et le Paulinisme* (1943) 109-129; C. EGGENBERGER, *Die Quellen der politischen Ethik des 1. Klemensbriefes* (1951) 79-104, who in particular focuses upon Dio Chrysostom. Cf. now also R. M. GRANT, "The Structure of Eucharistic Prayers", *Antiquity and Humanity* (2001) 329-332.

[783]Cf., e.g., Cic. *Nat. D.* 2.38.98-47.120. Here, just like Clement Cicero exhorts his audience to contemplate the fact that the different parts of the universe reveal such an order and stability: "But not only are these things marvelous, but nothing is more remarkable than the stability and coherence of the world, which is such that it is impossible even to imagine anything better adapted to endure. For all its parts in every direction gravitate with a uniform pressure towards the centre. Moreover bodies conjoined maintain their union most permanently when they have some bond encompassing them to bind them together; and this function is fulfilled by that rational and intelligent substance which pervades the whole world as the efficient cause of all things and which draws and collects the outermost particles towards the centre" (2.45.115). He goes on to say that "this harmonious combination of nature" serves the well-being of the world (2.46.119). We note the striking parallel to *1 Clem.* 20:11 where God's arrangement of the universe in peace and harmony reveals the goodness of God toward all his creation. Regarding the significant conception of harmony of the cosmos, see e.g., Arist [*Mund.*] 5.

[784]W. C. VAN UNNIK, "Is I Clement 20 Purely Stoic?", *Sparsa Collecta* 3 (1983) 54-56 points to *1 Enoch* 2-5; *T. Naph.* 3; *As. Mos.* 12:9-10; *Pss. Sol.*18:12-14, 54-56, O. ANDRÉN, *Rättfärdighet och Frid* (1960) 134 refers to Ps 18; Jer 8:7.

[785]H. E. LONA, *Der erste Clemensbrief* (1998), concludes by stating that "es lässt sich nicht bestreiten, dass nicht die Stoa hier die Grundlage bildet, sondern die LXX und die Welt des hellenistischen Judentums" (272), and "Die aus 1 Clem 20 gewonnenen Ergebnisse weisen auf das hellenistische Judentum als die Grundlage für dieses Verständnis hin" (274).

the passage tend to argue that the main function is, as indicated above, to demonstrate that the whole universe and all things created within it submit to God's established order from which peace and harmony proceed. In other words, the function of the chapter is chiefly to show that God's sovereign rule is manifested through good order in the universe, that the peace and harmony of nature is the effect of nature's submission to the divine will.[787]

Although these scholars rightly stress the theocratic aspect of chapter 20, the continuation of the letter indicates that Clement's basic purpose with the chapter is to present the harmony and peace of nature as a model for the Church to imitate. Immediately after the description of the order and peace and harmony of the universe, Clement warns the Corinthians that the many good works (εὐεργεσία) of the Creator will become a judgment on them if they not do "good and virtuous deeds before him in concord" (μεθ᾽ ὁμονοίας, 21:1). The basic point here seems to be that the good works of God require an adequate response from man. More concretely Clement means that the good order in nature where peace and harmony exist must be reflected among the Christians at Corinth as well. Both the words εὐεργεσία and μεθ᾽ ὁμονοίας function as catchwords and link the warning to the preceding chapter (εὐεργεσία 20:11, ἐν ὁμονοίᾳ, 20:3, 10f.). To do these works implies not to "be deserters from his [God's] will" (θέλημα αὐτοῦ, 21:4).[788] It is hardly necessary to say that the expression the "will of God" points back to chapter 20, where, as we have already seen, the conception of God's will was fundamental with regard to the creation of peace and harmony of nature. Thus, it follows that in this connection submission to God's will means to live in peace and harmony just as the different elements of nature submitting to God's rule live

---

[786]Cf. W. C. VAN UNNIK, "Is I Clement 20 Purely Stoic?", *Sparsa Collecta* 3 (1983) 53f., concludes: "I do not want to question the value of these parallels offered by Knopf and Sanders from the Stoic tradition. The same root ταγ- which is so favorite to Clement is found there, and the ὁμόνοια is praised by Stoics and Christian alike. Yet I cannot help thinking that there is a marked difference: among the Stoics the order seems more or less established in itself and makes men think that there must be behind it an organizing power, and that it is from the order of nature that the divine power can be known; in 1 Clement the order is established by the command of the Creator and reveals the *will* of God, the keynote of the passage being not so much the order in nature as the command of God ... The Stoa starts from the phenomena and finds in them the (pantheistic) God; the Christian author knew, that God 'spoke, and it was done; He commanded, and it stood fast' (Ps. 33:9), for him the τάξις is not a good in itself, but the result of God's will. The point of view from the Stoics is anthropocentric, that of 1 Clement theocentric, his 'theos' being the God of the Old Testament". See further W. ELTESTER, "Schöpfungsoffenbarung und natürliche Theologie im frühen Christentum", *NTS* 3 (1956/57) 110; O. ANDRÉN, *Rättfärdighet och Frid* (1960) 130-137; A. HALL, "I Clement as a Document of Transition", *CDios* 81 (1968) 682-692; J. W. WILSON, *The First Epistle of Clement* (1976) 74; B. E. BOWE, *A Church in Crisis* (1988) 108f; H. E. LONA, *Der erste Clemensbrief* (1998) 265f.

[787] A. HALL, "I Clement as a Document of Transition", *CDios* 81 (1968) 690; J. W. WILSON, *The First Epistle of Clement* (1976) 74f.

[788]We note that Clement makes use of the appeal to τὸ δίκαιον in this connection which is a common appeal in deliberative rhetoric, see chaps. 2.3.1 and 2.3.2.

in peace and harmony. In the following verses (21:5-9) Clement to some extent gives practical applications of the principles outlined in vv. 1-4 and exhorts his audience to a particular course of action which serves to remove the present strife and establish concord instead. It is hardly an accident that he first gives an exhortation in the negative which is obviously directed against the instigators of στάσις, i.e. to "offend foolish and thoughtless men, who are exalted and boast in their pride of their words, rather than God" (21:5),[789] before he gives positive exhortations mainly dealing with the proper relations in the household which aim to strengthen order and concord among the Christians (21:6-8).[790]

Also the introduction to "the hymn of universe" suggests that the main function of *1 Clem.* 20 is to present the peace and harmony of the universe as an example to imitate. In 19:2b Clement exhorts the Corinthians to focus upon "the Father and Creator of the whole world" and to hold fast to his magnificent gifts of peace (αὐτοῦ δωρεαῖς τῆς εἰρήνης). The description of the order and peace and harmony of the universe that follows in chapter 20 is thus an explanation of what the author means by the Creator's magnificent δωρεά τῆς εἰρήνης, i.e. the peace given man in creation and which is manifested through the peace and harmony of the universe. In other words, when Clement exhorts the Corinthians to hold fast to the gifts and benefits of God, the order of the universe in peace and harmony serves as a model for the proper relationship between the Christians at Corinth. This is in our view the main function of chapter 20.[791]

The reason why it was necessary to discuss and determine the function of *1 Clem.* 20 is connected with the aim of this chapter in the present investigation, i.e. to recognise political terms and *topoi* connected with the question of domestic concord. For, as indicated above, Clement uses a common *topos* in deliberative rhetoric urging concord

---

[789]Some of the same adjectives and participles are also used in other places in the letter depicting seditious man: ἄφρων (3:3); ἐπαιρομένων (16:1); ἐγκαυχωμένοις ἐν ἀλαζονείᾳ (13:1). For boasting as a *topos* connected with στάσις, see our discussion, pp. 131-136.

[790]For the need for proper relationships between the different groups of the household in order to create and maintain concord, see chap. 3.5.2.9.

[791]This is also a common point of view among scholars who emphasize the Stoic influence on *1 Clem.* 20; e.g., R. KNOPF, *Die zwei Clemensbriefe* (1920) 74; L. SANDERS, *L'hellénisme de Saint Clément de Rome et le Paulinisme* (1943) 125: "Clement propose a l'imitation de ses lecteurs la concorde qu'il leur fait contempler dans l'univers"; R. M. GRANT, *The Apostolic Fathers vol 1: An Introduction* (1964) 36: "Peace and harmony are characteristics of God's universe (ch. 20), and he requires Christians to express the same virtues in their lives (ch. 21-23), and 104: "And in chapter 20 he takes as a model the peace and harmony of the universe"; O. B. KNOCH, *Eigenart und Bedeutung der Eschatologie im theologischen Aufriss des ersten Clemensbriefes* (1964) 66. Scholars do not need, however, to assume a Stoic influence to assert that the main purpose of *1 Clem.* 20 is to serve as a model for the Christian community. W. C. VAN UNNIK, "Is I Clement 20 Purely Stoic?", *Sparsa Collecta* 3 (1983), who argues for the Jewish theology of *1 Clem.* 20, seems to assert that "the law in nature as an example of man" is the main point of the chapter (56). See also H. E. LONA, *Der erste Clemensbrief* (1998) 275f. With respect to the argumentative function, which is our main concern in this connection, we should underline that it is of no importance whether *1 Clement* reflects mainly a Stoic or a Jewish impact. These two traditions are not mutually exclusive alternatives. The author may well make use of both to enhance his purpose.

by his appeal to the peace and harmony of nature as an example to imitate.[792] A passage from Dio Chrysostom *Or.* 40 is especially illuminating with a view to *1 Clem.* 20, both regarding the overall stress upon the harmony of universe, and regarding its key terms and function. Just like Clement, Dio exhorts the audience to contemplate the order and concord of the universe:

> *Do you not see in the heavens as a whole and in the divine and blessed beings that dwell therein an order and concord and self-control (τάξιν καὶ ὁμόνοιαν καὶ σωφροσύνην) which is eternal ... Furthermore, do you not see also the stable, righteous, everlasting concord (τὴν ἀσφαλῆ καὶ δικαίαν δι᾽ αἰῶνος ἁρμονίαν) of the elements ... you should observe that these things, being by nature indestructible and divine and regulated by the purpose and power of the first and greatest god, are wont to be preserved as a result of their mutual friendship (φιλία) and concord (ὁμόνοια) for ever, not only the more powerful and greater, but also those reputed to be the weaker. But were this partnership to be dissolved and to be followed by sedition (στάσις), their nature is not so indestructible or incorruptible ... For the predominance of the ether of which the wise men speak ... taking place as it does with limitation and gentleness within certain appointed cycles, occurs no doubt with entire friendship and concord (μετὰ πάσης φιλίας καὶ ὁμονοίας). On the other hand, the greed (πλεονεξία) and strife (διαφορά) of all else, manifesting itself in violation of law, contains the utmost risk of ruin, a ruin destined never to engulf the entire universe for the reason that complete peace (εἰρήνη) and righteousness (δικαιοσύνη) are present in it and all things everywhere serve and attend upon the law of reason, obeying and yielding to it (Or. 40.35-37).*

Dio goes on by giving examples of the harmony of the universe he has described: the sun gives place to the night and the moon and stars, and vice versa; the earth is content with its lowest place; and the water with being poured about it. What follows this shows that Dio's purpose in paying attention to the harmony of the universe is the same as Clement's, i.e. the universe serves as a model for the audience. Taking his departure in the fact that these entities in the universe submit to their partnership free from hostility, he asks if it is not possible that the towns of ordinary mortals, i.e. Prusa and Apameia, could maintain peace and be good neighbours of one another (*Or.* 40.38f.). In other words, when Dio urges his home city Prusa to cease their strife with the neighbouring city Apameia and to live in harmony instead, he uses the harmony of the universe as an

---

[792]Cf. M. M. MITCHELL, *Paul and the Rhetoric of Reconciliation* (1991) 132 n. 405: "One of the most common *topoi* in literature about concord is the appeal to the κοινωνία of the planets and stars in the orderly running of the cosmos", and K. THRAEDE, "Homonoia (Eintracht)", *RAC* 16 (1994) 2: "Bei all dem ist in Reden περὶ ὁμονοίας zweierlei wichtig; erstens dient hier die H.[omonoia] des Weltalls (ἁρμονία, σύνδεσμος, συμφωνία usw.) als mahnendes Vorbild ... der gewünschten H.[omonoia] zwischen Menschen".

example to follow.[793] Although this is the best and most explicit illustration offered by Dio, others are also found.[794]

Here, however, as a second and final example of this *topos* in deliberative rhetoric that urges concord, we will focus upon a passage found in one of Aelius Aristides' discourses on concord. Similar to Clement and Dio Chrysostom, Aristides describes the order and harmony of universe, an order and harmony in accordance with divine government.

> ... the sun proceeds in its course ever preserving its proper place, and the phases of the moon and the motion of the stars go on ... and again their harmonies are preserved, since agreement prevails among them, and there are no differences present nor do they arise, but all things have yielded to the law of nature and they use one will concerning all their duties ... (Or. 23.77).

Aristides goes on to reveal his purpose in focusing on the order and harmony of universe. He states: "if imitation of the gods is an act of men of good sense, it would be the part of men of good sense to believe that they are all a unity" (*Or.* 23.77). The basic point in the argumentation is that just as the gods reveal their will in the harmony of the universe, good men ought to reflect this harmony in their relationships. In other words, the order and harmony of the universe is an example to imitate just as it is for Clement.[795]

According to Clement, living in harmony with the exhortation given in chapter 21 is an expression of the fear of God which "gives salvation to all who live holily in it with a pure mind" (21:8). Thus he appeals to the greatest benefit for the Corinthian Christians in order to persuade them. As we have seen, this is a hallmark of deliberative rhetoric. Further, by means of two quotations from the Psalms Clement attempts to show that his teaching is confirmed by Scripture.[796] Among other things, these passages say that the fear of the Lord means that one should make the tongue cease from evil, and that one should do good and seeks peace (εἰρήνη, 22:3-5). According to Clement instigators of sedition lack all these qualities. They use their tongue for self-praise, they are evil, and instead of peace they cause sedition.[797] In other words, the mentioned

---

[793]Dio goes on to describe how small animals live in co-operation without any quarrel; birds, ants and bees, and this is the case for herds of cattle, droves of horses, goats and sheep as well (*Or.* 40. 40-41). In particular Clement's statement that "the smallest of animals meet together in concord and peace" (20:10) is interesting in light of Dio's emphasis on this fact. To this and other similarities between 1 *Clem.* 20 and Dio Chrys. *Or.* 40.38-40, see the detailed discussion in C. EGGENBERGER, *Die Quellen der politischen Ethik des 1. Klemensbriefes* (1951) 74-86. Eggenberger argues for a literary dependence on Dio Chrysostom. It is, however, more likely that the similarities reflect common traditions.

[794]Dio Chrys. *Or.* 38.11; 48.14f.

[795]For an appeal to the harmony of universe as an argument for establishing concord among men, cf. also Aristid. *Or.* 24.42; 27.35. See further Philo *Jos* 145; *Congr* 133; *Spec Leg* 2.141, Luk. *Bellum Ciuil.* 2.272-73.

[796]Pss 34:11-17; 32:10.

[797]1 *Clem.* 14:1-4; 21:5; 57:1

manifestations of fearing God are directly related to the topic of sedition.[798] Clement concludes this section by stating in 23:1a that God has compassion on all who fear him which in this connection means to live in a manner consistent with his admonitions presented above (*1 Clem.* 21), and that God gives his favours (χάρις) to those who come to him with a simple mind (23:1b). In order to experience the compassion of God the Christians in Corinth must re-establish concord in the Church. This is the aim of the exhortation of chapter 21.

3.6.1.3. Political Terms and topoi in 1 Clement 23:1-36:6

The last part of 23:1 functions as a transition to a new topic, i.e. resurrection in the future. Because God gives favours to those who come to him with a simple mind, Clement exhorts the Christians not to be double-minded (μὴ διψυχῶμεν) regarding his great gifts (δωρεά, 23:2). He quotes a passage from an unknown source which says, "wretched are the double-minded (δίψυχος)". This refers to people who say that although they had heard about "these things" long ago, none of them had happened to them (23:3). Clement calls people with such thoughts fools and argues by pointing to the rapid maturation of the fruit of a vine that God will quickly and suddenly accomplish his will (23:4f.). That it is the resurrection which is in question is evident from 24:1 where Clement admonishes his audience to consider how God continually points out to them through nature that a resurrection will take place in the future. He mentions the resurrection of day and night, of the crops, and of the bird Phoenix.[799] After mentioning how God shows the greatness of his promise even through a bird, he asks whether it is so great and wonderful that God will raise up those who served him in holiness (26:1)? He then alludes to Pss 27:7, 3:6, 87:11, 22:4 and Job 19:26 as proof for his argumentation (26:2f.).[800]

In 27:1-28:4 Clement draws the following conclusion from 23:2-26:3: Christians must be bound to God in the hope of a resurrection and renew their faith in him. Because of God's omnipotence and omnipresence he exhorts the Corinthians to fear him and abstain from foul desires and evil deeds (φαύλων ἔργων μιαρὰς ἐπιθυμίας) in order to be shielded by his mercy from the coming judgments (28:1). What concrete deeds Clement has in mind is not said explicitly, but it is reasonable to assume that he is thinking primarily of the present strife and sedition. The fact that Clement uses the adjective μιαρός in 1:1 to depict the present στάσις and that he uses φαῦλοι in 36:6 to refer to the enemies of God who oppose his will points in this direction. Additionally, we have seen that the instigators of the sedition who hypocritically claimed to seek peace were lacking the fear of God.

---

[798]Regarding self-praise, see pp. 131-136, and regarding peace, see chap. 3.4.

[799]Regarding the tradition of the widespread myth of the bird Phoenix, see the excursus in A. LINDEMANN, *Die Clemensbriefe* (1992) 88f.

[800]See D. A. HAGNER, *The Use of the Old and New Testaments in Clement of Rome* (1973) 58f., 52f.; A. LINDEMANN, *Die Clemensbriefe* (1992) 90.

After Clement has argued that it is not possible to escape from the omnipresent God (28:2-4), he goes on to give a positive exhortation for his audience to seek and love God "who has made us the portion of his choice for himself" (29:1). The passage cited marks a transition to a new topic: Because God who chose his people is holy, the Corinthian Christians should live in a holy way (30:1). When Clement specifies what this means, he warns on the one hand against different vices and on the other hand he exhorts the Corinthians to practice different virtues that to a great extent belong to the traditional catalogues of vices and virtues respectively (30:1-8).[801] However, some of his paraenesis is particularly relevant to the present state of affairs in the Corinthian Church. First we note that he warns against νεωτερισμός, a term which in antiquity belonged to the semantic field of concord.[802] Secondly, we note that he warns against ὑπερηφανία. The topic of ὑπερηφανία occurs relatively frequently in the letter and is associated with men involved in sedition (in addition to 30:1: 30:2; 35:5; 49:5; 57:2). It appears that according to Clement seditious behaviour is an expression of ὑπερηφανία. His remarks in the prayer at the end of the *probatio*,[803] i.e. that God will humble the pride of the arrogant (ὕβριν ὑπερηφάνων, 59:3), reflect this opinion. In this connection it is not necessary to discuss the *topos* of *hybris* in antiquity in detail, but a few remarks are appropriate in order to indicate that Clement reflects a commonplace in depicting men involved in sedition as arrogant.[804]

In his *Rhetorica* Aristotle discusses the nature of *hybris*. An important aspect appears to be that *hybris* consists in causing injury or annoyance whereby the victim is disgraced. The motivation for those who insult or dishonour others is primarily the desire to feel and demonstrate their superiority over those who are insulted (*Rh.* 2.2.5-6).[805] Throughout antiquity, *hybris* was closely associated with the term κόρος, "fullness", "satiety", or "having too much".[806] This means that it was often the wealthy and powerful – people who are, or claim to be, in a position of superiority over others – who behaved in a hybristic way.[807] Although this was the norm, hybristic behaviour

---

[801]Cf. A. LINDEMANN, *Die Clemensbriefe* (1992) 96.

[802]For the use of this term expressing sedition in a political body, see Dion. Hal. *Ant. Rom* 6.1.1.

[803]For the definition and function of the *probatio* in *1 Clement*, see pp. 232-277.

[804]For detailed studies, see J. J. FRAENKEL, *Hybris* (1941); K. J. DOVER, *Greek Popular Morality in the Time of Plato and Aristotle* (1974); N. R. E. FISHER, "Hybris and Dishonour I", *GaR* 23 (1976) 177-193; *idem*, *Hybris. A Study in the Values of Honour and Shame in Ancient Greece* (1992); D. M. MACDOWELL, "Hybris in Athens", *GaR* 23 (1976) 14-31. For the use of the *hybris topos* in 1 and 2 Corinthians, see C. FORBES, "Comparison, Self-Praise and Irony", *NTS* 32 (1986) 1-30; P. MARSHALL, *Enmity in Corinth* (1987) 182-218, 364-381; S. M. POGOLOFF, *Logos and Sophia* (1992) 223-234.

[805]In other words, Aristotle discusses the nature of *hybris* within the context of honour and shame, emphasized by N. R. E. FISHER, "Hybris and Dishonour I", *GaR* 23 (1976) 177-193. For the main characteristics of an honour-shame culture, see the present investigation, chap. 5.4.1.2.

[806]For references to texts, see P. MARSHALL, *Enmity in Corinth* (1987) 183.

[807]Arist. *Eth. Nic.* 4.3.21-22; 4.3.36; *Rh.* 2.16.1-4; *Pol.* 4.9.4-6. Cf. N. R. E. FISHER, "Hybris and Dishonour I", *GaR* 23 (1976) 182f. Authors who are near contemporaries of *1 Clement* describe the behaviour of tyrants and corrupt politicians as hybristic; Dion. Hal. *Ant. Rom.* 6.58.3; 7.45.2; 7.45.4; Plut. *Alc.* 4.5.1; Dio Chrys. *Or.* 1.82.

was also at work, according to N. R. E. Fisher, "within a relationship of equality when one party's claim to be superior and to treat the other as an inferior is naturally resented".[808] Fisher has even demonstrated the following:

> … people in an inferior position are often accused of hybris if they attempt merely to assert a position of equality, or reduce the status-gap; verbal freedom ("cheek", "insolence"), or disobedience on the part of slaves, women or children, unrest or revolts on the part of organized slaves or helots, disobedience or revolts of citizens against their magistrates or rulers, or of subject cities or countries against imperial powers, are all regularly described as hybris.[809]

Given this basic definition of the nature of *hybris* it is easy to imagine that hybristic behaviour could lead to strife in a political body.[810] Aristotle probably reflects a common experience when he states in *Pol.* 5.2.4 that when people "in office show insolence and greed (ὑβριζόντων καὶ πλεονεκτούντων), people rise in revolt against one another … for men form factions both when they are themselves dishonoured and when they see others honoured". A connection between *hybris* and sedition is also reflected by Dio Chrysostom in *Or. 1*. When he pictures tyranny's throne he says that it is ornamented with arrogance (ἀλαζονεία, 1.79) and attended by, among other things, insolence (ὕβρις) and faction (στάσις, 1.82). Further, in another discourse Dio depicts Agamemnon as both a hybrist, i.e. he was arrogant (ὑπερήφανος) and overbearing (ὑβριστής), and as one who breeds envy (φθόνος) and jealousy (ζηλοτυπία, *Or* 61.12f.).[811] These examples should suffice to indicate why Clement found it appropriate to depict men involved in sedition as being ὑπερήφανος and showing *hybris*. These vices belonged to the semantic field of concord.[812] In other words by depicting seditious behaviour as arrogant and as an expression of *hybris* he is employing a commonplace.[813]

Further, when Clement specifies what it means to join "to those to whom is given grace from God",[814] it is symptomatic of his overall purpose in the letter that he first exhorts the Corinthians to "put on concord" (ὁμόνοια, 30:3). We hardly need to remind the reader of the fact that ὁμόνοια was a technical term used in antiquity when one dealt

---

[808]N. R. E. FISHER, "Hybris and Dishonour I", *GaR* 23 (1976) 183.

[809]*Ibid.* 184 with cited texts.

[810]P. MARSHALL, *Enmity in Corinth* (1987), remarks that "one of the most common characteristics of hybris is that denoted by στάσις, 'discord', and similar notions of division and disorder. Hybris results in either political or social factions and together with κέρδος 'gain', is the most obvious cause of faction between the dominating classes and the disadvantaged" (187).

[811]Considering the association of ζῆλος καὶ φθόνος with sedition, see chap. 3.5.1.2.

[812]It is not possible, however, on the basis of the *hybris topos* to draw any conclusion regarding whether Clement had a special strata of the Church in mind when he warns against arrogance and *hybris*. Though *hybris* includes the notion of superiority, behaviour that was regarded as hybristic could also take place among equals and people in an inferior position.

[813]So also H. O. MAIER, "1 Clement and the Rhetoric of Hybris", *StPatr.* 31 (1997) 136-142.

[814]*1 Clem.* 30:3.

with the question of unity in a political body.[815] The following two participles, ταπεινοφρονοῦντες and ἐγκρατευόμενοι, express how to establish the state of concord. Here Clement reveals why he puts so much stress upon the need for ταπεινοφροσύνη throughout the letter. It generates concord.[816] The subsequent passage indicates also that Clement makes a connection between gossip and speaking evil and the lack of concord in the Corinthian Church (30:3). The fact that he goes on to quote Job. 11:2f., which among other things warns the "good speaker" (ὁ εὔλαλος)" against believing that he is righteous and exhorts the Christians not to be talkative, suggests the possibility that the instigators of the sedition were gifted speakers and used their eloquence to argue for their point of view. Thus eloquence functioned as a divisive factor.[817] It is a reasonable assumption that Clement reflects a commonplace regarding the connection between rhetoric and strife.[818] Further, he warns against self-praise, "for God hates those who praise (αὐτεπαινετός) themselves" (30:6). Previously in this investigation we have attempted to show that self-praise was connected with strife and sedition in a political body.[819]

After Clement has summarized what characterises those who live in a holy way and are blessed by God (30:8), he again presents examples from the Old Testament, i.e. Abraham, Isaac, and Jacob (31:1-32:2). These examples from the life of the Patriarchs aim to demonstrate that a man who possessed certain virtues, who followed "the paths of blessing" (31:1), received the blessing of God in different ways. Their blessing, however, was not a result of their good works, but was ultimately rooted in the will of God (32:3).

In the following passage Clement wants to prevent any possible misunderstanding to the effect that good works are for this reason unnecessary (33:1-36:6). The acts of God in creating and maintaining the universe show in fact that good works are pleasing to him (33:2-6), and that the "Lord himself adorned himself with good works and rejoiced" (33:7).[820] Therefore, having God himself as a pattern (ὑπογραμμός), Clement exhorts the Corinthians to "follow his will (θέλημα) without delay" and to "work the work of righteousness (ἔργον δικαιοσύνης) with all our strength" (33:8). In the next chapter he develops this topic. However, the argumentation here takes its departure in a passage from Scripture which says that each one will be rewarded according to his work (34:1). On this basis Clement urges his audience to do good works and to be subject to God's will (ὑποτασσώμεθα τῷ θελήματι αὐτοῦ, 34:4f.). Additionally, he presents the multitude of angels who serve his will as an example to imitate (34:6).[821] We note that when Clement applies the example of the angels to the Corinthian

---

[815]See chaps. 3.3.1 and 3.4.

[816]Regarding ταπεινοφροσύνη, see our discussion, pp. 126-131.

[817]For the connection between eloquence and sedition, see pp. 133-136.

[818]See pp. 133-136.

[819]Cf. pp. 131f.

[820]The context indicates that the phrase "good works" refers back to 33:2-6, and thus the title 'Lord' designates God, not Christ, cf. R. Knopf, *Die zwei Clemensbriefe* (1920) 101.

[821]Clement combines two passages of the Scripture: Dan 7:10 and Isa 6:8.

Church, he does not explicitly focus upon the need to serve the will of God as we would expect from 34:6, but rather stresses the aspect of concord. He says we must gather together with concord at the same place (ἐν ὁμονοίᾳ ἐπὶ τὸ αὐτὸ συναχθέντες)[822] and cry "as it were with one mouth, that we may share in his [God's] great and glorious promises" (34:7).[823] However, as we have seen previously in this investigation Clement makes a close connection between obeying the will of God and concord in as much as the first secures the latter.[824] In the light of the manner in which he applies the example of angels who serve the will of God, it is reasonable to assume that, when he exhorts the Corinthians to do the "work of righteousness", to do "good works", and be subject to God's will, he is primarily thinking of behaviour which secures concord among the Corinthian Christians.

Clement goes further and lists the gifts of God, i.e. "life in immortality, splendour in righteousness, truth in boldness, faith in confidence, continence in holiness" (35:2), before he deals with how they may be gained (35:5-12). The first part of the answer focuses in general upon doing things which are consistent with his "faultless will" and thus "well-pleasing and acceptable to him" (35:5a). In 35:5b by means of a catalogue of vices he specifies to some extent in a negative way what this means. The similarity of this list, both regarding words and order, with Rom 1:29-31 indicates that he is relying on this passage. We should note, however, that at the end of the list he adds κενοδοξία and ἀφιλοξενία, which are not found in Rom 1.[825] The reason for this is probably that he believed these vices to be pertinent to the sedition facing the Corinthian Church. Striving for honour (δόξα, τιμή) was, as will be shown in the next chapter of the present work, often regarded in antiquity as a cause of sedition in a political body. It is likely that Clement considered such striving to be an important feature of the sedition in the Corinthian Church as well.[826] Regarding φιλοξενία we have noted that according to him the practise of this virtue was one of the praiseworthy characteristics of the Corinthian Church before the sedition took place. It is likely that he believed that this was a contributing factor in bringing about a state of peace and concord.[827]

Regarding the other vices listed in 35:5b we will argue that although Clement appears to depend on Rom 1 and thus expresses traditional Christian paraenesis, at least some of the vices are directly related to the issue of unity and sedition in a political body. In other words at least some of the vices belong to the semantic field of con-

---

[822]Regarding concord as a political term, see chaps. 3.3.1 and 3.4.

[823]The phrase ἐπὶ τὸ αὐτὸ συνάγεσθαι is *terminus technicus* expressing the whole local Church gathered in one place, cf. 1 Cor 11:20; 14:23; *Barn.* 4:10; Ign. *Eph.* 13:1 and W. C. van Unnik, "1 Clement 34 and the 'Sanctus'", *VigChr* 5 (1951) 229-231.

[824]Cf. the present investigation, pp. 155-157; 163.

[825]For a synopses and a comparison between *1 Clem.* 35:5 and Rom 1:29-31, cf. D. A. Hagner, *The Use of The Old and New Testaments in Clement of Rome* (1973) 214-216.

[826]See chaps. 5.4.1.3 and 5.4.2.

[827]See n. 563.

cord.[828] First of all we have in mind some vices which occur elsewhere in the letter, i.e. ἔρις,[829] ὑπερηφανία,[830] and ἀλαζονεία.[831] More interesting than the isolated occurrences of these vices elsewhere in the letter is the fact that all these three vices, especially ἔρις, are associated with the question of concord. We have also seen that this is not extraordinary for Clement, but rather that he reflects the conventional language of his literary milieu.[832]

In addition to the three vices just mentioned, some remarks are also appropriate regarding a fourth, i.e. πλεονεξία. Because this is the only occurrence of the term in the letter we must be more cautious in assuming that it relates directly to the trouble facing the Corinthian Church. In spite of this caution, there are features which might indicate that Clement also viewed this vice as linked with the current problem in the Corinthian Church. Specifically we have in mind clear examples in the literature of antiquity of πλεονεξία being linked with strife and sedition in a political body. Polybius, for instance, when dealing with the Roman constitution, writes the following:

> *For, there being two things to which a state owes its preservation, bravery against the enemy and concord (ὁμόνοια) among the citizens, Lycurgus by doing away with the lust for wealth (πλεονεξία) did away also with all civil discord (διαφορά) and broils (στάσις, Hist. 6.46.7f.).*

This passage where πλεονεξία is regarded as a cause for discord reflects a basic idea of Polybius' political thought. He views πλεονεξία as the greatest threat to the ideal of concord and considers it as the main reason for increased problems in a city.[833] A similar point of view is reflected by Diodorus Siculus. In a discourse Scipio Nasica delivered in the Senate of Rome according to Diodorus Siculus, he spoke as follows:

> *Furthermore, so long as Carthage survived, the fear that she generated compelled the Romans to live together in harmony (ὁμονοέω) and to rule their subjects equitably and with credit to themselves – much the best means to maintain and extend an empire; but once the rival city was destroyed, it was only too evident that there would*

---

[828]Contra R. KNOPF, *Die zwei Clemensbriefe* (1920) 105: "Da der Lasterkatalog ganz allgemein gehalten und aus Rm 1 übernommen ist, muss man darauf verzichten, in ihm irgendwelche Anspielung auf die Gemeindeverhältnisse in Korinth zu sehen". We may ask, however, why Clement incorporated this catalogue at all if he did not find anything of the content relevant to the situation of the recipients of the letter. Cf. also A. LINDEMANN *Die Clemensbriefe* (1992) 109, who is more positive in his estimation that in Clement for certain of the vices "ein aktueller Bezug intendiert sein dürfte" (109). Similarly H. E. LONA, *Der erste Clemensbrief* (1998) 386f.

[829]*1 Clem.* 3:2; 5:5; 6:4; 9:1; 14:2; 35:5; 44:1; 46:5; 54:2.

[830]*1 Clem.* 30:1f.

[831]*1 Clem.* 13:1; 14:1; 16:2; 21:5; 57:2.

[832]See chaps. 3.5.1.1.2; 3.5.2.10, pp. 131-136; and the present chap., pp. 167-169.

[833]Cf. E. SKARD, *Zwei religiös-politische Begriffe* (1932) 68f., 74-77 with cited texts. Skard summarizes: "der Gegensatz der ὁμόνοια ist besonders die πλεονεξία, die Selbstsucht, die den Staat ins Verderben stürzt" (69), and "Die Ursachen des kommenden Niederganges sieht er in der πολυτέλεια und der πλεονεξία" (76). For the connection between πλεονεξία and στάσις, see also K. THRAEDE, "Homonoia (Eintracht)", *RAC* 16 (1994) 181f.

be civil war (ἐμφύλιος πόλεμος) at home, and that hatred for the governing power would spring up among all the allies because of the rapacity (πλεονεξία) and lawlessness to which the Roman magistrates would subject them (34/35.33.5).

As a final example of a similar connection between strife and πλεονεξία we point to Dio Chrys. *Or.* 77/78.39. Here Dio describes the ideal man as one who does not arouse "strife (στάσις) or greed (πλεονεξία) or contentions (ἔρις) and jealousies (φθόνος) and base desires for gain, but reminding man of sobriety (σωφροσύνη) and righteousness (δικαιοσύνη) and promoting concord (ὁμόνοια)". Although Dio does not state explicitly that πλεονεξία generates sedition, it seems clear that he holds that sedition is associated with πλεονεξία in as much as the term is linked with other terms commonly used to depict discord in a political body.[834] The above-quoted passages should suffice to show that πλεονεξία belonged to the semantic field of ὁμόνοια.[835] Thus, it is likely that Clement also considered this vice to be relevant to what he regarded as the problem at Corinth.[836]

After Clement has presented the catalogue of vices which the Christians must desist from in order to "receive a share of the promised gifts" (35:4), he goes on to argue that God hates not only those who behave in this way, but using an allusion to Rom 1:22 followed by a quotation of Ps. 50:16-23, he argues that God also hates those that applaud these things (35:6-12). In the next chapter he gives the words of the Psalmist regarding the sacrifice of praise in which the way to the salvation of God is to be found (35:12). In a christological interpretation he states that Jesus Christ is the way to salvation. In order to show the majesty of Jesus, he alludes to and quotes different passages from the Psalms and Hebrews which end with the quotation from the Psalmist who says that the Son, that is Christ, shall sit on the right hand of God until he makes his enemies a footstool for his feet (36:5).[837] Characteristically Clement emphasizes his attitude to the will of Christ when in 36:6 he identifies the enemies as "those who are wicked and oppose his will" (οἱ φαῦλοι καὶ ἀντιτασσόμενοι τῷ θελήματι αὐτοῦ). As we have mentioned many times in this chapter, throughout the letter Clement stresses the need to submit to the will of God, which would guarantee the existence of peace and concord in the Corinthian Church. The instigators of the sedition as well as the majority of the congregation who have silently accepted and supported them behave against the will of God.[838] Here he underlines in a similar way the need to be obedient to the will of Christ. If not, one is his enemy. In as much as it is reasonable to assume that Clement holds that the will of Christ is consistent with the will of God there is no actual difference between his emphasis upon the need to adhere to the will of God or to the will of

---

[834]See chaps. 3.5.1.1.1; 3.5.1.1.2; 3.5.1.2; 3.5.2.5; 3.5.2.16; 3.4 respectively.

[835]For further references, see, e.g., Plut. *Mor.* 479 A; Dio Cass. 45.24.

[836]Contra H.E. LONA, *Der erste Clemensbrief* (1998) 385.

[837]The quotations in the order they occur in *1 Clem.* 36: Heb 1:3f; Ps 103:4; Heb 1:5; Ps 2:7f; 109:1. See D. A. HAGNER, *The Use of The Old and New Testaments in Clement of Rome* (1973) 178-184, for allusions and further discussions.

[838]E.g., 1:1; 3:4; 21:4; 44:4.

Christ. Thus his description of Christ's enemies is directly related to the issue of sedition.[839]

3.6.1.4. The Army

In chapter 37 Clement uses the image of an army as a metaphor for the Church. The Christians are soldiers who ought to serve in the army following God's "faultless commands" (37:1). Different suggestions have been offered as to why he introduces the military metaphor which at first seems to occur quite abruptly. Some scholars are of the opinion that it ought to be seen in connection with the reference to ἐχθροί in 36:6,[840] others that Clement here repeats and expands his previous exhortations in more concrete terms to strive (ἡμεῖς οὖν ἀγωνισώμεθα, 35:4).[841] Both these suggestions are possible, but it seems more likely that it is Clement's emphasis at the end of 36:6 on the enemies who oppose God's will that led him to introduce the army metaphor. The fact that he says that to serve in the army is in accordance with God's "faultless commands" (ἐν τοῖς ἀμώμοις προστάγμασιν αὐτοῦ) indicates that the stress is upon the will of God.[842]

In 37:2-4 Clement expands the military metaphor and gives the reason why the army serves as an appropriate metaphor for Christian communities. The soldiers are praised because they fulfil their duties in good order (εὐτάκτως), readily yielding (εἰκτικῶς),[843] and in submissiveness (ὑποτεταγμένως). It is evident that he places an emphasis on order and submission to the command of the generals. This aspect is further emphasized in 37:3:

> Not all are prefects (ἔπαρχος), nor tribunes (χιλίαρχος), nor centurions (ἑκατόν-
> ταρχος), nor in charge of fifty men (πεντηκόνταρχος), or the like, but each carries
> out in his own rank (ἐν τῷ ἰδίῳ τάγματι) the commands (ἐπιτασσόμενος) of the
> emperor and of the generals.

The last category of military officers enumerated by Clement, i.e. πεντηκόνταρχος, does not occur in the Roman imperial army, but the three other categories have Latin equivalents. ἔπαρχος is the *praefectus praetorio*, the highest office of the praetorian

---

[839]Cf. also A. LINDEMANN, *Die Clemensbriefe* (1992): "den Hörern in Korinth soll klar sein, dass die Rädelsführer der στάσις sich Gottes Willen widersetzen" (112).

[840]L. SANDERS, *L'Hellénisme de Saint Clément de Rome et le Paulinisme* (1943) 82; A. LINDEMANN, *Die Clemensbriefe* (1992) 114.

[841]B. E. BOWE, *A Church in Crisis* (1988) 126.

[842]For other use of the military metaphor, see 2 Cor 10:3; Eph 6:10-17; 1 Tim 1:18; 2 Tim 2:3f; Ign. *Pol.* 6:2.

[843]Uncertain reading in Codex A which has ειεκτι... The end of the word has disappeared, but it seems that it continues with an ω or a ικ, K. LAKE, *The Apostolic Fathers* (1959) 72. A¹ has εὐεικτ... H reads ἐκτικῶς and S leniter. In spite of the fact that the reading of A is uncertain, we follow J. A. Fischer and read εἰκτικῶς which gives a good meaning. For further discussion, cf. A. LINDEMANN, *Die Clemensbriefe* (1992) 115, and H. E. LONA, *Der erste Clemensbrief* (1998) 409.

guard in Rome.[844] χιλίαρχος and ἑκατόνταρχος are Greek designations for the *tribunus militum* (officers of high rank, 6 in each legion), and the *centurio* (leader of a division of 100 soldiers) respectively.[845] Although the last category, i.e. πεντηκόνταρχος, might be inspired by the organisation of the people of God during the time in the desert when the armies of Israel were divided under chiefs into units of 1000, 100, 50 and 10,[846] the equivalence in Latin terminology indicates that it is primarily the Roman army which serves as a model for Clement.[847] In other words, in his view, the Roman army with its order and discipline is a fitting analogy to the proper condition within the Christian Community.

In viewing the life of the Christians as service in the army, it is likely that Clement reflects a commonplace in the ancient world. The duty of a man's life was compared with the military service of a soldier.[848] We quote a text from Epictetus in *Diss.* 3.24.31-36 in order to give an impression of how this military metaphor functioned in an argumentation:

> *Do you not know that the business of life is a campaign? One man must mount guard, another go out on reconnaissance, and another out to fight. It is not possible for all to stay in the same place, nor is it better so ... So also in this world; each man's life is a kind of campaign, and a long and complicated one at that. You have to maintain the character of a solider, and do each separate act at the bidding of the General, if possi-*

---

[844]J. B. LIGHTFOOT, *The Apostolic Fathers. I: Clement 2* (1989, first pr. 1889) 114f.; R. J. BRICKSTOCK, "Praefectus praetorio", *A Dictionary of Ancient History* 519.

[845]J. B. LIGHTFOOT, *The Apostolic Fathers. I: Clement 2* (1989, first pr. 1889) 114f.; A. LINDEMANN, *Die Clemensbriefe* (1992) 115.

[846]It is in particular A. JAUBERT, "Les sources de la conception militaire de l'Eglise en I Clement 37", *VigChr* 18 (1964) 74-84, who has argued that Clement refers to the Jewish military by pointing to Jewish texts where the rank "in charge of fifty" is used for Israel's leadership or army; Exod 18:21, 25; Deut 1:15; 1 Macc 3:55; Joseph. *Ant* 3.4.1, and from Qumran; 1QS 2,21-22; 1Qsa 1:14; 1:29-2:1; 1QM 3:13-4:5; CD 13:1-2, 81-82. Following Jaubert, B. E. BOWE, *A Church in Crisis* (1988) 127-129, attempts to demonstrate that, since it is not the Roman army which is the model for Clement, but the "sacral and priestly conception of the people of the dessert", the function of the model of the army in 1 Clem 37 has almost nothing to do with "'blind military obedience' to superior officers, or the efficiency and discipline of the Roman army" (128). For the Jewish background, see also R. M. GRANT and H. H. GRAHAM, *First and Second Clement* (1965) 65; H. E. LONA, *Der erste Clemensbrief* (1998) 410f.

[847]In addition to the above-mentioned Latin equivalence in terminology, we should note, however, that many of the Jewish texts also operate with a leader "in charge of ten soldiers" (δεκάδαρχος). If Clement primarily relies on the Jewish model, why does he not also include this rank? The fact that Clement calls the officers "our generals" in the same way as he calls Roman officials "our rulers" in 60:2 points in the direction that he has the Roman army in mind, cf. J. S. JEFFERS, *Conflict at Rome* (1991) 140. For the view that it was primarily the Roman army Clement used as model, see further J. B. LIGHTFOOT, *The Apostolic Fathers I: Clement. II* (1989, first pr.1889) 114f.; L. SANDERS, *L'Hellénisme de Saint Clément de Rome et le Paulinisme* (1943) 82f; J. A. FISCHER, *Die Apostolischen Väter* (1966) 73 n. 220; K. WENGST, *Pax Romana and the Peace of Jesus Christ* (1987) 108; A. LINDEMANN, *Die Clemensbriefe* (1992) 115; G. SCHNEIDER, *Clemens von Rom* (1994) 155 n. 216.

[848]Cf. R. KNOPF, *Die zwei Clemensbriefe* (1920) 108f.; L. SANDERS, *L'Hellénisme de Saint Clément de Rome et le Paulinisme* (1943) 82-84; M. DIBELIUS and H. CONZELMANN, *The Pastoral Epistles* (1972) 32f. Important texts are Epict. *Diss.* 1.14.15; 16.3-5; 3.24.31-36; 3.26.29-30; Sen. *Ep.* 107.9f.

*ble divining what He wishes. ... You have been given a post in an imperial city, and
not in some mean place; not for a shorter time either, but you are a senator for life.*

Here, the senator's duty is compared with the service of a soldier. Just as in Clement
37:1-3, the aspect of loyalty and submitting to the command of the General is focused
upon. By fulfilling their duties at the different places they have been assigned to, they
contribute to the working of the whole. In a similar way the senator contributes to the
work of the whole when he carries out his duty.[849]

More interesting in this connection is the fact that Aelius Aristides also uses this
topos in one of his discourses on concord. Admittedly, the stress is not so much upon
the super/subordination, i.e. the solider-general relation, but primarily upon the relationships between the leaders. In spite of that, the aspect of good order among soldiers
is also present. Aristides writes:

> *I believe that just as everyone would most certainly think that generals should be bet-
> ter than their soldiers, or at least not worse, so also the cities which have the chief voice
> in the Council should not be less intelligent than the mass of inferior cities. It is not the
> case that good order and discipline are fitting for soldiers, yet dishonorable for gener-
> als; but if the masses are going to maintain order, their leaders must first take the lead
> in this, since it is impossible for the army to be harmonious when the generals engage
> in disruptive faction against one another (Or. 23.34).*

Aristides compares the leading cities with generals, and inferior cities with soldiers. He
argues that "good order and discipline" is not fitting just for soldiers, but it is a precondition for the harmony of the army that there is good order among generals as well. It
seems that Aristides assumes that the lack of good order leads to factions. In other
words, in this passage Aristides applies the ideal picture of the army, an army marked
by order and discipline and free from factions among its leaders, as an example to imitate for the cities fighting for first rank. By following this example, the cities will achieve
concord. Aristides' use of the military metaphor in this context attests that Clement's
use of this *topos* is appropriate and in line with deliberative rhetoric urging concord in a
political body.

3.6.1.5. σύγκρασίς τίς ἐστιν ἐν πᾶσιν

In his subsequent development of the military metaphor Clement places less emphasis
on hierarchy and order and more on interdependence and mutuality. This is not to say
that the aspect of order and discipline is not present – it is rather a question of interdependence and mutuality within the assigned rank of each individual (ἕκαστος ἐν τῷ
ἰδίῳ τάγματι, 37:3). The following statement, however, shows that Clement changes
the focus more in the direction of interdependence and mutuality: "The great cannot

---

[849]B. E. Bowe, *A Church in Crisis* (1988) 128, when commenting on the same passage lays too little stress on subordination and obedience in this passage when she says that "it is not so much the ideas
of super/subordination which are underscored but the conviction that each one contributes to the
working of the whole by faithfulness to an 'assigned place'".

exist without the small, nor the small without the great; there is a certain mixture among all (σύγκρασίς τίς ἐστιν ἐν πᾶσιν), and herein lies the advantage" (37:4). The main point for him is not order or military discipline in itself, but that the order serves to promote concord. This seems to be evident from the fact that in the statement just cited he reflects the widespread political idea in antiquity of ἡ μικτὴ πολιτεία, "the mixed constitution" which was connected with the conception of concord.[850]

A primary point in this political theory is that any political body, not just the more formal body which is the political constitution,[851] but any political body of different people, must contain a balance, a mix of "great and small" or opposite features which complement each other in an appropriate balance.[852] Though this theory emerged in the Greek arena, its basic conceptions were adopted and continued into the period of the Empire and were, as Cicero testifies, prevalent at the end of the Republic.[853] In the light of the important role of concord for the well-being of the city which has been discussed above, it is not surprising, as already indicated, that the question of concord was an important feature in the political theory of ἡ μικτὴ πολιτεία. This is evident from the fact that the Roman state is depicted as the ideal state because of its mixed constitution and because the different parties maintained concord by co-operating; and likewise Sparta is both praised for its concord and regarded as a *typos* for the mixed constitution.[854] The connection between the mixed constitution and concord is made explicit by Plutarch when he praises Cleisthenes for having "expelled the Peisistratidae and destroyed their tyranny, instituted laws, and established a constitution best attempered for the promotion of harmony and safety" (πολιτείαν ἄριστα κεκραμένην πρὸς ὁμόνοιαν καὶ σωτηρίαν, *Per.* 3.1).[855] It is notable that in this passage the same word stem for "mix" occurs as in *1 Clem.* 37:4 – Plutarch uses the verb while Clement uses the noun. In *Mor.* 474 A-B, which reflects the doctrine of the proper mix, the noun σύγκρασις occurs. In order to illustrate the condition of human affairs Plutarch compares it with the mixed universe, the mix of low and high notes in music, the mix of

---

[850]To the political theory of the mixed constitution, see P. ZILLIG, *Die Theorie von der gemischten Verfassung in ihrer literarischen Entwicklung im Altertum und ihr Verhältnis zur Lehre Lockes und Montesquieus über Verfassung* (1916) 55; K. VON FRITZ, *The Theory of the Mixed Constitution* (1954); N. WOOD, *Cicero's Social and Political Thought* (1988) 159-175. For Paul's application of this political theory in 1 Corinthians, see M. M. MITCHELL, *Paul and the Rhetoric of Reconciliation* (1991) 114f.

[851]Aristotle, for instance, says that the lawgiver Solon was considered to be a good lawgiver because he had established the "traditional democracy with a skillful blending of the constitution (μίξαντα καλῶς τὴν πολιτείαν): the Council on the Areopagus being an oligarchic element, the elective magistracies aristocratic and the law-courts democratic" (*Pol.* 2.9.2. Cf. also 4.7.6).

[852]For the need of cooperation between the greater and lesser components within a city, cf., e.g., Soph. *Aj.* 158-162; Eur. frg. 21; Pl. *Leg.* 10.902 D-E. See the discussion in L. SANDERS, *L'Hellénisme de Saint Clément de Rome et le Paulinisme* (1943) 82-84.

[853]Cf. the discussion with cited texts in N. WOOD, *Cicero's Social and Political Thought* (1988) 159-175.

[854]Concerning Rome; Polyb. *Hist.* 6.10.12-14; 6.12-14; Sparta; Polyb. *Hist.* 6.10.6; Arist. *Pol.* 2.3.10. See further the discussion in E. SKARD, *Zwei religiös-politische Begriffe* (1932) 75.

vowels and consonants in grammar. Human affairs "contain the principles of opposition to each other".[856] As a proof of this philosophy Plutarch quotes Euripides:[857]

The good, and bad cannot be kept apart,
But there's some blending (ἔστι τις σύγκρασις), so that all is well.[858]

The parallel to *1 Clem*. 37:4 b is striking both in terms and content. We do not maintain
that Clement depends on Plutarch or Euripides, but that he reflects the common tradition concerning the mixed constitution seems clear. In the continuation of Plutarch's
argument the connection between the proper mix and concord is obvious:

> ... *like musicians who achieve harmony by consistently deadening bad music with*
> *better and encompassing the bad with the good, we should make the blending of our*
> *life harmonious and conformable to our own nature (Mor. 474 B).*

Although the idea of the mixed constitution is not explicitly linked with concord in the
fragment of Euripides just quoted, he is dealing with the well-being of the city. He
argues that the well-being of a city is dependent on the proper mix of rich and poor, the
good and bad, which are mutually complementary with each other. In view of how vital
concord was perceived to be concerning the well-being of the city, it seems reasonable
to assume that a connection between σύγκρασις and concord is implied.[859]

On this basis it is reasonable to conclude with W. Jaeger that the term σύγκρασις
was a technical term for the "mixed constitution" in Greek political thought which
expressed the interdependence and mutuality of the different social elements. In this

---

[855]For an introduction to the emergence of the Athenian democracy and the role of Cleisthenes,
see H. MONTGOMERY, "Demokrati under Debatt", *I Skyggen av Akropolis* (1994) 99-127. Regarding the
connection between concord and a mixed constitution in Roman politics, cf. Cic. *Rep*. 2.42: "and this
perfect agreement and harmony is produced by the proportionate blending of unlike tones, so also is a
State made harmonious by agreement among dissimilar elements, brought about by a fair and reasonable blending together of the upper, middle, and lower classes, just if they were musical tones. What
the musicians call harmony in song is concord in a State, the strongest and best bond of permanent
union in any commonwealth", and the summary of N. WOOD, *Cicero's Social and Political Thought*
(1988) 161: "The ancients sought an immortal form of constitution, one that would be relatively
impervious to the passage of time and generate conditions of lasting unity, order, and stability. In the
opinion of ancient theorists, the properly mixed constitution was an ingenious contrivance for the
political implementation of these principles".

[856]For the analogy of the mixed and harmonious universe with the mixed social constitution, see
Arist. [*Mund*.] 4.395b.18-5.397b.8. Note the term κρᾶσις in 5.396b.25: "so in the same way the complex of the Universe, I mean heaven and earth and the whole cosmos by means of the mixture of the
most opposite elements (τῶν ἐναντιωτάτων κράσεως) has been organized by a single harmony". For
further examples of the image of the concordant music, see, e.g., Arist. [*Mund*.] 6.399a. 12-18; Dio
Chrys. *Or. 39.4*; Plut. Mor. 479 A; Ignat. *Eph*. 4:2.

[857]Eur. frg. 21.

[858]Quoted again in *Mor*. 25 C-D; 369 B.

[859]For further references where the verb is used to depict the mixed constitution, see M. M.
MITCHELL, *Paul and the Rhetoric of Reconciliation* (1991) 115 n. 306.

context it is significant that this interdependence and mutuality was seen as a means of achieving and maintaining concord.[860]

3.6.1.6. σῶμα, ἀλλὰ πάντα συνπνεῖ

Clement goes on to present the image of the human body in order to illustrate the interdependence of the "small" and "great":

> ... *the head (κεφαλή) is nothing without the feet (πούς), likewise the feet are nothing without the head; the smallest members of our body (ἐλάχιστα μέλη τοῦ σώματος) are necessary and valuable to the whole body, but all work together (συμπνέω) and are united in a common subjection to preserve the whole body (εἰς τὸ σώζεσθαι ὅλον τὸ σῶμα) (1 Clem. 37:5).*

Just as the different members of the body work together and depend on each other to preserve the whole body, he exhorts the Christians to behave in such a way that the whole body will be preserved in Christ Jesus (σωζέσθω οὖν ἡμῶν ὅλον τὸ σῶμα ἐν Χριστῷ Ἰησοῦ) by subordinating themselves according to their individual χάρισμα. In other words, he is applying the image of the body to the Christian Community. Although it is not certain, the similarity in terms and structure compared to 1 Cor 12 indicates that Clement was influenced by Paul in his use of this metaphor.[861] More important than achieving a decisive answer to this question is the fact noted by several scholars that the body metaphor was commonly applied to a political unit.[862] Aristotle

---

[860]Without mentioning any text reference W. JAEGER, *Early Christianity and Greek Paideia* (1961) 20f. says: "The Greek word which we have translated by 'proper mixture' is a special kind of mixture, which the Greek language calls *krasis* and so distinguishes from a mere juxtaposition of mixed elements without their mutual penetration ... It was a word of an almost technical meaning, which had a long and interesting history. It was used in Greek medical thought to mean a thing that, though composed of two or more elements, has coalesced into an indissoluble and well balanced unity. Political and social thinkers came to use the word in order to describe their ideal of political unity as a healthy blend of different social elements in the polis". For the synonym term μικτή, cf. M. M. MITCHELL, *Paul and the Rhetoric of Reconciliation* (1991) 113f., for many references to texts and discussions.

[861]So D. A. HAGNER, *The Use of the Old and New Testaments in Clement of Rome* (1973), who provides the most detailed comparison. We should note, however, that Hagner must admit that on certain points Clement's application of the body metaphor is more similar to Stoic than to Pauline usage (197f.). W. JAEGER, *Early Christianity and Greek Paideia* (1961) 22, simply states that Clement quotes 1 Cor 12:21f., and similarly R. M. GRANT and H. H. GRAHAM, *First and Second Clement* (1965): "Clement turns directly on 1 Corinthians 12:21-23, in which are set forth the mutual relations of head and feet, as well as the importance of the 'weaker'" (65). A. LINDEMANN, *Die Clemensbriefe* (1992), maintains that, although Clement of course knew 1 Cor 12, he "formuliert hier zunächst offenbar ohne direkte Bezugnahmen auf Paulus" (116). H. E. LONA, *Der erste Clemensbrief* (1998), says that "Der recht frei herangezogene Text ist 1 Kor 12,21b-22" (413).

[862]For relevant literature which points to the most important classical texts, see M. M. MITCHELL, *Paul and the Rhetoric of Reconciliation* (1991) 157 n. 554, and her own discussion of this *topos* in 1 Cor 12 (157-164). In addition, S. HANSON, *The Unity of the Church in the New Testament* (1946); E. SCHWEIZER and F. BAUMGÄRTEL, "σῶμα κτλ.", *TDNT* 7, 1024ff; H. CONZELMANN, *Der erste Brief an die Korinther* (1969) 248-255.

attests that this metaphor had emerged already during his life time,[863] and later sources reveal that it was commonly in use in the time of the late Republic.[864] Philo and Josephus show that it was common in Hellenistic Judaism as well.[865]

The classical example of the use of the body metaphor that all scholars take note of is the fable of Menenius Agrippa which was well-known even in the ancient world.[866] Characteristically Agrippa introduces his fable by saying the following:

> A commonwealth resembles in some measure a human body (ἀνθρώπειον σῶμα). For each of them is composite and consists of many parts; and no one of their parts either has the same function or performs the same services as the others (Dion. Hal. Ant. Rom. 6.86.1).

He goes on to describe a revolt (στάσις) of the feet, hands, shoulders, mouth, and the head against the belly because these members of the body thought that the belly was a burden and did not contribute to the common good of the body. However, as Agrippa says, if the different parts of the body no longer perform their office of providing food to the body, they would be destroyed within a few days by starvation. His main objective is to demonstrate that the proper mix of different members and the co-operation of these members are necessary for the well-being of the whole body. He proceeds to point out that this is exactly the case also in the commonwealth in as much as it is "composed of many classes of people not at all resembling one another" which all have particular services contributing to the common good (6.86.4). In line with this he urges the plebes to cease from στάσις against the senate (which is compared with the belly) and thereby contribute to what is beneficial to all (6.86.5).[867]

Although this is the deliberative discourse on concord where the body metaphor is taken farthest, it is nevertheless not difficult to point to other discourses on concord where the metaphor occurs in a more or less fully developed form. For instance, when Dio Chrysostom urges Nicea to cease from civil strife, he first states that neither abundance of riches nor numbers of men nor any element of strength is of advantage to a city without concord. Then he goes on to compare the city with a human body: "that body which is in sound health finds advantage in its height and bulk, while the body which is diseased and in poor condition finds a physical state of that kind to be most

---

[863] Arist. *Pol.* 1.1.11; 3.6.4; 5.2.7; *Eth. Nic.* 1.7.11. Cf.also Xen. *Mem.* 2.3.19.

[864] Plut. *Mor.* 426 A; 797 E; Dio Chrys. *Or.* 1.32; 3.104-107; 17.19; 33.16; 39.5; 50.3; Aristid. *Or.* 17.9; 24.18; 24.38-39; 26.43; Epict. *Diss.* 2.10.3f; 5.23-26; Sen. *De Ira* 2.31.7.

[865] E.g. Philo *SpecLeg* 3.131; Joseph. *Bell* 1.507; 2.264; 4.406f.

[866] Liv. *ab Vrbe Conditia* 2.32; Dion. Hal. *Ant. Rom.* 6.86; Plut. *Cor.* 6.2-4. Dionysius Halicarnassensis remarks that the discourse which the fable is a part of is quoted in all the ancient histories, *Ant. Rom.* 6.83.2. See further W. NESTLE, "Der Fabel des Menenius Agrippa", *Klio* 21 (1927) 350-360.

[867] This indicates that it is reasonable to classify Agrippas' discourse as a deliberative discourse on concord. Cf. the comment of Quint. *Inst.* 5.11.19: "Thus Menenius Agrippa is said to have reconciled the plebs to the patricians by his fable of the limbs' quarrel with the belly" (*nota illa de membris humanis adversus ventrem discordantibus fabula*), and E. SKARD, *Zwei religiös-politische Begriffe* (1932) 89: "Diese Rede ist ein echter λόγος προτρεπτικός εἰ ὁμόνοιαν".

perilous and productive of severest risk" (*Or.* 39.5).[868] Dio does not explicitly apply the image of strife against the different parts of the body as Agrippa does, but the image of the healthy body implies that the different parts co-operate and fulfil their services. The use of a diseased body as a metaphor for sedition in a political unit was common in antiquity.[869] Furthermore, when Aelius Aristides urges the divided Rhodians to live in concord, he first blames them because they destroy their city by their actions and because they "await the victory of Cleomenes Laconian who chopped up his body, beginning with his feet" (*Or.* 24.38).[870] Then he draws the following analogy:

> *And how shall you differ from the women who tore Pentheus apart (διασπάσασθαι), when you yourselves have torn apart with your hands the body of the city which you all share (αὐτοὶ τὸ κοινὸν σῶμα τῆς πόλεως ταῖς ὑμετέραις αὐτῶν χερσὶ διασπάσησθε, Or. 24.39)?*

A very similar application of the body metaphor is found in *1 Clem.* 46:7. Clement also defines sedition between the Christians as a tearing apart of the body, i.e. the church as the body of Christ where the Christians are μέλη τοῦ Χριστοῦ. Note that Clement even uses the same verb for tearing apart, i.e. διασπάω:

> *Why do we divide (διέλκω) and tear asunder (διασπάω) the members of Christ (τὰ μέλη τοῦ Χριστοῦ), and raise up strife against our own body (στασιάζομεν πρὸς τὸ σῶμα τὸ ἴδιον), and reach such a pitch of madness as to forget that we are members (μέλος) one of another (46:7)?*

The passages we have presented are taken from deliberative rhetoric urging concord and indicate that Clement reflects a common *topos* in this kind of rhetoric when he applies the body metaphor in his argument for concord among the Corinthian Christians. We should note, however, that it is not only his use of the metaphor that he has in common with other ancient literature that deals with concord in social units, but also (and this is the most important point), there is the fact of the striking similarities in the way that the metaphor is employed.

An important point in Clement's argumentation in chaps. 37-38 is that, just as the different parts of the bodies contribute to preserve the whole body (εἰς τὸ σώζεσθαι ὅλον τὸ σῶμα), so also each member of the Church at Corinth must contribute according to his χάρισμα in order to preserve "our whole body", i.e. the Church. What follows this shows that Clement does not use the term χάρισμα to refer to a spiritual gift, as Paul does in 1 Cor 12, but that he has in mind socio-economic gifts and certain virtues of individual members of the Church. He exhorts the strong to care for the weak, while the weak man for his part should respect the strong; and the rich man must

---

[868]For a similar use of the body metaphor, cf. Dio Chrys. *Or.* 34.23, where Dio prompts the Tarsans to regard the linen workers as μέρος αὐτῶν.

[869]See M. M. MITCHELL, *Paul and the Rhetoric of Reconciliation* (1991) 158 n. 564 for references.

[870]Here Aristides applies irony: "The victory of a faction is compared to the victory of the Spartan king Cleomenes, a suicide in 491 B.C., over his rival Demaratus (*cf.* Herodotus VI 75,3) because of which Cleomenes was said to have gone mad", C.A. BEHR, *P. Aelius Aristides* vol. 2 (1981) 370 n. 26.

bestow help on the poor, while the poor should give thanks to God that he provided someone to supply his needs (38:2).[871] The similarity to the fable of Agrippa is striking in as much as Clement applies the body metaphor to different social classes and underscores the notion that each individual must contribute his particular service to the common good (Dion. Hal. *Ant. Rom.* 6.86.5).[872]

Besides the admonition to different socio-economic groups to mutually support each other, Clement presents other exhortations that aim at preserving the whole community. He exhorts the wise man to "manifest his wisdom not in words but in good deeds" (38:2). This might be an allusion to eloquence, which can act as a dividing force, as we have seen previously in the present work.[873] Further, Clement admonishes the humble-minded man not to testify to his own humility, and to the pure in the flesh, i.e. the ascetic man, not to boast of himself. Concerning the latter we have attempted to show that to boast of oneself could generate strife in a political body.[874]

Another point we should note, which has already been touched upon, is the application of the body metaphor in order to motivate behaviour that is profitable for the whole community. In the quotation from Agrippa above this is expressed with the words "the common good" (τῷ κοινῷ χρείαν). Clement underscores this aspect when he says that the co-operation between the members of the body aims to preserve the *whole* (ὅλος) body. This means that the individual member must refrain from egoism and his own individual interest. Instead he should fulfil his duty according to his possessions and function with the common benefit in view. Clement then applies this aspect of the metaphor to the Corinthian Christians and urges them to act in such a way that the *whole* (ὅλος) body, i.e. the Church, may be preserved. This appeal to individual members of a social unit to use their gifts and possessions for the common advantage was quite commonly employed by ancient writers in connection with the body metaphor. As examples we cite a passage first from Epictetus and then one from Plutarch:

> *What, then, is the profession of a citizen? To treat nothing as a matter of private profit (ἰδίᾳ συμφέρον), not to plan about anything as though he were a detached unit, but to act like the foot or the hand, which, if they had the faculty of reason to understand the constitution of nature, would never exercise choice or desire in any other way but by reference to the whole (Epic. Diss. 2.10.4f.).*

And Plutarch reports the following of Aratus:

> *... he considered that the Greek states which were weak would be preserved by mutual support when once they had been bound as it were by the common interest (κοινῷ συμφέροντι), and that just as the members of the body (τὰ μέρη τοῦ σώματος) have*

---

[871]Regarding this passage, see further the present investigation, pp. 312f.

[872]We agree with K. WENGST, *Pax Romana and the Peace of Jesus Christ* (1987): "Here Clement is in fact closer than is Paul to an earlier Roman use of the imagery of the body and its members, namely the famous parable by Menenius Agrippa of the belly and the limbs".

[873]Cf. pp. 133-136.

[874]Cf. pp. 131f.

common life and breath because they cleave together in a common growth, but when
they are drawn apart and become separate they wither away and decay, in like man-
ner the several states are ruined by those who dissever their common bonds, but are
augmented by mutual support, when they become parts of a great whole and enjoy a
common foresight (Arat. 24.5).[875]

We note that Plutarch expresses the unity that exists between the members of the body by stating that they share the same breath (συμπνέοντα διὰ τὴν πρὸς ἄλληλα συμφυΐαν). Exactly the same term for describing the ideal unity between the members is used by Clement as well in the clause ἀλλὰ πάντα συνπνεῖ (37:5). The verb συμπνέω means "breathe together"[876] and was originally used in Greek medicine where it expressed the idea that "one pneuma permeates and animates the whole organism of the body", but was subsequently taken over by philosophical and political think-ers.[877] The verb was used by these thinkers to depict the unity between the members of a political body. Dio Chrysostom, for instance, in one of his discourses on concord writes the following:

… *only by getting rid of the vices that excite and disturb men, the vices of envy, greed,*
contentiousness, the striving in each case to promote one's own welfare at the expense
of both one's native land and the common weal – only so, I repeat, is it possible ever to
breathe (συμπνέω) the breath of harmony in full strength and vigour and to unite
upon a common policy (Or. 34.19).[878]

In other words, when Clement uses this term he once more demonstrates his familiar-ity with traditional political language related to the question of concord.[879]

To summarize, in a manner consistent with ancient literature that deals with con-cord and sedition within social units, and especially with deliberative rhetoric urging concord, Clement applies the body metaphor in order to combat strife and factional-ism. It is not just the occurrence of this *topos* that he has in common with ancient polit-ical literature, but when the *topos* is used striking parallels are revealed: the appeal to

---

[875]For additional texts cited, cf. H.-J. KLAUCK, *Herrenmahl und hellenistischer Kult* (1982) 339f.; M. M. MITCHELL, *Paul and the Rhetoric of Reconciliation* (1991) 160. Cf. the comment of W. JAEGER, *Early Christianity and Greek Paideia* (1961), upon Paul's use of this *topos* in 1 Cor 12:7: "In 1 Cor. 12.7 Paul places the emphasis not on the gift (*charisma*) that each individual has been given by the Holy Spirit but on the fact that it was given to him to make the best use of it. This distinction between the special virtue or excellence of each citizen and the use he makes of that virtue or excellence for the common good is also found in Greek political thought from the beginning; it was natural that this problem should be raised again in the early Christian community as soon as serious differences arose" (115 n. 10).

[876]H. G. LIDDELL and R. SCOTT *A Greek-English Lexicon* (1973) 1684.

[877]W. JAEGER, *Early Christianity and Greek Paideia* (1961) 22.

[878]The same author also uses the similar thought of sharing one soul as an expression for concord. "When a city has concord, as many citizens as there are, so many are the eyes with which to see that city's interest, so many the ears with which to hear, so many the tongues to give advice, so many the minds concerned in its behalf; why it is just as if some god had made a single soul (μία ψυχή) for so great and populous a city" (Dio Chrys. *Or.* 39.5). For further references where συμπνέω expresses the unity in a political body, see Arist. *Pol.* 5.2.10; Pl. *Leg.* 4. 708 D.

different members of the political body to fulfil their duty according to their socio-economic gifts or appointed position; and the appeal to behave in a way which is beneficial not for the individual member, but for the whole community as a whole.

In chapter 39:1 Clement characterises certain people as "foolish, imprudent, silly, and uninstructed men (ἄφρονες καὶ ἀσύνετοι καὶ μωροὶ καὶ ἀπαίδευτοι) … wishing to exalt themselves in their own conceits". These people appear to be the instigators of sedition,[880] and their behaviour implies that they are not concerned with the common good of the whole body. From what we shall argue later in the present investigation it is likely that all the terms Clement uses to depict these people carry socio-political connotations. They depict people of low status and honour.[881] According to him, the behaviour of these men is rooted in false imagination of the power and strength of mortal men. By means of allusions and quotations from different passages from Job he shows that the Lord has only to breathe upon mortal men who behave against his will and they will die.

3.6.2. Political Terms and topoi Related to Concord in 1 Clement 40:1-61:2 (ὑπόθεσις / quaestio finita)

3.6.2.1. εὐτάκτως, τάξις, τάγμα

1 Clem. 40:1 functions as a transition to the second main part of the *probatio.* Or more precisely (as we shall argue in chapter 4, *Compositional Analysis*), as a transition to the ὑπόθεσις section. At the same time, 40:1 functions as a transition to a new text sequence at a higher level, i.e. 40:1-43:6 in which the topic of *order* plays an important role.[882] Because of the things which are manifested to the Corinthians, including everything Clement has written so far in the letter, he asserts that one "ought to do in order (τάξει ποιεῖν) all things which the Master commanded" concerning religious service (40:1). He refers to the orderly aspect of the service at the Temple in Jerusalem. God by his supreme will has allocated places and appointed different services to different persons in order that the service should take place according to his will (40:2-5). The orderly service in the Temple of Jerusalem functions obviously as an example to imitate, since in 41:1 Clement exhorts each Christian to please "God in his own rank (ἐν τῷ ἰδίῳ τάγματι)" and not to transgress "the appointed rules of his ministration".

---

[879] Cf. W. Jaeger, *Early Christianity and Greek Paideia* (1961) 23: "Both the idea of *synkrasis* and that of *sympnoia* belong together and reveal their origin from the same philosophical source, which was concerned with the problem of political harmony in human society. Clement needed it for his purpose of establishing firmly in the rapidly growing church the ideal of an *ordo Christianus*, which assigns to each member of his community his own place and way of cooperating according to his ability". The political aspect of συμπνέω is also noted by A. Lindemann, *Die Clemensbriefe* (1992) 116, and H. E. Lona, *Der erste Clemensbrief* (1998) 414f.

[880] Cf. *1 Clem.* 3:3.
[881] Cf. pp. 294-299.
[882] Cf. pp. 232f. and 259f.

After this exhortation he again turns his attention to the order of the Temple service. The actual sacrifices are offered in one particular place, at the altar, after the High Priest and the other ministers have inspected it (41:2). In order to emphasize how vital it is to behave consistently with the instruction given by God concerning the service, he states that those who act contrary to this will suffer the penalty of death (41:3).[883] Then he goes on to interpret what this means for the Christians: "You see, brethren, that the more knowledge we have been entrusted with, the greater risk (κίνδυνος) do we incur" (41:4). It is uncertain if he means that God will punish those who disturb the order of the Corinthian Church with death.[884] It appears to be clear, however, from his reference to the great risk associated with the present disorder that he intends to give a warning to the Corinthian Church.[885] Previously in our investigation we have seen that an appeal to a present or impending risk to the audience, if they behave in a particular manner, was typical of deliberative rhetoric.[886]

Farther on in chapter 42 Clement focuses upon the good order of apostolic times. Analogous to the view that Christ was sent from God, the apostles were sent from Christ. He emphasizes that both these events were in agreement with the appointed order of God's will. As for the apostles, they appointed bishops and deacons among the converts at the places where they worked. This was not, however, a new idea, since according to Clement it had been written of bishops and deacons in Scripture many years ago (42:5).[887] In addition to Isa 60:7 he presents the story of the strife that arose over the priesthood among the Israelites (43:1-6).[888] In order to overcome the conflict Moses collected rods from each tribe and said that God had chosen for his priesthood and ministry the tribe which owned the rod which God let blossom. Thus God chose Aaron. Clement makes a point of the fact that Moses acted in this way although he knew beforehand that this was going to happen. According to him, the reason for this was that "there should be no disorder (ἀκαταστασία) in Israel" (43:6). In other words, this happening should demonstrate both that God himself has established an order among the people of God, and that Moses, his faithful servant, is an example to

---

[883]Regarding the death penalty for transgressing the cultic order, see, e.g., Exod 12:15; 31:14; Lev 7:20f; 17:8f.

[884]Cf. A. VON HARNACK, *Einführung in die Alte Kirchengeschichte* (1929) 115.

[885]Contra A. LINDEMANN, *Die Clemensbriefe* (1992), who holds that Clement did not intend "den Hörern konkret zu drohen" (125). Both the introduction to the section which deals with the need for order in 40:1 and the explicit exhortation in 41:1 point in the direction of Clement warning the Corinthian Christian in 41:4 against the consequence of disorder.

[886]Cf. chaps. 2.3.1; 2.3.2.

[887]Clement alludes to Isa 60:17. He has, however, altered a number of words. The most important is that the LXX refers to ἄρχοντας and not διακόνους as Clement does. Since Clement's variant is important for his argumentation he might have deliberately changed it to fit his purpose. So A. LINDEMANN, *Die Clemensbriefe* (1992) 127. Other explanations, however, could be offered for the change of the LXX text. It is possible that Clement quoted "from memory, and mistakenly remembering διακόνους for ἄρχοντας", or that he employed an unknown text variant. Cf. D. A. HAGNER, *The Use of The Old and New Testaments in Clement of Rome* (1973) 67.

[888]Num 15-17.

follow in as much as one aim of his leadership was that there should be no disorder among the people.

The apostles also knew that strife (ἔρις) would arise over the title of bishop (44:1). Therefore they appointed men as leaders of the Church and gave the instruction that, if these men died, other approved men should succeed their ministry (44:2). Because the order of the Church goes back in this way to the apostles and is ultimately rooted in the will of God, it is a great sin to remove men who have blamelessy fulfilled their ministry. This is exactly what the Corinthians have done, according to Clement (44:6). Thus a removal of some of the presbyters is in contravention with the apostolic order. Further, in chapter 45 he gives examples from the Old Testament of persecution of the just. It shows that the righteous never have been cast out (ἀποβεβλεμένοι) by holy men, but by the wicked (ἄνομοι) and unholy (ἀνόσιοι). The righteous, i.e. "those who served God with a holy and faultless purpose" (ἐν ὁσίᾳ καὶ ἀμώμῳ προθέσει δουλεύοντας τῷ θεῷ, 45:7), "were killed by men who had conceived foul and unrighteous envy" (μιαρὸν καὶ ἄδικον ζῆλον, 45:4).[889] In Clement's view, the removal of the presbyters in the Corinthian Church who had served God blamelessly in their ministry is obviously a parallel to the fate of the examples given from the Old Testament. We note also that Clement interprets ζῆλος as an underlying motive for the persecution of the righteous in Old Testament times. Previously we have seen that he takes the view that this vice, together with other vices, has caused the problems in the Corinthian Church. We have also seen that in antiquity ζῆλος belonged to the semantic field of concord.[890]

However, according to Clement, those of the righteous who endured received their wage in that they inherited "glory (δόξα) and honour (τιμή) ... were exalted, and were enrolled by God in his memorial for ever and ever" (45:8).

From our outline of the content of *1 Clem.* 40-45 it is clear that Clement emphasizes the aspect of order and structure. This is also reflected elsewhere in the letter. In 37:2f. soldiers are praised, and serve as an example for community life in the Corinthian Church, because they fulfil their duties in good order (εὐτάκτως) and in their appointed rank (τάγμα, 37:2f.). Previously we have seen that the topic of obedience and submission is significant in *1 Clement*, and that Clement's appeal for obedience to the established leader in order to achieve and maintain concord was a *topos* in the ancient world. His emphasis upon order is of course connected with this subject.

On this basis and with the main task of the present chapter in mind, it is interesting to observe that "good order" was considered to be a significant element in the conception of the ideal *polis*. Dio Chrysostom, for instance, says that the Stoics compare the orderly constitution of the universe to a city, "because of the arrangement and orderliness of its administration" (τὴν τάξιν καὶ τὴν εὐκοσμίαν τῆς διοικήσεως).[891] Immediately following this he says that the true city is "under royal governance in

[889]Clement refers to the fate of Daniel, cf. Dan. 6:16 and of Ananias, Azarias and Misael, cf. Dan 3:19ff., *1 Clem.* 45:6.
[890]See chap. 3.5.1.2.
[891]Dio Chrys. *Or* 36.31.

accordance with law, in complete friendship and concord".[892] Thus it follows that proper arrangement and good order are essential features in a *polis* free from discord. Also, in another discourse he praises the inhabitants of Prusa by presenting elements in their way of living that have contributed to the well-being of the city. Among other things, he says that they are "superior to the other self-governed communities in orderly behaviour" (εὐταξία), in obedience to their leaders, and in temperance (σωφρο-σύνη) in daily living. He also states that they have made the city truly Hellenic, free from discord.[893] Furthermore, in a discourse directed to the citizens of Tarsus, Dio refers to a sizeable group of citizens who are treated as if they do not belong to the con-stitution, and says that some people assert that this group of citizens are "responsible for the tumult (θόρυβος) and disorder (ἀταξία)" in the city. He warns against such behaviour and says that such conditions are harmful to a city, that there is "nothing more conducive to strife (στάσις) and disagreement" (διαφορά).[894] Here it appears that strife (στάσις) and disagreement (διαφορά) designate the same phenomena as Dio above refers to as tumult (θόρυβος) and disorder (ἀταξία). This means that in this passage ἀταξία and στάσις are synonyms.[895]

The close connection between good order and concord is also obvious in a passage of Aelius Aristides when he exalts the goddess Athena:

> *Through her agency, folly, wantonness, cowardice, disorder, faction, crime (ἀταξία καὶ στάσις καὶ ὕβρις), scorn of gods, and all such conduct that one could name is banished, and there enters in its place intelligence, moderation, courage, concord, good order (σωφροσύνη καὶ ἀνδρεία καὶ ὁμόνοια καὶ εὐταξία), success, and honor of the gods and from the gods (Or. 37.27).*

The same author links harmony and order elsewhere. He says that "a well lived life takes place whenever harmony and order prevail throughout. This adornment is truly proper to cities. This preserves both individual man and city" (*Or.* 27.41).

These examples from Dio Chrysostom and Aelius Aristides should suffice to dem-onstrate that good order was connected to the ideal of concord. εὐτάκτως, τάξις, and τάγμα belonged to the semantic field of ὁμόνοια. In spite of the fact that it is not expressed explicitly, it is reasonable to assume that good order was viewed as a precon-dition in order to preserve concord. Good order and concord were interrelated to such a degree that it is difficult to distinguish between them. They could even function as synonyms.[896] Thus, when Clement emphasizes the need for order, particularly the need for order in the religious service, he probably reflects a *topos* related to the ques-tion of concord. Just as good order was essential to the well-being of the city in general,

---

[892]Dio Chrys. *Or.* 36.31f.

[893]Dio Chrys. *Or.* 44.10.

[894]Dio Chrys. *Or.* 34.21f.

[895]Cf. also Dio Chrys. *Or.* 40.35, where he exhorts his audience to see the eternal "order and con-cord and self-control" (τάξιν καὶ ὁμόνοιαν καὶ σωφροσύνην) of the heavens. Although we will not assert that these terms are used as synonyms, the linking of them by means of the conjunction καί indicates that they are interrelated.

particularly with regard to the establishment and maintenance of concord, good order was of the greatest importance for the city of God in order to achieve and maintain concord.[897] Therefore we are of the opinion that the relatively strong emphasis Clement places upon good order must be viewed in the light of the overall purpose of the letter, i.e. to promote peace and harmony. To state it negatively, good order is not an aim in itself, but is rather a means of achieving something else, i.e. concord.

3.6.2.2. Political Terms and topoi in 1 Clement 46:1-48:6

In order to re-establish concord Clement exhorts the Corinthians in 46:1 to cleave to the examples (ὑπόδειγμα) of the righteous mentioned in 45:5-7 and gives additional quotations from authoritative Scriptures to demonstrate the benefit of doing so (46:2-3).[898] In 46:4 he again exhorts them to cleave to those who live according to the will of God, i.e. "the innocent and righteous, for these are God's elect", before he describes the present situation in Corinth by means of three rhetorical questions (46:5-7). From the context it is reasonable to assume that the description of life in the Corinthian Church in 46:5-7 is an expression of "das negative Gegenbeispiel" in 46:2-4.[899] He asks why there are "strife (ἔρις) and passion (θυμός) and divisions (διχοστασία) and schisms (σχίσμα) and war (πόλεμος)" among them. This means that when he explicitly describes the consequence of not cleaving to the righteous and the holy, he emphasizes their lack of concord. Previously in this chapter we have dealt with four of the five substantives he uses here to depict the present state of affairs in the Corinthian Church. We saw that all of them, in particular ἔρις and σχίσμα, were commonly used when one discussed discord in a political body in antiquity. In Clement's cultural milieu they belonged to the semantic field of ὁμόνοια.[900]

Clement goes on to focus on the oneness of God and asks if we do not have "one God, and one Christ, and one Spirit of grace poured out upon us? And is there not one calling in Christ?" (46:6).[901] He obviously attempts to make the Corinthian Christians conscious of the contrast between the fact that there is strife among them and the fact that God is one and that they all share a common calling. This fact must be reflected in the unity of his people. Similar appeals to the oneness of God in order to create and

---

[896]Cf. M. M. MITCHELL, *Paul and the Rhetoric of Reconciliation* (1991) 174f.: "The opposite of κατὰ τάξιν, ἀταξία, is another synonym for στάσις in ancient literature". She quotes Aristid. *Or.* 26.103, and refers to Arist. *Pol.* 2.2.11; 5.2.6; Philo *Jos* 143; 145, Dio Chrys. *Or.* 34.21; Plut. *Mor.* 304 F; Philostr. *VS* 488; App. *BCiv.* 4.12.94.

[897]When discussing how the conception of ὁμόνοια is reflected in *1 Clement*, K. THRAEDE, "Homonoia (Eintracht)", *RAC* 16 (1994) rightly notes that "H.[omonoia] findet man infolgedessen im Sinne von εὐταξία übernommen" (245).

[898]The source of the quotation in 46:2 is not certain. For different suggestions, see D. A. HAGNER, *The Use of the Old and New Testaments in Clement of Rome* (1973) 89-91.

[899]Cf. A. LINDEMANN, *Die Clemensbriefe* (1992) 136.

[900]See chaps. 3.5.1.1.2; 3.5.1.1; 3.5.2.13; 3.5.1.4 respectively.

[901]Regarding the discussion whether the triadic formula is dependent on Eph 4:4-6 or not, see D. A. HAGNER, *The Use of the Old and New Testaments in Clement of Rome* (1973) 223.

maintain unity among Christians were quite common in Early Christianity.[902] With regard to the purpose of the present chapter it is interesting to note that appeals to oneness are also found in Graeco-Roman texts that urge concord.[903]

In the last two rhetorical questions Clement applies the σῶμα metaphor twice in his combate against Corinthian factionalism. First he asks why the Corinthians "divide and tear asunder the members of Christ" (διέλκομεν καὶ διασπῶμεν τὰ μέλη τοῦ Χριστοῦ) (46:7). Here the σῶμα Χριστοῦ is used as a metaphor for the Church. In the continuation of the same question he explicitly refers to the Corinthian Church as a σῶμα when he asks why the Corinthian Christians raise up strife (στασιάζω) against their own body (τὸ σῶμα τὸ ἴδιον) and reach such madness (ἀπόνοια) that they forget that they are members (μέλη) one of another (46:7). In our discussion above we saw that the σῶμα metaphor was commonly applied to a political body in combating factionalism. When μέλη of the same body revolt against each other (στασιάζω) instead of co-operating, it was dangerous for the whole body.[904] In addition to the σῶμα *topos* we have also pointed out that the terms διασπάω and ἀπόνοια occurred when one discussed discord in a political body.[905]

It is interesting to note that when Clement describes the occurrences in the Corinthian Church in his own terms without any allusion to biblical passages as he does in 46:5-7 (except for the triadic formula in 46:5), he places a strong emphasis on political language related to the question of concord. This reveals, in our opinion, the 'heart' of Clement. He is first of all concerned with the topic of concord.

In order to show how cruel the instigators of the sedition's action are, Clement applies the words of Jesus to them. These consist of allusions to different Jesus logia,[906] one of which says that it would be better for a man that a millstone should be hung on him and be cast into the sea than that he should turn aside one of his elect (46:8). According to Clement, it is exactly this which has taken place in the Corinthian Church: "Your schism (σχίσμα) has turned aside many, has cast many into discouragement, many to doubt, all of us to grief; and your sedition (στάσις) continues" (46:9). Here in a manner characteristic of deliberative rhetoric he argues that his addressees are facing a present or impending danger because of their current behaviour. Once again he depicts the present conflict by using two common terms for discord in a political body, i.e. σχίσμα and στάσις which belonged to the semantic field of ὁμόνοια.[907]

---

[902]Eph 4:4-6; 1 Cor 3:16; 6:11; 8:6; 12:4-13; Ign. *Magn.* 7:1-2; and W. R. SCHOEDEL, *Ignatius of Antioch* (1985) 116f.

[903]M. M. MITCHELL, *Paul and the Rhetoric of Reconciliation* (1991) 90 n. 141. She refers to Dio Chrys. *Or.* 41.10; Aristid. *Or.* 23.62; 24.31; Sal. *Rep.* 10.8; Philo *Virt* 35.

[904]Cf. chap. 3.6.1.6.

[905]Regarding διασπάω, see pp. 180f., and regarding ἀπόνοια, see p. 107.

[906]See the detailed discussion in D. A. HAGNER, *The Use of the Old and New Testaments in Clement of Rome* (1973) 152-164.

[907]Regarding σχίσμα, see chap. 3.5.2.13, and regarding στάσις, see chap. 3.5.1.1.1.

Clement goes on to remind the Corinthian Christians of how the apostle Paul combated partisanship (πρόσκλισις) in the Church in his time (*1 Clem.* 47).[908] However, the former πρόσκλισις was not so grave as the present one because they "were partisans of Apostles of high reputation" in contrast to the instigators of the present sedition who have caused a diminishing of their previous love for the brethren (φιλαδελφία, 47:3-6). This indicates that Clement holds that there is a connection between φιλαδελφία and concord. We have previously dealt with the concept of φιλαδελφία in antiquity and concluded that true φιλαδελφία implied concord.[909] Clement continues by stating that it is "extremely shameful" (λίαν αἰσχρά) [910] that the steadfast (βέβαιος) and ancient Church on account of one or two persons should revolt (στασιάζω) against the presbyters (47:6). The adjective βέβαιος was appropriate when one discussed unity and refers here to a time when the Church was free from sedition.[911] Regarding the verb στασιάζω, it should not even be necessary to mention that this was the principal verb used in antiquity when one dealt with the political problem of sedition in a social unit. Clement concludes this chapter by once again using a convention of deliberative rhetoric when he explicitly points to the danger (κίνδυνος) the present state of affairs represents for the Corinthian Church (47:7).[912]

On this basis Clement exhorts the Corinthians to "quickly put an end" to the present state of affairs and to beseech God to restore the "holy and seemly practice of love for the brethren" (φιλαδελφία, 48:1). We observe that he uses the term φιλαδελφία to describe the ideal relationship between the Corinthians that should replace the present schism. One might have expected him to use the terms "concord and peace" instead, but, as we have just stated above, the concept of φιλαδελφία was closely related to concord. To express it more accurately, concord was a precondition for true φιλαδελφία.[913] Furthermore, he gives a reason for his exhortation: The proposed course of action is the gate of righteousness (πύλη δικαιοσύνης, 48:2).[914] This gate is open in Christ. It is characteristic of Clement's aims in the letter that in his next consideration of the πύλη δικαιοσύνης he emphasizes that it is those who enter the gate ἐν ὁσιότητι καὶ δικαιοσύνη and accomplish all things without disorder (ἀταράχως) who are blessed (48:4). All these qualities, particularly righteousness and order, belonged to the semantic field of concord.[915] Although Clement does not state it explicitly, it is likely that the qualities he says a man must possess in what follows are also a precondition for him to be blessed. Among other things he mentions faithfulness

---

[908]For references to πρόσκλισις as a political term depicting discord in a political body, see W. BAUER, *A Greek-English Lexicon of the New Testament* (1979) 716.

[909]Cf. chap. 3.5.2.12.

[910]For the appeal to what is shameful in deliberative rhetoric, see the present study, pp. 40f.

[911]See our discussion, pp. 111f.

[912]Regarding this fundamental appeal in deliberative rhetoric, see chaps. 2.3.1 and 2.3.2.

[913]See chap. 3.5.2.12.

[914]In *1 Clem.* 48:2b-3 the author quotes Ps 117:19f. in which the expression πύλη δικαιοσύνης is to be found.

[915]Regarding δικαιοσύνη, see chap. 3.5.2.16, and regarding εὐτάκτως, see chap. 3.6.2.1.

(πιστός) and the need to be wise in the discernment of arguments. We have argued both that πιστός was associated with concord[916] and also that Clement's focus upon the need to be wise in discernment of arguments is connected with the situation in the Corinthian Church in as much as it appears that the instigators of the sedition were skilled in eloquence.[917] Clement concludes this chapter by pointing out the appropriate behaviour of men who seem to be great, i.e. they must practise ταπεινοφροσύνη and "seek the common good of all" (τὸ κοινωφελὲς πᾶσιν) and not their own benefit (48:6). ταπεινοφροσύνη is a vital topic in the letter and in view of Clement it is a means of overcoming the current strife in the congregation.[918] We have also seen that a characteristic of seditious people was that they sought their own interest and benefit. The ideal leader or politician should instead sacrifice all private wishes in order to do what is the common good for the political body as a whole.[919]

3.6.2.3. ἀγάπη

In chapters 49-55 Clement focuses upon the attitude of ἀγάπη and presents examples of people who acted in loving self-sacrifice to benefit others. To practice love is obviously the proper way to seek the common good. Beside the fact that an attitude of love benefits others, it also unites Christians with God (49:4). Probably inspired by Paul, as an expression of the greatness of love, he introduces an "Encomium to Love" (49:2-6). The similarities to 1 Cor 13:4-7 are evident in both structure and content.[920] We note, however, that Clement explicitly links love with concord, something Paul does not do. Or more precisely, he begins in the negative by saying that love and sedition exclude each other; "love admits no schism, love makes no sedition" (ἀγάπη σχίσμα οὐκ ἔχει, ἀγάπη οὐ στασιάζει), before he states in the positive that "love does all things in concord" (ἀγάπη πάντα ποιεῖ ἐν ὁμονοίᾳ, 49:5). This connection between love and concord or absence of strife is subsequently applied in the principle of love to the Corinthian Church as well. Clement exhorts them to pray that they may be found in love, that is "without human partisanship" (δίχα προκλίσεως ἀνθρωπίνης, 50:2).[921] He says later that the Corinthians are blessed if they perform the commandments of God in the concord of love (ἐν ὁμονοίᾳ ἀγάπης), that through love their sins may be

---

[916]Cf. chap. 3.5.2.4.

[917]See pp. 133-136.

[918]See our discussion, pp. 126-131.

[919]See the present study, pp. 43f.

[920]See the table and discussion in D. A. HAGNER, *The Use of the Old and New Testaments in Clement of Rome* (1973) 200. Hagner concludes that "it cannot be questioned that he is dependent upon Paul". We should note, however, that the phrase ἀγάπη … πάντα μακροθυμεῖ (1 Cor 13:4 = 1 Clem 49:5) is the only accurate parallel between them, also noted by B. E. BOWE, *A Church in Crisis* (1988) 143. H. E. LONA, *Der erste Clemensbrief* (1998) 526f., comments that although Clement is influenced by 1 Cor 13, the author is free in his adaptation of the Pauline tradition. L. SANDERS, *L'Hellénisme de Saint Clément de Rome et le Paulinisme* (1943), has collected Hellenistic parallels to this hymn and argues that Clement is influenced by Pythagorean and Stoic themes (93-108).

[921]For references to πρόσκλισις as a political term depicting discord, see above n. 908.

forgiven (50:5). After drawing this connection between love and the forgiveness of sins, he quotes Ps 32:1f. in order to show the blessings of forgiveness, and on this basis to encourage the Christians to pray that their sins may be forgiven (51:1). Then he goes on to demonstrate that forgiveness depends on repentance and love. When he applies the principle of love to the Corinthian Christians he also states that the leaders of sedition and disagreement (ἀρχηγοὶ στάσεως καὶ διχοστασίας) must consider the common hope (51:1), since "those who live in fear and love (μετὰ φόβου καὶ ἀγάπης πολιτευόμενοι) are willing to suffer torture themselves rather than their neighbours, and they suffer the blame of themselves, rather than that of our tradition of noble and righteous harmony" (δικαίως ὁμοφωνία, 51:2).[922] In other words, if the instigators of the sedition are filled with love, they will have the common good in view and confess their sin so as to contribute to the disappearance of the sedition. Also in this connection Clement uses the appeal to what is good in this argumentation as is characteristic in deliberative rhetoric.[923] With respect to the instigators of the sedition he argues by referring to examples from the Old Testament that it is "better (καλόν) for man to confess his transgressions than to harden his heart" (51:3). Furthermore, after he has presented Moses as an example of great love (53:2-5), he applies the principle of love to the Corinthian Church and once more links love and concord. If a man is noble, passionate, and filled with love (ἀγάπη), he will voluntarily leave the Church if he is the cause of sedition (στάσις), strife (ἔρις), and divisions (σχίσμα). The overall criterion for the behaviour of a man filled with love is that the community should live in peace together with the presbyters set over it (54:1f.). Clement also points to examples of loving self-sacrifice among the gentiles and says, among other things, that many kings and rulers have departed from their own cities in order that sedition (στασιάζω) might have an end (55.1). He does this before turning to examples from the Christian and Jewish tradition of the same thing. Also in the *peroratio* where Clement summarizes the content of the letter, there is a connection between love and unity.[924] He states that he has reminded the Corinthian Christians, among other things, that they ought to live together in love and peace (ἐν ἀγάπη καὶ εἰρήνη, 62:2).

So far we may conclude our discussion of the virtue of ἀγάπη by stating that it plays an important role in *1 Clement* and that Clement holds that the realisation of love will abolish strife and sedition and secure concord in the Corinthian Church. Indeed ἀγάπη is an important term in the New Testament and Clement's use of it must, of course, be viewed against this background. However, his application of this term, i.e. the explicit linking of this term to concord, must be primarily understood in the light of Graeco-Roman and Hellenistic-Jewish literature. We should in particular pay attention to Graeco-Roman literature in as much as in this literature throughout the time

---

[922]For references for ὁμοφωνία used as a political term expressing concord, see H. G. LIDDELL and R. SCOTT, *A Greek-English Lexicon* (1973) 1228.

[923]Cf. chaps. 2.3.1 and 2.3.2.

[924]For the definition and function of the *peroratio* in *1 Clement*, see pp. 226-232.

from Plato to Dio Chrysostom we will find that love is associated with concord.[925] Admittedly we have not found texts where the noun ἀγάπη occurs in such a context, but the verb ἀγαπάω and other terms for love occur (φιλέω, φιλία, and ἔρως).[926] Plato, for instance, writes in *Leg.* 3.678 E:

> *Ath. Moreover, civil strife (στάσις) and war (πόλεμος) also disappeared during that time, and that for many reasons.*
>
> *Clin. How so?*
>
> *Ath. In the first place, owing to their desolate state, they were kindly disposed and friendly towards one another (ἠγάπων καὶ ἐφιλοφρονοῦντο ἀλλήλους) …* [927]

Furthermore, the connection between concord and love is obvious when Plato discusses the main task of a politician:

> *This, then, is the end, let us declare, of the web of the statesman's activity, the direct interweaving of the characters of restrained and courageous men, when the kingly science has drawn them together by friendship and community of sentiment into a common life (ὁμονοίᾳ καὶ φιλίᾳ κοινόν, Pl. Plt. 311 B-C).*

Furthermore, Aristotle's discussion of φιλία in *Nicomachean Ethics* clearly reveals a connection between this term and concord. When he says that "concord (ὁμόνοια) seems to be a friendly feeling (φιλικός)" he links φιλία and ὁμόνοια to such a degree that it is hardly possible to distinguish between them.[928] In addition to a similar explicit connection between φιλία and ὁμόνοια he used the term στάσις as an antonym of these terms earlier in the same work:

---

[925]This is emphasized and demonstrated by M. M. MITCHELL, *Paul and the Rhetoric of Reconciliation* (1991) 165-171. Several of the texts used below have been discussed by Mitchell. Above we said that Clement was probably inspired by Paul to present the hymn of love. However, why he found this hymn appropriate, and not least his adaptation of the hymn to the situation at the Corinthian Church and his explicit linking of love and concord in other parts of the letter must be seen to a great extent in the light of his broader literary milieu.

[926]We must restrict ourselves from entering into a discussion of the frequency and the semantic meaning of these terms. However, regarding the terms ἀγάπη / ἀγαπάω and φιλία / φιλέω we should note that there are scholars who argue against the traditional view of C. Spiq, who emphasizes the uniqueness of this term in the NT both regarding frequency and semantic meaning. They assert that ἀγαπάω was used more frequently than φιλέω already in Graeco-Roman literature and that the terms commonly had the same meaning, cf. the references in M. M. MITCHELL, *Paul and the Rhetoric of Reconciliation* (1991) 165 n. 608. Furthermore, J. P. Low and E. A. NIDA, eds., *Greek -English Lexicon of the New Testament* (1989), subsume these terms under the same semantic field and argues that it would "be quite wrong to assume that φιλέω and φιλία refer only to human love, while ἀγαπάω and ἀγάπη refer to divine love. Both sets of terms are used for the total range of loving relations between people, between people and God, and between God and Jesus Christ" (294).

[927]When Plato deals with the goodess of ἔρως in the *Symposium* he says, among other things, that it "makes peace (εἰρήνη) among men" (197 C). Cf. also 186 E; 187 C where ἔρως and ὁμόνοια are linked with the conjunction καί.

[928]Arist. *Eth. Nic.* 9.6.1.

> Moreover, friendship (φιλία) appears to be the bond of the state; and lawgivers seem
> to set more store by it than they do by justice, for to promote concord, which seems
> akin to friendship (ἡ γὰρ ὁμόνοια ὅμοιόν τι τῇ φιλίᾳ ἔοικεν εἶναι), is their chief
> aim, while faction (στάσις), which is enmity (ἔχθρα), is what they are most anxious
> to banish.[929]

A similar association between concord and love is reflected in Athenaeus' *Deipnosophists* when discussing love (ἔρως), a subject on which "very many philosophical
speeches (λόγος) were given". He reports the following:

> Pontianus said that Zeno of Citium conceived Eros (Ἔρως) to be a god who prepared
> the way for friendship (φιλία) and concord (ὁμόνοια) and even liberty, but nothing
> else. Hence, in his Republic, Zeno has said that Eros is a god who stands ready to help
> in furthering the safety of the State (13.561 C).

That love was associated with concord in Stoic ethics is also reflected in Arius Didymus'
account of it. He defines friendship in terms of harmony and concord. His argumentation is recorded in *Stob.* 2.106.12-17 as follows:

> Moreover they hold the view that every fool is also at enmity with the gods. For enmity
> is lack of harmony with regard to the affairs of life and discord, just as friendship is
> harmony and concord. But the morally bad are in disharmony with the gods with
> regard to the affairs of life. So every fool is at enmity with the gods.[930]

If we leave philosophical considerations, and instead pay attention to actual discourses
which deal with concord in a political body we will see that love/friendship and concord are linked in a similar way. First we turn to a fragment of Philip's speech to his sons
as reported by Polybius.[931] In this speech Philip urges his sons to live in concord. First
he states that when brothers give "way to wrath (ὀργή) and discord (φιλονικία)" it
leads to destruction not only of themselves, but also of their family and their cities. In
contrast to such behaviour he points to brothers who have "studied even in moderation
to love (στέργω) each other". The fruit of love is the preservation of all things.[932] Here
love appears to function as an antonym of "wrath and discord".

In Dio Chrysostom we find a similar clear connection between love and concord.
In one of his discourses on concord, for instance, he prays to the gods that they may
implant "a passionate love (ἔρως), a singleness of purpose (μία γνώμη), a unity of
wish and thought" and cast out the opposite, i.e. "strife (στάσις) and contentiousness

---

[929]Arist. *Eth. Nic.* 8.1.4. Cf. also *Pol.* 2.1.16 and the summary statement of A. MOULAKIS, *Homonoia* (1973): "Die vollkommene *homonoia* wird als die vollkommene *philia* der allumfassenden politi-
chen Gemeinschaft, die höchste und allumfassendste Form der *philia* sein, das harmonische
Zusammenleben von Menschen, die in Eintracht zu ihrem waren selbst – i.e. ihrem *nous* – stehen und
dadurch die noetische Ornung der Seele in der Gesellschaft realisieren" (102). See also K. THRAEDE,
"Homonoia (Eintracht)", *RAC* 16 (1994) 186f.
[930]According to M. SCHOFIELD, *The Stoic Idea of the City* (1991) 47. For further discussion on the
connection between love and concord in Early Stoic tradition, see *ibid.* 46-48.
[931]Polyb. *Hist.* 23.11.1-8.
[932]Polyb. *Hist.* 23.11.2.

(ἔρις) and jealousy" (φιλονικία, *Or.* 39.8). Here ἔρως obviously belongs to a cluster of terms which designate concord in contrast to a cluster of antonyms. And as one of many possible examples of Dio's linking of φιλία and ὁμόνοια we present a passage from the discourse where he urged the Nicomedians to live in concord with the Nicaens. When he gives an outline of the subject he is going to deal with, he makes the following points: first he intends to talk about concord (ὁμόνοια) in general, "and then over against that to set off strife (στάσις) and hatred (ἔχθρα) in contradistinction to friendship (φιλία) ... for when concord (ὁμόνοια) has been proved to be beneficial to all mankind ...".[933] Here concord and friendship are used interchangeably and function almost as synonyms. Also, the close connection between φιλία and ὁμόνοια is evident through the many occurrences of these terms coupled with the conjunction καί in the discourses of Dio.[934]

The same connection is also found in Aelius Aristides' *Or.* 23 when he argues for the advantage of concord by saying that "friendship and concord (φιλία καὶ ὁμόνοια) with one another is naturally the cause of great good for the nation, the leading cities, and each individual city in common, and on the contrary faction (στάσις) the cause of the most extreme evils".[935]

If we observe the writings of Hellenistic Judaism, we will see that in spite of the fact that the linking of love and concord does not occur so frequently in this literature, examples may be found. In Sir 25:1 we read that among the three things mentioned which are lovely in the sight of God and men are the concord of brethren and the friendship of neighbours (ὁμόνοια ἀδελφῶν, καί φιλία τῶν πλησίον). In 4 Macc 13:23-14:3 the love of the seven brothers for one another is referred to as concord:[936]

> The ties of brotherly love, it is clear, are firmly set and never more firmly than among the seven brothers; for having been trained in the same Law and having disciplined themselves in the same virtues, and having been reared together in the life of right-eousness, they love one another all the more (μᾶλλον ἑαυτοὺς ἠγάπων). Their common zeal for beauty and goodness strengthened their goodwill and fellow feeling for one another (ὁμόνοια), and in conjunction with their piety made their brotherly love (φιλαδελφία) more ardent ... O reason, more kingly than kings, more free than free-men! How holy and harmonious the concord (συμφωνία) of the seven brothers for piety's sake!

We have attempted to demonstrate that love and concord were commonly linked with each other in the ancient world. Love is associated to such a degree with concord that in

---

[933]Dio Chrys. *Or.* 38.8.
[934]In discourses on concord: Dio Chrys. *Or.* 38.15; 39.2 (together with peace): 40.36, 37; 41.13, others; 26.8; 34.45; 36.32. Cf. also 4.42.
[935]Aristid. *Or.* 23.53, see also 23.72.
[936]Cf. M. M. MITCHELL, *Paul and the Rhetoric of Reconciliation* (1991) 167. In addition to 4 Macc 13:23-26; 14:3 she cites Ps.-Phoc. *Sent.* 219 where love and concord are coordinated. Mitchell also refers to many texts, both Graeco-Roman and Hellenistic-Jewish, where love and friendship designate political associations and alliances (167 n. 619).

some cases it is not possible to distinguish between the meaning of the terms. This is especially the case in Dio Chrysostom's discourses on concord where the word pair φιλία and ὁμόνοια occur frequently. In the light of this, it is fair to assume that when Clement underlines the need for love in combating sedition and when he explicitly links concord and love, he is using this political *topos*. We stated above that he was probably influenced by 1 Cor 13 where Paul applies this *topos* in a similar way. However, the fact that in contrast to Paul Clement explicitly expresses that "love admits no schism" and "does all things in concord"[937] suggests that he was also familiar with this *topos* from his wider cultural milieu. It appears that he deliberately makes use of both a commonplace in antiquity and of an Early Christian letter which had great authority and was already known to the Christians in Corinth. By using a well-known text of Paul he masterfully combines theological argumentation with a commonplace of the cultural environment. By drawing on *both* these traditions his argumentation becomes more powerful than it would have been if he had used just one of them. This is, in our opinion, an example of Clement's rhetorical skill.

3.6.2.4. Political Terms and topoi in 1 Clement 56:1-61:3

In 56:1 Clement admonishes the Corinthians to pray for those who have fallen into any transgression that they might be given the meekness and humility to submit to the will of God. This implies that one should receive the correction (παιδεία) or the admonition (νουθέτησις) given in the letter (56:2).[938] In conformity with deliberative rhetoric he attempts to persuade the audience to accept his point of view by emphasizing the goodness and usefulness of his admonition (καλή ἐστιν καὶ ὑπεράγαν ὠφέλιμος, 56:2).[939] He also gives the reason why his admonition is good and beneficial – it unites the Corinthians to the will of God. As we have already noted many times, according to him following the will of God would secure concord among the Corinthian Christians.[940]

After Clement has quoted different passages from the Old Testament (56:3-15), which aim to show that God protects those who receive correction (παιδευόμενος) from him (56:16), for the first and only time he explicitly addresses those "who laid the foundation of the sedition" (στάσις, 57:1).[941] He applies what he has stated in the preceding chapter and exhorts them to "submit (ὑποτάσσω) to the presbyters, and receive the correction of repentance" (παιδεύθητε εἰς μετάνοιαν, 57:1). The concrete solution to the sedition in Corinth is, in other words, in line with the correction of God, i.e. submission to the presbyters.

Although the removal of the presbyters is a significant topic in the letter, we shall argue that the topic of office or order is not its principal theme. The principal topic is

---

[937] 1 Clem. 49:5.

[938] νουθέτησις must here depict the sum of all exhortations given in the whole letter.

[939] Cf. chaps. 2.3.1 and 2.3.2.

[940] See the present study, e.g., pp. 156-158; 161f.

[941] For στάσις as a political term belonging to the semantic field of concord, cf. chap. 3.5.1.1.1.

concord. To emphasize this we assert that Clement focuses upon order and office because it is a precondition for concord in the Church.

In 57:2 Clement further underlines the aspect of submission and at the same time warns against vices which are not consistent with a submissive attitude: "Learn to be submissive (μάθετε ὑποτάσσεσθαι), putting aside the boastful (ἀλαζονεία) and the haughty (ὑπερήφανος) self-confidence of your tongue" (57:2). In other words, to submit is not a single act, but a permanent attitude of not boasting and not being haughty. Previously in this investigation we have seen that everything that Clement focuses on here are terms and *topoi* associated in antiquity with concord in a political body.[942] Further, in conformity with deliberative rhetoric he argues that his exhortation is for the benefit of the audience. Concerning the leaders of the sedition he argues that "it is better (ἄμεινον) for you to be found small but honourable in the flock of Christ, than to be pre-eminent in repute but to be cast out from his hope" (57:2). As a proof of the terrible fate of those who do not respond adequately to his exhortation he quotes Prov 1:23-33. Here the most excellent Wisdom says that those who do not pay attention to her counsels will be ruined, but those who are obedient to her words will live in safety (57:3-7). On this basis he exhorts the Corinthians to be obedient (ὑπακούω) to the holy and glorious name of God and thus escape from the threats of Wisdom (58:1).[943] In 58:2 Clement continues to exhort the leaders of the sedition and urges them to "receive our counsel (συμβουλή)". συμβουλή was, as has been pointed out, a technical term for the advice given in deliberative rhetoric.[944] It is fair to assume that Clement uses the term συμβουλή in a similar technical sense. This means that the συμβουλή in 58:2 not only refers to the immediate context, but also includes all the other exhortations or advice given in the letter. In conformity with the γένος συμβουλευτικόν, he again argues that to follow this advice is beneficial for the audience. They will not regret doing so, since all who have "performed the decrees and commandments given by God shall be enrolled and chosen in the number of those who are saved through Jesus Christ" (58:2). However, he does not confine himself to pointing to the benefit of receiving the συμβουλή, but also clearly makes the Corinthians aware of the danger of doing the opposite. He warns that "if some be disobedient to the words which have been spoken by him [Jesus Christ] through us, let them know that they will entangle themselves in transgression and no little danger" (κινδύνῳ οὐ μικρῷ, 59:1).[945] A warning about danger connected to a particular kind of action was, as we have seen before, a hallmark of political rhetoric.[946]

A consequence of not taking notice of the advice given by Clement is that one would be excluded from the number of those who are saved through Jesus Christ

---

[942]ὑποτάσσω, chap. 3.5.2.8; ἀλαζονεία, pp. 131-136; ὑπερήφανος, pp. 168-169.

[943]It is likely that ὀνόματι αὐτοῦ refers to the name of God. See A. LINDEMANN, *Die Clemensbriefe* (1992) 161.

[944]Cf. the present investigation, n. 65.

[945]From the context it seems to be clear that κίνδυνος refers to the eschatological danger, i.e. the danger of not achieving salvation through Christ.

[946]Cf. chaps. 2.3.1 and 2.3.2.

(58:2). On this basis Clement says in 59:2 that he will pray to God that he might save all who belong to his elect. From what he has just said in 58:2 this means that he will pray that the Corinthians, and in particular the instigators of the sedition, will behave consistently with the exhortations or the advice given in the letter. The concrete prayer follows in 59:3-61:3. It is beyond the task of this investigation to enter into the many questions in the research regarding this prayer.[947] We will restrict ourselves to asserting that we hold that it is likely that Clement took his departure in features of the liturgy and partly adapted these to the situation in the Corinthian Church.[948] That he adapted the prayer to a certain degree for his purposes implies that much of its content is relevant to what he considered to be the problem among the Christians at Corinth. Most explicit is the petition that God may give ὁμόνοια and εἰρήνη to them and all who dwell on the earth (60:1:4) and the prayer for εὐστάθεια (firmness).[949]

3.7. Political Terms and topoi Related to Concord in 1 Clement 62:1-65:2 (peroratio and Epistolary Postscript)

After the prayer Clement gives a summary of the letter. He says that he has written sufficiently about the matters which befit worship and which are particularly helpful for a virtuous life for those who wish to live in piety (εὐσεβῶς) and righteousness (δικαίως, 62:1). In 62:2 he explains that he has "touched on every aspect of faith (πίστις) and repentance (μετάνοια) and true love (ἀγάπη) and self-control (ἐγκράτεια) and sobriety (σωφροσύνη) and patience (ὑπομονή)". Previously we have seen that of these virtues, the ones which play the most important roles in the letter, i.e. πίστις, ἀγάπη, and σωφροσύνη, belonged to the semantic field of ὁμόνοια in antiquity.[950] Additionally, Clement states that he has reminded the Christians at Corinth, among other things, that they must please "God with holiness in righteousness" (ἐν δικαιοσύνῃ), that they must live in concord (ὁμονοέω) in love and peace (ἐν ἀγάπῃ καὶ εἰρήνῃ, 62:2). At the risk of repeating ourselves unnecessarily we again mention that these terms were associated with the question of unity in a political body in Clement's cultural milieu.[951] In other words, when he himself offers a *recapitulatio*[952] of the letter he uses several terms which belong to the semantic field of ὁμόνοια.

---

[947]For an introduction to questions considered in the research, cf. A. LINDEMANN, *Die Clemensbriefe* (1992) 162 -176.

[948]So also P. MIKAT, "Zur Fürbitte der Christen für Kaiser und Reich im Gebet des 1. Clemensbriefes", *Festschrift für Ulrich Scheuner* (1973) 455-471; A. LINDEMANN, *Die Clemensbriefe* (1992) 168.

[949]Regarding εὐστάθεια as political term associated with concord, cf. W. C. VAN UNNIK "Studies over de zogenaamde eerste brief van Clemens", *Mededelingen* (1970) 164f.; B. E. BOWE, *A Church in Crisis* (1988), who states that εὐστάθεια is a technical term for political stability and that "this term appears as the opposite of στάσις and, almost as a synonym for 'peace and concord'" (63). For other topics in the prayer associated with concord, see the present study, pp. 272ff.

[950]πίστις, chap. 3.5.2.4; ἀγάπη, chap. 3.6.2.3; and σωφροσύνη, chap. 3.5.2.5.

[951]δικαιοσύνη, chap. 3.5.2.16; ὁμόνοια, chap. 3.4; ἀγάπη, chap. 3.6.2.3; εἰρήνη, chap. 3.4.

[952]For the definition and function of the *recapitulatio* in *1 Clement*, see 226f.

At the end of this chapter Clement expresses confidence that the receivers of the letters have studied τὰ λόγια τῆς παιδείας τοῦ θεοῦ (62:3). Throughout the whole letter he has attempted to demonstrate that his argumentation for concord and peace is in line with the Scriptures. Thus it follows that, if the Corinthians seek to live according to τὰ λόγια τῆς παιδείας τοῦ θεοῦ, they must re-establish concord and peace. In this connection some remarks on the term παιδεία are in place. This noun or the verb παιδεύω are found throughout the letter.[953] Often Clement reflects the LXX's use of the term where it commonly depicts God's correction of the sinner in order to change his mind.[954] However, in 62:3 the term παιδεία has the broader meaning "teaching" or "education", and the expression τὰ λόγια τῆς παιδείας τοῦ θεοῦ depicts "the sum total of all the Logia of the written tradition".[955] Also in 39:1 Clement refers to the instigators of the sedition as ἀπαίδευτοι. This must mean that he views their engagement in strife and sedition as a sign that they do not posses proper παιδεία. In positive terms, it appears that he holds that there is a connection between proper παιδεία and concord. We do not believe that this is an accident. As we have noted previously in this investigation Dio Chrysostom states explicitly that the proper παιδεία of the citizens will effect concord in the city.[956] In the light of the fact that concord was associated with the concept of παιδεία in Greek education, it is not surprising that Clement makes a similar connection.[957] But of course, he transforms the classical concept of παιδεία into a Christian setting. For the citizens of God proper παιδεία is not ultimately based on the classical Greek παιδεία, but on τὰ λόγια τῆς παιδείας τοῦ θεοῦ or the παιδεία in Christ (21:8). In this process of transformation, however, it appears to be clear that Clement takes up and incorporates into the Christian concept of παιδεία an important feature of the classical Greek παιδεία, i.e. the connection between proper παιδεία and concord.[958]

---

[953]The noun; 16:5; 21:6, 8; 35:8; 56:2,16; 62:3; the verb; 21:6; 56:3, 4, 5, 16 (2x); 57:1; 59:3.

[954]E.g., in 16:5 and the seven times it occurs in *1 Clem.* 56.

[955]W. JAEGER, *Early Christianity and Greek Paideia* (1961) 116f. n.15.

[956]See p. 121. That it was a common point of view among the Greeks that they considered proper παιδεία to be a means and even a precondition for concord is also reflected in W. JAEGER, *Early Christianity and Greek Paideia* (1961). Here the author focuses upon how certain Early Christian writings make use of and adapt the classical concept of παιδεία. When W. Jaeger states regarding Clement that "To a man of Greek education the word paideia must have suggested itself most naturally for what he [Clement] was trying to achieve by his letter" (24), he obviously holds that there is a connection between the main task of the letter – to appeal for peace and concord – and the classical concept of paideia. P. STOCKMEIER, "Der Begriff παιδεία bei Klemens von Rom", *StPatr.* 7, part 1, (1966) 401-408, follows W. Jaeger: "Mit Recht ordnet darum W. Jaeger die Anliegen, Friede und Eintracht in der Gemeinde von Korinth wieder herzustellen, der klassischen Paideia zu" (405).

[957]For an extensive introduction to the concept of Greek Paideia, see W. JAEGER, *Paideia: The Ideals of Greek Culture.* 2 vols. (1946-47).

[958]Cf. P. STOCKMEIER, "Der Begriff παιδεία bei Klemens von Rom", *StPatr.* 7. part 1, (1966) 405: "Die Ungebildetheit wird so zum Signum der Aufrührer. Wenn darüber hinaus auch nicht ausdrücklich von Bildung im profanen Sinn die Rede ist, das Paideia-Motiv in seiner umfassenden Bedeutung trägt weithin die Argumentation. Damit erscheint aber der Klemens-Brief als Zeugnis einer Synthese zwischen griechischer Bildung und Christentum".

Symptomatic of the abundant argumentation by use of examples in the letter, in 63:1 he once more appeals to the Corinthian Christians to follow the "so many and so great examples" who "were well-pleasing in their humility towards God ... and toward all man" (62:2). This implies that they are to "bow the neck, and take up the position of obedience" (ὑπακοή) in order to remove the vain sedition (μάταια στάσις) and thus gain the goal (σκοπός) set before them (63:1).[959] Such behaviour is not only consistent with the many great examples, but it will also create happiness among the Romans if the Corinthians "root out the wicked passion" (ὀργή) of their jealousy (ζῆλος) in line with "the entreaty for peace and concord" (περὶ εἰρήνης καὶ ὁμονοίας) he has presented in this letter (63:2). ὀργή is used as a synonym for στάσις.[960] Previously we have seen that Clement considered that ζῆλος is a underlying reason for sedition and that this term belonged to the semantic field of concord in antiquity. We note that Clement again uses the word pair εἰρήνη καὶ ὁμόνοια when he summarizes the topic of the letter.[961] His statement in 63:2 about the joy and gladness the Corinthians will cause among the Romans, if they re-establish concord and peace, functions as an implicit exhortation. This means that the last two exhortations in the letter (60:1-2) explicitly deal with the topic of concord, a fact that is significant regarding the main purpose of the letter. This is also confirmed by the author himself when he writes in 63:4 that "our whole care has been and is directed to your speedy attainment of peace" (εἰρηνεύω).

After the *recapitulatio*, and after he has introduced the representatives from the Roman Church (63:4), together with the exhortations to peace and concord which follow, Clement moves on to a brief prayer for the Corinthian Christians (*1 Clem.* 64).[962] Here he lists different virtues that God may give them.[963] Although these virtues reflect traditional Christian paraenesis, they are also relevant to what he considered to be the seminal problem in the Corinthian Church. This at least is the case regarding πίστις, εἰρήνη, and σωφροσύνη which we have attempted to show belonged to the semantic field of ὁμόνοια.[964]

Before a final blessing and doxology (65:2), Clement says that the Corinthians must quickly send back the Roman messengers so that they could bring the good news that the Corinthian Church again lives in "peace and concord (εἰρήνη καὶ ὁμόνοια) which we pray for and desire" (65:1). If the Corinthians still, contrary to all expectations, have not grasped the main intention of the letter, he uses the very end of the letter

---

[959]For a similar connection between concord and σκοπός, see 19:2. In 63:1 σκοπός primarily refers to eschatological salvation, cf. 6:2; 51:1. However it appears that Clement means that in order to be saved one must abstain from στάσις.

[960]So also A. LINDEMANN, *Die Clemensbriefe* (1992) 178.

[961]For these terms used as political terms urging concord, see the present study, chap. 3.4.

[962]The prayer appears to reflect liturgical language, cf. R. KNOPF, *Die zwei Clemensbriefe* (1920) 136-147; A. LINDEMANN, *Die Clemensbriefe* (1992) 179f.

[963]The catalogue is similar to that one in *1 Clem.* 62:2, but Clement adds φόβος and ἁγνεία.

[964]πίστις, see chap. 3.5.2.4; εἰρήνη, see chap. 3.4; σωφροσύνη, see chap. 3.5.2.5.

to make it clear. The overall aim of the letter is to urge them to re-establish εἰρήνη καὶ ὁμόνοια. This is what the Roman Church prays for and desires.

3.8. Summary

The intention of this chapter has been to point out that political terms and *topoi* occur throughout the whole letter. We have, however, not dealt with political terms and *topoi* in general, but have as a rule confined ourselves to those related to the value of concord which was highly esteemed in antiquity, and we have attempted to show that much of the content of *1 Clement* is related to this concept. Thus it follows that a precondition for discussing a particular term has been that we must have been able to observe its association with the concept of concord in other literature of antiquity apart from *1 Clement*. Therefore, with only a few exceptions, we have not discussed terms in *1 Clement* which are associated with concord in this letter, but are not, as far as we have been able to observe, used in connection with concord elsewhere in the literature of antiquity. In spite of this limitation we have dealt with the majority of terms and the most important ones that belong to "the language of unity and sedition in *1 Clement*". In this task the extant discourses περὶ ὁμονοίας have been of great importance as literature for comparison. At the same time other types of literature which deal with concord in a political body have also been considered.

As a theoretical basis for the investigation we have applied elements of the theory of semantic fields. This theory underlines the need to consider a term or linguistic unit in both its syntagmatic and its paradigmatic relations. A semantic field is, among other things, established by semantic relations of sameness or similarity of meaning and of opposition or incompatibility of meaning between different linguistics units. This means that these relations might be expressed in terms of synonymy, antonymy, and hyponymy. In other words, when we have attempted to point out terms associated with the concept of concord in this third chapter, we have focused upon the semantic field of concord.

A primary reason for taking our departure in the concept ὁμόνοια is the fact that Clement uses this term, together with εἰρήνη, when he gives a specification of the letter at its end: it is as an appeal for ὁμόνοια καὶ εἰρήνη (63:2). As we have seen, ὁμόνοια was regarded as vital for the well-being of different political bodies. It was in particular applied to a city and to relations among different cities. Regarding the phrase ὁμόνοια καὶ εἰρήνη, which occurs five times in *1 Clement*, we have seen that it was commonly used in deliberative rhetoric to advise individuals and groups to cease from sedition and to establish unity instead. This indicates that Clement applied conventional political terms, either consciously or otherwise, when he dealt with the occurrences in the Corinthian Church. On the basis of this assumption we have focused upon several terms in *1 Clement* in order to establish that there is a likelihood that in antiquity these were related to or belonged to the semantic field of ὁμόνοια.

The investigation has aimed to demonstrate that this was the case for many stock terms and conceptions in *1 Clement*. We shall group the terms in the positive and the negative semantic fields of ὁμόνοια, mentioning the terms in each group in the order they are dealt with in the present chapter.

1. Synonyms of the concept of ὁμόνοια:
   εἰρήνη, πίστις, σωφροσύνη, ὑποτάσσω, household duties, εἰρήνη βαθεῖα, ἀδελφότης, κοσμέω, δικαιοσύνη, σῶμα, σύγκρασις, συμπνέω, εὐτάκτως, τάξις, τάγμα, ἀγάπη, παιδεία.

In addition we should mention the ταπεινο-word group. Although this word group primarily reflects a Jewish Christian tradition, we have seen that ταπεινός could designate a virtue in antiquity as well, and of significance with regard to the aim of this chapter, it was linked with other virtues associated with concord.

2. Antonyms of the concept of ὁμόνοια:
   στάσις, ἔρις, ζῆλος, φθόνος, διωγμός, ἀκαταστασία, πόλεμος, αἰχμαλωσία, συμφορά, ἀλαζονεία, σχίσμα, ὑπερηφανία, πλεονεξία.

Beside these synonyms and antonyms we have seen that the following terms were associated with concord:
   ἀνόσιος, ἀπόνοια, βέβαιος, ἀσφαλῆς, δόξα.

In addition to these terms, we have seen that Clement applies *topoi* or common appeals for concord which are found in deliberative rhetoric urging concord or are reflected in other literature that deals with the subject:

1. The appeal using the argument that strife and sedition is a contradiction to the status of being beloved of God in as much as concord is in line with the will of God.

2. The appeal to follow the established law of a society. In *1 Clement* it is the commandments of God that are the established law of the church, the *polis* of God.

3. The appeal to establish and maintain proper relations among the different members of the household.

4. The appeal to imitate the order and harmony of the universe.

5. The appeal to imitate the order and discipline of the army.

6. The appeal to strive for the common good instead of one's own interest.

7. The application of the body metaphor to a political unit, the Church, with an implicit appeal expressing the need for co-operation between different members in order to preserve the whole body. In line with the famous fable of Agrippa the author of *1 Clement* applies the body metaphor to different social

classes and underlines that each individual must contribute with one's particular service to the common good.

8. The application of the commonplace that strife and faction destroy political bodies.

In other words, these appeals or arguments for concord are not a product of Clement's creativity in that they have almost direct parallels in other ancient texts which urge concord in a political body. They are commonplaces which were a part of the reservoir of arguments or *topoi* which was at one's disposal when one wanted to argue for social and political concord in antiquity.

Many of the terms which belong to the semantic field of concord occur frequently and, as is the case for the *topoi* as well, they are spread throughout the entire letter. However, the most concentrated application of terms and *topoi* related to concord occur in *1 Clem.* 1-3 where the author first praises the Corinthian Church for the previous state of affairs as characterised by concord before he moves on to describe the subsequent situation of strife and sedition. This observation is significant insofar as these chapters constitute the *exordium* and the *narratio* of the letter and thereby indicate its main theme.[965] As we have pointed out, it is consistent with this observation that in the passages of the letter where the author argues using his own words and where he applies the many quotations from and allusions to the Old Testament to the Corinthian Church, the frequency of political terms and *topoi* related to concord are comparatively much higher than they are in the other parts of the letter.

The fact that *1 Clement* contains many political terms and *topoi* related to ὁμόνοια suggests that concord is the fundamental theme in the letter. It means that the whole letter ought to be interpreted from this perspective. This conclusion indicates that the basic subject of the letter is of such a nature that it is appropriate for the author to employ the deliberative genre to communicate his message. We may be even more precise. The many terms and *topoi 1 Clement* has in common with extant discourses urging concord indicate that the letter ought to be included in a certain type of deliberative rhetoric, i.e. συμβουλευτικός λόγος περὶ ὁμονοίας. However, as noted in the introductory chapter, there still remains one important step in the process of determining the genre. The compositional analysis must demonstrate that it is likely that concord is the main theme of the letter. In other words, if the compositional analysis shows that the sub-texts on different levels are in one way or another integrated in Clement's argument for concord, this will be the definitive confirmation of the fact that the main topic of the letter is appropriate for deliberative rhetoric and that *1 Clement* is indeed an example of deliberative rhetoric urging concord.

---

[965]Regarding the delimitation and function of these parts of the letter, see the present study, pp. 218-226.

4. Compositional Analysis of 1 Clement

In this chapter we shall examine the compositional structure of *1 Clement*. Its composition has puzzled many scholars. In general there is agreement that the letter contains two main parts besides an introduction and a conclusion,[966] but there is no agreement where the first main part ends and where the second begins. The two most common suggestions are that the second part begins with 37:1[967] or 40:1.[968] The question that has been most puzzling for scholars, however, is what the structure of the first main part is. Linked to that question is that of its relationship to the second main part. It is commonly held that the first part has no leading theme and that much of its content has no relevance to the main purpose of the letter.[969] Thus it follows that it is difficult to discover a direct connection with the second part.[970] As far as we know, G. Brunner is the only scholar who has seriously challenged this common view.[971] He argues that the topic of "Ordnung" (order) is the leading theme and that the two parts have an almost parallel structure in that the different sub-texts correspond to each other.[972] In other words, there are close, discernible links and parallels between the two parts. The parallel structure implies, according to Brunner, that the two parts stand "gleichwertig nebeneinander" and that one can no longer set the concrete treatment of the occur-

---

[966]J. FULLENBACH, *Ecclesiastical Office and the Primacy of Rome* (1980), says that "this opinion is held by almost all scholars" (8).

[967]So A. VON HARNACK, *Einführung in die alte Kirchengeschichte* (1929) 52 n. 1; J. A. KLEIST, *The Epistles of St. Clement of Rome* (1946) 5; K. BIHLMEYER, *Die Apostolischen Väter* (1956) xxvi. There appears to be an error in Bihlmeyer. First he states that the first main part consists of chaps. 4-36. Then it is stated that chaps. 36-61 constitute the second main part. It should probably have been 37-61. Further O. B. KNOCH, *Eigenart und Bedeutung der Eschatologie im theologischen Aufriss des ersten Clemensbriefes* (1964) 39; B. ALTANER-A. STUIBER, *Patrologie* (1966) 45; J. A. FISCHER, *Die Apostolischen Väter* (1966) 4; G. SCHNEIDER, *Clemens von Rom* (1994) 11.

[968]For the view that it begins in 40:1, see R. KNOPF, *Die zwei Clemensbriefe* (1920) 41 (previously, "Der erste Clemensbrief", *TU* 20 (1901) 158, where he was of the opinion that it begins in 39:1); R. M. GRANT and H. H. GRAHAM, *First and Second Clement* (1965) 14; G. BRUNNER, *Die theologische Mitte des ersten Klemensbriefes* (1972) 54; P. VIELHAUER, *Geschichte der urchristlichen Literatur* (1975) 531; E. BAASLAND, "1. Klemensbrev", *De Apostoliske Fedre* (1985) 120; N. HYLDAHL, "Første Klemensbrev", *De Apostoliske Fædre* (1985) 52; A. LINDEMANN, *Die Clemensbriefe* (1992) 14 (Lindemann argues that the first main part ends with 38:4. He views chap. 39 as a transition between the two main parts); O. B. KNOCH, "Im Namen des Petrus und Paulus", *ANRW* 2.27.1 (1993) 13f.; H. E. LONA, *Der erste Clemensbrief* (1998) 26.

rences in Corinth against the general approach taken in the first part.[973] Further, Brunner argues that due to an increasing awareness of the idea that a local Church is part of the universal Church a "one dimensional" approach would not have dealt adequately with the issue. Clement sees the solution to the Corinthian crisis as a "paradigm" for the universal Church. This explains, according to Brunner, why Clement must apply a two

[969]According to W. WREDE, *Untersuchungen zum ersten Klemensbrief* (1891), in several chapters Clement seems to "völlig zu vergessen, was ihn eigentlich zum Schreiben veranlasste; es verschwindet jede durchsichtige Beziehung auf den praktischen Zweck der Briefes" (2). R. KNOPF, "Der erste Clemensbrief", *TU* 20 (1901), asserts that "viele seiner Ausführungen in gar keinen strengen Zusammenhang zu der Veranlassung des Briefes gebracht sind" (160), and complains that after a concrete beginning, Clement introduces topics which do not relate to each other at all (177f.). Knopf explains this absence of thematic unity by suggesting that this section is made up of a number of previously existing homilies (179). W. BAUER, *Rechtgläubigkeit und Ketzerei im ältesten Christentum* (1964), adopts the position of Knopf and holds "dass der Hauptteil des Briefes mit dem von ihm deutlich ausgesprochenen Zweck wenig oder nichts gemein hat" (98). The difficulties in finding a unifying theme in the first main section is also reflected in different overviews of the structure of the letter provided by several scholars in a variety of introductions to and commentaries on the letter. This section is either described in very general terms without any references to a theme, as "allgemeine Ermahnungen", B. ALTANER-A. STUIBER, *Patrologie* (1966) 45; as "The nature of the Christian life", R. M. GRANT and H. H. GRAHAM, *First and Second Clement* (1965) 14; as "Allgemeiner Ausführungen", J. A. FISCHER, *Die Apostolischen Väter* (1966) 4; as "Paränesen", P. VIELHAUER, *Geschichte der urchristlichen Literatur* (1975) 531; as "hvordan den kristne skal leve", N. HYLDAHL, "Første Klemensbrev", *De Apostoliske Fædre* (1985) 52; as "die Hinführung zum Thema", A. LINDEMANN, *Die Clemensbriefe* (1992) 14; or one does not offer any heading for the first section at all, K. BIHLMEYER, *Die Apostolischen Väter* (1956) xxvi; G. SCHNEIDER, *Clemens von Rom* (1994) 10; H. E. LONA, *Der erste Clemensbrief* (1998) 25.

[970]J. FULLENBACH, *Ecclesiastical Office and the Primacy of Rome* (1980) 8, summarizes as follows: "The first part poses a considerable problem for many scholars with regard to its inner structure as well as its relationship to the second part. It seems to be difficult to discover a leading theme in the first part and, consequently, to find a direct connection to the second part".

[971]G. BRUNNER, *Die theologische Mitte des ersten Klemensbriefes* (1972) 46-58. However, without offering a detailed discussion of the structure of the letter, other scholars have also pointed out that there are some corresponding links between the two main parts; K. J. LIANG, *Het Begrip Deemoed in 1 Clemens* (1951) 64-68; O. B. KNOCH, *Eigenart und Bedeutung der Eschatologie im theologischen Aufriss des ersten Clemensbriefes* (1964) 39; E. BAASLAND, "1. Klemensbrev", *De Apostoliske Fedre* (1984) 119f; H. E. LONA, *Der erste Clemensbrief* (1998), argues that in the first part of the letter three thematic units are to be found, and that these units constitute a "gegliedert aufgebauten Gedankengang, der darauf abzielt, die theologische Grundlage für den zweiten Teil des Briefes zu schaffen" (27).

[972] See the figure in G. BRUNNER, *Die theologische Mitte des ersten Klemensbriefes* (1972) 54. Brunner's suggestion is adopted by J. W. WILSON, *The First Epistle of Clement* (1976) 15.

[973]G. BRUNNER, *Die theologische Mitte des ersten Klemensbriefes* (1972) 57: "Wenn jeder der Teile, wie wir herausgearbeitet haben, im anderen Abschnitt für Abschnitt seine Entsprechung findet, dann ist er nicht mehr möglich, entweder den ersten als Vorspann des zweiten, oder den zweiten als Nachwort zum ersten zu verstehen, beide Teile stehen vielmehr von da an gleichwertig nebeneinander. Man kann nicht mehr den konkreten Anlass gegen die weitschweifige Form, die korinthischen Vorfälle gegen die allgemeine Unterweisung ausspielen und dann aus dem einen die klare Absicht des Verfassers ableiten".

dimensional approach.[974] However, he emphasizes that the "Doppelantwort" the letter gives does not have to be understood in terms of the first being a response to the general problem of the universal Church and the second being a response to the concrete situation in Corinth, "sondern dass in jeder der beiden Hälften der Doppelantwort Allgemeines und Besonderes ineinander verschränkt sind".[975] He believes that Clement himself was not concerned with a distinction between a general and a specific part.

In the subsequent compositional analysis of *1 Clement* we shall attempt to demonstrate that contrary to the commonly held view there is a leading theme in the first part that provides a direct connection with the second part. We will argue, however, that the unifying theme is not 'order' as Brunner maintains, but 'concord'. Further, we shall attempt to show by taking tools from ancient rhetoric as our starting point that it is possible to give a more adequate explanation of the structure of the letter than the suggestion provided by Brunner.[976] Lastly, if the compositional analysis shows that concord is the basic theme of the letter, this will be the definitive confirmation of our findings in chapters 2 and 3 that *1 Clement* is in fact deliberative rhetoric urging concord.

4.1. Remarks Regarding the Approach

4.1.1. Dispositio in Ancient Rhetoric

As already indicated above and outlined in the methodological considerations in chapter 1, we shall take tools from ancient rhetoric as our starting point in the process of examining the composition of *1 Clement*. *Dispositio* was the second step in the process of creating a discourse and it aimed at structuring the arguments found under *inventio* in a way that serves the purposes of the orator. Concerning the relation between *inventio* and *dispositio* H. Lausberg comments that "Die *dispositio* ist die notwendige Ergänzung zur *inventio*, die ohne *dispositio* ein beziehungsloser Vorgang wäre".[977] There were discussions among the theorists of ancient rhetoric regarding the number

---

[974]*Ibid.* 58: "Am Fall 'Korinth' ist die Gesamtsituation zum Bewusstsein gekommen. Deshalb muss dieser 'Fall Korinth' nun von der Gesamtsituation von Gemeinde, Kirche, Christentum her beurteilt und damit zum Paradigma, zum 'Besonderen' gemacht werden. ... Die Zweiteilung, durch die ein 'Allgemeines' und ein 'Besonderes' geschaffen wird, signalisiert also eine ganz bestimmte historische Sachlage, nämlich die Notwendigkeit der Unterscheidung von Allgemeinem und Besonderem, von Anwendungsbereich und paradigmatischem Fall, was nur als 'Schaffung' von Gesamtkirche und Einzelgemeinde interpretiert werden kann".

[975]*Ibid.* 58.

[976]Because several important passages in the first part of the letter have no parallels in the second part, the parallel structure between the two main parts is not so obvious as Brunner argues, and therefore his suggestion is not as adequate as he maintains. See the critique in H. E. LONA, *Der erste Clemensbrief* (1998) 27 n. 1.

[977]H. LAUSBERG, *Handbuch der literarischen Rhetorik* (1990) 244. This means that *dispositio* in ancient rhetoric corresponds to *syntagma* in modern text-linguistic, while *inventio* in ancient rhetoric corresponds to *paradigma* in modern text-linguistic, D. HELLHOLM, "Amplificatio in the Macro-Structure of Romans", *Rhetoric and the New Testament* (1993) 126.

of the *partes orationis* with suggestions varying from two to seven.[978] The following five parts are commonly mentioned:

1. *Exordium/principium / προοίμιον*[979]
2. *Narratio/διήγησις*[980]
3. *Propositio/partitio/πρόθεσις*[981]
4. *Probatio/confirmatio/πίστις*[982]
5. *Peroratio/conclusio/ἐπίλογος/epilogus*[983]

The *exordium* functions as an introduction to an oration or a piece of writing. It aims to make the listener or reader attentive, well-disposed and receptive. Often it consists of three parts, of which the order may change:[984]

a. *benevolum parare*: to arouse the goodwill of the audience.
b. *attentum parare*: to arouse the attention of the audience.
c. *docilem parare*: to arouse the receptivity of the audience by means of a short summary of what the orator is going to deal with.

The *narratio* consists of a report of what has been done or is supposed to be done and which is important for the case in question. It should be clear (*perspicua*), short (*brevis*), and credible (*verisimilis*).[985] The *propositio* functions as a transition between the *narratio* and the argumentative text, the *probatio*. It points out the topic of the argumentation, i.e. what the orator intends to demonstrate. "Some definite problem is set for the auditor on which he ought to have his attention fixed ... the matters which we intend to discuss are briefly set forth in a methodical way".[986] As is the case regarding a *narratio*, one of the main features of the *propositio* is its *brevitas* which "is secured when

---

[978]For the discussion, see Quint. *Inst.* 3.9.1-5. Cf. also the table of different suggestions with texts cited by H. LAUSBERG, *Handbuch der literarischen Rhetorik* (1990) 148f.; further H. HOMMEL, "Griechische Rhetorik und Beredsamkeit" (1981) 367-369.

[979]Cic. *Inv. Rhet.* 1.15.20; [*Rhet. Her.*] 1.3.4; 3.9.16; *De Or.* 2.78.315; Arist. *Rh.* 3.13.3; [*Rh. Al.*] 28.1436a.32; Quint. *Inst.* 4.1.1.

[980]Pl. *Phaedr.* 266 D-E; Cic. *Inv. Rhet.* 1.14.19; 1.19.27; *De Or.* 2. 80.326; [*Rhet. Her.*]1.3.4; 3.9.16.

[981]Quint. *Inst.* 3.9.1-2; 4.5.1; Cic. *Inv. Rhet.* 1.14.19; 1.22.31; Arist. *Rh.* 3.13.2.

[982]Quint. *Inst.* 3.9.1; Cic. *Inv. Rhet.* 1.14.19; 1.24.34; *De Or.* 2.81.331; *Part. Or.* 1.4; 7.27; [*Rhet. Her.*] 1.3.4; 3.9.16; Arist. *Rh.* 3.13.4.

[983]Cic. *Part. Or.* 1.4; 8.27; 15.52; Cic. *Inv. Rhet.* 1.14.19; 1.52.98; [*Rhet. Her.*]1.3.4; 2.30.47; 3.9.16; Arist. *Rh.* 3.13.3; 3.19.1; Quint. *Inst.* 3.9.1; 6.1.8.

[984]Arist. *Rh.* 3.14.6f.; [*Rh. Al.*] 29.1436a.33ff.; Cic. *Inv. Rhet.* 1.15.20; *Part. Or.* 8.28; *Top.* 26.97; [*Rhet. Her.*] 1.3.4; Quint. *Inst.* 10.1.48. For more detailed discussions, see Arist. *Rh.* 3.14-15; [*Rh. Al.*] 29.1436a.36-1438a.3; Cic. *Inv. Rhet* 1.15-18; [*Rhet. Her.*] 1.3.4-7.11; Quint. *Inst.* 4.1; and further H. LAUSBERG, *Handbuch der literarischen Rhetorik* (1990) 150-163; J. MARTIN, *Antike Rhetorik* (1974) 60-75; M. FUHRMANN, *Die antike Rhetorik* (1995) 83-86.

[985]Quint. *Inst.* 4.2.31; 4.2.86; Cic. *Inv. Rhet.* 1.19.27; *Part. Or.* 9.31. For more detailed discussions see, Arist. *Rh.* 3.16; [*Rh. Al.*] 30-31.1438a.3-1438b.29; Cic. *Inv. Rhet.* 1.19-21; [*Rhet. Her*] 1.8-9; Quint. *Inst.* 4.2-3; and further H. LAUSBERG, *Handbuch der literarischen Rhetorik* (1990) 163-190; J. MARTIN, *Antike Rhetorik* (1974) 75-89; M. FUHRMANN, *Die antike Rhetorik* (1995) 86-89.

[986]Cic. *Inv. Rhet.* 1.22.31.

no word is used unless necessary. It [*propositio*] is useful in this place because the attention of the auditor should be attracted by the facts and topics of the case, and not by extraneous embellishments of style".[987] The *probatio* constitutes the main bulk of a discourse and contains the argument or proof which should lend credit and support to the case. Theoretically there could be only one proof, but usually a series of different kinds of proofs are combined.[988] The appropriate place for the *peroratio* was a matter for discussion among theorists of ancient rhetoric, but most of them placed it after the *probatio*. It consists first of all of a recapitulation (ἀνακεφαλαίωσις) of the main points of the *probatio*. At this last part of an oration the rhetor is advised to play upon the feelings of the audience in order to arouse emotions for his case and against that of the opposition.[989]

The *dispositio* of the ancient rhetorical handbooks reflects the common structure of a discourse. However, deviation from this conventional scheme, the *ordo naturalis*,[990] could appear when it serves the case of the orator.[991] This reminds us that when one attempts to discover the rhetorical *dispositio* of an ancient writing, one must apply the scheme with care and not force rhetorical structures onto the texts which in fact do not exist. A further important point concerning the present study is that the theoretical considerations on *dispositio* of ancient rhetoric had a judicial setting as their origin. This fact makes it reasonable to assume that features of the conventional *dispositio* are not necessary or useful in epideictic and deliberative rhetoric. Aristotle, for example, confines the *narratio* to judicial rhetoric, and asks how it is possible to use a *peroratio* in epideictic rhetoric. Also, regarding the deliberative genre he argues that *exordium* and

---

[987]Cic. *Inv. Rhet.* 1.22.32. In addition, see Cic. *Inv. Rhet.*1.23; [*Rhet. Her.*] 1.10.17; Quint. *Inst.* 3.9.1-5; 4.4-5. See further H. Lausberg, *Handbuch der literarischen Rhetorik* (1990) 189f.; J. Martin, *Antike Rhetorik* (1974) 91-95; M. Fuhrmann, *Die antike Rhetorik* (1995) 89.

[988] D. Hellholm,"Amplificatio in the Macro-Structure of Romans", *Rhetoric and the New Testament* (1993) 130f. See further Arist. *Rh.* 3.17; [*Rh Al.*] 32-33.1438b.29-1439b.15; Cic. *Inv. Rhet.* 1.24.33-41.77; *Part. Or.* 9.33-14.51; [*Rhet. Her.*] 3. 9-10; Quint. *Inst.* 5.1-14; and further H. Lausberg, *Handbuch der literarischen Rhetorik* (1990) 190-236; J. Martin, *Antike Rhetorik* (1974) 95-137; M. Fuhrmann, *Die antike Rhetorik* (1995) 89-97.

[989]Arist. *Rh.* 3.19; [*Rh. Al.*] 20-21. 1433b.30-1434a.30; Cic. *Inv. Rhet.* 1.52; *Part. Or.* 17.59-60; [*Rhet. Her.*] 2.30.47; Quint. *Inst.* 6.1.1-8; and further H. Lausberg, *Handbuch der literarischen Rhetorik* (1990) 236-240; J. Martin, *Antike Rhetorik* (1974) 147-166; M. Fuhrmann, *Die antike Rhetorik* (1995) 97f.

[990] H. Lausberg, *Handbuch der literarischen Rhetorik* (1990) 245:"So gilt die den Geboten der *ars* entsprechende Abfolge *exordium-argumentatio-peroratio* ... bei manchen Theoretikern als *ordo naturalis* (während die Abweichung von ihr als *ordo artificiosus* bezeichnet wird)".

[991]H. Lausberg, *Handbuch der literarischen Rhetorik* (1990) 247: "Der *ordo artificialis* oder *ordo artificiosus*... besteht in der durch die Rücksicht auf die *utilitas* bedingten ... absichtlichen ('kunstvollen') Abweichung vom *ordo naturalis*, die dem *ordo naturalis* bei Vorliegen besonderer Umstände ... vorgezogen wird"; J. Martin, *Antike Rhetorik* (1974) 218: "Die Umkehrung des *ordo naturalis* zum *ordo artificiosus* geschieht, wenn es notwendig oder nützlich ist, auf mancherlei Art, am sinnfälligsten in der geänderten τάξις der Redeteile. Das Proömium z.B. kann unterbleiben, wenn eine seiner drei Aufgaben nicht erfüllt zu werden braucht".

peroratio "are only admissible when there is a conflict of opinion".[992] In other words, when one attempts to identify the *dispositio* in actual deliberative and epideictic letters and discourses, one cannot expect to find all the features of *ordo naturalis*. In fact, if one asserts that all the features are to be found in an ancient letter or discourse, this could indicate that the actual text belongs to *genus judiciale*.

4.1.2. Tools from the Status Theory of Ancient Rhetoric and Text-Linguistics

In spite of the considerations on *dispositio* which are found in the ancient rhetorical handbooks, this is the part of the rhetorical system which was most neglected by the theorists. An explanation of this circumstance appears to be that the *inventio* already offered certain principles for structuring a discourse.[993] What we should note in this connection is that, due to the rather superficial treatment of the *dispositio*, it deals mainly with the macro-structure on one level.[994] To use the words of D. Hellholm:

> ... the rhetorical *dispositio* remained one-dimensional, that is, the text could be delimited on one level only by the applicable rules; no hierarchical text-delimitation was provided for by the ancient theoreticians. This means that if one wants to employ a hierarchical multi-level delimitation of texts, one has to go beyond the *dispositio* of ancient rhetoric ...[995]

---

[992] Arist. *Rh.* 3.13.3. According to Aristotle only two parts are necessary, i.e. the πρόθεσις and the πίστεις (*Rh.* 3.13.1); and further J. MARTIN, *Antike Rhetorik* (1974) 79: "Wie beim Proömium ist auch bei der *narratio* die Frage heftig umstritten worden, ob sie an einem bestimmten Platz für alle Fälle festgebannt und ob sie überhaupt notwendig ist und nicht unterbleiben kann. Für die meisten epideiktischen Reden hat nun Aristoteles [*Rhet.* III.13.1414a 37f.; 16.1416b 26f.; 1417b 12ff] schon festgehalten, dass sie keine *narratio* benötigen, weil die Tatsachen als bekannt vorausgesetzt und nur kurz angedeutet werden müssen. Ferner hat die διήγησις nur in der Gerichtsrede ihren Platz und ist auch da in der Rede des Verteidigers geringer als in der des Klägers ...".

[993] D. HELLHOLM, "Amplificatio in the Macro-Structure of Romans", *Rhetoric and the New Testament* (1993) 126, who refers to H. F. PLETT, *Einführung in die rhetorische Textanalyse* (1975) 16 and M. FUHRMANN, *Die antike Rhetorik* (1984) 78.

[994] We said "mainly" because a few additional considerations on the structuring of the *probatio* section are to be found. In the chapter dealing with the *dispositio* within the *probatio*-section Aristotle discusses the strategic order of the *confirmatio* and the *refutatio* respectively: "In both deliberative and forensic rhetoric he who speaks first should state his own proofs and afterwards meet the arguments of the opponent, refuting or pulling them to pieces beforehand. But if the opposition is varied, these arguments should be dealt with first, as Callistratus did in the Messenian assembly; in fact, it was only after he had first refuted what his opponents were likely to say that he put forward his own proofs. He who replies should first state the arguments against the opponent's speech, refuting and answering it by syllogism, especially if his arguments have met with approval" (Arist, *Rh.* 3.17.14-15). Hermogenes reports that some rhetoricians "put the counter proposition (*antithesis*) before its refutation (*lysis*)", and regarding Demosthenes he states that he varies the order according to what he regarded to be "most beneficial to his own point of view" (Hermog. *Id.* 238). However, as Hellholm rightly notes, before he cites the above mentioned examples of the discussion regarding the syntagmatic position of sub-texts in a *probatio* "one has to be aware that they [*confirmatio* and *refutatio*] were treated foremost paradigmatically as can be seen in the modern handbooks, where these concepts mostly are found in the sections addressing the *inventio*", D. HELLHOLM, "Amplificatio in the Macro-Structure of Romans", *Rhetoric and the New Testament* (1993) 134.

We agree with Hellholm, if we add that the *dispositio* offers no further discussion from a syntagmatic point of view. However, from a paradigmatic point of view the delibera-tions on what features constitute an *exordium* provide tools for a further delimitation of the *exordium*.[996] An indication of the need to go beyond the *dispositio* of ancient rheto-ric is the fact that major scholars who apply the *dispostio* of ancient rhetoric to New Tes-tament scriptures make almost no reference at all to rhetoric when it comes to delimiting the *probatio* section into further sub-texts or proofs.[997] This, however, does not mean that the area of ancient rhetoric does not provide us with additional, relevant tools. The status theory developed by Hermagoras of Temnos[998] and consolidated by later theorists of ancient rhetoric, above all by Hermogenes of Tarsos,[999] contains addi-tional, relevant material regarding the structuring of the *probatio*.[1000] In this theory one differentiates between two levels of treating a question: (1) θέσις/*quaestio infinita* or *quaestio generalis* which involves an abstract, theoretical, general approach to a ques-tion;[1001] and (2) ὑπόθεσις/*quaestio finita* or *quaestio particularis* which gives a con-crete, non-theoretical, practical treatment of a question. In other words, "*Definite* questions involve facts, persons, time and the like".[1002] Cicero was of the opinion that *quaestio infinita* in fact was a part of the area of philosophy, rather than rhetoric. From a logical point of view, however, one must first discuss a question theoretically and in principle before one moves on to a concrete question under discussion.[1003] This is in

---

[995]*Ibid.* 129.

[996]That also Hellholm from a paradigmatic point of view holds the considerations on the *exor-dium* to be useful in delimiting sub-texts on grade two seems to be evident. Later on he states that the three parts of the *exordium* "are from a paradigmatic point of view entirely *langue*-determined, from a syntagmatic point of view they are so only to some extent", D. HELLHOLM, "Amplificatio in the Macro-Structure of Romans", *Rhetoric and the New Testament* (1993) 129.

[997]E.g., H. D. BETZ, "The Literary Composition and Function of Paul's Letter to the Galatians", *NTS* 21 (1975) 353-379; *idem, Galatians* (1979); G. A. KENNEDY, *New Testament Interpretation through Rhetorical Criticism* (1984); D. F. WATSON, *Invention, Arrangement and Style* (1988); M. M. MITCHELL, *Paul and the Rhetoric of Reconciliation* (1991).

[998]G. A. KENNEDY, *The Art of Persuasion in Greece* (1963) 303-321; *idem, Greek Rhetoric under Christian Emperors* (1983) 76-86; R. NADEAU, ed., "Hermogenes' On Stases", *Speech Monographes* 31 (1964) 373-381.

[999]R. NADEAU, "Hermogenes' On Stases", *Speech Monographes* 31 (1964) 382-424; G. A. KENNEDY, *The Art of Rhetoric in the Roman World 300 B.C.-A.D. 30* (1972) 619-633; *idem, Greek Rhet-oric under Christian Emperors* (1983) 76-86.

[1000]For the *stasis* or status theory in general, see J. MARTIN, *Antike Rhetorik* (1974) 28-52; H. LAUSBERG, *Handbuch der literarischen Rhetorik* (1990) 61-85; M. FUHRMANN, *Die Antike Rhetorik* (1995) 99-113.

[1001]Cf., e.g., Quint. *Inst.* 3.5.5: "*Indefinite* questions are those which may be maintained or impugned without reference to persons, time or place and the like"; see further J. MARTIN, *Antike Rhe-torik* (1974) 15-18; H. LAUSBERG, *Handbuch der literarischen Rhetorik* (1990) 61-63; M. FUHRMANN, *Die antike Rhetorik* (1995) 99f.

[1002]Quint. *Inst.* 3.5.7. See further J. MARTIN, *Antike Rhetorik* (1974) 15-18; H. LAUSBERG, *Hand-buch der literarischen Rhetorik* (1990) 63f.

[1003]H. LAUSBERG, *Handbuch der literarischen Rhetorik* (1990) 62; D. HELLHOLM, "Amplificatio in the Macro-Structure of Romans", *Rhetoric and the New Testament* (1993) 132.

line with Quintilian who argues that "it is from the *indefinite* question that the *definite* is derived"[1004] and "we cannot arrive at any conclusion on the special point until we have first discussed the general question".[1005]

As already indicated, these two approaches to a question are not a part of the syntagmatic *dispositio*, but of the basically paradigmatic status doctrine of the *inventio*. This implies that from a syntagmatic point of view the status theory does not offer any rules for how the *quaestio infinita* and the *quaestio generalis* are sequentially arranged. However, in the light of the opinion of Quintilian just referred to it is logical that "als amplifikatorischer Hintergrund und als Argumentations-Stütze werden den *quaestiones finitae* gerne *quaestiones infinitae* vorgeschaltet".[1006] In the following compositional analysis of *1 Clement* we will attempt to show that the *probatio* section can be delimited into a θέσις with a following ὑπόθεσις.

We cannot, however, leave the analyses of the *probatio* section at this low text level. In order to get a more accurate understanding of the argumentative structure of the text we must go further and delimit the θέσις and ὑπόθεσις into their respective sub-texts. D. Hellholm argues that according to the levels of complexity in an argumentation one must differentiate

> ... between at least (a) the micro-structural level of individual propositions and speech-acts – that is, the individual proof as such; (b) the intermediate level of groupings of propositions and speech-acts – that is, the functional integration of themes and illocutions created by the cluster of proofs with regard to a specific thesis; and (c) the macro-structural level of a hierarchical conjunction of arguments – that is, the functional integration of the intermediate themes and speech-acts into the global argumentation with regard to the overarching thesis of the given text.[1007]

The problem is that neither the *dispositio* of ancient rhetoric nor the status theory provides any tools from a syntagmatic point of view in delimiting the θέσις and ὑπόθεσις into further sub-texts.[1008] This means that one must go beyond the theory of ancient rhetoric when one seeks for analytical tools in the further process of delimiting the *probatio* section. In this connection we shall apply some insights from the field of linguistics. More precisely, we will take as our starting point the method D. Hellholm

---

[1004]Quint. *Inst.* 3.5.8.

[1005]Quint. *Inst.* 3.5.13. Additionally, Quintilian shows that Cicero in later works presuppose that *quaestio infinita* belongs to the domain of the rhetoric as well (*Inst.* 3.5.15).

[1006]H. LAUSBERG, *Handbuch der literarischen Rhetorik* (1990) 64; D. HELLHOLM, "Amplificatio in the Macro-Structure of Romans", *Rhetoric and the New Testament* (1993) 133.

[1007]D. HELLHOLM, "Enthymemic Argumentation in Paul", *Paul in His Hellenistic Context* (1995) 122.

[1008]We have already mentioned that the *dispositio* of ancient rhetoric operated with a delimitation of the *probatio* in sequential sections of a *confirmatio* and a *refutatio* respectively (see n. 994 above). But since Clement does not arrange his proofs in such sections, these considerations in the *dispositio* do not offer a suitable tool for the present study.

has applied in a number of works.[1009] To a great extent he builds upon and further develops the linguistic text analysis of E. Gülich, W. Raible, and K. Heger.[1010]

The approach provided by Hellholm takes the linear text-structure as a starting point, beginning with the text as a whole, and continues by delimiting the text into sub-texts on higher levels. Such a delimitation of a text should ideally proceed until one ends up with the smallest syntagmata. In other words this "analysis represents a syntagmatic approach proceeding in a descending manner from the larger to the smaller units".[1011]

It is neither fruitful nor necessary to reiterate Hellholm's detailed considerations. We will, however, present a primary feature in his approach, i.e. the need to pay attention to markers or signals on the surface level of a text in the process of delimiting it into its functional text-sequences or sub-texts on different levels. This is due to the fact that the receiver of a text is not provided with a macro-structure, but must construct a structure from indications in the text itself. In this process of making the structure explicit the reader or listener is assisted by certain signals or delimitation markers on the surface level of the text. We confine ourselves to mentioning those which are relevant to the present work.[1012]

1. *Substitution on meta-level (SM)*: A *substitution on meta-level* functions macrosyntagmatically to delimit text-sequences of the macrostructure of a text. These substitutions are often manifestations of various generic concepts such as 'narrative', 'gospel', 'apocalypse', etc., "or of whole texts or their subordinate text-sequences in terms of external features of organization (e.g., chapter, section, etc.) or in terms of content-related features (e.g., vision, instruction, comparison, etc.)".[1013] In other words, a meta-communicative part of a sentence, noun or verb serves as substitution[1014] for a text or a text sequence. They occur at the beginning or at the end of the text-sequence they delimit. Besides having the function of delimiting the texts into text sequences on the surface-level, a

---

[1009]D. HELLHOLM, *Das Visionenbuch des Hermas als Apokalypse* (1980); *idem*, "The Problem of Apocalyptic Genre and the Apocalypse of John", *Semeia* 36 (1986) 13-64; *idem*, "Enthymemic Argumentation in Paul", *Paul in His Hellenistic Context* (1995) 119-179; *idem*, "Substitutionelle Gliederungsmerkmale und die Komposition des Matthäusevageliums", *Texts and Contexts* (1995) 11-76; and the already mentioned article "Amplificatio in the Macro-Structure of Romans", *Rhetoric and the New Testament* (1993) 123-151.

[1010]For the titles of their works, see the bibliography in D. HELLHOLM, *Das Visionenbuch des Hermas als Apokalypse* (1980); *idem*, "The Problem of Apocalyptic Genre and the Apocalypse of John", *Semeia* 36 (1986) 13-64.

[1011]D. HELLHOLM, "Amplificatio in the Macro-Structure of Romans", *Rhetoric and the New Testament* (1993) 131.

[1012]For different type of markers and their function, cf. D. HELLHOLM, *Das Visionenbuch des Hermas als Apokalypse* (1980) 77-95; *idem*, "The Problem of Apocalyptic Genre and the Apocalypse of John" *Semeia* 36 (1986) 38-42; *idem*, "Substitutionelle Gliederungsmerkmale und die Komposition des Matthäusevangeliums", *Texts and Contexts* (1995) 17-32; *idem*, "Enthymemic Argumentation in Paul", *Paul in His Hellenistic Context* (1995) 124f. See also B. C. JOHANSON, *To all the Brethren* (1987) 24-33.

substitution on meta-level also "informs the receiver of the function of the text".[1015]

2. *Substitution on abstraction-level (SA)*: When an author refers to or reiterates the content of textual units, e.g., clauses, sentences or larger text sequences, by means of abstract nouns, pronouns and/or verbs he makes use of this kind of substitution. For example, when one draws the conclusion after an argumentation sequence by stating that "this proof ...", the pronoun "this" functions as a substitution for the foregoing argumentative section.[1016] To give an example from *1 Clement*, the expression προδήλων οὖν ἡμῖν ὄντων τούτων in 40:1 refers to the foregoing and is thus a SA. A distinguishing feature of this kind of substitution is that it "involves substituting expressions that have a wider range of meaning in relation to that which they substitute",[1017] but it cannot stand on a pure meta-level in relation to a substituted textual unity.[1018] From what we have said about the SA it follows that its function as a delimitation marker is to indicate the end of a passage.

3. *Sentence and text connectors: Adverbs and conjunctions*: This group of markers links together clauses or text-sequences. The most common are οὖν, δέ, καί, ἀλλά and γάρ. With respect to *1 Clement* the inferential conjunction οὖν occurs often and is thus the most important. Adverbs and conjunctions function on their own as delimitation markers of clauses and text-sequences on a

---

[1013]B. C. JOHANSON, *To all the Brethren* (1987) 27; D. HELLHOLM, "Substitutionelle Gliederungsmerkmale und die Komposition des Matthäusevageliums", *Texts and Contexts* (1995), by referring to E. Gülich and W. Raible says: "'Wird nun bei einer Substitution ein Text als Ganzes oder werden Teile des Textes als Bestandteil eines Kommunikationsprozesses bezeichnet', so sprechen wir mit E. Gülich und W. Raible von 'Substitution *auf Metaebene*'. 'Hierbei werden metakommunikative Nomina, gegebenenfalls in Verbindung mit metakommunikativen Verben ... verwendet, beispielsweise dann, wenn ein Text oder Teiltext als 'Rede' oder 'Erzählung' bezeichnet wird'" (25).

[1014]D. HELLHOLM, *Das Visionenbuch des Hermas als Apokalypse* (1980), quotes the founder of the "substitutionalen Textlinguistik" R. Harweg's definition of substitution: "'die Ersetzung eines sprachlichen Ausdrucks durch einen bestimmten anderen sprachlichen Ausdruck. Der erstere dieser beiden Ausdrücke, der ersetzte oder zu ersetzende, heisst *Substituendum*, der letztere, der ersetzende, *Substituens*'" (84).

[1015]D. HELLHOLM, "The Problem of Apocalyptic Genre and the Apocalypse of John" *Semeia* 36 (1986) 39.

[1016]D. HELLHOLM quotes Gülich and Raible: "'Eine solche Substitution auf Abstraktionsebene läge z.B. vor, wenn eine grössere Anzahl von Sätzen oder Textabschnitten zusammengefasst würde durch «*Diese Ereignisse* veranlassten X usw»'" ("Substitutionelle Gliederungsmerkmale und die Komposition des Matthäusevageliums", *Texts and Contexts* (1995) 31).

[1017]B. C. JOHANSON, *To all the Brethren* (1987) 27.

[1018]A *SA* "ist ein Typ von Wiederaufnahme gemeint, 'bei welcher das Substituens einen grösseren Bedeutungsumfang hat als das Substituendum' [quotation of Gülich/Raible], allerdings ohne auf einer reinen Metaebene im Verhältnis zum ersetzten Textabschnitt zu stehen" (D. Hellholm, "Substitutionelle Gliederungsmerkmale und die Komposition des Matthäusevageliums", *Texts and Contexts* (1995) 31).

higher level, but often occur together with other delimitation markers on lower levels.[1019]

4. *Semantic Markers (SemM):* Theme-indicating words, clauses or sentences may function as markers for text sequences. These markers could therefore be called semantic markers. A SemM "may be seen as governing a text-sequence thematically in so far as the propositions of that text-sequence 'satisfy' it directly or indirectly".[1020] It usually occurs at the beginning of the text-sequence it governs, but it could also occur medially or finally.[1021] This type of marker plays a limited role in the works of D. Hellholm, and he does not discuss it in his methodological considerations. The reason for this appears to be that he, in line with Gülich and Raible, stresses the importance of paying sufficient attention to the surface-level of the text in the process of delimiting it into text-sequences. Further, we note that the linguistic theory Hellholm depends on takes narrative texts as a starting point. The object of the present study is not, however, a narrative text, but an argumentative one. Although it is of great importance to identify the markers on the surface-level of *1 Clement*, we cannot expect to find so many markers of this type in letters as in narrative texts. Therefore, we must to a rather large extent rely on SemM in the compositional analysis of *1 Clement*. We shall see that text-sequences on different levels are marked out by theme-indicating words, clauses or sentences. Often a SemM occurs together with Sentence and text connectors.

5. *Direct address (Da), in particular the vocative ἀδελφοί:* In relation to the markers Hellholm operates with, it seems useful to add direct address (Da) as an indicator. Clement frequently addresses his audience directly, and the vocative ἀδελφοί in particular occurs frequently. Da could have many functions, but in this connection we should note that it often, although not always, indicates a transition in the text.[1022] Standing alone, this marker is in use on a high level, but in combination with other markers it is in use on low levels as well.

4.1.3. Limitations Regarding the Present Study

From what we have just said it follows that we will combine tools from ancient rhetoric and modern linguistics in working out the compositional analysis of *1 Clement*. Insofar as we take ancient rhetoric as our starting-point we will draw upon this to the extent that it offers relevant tools. In the process of delimiting the text into smaller units not addressed by ancient rhetoric we shall rely on tools from modern linguistics. According

---

[1019] Cf. D. HELLHOLM, *Das Visionenbuch der Hermas als Apokalypse* (1980) 95.

[1020] B. C. JOHANSON, *To all the Brethren* (1987) 29, who refers to the linguistic scholar T. A. van Dijk.

[1021] B. C. JOHANSON, *To all the Brethren* (1987) 29, who refers to a work of J. P. Louw.

[1022] J. L. WHITE, *The Form and Function of the Body of the Greek Letter* (1972) 29.

to what we have noted regarding the *dispositio* and the *status* theory of ancient rhetoric and the text-linguistic method employed by Hellholm, a compositional analysis of *1 Clement* should proceed with the following steps:

1. Distinguish between the different sub-texts on grade one, that is the prescript and the postscript on the one hand, and the body of the letter on the other.

2. Delimit these sub-texts on grade one into sub-texts on grade two. Here we shall use the *dispositio* of ancient rhetoric as a means of delimiting the body of the letter – that is the middle sub-text on grade one.[1023]

3. Delimit the sub-texts on grade two into sub-texts on grade three. At this level the *dispositio* of ancient rhetoric does not provide any help with respect to *1 Clement*. Regarding the *probatio* section the distinction between θέσις and ὑπόθεσις of the mainly paradigmatic status theory is relevant.

4. Continue the process of decoding the letter until we end up with the smallest syntagma. To the extent that the system of ancient rhetoric does not offer any relevant tools at these levels, we must rely on tools from modern linguistics.

A compositional analysis of *1 Clement* following these steps would have been a full scale analysis. Although this may have been preferable, such an analysis does not fall within the scope of the present study. We must in this connection confine ourselves to what is necessary in order to grasp the essential argumentative structure of the letter, particularly in the *probatio* section. This means that as a rule we will not delimit the text further than what D. Hellholm called the "intermediate level" above, i.e. "the functional integration of themes and illocutions created by a cluster of proofs with regard to a specific thesis". How many levels of sub-text we must operate with in order to do this will vary depending on the levels of complexity in the argumentation. Concerning the other sub-texts on grade one, *exordium, narratio* and *peroratio*, we confine ourselves to grade 2 or 3. This is sufficient in order to discover what we described above as "the essential argumentative structure" for these parts. Furthermore, the *dispositio* of ancient rhetoric provides relevant tools for these levels.

4.2. Compositional Analysis of 1 Clement

4.2.1. Sub-Texts on Grade One

1 Clement is quite clearly a letter because it contains the appropriate parts of the Greek letter: epistolary prescript (prescript), a corpus, (1:1-64:1) and a postscript, (65:1-

---

[1023]This is in line with our discussion in chap. 1.3 where we emphasized that we will confine ourselves to using tools from ancient rhetoric in this investigation as far as such tools are provided. The reason for going beyond ancient rhetoric and for using tools from modern text linguistics in the task of delimiting sub-texts on higher levels is noted above.

2).[1024] Taking as our starting point the literary frame of a letter, these three parts constitute the sub-texts on grade one: (1ST1) epistolary prescript, (1ST2) letter corpus, 1:1-64:1, (1ST3) epistolary postscript, 65:1-2.[1025]

In the epistolary prescript (1ST1) we find conventional features of ancient epistolography: the name of the sender, *superscript* (1ST11), the name of the addresses, *adscript* (1ST12), and salutation, *salution* (1ST13). The letter is from "the Church of God which sojourns in Rome to the Church of God (τῇ ἐκκλησίᾳ τοῦ θεοῦ) which sojourns in Corinth".[1026] We note that in spite of the sedition in the Corinthian Church, Clement uses the singular ἐκκλησία. This use already indicates Clement's intention to call them to unity. According to him, the Corinthians are one church. As we shall show below, in the letter corpus he exhorts the Corinthians to behave in a manner that manifests this oneness.

In the epistolary postscript, 65:1-2 (1ST3), before a final blessing and doxology,[1027] Clement instructs the Corinthians to send the Roman messengers back "in peace" in order to inform the Roman Christians about the re-established "peace and concord" (εἰρήνην καὶ ὁμόνοιαν) of the Corinthian Church.[1028] This means that at the very end of the letter in the epistolary postscript Clement reveals what we consider to be the main purpose of the letter, i.e. to urge the Corinthians to live in concord. In other words, both the epistolary prescript (1ST1) and the epistolary postscript in particular, 65:1-2 (1ST3), function as a part of Clement's strategy in his appeal for concord.

We have seen that Clement applies deliberative arguments in the remaining sub-text on grade one, the letter corpus, 1:1-64:1 (1ST2). This fact makes it reasonable to

---

[1024]On Greek epistolography, see J. SCHNEIDER, "Brief", *RAC* 2 (1954) 563-585; H. KOSKENNIEMI, *Studien zur Idee und Phraseologie des griechischen Briefes bis 400 n. Chr.* (1956); W. G. DOTY, "The Classification of Epistolary Literature", *CBQ* 31 (1969) 183-199; *idem, Letters in Primitive Christianity* (1973); J. L. WHITE, *The Form and Function of the Body of the Greek Letter* (1972); *idem, Light from Ancient Letters* (1986); F. J. EXLER, *The Form of the Ancient Greek Letter of the Epistolary Papyri* (1976); S. K. STOWERS, *Letter Writing in Greco-Roman Antiquity* (1986); D. E. AUNE, *The New Testament in its Literary Environment* (1987) 158-174; M. L. STIREWALT, *Studies in Ancient Greek Epistolography* (1993).

[1025]ST stands for Sub-Text.

[1026]Regarding the prescript see E. PETERSON, "Das Praescriptum des 1. Clemens-Briefes", *Pro regno, pro sanctuario* (1950) 351-357; A. LINDEMANN, *Die Clemensbriefe* (1992) 25. We agree with Lindemann when he states that Peterson's suggestion that *1 Clement* is a "catholic epistle" "ist freilich unbegründet, da der Brief sehr konkret auf die besonderen korinthischen Probleme Bezug nimmt" (25).

[1027]For similar wishes for grace in some of the Pauline epistles, see the discussion in A. LINDEMANN, *Die Clemensbriefe* (1992) 181.

[1028]For a study of the literary structure and *topoi* and the social conventions related to envoys in the New Testament, see M. M. MITCHELL, "New Testament Envoys", *JBL* 111 (1992) 641-662. Mitchell notes the similarities between 1 Thess 3; 2 Cor 7; 3 John 3-4; Acts 15; and *1 Clem* 65, cf. 656.

analyse the middle part of the letter in regard to the *dispositio* of ancient rhetoric when we go on to delimit it into further sub-texts.[1029]

4.2.2. Sub-Texts on Grade Two

When we delimit the sub-texts on grade two we must in some cases go on to grade three, at least with respect to the *exordium* and *peroratio*, because the sub-texts on grade two are constituted by sub-texts on grade three. Those parts of the text which make up grade three will be pointed out.

2ST21 Exordium, 1:1-2:8

As already noted, the *exordium* was the first part of the *dispositio* of ancient rhetoric. It was not compulsory in deliberative rhetoric, especially in cases where the audience had requested deliberation and when it was prepared for the discourse.[1030] However, if the audience in the view of the orator did not consider the actual situation, which was the point of departure for the oration, seriously enough or if it paid too little attention to the actual circumstances, an *exordium* was useful to prepare it for the deliberation.[1031] This seems to be the case regarding *1 Clement*, and as we will attempt to show, *1 Clem.* 1-2 contains the main characteristics of an *exordium*. The many appeals throughout the letter to the present or immediate danger facing the Corinthian Church, if the present state of strife continues, indicate that the Corinthian Christians, in Clement's view, did not consider the situation to be so serious as it in fact was.[1032] Thus an *exordium* in order to arouse the goodwill, attention and receptivity of the audience was in place.

According to ancient rhetorical theory there are many ways to capture the attention of the audience. Among them we mention that the orator can give the impression that what follows is an important, incredible, scandalous or alarming matter. Further, he

---

[1029]Cf. G. A. KENNEDY, *New Testament Interpretation through Rhetorical Criticism* (1984) 86f.: "Although an epistle requires a salutation and a complimentary close, its body can take the form of a deliberative, epideictic, or judicial speech with the traditional parts and all the inventional and stylistic features of an oration. On delivery a letter was usually read aloud; thus audience perception of its contents followed the pattern of speech"; M. M. MITCHELL, "Brief", *RGG* 4 (1998), who states that "In der neuesten Forschung wurde auch die Verwendung rhetorischer Formen im B.[rief]korpus nachgewiesen" (1759), and the discussion in the present investigation, pp. 26-30. We agree with H. E. LONA, *Der erste Clemensbrief* (1998), when he underlines that *1 Clement* is a real letter (20-23). We cannot follow him, however, when he draws the conclusion on the basis of the communication situation that the genre of *1 Clement* should not be defined in rhetorical terms. Though Lona describes *1 Clement* as "ein rhetorisches Werk" (21), and underlines the importance of paying attention to the rhetorical character of the letter in the interpretation, he criticizes W. C. van Unnik's determination of the letter as γένος συμβουλευτικόν on the basis of the communication situation of the letter. See the present investigation 13f. In our opinion, Lona's discussion of the genre, where he defines *1 Clement* as "ein echter Privatbrief" (22), lacks a consideration of the relationship between epistolography and rhetoric.

[1030]Quint. *Inst.* 3.8.6; Arist. *Rh.* 3.14.12; Quint. *Inst* 4.1.72.

[1031]Arist. *Rh.* 3.14.12.

[1032]For explicit appeals to the danger, see *1 Clem.* 14:2; 47:7; 59:1. For implicit appeals, see, e.g., *1 Clem.* 46:8; 51:2-5; 57:1-58:2.

can communicate that the matter is related to the welfare of the audience or to the worship of the gods.[1033] Clement makes use of several of these methods in 1:1. In light of the negative connotations of the term στάσις in the cultural milieu of the audience,[1034] the use of this term in describing the occurrences in the Corinthian Church which caused the letter to be written indicates in itself that what he is going to deal with is of great importance and is related to the welfare of the audience. When he further depicts the στάσις as abominable and unholy, alien and foreign to the elect of God, besides underlining the importance of the matter, he creates the impression that what follows is a scandalous and alarming matter, and that it is related to the worship of God. Moreover, when Clement states that the στάσις in the Corinthian Church has caused the previous good reputation of the Corinthian Christians to be much slandered, he reinforces the impression that what follows is of great importance, particularly in the light of the emphasis that was placed on having a good reputation in the ancient world.[1035] Thus it is reasonable to assert that 1:1 functions as an *attentum parare* (3ST211).

If an orator can succeed in gaining the attention of the audience, he has to a great extent secured its receptivity as well.[1036] In spite of this, according to ancient rhetorical theory there is a more explicit way to arouse receptivity – namely for the orator to provide a brief summary of what he is going to deal with in plain language.[1037] Admittedly, Clement does not offer an explicit summary. However, when he apologizes in 1:1 for the fact that the Roman Church was not able at an earlier point of time to pay attention to "the questions disputed among you, beloved, and especially the abominable and unholy sedition (στάσις)", he indirectly gives a brief summary of the main topic of the letter. From this statement the recipients will know that in what follows the letter will deal predominantly with questions in one way or another related to the subject of στάσις. In other words, although 1:1 primarily functions as an *attentum parare*, at the same time a part of it also functions as a *docilem parare*. It is important to pay sufficient attention to this feature of the rhetorical *disposito* because it provides help in attempting to grasp what the author considered to be the overall topic of the letter. Our understanding of the actual part of 1:1 as *docilem parare* with the implications mentioned regarding the main subject of the letter is further consistent with the continuation of the *exordium* which contains many terms and *topoi* related to στάσις or its antonym ὁμόνοια (and εἰρήνη).[1038] Just as the orator had many means at hand in order to arouse attention, he could also arouse the good will of the audience in many ways. He

---

[1033]Arist. *Rh.* 3.14.7; [*Rh. Al.*] 29.1436b.5-15; Cic. *Inv. Rhet.* 1.16.23; Quint. *Inst.* 4.1.33-34; 10.1.48.

[1034]Cf. our discussion of στάσις chap. 3.5.1.1.1.

[1035]This is connected with the fact that the culture of antiquity was a 'honour-shame culture', see chap. 5.4.1.2.

[1036]Cic. *Inv. Rhet.* 1.16.23; [*Rhet. Her.*] 1.4.7; Quint. *Inst.* 4.1.34.

[1037]Arist. *Rh.* 3.14.6; Cic. *Inv. Rhet.* 1.16.23; Quint. *Inst.* 4.1.34; 10.1.48.

[1038]See chaps. 3.5.1-3.5.2.16 in the present work. Also the many terms and *topoi* related to the topic of στάσις or ὁμόνοια in other parts of the letter indicate that it is appropriate to regard the actual part of 1:1 as *docilem parare*, see chap. 3 in the present investigation.

could, for example, start by focusing on the audience and praise them for certain actions.[1039] This is exactly the strategy Clement makes use of in the bulk of the *exordium* in 1:2-2:8. Here he praises the Corinthians for their noble life in the past, first by means of four stylised rhetorical questions (1:2),[1040] before he changes to direct statement in 1:3. Among other things, the Corinthian Christians are commanded for their steadfast faith, gentleness and piety, hospitality, knowledge, obedience to the laws of God, obedience to the rulers and older persons, for teaching both the youth and the women to observe "the rule of obedience", for humility, for "yielding subjection rather than demanding it", for paying attention to the words of Christ, for the existence of a "rich peace", for their desire to do good, for having been full of holy plans, for having striven "on behalf of the whole brotherhood that the number of his elect should be saved", and for having been "sincere and innocent". Further, Clement praises them for the absence of "all sedition and all schism", and for their adornment by "virtuous and honourable citizenship". It is a fair supposition that his praise of the previous life of the Corinthian Christians aroused their good will and thus opened their hearts for the subsequent argumentation. Therefore 1:2-2:8 ought to be perceived as a *benevolum parare* (3ST212).

It is hardly an accident that Clement in his appeal for concord finds it useful in respect to his rhetorical strategy to use so much space on a *benevolum parare* in the *exordium* – that is to say Clement appears to reflect a common practice in deliberative rhetoric urging concord. That a *benevolum parare* was common in this kind of rhetoric is explicitly expressed by Aelius Aristides in the *exordium* to one of his discourses on concord:

> *I believe that it is incumbent upon whoever wishes to create a common friendship (φιλία κοινή) for the cities with one another, not to laud some of them and slander others, but to mention them all with praise, so that, to begin with, by being pleased you may all more eagerly accept his advice (συμβουλή), and one part of concordant (ὁμόνοια) behavior may already be accomplished. For if you accept being praised in common and none of you regards the praise of the others as an act of dishonor toward himself, but each of you is delighted by the attributes of one another as if they were your own, first of all right from the start you shall give a demonstration of concord, and next you will gradually become accustomed also to praise one another and to have thoughts which are expedient for all of you in common. But to come to advise concord (συμβουλεύσων ὁμονοεῖν) and at the same time to hesitate to praise you, seems to me to be a kind of cowardice, and even the act of one who is destroying his*

[1039]Cic. *Inv. Rhet.* 1.16.22; [*Rhet. Her.*] 1.5.8; Quint. *Inst.* 4.1.16.

[1040]The questions are introduced with "For who has stayed with you" and continues with similar structural patterns

οὐκ ἐδοκίμασεν ... πίστιν
οὐκ ἐθαύμασεν ... εὐσέβειαν
οὐκ ἐκήρυξεν ... φιλοξενίας ἦθος
οὐκ ἐμακάρισεν ... γνῶσιν.

argument (ὑπόθεσις), *and either has badly attempted it, or does not know in what*
way it is proper to deal with it (Or. 23.6-7).

Clement knows "in what way it is proper to deal with" advising concord and thus
praises the Corinthian Christians in the *exordium* in order that they "all more eagerly
[should] accept his advice". We further note that, in line with the proposition of Aristides, he does not praise only a part of the Church but addresses praise to all its members. This is explicitly expressed by the emphatic πᾶς which emphasizes that every
single member of the Church acted in a praiseworthy manner. πάντες were humble-
minded (2:1), a profound and rich peace was given πᾶσιν (2:2).[1041] Besides arousing
good will, Clement's praise of the entire Church functions as a unifying feature in line
with Aristides. When all the members of the Church are commanded for a certain type
of behaviour in the past, this has the effect of strengthening the communal bond
between the individual members of the Church. This is all the more the case, as we have
seen previously in this study, when Clement deals predominantly in his praise with
communal behaviour related to the topic of concord.[1042] Furthermore, his description
of the ideal past of the Corinthian Christians' functions also as a paradigm or a
reminder of how they should be behaving towards each other.

To the extent that Clement praises his audience in 1:2-2:8, this passage reflects a
principal feature of epideictic rhetoric. The basic subject of this kind of rhetoric is
praise or blame.[1043] But unlike *1 Clem.* 1:2-2:8 the main temporal frame of epideictic
rhetoric is present time. In spite of the fact that the focus in *1 Clem.* 1:2-2:8 is on past
time, the obvious tone of praise during the whole passage makes it reasonable to say
that it at least reflects a basic element of epideictic rhetoric. That features of epideictic
rhetoric occur in deliberative rhetoric is not, however, surprising. There is namely a
close connection between these two types of rhetoric. To use the words of Aristotle:
"Praise and counsels have a common aspect; for what you might suggest in counselling
becomes encomium by a change in the phrase".[1044] So when Clement makes use of
praise this is not only a strategy to attain goodwill, but it is also a means of creating
adherence to the course of action he explicitly advises later on in the letter. Thus the
pure existence of epideictic rhetoric in *1 Clement* does not negate the view that the
overall genre of the letter is of the deliberative type. The epideictic elements must be
read and understood in the light of the main genre of the letter.

In addition to praise, a common way of making the audience well-disposed to the
rhetor was to shape the impression that he was a good man. This was in fact regarded to

---

[1041] In addition to these two occurrences, a form of πᾶς, πᾶσα, πᾶν is used seven more times in
1:3-2:7. In most cases the use of πᾶς serves to emphasize the praiseworthy quality of the previous
behaviour.

[1042] See the present study, chaps. 3.5.2.4-3.5.2.14.

[1043] For the main characteristics of epideictic rhetoric, see Arist. *Rh.* 1.3.3-5; [*Rh. Al.*] 3.1425b.36-
39; Cic. *Inv. Rhet.* 1.5.7; 2.4.12; 2.51.155-56; *Top.* 24.91; [*Rhet. Her.*] 3.6.10; Quint. *Inst.* 3.4.6-8; and
further J. MARTIN, *Antike Rhetorik* (1974) 177-210; H. LAUSBERG, *Handbuch der literarischen Rhetorik*
(1990) 129-138; M. FUHRMANN, *Die antike Rhetorik* (1995) 81-83.

[1044] Arist. *Rh.* 1.9.35.

be of great significance in the process of persuading an audience.[1045] It was important for the orator to show through the discourse that he had a good character, i.e. *ethos*, and that he had the well-being of the audience in view. Among other things, he could give the impression that he has "undertaken the case out of a sense of duty to a friend or relative".[1046] He must be free from suspicion of having personal interest and ambition in the case.[1047] It appears that Clement applies this strategy. In his apology for not having written before in 1:1 when he says that due to "sudden and repeated misfortunes and calamities" which had faced the Church of Rome he was only now able to write the letter, he creates the impression that the Roman Church interferes in the affairs of the Corinthian Church out of duty. And at the same time when he addresses the Corinthian Christians as "beloved" (ἀγαπητοί, 1:1), he indicates that he undertook the case out of a sense of duty to friends.

We have already mentioned that in order to gain attention the orator could provide a brief summary of what he is going to deal with. In addition to such an explicit *docilem parare* the whole *exordium* as such could briefly indicate the topics which the rhetor is going to develop further in the *probatio* and reiterate in the *peroratio*. In other words, there should be a close connection between *exordium*, *probatio* and *peroratio*.[1048] This is evident in the case of *1 Clement*. *1 Clem.* 1:1-2:8 contains several topics which are further developed in the *probatio* and reiterated in the *peroratio*:

1. στάσις, in the *exordium* 1:1; 2:6, in the *probatio*, e.g., 14:2; 46:7; 46:9; 49:5; 51:3; 54:2; 57:1, in the *peroratio* 63:1.

2. πίστις, in the *exordium* 1:2, in the *probatio* e.g. 5:6; 10:7; 22:1; 26:1; 27:3; 32:4; 35:2, in the *peroratio* 62:2; 64.

3. εὐσέβεια, in the *exordium* 1:2, in the *probatio* 11:1; 15:1; 32:4; 50:3, in the *peroratio* 62:1.

4. φιλοξενία in the *exordium* 2:2, in the *probatio* 10:7; 11:1; 12:1; 35:5.

5. "obedience to the law of God" in the *exordium* 2:3, in the *probatio* 20:5; 37:1; 40:4,5; 50:5; 58:2.

6. ταπεινοφροσύνη in the *exordium* 2:1, in the *probatio* 16:1, 2, 17; 17:2; 19:1; 21:8; 30:3,8; 31:4; 38:2; 44:3; 48:6; 56:1; 58:2, in the *peroratio* 62.2.

7. ὑποτάσσω in the *exordium* 1:3; 2:1, in the *probatio* 20:1; 34:5; 38:1; 57:1; 57:2; 61:1.

[1045]Arist. *Rh.* 1.2.3-4; 3.14.7; Quint. *Inst.* 4.1.7.

[1046]Quint. *Inst.* 4.1.7.

[1047]Cic. *Inv. Part. Or.* 8.28; Quint. *Inst.* 4.1.7-10.

[1048] Aristotle's comparison of the function of the *exordium* with the prelude in flute playing is well known. Just as "flute-players begin by playing whatever they can execute skilfully and attach it to the key-note ... the speaker should say at once whatever he likes, give the key-note and than attach the main subject" (Arist. *Rh.* 3.14.1). See further Quint. *Inst.* 4.1.23-27; Cic. *De Or.* 2.80.325.

8. εἰρήνη in the *exordium* 2:2, in the *probatio* including the synonym ὁμόνοια 9:4; 11:2;15:1; 16:5; 19:2; 20:1, 3, 9, 10, 11; 21:1; 22:5; 30:3; 34:7; 49:5; 50:5; 60:3, 4; 61:1,2, in the *peroratio* 63:2; 64:1; 65:1.

9. "an honourable citizenship" in the *exordium* 2:8, in the *probatio* 6:1; 21:1; 44:6; 51:2; 54:4; 55:1.

Although the term ἀγάπη does not occur in the *exordium*, the aspect of love is evident in 2:4-5. Here Clement praises the Corinthian Christians for their communal solidarity in the past – they "strove on behalf of the whole brotherhood", they "bore no malice to one another" and they behaved kindly. The topic of love, explicitly expressed by the term ἀγάπη is further developed in the *probatio* 21:7, 8; 33:1; 49:1, 2, 4, 5 (9x), 6 (2x); 50:1,2, 3, 5 (2x); 51:2; 53:5; 54:1; 55:5 and reiterated in the *peroratio* 62:2 (2 x). In other words, in line with ancient rhetorical theory he uses the *exordium* to indicate briefly the topics he will develop further in the *probatio*. We should note, however, that not all of these topics are of the same importance. If it is correct, as we has argued above, to consider 1:1 as *docilem parare*, this indicates that the topic of στάσις or its antonym ὁμόνοια (and εἰρήνη) is the main topic of the letter. This means that the other topics should be subsumed under this one. Such a point of view is also consistent with the fact that many of these terms belong to the semantic field of ὁμόνοια.[1049]

To sum up, it seems reasonable to consider *1 Clem.* 1:1-2:8 as an *exordium*. This passage contains the main functions of an *exordium* according to ancient rhetorical theory. 1:1 functions both as an *attentum parare* and as an implicit *docilem parare*, and the bulk of the *exordium* (1:2-2:8) functions as a *benevolum parare*.[1050] The implicit *docilem parare* indicates that the question of στάσις or its antonym ὁμόνοια (and εἰρήνη) is the main topic of the letter. This is consistent with the fact that many of the terms and *topoi* Clement applies in the *benevoulm parare* in antiquity belonged to the semantic field of ὁμόνοια. Furthermore, we have seen that Clement reflects a common

---

[1049] στάσις, see chap. 3.5.1.1.1; πίστις, see chap. 3.5.2.4; "obedience to the law of God", see chap. 3.5.2.7; ταπεινοφροσύνη, see chap. 3.5.2.10 pp. 126-131; ὑποτάσσω, see chap. 3.5.2.8; εἰρήνη, see chap. 3.4; "an honourable citizenship", see chap. 3.5.2.14; ἀγάπη, see chap. 3.6.2.3.

[1050] B. E. BOWE, *A Church in Crisis* (1988), when analysing the epistolary formulas in *1 Clement* in the light of Graeco-Roman epistolography and the Pauline letters, holds that the placement of 1:2-3:1 "is exactly that of the Pauline thanksgiving period" (44), and that it "serves as a skillful [*sic.*] *captatio benevolentiae*" (43-46). We agree with many of Bowe's observations. However, when she states that the placement of *1 Clem.* 1:2-2:8 corresponds exactly to the thanksgiving period of the Pauline letters, after the prescript and prior to the letter corpus, she does not discuss the placement and function of *1 Clem.* 1:1. It is this verse in fact which comes immediately after the prescript, and not the period that she depicts as *captatio benevolentiae*. Furthermore, in spite of the fact that *1 Clem.* 2:1-2:8 functions as *captatio benevolentiae*, the explicit, common thanksgiving formula is lacking, as Bowe also remarks. In our opinion these facts illustrate the problem of confining oneself solely to ancient epistolography in pointing out the macro-structure of the letter. As we have attempted to show, the rules of the *dispositio* of ancient rhetoric offer analytical tools which enable us to deal more accurately with the delimitation of *1 Clem.* 1:1-2:8.

practice when in his appeal for ὁμόνοια in the *exordium* he praises *all* the members of the audience in order to strengthen their bond of unity.

2ST22 Narratio, 3:1-4

3:1 functions as a transition from the praise of the noble past to the present scandalous situation in the Corinthian Church. One could perhaps regard 3:1a, where Clement states that "all glory and enlargement was given" to them, as a kind of summary of the praise of 1:2-2:8 and conclude that it therefore should be considered as a part of the *benevolum parare*. However, at the same time, Clement takes his departure in the noble situation of the past when by means of a quotation from Deut 32:15 he changes the focus in 3:1b toward the "fall" and what consequences that has for the congregation. Therefore, we have not taken 3:1a as a part of the *exordium*. In any case, the most important point in this connection is that in 3:1-4 Clement seems to offer a brief narration of what has taken place and how this still influences the communal life. He says that "jealousy and envy, strife and sedition, persecution and disorder, war and captivity" arose, and that certain groups of the congregation have risen against each other (3:2). According to Quintilian the *narratio* is "the persuasive exposition of that which either has been done, or is supposed to have been done ... a speech instructing the audience as to the nature of the case in dispute".[1051] It appears that it is reasonable to maintain that *1 Clem.* 3:1-3 is consistent with Quintilian's understanding. Although the quotation of Deut 32:15 does not provide any information about what actually took place, except that Clement considered it as apostasy from God, he is more concrete in what follows this. First, in 3:2 he focuses upon certain vices and the situation in the Church, before he describes different groups of people involved in the strife in 3:3. Later on in the investigation we shall argue that the terms Clement employs show that he considers the conflict primarily in socio-political terms. According to him it was a conflict between people of varying socio-economic status in which striving for honour appeared to play an important role.[1052] In other words, he both provides a *narratio* of the occurrences that have taken place, mainly in 3:3, and reveals what he considers to be the nature of the case in dispute.

As already mentioned, a *narratio* was not necessary in deliberative rhetoric, which was oriented towards the future since from a logical point of view, as Aristotle comments, no one narrates things to come.[1053] But, continues Aristotle, if reminding the audience of the past causes them to "take better counsel about the future" a *narratio* is in place in deliberative rhetoric as well.[1054] To take good counsel about the future, from the perspective of the orator, means in this connection that the audience follows his advice. That the rhetor should present the facts in a way which best serves his case is

---

[1051]Quint. *Inst.* 4.2.31.

[1052]See the present study chap. 5.

[1053]As noted by M. M. MITCHELL, *Paul and the Rhetoric of Reconciliation* (1991) 201 n. 87, this philosophical theme occurs also in deliberative speeches: Isoc. *Or.* 8.8; Dio Chrys. *Or.* 26.

[1054]Arist. *Rh.* 3.16.11. Cf. Cic. *Part. Or.* 4.13.

common for any *narratio*.[1055] Furthermore, Aristotle notes that such a *narratio* "may be done in a spirit either of blame or of praise".[1056] The whole passage of *1 Clem.* 3:1-4 is written in a tone of blame. Already the quotation and application of Deut 32:15 to the Corinthian Church at the beginning of the passage strikes the tone of blame, and the terms Clement uses to describe the present situation in the Corinthian Church carry negative connotations, as we have seen.[1057] *I Clem.* 3:3 is to some extent more of a "neutral" description of what Clement regarded as having taken place, but when he turns to the present situation of the Church in 3:4 the spirit of blame is again unmistakable. When he says that "righteousness and peace", terms with clearly positive connotations,[1058] are far removed, it is likely that the Corinthian Christians will perceive this as blame. This is even more the case when Clement asserts that their behaviour implies that they no longer practise the fear of God, that they do not live in accordance with the laws of God, and do not "use their citizenship worthily of Christ". On the contrary, they live according to their own lust and have "revived the unrighteousness and impious envy, by which also 'death came into the world'". Thus, in line with Aristotle, Clement's *narratio* is written in a spirit of blame.

As in the case of the *exordium*, the *narratio* also reflects features of epideictic rhetoric, especially in 3:4 where Clement blames the Corinthian Christians and uses the present tense to do so. Further, the elements of epideictic rhetoric in the *narratio* function in a similar way as in the *exordium*: The condemnation should lead the Corinthian Christians to cease from behaviour which later in the letter he explicitly discourages.[1059]

Furthermore, in the *narratio* when Clement, probably consciously, contrasts the "fall" and its consequences with the noble past (1:2-2:8), this serves to amplify the scandalous nature of the present behaviour of the Corinthian Christians. When he emphasizes the noble community life in the past so much, the present occurrences at the Corinthian Church are put more clearly into focus. He obviously attempts to make the Corinthians Christians realize the scandalous nature of their present behaviour. He attempts to demonstrate that their present state of living is inconsistent with being Christians. If he succeeds in this task, the effect of the *narratio* will be that the audience, from his perspective, "may take better counsel about the future". This function of the *narratio* may explain why Clement chose to make use of it although he writes in the frame of deliberative rhetoric.[1060]

Above we have argued that it is reasonable to label 3:1-4 a *narratio*. On the basis of the fact that it is, strictly speaking, only 3:1-3 that deals with the past, one could perhaps argue that it is more correct to limit the *narratio* to this passage. Against such a

---

[1055]Cic. [*Rhet. Her.*] 1.8.12; *Inv. Rhet.* 1.21.30; Quint. *Inst.* 4.2.31.

[1056]Arist. *Rh.* 3.16.11. Cf. Cic. *Part. Or.* 4.13.

[1057]Cf. chaps. 3.5.1-3.5.1.4.

[1058]See chaps. 3.4 and 3.5.2.16.

[1059]For the relation between deliberative and epideictic rhetoric, see above, p. 221.

[1060]For other examples of *narratio* in deliberative rhetoric, see, e.g., Isoc. *Or.* 8.2; *Ep.* 1.5; 3.2-3; Dion. Hal. *Ant. Rom.* 6.83.3; Aristid. *Or.* 24.3.

suggestion we will maintain that although 3:4 describes the *present* behaviour of the Corinthian Christians this behaviour is closely connected to what Clement deals with in 3:1-3. The things he blames the Corinthian Church for in 3:4 are in fact an underlying cause of the upheaval in the past. Furthermore, one should note that the στάσις which emerged in the past still continues. In other words, 3:4 is so closely related to the occurrences described in 3:1-3 that it ought to be regarded as a part of the *narratio*. One should further note that although the past is the proper temporal focus for a *narratio*, the *narratio* may also deal with the present situation which promotes the rhetorical invention. One cannot operate with definite demarcations between the past and the present, in so far as the present situation to a high degree depends on action in the past. That a *narratio* could deal with the present situation is confirmed by Arist. [*Rh. Al.*] 30.1438a 3-6: "After this [the proposal] we must either report or remind our hearers of events that have occurred before, or arrange in groups and exhibit the *facts of the present*, or forecast what is going to occur".

Clement ends the *narratio* by maintaining that the occurrences in the Corinthian Church are connected with the fact that they are marked by "unrighteousness and impious envy". In order to amplify the dangerous consequences of this envy, Clement adds, by quoting Wis 2:24, that it was because of envy that "'death came into the world'" (3:8). Here we note that the assertion that envy leads to death is one that Clement is going to prove in the following. Thus, the end of *1 Clem.* 3:4 functions as a transition to the *probatio* section.[1061]

2ST23 *Probatio, 4:1-61:3*

In the main part of the letter, *1 Clem.* 4:1-61:3, the author attempts to persuade the Corinthians by means of different strategies to cease from the present strife and to re-establish concord. On the surface-level it begins abruptly with a quotation formula: γέγραπται γὰρ οὕτως. A further delimitation of this section into sub-units follows later on.

2ST24 *Peroratio, 62:1-64:1*

According to ancient rhetorical theory the last part of a discourse, the *peroratio*, should commonly contain four parts: a *recapitulatio*, an appeal or appeals that dispose the audience favourably towards the orator, an emotional appeal (*adfectus*) and an amplificatio.[1062] In the *recapitulatio* the orator seeks to remind the audience about the main

---

[1061]Our attempt to delimit the beginning of the letter corpus in line with the rules of ancient rhetoric differs greatly from the delimitation provided by E. Baasland in his introduction to *1 Clement* in a Norwegian edition of the Apostolic Fathers. As far as we know Baasland is the only scholar who has attempted to outline the rhetorical structure of the letter based on ancient rhetoric prior to the present proposals. He operates with the following delimitation of chaps. 1-3: *exordium*, 1:1; *narratio*, 1:2-2:8; *propositio*, 3:1-4, E. BAASLAND, "1. Klemensbrev", *De Apostoliske Fedre* (1984) 119.

[1062]While the majority of the theorists regarded these features as three or four distinguished parts of the *peroratio*, Arist. *Rh.* 3.19.1; Cic. *Inv. Rhet.* 1.52.98-99; [*Rhet. Her.*] 2.30.47, others, Quint. *Inst.* 6.1.1-2 for instance, viewed them to be different types of *peroratio*.

points of the *probatio* in order that the audience should have these main points fresh in memory before making up its mind about the issue in question. This means that when one attempts to grasp the basic content and purpose of a discourse or a letter this section is of great importance. Here the orator or the author himself offers a summary of what he considers to be the basic topics of his argumentation and what he is aiming at with the argumentation. At the very end of the speech the orator appeals to the audience's feelings, arousing positive ones for himself and his case and negative ones for the opponent and his case. Although persuasion by means of *pathos* could appear in every part of a discourse, the use of *pathos* in the *peroratio* would be heavier than elsewhere in the discourse.[1063] The considerations on how to elicit *pathos* are given in a context of judicial rhetoric.[1064] Therefore one should not expect the actual rules to be used in the other types of rhetoric in full scale. However, this does not mean that the recommendation that *pathos* should be used in the *peroratio* is not appropriate for deliberative and epideictic rhetoric.

We shall argue that 62:1-64:1 comprises the *peroratio* in *1 Clement*. On the surface-level of the text in 62:1 there is a *SA* which serves to set this sub-text, 62:1-63:4 (2ST24), apart from the former of the same level, 4:1-61:3 (2ST23): περὶ μὲν τῶν ἀνηκόντων τῇ θρησκείᾳ … ἱκανῶς ἐπεστείλαμεν ὑμῖν. By means of this *SA* Clement refers to the content of the whole foregoing argumentation.[1065] The term ἱκανῶς (sufficiently) indicates the end of the *probatio* section. In addition to this *SA* on the surface-level, certain epistolary features and rhetorical elements in *1 Clem.* 62:1-64:1 also indicate that *1 Clem.* 62:1 introduces a new section of the letter.[1066] Regarding conventional epistolary features we note that the transition from body-middle to body-closing within a letter is often begun with a vocative.[1067] Further, it has been pointed out that the body-closing of a letter commonly employs the following formulae: "(1) the motivation for writing form of the disclosure formula; (2) responsibility state-

---

[1063]Quint. *Inst.* 4.1.28; 6.1.9-10; 6.1.51-52.

[1064]The emotional appeal was generally composed of two sections: (1) the *indignatio* in which the orator sought to elicit negative *pathos* for the opponent and his case (Cic. *Inv. Rhet.* 1.52.98; for further considerations on how to achieve this, see Arist. *Rh.* 3.19.1-4; Cic. *Inv. Rhet.* 1.53-54; Quint. *Inst.* 6.1.9-20); (2) the *conquestio* in which the orator attempted to elicit positive *pathos* for himself and his case (Cic. *Inv. Rhet.* 1.52.98; for further deliberations on how to attain this, see Arist. *Rh.* 3.19.1-4; Cic. *Inv. Rhet.* 1.55f.; Quint. *Inst.* 6.1.21-35).

[1065]See below, pp. 229f.

[1066]For an epistolary analysis of the body-closing of *1 Clement*, see B. E. BOWE, *A Church in Crisis* (1988) 48-57. In many respects we agree with Bowe's observations. However, we can not support her when she holds that the body-closing already begins in 58:1. The admonition in 58:1-2 is linked with the preceding quotation of Prov 1:23-33. Clement even makes an explicit reference to this passage from Proverbs when he says in the exhortation that one must "be obedient to his most holy and glorious name, and escape the threats which have been spoken by wisdom aforetime to the disobedient" (58:1). 58:1-2 is an application and conclusion of the preceding argumentation and belongs thus to the letter body. Further, taking one's departure in the study of ancient epistolography one cannot, as Bowe does, include the prayer in 59:1-61:1 in the body-closing.

[1067]A vocative signals a transition anywhere within the letter body, J. L. White, *The Form and Function of the Body of the Greek Letter* (1972) 15.

ments; (3) the polite requests for a letter formula; (4) formulaic references to a coming visit; (5) conditional clauses employed formulaically as a threat".[1068]

In 62:1 Clement applies a double vocative when he addresses the receivers of the letter as ἄνδρες ἀδελφοί. Further, the statement in 62:1-2 where Clement explicitly summarizes topics he has dealt with, might be conceived as a disclosure-motivation for writing. However, 63:4 is a more explicit disclosure-motivation formula. Here Clement directly states that the purpose of the letter was that "our whole care has been and is directed to your speedy attainment of peace".

63:1f. could be taken as containing a responsibility statement. These statements occasionally involved an exhortation from the letter writer to do something and an additional reference to a benefit either for the addressees or for the author if the addressees should follow the exhortation.[1069] Although an explicit exhortation is not found in 63:1-2, Clement's appeal that it is "right that we should respect so many and so great examples" functions as an exhortation to behave in a certain way. As is characteristic of responsibility statements, Clement points to the benefit for the addressees connected with such behaviour: The Corinthian Christians will "gain without any fault the goal set before" them (63:1). Clement not only points to the benefits gained by the Corinthian Christians. He goes on to refer to the benefit of the Roman Church if the Corinthians are "obedient to the things which we have written through the Holy Spirit".[1070] They will experience the "benefit" of "joy and gladness" (63:2).

A similar responsibility formula is found in 65:1. Here Clement exhorts the Corinthians to send back the messengers "in peace with gladness" in order that they can report the re-establishing of "peace and concord" which in turn involves a "benefit" for the Roman Christians, i.e. that it would make them joyful (ἡμᾶς χαρῆναι). At the same time 63:2 is also a disclosure formula. When he exhorts Corinthian Christians to send back the messengers in order that they can report the "peace and concord" he adds an attribute which reflects the intention of the letter. He depicts the "peace and concord" as something the Romans Christians "pray for (εὐκταῖος) and desire (ἐπιπόθητος)".

Therefore, on the basis of the conventional features of the letter-closing in ancient letter writing which are found in *1 Clem.* 62:1-64:1 it is reasonable to consider this passage as a letter closing.[1071] The letter-closing has two main functions, though these are not always separable: "(1) as a means of finalizing the principal motivation for writing

---

[1068]*Ibid.* 41.

[1069]*Ibid.* 28.

[1070]This functions as an implicit exhortation.

[1071]Here we shall point out that the term "letter-closing" is not a term that occurs in ancient epistolography, but is a modern one. We have already mentioned that although we cannot support B. E. Bowe, *A Church in Crisis* (1988) in her definition of the letter-closing in *1 Clement*, we agree with many of her observations. She operates with the following delimitation of the passages we consider as the letter-closing: 62:1-2 disclosure formula; 62:3 confidence expression; 63:1 responsibility statement; 63:2 benefit formula; 63:3 dispatch of emissaries; 63:4 disclosure formula; 64:1 blessing and doxology; 65:1 responsibility and benefit formulae; and 65:2 blessing and doxology (49).

(by accentuating or reiterating what was stated earlier in the body); (2) as a means of forming a bridge to further communication".[1072] This means that these two basic functions correspond to the *recapitulatio* and the emotional appeal which constitutes a *peroratio*. Therefore, although 62:1-64:1 reflects conventional epistolary features it is also fruitful to consider this part of the letter within the frame of *dispositio* of ancient rhetoric.[1073]

According to Aristotle a *recapitulatio* is not necessary in deliberative rhetoric unless there is a conflict in opinion.[1074] It should go without saying that this was exactly the case regarding Clement's audience; there was strife and different opinions. Also, we can take it for granted that there would be different reactions to his advice regarding the solution to the conflict. Due to this fact it is not surprising that he found it useful to employ a *recapitulatio* (62:1-3).

There are different kinds of *recapitulatio*. Clement employs the method that was the most common among the speakers, i.e. the method which consists of touching briefly upon main points of the *probatio* by means of a summary.[1075] He not only mentions the main topics in an indirect manner, but he even introduces the *recapitulatio* by stating explicitly that he has now touched sufficiently upon the things which befit the worship and "are most helpful (ὠφέλιμος)[1076] for a virtuous life to those who wish to guide their steps in piety and righteousness" (62:1). In what follows he goes on to list the concrete topics he has dealt with.

> For (γάρ) we have touched on every aspect of faith (πίστις) and repentance (μετάνοια) and true love (ἀγάπη) and self-control (ἐγκράτεια) and sobriety (σωφροσύνη) and patience (ὑπομονή) ... (62:2).

Further, Clement says, we have

> ... reminded you that you are bound to please almighty God with holiness in righteousness (δικαιοσύνη) and truth and long-suffering, and to live in concord (ὁμονοέω), bearing no malice, in love (ἀγάπη) and peace (εἰρήνη) with eager gentleness (ἐπιεικείας), even as our fathers, whose example we quoted, were well-pleasing in their humility (ταπεινοφρονοῦντες) towards God ... and towards all men (62:2).

[1072]J. L. WHITE, *The Form and Function of the Body of the Greek Letter* (1972) 25.

[1073]Cf. D. F. WATSON, *Invention, Arrangement, and Style* (1988) 68: "It can be safely concluded that just as the body-opening and body-middle correspond to the *exordium-narratio* and *probatio* respectively, the body closing corresponds to the *peroratio*".

[1074]Arist. *Rh.* 3.13.3. [*Rh. Al.*], however, holds that a *recapitulatio* "should be employed at every part of a speech and with every kind of speech. It is most suitable for accusations and defences, but also in exhortations and dissuasions" (36.1444b.21ff.).

[1075]For the different types of *recapitulatio*, see Cic. *Inv. Rhet.* 1.52.98-100.

[1076]As is characteristic of deliberative rhetoric Clement emphasizes that what he has dealt with is useful for the audience. It appears to be no accident that he mentions exactly this aspect in the *peroratio*.

In this summary he enumerates some of the most important topics of the *probatio*.
Consistent with ancient rhetorical theory many of the topics were introduced in the
exordium and *narratio*, developed further in the *probatio* and reiterated in the
peroratio.[1077] We observe that when Clement comes to topics which are explicitly
related to the community life of Christians, he uses the verb ὁμονοέω. And when he
further describes this way of living, he uses the terms ἀγάπη and εἰρήνη which are
closely associated with the ideal of concord.[1078] Previously in the investigation we have
seen that this is also the case for the majority of the other topics Clement enumerates in
the *recapitulatio*.[1079] Furthermore, we note that he also refers to the many examples of
the fathers he has quoted. Proof by means of examples, and particularly historical
examples from Scripture, play a dominant role throughout the whole *probatio*, as we
have pointed out earlier.[1080]

Clement does not, however, restrict himself to enumerating the topics he has dealt
with. After he has referred to the quoted examples of the fathers and praised the Corinthian Christians for their great knowledge of Scripture he gives a last exhortation in his
plea for concord. It is right (θεμιτόν), argues Clement, to follow "so many and so great
examples" and be obedient, thereby abolishing the vain sedition (ματαίας στάσεως,
63:1). Here he briefly reiterates what he has argued in the *probatio*. He does not, as recommended by Cicero, "run briefly over all the arguments", but he confines himself to
presenting his main argument "as briefly as possible, so that it may appear to be a
refreshing of the memory of the audience".[1081] In other words, in line with ancient
rhetoric, Clement both gives an explicit summary of the main topics of the *probatio* and
briefly reiterates what he probably considered to be the most persuasive argument for
concord.

From what we have just stated it follows that the *recapitulatio* constitutes the main
bulk of the *peroratio*. However, other features seem to occur also. In 62:3 Clement states
that it has been a pleasure to remind the Corinthian Christians of the things he has
dealt with because of their good character. He knew that he was "writing to men who
were faithful (πιστός) and distinguished (ἐλλογιμώτατος)[1082] and had studied
(ἐγκύπτω) the oracles of the teaching of God". On the basis of what he has stated in
the *narratio* and in the *probatio* about the present situation in the Corinthian Church, it
might appear quite surprising that he describes them with the terms πιστός and
ἐλλόγιμος. He has commanded them twice in the *probatio* (45:1-2; 53:1) regarding
their knowledge and good understanding of the Scriptures. What we should note in
this connection, and what might explain the fact that Clement, in spite of what he has
stated previously in the letter, describes them in such a positive way, is that he expresses
confidence in his addressees by doing so. This is a means to "dispose the hearer favour-

---

[1077]See above, pp. 222f.
[1078]ἀγάπη, see chap. 3.6.2.3; εἰρήνη, see chap. 3.4.
[1079]Cf. chaps. 3.5.2.4; 3.5.2.5; 3.5.2.16; 3.5.2.10, pp. 126-131.
[1080]For proof by examples in *1 Clement*, see our discussion, chap. 2.4.2.
[1081]Cic. *Inv. Rhet.* 1.52.98-100.

ably towards"[1083] himself which was considered to be a part of the *peroratio*. To make the audience respond favourably towards the rhetor is of course important in the other parts of the oration as well, particularly in the *exordium*. Previously in the study we have pointed out that the bulk of Clement's *exordium* serves this function. This is also the case for two expressions of confidence in the *probatio* section (45:1-2; 53:1). Thus 62:3 functions as a reinforcement of the good relations Clement has attempted to establish and maintain previously in the letter. It is hardly an accident that this part of the *peroratio* is placed right before the last appeal for concord in the letter (*1 Clem.* 63:1-3).

Besides its functions within the *peroratio*, his praise of the Corinthians, particularly of their diligence in studying the Scriptures, serves to further express confidence that their proper understanding of the Scriptures will lead to a solution to the present crisis. Such a confidence in their understanding of the Scriptures must imply that Clement attempts to give the impression that they share his understanding. If he succeeds, there should be a strong likelihood that the Corinthians would follow the many examples from the Scriptures he has referred to throughout the letter and would thereby cease from the present strife and sedition. Thus the expression of confidence in their knowledge of Scripture in 62:3 prepares the audience for his last appeal to respect the "many and so great examples" in order to re-establish concord.[1084]

Clement also makes use of *pathos* in the *peroratio*, though to a limited degree. When he states that acceptance of his advice will lead to "joy and gladness" in the Roman Church (63:2), he plays on the feelings of the Corinthian Christians in as much as they are unlikely to want to disappoint their Roman brothers. Further, the short remark that the letter is written "through the Holy Spirit" (διὰ τοῦ ἁγίου πνεύματος) is intended to give divine authority to its content (63:2). Here Clement applies one of several specific topics for amplification, namely the topic of authority. This topic should demonstrate that the case under discussion greatly concerns the gods, the forefathers, and

---

[1082] ἐλλόγιμος means "to be taken into account", "reputable, eminent", W. BAUER, *A Greek-English Lexicon* (1979) 252. In *1 Clem.* 44:3 the term has the latter meaning. Here the term designates members of the Church who are probably characterised in this way because of their good Christian life. In 57:2 the terms depicts those who turn from the instigators of the sedition and submit to the presbyters, and thus it refers to a proper Christian way of living. Also, in 58:2 the term occurs in connection with the question of concord. Clement exhorts his audience to "receive our counsel" which implies that the Corinthian Christians must live according to God's commandments. If they do so they will be "ἐλλόγιμος (chosen) in the number of those who are saved through Jesus Christ". This means that the term depicts those who live an honourable Christian life within the body of the elect in general. However, it also appears that Clement links this term more concretely with behaviour which contributes to concord among the Christians. The fact that he links ἐλλόγιμος with πιστός, a term associated with the value of concord, points in the same direction. For πιστός as a term associated with concord, see chap. 3.5.2.4.

[1083] Arist. *Rh.* 3.19.1.

[1084] For further discussion on the confidence expressions in *1 Clem.* 62:3 in the light of ancient epistolary conventions, see B. E. BOWE, *A Church in Crisis* (1988) 50-53. She concludes: "Therefore, Olson's conclusion proves true in *1 Clement*: 'Whatever the emotion behind the expression, the function is to undergird the letter's request or admonitions by creating a sense of obligation through praise'" (53).

other authoritative groups.[1085] Similarly, the appeal to follow the great examples of the Holy Scriptures reflects the same topic. Furthermore, a divine sanction of the content of the letter probably shaped a certain fear of what would happen if one failed to follow his advice.[1086]

4.2.3. Sub-Texts on Grade Three

We have indicated above the sub-texts on grade three for a certain part of the letter. In what follows we confine ourselves to a further delimitation of the bulk of the letter, i.e. the *probatio*-section.

3ST231 Quaestio infinita/θέσις, 4:1-39:9

In this section Clement deals with and exhorts his audience to certain virtues and behaviour which secure concord, and warns against vices and behaviour that lead to sedition. He does so without relating these to the concrete situation among the Corinthian Christians. He discusses the question of concord in a general way. We can describe this part of the letter as the *principle* of concord for a Christian community. That this is a relevant description and that it is adequate to consider 4:1-39:9 as a θέσις will be substantiated in the delimitation of this passage below.

3ST232 Quaestio finita/ὑπόθεσις, 40:1-61:3

In chapters 40:1-61:3 Clement focuses more on the concrete situation in the Corinthian Church and advises a particular course of action in order to solve the crisis in the Church and re-establish concord.[1087] That this is an adequate summary of 40:1-61:3 will be substantiated in the delimitation of this passage later on. Therefore it is appro-

---

[1085]Cic. *Inv. Rhet.* 1.52.101.

[1086]For the appeal to this emotion in order persuade the audience, see Arist. *Rh.* 2.1.8.

[1087]That *1 Clement* consists of two main parts, one general or "paraenetic" section and one that focuses more on the specific problem in the Corinthian Church is commonly mentioned by scholars. For literature references, see nn. 966-968. There is however, as mentioned above, no agreement as to whether the second part dealing with the concrete situation in the Corinthian Church begins in 37:1 or 40:1. As indicated above we are of the opinion that the second main section that deals more concretely with the particular situation in the Corinthian Church begins in 40:1. Chaps. 37 -38 consist mainly of general teaching and paraenesis dealing with the need for mutual subordination and interdependence in order to establish concord in a Christian community. Admittedly, chap. 39 appears to focus to a certain extent more directly upon the concrete situation in the Corinthian Church and therefore could be viewed as a transition to the ὑπόθεσις, 40:1-61:3. Another question one must consider is whether or not chaps. 40:1-43:6 ought also to be included in the first main part in view of the fact that in these chapters Clement does not make any specific reference to the situation in Corinth and that the focus upon the need for order in their religious service is rather general. The reason why we, in spite of this fact, include 40:1-43:6 in the second section is that the topic of order in religious services is so closely connected to what Clement considers to be the concrete problem of the Corinthian Church; the removal of the presbyters has caused disorder and sedition in the Church (44:3-6). Furthermore, 44:1, which introduces a new sub-text, shows that the following is closely related to the preceding. And finally, the *SA* clause ὄντων τούτων in 40:1 indicates that the ὑπόθεσις section begins with this verse.

priate to categorize this section as the ὑπόθεσις.[1088] Here Clement applies the principles of concord he has discussed in the θέσις-section to the concrete situation in the Corinthian Church.

On the surface-level of the text two *SAs* are found in 40:1. These indicate that a new section begins at this point. The first *SA* is ὄντων τούτων. It is reasonable to argue that ὄντων τούτων not only refers to the very close context, that is chapter 39, but that it is used anaphorically for the whole θέσις-section.[1089] The things which are manifested to them include therefore everything Clement has stated about the need for a community life which leads to concord and the behaviour which serves this purpose. The second *SA* is the abstract τὰ βάθη τῆς θείας γνώσεως. The depths of the divine knowledge which the Christians have looked into (ἐγκύπτω)[1090] ought not to be restricted to the quotation from Job in 39:3-9,[1091] but it is likely that by that phrase Clement includes what he has written in chapters 4-39 insofar as throughout these chapters he seeks support in Scripture for his exhortations to behaviour which leads to concord.[1092] Furthermore, the fact that in the *peroratio* he states that the letter is written through the Holy Spirit (63:2), also indicates that he regards the whole letter as an expression of divine knowledge.

As already mentioned, we are of the opinion that the *probatio*-section consists of a θέσις followed by a ὑπόθεσις. Before we go further and delimit these two main parts of the *probatio* into further sub-texts, it is interesting to note that we find examples of a similar delimitation of the *probatio*-section in a θέσις with a following ὑπόθεσις in other discourses on concord. First let us observe the discourse Dio Chrysostom addressed to Nicomedia on concord with Nicaea (*Or.* 38). After an *exordium* (38.1-6), he states what he is going to argue in a *propositio* (38.7-9): "that you [men of Nicomedia] must achieve concord with the Nicaeans" (38.7), and how he is going to structure the discourse:

[1088]Of course we are aware that the rather long prayer in 58:2-61:3 does not fulfil the criteria for a ὑπόθεσις. The reason why after some hesitation we have chosen to regard the prayer as an integrated part of the *probatio* is that it clearly has an argumentative function in Clement's appeal for concord.

[1089]For similar use of a *SA* in Didache, see *Did.* 7:1; 11:1 and D. HELLHOLM, "Från Judisk Två-vägslära till Kristen Dopkatekes", *Ad Acta* (1994) 134f.

[1090]The verb occurs also in 45:2; 53:1; 62:3 where it expresses the proper understanding of the Scripture.

[1091]Contra A. LINDEMANN, *Die Clemensbriefe* (1992) 122, who is of the opinion that ὄντων τούτων and the phrase "depths of the divine knowledge" refers to the quotation of Job in *1 Clem.* 39:2-9.

[1092]R. M. GRANT and H. H. GRAHAM, *First and Second Clement* (1965) 69, support this interpretation. It is argued that ὄντων τούτων and "the depths of the divine knowledge ... consists of the whole argument up to this point, based on the Old Testament revelation and confirmed by the teaching of Christ and the apostle Paul". More recently H. E. LONA, *Der erste Clemensbrief* (1998) 428 states: "Die zwei Partizipialsätze (προδήλων ... γνώσεως) stellen zunächst eine Verbindung zum ersten Teil des Schreibens dar, indem sie die bisherige Darlegung als Zugang zur göttlichen Erkenntnis bewerten und zur Grundlage für die folgenden Bestimmungen machen".

> *But I want to break up my address, and first of all to speak about concord in itself in*
> *general, telling both whence it comes and what it achieves, and then over against that*
> *to set off strife and hatred in contradistinction to friendship. For when concord has*
> *been proved to be beneficial to all mankind, the proof will naturally follow that this*
> *particular concord between these particular cities is both quite indispensable for you*
> *and quite profitable as well (38.8).*

The following *probatio*-section shows that he follows this structure. In 38.10-20 he
speaks about concord in general, before he deals in 38.21-51[1093] with the concrete
strife between Nicomedia and Nicae and gives his advice in order to establish concord.[1094] This means that that it appears reasonable to consider 38.10-20 as a θέσις
and the subsequent passage as a ὑπόθεσις.

Aelius Aristides' discourse on concord addressed to the Rhodians (*Or.* 24) reflects a
similar structure in the *probatio*-section. This discourse appears to consist of an
exordium (24.1-3), a *probatio* (24.4-57), and a *peroratio* (24.58-59).[1095] In this connection it is sufficient to note that the first main section of the *probatio* deals with concord
in general (24.4-21). Aristides, to a great extent by using different types of examples,
aims to demonstrate that in general "concord is the greatest good for cities" (24.4).
Though in the remaining part of the *probatio* (24.22-57), we also find general considerations on concord, this part is more related to the concrete situation of the audi-

---

[1093]Cf. the introduction to the concrete affairs in the beginning of 38.21: "First of all, then, men of
Nicomedia, let us inspect the reasons for your strife".

[1094]Though she does not deal with the composition of this discourse of Dio Chrysostom in rhetorical terms, B. E. Bowe, *A Church in Crisis* (1988) 72, comments that Dio here first deals with concord in general before he gives specific exhortation. Further, she maintains that Aristid. *Or.* 23 reflects
the same structure. Before she quotes *Or.* 23.27 she says that "having introduced his topic, and spoken
in general about the situation he encounters, he then proceeds to apply the general to the particular"
(72). This is not, however, an adequate description of the structure of this oration. 23.8-26 consists not
of a general treatment of concord, but is a praise of Asia's leading cities. In the following *probatio*
(23.27-79), Aristides discusses the advantage of concord in general and gives concrete advice interchangeably. For the delimitation of this discourse, cf. C. A. Behr, *P. Aelius Aristides. The Complete
works* vol. 2 (1981) 365f. By and large we follow Behr, but we think 23.8-23 ought to be regarded as an
enlarged *exordium*. We agree with Bowe that there is an interesting similarity between the composition
of Dio Chrys. *Or.* 38 and *1 Clement* which may cast light on the macro-structure of *1 Clement*. But
when she infers on the basis of this similarity and the alleged similarity with Aristid. *Or.* 23 that "the
structure of the letter is devised to place greater emphasis on the general situation and to view the particular incident as less significant" we cannot follow her (72). As far as we can understand, Dio Chrysostom's statement in *Or.* 38.3 which says that he will first offer advice "on the weightiest matter of all"
does not solely refer to his general treatment of concord, but includes both the general treatment and
the specific application to the concrete situation. Neither Dio Chrysostom nor Aelus Aristides makes
any distinction of importance with respect to the general and the concrete treatment of concord.

[1095]C. A. Behr, *P. Aelius Aristides. The Complete works* vol. 2 (1981) 369, gives the following
delimitation of this discourse: 1-3 Proem; 4-21 Concord and indisputable good: traditional evidence;
22 Faction injurious to Rhodes' freedom; 23-27 Examples from history; 28-40 Appeal for settlement of
the present dispute; 41-44 Praise of concord; 45-57 Rhodes' glorious tradition opposes faction; 58-59
Peroration.

ence.[1096] In other words, 24.4-21 could be regarded as a θέσις and 24.22-57 as a ὑπόθεσις.

Also in Paul's letter to the Romans the theoretical part of the *probatio* (1:18-11:36) can be delimited into a θέσις (1:18-8:39) and a ὑπόθεσις part (9:1-11:36) as has been proposed by D. Hellholm.[1097]

4.2.4. Sub-Texts on the Fourth and Following Grades

4.2.4.1. Sub-Texts on the Fourth and Following Grades within the quaestio infinita Section (4:1-39:9)

4ST2311 ζῆλος and ἔρις leads to death, 4:1-6:4

4:1-6:4 (4ST2311) constitutes the first section of proof in the *quaestio infinita/*θέσις part. 4:1 is introduced with a "for (γάρ) it is written" formula where γάρ points back to the assertion in the *narratio* which says that unrighteousness and impious envy (ζῆλος) caused that "'death came into the world'" (3:4). In the *narratio* where Clement deals with the past and present occurrences in the Corinthian Church which shaped the exigency the letter responds to, he states that the Corinthian Christians are coloured by ζῆλος. If in what follows he succeeds in proving that ζῆλος in fact leads to death, this will be an important step towards making the audience ready to accept his advice.

It is exactly this strategy that Clement applies in 4:1-6:4. Here he attempts to prove that the assertion at the end of 2:7 is valid. This means that the assertion that unrighteousness and impious envy (ζῆλος) caused that "'death came into the world'" functions as a thesis for the following argumentation.

As proofs Clement uses many historical examples from the Scriptures, the Christian tradition, from life in the household, and from political history, 4:1-6:4. This section of proof consists of four parts. (1) Examples taken from the Old Testament, 4:1-13 (5ST23111). After the first example to which he devotes most space, the Cain and Abel story, in 4:7 he addresses the readers directly (ὁρᾶτε, ἀδελφοί) and offers a preliminary conclusion; "jealousy and envy (ζῆλος and φθόνος) wrought fratricide". This first subsection of proof contains altogether seven examples which intend to demonstrate the crucial consequence of ζῆλος and φθόνος.[1098] (2) Examples from the Christian tradition, 5:1-6:2 (5ST23112). Also these examples aim to show the evil consequences of ζῆλος and φθόνος: Peter and Paul "were persecuted and contended unto death" (5:2), many Christians were tortured (6:1), women were persecuted (6:2). (3) Examples from the household; it has "estranged wives from husbands", 6:3

[1096]The change from the general to the more concrete is reflected in 24.22 where Aristides argues that the present strife is a threat to their freedom.

[1097]D. HELLHOLM, "Amplificatio in the Macro-Structure of Romans", *Rhetoric and the New Testament* (1993) 133 and 138-140.

[1098]In addition to the Cain and Abel story, Clement uses the Jacob and Esau story, the evil consequences of ζῆλος and φθόνος for Moses, Aron and Miraim, Dathan and Abiram, and David.

(5ST23113). (4) The consequences of ζῆλος from the political area, 6:4 (5ST23114). When Clement states that "jealousy and strife" (ζῆλος καὶ ἔρις) have caused great cities to become destroyed and mighty nations to have been rooted up, he reflects a common experience in Greek political history.[1099] This statement functions also as an amplification: ζῆλος and φθόνος have not only caused death for members of the people of God, but have even caused "death" for great cities and mighty nations.

By means of these examples which reflect experience from a wide range of areas, from Holy Scripture, from the Christian tradition, from family life and from political history, Clement attempts to demonstrate his assertion in 2:7b. Experience from different times and from areas of fundamental importance to the Corinthian Christians demonstrates that ζῆλος and φθόνος are dangerous vices which ultimately lead to death and destruction.

We should pay attention to some aspects of Clement's use of example in this section. First we observe that his use of example is remarkably in line with Aristotle's considerations on how to apply example as proof.[1100] When the orator has no enthymemes at hand and the example is placed first, he underlines the need to use many examples. In the opposite case, when the orator uses an enthymeme first, it is sufficient to present just one example. In the latter case the example functions as evidence. Clement does not use an enthymeme here, but instead uses a great number of examples. Secondly, we note that in line with rhetorical theory and practice he takes examples both from their forefathers, the examples taken from the Old Testament, and from recent history.[1101]

Previously in the present study we have seen that when Clement maintains that ζῆλος and φθόνος could have such serious consequences within different political bodies, he reflects a thought common in his cultural milieu. ζῆλος and φθόνος were perceived as a root of civil strife which could develop into war and death.[1102] That Clement associates ἔρις with ζῆλος is obvious from 6:4 where he explicitly links these terms. Thus on the basis of the *docilem parare* where he indicates that στάσις is the main theme of the letter it is understandable that he focuses upon the serious consequences of ζῆλος and φθόνος. In other words, there is consistency between the overall topic of the letter and what he deals with in this section of proof.

When Clement has stated in the *narratio* that ζῆλος and φθόνος have arisen among the Corinthian Christians and when he further attempts to demonstrate the evil consequences of these vices in 4:1-6:4, this appears to be a deliberate strategy in his appeal for concord. For if he first succeeds in making the Corinthians aware of the dangerous situation they in fact are facing, they would be more ready to accept his subsequent advice to follow a certain way of behaviour. In this strategy for making them open to correction, he probably consciously tries to stir up the emotion of fear among

---

[1099]For the destructive effects of ζῆλος and ἔρις, see chaps. 3.5.1.2 and 3.5.1.1.2 respectively.

[1100]Aristotle distinguishes between examples used as evidence (μαρτύριον) and as demonstrative proofs (ἀπόδειξις, *Rh.* 2.20.9).

[1101]Cf. chap. 2.4.1.

[1102]Cf. chap. 3.5.1.2.

them. This emotion is one of "those affections which cause men to change their opinion in regard to their judgements".[1103] Fear for what consequences ζῆλος and φθόνος could have for the Corinthian Church should make them realize that they are in fact in trouble and thus need correction. That this was the intended function of 4:1-6:4 seems to be confirmed in what follows in 7:1 where Clement states that he has dealt with these things for the purpose of admonition, before he goes further in the following passage to explicitly exhort the Corinthians to do the things which please God (7:2ff.). To follow his proposed way of behaviour implies repentance (7:5ff.).

If we turn our attention to other deliberative discourses and letters urging concord, we find a similar strategy in some of them. Before one advises a particular kind of action, one first seeks to demonstrate that the audience in fact is facing trouble and thus that a change of behaviour indeed is required.[1104] Let us first focus upon Dio Chrysotom's *Or. 34*. In a *partitio* he outlines the structure of the discourse under three heads:

> ... *first of all I wish to point out to you one thing, in case you are not fully aware of it – that you need good judgement in the present emergency, and that your problems are such as to merit counsel and much foresight; secondly, that no man in this company can readily advise you as to the proper course of action, some being really ignorant of your true advantage and some ... looking rather to their own interests. Next I shall indicate my own opinion with reference to these affairs and suggest by what cause of action on your part at the moment and by what general policy in your leadership of the city, things will, as I believe, work out in all respects to your advantage for the future also (Or. 34.6f.).*

We observe that Dio first focuses upon the fact that the audience is facing an emergency, that the problem is of such a character that counsel is in place. Further, his focus on the fact that no members of the audience possess the ability to offer proper advice emphasizes the fact that they are in real trouble and need correction. After attempting to make the audience realize their real situation, Dio goes further and offers advice regarding the proper course of action in the future.[1105] In other words, before he gives his advice he first demonstrates that the audience is facing the evil of στάσις, political discord in both external and internal affairs (34.7-26).

A similar pattern is found in *Or. 38* where he says in the *partitio* that he first of all wants to "speak about concord (ὁμόνοια) itself in general, telling both whence it comes and what it achieves, and then over against that to set off strife (στάσις) and hatred (ἔχθρα) in contradistinction to friendship" (38.8). In line with this he first points to the blessings of concord in contrast to the evils of στάσις (38.10-20).[1106]

[1103] Arist. *Rh.* 2.1.8.

[1104] This has already been pointed out by M. M. MITCHELL, *Paul and the Rhetoric of Reconciliation* (1991) 208f. In what follows we depend on the texts she has systematized for this purpose.

[1105] For the macro-structure of this discourse, see C. P. JONES, *The Roman World of Dio Chrysotom* (197) 76-82.

[1106] For the arrangement of the whole discourse, cf. *Ibid.* 85; M. M. MITCHELL, *Paul and the Rhetoric of Reconciliation* (1991) 208 n. 116.

στάσις, "of which wars and battles constitute departments and subsidiary activities" (38.11), represents a great danger. Also, in order to show that the audience need correction he maintains that there are members of the audience who love this kind of activity. Moreover, στάσις is widespread and its effects "are continually at work in communities and in nations, just like the diseases in our bodies" (38.12).[1107] Thus it should be beyond any doubt that the audience is facing a situation which needs correction for their own advantage.

As a last example of this strategy in deliberative argument for concord, we shall pay attention to the speech of Titus Lauicus reported by Dionysius Halicarnassensis. First he refers to the dangerous consequence of the present disobedience and discord among the Romans, i.e. overthrow and ruin of the commonwealth (*Ant. Rom.* 6.35f.). This implies that the audience in fact needs correction. Then he moves on to point out the advantage for the Romans, if they all could be of one mind (μιᾷ πάντες γνώμῃ): "For the power of the commonwealth when harmonious will be sufficient both to give security to our allies and to inspire fear in our enemies, but when discordant, as at the present, it can effect neither" (*Ant. Rom.* 6.35.2). Then Titus Lauicus gives concrete advice on the Volscians and the Latins: "As to the answers to be now given to them, this is the advice I have to offer". In this advice he argues for courses of action which would be the best for the audience and which would be most just (*Ant. Rom.* 6.36.2f.).

There are also other deliberative arguments for concord which reflect a similar structure, but the above-mentioned should suffice to illustrate our point in this connection.[1108] Clement appears to reflect a common structure in deliberative argument for concord made by others, in as much as at the beginning of the letter he tries to show the Corinthian Christians that they in fact are facing trouble and thus need correction. Admittedly, he does not explicitly discuss the dangerous consequences of sedition in contrast to the blessings of concord, as the actual comparative literature does. Instead he emphasizes how dramatic one of the underlying causes of στάσις – ζῆλος and φθόνος – could be. In this matter he to some extent resembles the structure of Dio Chrysostom's *Or.* 38. While Dio first deals with the subject of concord in general, "telling both whence it comes and what it achieves", Clement deals with an underlying cause of the antonym στάσις. In spite of these differences, the basic function of *1 Clem.* 4:1-6:4 and the focus upon the negative consequences of στάσις in the above-mentioned deliberative argument for concord is quite similar. In all cases it should demonstrate that the members of the actual audience are in real trouble which should further make them realize that they are in need of correction. Thus the orator has created a good basis for the advice that follows.

[1107]Cf. also 38.3 where he says there are things of "greater matters" which deserve correction.

[1108]Cf. Dem. *Ep.* 1; Dion. Hal. *Ant. Rom.* 4.26.1-4; 6.49.3-55.3; Aristid. *Or.* 24; Pl. *Ep.* 8, and the comments on these text in M. M. MITCHELL, *Paul and the Rhetoric of Reconciliation* (1991) 208f.

4ST2312 Exhortations to certain virtues which are according to the will of God and which promote concord, 7:1-39:9

4:1-6:4 is set apart from the following sub-text on the same level by means of a *SA*, two *SMs*, and a *Da* in 7:1: Ταῦτα, ἀγαπητοί, οὐ μόνον ὑμᾶς νουθωτοῦντες ἐπιστέλλομεν, ἀλλὰ καὶ ἑαυτοὺς ὑπομιμνῄσκοντες ("We are not only writing these things to you, beloved, for your admonition, but also to remind ourselves").[1109] ταῦτα functions as a *SA*. It is reasonable to hold that this *SA* is used both anaphorically and cataphorically. In other words, it both points back to the former sub-text at the same level in 4:1-6:4 (4ST2311) and points forward to the following exhortations given in 7:1-39:9 (4ST2312). The terms νουθωτοῦντες and ὑπομιμνῄσκοντες are *SMs*. Concerning this group of markers we remind the reader that it "informs the receiver of the function of the text".[1110] Clement informs the Corinthian Christians by means of this *SM* that 4:1-6:4 should be taken as an admonition. However, this *SM* not only refers to this passage, but also to the following passage at the same level in as much as its basic content is made up of exhortations to live in accordance with the will of God. In this section, which ends in 39:9, Clement gives many exhortations to various virtues and ways of living which constitute an expression of what it means to live according to the will of God. One must observe, however, that he does not focus upon concrete actions that aim to put an end to the present strife and sedition, but rather that he restricts himself in this section to focusing upon general virtues which are according to the will of God and at the same time promote concord. This is consistent with the fact that in the former sub-text on the same level, 4:1-6:4, he dealt with vices associated with στάσις. Although he undoubtedly gives many exhortations in 7:1-39:9 to a specific group of people at a particular time and place, he does not deal with the concrete situation in the Corinthian Church or present concrete advice in order to resolve the strife. This general treatment of concord justifies our viewing this section as part of a θέσις.

In the following we will attempt to outline the argumentative structure and the different sub-sections of 7:1-39:9.

5ST23121 Introduction to the exhortations, 7:1-4

As just mentioned, a number of delimitation markers are found in 7:1. Two of these are *SMs* which reveals the intended function of both this and the former sub-text at the same level: they should admonish. The description of the negative consequences of ζῆλος and φθόνος should demonstrate that the Corinthian Christians in fact are in need of correction and thus functions as an implicit admonition to them to change their behaviour. After expressing the function of the passage by means of the *SMs*, Clement goes on in 7:1-4 to give explicit exhortations which admonish the Corinthians

---

[1109]A. LINDEMANN, *Die Clemensbriefe* (1992) 43: "Mit dem einleitenden ταῦτα ... ἐπιστέλλομεν setzt der Vf ein deutliches Gliederungssignal: Der Argumentationsgang 3:1b-6:4b ist abgeschlossen". We do not, however, agree with Lindemann that this "Arrgumentationsgang" begins in 3:1b, but in 4:1 as we have argued above.

[1110]D. HELLHOLM, "The Problem of Apocalyptic Genre and the Apocalyps", *Semeia* 36 (1986) 39.

to "come to the glorious and venerable rule" of their tradition and to do "what is good and pleasing and acceptable in the sight "of their Maker (7:2-3). In other words, he exhorts them to live according to the will of God. For the Corinthian Christians this implies that they must repent. The term μετάνοια is introduced in 7:4. 7:1-4 (5 ST23121) functions thus as an introduction to the rather large passage (7:5-39:9) in which Clement gives them many exhortations to virtues which manifest the will of God and secure concord among Christians (7:2).

5ST23122 Repentance is possible, 7:5-8:5

As just noted, the admonition to live according to the will of God, implies repentance for the Corinthian Christians. In the sub-section 7:5-8:5 (5 ST23122) Clement seeks to demonstrate that μετάνοια is possible and according to the will of God. μετάνοια functions as a *SemM*. In 7:5 he maintains that the Master in all generations "has given a place of repentance to those who will turn to him" (6ST231221). In order to prove this assertion he presents examples from the Old Testament in 7:6f. and quotes passages from the Scriptures in 8:1-4 (6ST231222). Besides proving that repentance is according to the will of God, the end of the quotations of Isa 1:16-20 also indicates the grim consequence for those who oppose repentance: "'a sword shall devour you'" (8:4). It is reasonable to assume that this quotation gave rise to some fear among the Corinthian Christians of what would happen to them if they failed to follow his exhortations. Hence the quotation in addition to its main purpose functions as proof by *pathos* of Clement's overall purpose with the letter. 8:5 constitutes the conclusion of this sub-section: "Thus desiring to give all his beloved a share in repentance, he established it by his Almighty will" (6ST231223).

5ST23123 The need for obedience, 9:1-12:8

On this basis Clement goes on in 9:1 to exhort the Corinthians to obey God's will: "Wherefore let us obey his excellent and glorious will" (Διὸ ὑπακούσωμεν τῇ μεγαλοπρεπεῖ καὶ ἐνδόξῳ βουλήσει αὐτοῦ). In this statement two delimitation markers which set the present sub-text 9:1-12:8 (5 ST23123) apart from the former on the same level (5 ST23122) are found, i.e. the conjunction διό and a *SemM*, which introduces the *topic of obedience* (ὑπακούω). That the topic of obedience is the central theme in 9:1-12:8 is evident in as much as the bulk of this section consists of examples taken from the Old Testament that express the virtue and its synonym πιστός. The conclusion he draws in 12:8 on the basis of a list of examples represents the end of this section of proof.

In 9:1b Clement reveals what obedience implies for the Corinthian Christians at the present time, i.e. that they turn to God's pity and cease from the "vain toil and strife (ἔρις) and jealousy (ζῆλος) which leads to death". This shows that the exhortation to obedience and its synonym πιστός is explicitly related to his overall argument for concord.[1111] Further, we note that the remark he makes about the consequence of strife (ἔρις) and jealousy (ζῆλος), that they lead to death, functions as an implicit appeal to the danger connected with the present state at issue. As we have pointed out earlier, this is a common appeal in deliberative rhetoric. In order to persuade the Corinthians to repent and become obedient to the will of God, which in turn will lead to abandoning strife, Clement presents examples both of the advantage of being obedient and faithful and of the opposite.

More precisely, the argumentative structure of this section of proof is as follows: (1) An admonition to obey the will of God which implies that one ceases from strife (ἔρις) and jealousy (ζῆλος) in 9:1 (6 ST231231); (2) proof by examples taken from the Old Testament in order to demonstrate on the one hand the great advantage connected with being faithful and obedient to the will of God and on the other hand the risk of not doing so in 9:2-12:8 (6ST231232). The latter could be further divided into the following sub-sections: (1) An introduction to the examples in 9:2 (7ST2312321); (2) a section of positive examples, i.e. Enoch, Noah, Abraham, and Lot in 9:3-11:1 (7ST2312322); (3) a section containing a warning example, i.e. Lot's wife in 11:2 (7ST2312323); (4) a section containing a positive example, i.e. Rahab the harlot in 12:1-8 (7ST2312324).[1112]

As already indicated, the main function of the examples is to give support to the exhortation to obey the will of God and thus cease from strife and jealousy (9:1). On the one hand, examples from God's dealing with his people in the Old Testament demonstrate the great advantage of being faithful and of obeying the will of God: death did not befall Enoch; God saved the world through Noah's faithfulness; God's blessing of Abraham and his house; Rahab the harlot was saved. On the other hand, the fate of Lot's wife who Clement describes as "a warning to all generations" in 11:2 demonstrates the opposite. Or to use the words of Clement, these examples should make it clear that the Master "does not forsake those who hope in him [that is those who obey him], but delivers to punishment and torture those who turn aside to others" (11:1). This means that Clement, as is characteristic of deliberative rhetoric, appeals both to the advantage to the audience, if they follow the proposed cause of action, and to the danger they are facing, if they do not follow the proposed advice. Furthermore, the examples are likely to have stirred the emotions of the audience. First of all, we believe, the warning example about Lot's wife would lead to a certain fear among the Corinthian Christians of the consequence of not paying attention to the admonition.

Before we go further we will reiterate that Clement's exhortation and argumentation for the need of being faithful and obedient to the will of God is closely related to the main topic of the letter. That is to say, obedience and faithfulness should be manifested in a community life free from strife and jealousy. In other words, when he focuses upon the need for obedience he underlines one particular aspect of how this obedience

---

[1111]Previously we have seen that obedience and faithfulness, which are used as synonyms in this section, belonged to the semantic field of ὁμόνοια in antiquity. See chaps. 3.5.2.8 and 3.5.2.4.

[1112]The fact that Clement presents two sections of positive examples and only one of negative examples, shows that the emphasis is on the positive.

should be manifested, i.e. to live in concord.[1113] Therefore it is reasonable to conclude that Clement does not focus upon the need for obedience for its own sake, but because obedience to the will of God will lead to concord. To express it in other words, the topic of obedience is subsumed under the cardinal theme of the letter, and the appeal for obedience to the will of God is an integrated element in his overall argumentative strategy in persuading the Corinthian Christians to receive his advice.

5ST23124 The need for humility, 13:1-19:1

After having exhorted the Corinthians to obey the will of God, which implies ceasing from the present strife, and having proved the need for and advantages of this by means of historical examples taken from the Old Testament, Clement now goes on to focus upon an attitude which he holds to be a consequence of obeying God's will: ταπεινοφρονέω, to be humble.[1114] The exhortation to be humble-minded (ταπεινο-φρονέω,) in 13:1 functions as a SemM in as much as this is the basic topic in 13:1-19:1.[1115] In addition to this SemM the conjunction οὖν and the DA ἀδελφοί are markers in 13.1 which serve to set this sub-text (5ST23124) apart from the former one at the same level, i.e. 9:1-12:8 (5 ST23123). This sub-text (5ST23124) ends in 19:1 where Clement concludes a list of biblical examples of humility by focusing upon its effect upon the people of God: the humility (and obedient submission) of so many famous men have rendered better both the past generations and the present. The key word ταπεινοφρονέω, functions as a frame for the whole text sequence.

The exhortation to be humble-minded in 13:1, which functions as a SemM, introduces a new topic in the probatio-section. The topic of humility was however touched upon in the exordium where Clement emphasized this aspect of the Corinthians' noble life in the past.[1116] He not only exhorts them to be humble-minded, but also points out what it means for the Corinthian Christians to practice this virtue, i.e. that they put aside (ἀποτίθημι) "all arrogance (ἀλαζονεία) and conceit and foolishness (ἀφρο-σύνη) and wrath" (ὀργή, 13:1). Such a contrast between humility and arrogance is also found in the exordium where Clement praises the Corinthian Christians, among other things, for the fact that they had formerly not been arrogant at all. Previously in the investigation we have seen that ἀλαζονεία belonged to the semantic field of con-

---

[1113]This is evident from what we have noted previously regarding the terms strife (ἔρις) and jealousy (ζῆλος) which belong to the semantic field of concord. ἔρις is even used as synonym for στάσις both in 1 Clement and in other ancient literature that deals with the topic of unity and sedition in political bodies. See pp. 86f., 91f.

[1114]Cf. A. LINDEMANN, Die Clemensbriefe (1992) 53: "Der Vf leitet sie jetzt aus dem Vorangegangenen ab, ohne dass der sachliche Zusammenhang ohne weiteres sichtbar würde, da die in Kap. 9-12 erwähnten biblischen Gestalten sich ja nicht durch "Demut" ausgezeichnet hatten; offenbar ist gemeint, dass aus Glauben und Gehorsam die Demut als sittliche Haltung folgen soll". Similarly H. E. LONA, Der erste Clemensbrief (1998) 210.

[1115]The term occurs seven times in 13:1-19:1 (13:1; 13:3; 16:1, 2, 17; 17:2; 19:1).

[1116]1 Clem. 2:1.

cord.[1117] We have also seen that although Clement's use of ταπεινοφρονέω, primarily reflects a Jewish use of this term, there are also examples that show that ταπεινο-φρονέω, in the Greek tradition was connected with behaviour which promoted concord.[1118] The most important point in this connection is, however, to note that the exhortation in 13:1 introduces a *new argumentative sequence.* This sequence serves to give support to the exhortation in 13:1 and to make clear what it means for the Corinthian Christians to practise humility. The argumentative structure of 13:1-19:1 could be outlined in the following way:

After the exhortation in 13:1a Clement quotes from Scripture and refers to logia of Jesus in order to show that he has support for the exhortation (13:1b-13:4). Thus 13:1-13:4 (6ST231241) could be regarded as an argumentative sub-sequence of 13:1-19:1. His remark in 13:3 about how the Christians must respond to the material he has presented shows how closely he holds the connection to be between obedience toward the will of God and humility: "With this commandment and with these injunctions let us strengthen ourselves to walk in obedience (ὑπήκοος) to his hallowed words and let us be humble-minded (ταπεινοφρονέω)".[1119] Furthermore, the quotation of Isa 66:2, where the prophet says that God will look on those who tremble at his words, serves to emphasize the need for obeying the words of God (13:4).

After having demonstrated both that his exhortation in 13:1 is in line with the Scriptures and the teaching of Jesus, and that God will look favourably on those who have respect for his words, Clement continues his argumentation in 14:1 on this basis. The conjunction οὖν, which expresses an inference from the preceding passage, and the double *DA* ἄνδρες ἀδελφοί in this verse serve as delimitation markers on the surface-level and indicate the beginning of a new sub-text, i.e.14:1-5 (6ST231242).[1120] From the preceding text Clement draws the inference (οὖν) that it is "right (δίκαιος)[1121] and holy (ὅσιος), my brethren, for us to obey (ὑπήκοος) God rather than to follow those who in pride and unruliness (ἐν ἀλαζονείᾳ καὶ ἀκαταστασίᾳ) are the instigators of an abominable jealousy" (ζῆλος, 14:1). In other words, to a certain extent he reiterates the exhortation in 13:1: to obey God and to be humble-minded means that one turns away from those who ἐν ἀλαζονείᾳ καὶ ἀκαταστασίᾳ cause jealousy which in turns leads to sedition. Furthermore, in 14:2 he adds an argument which serves to strengthen his statement in 14:1. Here in a manner so characteristic of deliberative rhetoric urging concord he warns of a present or immediate danger facing the members of the audience if they do not pay attention to the proposed course of action.[1122] He says that one "shall incur no common harm (βλάβη), but great danger (κίνδυνος μέγας)", if one follows those who launch out into strife and sedition (εἰς

[1117]Cf. pp. 131-136.

[1118]See pp. 126-131.

[1119]Cf. what we have said above regarding the connection between obedience and humility.

[1120]For this delimitation, see below.

[1121]For the appeal to the right in deliberative rhetoric, see chaps. 2.3.1; 2.3.2.

[1122]Cf. chaps. 2.3.1; 2.3.2.

ἔριν καὶ στάσεις). By qualifying the danger with the adjective "great" Clement emphasizes this aspect of the appeal. Furthermore, his emphasis on the danger connected with joining those who rush into strife and sedition serves also to arouse the emotion of fear in the audience. Thus, this is another example of his use of *pathos* in his argumentation. Moreover, 14:1-2 shows clearly that the exhortation to be humble-minded and to put aside arrogance in 13:1 must imply that the Corinthian Christians should abandon strife and sedition. In other words, his exhortation to humility and obedience toward God is closely related to the main topic of the letter as it is outlined in the *docilem parare* in 1:1. In as much as he admonishes the Corinthians in 14:3 to be "kind (χρηστεύομαι) to one another" it appears that he holds that such an attitude will encourage the way of behaviour proposed in 14:1.[1123] The rest of this argumentative sequence consists of quotations from the Old Testament which aim to demonstrate on the one hand the blessings or advantages to those who follow God's law and are kind and peaceable (εἰρηνικός) and on the other hand to show the disadvantages or the dangers associated with the opposite course of action (14:4-5). Thus the quotation from Scripture serves to support Clement's statement in 14:1-3, which, as mentioned above, reflects the common reference to the danger associated with sedition in a political body.

On the basis of the argumentation in 14:1-5, and in particular 14:5b, Clement goes on to exhort the Corinthians to adhere to men "whose peacefulness is based on piety (μετ᾽ εὐσεβείας εἰρηνεύουσιν) and not to those whose wish for peace is hypocrisy" (15:1). The inferential particle τοίνυν functions as a delimitation marker indicating that a new text-sequence begins at this point. This sub-text includes 15:1-16:1 (6ST231243). That the exhortation is introduced with this particle also indicates that what follows is an inference from what precedes it. However, in as much as the topic of ὑπόκρισις does not occur in the preceding text, this is strictly speaking the case only regarding the first part of the exhortation. The warning against those whose wish for peace is hypocrisy, however, is closely connected to the first part of the exhortation in as much as ὑπόκρισις is an antonym of εὐσέβεια. Thus an exhortation to cleave to those whose peacefulness is based on piety must in turn encourage behaviour that rejects those whose desire for peace is hypocritical. The reference to those who are hypocritical in their wish for peace is probably an indirect reference to the instigators of sedition in Corinth.[1124] Yet we note that Clement does not explicitly apply the term ὑπόκρισις to any group of people in the Corinthian Church. In accord with the rules of a θέσις, the exhortations Clement uses are general in their content and are not applied to a concrete case in question.

Although the exhortation in 15:1 is an inference from what precedes it, Clement quotes passages from the Scriptures, as he typically does, in order to make it more per-

---

[1123]Clement has already pointed out that being kind is in accord with the teaching of Jesus (13:2).

[1124]A. LINDEMANN, *Die Clemensbriefe* (1992) 58: "Vorausgesetzt ist jetzt, dass auch die Rädelsführer der korinthischen στάσις Frieden wollen, aber eben nicht μετ᾽ εὐσεβείας, sondern μεθ᾽ ὑποκρίσεως".

suasive (15:2-7). By means of these quotations he aims to show that hypocrisy was present among the people of God in Old Testament times. The most important point for him, however, is to show that God does not accept it and will punish "the deceitful lips" (15:5). Thus the quotations serve to underline the need to cleave to those who really promote peace, or to use his own words: "to those whose peacefulness is based on piety", and to turn away from those who only desire peace hypocritically.

The last quotation from Scripture contains a promise of salvation for the πτωχός and πένης (15:6f.). So when Clement states in 16:1, that "For Christ is of those who are humble-minded" (ταπεινοφρονούντων γάρ ἐστιν ὁ Χριστός), it seems that he has these in mind. In the immediate context the conjunction γάρ refers to the promise of salvation for these people, i.e. the humble-minded.[1125] However, this γάρ could also refer back to the whole preceding passage, 13:1-15:7, and add a new proof to his argumentation. The simple fact that the key term ταπεινοφρονέω is found in 13:1 and 13:3 points in this direction. Furthermore, when Clement contrasts the humble-minded in 16:1 with "those who exalt themselves (ἐπαίρω) over His [Christ's] flock", the latter group of people probably refers to those who are arrogant (13:1), "those who in pride and unruliness are the instigators of an abominable jealousy" (14:1) and "rush into strife and sedition" (14:2), and "whose wish for peace is hypocrisy" (15:1).[1126] If we are right in these suggestions, the statement introduced with γάρ serves to strengthen Clement's argumentation for concord in 13:1-15:7. If Christ and his salvation are restricted to those who are humble-minded this is a strong argument for the need to practise humility. In other words, it gives support to the exhortation in 13:1, which introduces the topic of being humble-minded and the similar exhortation in 14:3. Insofar as being humble-minded is inconsistent with strife and sedition it is ultimately a strong argument for concord as well. Our understanding of the function of 16:1 in Clement's argumentative strategy implies that, in contradiction of the commonly held view that this verse constitutes the beginning of the section which deals with the humility of Christ,[1127] we should maintain that it constitutes the end of the text sequence 15:1-16:1.

We have attempted above to show that in 13:1-16:1 Clement argues that the practice of being humble-minded and obedient to the word of God, qualities that are closely interconnected,[1128] must lead to one's turning away from those who rush into strife and sedition. In other words, if the Corinthian Christians seek to practice humility, it is a contradiction at the same time to be involved in activities which lead to strife in the

---

[1125]So also R. KNOPF, *Die zwei Clemensbriefe* (1920) 67; A. LINDEMANN, *Die Clemensbriefe* (1992) 60.

[1126]Cf. A. LINDEMANN, *Die Clemensbriefe* (1992), who holds that "Die ἐπαιρόμενοι sind wieder die Rädelsführer, von deren Hochmut Gott gegenüber in Kap. 15 die Rede gewesen war" (60).

[1127] J. A. FISCHER, *Die Apostolischen Väter* (1966) 4; A. LINDEMANN, *Die Clemensbriefe* (1992) 59f.

[1128]From 14:3 it appears that Clement holds that to be obedient to the word of God necessarily means that one is humble-minded.

community. It is hardly an accident that he has established such a connection between being humble-minded and concord. Besides the fact that humility was a significant virtue in the Jewish-Christian tradition, it was not difficult to find biblical examples of highly esteemed people who practised humility. In the following sub-text within 13:1-19:1, i.e. 16:2-19:1 (6ST231244), he presents a number of such examples.

First he focuses upon the humility of Christ in 16:2-16:17 (7ST2312441). In contrast to those who are marked by arrogance (ἀλαζονεία) and pride (ὑπερηφανία) Christ was humble-minded (ταπεινοφρονέω, 16:2). It is hardly an accident that Clement contrasts arrogance and pride with being humble-minded. Pride and arrogance were, as we have seen, according to him a characteristic trait of people involved in strife and sedition.[1129] In order to prove the statement in 16:2, he quotes the rather long LXX texts of Isa 53:1-12 with only slight modifications,[1130] and also Ps 21:7-9. The content of these passages is directly applied to Christ. In the summary statement in 16:17, beginning with the direct address ὁρᾶτε, ἄνδρες ἀγαπητοί,[1131] Clement himself quite directly expresses the function of the quotations from Scripture and the reason for focusing upon the humility of Christ. Firstly, the quotations from the Old Testament should demonstrate that "the Lord was thus humble-minded". Secondly, the basic reason for dealing with the humility of Christ in this connection is that he is an example (ὑπογραμμός) to imitate. After describing Christ as an example and referring to his humility, he expresses the call to imitate him by means of a rhetorical question; "what shall we do, who through him have come under the yoke of his grace?" (16:17). That this is the conclusion Clement wants the Corinthians to draw is also indicated when he introduces examples in 17:1 from the Old Testament using the words μιμηταὶ γενώμεθα. Thus the example of Christ functions as proof of the need to practise humility and therefore strengthens the preceding argumentation and exhortations to cease from strife and sedition.

After using the example of Christ, Clement moves on to use examples from the Old Testament in 17:1-19:1 (7ST2312442). As just mentioned above, he introduces these with an exhortation to imitate the examples that follow (μιμηταὶ γενώμεθα, 17:1). More specifically, he exhorts his audience to imitate the prophets Elijah, Elisha and Ezekiel and additionally "the famous men of old" (17:1). Among the latter group he pays attention to Abraham (17:2), Job (17:3-4), Moses (17:5-6), and David (18:1-17). It is only in the description of Abraham that Clement employs the term ταπεινοφρονέω (17:2). However, the quoted passages from Scripture is obviously intended to demonstrate the humility of these men. That this was his intention is evident from 19:1 where he refers in a summary statement to "the humility and obedient

---

[1129] *1 Clem.* 14:1.

[1130] See the discussion in D. A. HAGNER, *The Use of the Old and New Testaments in Clement of Rome* (1973) 49-51.

[1131] The imperative ὁρᾶτε constitutes the transition to a summary several times in the letter (4:7; 12:8; 21:1; 23:4; 41:4). Cf. A. LINDEMANN, *Die Clemensbriefe* (1992) 64.

submission (τὸ ταπεινόφρον καὶ τὸ ὑποδεὲς διὰ τῆς ὑπακοῆς) of so many men of such great fame".

Furthermore, Clement also expresses the purpose of focusing upon the humility and obedient submission of so many "famous men of old"; their examples "have rendered better" not only the present generation, but also the generations from the past who have received the words of God in fear and truth (19:1). Although he does not state it explicitly, there is no doubt that his use of the examples of those who rendered better both people of the past and in the present times serves as an implicit appeal to the Corinthian Christians to imitate their examples. Since both Christ and the most famous men of God's people were humble-minded, the Corinthians should imitate their practice. This means, as was the case regarding the example of Christ, that these noble examples from the Old Testament are intended to strengthen Clement's argumentation, in particular his exhortation to be humble-minded in 13:1-16:1. Taking into consideration how he has described the implications of being humble-minded in 13:1-16:1 it is fair to assume that by using the phrase "render better" he primarily means to live in concord and peace. That this suggestion is correct seems to be confirmed in 19:2a.[1132]

5ST23125 Exhortations to unity in peace, 19:2-22:8

In 19:2-22:8 (5ST23125) Clement changes the focus from the many "great and glorious deeds" of famous men to the good deeds of God towards his creation, in particular to the peace and harmony of the universe. The main line of argumentation in this text-sequence is that the order and peace and harmony of nature established by God should be reflected in a community life of peace and harmony.

On the surface-level this sub-text is delimited from the former one at the same level (5 ST23124) by means of a *SA* in 19:2. It appears reasonable to argue that the expression πολλῶν οὖν καὶ μεγάλων καὶ ἐνδόξων μετειληφότες πράξεων encompasses what is said about the examples of humility in 13:1-19:1. Thus it functions as a *SA*. Furthermore, the conjunction οὖν also functions as a delimitation marker on the surface-level of the text. In addition to these delimitation markers on the surface-level, there is also a *SemM*. The exhortation in 19:2b to fasten one's gaze on and hold fast to the Father and Creator's "excellent gifts of peace, and to his good deeds to us" functions as a *SemM* in as much as the text that follows focuses upon these gifts and how the Corinthians ought to respond to them.

In 19:2a on the basis (οὖν) of the "many great and glorious deeds" he has just dealt with, i.e. the examples of humility,[1133] Clement exhorts the Corinthians to "hasten on to the goal of peace (εἰρήνης σκοπός)" which was given (παραδεδομένος) from the beginning (ἐξ ἀρχῆς). In our opinion it is reasonable to assume that the phrase ἐξ ἀρχῆς refers to the time before the strife and sedition took place in the Corinthian

---

[1132]See the discussion below.

[1133]Cf. R. KNOPF, *Die zwei Clemensbriefe* (1920) 74.

Church,[1134] and is not a reference to the beginning of Creation.[1135] Supporting this is the fact that in his exhortation to peace Clement does not take his departure in the good deeds of God, but in great deeds of human beings.[1136] Furthermore, we should note the similarity in phraseology with *1 Clem.* 2:2 where the author deals with the peace of the Corinthian Church before the present strife arose. Here he says that a deep peace (εἰρήνη βαθεῖα) was given (ἐδέδοτο) to them. This means that both in 2:2 and in 19:2a he uses the medium of the verb (παρα)δίδωμι with εἰρήνη as object. This fact also indicates that "the goal of peace (εἰρήνης σκοπός), which was given (παραδεδομένος)" from the beginning (ἐξ ἀρχῆς) refers to the former peace of the Corinthian Church. In other words, he concludes the list of examples of humility by exhorting the Corinthian Christians to imitate the great deeds of these men and to re-establish the former peace of the Corinthian Church.

In 19:2b Clement turns his attention from the glorious deeds of men towards God's good deeds to mankind. More precisely, he focuses upon the Creator's "splendid and excellent gifts of peace" (αὐτοῦ δωρεαῖς τῆς εἰρήνης εὐεργεσίαις). In other words, in 19:2 the author both brings to a definitive conclusion the examples of humility in the former sub-text by exhorting the Corinthians to re-establish peace in the Church, and changes the focus to God's gifts of peace. Thus 19:2 could be viewed as a transition to a new topic.

After the exhortation in 19:3 to contemplate the Creator, Clement continues by describing God's "excellent gifts of peace" as they are manifested according to his will in the order and the peace and harmony of the universe (20:1-12). The different parts of the universe – among others, day and night, sun and moon, the stars, and the seasons – co-operate and accomplish their duties in peace and harmony in submission to the command of God. Characteristic of Clement's emphasis upon these aspects is the summary statement in 20:11 where he concludes that "all these things did the great Creator and Master of the universe ordain to be in peace and concord (ἐν εἰρήνῃ καὶ ὁμονοίᾳ)". The doxology in 20:12 constitutes the end of this text sequence, 19:2-20:12 (6 ST231251).

In 21:1-22:8 (6 ST231252) Clement draws a conclusion regarding what consequences God's gifts of peace or his many good works must have for the community life of the Christian. The introduction to verse 21:1 with the emphasized *DA* ὁρᾶτε, ἀγαπητοί indicates clearly that a new text sequence begins at this point. First he warns

[1134]So also E. BAASLAND, "1. Klemensbrev", *De Apostoliske Fedre* (1984) 155.

[1135]Contra, e.g., R. KNOPF, *Die zwei Clemensbriefe* (1920) 74; A. LINDEMANN, *Die Clemensbriefe* (1992) 68. These scholars argue that the focus upon God's "excellent gifts of peace" manifested in the universe must mean that the phrase ἐξ ἀρχῆς refers to the beginning of the creation. H. E. LONA, *Der erste Clemensbrief* (1998), is of the opinion that the expression "bezieht sich wahrscheinlich auf die für den Vf. über allem stehende Offenbarung Gottes in der Schrift, d.h. im AT" (246).

[1136]A. Lindemann does not reflect upon this point at all. R. KNOPF, *Die zwei Clemensbriefe* (1920), admits that the transition from the good deeds of man in history, that is the examples of humility, to the good deeds of God is abrupt (schroff), but argues that "schon die Liturgie band beides zusammen, den Gott der Natur und den heiligen Geschichte" (74).

the Christians that the Creator's "many good works" (εὐεργεσία) might bring condemnation (εἰς κρίμα) upon them. This will be the case if they do not do "good
(καλός) and virtuous (εὐάρεστος) deeds before him in concord (μεθ᾽ ὁμονοίας),
and be citizens (πολιτευόμενοι) worthy of him" (21:1). As we have argued previously,
Clement's focus on concord specifically when he draws connection between the good
deeds of the Creator and the community life of the Christians shows that he uses the
order, peace and harmony of the universe as an example to imitate as is usual in deliberative rhetoric urging concord.[1137] In order to strengthen his warning in 21:1 he
quotes Prov 20:27 which states that the Lord discerns even the inward part of man and
then uses this thought to exhort the Corinthians to observe how close the Lord is
(21:2f.). On this basis Clement broadly reiterates the statement in 22:1 by arguing that
it is not right to desert the will of God (21:4). Then subsequently in 21:5-8, Clement
specifies what that means, though he does not deal explicitly with the situation in the
Corinthian Church. It is notable that he first exhorts his audience to give offence to
people "who are exalted and boast in the pride of their words, rather than God" (21:5),
in as much as such behaviour was associated with discord.[1138] Than he focuses upon
the duties of different groups of the household (22:6-8). As we have previously seen,
this topic was linked to the question of concord. In other words, when Clement specifies what it means to adhere to the will of God, he focuses upon behaviour, which in
antiquity was regarded as significant in the establishment and maintenance of concord
in a political body. In 21:9 he takes up the theme from 21:2-3 and emphasizes that
nothing is hidden from God. The aim here is probably to underscore the need to do
those things which are in accordance with the will of God, or to live in fear of God.
Subsequently in 22:1-8 he quotes Pss 33:12-18 and 31:10 in order to demonstrate that
what he has stated in 21:1-9 is confirmed by "the faith which is in Christ".[1139] As we
see, many terms and themes which occur in these quotations from the Psalms are also
found in *1 Clem.* 21:1-9.[1140] The confirmation of the fact that the statement in 21:1-8
has support in Scripture serves of course to give authority to and thus to emphasize the
need to follow Clement's exhortations.

5ST23126 Do not be double-minded regarding the gifts of God, 23:1-28:4

The indicative statement in 23:1 concerning God's gifts of salvation for those who fear
him is linked in many ways with the passage that precedes it. A similar description of
God as οἰκτίρμων κατὰ πάντα occurs in 20:11, and the deeds of the Creator are
depicted as εὐεργεσία in 21:1. Further, the expression φοβούμενοι αὐτόν is linked
with 21:6-8, particularly in 21:8 where the fear of God (ὁ φόβος αὐτοῦ) is said to give

---

[1137]Regarding the function of *1 Clem.* 20 within Clement's argumentation, see chap. 3.6.1.2.

[1138]See the present study, pp. 131-136.

[1139]It is not likely that the SM ταῦτα πάντα in 22:1 refers to any other passage than 21:1-9. The
quotations from the Psalms deal with topics which also are found in 21:1-9.

[1140]See A. LINDEMANN, *Die Clemensbriefe* (1992) 82.

salvation to all those who live in a holy way.[1141] On the basis of these links with the preceding passage it could on the one hand have been reasonable to view 23:1 as a summary statement which constitutes the end of a sub-text 19:2-23:1.[1142] On the other hand, the introduction of the expression "simple mind" (ἁπλοῦς διάνοια) appears to indicate that this verse introduces a new text-sequence in view of the fact that its antonym "to be double-minded (διψυχέω)" with respect to God's glorious gifts plays a significant role in what follows. Here Clement attempts to demonstrate that there is no reason to be double-minded by focusing upon one particular gift: i.e. a future resurrection. Further, Clement points out what this implies for the Corinthian Christians. Thus the exhortation in 23:2 not to be double-minded (διψυχέω) functions as a *SemM*. This means that, although somewhat hesitantly, we hold that 23:1 introduces a new argumentative sequence. In spite of this, the connection with the preceding sub-text is clear, with the sub-text 23:1-28:4[1143] (5ST23126) serving in many ways to strengthen his argumentation in 21:1-9.

In 23:2 Clement points to the consequences (διό) that follow from what is said about God in 23:1: He exhorts his addressees not to be double-minded (διψυχέω) concerning God's "excellent and glorious gifts". As a warning he quotes a passage from a non-canonical Scripture which states that the double-minded (δίψυχος) person is wretched. Then Clement goes on to pay attention to the process of growth in a vine. This process serves to show "how in a little time the fruit of the tree comes to ripeness" (23:3f.).[1144] Introducing it with ἐπ' ἀληθείας Clement clarifies what the metaphor of the vine should illustrate, i.e. God's will "shall be quickly and suddenly accomplished" (23:5). In other words, there should be no reason to be double-minded (διψυχέω) regarding God's "excellent and glorious gifts". God will complete his intentions. The quotation of Isa 13:22b in 23:5 intends to show that this also is confirmed in Scripture. Furthermore, the phrase "he shall come quickly and shall not tarry" in the quotation appears to indicate that the expression "excellent and glorious gifts" primarily refers to the *parousia*. Although the reference in 23:3 to old people who have experienced that what they have heard as children still has not happened is more vague, it might also point in the same direction. It is the *parousia* which has not taken place.[1145]

From the discussion above it follows that we consider 23:1-8 as a sub-text (6ST231261) in which Clement introduces the topic of not being double-minded regarding God's glorious gifts.

[1141]Cf. *ibid.* 83.

[1142]E. BAASLAND, "1. Klemensbrev", *De Apsotoliske Fedre* (1984), includes 23:1 in the-sub text 19:2-23:1, 120. As far as we know, no other scholars operate with this delimitation.

[1143]For delimitation markers which indicate that a new sub-text on same level begins in 29:1, see below.

[1144]The same quotation with some slight changes and an addition is also found in *2 Clem.* 11:2f. So far it has not been possible to locate the source of the quotation to any certain degree. The suggestion which appears to have the most support among scholars is that it is from the book *Eldad and Modad*. For a discussion see, D. A. HAGNER, *The Use of The Old and The New Testaments in Clement of Rome* (1973) 87f; H. E. LONA, *Der erste Clemensbrief* (1998) 289-294.

The exhortation in 24:1 to consider how the Master continually shows that a future resurrection will take place introduces a new sub-text, i.e. 24:1-26:3 (6ST231262). The *DA* ἀγαπητοί and the *SemM* ἀνάστασις are delimitation markers which serve to set this sub-text apart from the former one on the same level, i.e. 23:1-8 (6ST231261). In this section Clement explicitly focuses upon the future resurrection as one of God's "excellent and glorious gifts", and attempts to demonstrate that there is no reason to be double-minded with respect to the fact that it will take place.

First, Clement pays attention to certain phenomena of nature in which God foreshadows a future resurrection, i.e. the resurrection of day and night and the raising of much grain from one seed (24:2-5). Then he presents a widespread myth in the ancient world of the bird Phoenix as a sign of the resurrection (25:1-5).[1146] These examples taken from nature and from the myth of the Phoenix function as proofs of the fact that God is faithful and will fulfil the promise of a future resurrection. This is said most directly in regard to the myth of the Phoenix when Clement explicitly uses this myth in his argumentation. He asks if it is such a great and wonderful thing for the Creator to provide resurrection for those who have served him in holiness (τῶν ὁσίως αὐτῷ δουλευσάντων), "when he shows us the greatness of his promise even through a bird?" (26:1). In order to strengthen his argument concerning a future resurrection he quotes different passages from Scripture which all in one way or another deal with this topic (26:1-3).[1147]

After attempting to prove by means of examples taken from nature, from the myth of the bird Phoenix, and by means of quotations from the Scripture that God will effect a future resurrection, Clement points in 27:1-28:4 (6ST231263) to the consequences for the Corinthian Christians. The *SA* ταύτῃ τῇ ἐλπίδι refers to the future resurrection as the previous topic in chapters 24-26. Together with the conjunction οὖν in 27:1 it indicates both that a new sub-text is beginning and that this sub-text is connected with the preceding one. On the basis of the preceding argumentation the author shows that there is no reason to be double-minded. On the contrary, in 27:1 he exhorts the Corinthians to "be bound to him [God] who is faithful in his promises and righteous in his judgments" and to renew their faith in him (27:3). Further, he focuses upon God's omniscience and might (27:3b-7). Although Clement does not state it explicitly, the

---

[1145]That this is correct seems to be confirmed in 24:1 which explicitly introduces the topic of resurrection. The exhortation to consider that the Lord continually proves that a future resurrection will take place seems to presume that Clement already has dealt with matters related to this topic above. For a similar understanding of 23:3-5, cf. R. KNOPF, *Die zwei Clemensbriefe* (1920) 85-87; H. E. LONA, *Der erste Clemensbrief* (1998) 290. A. LINDEMANN, *Die Clemensbriefe* (1992), argues that the topic of resurrection first begins in 24:1 and that 23:3-5 more generally aims to show that "Gottes Gabe wird den zu ihm kommenden Menschen unverzüglich zuteil, ebenso umgekehrt Gottes Gericht den Zweiflern und Sündern"(84).

[1146]Regarding occurrences of this myth in antiquity, see the excursus in A. LINDEMANN, *Die Clemensbriefe* (1992) 88f.

[1147]Regarding the question of which LXX passages Clement quotes or alludes to, see D. A. HAGNER, *The Use of The Old and The New Testaments in Clement of Rome* (1973) 58f.

focus upon God's omniscience and might serves to strengthen his argumentation that there is no reason to be double-minded with respect to the Creator's glorious gifts. He has the power to realize his promise and intentions. In 28:1 however, he draws an explicit inference: positively one should fear (φοβέω) God, and negatively one should abstain from "foul desires of evil deeds" in order that one may be sheltered from future judgment by the mercy of God. This is followed by three rhetorical questions in 28:2, 4 and a quotation from Scripture in 28:3[1148] which amplifies the almighty and in particular the omniscient character of God. This serves to underline the need for following the exhortation given in 28:1.

In other words, Clement's purpose with the exhortation not to be double-minded in 23:2 and the additional argumentation for such an attitude is that he aims to make the Christians realize that they must be bound to God (27:1). This means that one should fear Him and cease from evil deeds (28:1). First we note that the aspect of fearing God links the purpose of the argumentation to 23:1 which constitutes the beginning of the sub-text 23:1-28:4. Furthermore, and more importantly, we note the connection between 19:2-22:8 (5ST23125) and 23:1-28:4 (5ST23126). We saw above in chapter 21 that when Clement applied the example of the order, peace and harmony of the universe to the community life of the Christians, he focused upon the need to do "good and virtuous deeds" (21:1) and to not desert God's will (21:5). When he specifies what that means, he mentions behaviour that was associated with the question of concord in a political body. Unfortunately, he does not specify what it means to fear God and abstain from evil deeds in 28:1. However, in the light of the meaning of similar expressions in chapter 21 it is reasonable to assume that Clement is primarily thinking of behaviour that promotes concord among the Christians. At least, one might say that it appears that his exhortation not to be double-minded, the argumentation in support of this, and the conclusion he draws regarding the Christians' attitude toward God in *1 Clem.* 26-27, all offer further support to the exhortation given in chapter 21. This indicates that, although the question of concord is not explicitly mentioned in 23:1-28:4, this sub-text also serves Clement's over-all argumentation in favour of concord and how it is to be achieved.

5ST23127 Live a life in holiness which is manifested in concord, 29:1-36:6

29:1 constitutes the beginning of a new sub-text (29:1-36:6, 5ST23127). The exhortation to "approach him in holiness of soul" (ἐν ὁσιότητι ψυχῆς) functions as a *SemM* in as much as the main content of 29:1-36:6 one way or another is related to the topic of holiness. Clement has already touched upon this topic in 26:1, but in 29:1-33 he deals with it in a much broader way. The conjunction οὖν in 29:1 indicates that the exhortation to be holy is an inference from what precedes it. On the basis of the fact that man

[1148]Clement puts forward an extensively altered quotation of the LXX text of Ps 138:7-10. See the discussions in A. LINDEMANN, *Die Clemensbriefe* (1992) 93f. and in H. E. LONA, *Der erste Clemensbrief* (1998) 322.

cannot escape from God and his judgments (*1 Clem.* 28), he now points to the positive alternative, i.e. to seek God in a holy life.

When Clement exhorts the Corinthians in 29:1 to "approach him in holiness of soul" (ἐν ὁσιότητι ψυχῆς), he further describes God as the one "who has made us the portion of his choice for himself". After presenting quotations from Scripture that aim to show that the holy God has chosen his people, based on this he exhorts the Corinthians to do all things which pertain to holiness (ποιήσωμεν τὰ τοῦ ἁγιασμοῦ πάντα, 30:1). The catalogue of vices, introduced by the participle φεύγοντες, outlines what that means in the negative (30:1b). Many of the vices mentioned were a part of traditional Christian paraenesis.[1149] However, we should note that νεωτερισμός is not found in the catalogues of vices in the New Testament. This is interesting with regard to the main topic of the letter in as much as νεωτερισμός belonged to the semantic field of concord in antiquity.[1150] Besides νεωτερισμός, among the other vices Clement refers to ὑπερηφανία was associated with sedition and strife.[1151] His stress on the latter in particular is evident from the fact that among the vices he mentions it is only with respect to ὑπερηφανία that he quotes from Scripture (Prov 3:34) in order to support his exhortation (30:2). Here it is said that in contrast to the proud (ὑπερήφανος), the humble (ταπεινός) receives grace from God. On this basis Clement further exhorts his audience to join "those to whom is given grace from God" (30:3). The most interesting point to note in this connection is that when he further specifies what that means, he focuses solely upon the need for concord, "let us put on concord" (ἐνδυσώμεθα τὴν ὁμόνοιαν, 30:3). The following participial clauses show how this is to be achieved: ταπεινοφρονοῦντες; ἐγκρατευόμενοι; and keeping oneself "far from all gossip and evil speaking, and be justified by deeds, not by words" (30:3). After a quotation from Scripture that warns the good speaker against imagining that he is right, Clement continues to exhort the Corinthians. He warns against self-praise, "for God hates those who praise themselves" (αὐτεπαινετός, 30:6). It is hardly an accident that Clement focuses so much upon this topic since in antiquity self-praise was considered to be a cause of strife and sedition.[1152] In order to strengthen the exhortations in this chapter he contrasts three vices associated with those who are accursed by God (τοῖς κατηραμένοις ὑπὸ τοῦ θεοῦ), i.e. θράσος, αὐθάδεια, τόλμα,[1153] with three virtues associated with those who are blessed by God (τοῖς ηὐλογημένοις ὑπὸ τοῦ θεοῦ), i.e. ἐπιείκεια, ταπεινοφροσύνη, πραΰτης (30:8). Those who are associated

---

[1149] A. LINDEMANN, *Die Clemensbriefe* (1992) 96; H. E. LONA, *Der erste Clemensbrief* (1998) 329f.

[1150] For the use of this term expressing sedition in a political body, see Dion. Hal. *Ant. Rom.* 6.1.1, quoted on p. 163, and the references listed by H. E. LONA, *Der erste Clemensbrief* (1998) 330. Lona correctly notes that" νεωτερισμός and στάσις gehören ... eng zusammen" (331).

[1151] See the present investigation, pp. 168-169.

[1152] Cf. the present study, pp. 131-136.

[1153] θράσος and αὐθάδεια are not found in the New Testament, but occur in connection with the teaching of "the two ways" in *Did.* 3:9 and 5:1 respectively. Clement seems to apply the three vices as synonyms. Cf. A. LINDEMANN, *Die Clemensbriefe* (1992) 97.

with the vices, τοῖς κατηραμένοις ὑπὸ τοῦ θεου, appear to be the same group of
people whom Clement says in 30:6 that God hates.

The discussion above in 29:1-30:8, which constitutes a sub-text (6ST231271)[1154]
of 29:1-36:6, shows that when Clement exhorts the Corinthians to carry out "deeds of
sanctification" he mainly focuses upon concord. After a general exhortation to concord, he goes on to exhort them on the one hand to practise virtues that promote concord, and on the other hand warns against vices which have the opposite effect. As a
feature of his argumentative strategy he labels those who behave in a manner that goes
against his exhortations as accursed by God, and those who follow them as blessed by
God (30:8). In other words, it seems clear from the context that those who behave in a
way that promotes concord live in a holy way and are blessed by God.

Against this background, Clement's exhortation to cleave to God's blessing
(εὐλογία) and to consider what the paths of blessing are (ὁδοὶ τῆς εὐλογίας) in 31:1
is natural. The exhortation in 31:1, in which the *SemM* εὐλογία and the conjunction
οὖν are found, constitutes the beginning of a new sub-text, i.e. 31:1-32:4 (6ST231272)
which deals with the topic of εὐλογία. In line with the exhortation in 31:1 Clement
presents examples from the great forefathers of Christians in order to demonstrate
where the path of blessing leads (31:2-4): Abraham was blessed because "he wrought
righteousness and truth through faith" (δικαιοσύνην καὶ ἀλήθειαν διὰ πίστεως);
Isaac behaved in confident knowledge; and "Jacob departed from his country in meekness (μετὰ ταπεινοφροσύνης) because of his brother". The aspect of πίστις which
seems to be implied in all examples is most explicitly expressed with respect to Abraham. However, the behaviour of Isaac and Jacob also presupposes this attitude. In this
connection πίστις carries the connotation of obedience and trust towards God which
was the basis of a certain kind of action.[1155] As has been already mentioned, πίστις
brought about that Abraham "wrought righteousness and truth". Previously in the
present investigation we have seen that both πίστις and δικαιοσύνη belonged to the
semantic field of concord.[1156] Further, it is striking that Clement describes Jacob with
the term ταπεινοφροσύνη in as much as this is not mentioned in connection with the
Jacob story in the Old Testament. The reason appears to be that the virtue of being
humble-minded is closely linked with the topic of concord in *1 Clement*, and that those
who are humble-minded are blessed by God, (30:8). In other words, when Clement
considers by means of historical examples what the paths of blessing are, he focuses
upon virtues that both in the letter and in its wider cultural setting were associated with
concord.

In 32:3f. it seems that Clement changes focus from the deeds of man as a condition
for being blessed towards a more Pauline conception of faith. πάντες in 33:3 refers to

---

[1154]Regarding the beginning of a new sub-text in 31:1, see below.

[1155]Cf. R. Knopf, *Die zwei Clemensbriefe* (1920) 96: "πίστις ist natürlich nicht der paulinische
Glauben, aber das Zutrauen zu Gott, das Bauen auf ihn und auf die Warheit seiner Verheissung liegt
doch darin".

[1156]See chaps. 3.5.2.4 and 3.5.2.16 respectively.

the descendants of Jacob who were not "renowned and magnified" through their own works, but through the will of God (διὰ τοῦ θελήματος αὐτοῦ). When he applies this principle to the Christians at the present time, he states that they are made righteous not by themselves, but "through faith (διὰ τῆς πίστεως), by which Almighty God has justified all men from the beginning of the world" (32:4). However, in the light of the above mentioned connotations of πίστις in 31:2, it is fair to infer that πίστις carries the connotation of obedience towards the will of God in 32:4 as well. In spite of this, it appears that this connotation is not stronger than the statement in 32:3-4 could lead the Corinthians to conclude that the obedience and the works of man could be seen as of lesser importance. Consequently Clement found it necessary in the subsequent passage to prevent a possible misunderstanding that it is not imperative to do good deeds.

The question in 33:1 introduces a new sub-text within 29:1-36:6. This text-sequence, 33:1-36:6 (6ST231273), deals with the need to do good. The doxology in 32:4 constitutes the end of the former sub-text, and the vocative ἀδελφοί, the conjunction οὖν and the term ἀγοθοποιία in 33:1 function as delimitation markers. Among these the *SemM* ἀγοθοποιία is the most important.

Clement denies that the consequence of what he has stated in 32:3f. is that one could abstain from doing good (ἀγοθοποιία) and forsake love (ἀγάπη). On the contrary, he emphasizes that one must "be zealous to accomplish every good deed (πᾶν ἔργον ἀγαθόν) with energy and readiness" (33:1). In order to persuade the Corinthians to follow his exhortation, he uses the deeds of the Creator as an example of good deeds (33:2-33:6). This shows that "the Lord himself adorned himself with good works" (33:7). In 33:8 he draws the conclusion for his addressees: "Having therefore this pattern let us follow his will without delay, let us work the work of righteousness with all our strength".

In chapters 34-35 Clement continues to argue for the need to do good works, but from a different perspective. Now he admonishes the Christians to do good works by focusing upon the thought that God is going to reward each one according to his work. Among other things in chapter 34, Clement exhorts the Corinthians to "be subject (ὑποτάσσω) to his will" (θέλημα, 34:5). Previously we have seen that the appeal to obey the will of God functions as a means of establishing concord.[1157] That this is the intended function in this case as well seems to be confirmed in what follows. After using the great multitude of angels as examples of the right attitude in serving the will of God and quoting a combination of Dan 7:10 and Isa 6:3 as proof from Scripture, Clement applies this example to the Christians: they also must gather in concord (ἐν ὁμονοίᾳ ἐπὶ τὸ αὐτὸ συναχθέντες)[1158] and cry to God as it were with one mouth (ἐξ ἑνὸς στόματος), that they may share in his great and glorious promises

---

[1157]See, e.g., pp. 156f.; 163.

[1158]ἐπὶ τὸ αὐτὸ συνάγεσθαι is a *terminus technicus* for the whole Church gathered in one place, see the present study, n. 823.

(34:7).[1159] In other words, when he specifies what it means to submit to the will of God he emphasizes the aspect of concord. By means of a quotation from 1 Cor 2:9 in 34:8 he goes on to give the reason for what he just has stated: God has prepared (great) things for those who wait for him.

What Clement means by the things God has prepared for those who wait for him becomes evident from what follows. It is the blessed and wonderful gifts of God (35:1) which he further specifies in 35:2, that he has in mind. After emphasizing the greatness of God's gifts, he exhorts the Christians to "strive to be found among the number of those that wait" in order that one may receive a share of these gifts (35:4). When in 35:5 he answers the question of how this shall take place, he again focuses upon behaviour that is "well-pleasing and acceptable" to God, and that follows his "faultless will" (ἄμωμος βούλησις) and "the way of truth" (ὁδὸς τῆς ἀληθείας).[1160] The following participle clauses in 35:5b specify what that means in the negative. It seems that Clement depends here on the catalogue of vices in Rom 1:29-32. We should note, however, that the two last vices in 35:5, κενοδοξία and ἀφιλοξενία, are not found in Rom 1.[1161] This is an interesting observation in as much as these vices belong to the semantic field of concord in *1 Clement*.[1162] Besides these vices, some that Clement uses in 35:5b are also clearly associated with the topic of concord elsewhere in the letter, and others of them in the literature of antiquity dealing with concord in a political body as well, i.e. πλεονεξία, ἔρις, ὑπερηφανία, ἀλαζονεία.[1163] 35:7-12 consists of a quotation of Ps 49:16-23 which serves to demonstrate that those who do not adhere to the proposed course of behaviour are hated by God who is also going to judge them.

In chapter 36:1 Clement gives a christologial interpretation of 35:12. Jesus Christ is the way of salvation. In 36:2 he describes different aspects of Jesus Christ, followed by quotations from Scripture (36:3-5) that serve to confirm what he has just said. This chapter seems to be a kind of brief christological excursus in relation to Clement's line of argumentation in this sub-text. However, we should note that his answer in 36:6 to his own question concerning the identity of the enemies of Christ to some extent connects chapter 36 to the two preceding chapters. The enemies are "those who are wicked and oppose his will" (θέλημα αὐτοῦ). Admittedly, in chapter 35 he writes about the

---

[1159]A. LINDEMANN, *Die Clemensbriefe* (1992), maintains that the phrase ἐν ὁμονοία συναχθέντες should not be taken as an adhortative. "Der Vf unterstreicht im Grunde nur die Notwendigkeit dessen, was in der Gemeinde ohnehin geschieht" (107). Regardless of whether one agrees with Lindemann or not, the angels function as examples for Christian community life. Cf. the conjunction οὖν in 34:7 which introduces the application to the Christians.

[1160]It should hardly be necessary to remind the reader that in the light of the use of these and similar expressions elsewhere in the letter a precondition for receiving a share of God's gift implies behaviour that promotes concord. See, e.g., pp. 117f.; 155f.

[1161]For a comparison of Rom 1:29-32 with *1 Clem.* 35:5, see L. SANDERS, *L'Hellénisme de Saint Clément de Rome et le Paulinisme* (1943) 74-78; D. A. HAGNER, *The Use of The Old and The New Testaments in Clement of Rome* (1973) 214-216.

[1162]See n. 563. Regarding striving for honour as a cause for sedition, see chap. 5.4.1.3.

[1163]πλεονεξία, see pp. 172f.; ἔρις, see chap. 3.5.1.1.2; ὑπερηφανία, see pp. 168-169; ἀλαζονεία, see pp. 131-136.

will of God. Yet it is a reasonable assumption that he uses the will of God and the will of Christ interchangeably.[1164] Thus in connection with the christological excursus Clement reiterates a basic point in chapter 35, i.e. the need to follow the will of Christ (God) in order to receive a share in his gifts, though now in the negative.

Before we go further, let us give a brief summary of the main line of argumentation in the sub-text 29:1-36:6 (5ST23127). Here Clement deals mainly with the consequences of living a life in holiness. In 29:1-30:8 (6ST231271), partly on the basis of the preceding text, 27:1-28:4, and partly on the basis of quotations from Scripture, he exhorts the Corinthians to live a holy life. When he specifies what that means, he focuses primarily upon concord, and exhorts them on the one hand to practise certain virtues in order to achieve it, and on the other hand warns against vices which have the opposite effect. Those practising the virtues proposed by Clement and who thus "approach him [God] in holiness of soul" (29:1) are described as blessed by God. On this basis he exhorts them to cleave to the blessing of God and thus makes the paths of blessing the topic in 31:1-32:4 (6ST231272). In as much as he links holiness with concord in 29:1-30:8, and characterises those practising the virtues that promote concord as blessed, it is not surprising that he also focuses upon virtues which are associated with concord in 31:1-32:4. This is even more evident in 33:1-36:6 (6ST231273) where he deals with the need to do good works. Although Clement's exhortations regarding good works are given different motivations, it is reasonable to see them as closely associated with the topic of holiness and the path of blessing. As already mentioned, we also find in this sub-text many virtues and vices which are associated with concord. Even more importantly, we find statements that explicitly deal with the need for concord. This means that, when Clement deals with the need for holiness and good works in 29:1-36:6, he to a great extent argues that these must be manifested in concord among the Christians. We note that this is done in a general manner without focusing upon the specific situation in the Corinthian Church. As is characteristic for a θέσις he deals in a general way with features that promote concord without discussing a concrete situation.

5ST23128 The need for subordination, mutuality and interdependence, 37:1-39:9.

The double *DA* ἄνδρες ἀδελφοί and the conjunction οὖν in 37:1 introduce a new sub-text which focuses both upon the need for subordination and the need for mutuality and interdependence in order to establish concord in 37:1-39:9 (5ST23128). After emphasizing in different ways the need to follow the will of God in 29:1-36:6, and describing those opposing the will of God as enemies at the end of this sub-text, Clement exhorts the Corinthian Christians to serve as in an army following God's faultless commands (37:1).[1165] He presents the order of the Roman army in 37:2-4 as an exam-

---

[1164] This is taken for granted by A. LINDEMANN, *Die Clemensbriefe* (1992) 112.

[1165] The introduction of the military metaphor ought to be understood against the background of a description of those who oppose the will of God as enemies, see the discussion in chap. 3.6.1.4.

ple to follow.[1166] In addition to the fact that the introduction of the term ἐχθρός prepares the audience for the military metaphor, there are other reasons which might explain why he uses the army as an example for community life. As we have seen previously, it was a commonplace in the ancient world to compare life's duties with the military service of a solider. Of even more significance, the order of the army is used as an example to imitate in deliberative rhetoric that urges concord.[1167] In 37:2f. it is order and submission which are highlighted.[1168] Although these features are important in 37:4 as well, the aspect of interdependence and mutuality is more accentuated. The expression "there is a certain mixture among all" (σύγκρασις τίς ἐστιν ἐν πᾶσιν) reflects the widespread ideal of the mixed constitution (μικτὴ πολιτεία) in which the mix of "great and small" in order to secure concord was an essential feature.[1169]

In 37:5 Clement uses the body as an example in order to illustrate the interdependence of the small and great, and concludes that "all [the members of the body] work together and are united in a common subjection to preserve the whole body". He then applies the example of the body to his addressees (38:1-3). Each individual Christian must be subject to his neighbour according to his rank in order to preserve the whole body in Christ. The following exhortations in 38:2a show that Clement is primarily concerned with relations between people of different socio-economic classes,[1170] but he also focuses upon the fact that people who have the gifts of certain virtues must not boast of themselves. When he applies the body metaphor in this way to the Christian community in his argumentation for a particular course of action which serves the well-being and thus the concord of the whole community, he reflects a common *topos* in deliberative rhetoric urging concord.[1171] His considerations about the fact that all men are created by God and thus have received their gifts from him in 38:3-4 serve to support the exhortations in 38:2.

In chapter 39 it appears that Clement focuses more concretely *upon the situation in Corinth*. Consequently, this chapter is a part of the transition to the ὑπόθεσις-section.[1172] In the list of terms describing the people who "mock and deride us (ἡμᾶς) wishing to exalt themselves" in 39:1 we find ἄφρων which Clement uses in 3:3 to depict the rebels. It is reasonable to view the three other terms, ἀσύνετος, μωρός, and ἀπαίδευτος, as synonyms of ἄφρων. The ἡμᾶς could be explained by the fact that Clement identifies himself with the receivers of the letter, as is frequently the case elsewhere in the letter. In spite of the suggestion that chapter 39 functions as a transition to the ὑπόθεσις-section, it ought with respect to its function in Clement's argumentative strategy to be

---

[1166]Cf. our discussion, pp. 174f.

[1167]Cf. chap. 3.6.1.4.

[1168]For order as a means of establishing concord, see chap. 3.6.2.1.

[1169]Cf. chap. 3.6.1.5.

[1170]See pp. 295-298.

[1171]Cf. chap. 3.6.1.6.

[1172]Regarding the other part of the transition to the ὑπόθεσις-section, see below, p. 260.

linked with the preceding text. The bulk of the chapter, i.e. 39:3-9 which contains several quotations from Job, aims to show the lack of power of mortal beings, who in this connection are those who exalt themselves (39:1).[1173] Notably, the topic of exalting oneself is reflected in Clement's warning against certain behaviours in 38:2b, i.e. the wise man shall not manifest his wisdom in words, the humble-minded one shall not testify to his own humility, and the pure in the flesh shall not be boastful. For this reason it is reasonable to assert that the main function of this chapter is to show the necessity of paying attention to Clement's exhortations in 38:2b.[1174]

4.2.4.2. Sub-Texts on the Fourth and Following Grades within the quaestio finita Section, 40:1-63:1

4ST2321 Order among the people of God according to the will of God, 40:1-43:6

We have already argued that the two *SAs* ὄντων τούτων and τὰ βάθη τῆς θείας γνώσεως function as markers which set the ὑπόθεσις in 40:1-61:3 apart from the θέσις. In addition to this function on level 3, they also indicate the beginning of the first sub-text of the ὑπόθεσις. Besides this type of marker on the surface-level, we also find the *SemM* πάντα τάξει ποιεῖν and the conjunction οὖν which serve to delimit the following sub-text, 40:1-43:6, from 37:1-39:9 preceding it on the same level. On the basis of the "things" which are manifested to the Corinthians, Clement focuses upon the need for doing all the things God has commanded to perform in due order (40:1).

He does not, however, restrict himself to exhorting the Corinthians to live in a state of order purely on the basis of what has already been said. He goes on to focus upon the order and the differentiation of tasks in the temple service in Jerusalem (40:1-5) in order to demonstrate how essential order must be for Christians. Clement emphasizes several times that this order was according to the will of God.[1175] In 41:1, introduced with the vocative ἀδελφοί, he applies the example of the order of the temple service to the Christians. Each one must please God in his own rank (ἐν τῷ ἰδίῳ τάγματι) and not transgress the designated rule of one's ministry. In 41:3 he states that those "who do anything contrary to that which is agreeable to" God's will will suffer the penalty of death. This serves to underline the need to act according to his exhortation.[1176] With the emphatic ὁρᾶτε, ἀδελφοί Clement draws the following conclusion from 40:1-41:3: "that the more knowledge (γνῶσις) we have been entrusted with, the greater risk do we incur" (κίνδυνος, 41:4). Because the Christians in fact have knowledge of the will of God concerning order in the community life, they are exposed to a great danger

---

[1173]Cf. A. LINDEMANN, *Die Clemensbriefe* (1992) 119.

[1174]*Ibid.* 118: "Das im Mittelpunkt stehende Schriftwort (V.3-9) unterstreicht einerseits die Dringlichkeit der in 38,2f ausgespochenen Mahnung, und es verurteilt andererseits zugleich den Hochmut der ἄφρονες (39:1)".

[1175]*1 Clem.* 40:2, 3, 4.

[1176]For the death penalty when one acted against God's commandments regarding the cult in Old Testament times, see for examples Exod 12:15; 31:14; Lev 7:20f; 17:8f, 14.

if they act against God's will.[1177] Clement does not specify what the danger consists of. There is no reason to believe that he means that those who transgress the commandments of the cultic order should be punished with the death penalty.[1178] He does not transfer the cultic order of the Old Testament and the penalties prescribed therein to the Corinthian Christians, but he uses this order as an example to illustrate the need for the individual Christian not to transgress the rules of his ministry. The most important point to note in respect to the argumentative structure is that Clement's warning of a great danger serves to underline the need to follow the exhortations in 40:1 and 41:1. Further, we remind the reader that the warning of danger associated with a certain course of action was common in deliberative rhetoric.[1179]

After using the cult of the Temple as an example of the view that order is according to the will of God in 40:1-41:4 (5ST23211), Clement goes on to focus upon order in apostolic and post-apostolic times in 42:1-43:6 (5ST23212). He stresses that the apostles, who were themselves appointed by Christ, appointed some of their first converts to be bishops (ἐπίσκοπος) and deacons (διάκονος, 42:1-4). Further, Clement emphasizes that when the apostles did so, this was not a new thing. The substantially changed quotation of Isa 60:17 in 42:5 intends to show that the appointment of bishops and deacons was witnessed to in the Scripture and thus not a new creation of the apostles. Regardless of one's position concerning the nature and historicity of Clement's depiction of the apostolic succession in this chapter, it is beyond doubt that he holds that according to the will of God there should be an order in the church which includes different offices.[1180] The focus upon how Moses handled the situation when "jealousy (ζῆλος) arose concerning the priesthood (ἱερωσύνη), and the tribes were quarrelling (στασιάζω) as to which of them was adorned with that glorious title" (43:2) serves also to demonstrate that when the apostles appointed bishops and deacons they did so in agreement with the Scripture. Furthermore, his argumentation for the view that the apostles acted in line with the Scripture when they appointed bishops and deacons supports and underlines the need to follow the exhortation to "be well pleasing to God in his own rank" (41:1).

Admittedly, in 40:1-43:6 Clement deals with the need for order and the differentiation of tasks among the people of God in general. On first sight this fact seems to indicate that this passage should be regarded as a part of the θέσις-section. It is, however, reasonable to argue that he presents the biblical examples of order because he considered the question of order to be crucial with respect to the concrete happenings in the Corinthian Church. More importantly, the passage that deals with strife concerning the

---

[1177] γνῶσις connects 41:1 with the beginning of this sub-text (40:1). Thus it is reasonable to consider 41:4 not only to be an application of 41:2-3, but also of the greater passage 40:1-42:3. Furthermore, it is likely that γνῶσις in 41:4 also refers to the content of the entire θέσις-section.

[1178] So also A. LINDEMANN, *Die Clemensbriefe* (1992) 125.

[1179] See chaps. 2.3.1 and 2.3.2.

[1180] We must refrain from entering into the discussion about the nature and historicity of apostolic succession in *1 Clement*. For an overview of the discussion, see J. FUELLENBACH, *Ecclesiastical Office and the Primacy of Rome* (1980) 25-146; H. E. LONA, *Der erste Clemensbrief* (1998) 471-481.

priesthood (43:1-6) should demonstrate that Scripture deals with a situation analogous to the one facing the Corinthian Church, i.e. the removal of some presbyters who were appointed to their service represented a breach of God's order and thus caused sedition. In other words, by means of the biblical examples presented in 40:1-43:6 Clement moves from a general treatment toward the concrete situation in the Corinthian Church. Thus 40:1-43:6 constitutes a transition from θέσις to ὑπόθεσις. For this reason we are of the opinion that it is appropriate to view 40:1-43:6 as a part of the ὑπόθεσις-section.

4ST2322 Clement blames the Corinthians for the present state of affairs, 44:1-47:7

After demonstrating that an order which presupposes an appointed leadership among the people of God is according to God's will, Clement turns more explicitly to the situation in Corinth. The expression ἔρις ἔσται περὶ τοῦ ὀνόματος τῆς ἐπισκοπῆς in 44:1 serves as a *SemM* in as much as in 44:1-47:7 (4ST2322) he mainly blames the Corinthian Christians for having removed some of the presbyters and for the present strife and sedition. This topic is introduced in the story about the Israelites who were quarrelling about the priesthood. Here the emphasis is upon the way Moses handled the conflict. He made provisions for the people of God to get priests and thereby contributed to ensuring "that there should be no disorder in Israel" (43:6). Further, the argumentative function of the story was to prove that when the apostles appointed bishops and deacons it was no novelty.

As already indicated, 44:1 is linked with what precedes it. Analogous to Moses, who by means of his leadership contributed to order among the Israelites, the apostles, who knew beforehand that a time would come when there would be "strife for the title of bishop", appointed bishops and deacons in order to secure order in the Church. Additionally, they gave instruction that if these appointed men died, "other approved men should succeed to their ministry" (44:2). By this argumentation Clement attempts once more to prove that the offices of deacons and bishops have apostolic and thus ultimately divine sanction. After having attempted to establish this fact, he draws the conclusion in the negative in 44:3-6. First, in vv. 3-5 he states as a general principle that it is not right (δικαίως) to remove legitimate and properly appointed presbyters from their office. In fact, it is not a small sin to "eject from the episcopate those who have blamelessly and holily offered its sacrifices" (44:4). Then when he has emphasized in this way the seriousness of removing legitimate presbyters from their office in general, he explicitly focuses in 44:6 upon the situation in Corinth: the Corinthians have removed some men in office in spite of their good service. In the light of what Clement has just stated, this statement about the occurrences in the Corinthian Church functions as a powerful condemnation. Some may be of the opinion that he is remarkably brief when he deals with the concrete occurrences in the Corinthian Church. However, there are several features that explain this: (1) the comparatively long θέσις which emphasizes the need for order and concord in general and the need to obey the will of God; (2) in particular his argumentation for the opinion that order, including the office of bishops, is according to the will of God (40:1-44:2); and (3) his condemnation of the removal of appropriately appointed presbyters in 44:3-4. All these have meant that it was not necessary to deal in greater detail with the situation in Corinth. There was probably no doubt among the readers that according to Clement the removal of the presbyters was a great sin and against the will of God. The statement in 44:6 constitutes the end of the first sub-text, i.e. 44:1-44:6 (5ST23221), of 44:1-47:7.

The *DA* ἀδελφοί in 45:1 indicates a transition to a new sub-text, i.e. 45:1-8 (5ST23222). After Clement has blamed the Corinthians because they have removed some of the bishops, he exhorts them in 45:1 to seek the things which lead to salvation. This must imply that the present state of affairs is having the opposite effect. What follows indicates that to seek the things which lead to salvation means that the Christians must live according to Scripture. Scripture shows, Clement argues, that it has never been the case that the "righteous have been cast out by holy men" (45:3). It is the other way around – the righteous have been persecuted by the wicked (ἄνομος, 45:4). In order to demonstrate this, he presents what happened to Daniel, Ananias, Azarias and Misael, men "who served God with a holy and faultless purpose" (45:6f.). It follows that the Corinthians, by removing some of the bishops from the office in which they served blamelessly, have placed themselves among the wicked and law-breakers. This functions as an additional condemnation of such behaviour in the Corinthian Church, and at the same time gives support to the exhortation in 45:1. At the end of this sub-text Clement describes the reward for those who served God's holy name and endured in confidence. They received glory and honour from God "and were enrolled by God in his memorial for ever and ever" (45:8).

As was the case in 45:1, the *DA* ἀδελφοί in 46:1, together with the conjunction οὖν, indicates a transition to a new sub-text in 46:1-46:9 (5ST23223). Clement makes explicit use of biblical examples in his argumentation and exhorts the Corinthians to cleave to the examples (ὑπόδειγμα) who endured and received their reward from God (46:1). In 46:2-4 he presents passages from authoritative scriptures which admonish the Christians to follow the holy (ἅγιος),[1181] the innocent and the elect, as a further argument for the exhortation in 45:1. In 46:4 he applies the quotations and reiterates the exhortation in 45:1 in a more specific way: "Let us then cleave to the innocent (ἀθῷος) and righteous (δίκαιος), for these are God's elect". δίκαιος refers to the examples in 45:3ff. After this positive argumentation for following biblical examples, Clement focuses upon the present situation of strife and sedition among the Corinthians in 46:5-7 by means of a number critical rhetorical questions. We find in these verses, as we have seen previously in our investigation, many terms and political *topoi* associated with concord.[1182] By using these standard terms and *topoi* related to concord, together with their very negative connotations, Clement seeks to make the Corin-

---

[1181]Previously Clement has argued that a holy life should be manifested first of all in concord among the Christians, *1 Clem.* 30.

[1182]ἔρις, see chap. 3.5.1.1.2; διχοστασία, see chap. 3.5.1.1.1 (στάσις); σχίσμα, see chap. 3.5.2.13; πόλεμος, see chap. 3.5.1.4; body metaphor, see chap. 3.6.1.6.

thians aware of how bizarre their present behaviour in fact is. It should hardly be necessary to say that these rhetorical questions function as a condemnation of the Corinthians' community life. In the argumentative structure in this sub-text the rhetorical questions describe "das negative Gegenbeispiel" to the course of behaviour expressed in 46:2-4.[1183] The quotations of and allusions to different logia of Jesus in 46:8, which among other things say that it was better for a man "that a millstone be hung on him, and he be cast into the sea, that he should turn aside (διαστρέφω) one of my elect", function as a strong warning. Clement emphasizes this warning when he continues in 46:9 by stating that the consequence of the Corinthian's schism (σχίσμα) in fact has been that it has turned many aside (πολλοὺς διέστρεψεν) and that the sedition (στάσις) still continues. Here he probably consciously applies *pathos* in the argumentation. He attempts to arouse fear among the Christians as to what would happen to them if they did not follow his exhortations.

In 47:1-7 (5ST23224) Clement continues to emphasize how blameful the present στάσις is by comparing it with the πρόσκλισις Paul dealt with in 1 Corinthians.[1184] At that point of time the Corinthians "were partisans of Apostles of high reputation, and of a man approved by them" (47:4), but now it is otherwise (47:5). He does not describe those who now have misled them, but leaves it to the readers to discern who they are. It is obvious, however, that he considers them to be bad persons. Indeed, he argues that although Paul blamed the Corinthians for that kind of πρόσκλισις, the present sedition is more serious and entails more guilt (ἁμαρτία) on their part (47:4). In other words, by means of a comparison with the strife which Paul combated, Clement seeks to amplify how blameworthy the ongoing strife really is. In 47:6f. he gives his explicit evaluation of the strife. First we note that he characterises it as shameful, extremely shameful (αἰσχρά, λίαν αἰσχρά, 47:6). This utterance must be evaluated in the light of an aspect we shall pay attention to later on in this study, namely that the Mediterranean culture was an honour-shame culture in which much of life was directed towards increasing one's honour and avoiding shame.[1185] Thus when Clement argues that the strife brings shame upon the Corinthian Church, this is a strong expression of the seriousness of the strife. At the same time it is a strong implicit appeal to cease from the present state of affairs. Further, the mention of the fact that the report of this shameful event has also reached others besides the Romans, must also be understood in light of the pivotal value of honour – that is to say, to have a good reputation was connected with honour, and the opposite with shame. Furthermore, Clement focuses upon two more negative effects of the strife, that the Corinthians are bringing

---

[1183]Cf. A. LINDEMANN, *Die Clemensbriefe* (1992) 136.

[1184]*Ibid.* 139: "πρόσκλισις ist gegenüber σχίσμα (so Paulus in 1 Kor 1,10; vgl. 1 Clem 46,9) bewusste Abschwächung".

[1185]Cf. chap. 5.4.1.2.

blasphemy on the name of the Lord and that they are creating danger (κίνδυνος)[1186] to themselves.

To summarize, in 44:1-47:7 Clement employs different strategies to make the Corinthians realize both how blameworthy their present strife is and how negative the consequences are for them. First he argues that the removal of the presbyters who have fulfilled their duties blamelessly is a contradiction to the order of the apostles and thus is a great sin (44:1-7). Further he draws an analogy between the actions of the Corinthians and those in the Old Testament who persecuted the servants of God (45:1-8); he applies traditional terms and *topoi* associated with concord, which carry negative connotations, followed by different logia of Jesus which function as a strong warning (chap. 46); he amplifies the seriousness of the situation by comparing the present strife with the former strife Paul combated in 1 Corinthians, and maintains that the present entails more guilt (ἁμαρτία) on their part (47:1-5). Finally, he states that the removal of the presbyters has brought shame upon the Corinthian Church and that they create danger to themselves.

4ST2323 Clement exhorts the Corinthians to cease from the present strife, 48:1-58:2

If by means of different strategies Clement has now succeeded in demonstrating how blameworthy the ongoing strife is and that it has very negative consequences for the Corinthians, he has laid a good basis for his subsequent appeal for concord. Therefore it is not surprising that in 48:1-58:2 (4ST2323) he exhorts them to put an end to the strife. Although we also find general exhortations to virtues that would promote concord, he is more concrete and focuses directly upon the situation in the Corinthian Church. The fact that he has laid a good foundation for his exhortations previously in the letter does not, however, mean that 48:1-58:2 consists solely of exhortations. The exhortations are interlinked with further argumentation for the need to follow the proposed course of action.

On the surface-level of the text the *SA* τοῦτο and the conjunction οὖν serve as indicators of delimitation and connection. τοῦτο refers to the foregoing chapter, in particular to vv. 6-8 which refer to the concrete occurrences in the Corinthian Church. In addition to these markers, the *SemM* ἐξαίρω delimits the following sub-text, 48:1-58:2 (4ST2323), from the former on the same level, i.e. 44:1-47:7 (4ST2322).

5ST23231 The exhortation to put an end to the sedition, 48:1-6

As already indicated, on the basis of the foregoing, in particular 44:1-47:7, Clement exhorts the Corinthian Christians in 48:1 to quickly put an end to the present state of affairs. Since τοῦτο refers back to 47:6, this exhortation implies that the persons involved in the upheaval against the presbyters must cease from their actions. The following exhortation to beseech God and beg for mercy indicates that putting an end to

---

[1186]The appeal to danger was, as we have seen, common in deliberative rhetoric, see chaps. 2.3.1 and 2.3.2.

the present situation implies the confession of sins and repentance (48:1). This is self-evident since Clement has described the removal of the presbyters as a sin. The fact that he exhorts the Corinthians to beg God to restore their love for the brethren is not surprising in as much as love for the brethren (φιλαδελφία) implies concord. As a further argument for these exhortations he maintains that "this is the gate of righteousness" which is open in Christ (48:2-4). He maintains that all those who enter this gate in holiness (ὁσιότης) and righteousness (δικαιοσύνη) are blessed. That Clement links blessings to these virtues is hardly an accident. Previously we have seen both that when he specifies what it means to live in a holy way he primarily focuses upon concord.[1187] We have also seen that δικαιοσύνη belonged to the semantic field of concord.[1188] It is likely that the opponents of Clement claimed to possess the qualities he mentions in 48:5.[1189] Otherwise it is difficult to understand the subsequent argumentation: "for (γάρ) the more he seems to be great, the more ought he to be humble-minded, and to seek the common good of all and not his own benefit" (48:6). The premise of this argumentation is that the opponents claim to possess the gifts mentioned in 48:6 and thus would seem to be great. The appeal to seek the common good was a standard appeal in deliberative rhetoric urging concord.[1190] As we have noted many times, to be humble-minded is in the argumentation of Clement a means of securing concord.[1191]

5ST23232 The greatness of love with application to the sedition in Corinth, 49:1-55:6

After exhorting the Corinthians to put an end to the present state of affairs in 48:1-6 (5ST23231), in 49:1-55:5 (5ST23232) Clement focuses upon the virtue of love and applies this to the situation in Corinth. The term ἀγάπη in 49:1 (which occurs 22 times in 49:1-55:5) serves as a *SemM*.

6ST232321 The greatness of love, 49:1-6

After the exhortation in 49:1, directed to ὁ ἔχων ἀγάπην ἐν Χριστῷ to perform the commandments of Christ, Clement focuses upon the nature and the effect of love (49:2-6). This passage, 49:1-6 (6ST232321)[1192] which constitutes the first sub-text of 49:1-55:5, is carefully structured and reflects the rhetorical skills of the author. In order to make the message effectual, among other things, he applies polyptoton, anaphora,

---

[1187]See above, pp. 252f.

[1188]Cf. chap. 3.5.2.16.

[1189]R. KNOPF, *Die zwei Clemensbriefe* (1920) 125 holds that "es muss angenommen werden, dass die Gegner der Amtsträger in Korinth sich des Besitzes dieser Gaben rühmten". Otherwise A. LINDEMANN, *Die Clemensbriefe* (1992) 141, who underscores that "eine direkte Polemik gegen konkrete Personen ist nicht zu erkennen". That the opponents of Clement claimed to posses the actual qualities does not mean, however, in the light of how he has described them elsewhere in the letter, that he agrees with the claim.

[1190]Cf. chap. 2.3.3.

[1191]Cf. pp. 126-131.

[1192]For delimitation markers that indicate that a new sub-text begins in 50:1, see below.

rhetorical questions, parallels, antitheses, and amplification by means of repetition.[1193] The similarities with 1 Cor 13, particularly in *1 Clem.* 49:5, are so obvious that it appears to be reasonable to deduce that Clement is influenced by Paul.[1194] We note however a significant difference, i.e. Clement explicitly stresses in the negative that σχίσμα and στάσις are contrasted with ἀγάπη, and in the positive that ἀγάπη does all things ἐν ὁμονοίᾳ (49:5). Such a stress upon the connection between love and concord appears not only to be an adaptation to the Corinthian situation, but also reflects a commonplace in antiquity.[1195] In the whole chapter, and in particular in 46:5, Clement praises the virtue of love by focusing on its effect. Thus this chapter contains the essential features of epideictic rhetoric. Though the objects of epideictic rhetoric were most often persons, gods or cities, Greek rhetoricians used epideictic rhetoric or more precisely the form of encomium to praise virtues as well.[1196] As previously noted in this investigation, there was a close connection between epideictic and deliberative rhetoric; the orator praised the behaviour or virtue he sought to encourage his audience to practise.[1197] This means that the encomium of love functions as an implicit exhortation to practise the virtue of love with the mentioned manifestations.

6ST232322 The principle of love applied to the situation in the Corinthian Church, 50:1-55:6.

The imperative and *DA* ὁρᾶτε ἀγαπητοί in 50:1 serve as delimitation markers and indicate that a new sub-text has begun. In 50:1 Clement concludes what the encomium of love should demonstrate, how great the love is.[1198] After he has underlined this fact, he goes on to apply the principles of love to Christians in general and to the Corinthian situation in particular (50:2-55:6). Therefore it is reasonable to view 50:1 as a transitional verse, concluding the praise of love and preparing for the application that fol-

---

[1193]For the structure and the rhetoric of chap. 49, cf. R. Knopf, *Die zwei Clemensbriefe* (1920) 125f., who asserts that "Der Verfasser ist sich sicher bewusst, ein Glanzstück seiner erbaulichen Redekunst zu geben"; A. Lindemann, *Die Clemensbriefe* (1992) 143-145; H. E. Lona, "Rhetorik und Botschaft in 1 Clem 49", *ZNW* 86 (1995) 94-103, *idem, Der erste Clemensbrief* (1998) 519-530.

[1194]Cf. the synopsis and discussion in L. Sanders, *L'Hellénisme de Saint Clément de Rome et le Paulinisme* 94f.; D. A. Hagner, *The Use of The Old and The New Testaments in Clement of Rome* (1973) 200f. See further A. von Harnack, *Einführung in die alte Kirchengeschichte* (1929) 117; A. Lindemann, *Die Clemensbriefe* (1992) 143-145; H. E. Lona, "Rhetorik und Botschaft in I Clem 49", *ZNW* 86 (1995) 94-103.

[1195]Cf. chap. 3.6.2.3.

[1196]Theon *Progymnasmata* 8.231.14-15 (Spengel 2.112 .14-15); Hermog. *Prog.* 7.35.20-21 (Spengel 2.11.20-21). The basic τάξις of a encomium consists of the following five features: prologue, birth and upbringing, acts (πράξεις), comparison (σύγκρισις) and epilogue, see J. G. Sigountos, "The Genre of 1 Corinthians 13", *NTS* 40 (1994) 247f. and the literature references in this article. Siogountos demonstrates that 1 Cor 13 ought to be classified as an encomium on love. In a note he terms *1 Clem.* 49:1-50:2 as an encomium of love, *ibid.* 260 n. 77. Cf. also J. Smit, "The Genre of 1 Corinthians 13 in the Light of Classical Rhetoric", *NT* 33 (1991) 193 -216, who concludes that 1 Cor 13 is epideictic rhetoric. And more recently H. E. Lona, "Rhetorik und Botschaft in I Clem 49", *ZNW* 86 (1995) 100; *idem, Der erste Clemensbrief* (1998) 522, defines the Gattung of *1 Clem* 49:1-6 as an ἐγκώμιον τῆς ἀγάπης.

[1197]Arist. *Rh.* 1.9.35f.

lows. In 50:2-55:6 he does not, however, restrict himself to drawing the consequences of what he said in 49:1-49:6, but this application is interlinked with subsequent argumentation for practising love.

7ST2323221 Pray that one must live in love without sedition, 50:1-7

First Clement exhorts the Corinthians to pray and beg for God's mercy that they may be "found in love, without human partisanship" (πρόσκλισις ἀνθρωπίνης, 50:2). In line with the emphasis he places upon the fact that strife and sedition are opposite to love, he not only exhorts them to pray for love in 50:2, but also that this love must be manifested in a community life without πρόσκλισις ἀνθρωπίνης. As a further argument for the need of love he makes a connection between practising love and being recognised among the pious (εὐσεβής) by means of a quotation from Scripture (50:3f.).[1199] Further, in line with the importance and the nature of love, Clement does not simply assert that those who fulfil the commandments of God are blessed, but states that those who do this ἐν ὁμονοίᾳ ἀγάπης so that their sins may be forgiven through love (δι' ἀγάπης) are blessed (50:5). The quotation taken from Scripture in 50:6 that follows aims primarily to show that those whose sins are forgiven are blessed. However, from what Clement has just stated about the role of love in 50:5 the quotation functions also as an implicit emphasis on the necessity of love. Further, the statement in 50:7, which makes it clear that God's blessing is for those who "have been chosen by God through Jesus Christ", functions in a similar way in as much as the Corinthians are likely to have considered themselves to be among the chosen ones. This means that 50:3-7 serves to strengthen the argument for following Clement's exhortation to pray that the Christians may practise "love, without human partisanship" (πρόσκλισις ἀνθρωπίνης, 50:2). An exhortation to pray for something functions, of course, also as an unexpressed exhortation to perform what one prays for.

7ST23233222 Love implies that one seeks the common good of all and therefore those who laid the foundation of the sedition should voluntarily leave the Church, 51:1-55:6

When Clement goes on in 51:1a to exhort the Corinthians to pray for forgiveness, which implies repentance, the conjunction οὖν points back to 50:5f. The term ἀφίημι serves as catch-word in 50:5 and 51:1a. Repentance implies also that "the leaders of sedition and disagreement" (ἀρχηγοὶ στάσεως καὶ διχοστασίας) must see the common hope (κοινὸς τῆς ἐλπίδος, 51:1b). That Clement explicitly mentions this group of people indicates that the exhortation in 51:1a is directed to them in particular.

[1198]A. LINDEMANN, *Die Clemensbriefe* (1992), holds that *1 Clem.* 50 is also a part of the encomium (142). Though they do not use the term "encomium", other scholars also see *1 Clem.* 49-50 as a unity characterising it "Lobpreis" or "Lob" der Liebe, so R. KNOPF, *Die zwei Clemensbriefe* (1920) 125; G. SCHNEIDER, *Clemens von Rom* (1994) 11. Whether one uses the rhetorical term "encomium" or not, we must distinguish between chap. 49 and 50. For in chap. 50 we do not find praise of love, but here Clement draws out the consequences of chap. 49.

[1199]Cf. 49:5 where Clement states that "Without love is nothing well pleasing to God".

In 51:2f. he presents arguments, introduced with two γάρ clauses, for following the exhortation. First, he applies the principle of love and asserts that those who live in love (and fear) are willing to suffer themselves, rather than see their neighbours do so (51:2). It appears that he holds that the action of the leaders of the sedition is a threat against the common eschatological hope of the Corinthian Christians.[1200] Their behaviour is thus not directed towards the common good of the whole community, but they are behaving according to their own purposes.[1201] Secondly, he argues, as is characteristic of deliberative rhetoric, that the proposed course of action benefits the audience: "it is better (καλόν) for man to confess his transgressions than to harden his heart" (51:3). In order to demonstrate the latter, he pays attention to what happened to men who hardened their hearts and rebelled (στασιάζω) against Moses.[1202] Korah and his flock "'went down into Hades alive' and 'death shall be their shepherd'",[1203] and Pharaoh and his army perished in the Red Sea[1204] (51:3-5). After these warning examples, he combines different quotations by David "the chosen" (ὁ ἐκλεκτός) in order to demonstrate the proper attitude towards the confession of sins (52:1-4).[1205] Although Clement does not deal explicitly with the consequences of David's confession, the attitude of David, this famous "chosen (ὁ ἐκλεκτός)" man, functions as a proof of the truth of the statement in 51:3. In other words, all the examples in 51:3b-52:4 aim to prove that the statement in 51:3, which in turn is an argument for the exhortation in 51:1, is valid. Following this Clement returns to the other argument that should support the exhortation in 51:1, i.e. that a life in love (and fear) is characterised by self-sacrifice (51:2). He presents Moses' behaviour when God intended to destroy the Israelites because of their iniquity as an example in order to demonstrate this (53:1-5). Moses' love for the people was manifested by his prayer that God should forgive the people, or that he himself should be wiped out together with them. Moses is an example that those who live in love are willing themselves to suffer for the benefit of others.

After using the example of Moses to demonstrate that those who live in love are willing to suffer even death if that could serve the well-being of others, Clement applies this principle to the Corinthian situation (54:1-4). Those among the Corinthians who consider themselves to be noble (γενναῖος), compassionate (εὔσπλαγχνος)[1206] and filled with love (ἀγάπη) should voluntarily depart from the Church if they were causing sedition (στάσις), strife (ἔρις) and divisions (σχίσμα). Further, they should obey the commands of the members (πλῆθος) of the Church and "let the flock of Christ

---

[1200]A. LINDEMANN, *Die Clemensbriefe* (1992) 149: "Gemeint ist offenbar, dass die Rädelsführer der στάσις durch Unbussfertigkeit auch die (Verwirklichung der eschatologischen) Hoffnung der anderen Gemeindeglieder gefährden".

[1201]It is hardly an accident that the focus upon the nature of love comes immediately after the appeal to the common good in 48:6.

[1202]The rebellion against Moses is previously used as a warning example in 4:12.

[1203]Quotations from Num 16:30b; 33a; Ps 48:15a.

[1204]Exod 14.

[1205]Pss 68:32-33a; 49:14f; 50:19a.

[1206]εὔσπλαγχνός refers to the behaviour of Moses in 53:1-5.

have peace with the presbyters set over it" (54:2). In other words, an attitude of love as it was expressed by Moses implies that one is willing to sacrifice one's own interest and ambitions in order to secure the well-being of others, i.e. the restoration of peace. As noted later on in the present study, voluntary exile in cases where it could contribute to peace was regarded in antiquity as patriotism.[1207] As further arguments for the proposed course of action Clement first points out to the Corinthians that those behaving in line with this principle will achieve "great glory (μέγας κλέος) in Christ" (54:3). This argument must be understood in the light of the pivotal value of honour in Mediterranean culture.[1208] Secondly, he underlines that this course of behaviour has been the right conduct both in the past and will be in the future for the citizens of the city of God (54:4).

In 55:1-6 Clement presents other examples of loving self-sacrifice to the benefit of others. First he focuses upon examples from the heathen (ὑποδείγματα ἐθνῶν). Many (πολλοί) kings and rulers have followed the advice of the oracles and voluntarily given themselves to death in a time of pestilence to save their subjects through their own blood. The second example is more directly related to the situation in Corinth: "Many (πολλοί) have gone away from their own cities, that sedition (στασιάζω) might have an end" (55:1). We will not enter into the discussion as to whether or not Clement is thinking of concrete historical persons.[1209] In this connection it is sufficient to note that the argumentative function of these examples is to give support to his proposed solution to the strife (54:2). In 55:2-3 he changes the focus to many (πολλοί)[1210] women among the Christians[1211] who in different ways have conducted themselves in loving self-sacrifice for the benefit of others, before he continues with two examples from the Old Testament. Both Judith and Esther, because of love of their people, delivered themselves to danger that their people could be saved (55:4-6).[1212] All the examples Clement presents in this chapter demonstrate that if one is filled with love one is willing to suffer oneself in order to secure the well-being of others. As such they function as support for Clement's solution to the strife. Moreover, the fact that Clement takes wide-ranging examples from the Old Testament, from contemporary Christians, and from the heathens, makes his argumentation more persuasive.

[1207]See pp. 288.

[1208]Cf. chap. 5.4.1.2.

[1209]Regarding this question, see the discussion in A. LINDEMANN, *Die Clemensbriefe* (1992) 154f.; H. E. LONA, *Der erste Clemensbrief* (1998) 561f. Lona comments that "Das Motiv von der Hingabe des Machthabers zugunsten des Volkes ist in der Antike weit verbreitet" (561).

[1210]πολλοί occurs 5 times in 55:1-3 and serves to underline that the number of people who acted in loving self-sacrifice indeed were great.

[1211]We cannot say for certain if ἐν ἡμῖν refers to the Roman Christians or to the Christians in general, but the description of the persecution of the Roman Christians in 6:1 might suggest that it refers to the first mentioned. So also R. KNOPF, *Die zwei Clemensbriefe* (1920) 132; A. LINDEMANN, *Die Clemensbriefe* (1992) 155.

[1212]Cf. Jdt 8-13; Esth 4:16.

5ST23233 Clement exhorts the Corinthians to receive correction and the leaders of the sedi-tion to submit to the presbyters, 56:1-58:2

In 56:1-58:2 (5ST23233) Clement focuses upon the need for correction, which implies that the instigators of the sedition should submit to the presbyters. One could discuss whether 56:1, in which Clement applies the example of Esther's prayer for her people to the Christians, should be regarded as a part of the former sub-text. The fact that Esther's prayer marks the starting point of the exhortation in 56:1 (καί) might suggest this. In spite of this, we are of the opinion that 56:1 should be regarded as an introduc-tion to the new sub-text. The intended effect of the prayer would be that the Christians should yield to the will of God. From what Clement has said previously this implies repentance and a willingness to correct one's behaviour. Thus it is reasonable to assert that 56:1 prepares for and serves as a transition to the topic of παιδεία which is intro-duced in 56:2. The exhortation in 56:2 to receive παιδεία functions as a *SemM* in as much as the basic argumentation in 56:1-58:2, as already indicated, serves to demon-strate the need for παιδεία.[1213] As is characteristic of deliberative rhetoric Clement appeals to the benefit to the audience if they follow the proposed course of action,[1214] the admonition (νουθέτησις) to receive παιδεία is "good (καλή) and beyond meas-ure helpful" (ὑπεράγαν ὠφέλιμος, 56:2). In the following γάρ-clause Clement gives the reason why it is useful. It unites the Christians to the will of God. Furthermore, in 56:3-16 he gives a number of quotations from the Scripture[1215] in order to prove that his assertion that the admonition is good and helpful is valid.[1216] In 56:16 he reaches the conclusion which is introduced with the emphatic βλέπετε, ἀγαπητοί. The admo-nition to receive παιδεία is "good (καλή) and beyond measure helpful" (ὑπεράγαν ὠφέλιμος) because the intention of God's παιδεία is to ensure that the Christians will obtain mercy.

On the basis of the argumentation above that παιδεία is useful for the Corinthian Christians, Clement goes on to clarify what παιδεία means for the leaders of the sedi-tion. The conjunction οὖν in 57:1 indicates that what follows is an inference from the preceding passage. Here for the first and only time in the letter Clement explicitly addresses (ὑμεῖς) those "who laid the foundation of the sedition" (καταβολὴ τῆς στάσεως) and admonishes them by means of two co-ordinated imperative clauses to "submit (ὑποτάσσω) to the presbyters, and receive the correction (παιδεύω) of repentance" (57:1). The fact that these two exhortations are given in the form of two co-ordinated clauses shows that Clement intends to convey that the reception of cor-rection implies that the actual men themselves should submit to the presbyters. Fur-thermore, he reiterates the exhortation in order to emphasize it: μάθετε ὑποτάσ-σεσθαι (58:2). The following participial clause expresses in the negative how the atti-

---

[1213]The noun παιδεία and the verb παιδεύω occur two and six times respectively.

[1214]See chaps. 2.3.1 and 2.3.2.

[1215]*1 Clem.* 56:3-4: Ps 117:18; Prov 3:12, *1 Clem.* 56:5: Ps 140:5, *1 Clem.* 56:6-15: Job 5:17-26.

[1216]Concerning the question whether Clement uses a Testimonium here, see D. A. HAGNER, *The Use of The Old and The New Testaments in Clement of Rome* (1973) 98f., 102f.

tude of submission should be manifested. It is hardly an accident that he focuses upon putting aside ἀλαζονεία and ὑπερηφανία in as much as these terms belonged to the semantic field of concord in antiquity.[1217] In line with his argumentation regarding the usefulness of receiving correction (57:2-16), Clement argues in 57:2b that it will benefit the leaders of the sedition if they follow the admonition in 57:1-2a. It is better (ἄμεινον) for them to be small (μικρός) within the Church than to have a pre-eminent reputation – in the sort of position that presbyters gain – with the result that they would be excluded from the Christian hope.[1218] On the one hand, the quotation of Prov 1:23-33 that follows should serve to demonstrate that those who do not obey and pay attention to the counsel of the *Wisdom* indeed have no hope (57:3-6). They shall "'eat the fruits of their own way'" because of their sins, "'they shall be put to death, and inquisition shall destroy the wicked'" (57:6-7a). On the other hand, the end of the quotation shows that those who hear, in the sense of obeying, shall dwell with confidence in his hope (57:7b).

In 58:1 Clement explicitly applies (οὖν) the words of the Proverbs to the Corinthians. If they desire to escape from the threats of *Wisdom* they must be obedient to God.[1219] Obeying God in this connection means that the founders of the sedition must follow the exhortation in 57:1 and submit to the presbyters. That both this exhortation and the many others in the letter are according to the will of God is self-evident for him. In 59:1, for instance, he states that God has spoken through the author of the letter and in 63:2 that the letter is written through the Holy Spirit.[1220] On the background of the future fate of those who are disobedient to God, he uses the imperative to exhort the Corinthians to δέξασθε τὴν συμβουλὴν ἡμῶν (58:2). It is reasonable to argue that σύμβουλος, in addition to its reference to submission to the presbyters in the immediate context, is used as a technical term for the whole letter.[1221] When Clement argues in favour of taking the advice by asserting that they will have nothing to regret if they do so (58:2), he implies that if they act otherwise they will regret it. He probably has the threats of *Wisdom* in mind. In contrast to the fate of the disobedient, he continues in the positive to focus upon the good future of those who in humility and gentleness have "performed the decrees (δικαίωμα) and commandments (πρόσταγμα) given by God". They "shall be enrolled and chosen in the number of those who

---

[1217]See pp. 131-136, and 168-169 respectively.

[1218]Clement's exhortations and argumentation in 57:1-2 imply that he considered it as possible that the instigators of the sedition could still remain in the Corinthian Church. At first sight this might appear to contradict 54:2 where Clement suggests voluntary exile as a solution to the sedition. However, to submit to the presbyters is an embedded consequence of what Clement suggests in 57:2. A. LINDEMANN, *Die Clemensbriefe* (1992) 159: "Aber wenn die Auflagen von 54,2 erfüllt worden sind, ergibt sich die in 57,1 geforderte Unterordnung ... als unmittelbare und notwendige Folge. Dass zwischen dem freiwilligen Exil von 54,2 und den Forderungen in 57,1.2. eine Alternative bestünde (so Grant zST), ist nicht zu erkennen".

[1219]The expression τῷ παναγίῳ καὶ ἐνδόξῳ ὀνόματι αὐτοῦ in 58:1 stands for God himself, so also A. LINDEMANN, *Die Clemensbriefe* (1992) 161.

[1220]In addition, see, e.g., 56:1 and 58:2.

[1221]For σύμβουλος as a technical term for deliberative rhetoric, see the present work, n. 65.

are saved through Jesus Christ" (τῶν σωζομένων διὰ Ἰησοῦ Χριστοῦ, 58:2). In other words, Clement in his argumentative strategy contrasts the great danger to the instigators of the sedition if they do not follow his advice and submit to the presbyters, with the great benefit they will achieve if they behave according to it. More concretely, 58:1-2 serves to prove that Clement's argumentation for submitting to the presbyters in 57:2 is valid. It should not be necessary to remind the reader that when Clement on the one hand explicitly warns of the danger connected with the present course of action being taken, and on the other hand appeals to the great benefit to the audience if they follow his advice, he reflects a key feature in deliberative rhetoric. Further, we note that when Clement does so, he plays on the feelings of the audience. By asserting that those who laid the foundation of the sedition will be excluded from the flock of Christ and by applying the threatening words of *Wisdom* to them, he would probably stir up fear among them. The warning of danger connected with the present course of action is especially effective when it is contrasted with the greatest benefit for the Christians, i.e. to be saved through Christ. It is hardly an accident that Clement makes such powerful use of *pathos* in his argument at the end of the *probatio*-section. *Pathos* is an effective means in the process of persuasion and it is perceived as a good rule to place the most persuasive argument at the end of the *probatio*-section.[1222]

4ST2324 A prayer for concord, 59:1-61:3

59:1f. serves as an introduction or a transition to the prayer in 59:3-61:3. In 59:1 Clement reiterates, and thereby emphasizes the point that those who do not follow "the words which have been spoken by him [God] through us" (τοῖς ὑπ᾽ αὐτοῦ δι᾽ ἡμῶν εἰρημένοις) entangle themselves in "no little danger" (κινδύνῳ οὐ μικρῷ). From what he has just said in 58.2 and what follows in 59:2 it seems obvious that κίνδυνος refers to the eschatological danger, i.e. the danger of not achieving salvation through Christ. This warning of the danger of not following Clement's advice links 59:1 with the foregoing. In spite of this, the main reason why we are of the opinion that this verse should be regarded as a part of the present sub-text is the fact that there is a *SA* on the surface-level of the text. In our view it seems to be obvious that the passage quoted above from 59:1 should be regarded as a substitution on abstraction level for the foregoing and thus indicates that a new sub-text begins at this point. There is also another reason for including the 59:1-2 in the sub-text 4ST2324. One can argue that 59:1-2 functions as a transition to the prayer. On the basis of the statement in 58:2, Clement says that the Romans will be innocent of this sin (ἁμαρτία), i.e. the continuation of sedition with its dangerous implications, and will pray that God "may guard unhurt the number of his elect that has been numbered in all the world through his beloved child Jesus Christ" (59:2). From what he has stated in 57:1-58:2 it is implied that he will pray that those who laid the foundation of the sedition will submit to the presbyters and thus establish concord in the Church. In other words, he indicates in this introduction to the

---

[1222]Cic. [*Rhet. Her.*] 3.10.18.

prayer that he intends to pray for things that could secure concord among the Christians. Furthermore, we note that when he presents a prayer it is in line with the exhortation found earlier in the letter to pray for people who live in sin that they will submit to the will of God (56:1).

We must refrain from entering into the discussion on which traditions Clement eventually depends on regarding the prayer. However, some comments are in place. The stylistic structure of the prayer indicates that Clement did not create it at the time of writing.[1223] It appears that the prayer reflects features of the Jewish prayer tradition[1224] and possible elements of the liturgy in the Roman Church.[1225] This does not mean, however, that he is simply using an already existing prayer. It seems reasonable to argue that he took already existing prayer traditions as a starting-point and adapted them in line with the purpose of the letter.[1226] To a certain extent this might explain the rather general content of the prayer. However, we should note that in the light of what he has said previously in the letter much of the content is related to what he indicated as the main topic of the prayer in 58:2, i.e. concord.[1227] Examples of this are (1) that God humbles the pride of the haughty (ὕβρις ὑπερηφάνων) and raises up the humble (ταπεινός) in 59:3, (2) the prayer for forgiveness of their "iniquities (ἀνομία) and unrighteousness (ἀδικία), and transgressions (παράπτωμα), and short-comings" (πλημμέλεια), and (3) that God must "guide our steps to walk in holiness of heart (ἐν ὁσιότητι καρδίας), to do the things which are good (καλός) and pleasing (εὐάρεστος)" for him in 60:1f. Most directly related to the main topic of the letter is the prayer that God may give "concord (ὁμόνοια) and peace (εἰρήνη) to us and to all that dwell on the earth" (60:4).

The fact that we find that so much of the content of the prayer is related to what we consider to be the main topic of the letter does not, however, explain why Clement introduces it between the *probatio* and *peroratio*. The suggestion of A. von Harnack, that by means of the prayer at the end of the letter Clement attempts to make the Corinthians think that they "mit den römischen Brüdern *eine* Gemeinde bilden" is not suffi-

---

[1223]Regarding the "sorgfältige Stilisierung und Strukturierung" of the prayer, see A. LINDEMANN, *Die Clemensbriefe* (1992) 165-168; H. E. LONA, *Der erste Clemensbrief* (1998) 583-588. R. KNOPF, *Die zwei Clemensbriefe* (1920) depicts the prayer as "einer der wertvollsten Teile des ganzen Briefes, überhaupt ein besonders kostbares Stück der ganzen urchristlichen Literatur" (137).

[1224]Cf. B. E. BOWE, "Prayer Rendered for Caesar ?", *The Lord's Prayer and other Prayer Texts* (1994) 85.

[1225]See for example P. DREWS, "Untersuchungen über die sogen. clementinische Liturgie im VIII Buch der apostolischen Konstitutionen", *Studien zur Geschichte des Gottesdienstes* (1906) 40-47; R. KNOPF, *Die zwei Clemensbriefe* (1920) 137; H. E. LONA, *Der erste Clemensbrief* (1998) 616-619.

[1226] So also P. MIKAT, "Zur Fürbitte der Christen für Kaiser und Reich im Gebet des 1. Clemensbriefes", *Festschrift für Ulrich Scheuner* (1973) 456; A. LINDEMANN, *Die Clemensbriefe* (1992) 168.

[1227]So also P. MIKAT, "Zur Fürbitte der Christen für Kaiser und Reich im Gebet des 1. Clemensbriefes", *Festschrift für Ulrich Scheuner* (1973) 459f. Also, H. E. LONA, *Der erste Clemensbrief* (1998), emphasizes that the main topics of the prayer are related to both the basic themes of and the purpose of the letter (588; 619).

cient.[1228] Obviously, the letter does not end with the prayer.[1229] Further, the attempt to create a state of unity between the Corinthians and the Romans is not limited to this prayer, but is reflected throughout the letter.[1230] R. Knopf explains both the occurrence and the placing of the prayer by viewing it as an analogy to the community prayer that followed the sermon in the Sunday service.[1231] This suggestion was recently taken up and further developed by J. Chr. Salzmann. Clement has delivered his sermon and now the prayer follows.[1232] A similar objection to the one we made against Harnack appears to be in place here as well, i.e. if Clement regarded the prayer as analogous to the prayer after the sermon in the Sunday service, it is more likely that he would have put it after the end of the *peroratio* which constitutes the end of a discourse.

In our opinion one should pay more attention to the persuasive force of the prayer when attempting to grasp why Clement makes use of it. In this connection it is interesting to note that Dio Chrysostom uses a prayer to the gods for concord in one of his discourses on concord. He ends *Or.* 39 with the following prayer:

> ... *I pray to Dionysus the progenitor of this city, to Heracles its founder, to Zeus Guardian of Cities, to Athena, to Aphrodite Fosterer of Friendship, to Harmony, and Nemesis, and all the other gods, that from this day forth they may implant in this city a yearning for itself, a passionate love, a singleness of purpose, a unity of wish and thought; and, on the other hand, that they may cast out strife and contentiousness and jealousy, so that this city may be numbered among the most prosperous and the noblest for all time to come (Or. 39.8).*

It is in itself an interesting observation that one finds a prayer for concord at the end of this deliberative discourse urging concord.[1233] However, Dio's foregoing considerations on why he uses the prayer is even more interesting. He depicts an appeal to the gods as the "most efficacious appeal. For the gods know what men mean to say even when they speak in whispers" (*Or.* 39.8). Furthermore, he says that a prayer to the gods is typical of one who is especially well-intentioned, and as an example he mentions good fathers who are concerned for their children: "Good fathers use admonition with their children where they can, but where persuasion fails they pray the gods on their behalf" (Or.39.8). It is reasonable that Clement uses the prayer in 59:3-61:3 for a simi-

---

[1228] A. VON HARNACK, *Einführung in die Alte Kirchengeschichte* (1929) 119f.

[1229] Also A. LINDEMANN, *Die Clemensbriefe* (1992) 168, opposes Harnack's suggestion on the basis of this fact.

[1230] This attempt is, among other things, reflected in the heavy use of the first person plural, the vocatives ἀγαπητοί (17 times: 1:1; 7:1; 12:8; 16:17; 21:1; 24:1,2; 35:1,5; 36:1; 43:6; 47:6; 50:1, 5; 53:1; 56:2, 16) and ἀδελφοί (14 times: 4:7; 13:1; 14:1; 33:1; 37:1; 38:3; 41:1, 2, 4; 45:1, 6; 46:1; 52:1; 62:1). For the group cohesion effect of using such language, see W. A. MEEKS, *The First Urban Christians* (1983) 85-94.

[1231] R. KNOPF, *Die zwei Clemensbriefe* (1920) 138.

[1232] J. CHR. SALZMANN, *Lehren und Ermahnen* (1994) 160-162.

[1233] Cf. also Dio Chrys. *Or.* 38:51 where Dio says at the end of the discourse that he will pray to the gods that the audience would take the most admirable resolutions, that is resolutions which secure concord.

lar reason, namely because he regarded it as an efficacious appeal in the sense that God has the power to answer it. In fact, in his opinion, a prayer to the Almighty God was probably regarded as the strongest of all means he could employ in order to persuade the Corinthian Christians.

Additionally, the prayer is an effective appeal in another sense. On the basis of what Clement has stated previously the appropriate response to the prayer would be that the instigators of the sedition would submit to the presbyters and thereby re-establish peace and concord. Therefore, if these men and those who supported them took part in the prayer, the prayer would function as a strong implicit appeal to follow Clement's advice. The prayer would be particularly efficient as an implicit appeal for concord, if the Corinthians were familiar with similar phrases from their liturgy. One would not pray to God and at the same time consciously oppose the things one prays for.[1234]

Furthermore, if prayer was commonly thought to be an expression of goodwill, the prayer would be a means of increasing the *ethos* of the letter writer. Thus, we believe, Clement uses a prayer not because of an association with the religious service, but first of all because it functions as an appeal to follow his proposed course of action and has the effect of enhancing his *ethos*.

The analysis of the macro-structural composition of *1 Clement* provided above gives us the following table of the composition of the letter:

1ST1   Epistolary prescript

    2ST11   Superscript
    2ST12   Adscript
    2ST13   Salution

1ST2   Letter corpus, 1:1-64:1

    2ST21   *Exordium*, 1:1 2:8

        3ST211   *Attentum et docilem parare*, 1:1
        3ST212   *Benevolum parare*, 1:2-2:8

    2ST22   *Narratio*, 3:1-4
    2ST23   *Probatio*, 4:1-61:3

        3ST231   *Quaestio infinita*/θέσις, 4:1-39:9
            The principle of concord for a Christian community. Clement deals with and exhorts the Corinthians regarding virtues and behaviour that secure concord, and warns against vices and behaviour that lead to sedition.

[1234]B. E. Bowe, "Prayer Rendered for Caesar ?", *The Lord's Prayer and other Prayer Texts* (1994) 88f., when discussing the function of the prayer, refers to G. B. Caird (*The Language and Imagery of the Bible*. Philadelphia: Westminster, 1980) and states that "He includes prayer in the category of 'cohesive language' whose function is to 'establish rapport, to create a sense of mutual trust and common ethos.' [G.B. Caird, 32]. All forms of worship, especially the more stylized forms, have this group binding function. A call to prayer is frequently an over invitation to the audience to identify with the speaker (or writer) and with the beliefs that they share in common". Similarly H. E. Lona, *Der erste Clemensbrief* (1998) 623.

4ST2311 ζῆλος and ἔρις leads to death, 4:1-6:4
   5ST23111 Examples from OT, 4:1-13
   5ST23112 Examples from the Christian tradition, 5:1-6:2
   5ST23113 Example from the household, 6:3
   5ST23114 Example from the political area, 6:4
4ST2312 Exhortations to certain virtues which are according to the will of God and which promote concord, 7:1-39:9
   5ST23121 Introduction, 7:1-4
   5ST23122 Repentance is possible, 7:5-8:5
      6ST231221 Assertion, 7:5
      6ST231222 Examples and quotations from the Scriptures, 7:6-8:4
      6ST231223 Conclusion, 8:5
   5ST23123 The need for obedience, 9:1-12:8
      6ST231231 Admonition to obey the will of God which implies that one cease from strife, 9:1
      6ST231232 Examples from the OT, 9:2-12:8
         7ST2312321 Introduction to examples, 9:2
         7ST2312322 Positive examples, 9:3-11:1
         7ST2312323 Warning example, 11:2
         7ST2312324 Positive example, 12:1-8
   5ST23124 The need for humility, 13:1-19:1
      6ST231241 Exhortation to humility, 13:1-13:4
      6ST231242 Admonition to obey God and abstain from sedition, 14:1-5
      6ST231243 Warning against those who hypocritically seek peace, 15:1-16:1
      6ST231244 Examples of humility, 16:2-19:1
         7ST2312441 Christ, 16:2-17
         7ST2312442 Examples taken from the OT, 17:1-19:1
   5ST23125 Exhortations to unity in peace, 19:2-22:8
      6ST231251 The concord of the Universe, 19:2-20:12
      6ST231252 Application to the Christians, 21:1-22:8
   5ST23126 Admonition to not be double-minded regarding the gifts of God, 23:1-28:4
      6ST231261 Introduction to the topic of not being double-minded 23:1-8
      6ST231262 A future resurrection, 24:1-26:3
      6ST231263 Application to the Corinthians, 27:1-28:4.
   5ST23127 A life in holiness, 29:1-36:6
      6ST231271 Exhortation to live a holy life which implies concord, 29:1-30:8
      6ST231272 The paths of blessing, 31:1-32:4
      6ST231273 The need to do good, 33:1-36:6
   5ST23128 The need for subordination, mutuality and interdependence, 37:1-39:9

3ST232 *Quaestio finita*/ὑπόθεσις, 40:1-61:3
   Clement deals explicitly with the problem of the Corinthian Church and exhorts the leaders of the sedition to submit to the presbyters
   4ST2321 Order among the people of God according to the will of God, 40:1-43:6

5ST23211 The cult of Temple as an example, 40:1-41:4

5ST23212 Order in the apostolic times, 42:1-43:6

4ST2322 Clement blames the Corinthians for the present state of affairs, 44:1-47:7

5ST23221 The Corinthian have removed some of the presbyters, 44:1-44:6

5ST23222 The Scripture shows that it is the law-breakers who have persecuted the righteous, 45:1-8

5ST23223 Clement exhorts the Corinthians to cleave to those who endured and blames the Corinthians for the present sedition, 46:1-46:9

5ST23224 Clement compares the present sedition with that which Paul dealt with in 1 Cor, 47:1-7

4ST2323 Clement exhorts the Corinthians to cease from the present strife, 48:1-58:2

5ST23231 Admonition to put an end to the sedition, 48:1-6

5ST23232 The greatness of love with application to the situation in Corinth, 49:1-55:6

6ST232321 The greatness of love, 49:1-6

6ST232322 The principle of love applied to the situation in the Corinthian Church, 50:1-55:6

7ST2323221 Exhortation to pray that one live in love without sedition, 50:1-7

7ST2323222 Love implies that one seeks the common good of all and therefore those who laid the foundation of the sedition should voluntarily leave the Church, 51:1-55:6.

5ST23233 Clement exhorts the Corinthians to receive correction and the leaders of the sedition to submit to the presbyters, 56:1-58:2.

4ST2324 A prayer for concord, 59:1-61:3

2ST24 *Peroratio*, 62:1-64:1

1ST3 Epistolary postscript, 65:1-2

4.2.5. Summary of the Compositional Analysis

1 Clement is clearly a letter. As such it contains conventional features of the Greek letter: epistolary prescript (prescript), a corpus (1:1-64:1) and a postscript (65:1-2). By taking our point of departure in the *dispositio* of ancient rhetoric we have attempted to show that it is adequate to operate with the following delimitation of the corpus of the letter: 1:1-2:8 *exordium*, 3:1-4 *narratio*, 4:1-61:3 *probatio* and 62:1-64:1 *peroratio*. The *exordium* consists of a *docilem parare* in which Clement indicates that the main topic of the letter is στάσις or its antonym ὁμόνοια (and εἰρήνη, 1:1), an *attentum parare* which intends to gain the Corinthian's attention (1:1), and a *benevolum parare* (1:2-2:8), which should serve to arouse the good will of the audience. In the *narratio* Clement briefly gives an exposition of the occurrences that have taken place and introduces his readers to the nature of the case in question. The *narratio* is written in a spirit of blame and contrasts the present situation with the noble past when the Corinthians lived in peace and concord. It appears that Clement attempts to make the Corinthians aware of the scandalous nature of their present behaviour and thereby bring it about that they should "take better counsel about the future" (Arist. *Rh*. 3.16.1). In the *pero-ratio* he both enumerates some of the most important topics of the *probatio* and briefly reiterates what it appears that he considered to be the most persuasive argument for concord, i.e. the appeal to follow the many and the great examples he has put forward throughout the letter (63:1).

We stated above that the *docilem parare* indicates that ὁμόνοια is the main topic of the letter. That this is the fundamental theme is further confirmed in the other parts of the letter-body. Due to the fact that the *probatio* constitutes the main bulk of the letter, as is the case in deliberative rhetoric in general, we have paid especial attention to the delimitation of this section. In line with what has just been said concerning the main topic of the letter it is argued that the sub-texts on different levels of the *probatio* in one way or another serve Clement's overall argument for concord in the Corinthian Church. This is also the case regarding the first main part of the *probatio* (4:1-39:9). Though Clement touches upon a number of topics, we have argued that the different topics are subsumed under the topic of concord. This means that we oppose both the commonly held view that it is not possible to find a leading theme in this part of the letter, and also the view of those scholars who assert that order is the leading theme.[1235] There is indeed a leading theme, i.e. concord.

We have seen that in 4:1-39:9 Clement focuses on the one hand upon virtues and behaviour that promote concord, and on the other hand upon vices and behaviour that have the opposite effect. Furthermore, we have pointed out that in this part of the letter he does not deal with the concrete situation in the Corinthian Church. Thus we can depict this section as *a treatise on the principles of concord for a Christian Community*. Because of this general approach we find it reasonable to characterise 4:1-39:9 as being a θέσις in line with the status theory of ancient rhetoric.

In the second main part of the *probatio* (40:1-61:3) Clement to a great extent applies the general principles of the θέσις to the situation in the Corinthian Church. This does not mean, however, that we do not find general deliberations on virtue and behaviour which should secure concord in this part as well. However, in contrast to the θέσις, in 40:1-61:3 Clement explicitly applies the general to a particular situation. He addresses the founders of the sedition directly and exhorts them to submit to the presbyters and thereby re-establish concord. Therefore it is reasonable to view this section as a ὑπόθεσις. This implies also that we hold, in contrast to what is commonly argued, that there is a direct connection between the two main parts of the letter. That it was appropriate to structure the *probatio* of deliberative rhetoric urging concord in a θέσις-section followed by a subsequent ὑπόθεσις-section is evident from the fact that we have seen that this structure is found in one discourse of Dio Chrysostom and in one of Aelius Aristides respectively. This "rhetorical" solution to the problem of the composi-

---

[1235]E.g., H. VON CAMPENHAUSEN, *Ecclesiastical Authority and Spiritual Power in the Church of the First Three Centuries* (1969) 94; G. HASENHÜTL, *Charisma* (1969) 284-290; G. BRUNNER, *Die theologische Mitte des ersten Klemensbriefes* (1972) 152-163; E. SCHWEIZER, *Church Order in the New Testament* (1979) 146-149.

tion of *1 Clement* offers an explanation that is both more adequate and more straight-forward than the suggestion by G. Brunner.[1236]

Furthermore, the fact that the compositional analysis has shown that concord is the most likely main theme of the letter definitely confirms the adequacy of describing *1 Clement* as deliberative rhetoric urging concord.

[1236]In fact, G. Brunner's position that a one dimensional approach, for example one similar to Paul's approach in 1 Corinthians, would not have been sufficient in the new historical situation is a mere postulate without further argumentation. For Brunner's view, see above pp. 205-207.

5. The Social-Historical Situation

5.1. Introductory Remarks

In our discussion on methodology we noted the significance of the communication situation in rhetorical analyses and stated that the analysis must demonstrate the appropriateness of rhetorical genre and content to the communication situation.[1237] So far in our investigation we have focused upon the question of genre, the language of unity and sedition and the composition of the letter. A main element has been our attempt to demonstrate that Clement employs many terms and *topoi* related to the concept of concord and to demonstrate that the sub-texts on different levels serve Clement's argumentation for concord. This fact, in addition to the fact that the main characteristics of deliberative rhetoric occur in the letter, indicates that *1 Clement* ought to be classified as συμβουλευτικὸς λόγος περὶ ὁμόνοιας.

In this work on the question of genre and on the compositional analysis we have deliberately moved at a literary level without paying attention either to the historical situation, or to what the letter itself says explicitly and implicitly about the underlying cause of the sedition. The only exception is that when we dealt with political terms and *topoi* in *1 Clem.* 3 we briefly stated that the terminology Clement employs in this chapter indicates that he considered the conflict in terms of socio-political categories in which striving for honour was an essential feature.[1238] This means that although we have dealt with certain elements connected to the communication situation, namely the question of genre and the basic type of argumentation,[1239] we have only to a very limited degree focused on the basic feature of the communication situation: the occurrences in the Corinthian Church which promoted the Roman Church to intervene – or what we refer to in this chapter as the *Social-Historical Situation*.

The reason why we did not deal more extensively with the question of the social-historical situation in connection with the discussion of 3:3 in the preceding chapter was to avoid a break with the literary approach taken in the rest of the chapter. Additionally, this question has been so extensively discussed in research on *1 Clement* that it deserves to be dealt with in a chapter of its own.[1240] Therefore in this chapter we shall

---

[1237]Cf. p. 22.

[1238]See pp. 149f.

[1239]Cf. chap. 2.4.2. The argumentative function of the examples is further dealt with in chap. 4. *Compositional Analysis of 1 Clement*.

[1240]See below.

deal explicitly with the situation in the Corinthian Church which in the view of the Roman Church made a rhetorical response necessary.

We must, of course, distinguish between the real historical situation and Clement's description and interpretation of the incident. Clement's presentation of the matter is his interpretation which is coloured by the intention of the letter. Nevertheless, we question the view that Clement's depiction is so one-sided and biased that one should dismiss in general what he says about the situation at Corinth.[1241] For if the gap between Clement's description of the occurrences and what actually happened was too wide, it is unlikely that the recipients would have responded so positively to the letter as we know they in fact did.[1242] When we focus in what follows upon the motives behind the conflict we shall primarily deal with what the letter itself says about the conflict, both explicitly and implicitly. We shall, however, pay attention to other ancient literature which reflects that what Clement considered to be the underlying cause of the strife was commonly regarded to be a source of sedition in a political body. Although this in itself does not confirm that Clement's depiction mirrors the real historical situation, it at least shows that Clement's description of what happened was reasonable.

The main purpose of the letter is to urge the Corinthian Christians to cease from present strife and sedition and return to the previous situation of concord (62:2; 65:1). According to Clement the sedition involves the removal of some of the legally appointed presbyters from their office (44:6; 47:6). That the removal of some presbyters is a primary element in the conflict seems to be clear, but Clement is unfortunately rather vague regarding the description of what actually took place in the Church at Corinth.[1243] At first sight, he neither offers any information about the underlying causes of the conflict nor any identification of the different groups involved. The latter would to a great extent have enhanced our understanding of the motives underlying the conflict. His apparent silence on these points may explain, on the one hand, the many suggestions proposed regarding the actual content of the conflict and the different groups involved, and on the other, the fact that some scholars hold a negative view concerning the possibility of saying anything at all with any certainty regarding this

---

[1241] A. von Harnack, *Einführung in die Alte Kirchengeschichte* (1929) 91, and in particular W. Bauer, *Orthodoxy and Heresy in Earliest Christianity* (1971) 96-99, who holds that "the picture that faces us of the conditions in Corinth is sketched from the perspective of Rome, which was doubtless one-sided and based on self-interest – to say the very least, a biased picture" (96) and that "Harnack is quite correct when he dismisses without further ado many things that *1 Clement* says in characterization of the situation" (98).

[1242] So also H. E. Lona, *Der erste Clemensbrief* (1998) 81. The reception of the letter in the Early Church is a testimony to its positive response. For the reception of the letter, see *ibid.* 89-109.

[1243] This need not be taken as a sign that Clement had little or no information about the occurrences in the Corinthian Church. So R. Knopf, "Der Erste Klemensbrief", *TU* 20 (1901) 174f. It is a fair supposition that Clement's apparent vagueness regarding the historical situation in Corinth must rather be explained by the simple fact that the recipients of the letter would understand quite well what he is writing about. Cf., e.g., B. Weiss, "Amt und Eschatologie im 1. Clemensbrief", *ThPh* 50 (1975) 71; J. Fuellenbach, *Ecclesiastical Office and the Primacy of Rome* (1980) 4; H. O. Maier, *The Social Setting of Ministry as Reflected in the Writings of Hermas, Clement and Ignatius* (1991) 88.

issue. Before we make our own contribution to this much discussed question in *1 Clement* research, it is time for a brief outline of the discussion among scholars on this point.

5.2. A Brief Outline of the History of Research on the Nature of the Strife[1244]

A. von Harnack attempts to minimise the seriousness of the strife. He argues that the strife was not more than a "ausgewaschenen Cliquenzank ... ohne jeden prinzipiellen Hintergrund".[1245] Other scholars have followed Harnack's reluctance to see any matters of great significance behind the strife.[1246] In particular we should note that two of the most recent special studies on *1 Clement* express considerable sympathy with Harnack's description. Although B. E. Bowe remarks that Harnack's description of the dispute "was, perhaps, a bit *too* minimal, given the reference to its broad publicity in *1 Clem* 47:7", she holds that the suggestion of Harnack is still "the most balanced presentation of the occasion of the letter" offered so far by scholars.[1247] H. O. Maier, who stresses the need to interpret *1 Clement* in the light of the wider social setting of the Church, holds that the strife refers to divisions among patrons of house churches. He holds that the dispute "over the title bishop is best understood as referring to a division within one or two of the Corinthian house churches which has resulted in the creation of an alternative meeting place, the exodus of members who are sympathetic with these persons and, presumably, the exclusion of members who are opposed to them".[1248] However, regarding the concrete reason why the strife arose, Maier is rather vague. He comments that the reason is not given and restricts himself to saying that it is possible that no theological matters were involved, and continues by referring to Harnack: "the division was merely between 'personal cliques'".[1249]

Notwithstanding this, the majority of scholars are inclined to see questions of a more principal nature behind the strife. The most common suggestion is that the strife reflects a conflict between the pneumatic members of the Church and those who emphasized ecclesiastical office. The instigators of the strife are regarded as pneumatics who opposed the increasing power of the office.[1250] Although we find slight differences in view among the advocates of this theory, for example F. Gerke, P. Meinhold, H. Opitz, G. G. Blum, J. Rohde, H. F. von Campenhausen, and E. Schweizer, they all agree

---

[1244]This review does not pretend to be complete regarding the issue. Our intention is to present the suggestions which have played the greatest role in the research on *1 Clement*. In our selection of literature we have in addition chosen to refer to what the most recent works, works published after 1980, say about the question.

[1245]A. von Harnack, *Einführung in die Alte Kirchengeschichte* (1929) 92.

[1246]See, e.g., A. Stuiber, "Clemens Romanus", *RAC* 3 (1957) 191; J. A. Fischer, *Apostolische Väter* (1966) 3.

[1247]B. E. Bowe, *A Church in Crisis* (1988) 21.

[1248]H. O. Maier, *The Social Setting of Ministry as Reflected in the Writings of Hermas, Clement and Ignatius* (1991) 93.

[1249]*Ibid.* 93. Although Maier is too vague regarding the nature of the strife, we have much sympathy with his emphasis upon the social setting of the conflict in the Corinthian Church.

that the basic motive behind the dispute was a conflict between a still existing charismatic tradition which went back to apostolic times and an increasing emphasis on order and hierarchy.[1250] R. Knopf and W. Telfer argue on the basis of 54:2, where Clement exhorts the leaders of the sedition to voluntarily leave the Church, that these persons had not originally belonged to the Corinthian Church. More precisely, they hold that these men were pneumatics who had invaded the community from the outside. They were so-called wandering charismatics who because of their spiritual gifts claimed the leadership of the Church.[1252] B. E. Bowe, in spite of appreciating the above-mentioned description by Harnack of the conflict as a "quarrel among cliques", expresses a high degree of agreement with R. Knopf at the end of her work.[1253] According to H. E. Lona there could be many motives for removing some of the presbyters,

---

[1250]K. Beyschlag, *Clemens Romanus und der Frühkatholizismus* (1966), comments regarding this suggestion that it "erscheint in fast allen Clemensdarstellungen in monotoner Wiederkehr" (4 n. 2), and J. Fuellenbach, *Ecclesiastical Office and the Primacy of Rome* (1980) 5, says that "the most common view is to see behind the dissidents 'pneumatics' who had a different understanding regarding office in the community and who as 'charismatics' opposed any consolidation of office in the congregation".

[1251] F. Gerke, *Die Stellung des ersten Clemensbriefes innerhalb der Entwicklung der altchristlichen Gemeindeverfassung und des Kirchenrechts* (1931) 66; P. Meinhold, "Geschehen und Deutung des ersten Clemensbriefes", *ZKG* 58 (1939): "Die Gegner des 1 Clem. haben sich für ihr pneumatisches Christentum auf Paulus berufen. Der spirituale Kirchenbegriff des Paulus stehet letzlich hinter dem Vorgehen gegen das Amt in Korinth" (99f.), and further; "Die Pneumatiker von Korinth sind, wie sich aus der Polemik des Clemensbriefes ergibt, von Paulus ausgegangen und haben, sich im Besitz der von Paulus 1. Kor. 12 aufgezählten Geistesgaben fühlend, die geistliche Leitung der Gemeinde beansprucht" (127); H. Opitz, *Ursprünge Frühkatholischer Pneumatologie* (1959) 11-20: "Die mehr oder weniger stark vertretenen Vermutungen, es handle sich um Pneumatiker, hat Meinhold in einer scharfsinnigen Analyse dahingehend präzisiert, dass er in ihnen Pauliner sieht, die, ausgerüstet mit Charismen glossolalischer Art, ein pneumatisches Gemeindeleben in Korinth im Sinne von 1. Kor. 12-14 wieder herzustellen trachten" (11). Characteristic of H. Opitz's opinion is the heading "Das Wesen der 'pneumatischen' Gegner in Korinth" (11); G. G. Blum, *Tradition und Sukzession* (1963) 45f.; J. Rohde, "Häresie und Schisma im ersten Clemensbrief und in den Ignatius-Briefen", *NT* 10 (1968), concludes regarding the opponents: "Tatsächlich waren sie aber Neocharismatiker, die sich in der Kraft des Pneuma gegen die Macht der Tradition und gegen die Entwicklungstendenzen ihrer Zeit, die auf das rechtlich geordnete Amt hin ausgerichtet waren, erhoben, um die Entwiclung wieder zur apostolichen Zeit zurückzuschrauben" (226); H. F. von Campenhausen, *Ecclesiastical Authority and Spiritual Power in the Church of the First Three Centuries* (1969), writes: "It looks as though the old turbulence and disruption, the religious arrogance and the chaotic craving for freedom, had still not died out. It is easy to understand how such a congregation would be all the more likely to come into conflict with the representatives of the presbyterial system in proportion as the latter had perhaps as yet not occupied their position for long, and may have been seeking to extend and reinforce their all too recent authority" (86); E. Schweizer, *Church and Order in the New Testament* (1979) 146.

[1252]R. Knopf, *Die zwei Clemensbriefe* (1920) 130f.; W. Telfer, *The Office of a Bishop* (1962) 57ff. Cf. *Did.* 11 and 13. For a discussion of the phenomena of "Wanderradikalismus" in Early Christianity, see G. Theissen, "Wanderradikalismus", *Studien zur Soziologie des Urchristentums* (1989) 79-105.

[1253]B. E. Bowe, *A Church in Crisis* (1988) 152f.

but all of them had in common that the consequences of institutionalizing the office could not be accepted.[1254]

Also G. Brunner holds that the strife was about the structure of the Church's leadership.[1255] *1 Clem.* 44, which Brunner regards as the centre of the whole letter, shows that the Corinthian dispute was about the ὄνομα τῆς ἐπισκοπῆς. However, it was not a conflict between charism and office which was the point of departure for the strife. It was caused by the fact that the Church was facing a new historical situation. At the end of the first century the Church was about to grow out of its household structures and into a public and juridical entity analogous to the state. This new situation needed new structures. According to Brunner the Church had to institutionalize authority and structure if it was to have a future. It was in this new situation, where the Church had to develop new structures, that the strife concerning office emerged in the Corinthian Church.[1256]

R. A. Campbell argues that the cause of the conflict has to do with "an attempt to introduce monoepiscopacy in the manner recommended by the pastorals".[1257] On the basis of 54:1f. Campbell maintains that the dispute "centres on one man", a bishop who "has sought to be more than a chairman of the presbyters, and has sought to centralize the worship of the church under his own presidency in the way later to be advocated by Ignatius".[1258]

Several of the scholars referred to above emphasize that the conflict was restricted to the question of office and that questions relating to dogma were not involved. In other words, the dispute was not a matter of heresy.[1259]

[1254]H. E. Lona, *Der erste Clemensbrief* (1998) 81.

[1255]G. Brunner, *Die theologische Mitte des ersten Klemensbriefs* (1972).

[1256]*Ibid.* 152-163. Further G. Brunner argues that Clement does not offer much information about what he considered to be the seminal problem at Corinth, because he intended to have a broader audience than the Corinthian Church. The letter carries characteristics of a "catholic" letter. It is argued that Clement uses the occurrences in the Corinthian Church for a broader purpose; he is first of all interested in presenting an understanding of the office which should be operative in the universal Church. This wider purpose has the consequence that the occurrences in the Corinthian Church have fallen into the background (100-107). Similarly R. Zollitsch, *Amt und Funktion des Priesters* (1974): "Es ist durchaus nicht unwahrscheinlich, dass erst Rom den Streit in Korinth von der grundsätzlichen Seite des Amtes her beleuchtete, um eine Basis für die Lösung des Streites zu haben" (82f.). Cf. E. Peterson, "Das Praescriptum des 1. Clemensbriefes", *Pro regno, pro sanctuario* (1950) 351-357, the first scholar to argue that *1 Clement* is a catholic letter.

[1257]R. A. Campbell, *The Elders* (1994) 214. See 211-216.

[1258]*Ibid.* 214.

[1259]F. Gerke, *Die Stellung des ersten Clemensbriefes innerhalb der Entwicklung der altchristlichen Gemeindeverfassung und des Kirchenrechts* (1931) 68; G. G. Blum, *Tradition und Sukzession* (1963) 45f.; J. Rohde, "Häresie und Schisma im ersten Clemensbrief und in den Ignatius-Briefen", *NT* 10 (1968) 224-226; H. F. von Campenhausen, *Ecclesiastical Authority and Spiritual Power in the Church of the First Three Centuries* (1969) 91f. In addition, see O. Knoch, *Eigenart und Bedeutung der Eschatologie im theologischen Aufriss des ersten Clemensbriefes* (1964) 38; J. A. Fischer, *Apostolische Väter* (1966) 3; A. Lindemann, *Die Clemensbriefe* (1992) 16; G. Schneider, *Clemens von Rom* (1994) 8.

Other scholars argue that although the term 'heresy' does not occur in the letter, the question of the apostolic order was a matter of doctrine for Clement. The distinction between ecclesiastic order and heresy emerged at a later point of time in Church history and thus is anachronistic regarding *1 Clement*.[1260] However, the foremost advocate of the view that the dispute was about doctrine, W. Bauer, argued from a different point of departure.[1261] According to Bauer, in line with 1 Cor 3:4f., there were two types of Christianity at the end of the first century, an "orthodox" and a "gnostic" party, represented by Cephas and by Apollon respectively. The dissidents were the Gnostic party which opposed the orthodox. A central feature of Bauer's theory was that the Church had a collegial leadership structure. People of different theological positions took part in this collegial leadership. The removal of some orthodox presbyters reflects a situation where the Gnostic party had increased its support and influence. Rome intervened, according to Bauer, in order to defend orthodox Christianity and by means of this, increase the power of the Roman Church.[1262]

In addition to the most common suggestions just mentioned, other theories have been proposed. A theory often referred to is the hypothesis of H. Lietzmann.[1263] He argues that the Early Christians adopted the practice of the Roman associations or clubs where the overseers where chosen for only a short period of time. The problem of the Corinthian Church emerged when certain of the elected leaders refused to give up their offices when the period was over. Younger members of the Church did not accept this and by pointing to the practice of the contemporary associations they succeeded in

---

[1260]A. DAVIDS, "Irrtum und Haresie", *Kairos* 15 (1973) 187, similarly B. WEISS, "Amt und Eschatologie im 1. Clemensbrief", *ThPh* 50 (1975) 75, and A. E. W. HOOIJBERG, "A Different View of Clement Romanus", *HeyJ* 16 (1975) 266-288, especially 276. The last work in particular deserves to be mentioned because of its original suggestion regarding the motives behind the conflict. Hooijberg argues that it was not a conflict between charism and office, but that the instigators of the sedition represented an Essene faction who removed some presbyters because they "wanted to sacrifice in relation to the 'last days' (the paschal lamb)" (282). A precondition for this thesis is that *1 Clem.* 40:2-5 represents the point of view of Clement's opponent in Corinth and not the opinion of the author. In chap. 41 Clement gives his response to the theological argument of the Essenes. 40:2-5 and chap. 41 should in other words be read as contrasting accounts. This theory has not, however, gained support among scholars. An important objection is that Clement reflects similar thoughts elsewhere in the letter as the alleged Essene faction does in 40:2-5. See, e.g., B. E. BOWE, *A Church in Crisis* (1988), who because of this fact characterises Hooijbergh's suggestion as "entirely speculative" (19).

[1261]W. BAUER, *Rechtgläubigkeit und Ketzerei im ältesten Christentum* (1964).

[1262]*Ibid.* 99-114. Bauer regarded *1 Clement* as the first step of the Roman Church in its attempt to combat heretical Christianity which in every place except Rome came into existence earlier and had more followers than what was later considered to be orthodox Christianity. Bauer's work, after it was translated into English, has been much discussed and criticised. For a presentation, evaluation and an introduction to the "Bauer debate", see T. A. ROBINSON, *The Bauer Thesis Examined* (1988). Also H. KÖSTER, *Einführung in das Neue Testament* (1980) 727, finds it reasonable to assume that the strife was connected with doctrine.

[1263]H. LIETZMANN, *Geschichte der Alten Kirche* vol 1 (1953) 201 ff.

removing the leaders and placing themselves in the offices they had held.[1264] Lietzmann does not see any issue of principle or doctrine behind the revolt of the young.
The motive was probably "einfach der Wunsch nach einer neuen Verteilung der
Machtverhältnisse".[1265] An important objection to Lietzmann's theory is that we find
no evidence that elected leaders in the Early Church held their office for a limited
period.[1266] There are, however, several scholars who through an other line of argumentation than that of Lietzmann draw the conclusion that the instigators of the rebellion were young people.[1267]

Furthermore, E. S. Fiorenza seems to find a connection between the sedition and
gender. She argues that at least some of the dissidents were wealthy women who did not
want their donations to be controlled by the existing leadership, and thus joined those
who removed the presbyters.[1268] Although it is likely that wealthy women had leading
positions in the Early Church, nothing in *1 Clement* itself indicates that the gender of
the dissidents was at issue.[1269]

Last but not least, the suggestions of L. Wm. Countryman and R. Garrison must be
mentioned. Countryman argues that the cause of the strife was the fact that rich recent
converts with a certain prestige claimed leadership due to their social status. In other
words, he asserts that rich Christians were the instigators of the sedition.[1270] R. Garrison is also of the opinion that in causing the conflict social tensions played a significant
role. However, he asserts that there is evidence "to suggest that Clement believed that it
was the discontented among the neglected poor who attempted to remove the wealthy
elders/presbyters from office permanently".[1271] By referring to *1 Clem.* 59:3f., Garrison maintains that Clement reprimands the wealthy for not taking care of the poor in
the community. The intended purpose of the letter is to reconcile the two groups and
restore the program of lovepatriarchalism.[1272] An interesting and important aspect of
Countryman's and Garrison's suggestions is that they, in spite of their rather brief and
superficial treatments of the question, see the conflict in social terms.

[1264]Lietzmann does not refer to any passages in *1 Clement* when he describes the conflict as a conflict between the young and the old, but he is probably referring to *1 Clem.* 3:3.

[1265]H. Lietzmann, *Geschichte der Alten Kirche* vol 1 (1953) 201.

[1266]J. Fuellenbach, *Ecclesiastical Office and the Primacy of Rome* (1980) 7; H. O. Maier, *The
Social Setting of the Ministry as Reflected in the Writings of Hermas, Clement and Ignatius* (1991) 89.

[1267]A. von Harnack, *Einführung in die alte Kirchengechichte* (1929) 106; K. Wengst, *Pax
Romana and the Peace of Jesus Christ* (1987); O. B. Knoch, "Im Namen des Petrus und Paulus", *ANRW*
2.27.1 (1993) 10.

[1268]E. S. Fiorenza, *In Memory of Her* (1983) 293.

[1269]Cf. B. E. Bowe, *A Church in Crisis* (1988) 20.

[1270]L. Wm. Countryman, *The Rich Christian in the Church of the Early Empire* (1980): "The prestige that fuelled the insurgency, therefore, is likely to have been social in origin, and the movement was
inaugurated to place a small number of important new converts in positions of power within the
church that would comport with their social prestige" (156), and previously he states that the schism
"was fomented by rich Christians" (154).

[1271]R. Garrison, *Redemptive Almsgiving in Early Christianity* (1993) 84.

[1272]*Ibid.* 117.

We have already indicated what we consider to be essential objections against some of the theories about the motives behind and the underlying causes of the conflict in the Corinthian Church. Furthermore, the most commonly held view, that the issue was a conflict between charism and office, might also be questioned. If Clement's opponents appealed to their charisms to support and legitimate their rising against the authority of office, it is difficult to explain why Clement does not refer to Paul's exhortations concerning the right use of the spiritual gifts in 1 Cor 14, or his teaching regarding their relative importance in 1 Cor 13:8f. This is even more striking as Clement applies 1 Cor 13 in an adapted form in 49:1ff.[1273] In addition we might also ask if this theory, as well as the theory of G. Brunner places too much emphasis on the issue of office.[1274] Previously in this work we have argued that ὁμόνοια (and εἰρήνη) is the cardinal topic of the letter and that Clement's focus upon office is a means of creating that condition. Concerning the theory that the instigators of the sedition were wandering charismatics, it is likely that Clement's exhortation to self-exile in 54:2 reflects the thought in antiquity that a patriot would voluntarily go into exile if this secured the peace of the country.[1275] Additionally, 57:1f. appears to imply that Clement is of the opinion that the leaders of the revolt could remain in the Church if they repent. Regarding R. A. Campbell's suggestion that the strife concerned an attempt to introduce monoepiscopacy, we would question his interpretation of 54:1f. It is more likely that Clement's appeal to leave the community is not directed to one particular "trouble-maker", but to any of the instigators of the sedition. The fact that Clement elsewhere in the letter explicitly accuses a few people (ὀλίγα πρόσωπα) of causing the sedition (1:1) appears to confirm such an understanding.[1276] Against the heresy theory of W. Bauer it has been rightly objected that there is nothing in *1 Clement* itself which suggests that theological issues were at the heart of the conflict.[1277] Although, as indicated above, we agree with L. Wm. Countryman that it is fruitful to consider the conflict in social terms, there are good reasons for questioning his conclusion that the instigators of the sedition were rich Christians who claimed leadership due to their social status. Among other things, it is difficult to understand why Clement would describe rich Christians with

---

[1273]So also H. O. MAIER, *The Social setting of the Ministry as Reflected in the Writings of Hermas, Clement and Ignatius* (1991) 89.

[1274]So also B. E. BOWE, *A Church in Crisis* (1988) 20.

[1275]Cic. *Mil.* 93. Cf. A. VON HARNACK, *Einführung in die alte Kirchengeschichte* (1929) 82: "Es ist ein antiker Gedanke, dass der Patriot sich selbst exilieren soll, wenn er dadurch dem Vaterlande den Frieden zurückzugeben vermag". For the commonplace in antiquity that exile, either voluntary or not, was a means to resolve conflicts, see A. W. ZIEGLER, *Neue Studien zum ersten Klemensbrief* (1958) 100f.; P. MIKAT, "Der 'Auswanderungsrat' (1 Clem 54,2) als Schlüssel zum Gemeindeverständnis im 1. Clemensbrief", *Geschichte* (1984) 365.

[1276]For further critic of R. A. Campbell, see D. G. HORRELL, *The Social Ethos of the Corinthian Correspondence* (1996) 248.

[1277]H. E. W. TURNER, *The Pattern of Christian Truth* (1954) 70f.; A. I. C. HERON, "The Interpretation of I Clement", *EkklPh* 55 (1973) 517-545. Further, Clement gives no information which should indicate that the new presbyters took part in an alleged collegial power structure of the Church before the revolt took place, cf. T. A. ROBINSON, *The Bauer Thesis Examined* (1988) 71f.

high social status as οἱ ἄτιμοι, ἄδοξοι, ἄφρονες, νέοι and why he, if he regarded the behaviour of the rich as the major problem in the Corinthian Church, urged the "weak" and "poor" to reverence the "strong" and "rich".[1278] Regarding R. Garrison's thesis that it was the neglected poor that revolted against the wealthy leaders of the Church, one might question if he does not draw a too extensive conclusion on the basis of Clement's prayer for the needy. Below it will become clear, however, that we have much sympathy with Garrison's suggestion, though our conclusion will be rooted both in a more extensive discussion and in a different line of argumentation.

This means, in our opinion, that on the one hand one may question all the major contributions regarding the precise reason for the strife in the Corinthian Church. On the other hand, we do not find the minimalist suggestion of A. von Harnack, followed in recent works, that the division was merely between personal cliques, as satisfactory. When B. E. Bowe concludes that "given the evidence present in *1 Clement*, the actual causes and motivation both for the deposition of the presbyters and for the general state of στάσις ('communal strife') in Corinth cannot be known", she is too cautious regarding the possibility of pointing out what Clement considered to be the underlying cause of the conflict.[1279] On the contrary, by paying sufficient attention to a particular part of the letter and by employing a particular methodology, we believe it is possible to demonstrate that Clement in fact quite directly stated what he supposed to be at stake in Corinth. Further, we intend to show that what Clement considered to be underlying causes of the conflict were often regarded to be causes of strife in a political body. Although (if we succeeded in doing this) this would not amount to a confirmation that Clement's perception of the conflict was consistent with the "historical situation", it would indicate that Clement's estimation of the conflict was reasonable.

This means that we are of the opinion that one must distinguish between what the letter reflects concerning the social-historical situation in Corinth and what actually took place. It is problematic with respect to methodology to draw a direct inference from Clement's perception of the conflict to the real situation in the Corinthian Church. The closest one can come to the "historical situation" is to show that Clement's interpretation of the conflict was plausible in the light of comparative sources.

5.3. 1 Clement 3:3 and the Social-Historical Situation

In our opinion Clement's description of the uprising in 3:3 is a key verse when one deals with the question of what he considered to have happened in the Corinthian Church. In contrast to several scholars, who hold that this verse offers little or nothing of interest regarding the actual question,[1280] we will argue that the description of the uprising in 3:3 and Clement's description of the instigators of sedition at other points in the letter offer both greater and different information than what it is traditionally believed to

---

[1278]For further critic of L. Wm. Countryman, see the present investigation, n. 73 p. 352, and D. G. Horrell, *The Social Ethos of the Corinthian Correspondence* (1996) 246f.

[1279]B. E. Bowe, *A Church in Crisis* (1988) 21, see also 18.

contain, thereby shedding light on a basic aspect of the reason for the sedition. According to Clement what took place was the following:

> ... *the worthless rose up against those who were in honour, those of no reputation against the renowned, the foolish against the prudent, the young against the old (οἱ ἄτιμοι ἐπὶ τοὺς ἐντίμους, οἱ ἄδοξοι ἐπὶ τοὺς ἐνδόξους, οἱ ἄφρονες ἐπὶ τοὺς φρονίμους, οἱ νέοι ἐπὶ τοὺς πρεσβυτέρους, 3:3).*[1281]

If we succeed in determining more or less accurately which persons these groups of terms refer to, we may also say something about the reason for the sedition.

5.3.1. A mere Rhetorical Cliché and Allusion to Isa 3:5?

As already mentioned, several scholars hold a negative view concerning the possibilities of drawing any conclusion from this verse regarding what Clement considered to be the underlying motive for the occurrences in the Corinthian Church. The argumentation of this group of scholars takes it departure partly in the stylistic form of the verse and partly in the common opinion that it appears to be reminiscent of the language of Isa 3:5.[1282] Since *1 Clem.* 3:3 is stylistically formed in four phrases with a contrast between the first and second terms in each, and since it is perhaps reminiscent of the language of Isa 3:5, B. E. Bowe, for example, describes this verse as a "rhetorical cliché using general language and terminology to speak of opposing groups", and therefore asserts that it gives no information of value regarding the different groups involved in the dispute.[1283] We wish, however, to question the implied assumption in this line of argument, namely that an author can not use an ornately formed style in a passage and at the same time reflect what he or she considers to be historical events. That Clement

---

[1280]A. von HARNACK, *Einführung in die alte Kirchengeschichte* (1929), in his comments to *1 Clem.* 3:2-4 says that "leider sagt der Brief nichts Konkretes über den Ausbruch der Zwistigkeiten und des Aufruhrs". According to him, if one can draw any conclusion at all on the basis of 3:2-4, the most one might suppose is "dass am 'Aufruhr' jugendliche Mitglieder der Gemeinde, die vorher kein Ansehen gehabt hatten, beteiligt gewesen sind" (106). Cf. also A. DAVIDS, "Irrtum und Häresie", *Kairos* 15 (1973) 168; B. E. BOWE, *A Church in Crisis* (1988) 18f.; H. O. MAIER, *The Social Setting of the Ministry as Reflected in the Writings of Hermas, Clement and Ignatius* (1991), when he focuses upon Clement's "less indirect references concerning the nature of the Corinthian dispute" he does not mention *1 Clem.* 3:3 at all (91f.); H. E. LONA, *Der erste Clemensbrief* (1998) 141f.

[1281]Cited without the quotations used in K. LAKE, *The Apostolic Fathers* vol. 1 (1959) 13.

[1282]E.g., B. E. BOWE, *A Church in Crisis* (1988) 18f. and H. E. LONA, *Der erste Clemensbrief* (1998) 141f. D. A. HAGNER, *The Use of the Old and New Testaments in Clement of Rome* (1973), is more careful when he says that Clement is probably dependent upon the LXX of Isa 3:5 for the two clauses beginning with οἱ ἄτιμοι and οἱ νέοι (208). For the allusion to Isa 3.5 see also 129. Hagner characterises the allusion to Isa 3:5 as being "of less importance" (22 n. 3).

[1283]So B. E. BOWE, *A Church in Crisis* (1988) 19. Unfortunately, Bowe does not expand on what she has in mind with "general language and terminology" commonly used in describing groups in opposition. Most likely it is the opposing groups in Isa 3:5 which also occur in *1 Clem.* 3.3 that she has in mind, but it could also be a possible allusion to the socio-economic use of these terms (see below). However, if the latter suggestion is right, we believe that Bowe would have drawn a different conclusion with respect to the value of *1 Clem.* 3:3 in attempting to uncover the conflict at Corinth.

applies an ornate style in 3:3 cannot in itself be used as an argument that this utterance should be understood as a cliché without any connection to the historical event it reports on.

Likewise, the alleged reminiscence of the language of Isa 3:5 does not necessarily imply that the language of *1 Clem.* 3:3 consists of rhetorical clichés without any connection to what he regarded as the historical situation. The decisive question regarding the evaluation and significance of the Isaian language in *1 Clem.* 3:3 is why Clement finds the language of Isaiah appropriate and why he alludes to it. Before we attempt to give an answer to this question, we shall present a synopsis of Isa. 3:5 and *1 Clem.* 3:3 in order to make clear the similarities and differences between the texts.

Isa 3:5	1 Clem. 3:3[a]
καὶ συμπεσεῖται ὁ λαός ἄνθρωπος πρὸς ἄνθπωπον ἄνθρωπος πρὸς τὸν πλησίον αὐτοῦ προσκόψει τὸ παιδίον πρὸς τὸν πρεσβύτην ὁ ἄτιμος πρὸς τὸν ἔντιμον	οὕτως ἐπηγέρθησαν οἱ νέοι ἐπὶ τοὺς πρεσβυτέρους οἱ ἄτιμοι ἐπὶ τοὺς ἐντίμους οἱ ἄδοξοι ἐπὶ τοὺς ἐνδόξους οἱ ἄφρονες ἐπὶ τοὺς φρονίμους

[a.] The order of the opposing groups in *1 Clem.* 3:3 is changed.

The similarity of language between Isa 3:5 and *1 Clem.* 3:3 might indicate that Clement depends on and alludes to the Isaiah passage, but the similarity in language in our view is not so striking that it is fair to assert with any degree of certainty that Clement is dependent on the language of the prophet.[1284] This circumstance alone should lead to a fair degree of caution in dismissing the value of *1 Clem.* 3:3 regarding Clement's perception of the occurrences, by simply referring to it as reminiscent of the language of Isa 3:5. In spite of this warning, the following discussion is based on the premise that the language of Clement is influenced by Isa 3:5. We intend to show that even if one accepts this premise, the statement in *1 Clem.* 3:3 is of great importance in attempting to discover what he considered to be a main feature of the conflict in the Corinthian Church.

After these comments it is time to return to the question introduced above: Why did Clement find the language of Isa 3:5 appropriate in his description of the present

---

[1284]Cf. A. LINDEMANN, *Die Clemensbriefe* (1992) who regarding the terms φρόνιμος, ἔνδοξος, ἄτιμος argues that "der Vf bei der Formulierung an 1 Kor 4,10 gedacht hat" (33). This means that Lindemann does not consider the word pair ἔντιμοι – ἄτιμοι to be an allusion to Isa 3:5. Regarding the word pair νέοι – πρεσβύτεροι he does not discuss any possible sources Clement could depend on. Considering the precise meaning of the νέοι Lindemann is of the opinion that it is not possible to say anything to any degree of certainty, but suggests that Clement introduced this term as a contrast to the removed πρεσβύτεροι (33).

state of affairs in the Corinthian Church? To this question at least three different answers might be given.

One answer may be that in general he considers the present situation in the Corinthian Church to be similar to that of the people described in Isa 3:5 in as much as the actions of both the people of God in the Old Testament and the Christians in Corinth involve apostasy from God. Such a point of view implies that the "language of uprising" in *1 Clem.* 3:3, at least the terms dependent on Isa 3:5, do not offer any information on what actually took place. Clement focuses upon the general situation – that what is taking place among the Christians in Corinth implies that they are under the judgement of God – without saying anything explicit about the actual situation at Corinth.

A *second* answer, which at the same time does not exclude the first one, is that Clement sees some kind of a parallel in the historical situation.[1285] In other words, in addition to the more general similarity that the actions involve the judgement of God, the allusion to Isa 3:5 also involves a more specific similarity regarding the historical realities. This means that in the view of Clement one feature of the strife was that younger members of the congregation rose up against the older.

A *third* answer might be that Clement found the language of Isa 3:5 appropriate for what took place in Corinth in the light of the use and meaning of the terms in his cultural environment. In what follows we shall attempt to demonstrate that this is the most plausible explanation to the question. Furthermore, it is to be hoped that the following attempt to read *1 Clem.* 3:3 in its Graeco-Roman context, in particular the terms describing the first three groups of people, will show that *1 Clem.* 3.3 both offers more and different information than what is traditionally believed regarding Clement's perception of the conflict in the Corinthian Church.

5.3.2. 1 Clement 3:3 in Its Graeco-Roman Context

In our attempt to read *1 Clem.* 3:3 in its Graeco-Roman context works which focus upon the stratification of the Early Christian communities offer valuable information. For our purpose it is not necessary to enter into the rather extensive scholarly discussion on the stratification of Early Christian communities in detail, either regarding the question of methodology or the concrete results.[1286] It suffices to note that the traditional view among scholars from the end of the nineteenth century until about 1960 – that the first Christians belonged solely to the lower classes – has been challenged in recent years.[1287] Gerd Theissen, in a number of articles on the Corinthian Church pub-

---

[1285]Cf. also D. A. HAGNER, *The Use of the Old and New Testaments in Clement of Rome* (1973), who states that "the words οὕτως ἐπηγέρθησαν οἱ ἄτιμοι ἐπὶ τοὺς ἐντίμους ... οἱ νέοι ἐπὶ τοὺς πρεσβυτέρους (cf. Is. 3.5) were particularly appropriate in describing the same type of historical reality in Corinth" (129).

[1286]For a an introduction and evaluation of the scholarly debate until ca. 1990, see B. HOLMBERG, *Sociology and The New Testament* (1990) 21-76. A more recent and comprehensive study is that of E. W. STEGEMANN and W. STEGEMANN, *Urchristliche Sozialgeschichte* (1995) 249-271.

[1287]For discussion and literature references, see B. HOLMBERG, *Sociology and The New Testament* (1990) 28-36.

lished in 1974 and 1975 provided both one of the first and one of the most fundamental contributions in challenging the "old consensus".[1288]

On the basis of prosopographical analyses of the Corinthian correspondence Theissen concludes that the "hellenistische Urchristentum ist weder eine proletarische Bewegung unterer Schichten gewesen, noch eine Angelegenheit gehobener Schichten. Charakteristisch für seine soziale Struktur ist vielmehr, dass er verschiedene Schichten umfasste".[1289] Although scholars have modified Theissen's interpretation on certain points, they have confirmed his basic opinion that the Christians of the Pauline communities represented "verschiedene Schichten".[1290]

With respect to our task it is interesting that the interpretations of 1 Cor 1:26-29 have played a key role in the discussions of the social status of those in the Pauline

---

[1288]G. THEISSEN, "Soziale Schichtung in der korinthischen Gemeinde", *ZNW* 65 (1974) 232-273, (reprinted in *Studien zur Soziologie des Urchristentums* (1989) 231-271); *idem,* "Die Starken und Schwachen in Korinth", *EvTh* 35 (1975) 155-172, (reprinted in *Studien zur Soziologie des Urchristentums* (1989) 272-289); *idem,* "Soziale Integration und sakramentales Handeln", *NT* 16 (1974) 179-206, (reprinted in in *Studien zur Soziologie des Urchristentums* (1989) 290-317). The first scholar to question that the Christians of the first century belonged solely to the lower classes was the classical historian E. A. JUDGE, *The Social Pattern of the Christian Groups in the First Century* (1960) 49-61; *idem,* "The Early Christians as a Scholastic Community", *JRH* 1 (1960) 4-15, 125-137. It seems that the works of Judge influenced New Testament scholars to a limited extent only in the sixties. For the impact of Judge on New Testament Scholars, see B. HOLMBERG, *Sociology and The New Testament* (1990) 40-44.

[1289]G. THEISSEN, "Soziale Schichtung in der korinthischen Gemeinde", *Studien zur Soziologie des Urchristentums* (1989) 267. For structural reasons Theissen considers that the stratification in the Corinthian Church was typical of the Hellenistic churches in general (231).

[1290]Cf., e.g., D. TIDBALL, *An Introduction to the Sociology of the New Testament* (1983) 90-103; C. OSIEK, *What Are They Saying about the Social Setting of the New Testament?* (1984) 47-64; W. A. MEEKS, *The First Urban Christians* (1983) 51-73. Meeks concludes regarding the Pauline Christians: "It is a picture in which people of several social levels are brought together. The extreme top and bottom of the Greco-Roman social scale are missing from the picture. It is hardly surprising that we meet no landed aristocrats, no senators, *equites* nor … decurions. But there is also no specific evidence of people who are destitute – such as the hired menials and dependent handworkers; the poorest of the poor, peasants, agriculture slaves, and hired agricultural day laborers, are absent because of the urban setting of the Pauline groups" (72f.). Regarding the Roman Church, see the careful prosopographical analysis of Rom 16 in P. LAMPE, *Die stadtrömischen Christen in den ersten beiden Jahrhunderten* (1989) 124-153. In one of the most recent works on the social history of Early Christians E. W. STEGEMANN and W. STEGEMANN, *Urchristliche Sozialgeschichte* (1995), by and large confirm the previous works considering the question of stratification (249-271). Regarding the Pauline Communities Stegemann and Stegemann conclude that "Zu den paulinischen Gemeinden hat kein *ordo*-Mitglied aus der Gruppe der Oberschicht gehört. Eindeutige Belege für reiche Christusgläubige besitzen wir nicht, doch kann nicht ausgeschlossen werden, dass einige Gemeindemitglieder in der Funktion von Patronen für ihre Glaubensgenossen tätig waren und zu wohlhabenden Kreisen gehörten, vielleicht auch zur lokalen Oberschicht unterhalb des Dekurionenadels. Einige Christusgläubige konnten als Gefolgsleute der Oberschicht (*retainers*) identifiziert werden, auch wenn im einzelnen nicht deutlich wird, auf welcher Stufe dieser Gruppe sie rangierten. Die überwiegende Mehrheit gehörte zweifellos zur Unterschicht, d.h. zu den relativ Armen bzw. relativ Wohlhabenden" (260). The authors draw a similar conclusion regarding the Churches of the New Testament after year 70 (269).

Churches.[1291] As will become clear below, in 3:3 Clement uses synonyms for some of the terms Paul uses to depict members of the Corinthian Church. Although the terms Paul employs in these verses, οἱ σοφοί, οἱ δυνατοί, οἱ εὐγενεῖς, τὰ ἀσθενῆ (the weak), τὰ ἰσχυρὰ (the strong), τὰ ἐξουθενημένα (the despised), and τὰ μὴ ὄντα (nothings), are seen in a theological light, the sociological implications of the concepts cannot, according to Theissen, be denied.[1292] Besides a prosopographical analysis Theissen adds to the texts already collected by J. Bohatec[1293] a number of Hellenistic references where the terms employed in 1 Cor 1:26-29 designate people of either high or low social status.[1294] The σοφοί are those who belong to the educated classes, the δυνατοί are influential people, and the εὐγενεῖς those of noble birth.[1295] In spite of certain nuances concerning the precise meaning of these terms Theissen's basic point of view prevails in recent scholarship.[1296]

In 1 Cor 4:10 Paul describes the same group of people as φρόνιμοι, ἰσχυροί, ἔνδοξοι and contrasts these groups respectively with μωροί, ἀσθενεῖς, ἄτιμοι.[1297] On the basis of Paul's use of such terms with apparent sociological connotations D. Sänger has provided a table of three sets of parallels and corresponding antonyms:[1298]

[1291] For a history of interpretation from the Early Church fathers to the present, see K. SCHREINER, "Zur biblischen Legitimation des Adels", *ZKG* 85 (1974) 317-357.

[1292] G. THEISSEN, "Soziale Schichtung in der korinthischen Gemeinde", *Studien zur Soziologie des Urchristentums* (1989) 232f. The assertion that the concepts have such an implication was not however a novelty. W. WUELLNER, "Ursprung und Verwendung der σοφός-, δυνατός-, εὐγενής-Formel in 1 Kor 1,26", *Donum Gentilicium* (1978) 165f., lists four of the common interpretations of the triad in 1 Corinthians 1:26. He notes that "(1) die älteste und dominierende Interpreation sieht in der triadischen Formel soziale, ökonomische Hinweise. (2) Man hat versucht, die triadische Formel rein rhetorisch oder stilistisch zu erklären. (3) Ein anderer neuerer Versuch, die Herkunft der drei genannten Eigenschaften zu erleutern, bezieht sich hauptsächlich auf den kynischen anti-εὐγενής topos, der in der Polemik gegen die Sophisten seinen Sitz haben mag. (4) Schliesslich hat man die eigenartige Komposition der drei genannten Eigenschaften aus einem bestimmten Teil der nachbiblischen liturgischen Tradition zur Erinnerung des Tages der Zerstörung des Tempels zu erklären versucht". But Theissen was one of the first scholars in recent times who emphasized the sociological implication of these conceptions in the reconstruction of stratification of the Early Christians.

[1293] J. BOHATEC, "Inhalt und Reihenfolge der 'Schlagworte der Erlösungsreligion' in 1 Kor 1.26-31", *ThZ* 4 (1948) 252-271, who pointed out several Jewish-Hellenistic and Classical sources where the actual terms express the socio-economic level of man; among others Arist. *Pol.* 4.10; Philo *Somn* 155; *Virt* 162; 173; *Det* 34; Pl. *Grg.* 465 B; *Lach.* 186 C; *Lys.* 221 E; *Resp.* 2.364 B; Epict. *Diss.* 4.1.10; Thuc. 2.65; Sen. *Controv.* 4.9. J. BOHATEC concludes that "Unter den δυνατοί und ἀσθενεῖς (Vers 26) sind die sozial und wirtschaftlich Starken und Schwachen zu verstehen. Dafür spricht nicht blossdie Nennung des πλούσιος neben dem ἰσχυρός in der Jeremiastelle, sondern auch der sonstige Gebrauch in der Profanliteratur" (261).

[1294] Pl. *Phdr.* 234 E; *Tht.* 176 C; Epict. *Diss.* 3. 9.14; 4.8.25; Eur. *Tro.* 612ff; Soph. *Aj.* 1094-7; Philo *Virt* 173f; *Som* 155. Cf. G. THEISSEN, "Soziale Schichtung in der korinthischen Gemeinde", *Studien zur Soziologie des Urchristentums* (1989) 233.

σοφοί = φρόνιμοι vs. μωροί
δυνατοί[1299] = ἰσχυροί vs. ἀσθενεῖς
εὐγενεῖς[1300] = ἔνδοξοι vs. ἄτιμοι

It is beyond the scope of this investigation to deal with the precise meaning of these terms in detail. For our purpose it is sufficient to point out that the terms are related to

[1295] After having discussed the parallel idiomatic uses of τὰ μὴ ὄντα in opposition to εὐγενεῖς Theissen concludes that "Die letzte der drei aufgezählten Kategorien (Weise, Mächtige, Hochgeborene) hat also eindeutig soziologischen Sinn. Da gerade dies Glied der Aufzählung über die Stichworte des vorhergehenden Kontextes hinausgreift, wird man schliessen dürfen, dass Paulus in dem neuen Abschnitt (1 Kor 1 26 ff.) einen sozialen Sachverhalt vor Augen hat und wahrscheinlich auch die ersten Kategorien soziologisch verstanden wissen will: Mächtige wären dann Leute mit Einfluss, Weise Angehörige gebildeter Schichten, nämlich 'Weise nach irdischen Massstäben', bei denen Weisheit auch Zeichen sozialen Status ist ... Über die soziologischen Implikationen von 1 Kor 26-29 kann m.E. kein Zweifel bestehen" (G. THEISSEN, "Soziale Schichtung in der korinthischen Gemeinde", Studien zur Soziologie des Urchristentums (1989) 233f.). That the Corinthian Church besides the poorer majority contained a fairly wealthy minority is further substantiated in his analysis of the relation between the "strong" and the "weak" in the conflict about the Lord's supper, 1 Cor. 11, idem, "Die Starken und Schwachen in Korinth", Studien zur Soziologie des Urchristentums (1989) 272-289.

[1296] For example B. HOLMBERG, Paul and Power (1978) 104-107; D. SÄNGER, "Die δυνατοί in 1 Kor 1:26", ZNW 76 (1985) 285-291; E. W. STEGEMANN and W. STEGEMANN, Urchristliche Sozialgeschichte. (1995) 58, 253; W. WITHERINGTON, Conflict & Community in Corinth (1995) 113-115; and some standard commentaries: H. CONZELMANN, Der erste Brief an die Korinther (1969) 66; E. FASCHER, Der erste Brief des Paulus an die Korinther (Kap.1-7) (1975) 106; G. D. FEE, The First Epistle to the Corinthians (1987) 80; and W. SCHRAGE, Der Erste Brief an die Korinther (1 Kor 1,1-6,11) 1991, who summarizes as follows: "σοφοί sind die Gebildeten, δυνατοί die wirtschaftlich, gesellschaftlich und finanziell Mächtigen, Vermögenden, Einflussreichen, wobei man wegen der Vielfalt der Möglichkeiten, worin einer δυνατός sein kann, keinen Aspekte isolieren oder ausschliessen kann (vgl. auch Apg 25,5), jedenfalls nicht nur an geistige Überlegenheit denken wird. Εὐγενεῖς sind die von vornehmer Herkunft, die aus angesehenen Familien Stammenden, die aristokratische Bourgeoisie" (208f.). For a more reculant or opposing view regarding the social meaning of the terms, see W. WUELLNER, "The Sociological Implications of 1 Corinthians 1.26-28 Reconsidered", StEv 4 (1973) 666-672; R. A. HORSLEY, "Wisdom of word and Words of Wisdom in Corinth", CBQ 39 (1977) 224-239; J. A. DAVIS, Wisdom and Spirit (1984) 75-77.

[1297] G. THEISSEN, "Soziale Schichtung in der korinthischen Gemeinde", Studien zur Soziologie des Urchristentums (1989) 234; D. SÄNGER, "Die δυνατοί in 1 Kor 1:26", ZNW 76 (1985) 287.

[1298] D. SÄNGER, "Die δυνατοί in 1 Kor 1:26", ZNW 76 (1985) 288.

[1299] Regarding the δυνατοί Sänger points out more precisely how people achieved power and influence. He argues that they became influential and powerful because of their wealth. Thus the δυνατοί are identical with the πλούσιοι (290). See further L. L. WELBORN, "On the Discord in Corinth", JBL 106 (1987) 97; S. M. POGOLOFF, Logos and Sophia (1992) 209. Cf also R. MacMULLEN, Roman Social Relations (1974), who underlines the significance of money in order to enter the upper class: "To pay for the enormously expensive role in the community that would, over the span of some generations, ennoble one's line; to pay the fees and voluntary subscriptions to the gymnasium through which one's culture and accent might satisfy polite circles; to maintain one's household in proper fashion – all required a handsome income. It was taken for granted by the aristocracy. Without it, social ambitions could never be treated seriously" (108).

socio-economic levels.[1301] The three sets of parallels in the table above depict people of high status. They are well educated, of good birth, and usually wealthy. The corresponding antonyms refer to people of low status. This means that it is reasonable to suppose that social tensions were present in the Corinthian Church at the time of Paul, although this is not expressed explicitly in 1 Corinthians. It is also likely that these tensions, which derived from the inequality of the members of the Church, were an important factor in the strife in the Corinthian Church.[1302]

In our view Clement's depiction of the conflict suggests that socio-economic factors were significant in the conflict at this point of time as well. For now, on the basis of the findings of G. Theissen and others, if we again turn our attention to the point of departure, i.e. to *1 Clem.* 3:3 and the way Clement depicts the different groups involved in the upheaval, it seems obvious that such factors played a fundamental role in the sedition. First we note that the terms Clement uses to depict the three first pairs of groups are found in the table above on socio-economic terms: [1303]

1. ἔντιμοι	—	ἄτιμοι
2. ἔνδοξοι	—	ἄδοξοι
3. φρόνιμοι	—	ἄφρονες

[1300]D. Sänger further notes that εὐγενής is not an equivalent term for wealthy, but that it refers primarily to "die Abstammung und die soziale Zugehörigkeit des Trägers" ("Die δυνατοί in 1 Kor 1:26", *ZNW* 76 (1985) 288). Among the upper class money alone was not a guarantee of honour. One thing a rich person might lack was *paideia*. Wealth was, however, one important factor for achieving honour and status (288). See also S. M. Pogoloff, *Logos and Sophia* (1992) 208. Cicero reflects the close connection between 'rich' and 'honourable' among the upper-class concept of morality at Rome. R. MacMullen, *Roman Social Relations* (1974) 117, comments: "In his mind the two words 'rich' and 'honorable' belong together and thus appear so regularly in his speeches arm in arm, like a happily married couple".

[1301]Here and elsewhere in the investigation the adjective "socio-economic" has a wide range of meanings expressing features which are related to class, status, levels, or other terms used to differentiate members of a political body. Conceptions used in studies of stratification of the Early Christians like class, status, and levels belong to the tool box of modern sociology. This means that one must be aware of the danger of anachronism in applying them to a political body in antiquity. An additional problem is that the conceptions are not unambiguously defined sociologically. Cf. E. W. Stegemann and W. Stegemann, *Urchristliche Sozialgeschichte* (1995), 62. For a discussion of methodology, see *ibid.* 58-94; W. A. Meeks, *The First Urban Christians* (1983) 53-55; B. Holmberg, *Sociology and The New Testament* (1990) 21-28, 64-73.

[1302]L. L. Welborn, "On the Discord in Corinth", *JBL* 106 (1987) 93-101, emphasizes that the difference in socio-economic status was the cause of the sedition. See also G. Theissen, "Die Starken und Schwachen in Korinth", *Studien zur Soziologie des Urchristentums* (1989) 272-289, and M. M. Mitchell, *Paul and the Rhetoric of Reconciliation* (1991) 92 n. 151: "Striving for higher social status is also clearly linked to partisanship at Corinth". However, she means that this was only one among many possible factors which contributed to the sedition. She also remarks that it is important to note that Paul does not himself explicitly describe the sedition in those terms (94f. n. 174).

[1303]Aristotle, [*Mund.*] 5.396b.3-5, includes "young and old" among opposite classes which are to be found in a city. The author operates with the following four opposite classes: poor and rich, young and old, weak and strong, bad and good (πενήτων λέγω καὶ πλουσίων, νέων γερόντων, ἀσθενῶν ἰσχυρῶν, πονηρῶν χρηστῶν).

It is not possible to distinguish between the first two groups. According to Sänger's table it follows that ἔντιμοι and ἔνδοξοι are both synonyms for εὐγενεῖς and designate people of noble birth, thereby belonging to the social elite, and that ἄτιμοι and ἄδοξοι designate people of lower classes. The term φρόνιμοι is a synonym for σοφοί and depicts those who belong to the educated class, versus the ἄφρονες. With the socio-economic meaning of these terms in view, it can hardly be said more explicitly that socio-economic factors were a major contribution to the conflict in the Corinthian Church than what Clement does in 3:3 when he says that οὕτως ἐπηγέρθησαν οἱ ἄτιμοι ἐπὶ τοὺς ἐντίμους, οἱ ἄδοξοι ἐπὶ τοὺς ἐνδόξους, οἱ ἄφρονες ἐπὶ τοὺς φρονίμους.

That socio-economic factors, according to Clement, were important elements in the conflict also appears to be reflected later in the letter. As a means of preserving the whole body, i.e. the Christian community, Clement exhorts the strong (ἰσχυρός) as follows:

> ... care for the weak (ἀσθενής) and let the weak (ἀσθενής) reverence the strong (ἰσχυρός). Let the rich man (πλούσιος) bestow help on the poor (πτωχός) and let the poor (πτωχός) give thanks to God, that he gave him one to supply his needs; let the wise (σοφός) manifest his wisdom (σοφία) not in words but in good deeds ... (38:2).

Because this passage belongs to the part of the letter that deals with concord in general without explicitly applying it to the concrete situation in the Corinthian Church,[1304] we must show some caution in using it as evidence that our interpretation of *1 Clem.* 3:3 is correct. However, it is beyond doubt that *1 Clem.* 38:2 testifies that Clement held that socio-economic tensions among Christians could lead to strife. It is also possible, and even likely, that without saying so he has the concrete situation in the Corinthian Church in mind. In addition to testifying that the distribution of goods was in question and that social tensions connected with this issue were a threat to a Christian community, this passage is a good illustration of the socio-economic use especially of the terms ἰσχυρός, ἀσθενής, but also of σοφός. Although the terms ἰσχυρός and πλούσιος do not have exactly the same meaning, they function as syntactic and partly as semantic parallel terms just as ἀσθενής and πτωχός do. The ἰσχυρός refers primarily to the socio-economically strong, corresponding to πλούσιος. And the ἀσθενής refers primarily to the socio-economically weak, corresponding to πτωχός.[1305] In spite of the fact that the term σοφός introduces a change in the structure of the text and of σοφός being structurally linked primarily with the subsequent terms that predominantly refer to spiritual qualities, it is nevertheless reasonable, for different reasons, to assume that this term also contains a socio-economic aspect depicting cultivated and well-educated

---

[1304]See chap. 4. *Compositional Analysis of 1 Clement.*

[1305]So A. LINDEMANN, *Die Clemensbriefe* (1992), who, although he argues that "es geht nicht nur um die soziale Stellung", thinks that it is clear "dass von Angehörigen unterschiedlicher Schichten innerhalb der christlichen Gemeinde die Rede ist" (117). For the use of these terms in Jewish-Hellenistic and Profane Greek with a socio-economic meaning, see the literature mentioned above, pp. 293-295.

men.[1306] As noted, σοφός is structurally linked predominantly with the subsequent terms, but it is also to some extent linked with the preceding terms in as much as the exhortations to both the ἰσχυρός and πλούσιος and the σοφός are introduced by the same pattern (the addressed group + the imperative) and the exhortation to all these groups encourages them to behave in a way which benefits others. Furthermore, the fact that Clement immediately goes on, among other things, to refer to those who act against the duties of mutual help as ἄφρονες, ἀπαίδευτοι (uninstructed), and μωροί (silly) points in the same direction.[1307] It is namely reasonable to view these terms as almost synonymous. Also, as we have seen above, ἄφρονες and μωροί are antonyms to the technical terms σοφοί and φρόνιμοι. And lastly, the terms are obviously linked in 13:1 where Clement, in quoting Jer 9:23-24, exhorts the wise man (ὁ σοφός) not to "boast in himself in his wisdom, nor the strong man (ἰσχυρός) in his strength, nor the rich man (ὁ πλούσιος) in his riches".

The fact that Clement gives an exhortation in 38:2 in such an explicit way as to how people of different status and honour ought to act towards each other in order to preserve the community, and that he so emphatically applies standard socio-economic terms depicting different classes, strengthens our understanding of *1 Clem.* 3:3. This conclusion, however, depends on whether Clement views the general exhortation in 38:2 in connection with the occurrences in the Corinthian Church.

To sum up, our attempt to read the language of *1 Clem.* 3:3 in its Graeco-Roman context, building upon works of G. Theissen and others, makes it likely that Clement applies standard socio-political terms when he describes the different groups of people involved in the strife. It is, we believe, primarily because he found these terms appropriate in their socio-political meaning for depicting the occurrences at the Corinthian Church that he to some extent uses the language of Isa 3:5. He describes the conflict mainly as a conflict between people of different social status.[1308] The fact that on the one hand he excludes certain pairs of opposing groups in Isa 3:5 which are not described in socio-political terminology and on the other hand adds other opposing groups by using terms commonly employed in a socio-political context in antiquity points in the same direction. But this point of view does not exclude the two other suggestions made above as to why Clement found it useful to allude to Isa 3:5: (1) that he saw a parallel in the historical situation – that the νέοι arose against the πρεσβύτεροι; and (2) that he, by means of the allusion, expressed the view that what was taking place is under the judgement of God. This means, to be clear, that we argue that *1 Clem.* 3:3 in spite of its stylistic form and its allusion to Isa 3:5 is of great importance and serves as a good starting point when one seeks to discover what Clement regarded to be at stake in the Corinthian Church.

[1306]For the structure of the text, see A. LINDEMANN, *Die Clemensbriefe* (1992) 117.
[1307]*1 Clem.* 39:2.

5.3.2.1. Inequality as Cause for Sedition in the Ancient World

That conflict between different socio-economic classes was often considered to play an important role in στάσις in the ancient world is well documented both in theoretical reflections on the nature of στάσις, in discourses, history writings, and in other types of literature. [1309] On the theoretical level Aristotle's dealing with στάσις and the cause of στάσις in the political life of the ancient city is illuminating. This expert on political life asserts:

> For party strife is everywhere due to inequality (πανταχοῦ γὰρ διὰ τὸ ἄνισον ἡ στάσις), where classes that are unequal do not receive a share of power in proportion … for generally the motive for factious strife is the desire for equality (Pol. 5.1.6-7). [1310]

It can hardly be stated more clearly that inequality between members of a political body, in this case a *polis*, was perceived to be an underlying cause of στάσις. Aristotle

---

[1308]L. Wm. COUNTRYMAN, *The Rich Christian in the Church of the Early Empire* (1980), correctly underlines the value of *1 Clem.* 3:3 for discerning the origins of the conflict, but is wrong when he argues that the terms Clement uses should not be understood in a literary sense and says that, "Instead, they must refer to status *within the Church*: the insurgents were people of no proven virtue (worthless), not well-known to other churches (of no reputation), and inexperienced in Christianity (foolish)" (156). The main reason for this misinterpretation seems to be that Countryman pictures a too homogeneous picture of the Corinthian Christian's economic level. It appears that he argues on the basis of 3:1 that all members are almost at the same level of social and economic prosperity (156). After this chapter was completed, D. G. HORRELL's *The Social Ethos of the Corinthian Correspondence* (1996) was published. Horell agrees with R. GARRISON, *Redemptive Almsgiving in Early Christianity* (1993) 84, 117, that a significant element in the conflict was tensions between rich and poor members of the community, though he admits that it is hard to substantiate this suggestion. However, and this is especially interesting in this connection, Horrell remarks in parenthesis that *1 Clem.* 3:3 "adds some textual support to it" (250, similarly 247). As far as we know, Horrell's brief remarks on 3:3 are the only ones in the history of research that indicate that this passage in *1 Clement* offers useful information about social tensions between members of different strata of the Corinthian Christians and that these tensions caused strife. But Horrell is remarkably brief when it comes to the importance of 3:3 with regard to the conflict i Corinth. In fact he does not offer any discussion of the terms used in this passage. We hope that our discussion of *1 Clem.* 3:3 in its Graeco-Roman context contributes to substantiate the suggestion that according to Clement social tensions between members of different social strata of the congregation was a significant aspect of the conflict.

[1309]This is emphasized by L. L. WELBORN, "On the Discord in Corinth", *JBL* 106 (1987) 85-11, who aims to investigate the bearing that present tensions between rich and poor has on the instance of faction in the Corinthian Church at the time of Paul in the light of the prevalent view of the ancient world that class conflicts were often at the root of στάσις. Welborn even argues that "what matters is that ancient writers assumed that where there was discord, opposition between rich and poor lay behind" (96).

[1310]Aristotle further develops this point of view in *Pol.* 5.2.1ff. Among other things, he argues that "those that desire equality enter on party strife if they think that they have too little although they are equals of those who have more, while those that desire inequality or superiority do so if they suppose that although they are unequal they have not got more but an equal amount or less … for when inferior, people enter on strife in order that they may be equal, and when equal, in order that they may be greater" (*Pol* 5.2.1-2).

goes further and discusses more precisely what kind of equality was at stake and what states of feelings gave rise to στάσις. People form factions in states in order to achieve gain (κέρδος) and honour (τιμή), or the opposite, to avoid dishonour and loss.[1311] It is obvious, says Aristotle, that the nature of gain and honour can create στάσις:

> ... *for when the men in office show insolence and greed, people rise in revolt against one another and against the constitutions that afford the opportunity for such conduct; and greed sometimes preys on private property and sometimes on common funds. It is clear also what is the power of honour (τιμή) and how it can cause party faction (στάσις); for men form factions both when they are themselves dishonoured and when they see others honoured ... (Pol. 5.2.4).*

That the question of property was commonly considered to be a cause of στάσις is also reflected previously in his *Politics* when Aristotle discusses different constitutional schemes. He refers to some persons who are of the opinion that the right regulation of property is of fundamental importance, for this question is, according to these people "universally the cause of party strife (στάσις)".[1312] In other words, both the feelings of inequality associated with honour and property possess the power to raise στάσις.

If we leave the theoretical considerations of Aristotle and turn to other types of ancient literature, we find that his opinion was not particular to him, but reflected a commonly held view.[1313] This is, for instance, the case in Thucydides' account of the violent upheaval at Corcyra in 427 B.C.E. Some of the people rose up against the oligarchy and brought several of the oligarchs to trial and prosecuted them for conspiracy to overthrow the democracy. The interesting point in this connection is the remarks of Thucydides that "some were in fact put to death merely to satisfy private enmity, and others, because money was owing to them, were slain by those who borrowed it".[1314] The enmity between rich and poor was obviously a feature in the revolt. That the question of property was at the root of the upheaval is also expressed explicitly by Thucydides who when reflecting upon the period of civil strife concludes: "The cause of all these evils was the desire to rule which greed and ambition inspire, and also, springing from them, that ardour which belongs to men who once have become engaged in factious rivalry".[1315]

If we move approximately four centuries later in time to Dionysisus Halicarnassensis, we find that this author also reflects the view that socio-economic tensions might cause στάσις. When Dionysius writes about Mamilius and Tarquinius who attempted to make war against Rome but did not get foreign support, he says that they changed their strategy and tried instead to "stir up in Rome itself a civil war ... by

---

[1311] Arist. *Pol.* 5.2.2. In addition to these two primary causes of στάσις Aristotle discusses other causes and lists insolence, fear, excessive predominance, contempt, disproportionate growth of power, election intrigue, carelessness, pettiness, and dissimilarity (*Pol.* 5.2.3).

[1312] Arist. *Pol.* 2.4.1.

[1313] Cf. L. L. WELBORN, "On the Discord in Corinth", *JBL* 106 (1987) 95-99.

[1314] Thuc. 3.81.4.

[1315] Thuc. 3.82.8.

fomenting a sedition (στάσις) of the poor against the rich" (στάσιν εἰσάγοντες τοῖς πένησι πρὸς τοὺς εὐπόρους).[1316] By playing consciously upon the great social tensions between the greater part of the common people and the rich "a conspiracy was formed against the aristocracy not only by needy freeman, but also by unprincipled slaves who were beguiled by hopes of freedom".[1317] Further, the same author gives an account of a speech by the wise man Agrippa Menenius, who was particularly commended for his political principles, directed to the senate. He says among other things the following:

> ... we are not the only people, nor the first, among whom poverty has raised sedition against wealth, and lowliness against eminence, but ... in nearly all states, both great and small, the lower class is generally hostile to the upper ... (Dion. Hal. Ant. Rom. 6.54.1).

That the question of distribution of possessions was considered to be the root of discord is also expressed in a pregnant way by Aelius Aristides in one of his discourses on concord:

> For where each has separate possessions, what is expedient for each is also separate. Hence faction, battles, and disputes. For 'this is not yours, but mine' begins every argument. But where men believe that possessions belong to all in common, they also have a common point of view about them (Or. 23.65).[1318]

It should not be necessary to mention other ancient texts to indicate that the socio-economic gap between high status groups and low status groups gave rise to upheaval and στάσις in different political bodies, above all in the city state.[1319] As we have argued above, Clement sees the conflict in the Corinthian Church from a similar perspective, i.e. that the socio-economic gap between different groups in the Church gave rise to στάσις. This might indicate that the distribution of goods was in question. If we are correct in suggesting this, a result of the στάσις was that peoples of the low status group succeeded in gaining leading positions in the Corinthian Church and thereby increased their power and influence regarding questions related to the distribution of

---

[1316]Dion. Hal. *Ant. Rom.* 5.53.1f.

[1317]Dion. Hal. *Ant. Rom.* 5.53.3.

[1318]We should note that the purpose of this speech was to curb "the discord caused by the struggles of the leading cities of Asia ... to outdo one another in their ambition for titles and other empty symbols of rank ... This amazing rivalry had become notorious" (C. A. BEHR, *P. Aelius Aristides. The Complete Works* vol 2 (1981), 365 n. 1). To hold the leading position was connected with both possessions and honour. The other discourse by Aristides on concord (*Or.* 24) was a response to a class struggle which broke out in Rhodes (*ibid.* 368 n. 1).

[1319]For further references to texts, cf. L. L WELBORN, "On the Discord in Corinth", *JBL* 106 (1987) 95-99; M. M. MITCHELL, *Paul and the Rhetoric of Reconciliation* (1991) 94. V. EHRENBERG, *The Greek State* (1969), summarizes: "The gravest cause for disunity was the struggle between rich and poor ... Inequalities of power and possessions did, however, drive the social groups time and again into conflict ... These social struggles, which in many places eventually became regular fights between parties – especially when the parties more and more attached themselves to foreign powers – directly threatened the Polis in its very existence as a community of citizens" (90, cf. also 47).

goods within the church. Since it appears that the majority of the Corinthian Church more or less supported the revolt, it is possible that they expected that the new presbyters would attend to their interests in a better way than the presbyters who had been removed. More accurately, perhaps the majority of the Church hoped that the new presbyters would represent the interest of the lower status classes in matters relating to the distribution of goods.

5.4. Striving for Honour and Status

In our discussion on *1 Clem.* 3:3 we attempted to show that Clement perceived the conflict in socio-economic categories, and that the distribution of goods was probably at issue. This indicates that the men who succeeded in removing the present presbyters and in taking their office acquired influence in these matters and were thus in a position to increase their own and their allies' wealth. However, there is another aspect which is closely related to the question of goods and to holding an office, which we have just mentioned above; i.e. the aspect of honour. Previously we have argued that it appears that Clement believes that there is a connection between the "glory and enlargement" (δόξα καὶ πλατυσμός) of the Corinthian Church and the present strife.[1320] We have also seen that the terms he uses to depict the first three opposing groups in 3:3 were not only related to wealth, but also to status and honour. The ἔντιμοι and the ἔνδοξοι designate people of noble birth belonging to the social elite, who were thus in positions that were connected with honour. Thus the rise of the ἄτιμοι and the ἄδοξοι could be viewed as a quest for increasing status and honour.

5.4.1. Patronage and the Role of Honour in Clement's Cultural Milieu

In order to substantiate this thesis we must use some space to give an outline of the role of honour in the culture of antiquity and how one gained it. However, since honour was closely related to the institution of "patronage" – the relationships of patron and client – which was so important in antiquity, we must first briefly point out some key features of these relationships.[1321]

5.4.1.1. Patronage

In this task we take our departure in one of the most important theoretical studies on patronage in general, i.e. the work of S. N. Eisenstadt and L. Roniger.[1322]

[1320]See p. 149.

[1321]Cf. H. MOXNES, "Patron-Client Relations and the New Community in Luke-Acts", *The Social World of Luke-Acts* (1991) 244.

[1322]S. N. EISENSTADT and L. RONIGER, *Patrons, Clients and Friends* (1984). The following quotations are taken from pp. 48f. For further literature see, e.g., R. P. SALLER, *Personal Patronage under the Early Empire* (1982).

1. Patron-client relations are based on "simultaneous exchange of different types of resources". The patron has access to resources of instrumental, economical and political character and can therefore offer support and protection to the clients. As repayment the clients can give promises and expressions of solidarity and loyalty. Patron-client relations are in other words relations based on exchange. The patron gives what the client needs, and in return gets what he wants from the client.

2. In the interaction between patron and clients a strong element of interpersonal obligation is prevalent – "an element often couched in terms of personal loyalty or reciprocity and attachment between patrons and clients". This solidarity is often linked to personal honour and obligations, but it is also evident, though very ambivalent, in a spiritual attachment between the patron and client.

3. Patron-client relations are seemingly binding and of long duration, ideally lasting for life. But in as much as these relations are, at least in principle voluntary, they can be abandoned voluntarily.

4. Patron-client relations are based on very strong elements of inequality and of differences in power. A very important aspect of these relations is that the patron has a monopoly on certain positions and resources that are of crucial importance to the client. Because the client has no direct access to the actual resources, he is forced to depend on the patron for the provision of them or to seek the mediation of the patron in order to get them.

From these basic features of patron-client relations one may see that they create a paradoxical combination of elements. First, and most important, inequality and asymmetry in power are combined with "seeming and mutual solidarity expressed in terms of personal identity and interpersonal sentiments and obligations". And further, potential coercion and exploitation from the patron is combined with seemingly voluntary relations and mutual obligations.

In a society like the Roman Empire, which did not have a central government and an efficient bureaucracy like modern Western democracies, the institution of patronage played an important role in interaction between people in different strata of society.[1323] It provided many of the services which today are mediated by impersonal governmental or private institutions. With respect to the present study it should suffice to mention a few of the areas where patron-client relations were at work.[1324] (1) The Roman emperor by giving peace and order functioned as a patron of the whole empire. In

---

[1323]R. P. SALLER, "Patronage and Friendship in Early Imperial Rome", *Patronage in Ancient Society* (1989) 49-62; *idem, Personal Patronage under the Early Empire* (1982); H. MOXNES, "Patron-Client Relations and the New Community", *The Social World of Luke-Acts* (1991) 241-268.

[1324]For a detailed discussion see R. P. SALLER, *Personal Patronage under the Early Empire* (1982); *idem,* "Patronage and Friendship in Early Imperial Rome", *Patronage in Ancient Society* (1989) 49-62; S. N. EISENSTADT and L. RONIGER, *Patrons, Clients, and Friends* (1984) 61-64; J. K. CHOW, *Patronage and Power* (1992) 41-82. The last work focuses especially upon Corinth.

return the people, that is the clients, in various ways expressed reverence and honour. (2) The emperor functioned further as a patron for a narrower circle of officials. (3) Officials who represented the central power functioned as brokers, and thus as patrons, toward the periphery. (4) Local notables gave benefactions to the common good for a city or local community and in return received different expressions of public honour. (5) Different ties of *amicitia* existed between the ruling class and other powerful sub-elites. A member of the ruling class, the patron, could for instance provide knowledge regarding "the working of the State, the relation of subjects and allies to Rome, the rules of senatorial procedure and the cases of precedent",[1325] and secure for the client a pub-lic office. In return the client should advance the interest of the patron. (6) Wealthy men functioned as patrons for clubs, and in return received different expressions of honour from the members of the club. (7) The head of individual households functioned as a patron for the members of the groups and received in return special privileges and expressions of loyalty. The oldest patron-client relationship and that most open to coercion was the relationship between a former master and his freedman.

This indicates that in the Roman Empire patron-client relations were at work in interaction between people at a wide range of levels including the emperor, officials, the common people and the local notables. We do not maintain that the institution of patronage regulated all behaviour in interaction between people, but it is certain that patronage provided *one* of the ways through which behaviour in societies of the Medi-terranean would have been organized.[1326] A statement of Seneca who had first hand information regarding patron-client relations in the early Roman Empire gives a vivid picture of the pervasiveness of such relations:

> Look at those whose prosperity men flock to behold; they are smothered by their bless-ings. To how many are riches a burden! From how many do eloquence and the daily straining to display their powers draw forth blood ... To how many does the throng of clients that crowd about them leave no freedom! In short, run through the list of all these men from the lowest to the highest – this man desires an advocate, this one answers the call, that one is on trial, that one defends him, that one gives sentence; no one asserts his claim to himself, everyone is wasted for the sake of another. Ask about the men whose names are known by heart, and you will see that these are the marks that distinguish them: A cultivates B and B cultivates C; no one is his own master (De Brev. Vit. 2.4).

In another treatise, *On Benefits*, the same author deals with how men ought to interact in the process of giving and receiving favours and services. The fundamental idea is

---

[1325]S. N. Eisenstadt and L. Roniger, *Patrons, Clients, and Friends* (1984) 62. Cf. also J. K. Chow, *Patronage and Power* (1992) 53.

[1326]Cf. H. Moxnes, "Patron-Client Relations and the New Community", *The Social World of Luke-Acts* (1991) 246: "Patron-client relationship, therefore, is a central concept needed for under-standing the way in which this type of society [the Roman Empire in the first century] functioned, both on the level of the administration of Rome and its provinces, and on the level of relations in small scale communities".

that a man who receives a favour is obliged to respond to his benefactor with gratitude and in kind. Seneca is harsh to those who do not repay their debt.[1327] He writes "Homicides, tyrants, thieves, adulterers, robbers, sacrilegious men, and traitors there always will be; but worse than all these is the crime of ingratitude" (*Ben.* 1.10.4).[1328] Further we note that Seneca emphasizes the unifying effect upon society of patron-client relations. They constitute "the chief bond of human society" (*Ben.* 1.4.2). In other words, a benefit of reciprocal exchange is that "it eased tensions and conflicts provoked by divisions and inequalities".[1329]

5.4.1.2. Honour

We have already stated that honour was closely related to the institution of patronage, and we have seen that commonly a client was obliged to give expressions of honour in return for benefactions. In short, to use the words of P. Garnsey and R. P. Saller; "benefaction and requital were matters of honour".[1330] Keeping in mind the importance of patronage in the Roman Empire, it follows that honour was an essential value in Clement's cultural milieu.

Scholars in cultural anthropology have described the Mediterranean as an 'honour-shame culture'. A premise of treating this area as a unity for study purposes was that it had and has a certain cultural and social unity in which the aspects of honour and shame were fundamental elements.[1331] A primary aspect of an honour-shame culture, according to scholars in cultural anthropology, is that unlike the modern culture of the West the group and the collective is more significant than the individual. The single person receives status from the group. People perceive themselves primarily in terms of their relations to other persons and groups. This does not mean that a person's own estimation of himself or herself does not have any impact on that individual's perception of his or her value. However, the degree of honour depends ultimately on the

---

[1327]The language of debt and repayment is frequently used in discussions on exchange between patrons and clients and between friends. See R. P. SALLER, *Personal Patronage under the Early Empire* (1982) 21, and the whole of chap. 1 regarding the language of exchange.

[1328]And similarly Cic. *Off.* 1.15.48: "To fail to requite one [a favour] is not allowable to a good man".

[1329]P. GARNSEY and R. P. SALLER, *The Roman Empire* (1987) 148. For the cohesive effects of patronage in Latin America, see R. KAUFMAN "The Patron-Client Concept and Macropolitics", *CSSH* 16 (1974) 286f.

[1330]P. GARNSEY and R. P. SALLER, *The Roman Empire* (1987) 149.

[1331]For an overview of the most important works in the field of social anthropology on the subject and the discussion among scholars on whether it is appropriate to call the Mediterranean culture a 'honour-shame culture', see H. MOXNES, "Honor and Shame", *BTB* 23 (1993) 168f. Moxnes concludes that "it is fair to say that the thesis of a specific Mediterranean honor and shame culture holds, even if many aspects have been modified" (169). Another premise for the development of the honour-shame model is that Mediterranean societies have undergone lesser change in social structures than many of the societies of the West during the last 2500 years. As an example of this stability one might pay attention to the continuation of patron-client relationships with their accent on honour. See S. N. EISENSTADT and L. RONIGER, *Patrons, Clients, and Friends* (1984), 50-81.

response and evaluation of others. To put it another way, if a person on the basis of his or her self-esteem claims honour, it is only real honour when the group recognises and confirms the claim.[1332] Thus interaction between people was to a high degree directed towards recognition and defence of one's own status and honour.

Honour could basically be achieved in two ways. A person might claim honour because of his status, e.g., because of inherited wealth or because of his noble family. In such cases the person does not need to do anything active in order to be honoured. Therefore one calls this honour *ascribed honour*. On the other hand, *acquired honour* is based on deeds which the group recognise as virtuous.[1333]

In cases where a person's claim for honour is not recognised by the group he identifies himself with, i.e. the significant others, he is put to shame. Such a culture might therefore be described as a culture of competition, competition to increase honour and avoid shame.[1334] One of the scholars who initiated the research on honour in the field of social anthropology, J. A. Pitt-Rivers, has offered the following summary of the concept of honour, its relation to shame, and the hallmarks of a honour culture:

> It is a sentiment, a manifestation of this sentiment in conduct, and the evaluation of this conduct by others, that is to say, reputation … It stands as a mediator between individual aspirations and the judgement of society. It can, therefore, be seen to reflect the values of a group with which a person identifies himself. But honour as a fact, rather than a sentiment, refers not merely to the judgement of others but to their behavior. The facets of honor may be viewed as related in the following way: honor felt becomes honor claimed, and honor claimed becomes honor paid.
>
> The same principles that govern the transactions of honor are present in those of dishonor though in reverse: the withdrawal of respect dishonors, since it implies a rejection of the claim to honor and this inspires the sentiment of shame. To be put to shame is to be denied honor, and it follows that this can only be done of those who have some pretension to it … Honor and dishonor, therefore, provide the currency in which people compete for a reputation and the means whereby their appraisal of themselves can be validated and integrated into the social system – or rejected, thus obliging them to revise it.[1335]

[1332] "Therefore, recognition from others is important. Although honour is also an inner quality, the value of a person in his or her own eyes, it depends ultimately upon recognition from the group or from important people in society – the 'significant others'" (H. Moxnes, "Honor and Shame", *BTB* 23 (1993) 168). See also J. A. Pitt-Rivers, "Honour and Social Status", *Honour and Shame* (1965) 21-23.

[1333] B. J. Malina, *The New Testament World* (1981) summarizes: "Honor can be ascribed or acquired. Ascribed honour befalls or happens to a person passively through birth, family connections, or endowment by notable persons of power. Acquired honour is honour actively sought and garnered most often at the expense of one's equals in the social contest of challenge and response" (47). Cf. also P. F. Esler, *The First Christians in their Social Worlds* (1994) 25-29.

[1334] H. Moxnes, "Honour and Righteousness in Romans", *JSNT* 32 (1988) 63. Cf. also *idem*, "Honor and Shame", *BTB* 23 (1993) 168; B. J. Malina, *The New Testament World* (1981) 27-48.

[1335] J. A. Pitt-Rivers, "Honor", in *Encyclopaedia of the Social Sciences*, 2d ed. (New York: Macmillan Co., 1968), 503-511, quotation 503f., according to H. Moxnes, "Honor, Shame and the Outside World", *The Social World of Formative Christianity and Judaism* (1988) 208.

If we turn our attention to classical studies, it becomes clear how fundamental the value of honour was in the ancient world.[1336] In his study on Homerian society M. Finley has showed that it was characterised by a warrior's quest for honour,[1337] a point of view which is confirmed by A. W. H. Adkins.[1338] The warrior was praised and honoured for being ἀγαθός. Regard was given to the things which society was most dependent on. Thus the warrior with his military skill offering safety and protection to the society was an object of honour. If the warrior failed, however, he was put to shame.[1339] Adkins traces the further development of ἀγαθός and notes that when society changed – when strategic military defence was a less threatening problem and society became more complex – a conflict developed between the warrior's ideal and softer ideals such as σωφροσύνη and δικαιοσύνη. One was in need of softer values to balance the traditional aggressive behaviour connected with warriors in order to prevent στάσις and preserve public life.[1340] However, the emphasis on the aspect of common good or what benefited the society was constant. The hallmark of the ἀγαθός πολίτης was that he was of great benefit to the political life of his home city. In order to gain honour he should use his talents and his possessions to secure the political security and rank of the city. The usual way to do so was by giving of his wealth to the city's expenses. In return the benefactor was paid back by means of different demonstrations of honour. The sources show that this system of city honour in exchange for benefactions was prevalent throughout antiquity.[1341] Common expressions of such honour of the city

---

[1336]Because, as we noted above, the Mediterranean societies have been more stable regarding social structures since classical times than many societies in the West, there has been a great deal of contact and mutual influence between studies in social anthropology and classical studies. Cf. H. MOXNES, "Honor, Shame and the Outside World", *The Social World of Formative Christianity and Judaism* (1988) 208.

[1337]M. I. FINLEY, *The World of Odysseus* (1978) (first. pr. 1954), e.g. 113-122.

[1338]A. W. H. ADKINS, *Merit and Responsibility* (1960) 30-49; *idem*, *Moral Values and Political Behaviour in Ancient Greece* (1972) 10-21.

[1339]Cf. A. W. H. ADKINS, *Moral Values and Political Behaviour in Ancient Greece* (1972): "Since it is by success, not by good intentions, that the group continues to exist, good intentions do not suffice: it is *aischron* to fail, whatever one's intentions, in those activities which are held to contribute to the defence of the *oikos*, or of the group for whose success one is held responsible in war" (13).

[1340]Cf. *ibid.* 112ff., in particular the chap. "*Arete* within the City", 126-133. Adkins summarizes: "*Arete* has traditionally commended the qualities conducive to success in war; and is still widely so used in the later fifth century. However, by this time, in some parts of society, even if the results are not apparent in the law-courts, thought and analysis are being devoted to the question of types of behaviour most likely to avert civic strife, *stasis*" (127). For the relation between σωφροσύνη and δικαιοσύνη and concord, see our discussion chaps. 3.5.2.5 and 3.5.2.16 respectively.

[1341]For a comprehensive collection of inscriptions, see F. W. DANKER, *Benefactor* (1982) 87-151, 202-286. Considering the constancy of the system of exchanging honour for benefactions Danker summarizes: "In brief, about eight centuries separate Homer and the flowering of Hellenistic Christian communities, yet the cultural phenomenon of interplay between people of excellence and those on whom they make their impact finds continuous celebration, with a fairly consistent pattern of themes and diction developing in the last five centuries preceding the reign of Caesar Augustus" (27).

elite were to reserve seats of honour for them at the public entertainment,[1342] one had one's name inscribed above the door of some important public building, statues were erected of those who were honoured,[1343] and they were offered public offices.[1344] With respect to the present investigation it is especially interesting to note how much honour was attached to the holding of a public office. Plutarch, for instance, writes that "not all men expect that the power derived from πλοῦτος, λόγος or σοφία will accrue to them, but no one who takes part in public life is without hope of attaining the reverence and repute to which old age leads" (*Mor.* 787 D). Further, "and deeming every public office to be something great and sacred, we must also pay the highest τιμή to one who holds an office" (*Mor.* 816 A).

This system could be expensive for the benefactor, but the love of honour was so strong that some were willing to use so much money in order to gain it that they were driven into poverty.[1345] In such an honour culture it became important to display one's status.[1346] Plutarch, for instance, despite being a part of this culture, could be critical of the extent to which people would go to make known their social status.[1347]

It is obvious that in as much as such honours were connected with being a benefactor to the city they were restricted to the rich. They bought honour at a high cost. How-

----

[1342]Cf. Dio Chrys. *Or.* 66.2; 75.7: "Furthermore, most beautiful are the rewards which it has established for their benefactions, having devised crowns and public proclamations and seats of honour, things which for those who supply them entail no expense, but which for those who win them have come to be worth everything". Plut. *Mor.*58 C reports on a practice where some persons take possession of these seats not because they believe they have any right to them, but because they could flatter the rich by giving up their seats.

[1343]Cf. Dio Chrys. *Or.* 31.108; 44.2; Plut. *Mor.* 820 D: "But if it is not easy to reject some favour or some kindly sentiment of the people, when it is so inclined, for men engaged in a political struggle for which the prize is not money or gifts, but which is a truly sacred contest worthy of a crown, a mere inscription suffices, a tablet, a decree, or a green branch …". Also Josephus offers an illustrative description of the wide range of demonstrations of honour. His report of an Athenian decree to honour the Jewish high priest Hyrcanus shows in addition that foreigners could be the objects of honour: "It has therefore now been decreed … to honour this man with a golden crown as the reward of merit fixed by law, and to set up his statue in bronze in the precincts of the temple of Demos and the Graces, and to announce the award of the crown in the theatre at the Dionysian festival when the new tragedies are performed, and the Panathenaean and Eleusinian festivals and at the gymnastic games; and that the magistrates shall take care that so long as he continues to maintain his goodwill toward us, everything which we can devise shall be done to show honour and gratitude to this man for his zeal and generosity" (Joseph. *Ant* 14.152-154).

[1344]H. Moxnes, "Honor and Shame", *BTB* 23 (1993) 172.

[1345]Cf. Dio Chrys. *Or.* 66.2f.

[1346]Regarding Corinth, cf. A. D. Clarke, *Secular and Christian Leadership in Corinth* (1993): "Corinth itself provides many suitable examples of inscriptions where honour is displayed either by the benefactor himself, or by a dependent friend on his behalf. Such inscriptions, often accompanied by statues, would be erected in the most prominent parts of the city in order to have the greatest effect. In Corinth such inscriptions are found in the public places; around the agora, in front of the Theatre, and along the main streets, for example the Lechaion Road" (24 n. 12). He further refers to a list of many benefactions mentioned in the inscriptions in J. H. Kent, *Corinth – The Inscriptions 1926-1950* (1966) 21.

ever, as mentioned above, the patron-client system not only regulated behaviour between the city elite and the inhabitants of the city.[1348] We noted that it was at work in lesser political bodies as well, e.g., associations and households. A man of some wealth, a freedman for example, could sponsor clubs and associations, and would receive honour and praise from the members in return. Likewise, a person of some wealth could function as patron of a household. He offered legal and economic support to different groups of the household in exchange for honour and necessary support in order to gain public office which again led to increasing status and honour.[1349] This means that although honour was dependent on money, there was no need to belong to the elite of society in order to be in a position which enabled one to "buy" honour.

B. J. Malina and J. H. Neyrey say that "honour indicates a person's social standing and rightful place in society" which among other things depends on gender.[1350] When a man on the basis of his gender and its connected position of power expects to be treated in a certain way that expresses honour, this kind of honour is to a very limited degree connected with wealth. The father of the household for example could according to the household codes expect that his wife and his children should obey him and thereby treat him honourably. If, on the other hand, they behave against the codes, they bring shame upon him. This means that if one behaves otherwise than what is considered to be consistent with the proper social order, one is acting dishonourably and the man who is not treated according to his place in society will suffer shame. It has been pointed out that a characteristic feature of the mentality of the people of the Mediterranean is "'their predisposition to regard offences against the social order or conditions that bring about social disorder as being preeminently deviant.' This presupposes that people who upset the social order are acting dishonorably".[1351] In other words, if the

---

[1347]"So of all kinds of love that which is engendered in states and peoples for an individual because of his virtue is at once the strongest and the most divine; but those falsely named and falsely attested honours which are derived from giving theatrical performances, making distributions of money, or offering gladiatorial shows, are like harlots' flatteries, since the masses always smile upon him who gives to them and does them favours, granting him an ephemeral and uncertain reputation" (Plut. *Mor.* 821 F).

[1348]For a summary of the patron-client relations, see J. K. CHOW, *Patronage and Power* (1992) 30-36 with literature references.

[1349]For discussion and references to texts related to Corinth, see *ibid.* 64-82. This illustrates a characteristic element in patron-client relations, i.e. that there is a mutual dependence between the patron and the clients. P. J. J. VANDERBROECK, *Popular Leadership and Collective Behavior in the Late Roman Republic (ca. 80-50 B.C.)* (1987), in explaining why the patron depends on the clients writes: "In pursuing a career at the top, it does not seem at first sight purposeful to mobilize the group of artisans and shopkeepers, because their vote hardly counted in the centuriate assembly which elected the highest magistrates. Yet support of the *plebs contionalis* was necessary: to reach the top one first had to be elected to the lower offices by the tribal assembly" (163).

[1350]B. J. MALINA and J. H. NEYREY, "Honor and Shame in Luke-Acts", *The Social World of Luke-Acts* (1991) 26.

[1351]Malina and Neyrey, *Ibid.* 27, quote Henry Selby, *Zapotec Deviance: The Convergence of Folk and Modern Sociology.* Austin, TX: University of Texas Press, 1974, 16. This illustrates that what one evaluated as honourable is what one considers valuable and worthy (*Ibid.* 26).

youths or children, for instance, do not obey the old and the father of the household, they are acting dishonourably and in fact are revolting against the social order.[1352]

To summarize, honour played a fundamental role in the cultural environment of Clement. The life of the city elite and of those of some wealth was to a high degree directed towards increasing their honour.[1353] The importance of honour might be traced back to the time of Homer, but what particular deeds and virtues were considered to be honourable changed in line with the changing needs of society. At the time of Clement honour was first of all linked to being a benefactor to the city and in that way contributing to the upkeep of public life and to the financing of the common good. As a repayment the benefactor received different expressions of honour, among other things the holding of a public office. In our connection it is important to stress that holding a public office was in Clement's wider cultural milieu associated with great honour. People, however, could also function as benefactors toward lesser political bodies, such as associations and households, and in return receive honour from the members of the actual body.

5.4.1.3. Honour as Cause of Strife and Sedition

On the basis of the significant role of honour in the societies of antiquity, it is not surprising that the sources testify that competition for honour might lead to strife. This is, for example, reflected in some of the discourses of Dio Chrysostom.

It was not only individuals who competed for honour, but also cities. In *Or.* 38 Dio deals with struggles between Nicomedia and Nicea over the right to use the title "first".[1354] Honour and glory were associated with bearing this title. Dio, however, in his appeal for concord between the cities condemns the futility of struggling over titles.[1355] In his argumentation he compares the present strife with the classic and destructive rivalry between Athens and Sparta which also was a struggle for primacy (38:24). Contrary to the Nicomedians who associated glory and honour with the title "first", Dio holds that a primacy which is not beneficial is vainglory and false glory.[1356]

We then move on to *Or.* 44, a discourse addressed to his hometown Prusa. The background to the discourse was honour offered to Dio by the city. Although he responds respectfully to this honour (44.1), he is somewhat reluctant to receive it as

---

[1352]Cf. what we noted above about the unifying effect of patronage on society, p. 304.

[1353]H. Moxnes, "The Quest for Honor and the Unity of the Community in Romans 12", *Paul in His Hellenistic Context* (1995) 204, describes the role of honour as follows: "Competition for honor among members of the elite was a major characteristic of life in the Hellenistic city. Honor and status in exchange for munificence towards the city, towards the 'common good', was a central feature in city culture and city life".

[1354]Dio Chrys. *Or.* 38.24. See further C. P. Jones, *The Roman World of Dio Chrysostom* (1978) 86.

[1355]Dio Chrys. *Or.* 38.21-30.

[1356]"Vainglory (κενοδοξία) has come to be regarded as a foolish thing even in private individuals, and we ourselves deride and loathe, and end by pitying, those persons above all who do not know wherein false glory (δόξα ψευδής) differs from the genuine; besides, no educated man has such a feeling about glory as to desire a foolish thing" (Dio Chrys. *Or.* 38.29).

can be seen from the fact that he attempts to redefine the common perceptions of what honour is. Real honour is not connected with status, proclamations or seats of honour, not even with "a portrait statue of beaten gold set up in the most distinguished shrines", but is expressed through goodwill, friendship and love: "For one word spoken out of goodwill (εὔνοια) and friendship (φιλία) is worth all the gold and crowns and everything else deemed splendid that men possess" (44.2). In other words, Dio emphasizes certain communal virtues instead of traditional external expressions of honour. Accordingly his picture of the ideal city consists of men who compete for character (ἀρετή), good repute (εὐδοκία) and "for being just and patriotic and not incapable of promoting … [their] country's welfare" (44.8). Further, Dio argues, such competition must be "without envy (φθόνος) and jealousy (ζηλοτυπία)". This means that for him true honour depends on men's love for the city and on their behaviour being directed to what is the common good of the city, and not on external demonstrations of honour.[1357] Dio's remark that this competition must be without envy and jealousy is probably a reaction to the fact that the traditional concept of honour was connected with these vices.[1358]

Furthermore, Plutarch probably reflects a common experience when he writes as follows:

> … in public life one must escape, not from one tyrant, the love of boys or women, but from many loves which are more insane than that: love of contention, love of fame, the desire to be first and greatest, which is a disease most prolific of envy, jealousy, and discord (φιλονεικίαν, φιλοδοξίαν, τὴν τοῦ πρῶτον εἶναι καὶ μέγιστον ἐπιθυμίαν, γονιμώτατον φθόνου νόσημα καὶ ζηλοτυπίας καὶ διχοστασίας, Mor. 788 E).

These experiences of Dio Chrysostom and Plutarch, that the love of honour contains the power to raise στάσις are not peculiar to their lifetime. As we have already observed, Aristotle testifies that in his lifetime also one had the same experiences. He says: "It is clear also what is the power of honour (τιμή) and how it can cause party faction (στάσις); for men form factions both when they are themselves dishonoured and when they see others honoured" (*Pol.* 5.2.4).

5.4.2. Patronage and Honour in 1 Clement

Before we consider whether the institution of patronage and the role of honour in the Mediterranean as outlined above might shed light on what Clement regarded to be an underlying motivation for the strife in the Corinthian Church, we shall briefly see to what extent these features are reflected in the letter in general.

[1357] Cf. *Or.* 48.7 where Dio Chrys applies the bees as an example of mutual love and solidarity. See also H. MOXNES, "The Quest for Honor and the Unity of the Community in Romans 12", *Paul in His Hellenistic Context* (1995) 212.

[1358] C. P. JONES, *The Roman World of Dio Chrysostom* (1978): "Desire for honor and glory was ubiquitous: cities struggled to be first in their province or to have a temple of the imperial cult, as individuals struggled to be the 'first men' of their city or to wear the gold crown and purple robe of office" (85).

After Clement has indicated the theme of the letter in 1:1a he stresses that the present sedition has caused the "venerable (σεμνός) and famous" (περιβόητος) name of the Corinthians to be much reviled (1:1b).[1359] Following this Clement gives the reason why the Corinthians' name was venerable and famous by focusing upon their noble community life in the past. Here he appears to reflect conventional aspects within an honour culture. Firstly, to have a good reputation was essential in such a culture.[1360] So, when he maintains that their previous good reputation has been much slandered, it reveals how seriously he viewed the present state of affairs. Further, in the context of an honour culture it is likely that such an assertion would have a strong argumentative appeal. Secondly, we should note that Clement makes a connection between sedition and a damaged reputation. Sedition implies an upset in one way or another of the previous order of the Church. On the basis that the Mediterraneans were inclined to consider behaviour that upset the existing social order to be dishonourable, as mentioned above, Clement appears to reflect conventional thoughts. Thirdly, in his praise for the Corinthians' community life in the past which secured them a good reputation, he pays attention to the fact that they lived in a manner consistent with the traditional household codes. In other words, the Corinthians upheld what was considered to be the proper social order and thereby behaved honourably.

In 47:5-7 Clement reiterates and reinforces the assertion that the present sedition is dishonourable. In 47:5 the topic of the Corinthians' previous fame reoccurs. The sedition has according to Clement diminished the respect due to the Corinthians' renowned love for the brethren (τὸ σεμνὸν τῆς περιβοήτου φιλαδελφίας). Further, he explicitly states that the removal of the presbyters has brought shame upon the Corinthians. He describes the report that has reached him about what has taken place as shameful (αἰσχρά) and even extremely shameful (λίαν αἰσχρά, 47:6). As was the case in chapters 1-3 Clement seems to play deliberately in his argumentation upon the great value of having a good reputation and in the negative of avoiding shame. Thereby his argumentation reflects the essential feature of an honour culture.

As a final example demonstrating that Clement appears to mirror the pivotal value of honour in the Mediterranean we turn to chapter 54. Here he exhorts the men involved in sedition to voluntarily depart and thereby contribute to the re-establishing of concord. What is interesting in this connection is the argument he uses in order to persuade them. If one follows the exhortation, he says that one will gain great glory (μέγα κλέος) in Christ (54:3). There is no doubt that this type of honour is different from what was traditionally regarded as an expression of honour. However, the simple fact that Clement appeals to a future glory as a reward makes it reasonable to assert that here also he reflects the great value of honour for men in antiquity.

On the basis of the observations above we maintain with a reasonable degree of certainty that Clement reflects the pivotal value of honour in the Mediterranean. But what about patron-client relations? Here *1 Clem.* 38 is of great interest. In this chapter, as

---

[1359]This statement functions as an *attentum et docilem parare*. See the present study, pp. 219.
[1360]Cf. above, pp. 305f.

noted above,[1361] as a means of preserving the Christian community he gives an exhortation with respect to how people of different status and honour ought to act towards each other. The strong (ἰσχυρός) must take care of the weak (ἀσθενής) and the weak must reverence the strong, the rich man (πλούσιος) should support the poor and the poor should give thanks to God because he has been given one to supply his needs (38:2). Previously we have argued that this passage appears to reflect the fact that matters of a socio-economic nature were at stake in the conflict and thus supports our understanding of *1 Clem.* 3:3.[1362]

What we shall emphasize in this connection is, however, that this exhortation, which expresses Clement's ideal or advice regarding how Christians of different social levels must interact in order to live harmoniously, reflects basic structures of patron-client relations. Above we have seen that a key feature of such relations is a reciprocal exchange of different types of resources based on a strong element of inequality and of differences in power.[1363] This feature is evident in Clement's advice in 38:2 as well. Firstly, the inequality and differences in power are expressed by referring to one group of people as strong (ἰσχυρός) and rich (πλούσιος) and to the other as weak (ἀσθενής) and poor (πτωχός). Previously we argued that it is reasonable, on the one hand, to view ἰσχυρός and πλούσιος as synonyms depicting those who were rich in economic terms and, on the other hand, ἀσθενής and πτωχός as synonyms depicting those who were poor in economic terms.[1364] Secondly, the aspect of reciprocity is clearly expressed in the exhortation to the ἰσχυρός and πλούσιος to take care of the ἀσθενής and πτωχός and to the latter to give expressions of respect in return and give thanks to God. Among other things this probably means that the ἀσθενής – πτωχός must show loyalty and obedience toward the ἰσχυρός – πλούσιος and thereby express honour due to his social position.

In the last two decades an immense number of works has been published that discuss the rise, development, and organisation of the Early Church – that is the period of the N.T. letters – in the setting of the Graeco-Roman household.[1365] These works demonstrate that in order to understand essential features of Early Christianity it is of the greatest importance that one pay sufficient attention to its household setting. Wealthy

---

[1361]See pp. 297.

[1362]We emphasize that this conclusion depends on Clement's making a connection between the general exhortation in 38:2, which belongs to the general θέσις section of the *probatio*, and the actual occurrences in the Corinthian Church.

[1363]See chap. 5.4.1.1.

[1364]See pp. 297-298.

[1365]For example R. BANKS, *Paul's Idea of Community* (1980); B. HOLMBERG, *Paul and Power* (1980); J. H. ELLIOT, *A Home for the Homeless* (1981); H.-J. KLAUCK, *Hausgemeinde und Hauskirche im frühen Christentum* (1981); A. J. MALHERBE, *Social Aspects of Early Christianity* (1983); W. A. MEEKS, *The First Urban Christians* (1983); J. STAMBAUGH AND D. BALCH, *The Social World of the First Christians* (1986); P. LAMPE, *Die stadtrömischen Christen in den ersten beiden Jahrhunderten* (1989). Important older works are F. V. FILSON, "The Significance of the Early House Churches", *JBL* 58 (1939) 105-112; E. A. JUDGE, *The Social Pattern of the Christian Groups in the First Century* (1960).

Christians invited other Christians to their home and thereby established a house-church. As the number of Christians increased there was no longer room for everyone in one house, and therefore already in the very early stages of Christianity a network of house-churches developed within a given city.[1366] The sources do not give a clear-cut picture concerning the interrelation between the churches either on the level of service or the level of leadership. It appears, however, that occasionally a full church assembly took place and that a kind of presbyterial collegium existed at least in Rome from the first half of the second century.[1367]

On the basis of the fact that traditional household codes are found in *1 Clement* (1:3; 21:6-8) and that there is a stress upon hospitality (11:1; 12:1:3) it is reasonable to assume that Clement presupposes that the house church was the social setting for the Corinthian Christians at the time of the composition of *1 Clement* as well.[1368]

In our connection it is interesting that research has established that a given house-church host functioned commonly as a patron for the members of the particular house-church and quite naturally played a central part in the leadership of the house-church. This means that the rather prosperous house-host and the overseer of a house-church were often one and the same person.[1369]

Further, this circumstance makes it reasonable to assume that the presbyters who were removed from their offices in Corinth were relatively wealthy house-hosts who functioned as patrons for the members of their respective house-churches.[1370] The suggestion that the presbyters were wealthy is, furthermore, consistent with our interpretation of 3:3. The instigators of the sedition belonged according to this interpretation to the lower strata of the church.

If the suggestion above is correct, this means that those who revolted against the presbyters were clients who did not behave according to the rule of patronage. Instead of showing them honour by being loyal and obedient as a repayment for the benefaction received from the patron, they did the opposite. Thereby, according to the rule of patronage, which also is reflected in Clement, they brought shame upon the Corinthian

[1366]Cf. the archaeological data on the size of private homes collected and discussed by J. MURPHY-O'CONNOR, *St. Paul's Corinth* (1983) 153-161. He maintains that no more than fifty people could have gathered comfortably together in a private home of moderate size.

[1367]Cf. 1 Cor 14:23; Rom 16:5: 23. For discussion see, e.g., R. BANKS, *Paul's Idea of Community* (1980) 38. For Rome in the second century, see *Herm. Vis.* 2.2.6; 2.4.2-3; 3.9.7, and the discussion in P. LAMPE, *Die stadtrömischen Christen in den ersten beiden Jahrhunderten* (1989) 338. Lampe traces further the evidence for the development from presbyterial collegium toward a monarchic episcopacy (339-344).

[1368]So also R. E. BROWN and J. M. MEIER, *Antioch & Rome* (1983) 173; H. O. MAIER, *The Social Setting of Ministry as Reflected in the Writings of Hermas, Clement and Ignatius* (1991) 93.

[1369]Cf. the discussion of texts and references to literature regarding the prosperity of the leaders in the Early Church in H. O. MAIER, *The Social Setting of the Ministry as Reflected in the Writings of Hermas, Clement and Ignatius* (1991) 45f.

[1370]So also R. A. CAMPBELL, *The Elders* (1994) 215 (though we do not agree that the 'rebell' was a bishop who attempted to introduce monepiscopacy); D. G. HORRELL, *The Social Ethos of the Corinthian Correspondence* (1996) 250.

Church. Against this background Clement's exhortation in 38:2 makes good sense. The ἰσχυρός – πλούσιος is the patron of the church while the ἀσθενής – πτωχός is the client. In order to ease tensions and conflicts between unequal members Clement exhorts them to follow the rule of patron-client relations, an exhortation which reflects a traditional view of the effect of patron-client relations upon social units.[1371]

On the basis of the discussion above it should be determined at least beyond a low level of probability that Clement reflects both basic features of patron-client relations and the pivotal value of honour so characteristic of the societies of the Mediterranean. When he appears to reflect such conventional conceptions regarding patronage and not least honour, it is a fair supposition that he was also familiar with the common expressions of honour and with the experience of Aristotle, Dio Chrysostom and Plutarch that love of honour was commonly a source of sedition and strife in a political body. This means that he probably knew that holding a public office was connected with great honour. To use the words of Plutarch quoted above, Clement probably knew that one must "pay the highest τιμή to one who holds an office".[1372] Thus it is possible that he regarded striving for honour as one underlying motive which the instigators of the sedition had for removing some of the presbyters and placing themselves in their office. We have seen, however, that he opposes these ambitious men by arguing that the result of their action in fact has the opposite effect. Their actions have caused the famous reputation of the Corinthian Church to be much slandered and the Corinthians to be put to shame.

Furthermore, one more feature ought to be mentioned in this connection which seems to support our interpretation that Clement considered striving for honour to be an important aspect of the conflict. As noted above, his appeal to the fact that the instigators of the sedition would gain "great glory (μέγα κλέος) in Christ" (54:3), if they should depart and thereby contribute to bringing about an end to the sedition, appears to reflect the high value of honour in general. The appeal to the great glory in Christ might also be seen against a more specific background. It is possible that Clement here implicitly contrasts the honour the new presbyters believed they would gain by holding a leading position in the Church with glory in Christ. If this is the case, he argues that instead of seeking glory by means of holding an office the instigators of the sedition should be concerned with gaining glory in Christ.

We do not, of course, maintain that on the basis that striving for honour was associated with sedition, and that holding a public office was honourable, one can draw the definitive conclusion that Clement holds that this matter was at stake in Corinth as well. Yet the essential value of honour in the Mediterranean in general and the common experience that striving for honour caused sedition in particular, together with internal evidence in the letter, indicate both that our interpretation of Clement is reasonable and that Clement's perception of the conflict was plausible.[1373]

[1371]Cf. p. 304.
[1372]*Mor.* 816 A.

5.5. Conclusion with regard to the Social-Historical Situation

Building upon studies of the social world of the Early Christians, in particular G. Theissen's articles on the Church at Corinth, we have attempted to demonstrate that when Clement depicts the different people involved in the strife at the Corinthian Church in 3:3, he employs standard terms describing people of different socio-economic status. This indicates that he considered tensions between different social groups, between high status and low status groups, to be a major cause of the conflict. That the distribution of goods was in question appears, moreover, as we have seen, to be consistent with 38:2 where he explicitly deals with how people of different economic status should mutually support each other in order to live harmoniously. On the basis of these observations we have argued that Clement appears to hold that the lower class rose against the more wealthy and powerful in order to increase their influence and power in the Church. Thus the removal of some presbyters reflects a struggle for power. Further, we have seen that it was a common experience in antiquity that the socio-economic gap between high status groups and low status groups gave rise to upheaval and sedition in different political bodies, especially in the city state. Though this circumstance does not prove that Clement's perception of the conflict was consistent with the historical situation, it shows that Clement's perception was reasonable.

Closely related to the quest for increased influence and power was the striving for honour. We have noted that scholars in social anthropology have described the Mediterranean as an "honour-shame culture" and that scholars in the classics have confirmed that honour was a pivotal value in antiquity. In the city life of antiquity much behaviour was directed towards increasing one's honour and avoiding shame, and thus it became significant to demonstrate one's status and honour. Of interest, with regard to *1 Clement*, is the fact, as we have pointed out, that holding a public office was connected with honour and status. Therefore, in light of the great value of honour, it is a reasonable suggestion that the removal of some of the presbyters not only ought to be seen as a quest for power and influence in itself, but that *to hold an office in the Church was regarded as honourable in a way that was analogous to holding a public office in a city.* The fact that many of the terms Clement uses to depict the opposing groups in 3:3 were not only related to wealth, but also to status and honour indicates that he holds that the quest for honour was at stake. Therefore, we have argued, that when he reports on the uprising of the ἄτιμοι and the ἄδοξοι he indicates that the competition for honour was a significant element in the conflict. We have argued also that the way in which

---

[1373]The experience that quest for honour could lead to strife in a Christian Community appears to be evident in the *Shepherd of Hermas*. In *Sim.*8.7.4 the Shepherd informs his readers that some members of the Church "had some jealousy (ζῆλος) among themselves over the first place (περὶ πρωτείων) and some questions of reputation (περὶ δόξης τινός). But all these are foolish, who quarrel (ζῆλος) among themselves about the first place (περὶ πρωτείων)". See also *Herm. Vis.* 3.9.7-10. The context shows that it was among the leaders of the Church that the quest for honour caused sedition. See H. O. MAIER, *The Social Setting as Reflected in the Writings of Hermas, Clement and Ignatius* (1991) 64. P. LAMPE, *Die stadtrömischen Christen in den ersten beiden Jahrhunderten* (1989), suggests that πρωτεῖος refers to ecclesiastical offices (336).

Clement introduces the description of the strife in 3:1 indicates that he makes a connection between glory and the present strife.

Furthermore, we have presented evidence that demonstrates that it appeared to be a common experience that striving for honour led to sedition in a political body. Though this fact neither confirms our interpretation of Clement, nor the view that what we consider to be Clement's perception of the conflict was consistent with the historical situation, it does demonstrate that when Clement, as we understand him, indicates that striving for honour was an underlying cause of the sedition, this perception was reasonable.

For a modern Western reader it is not obvious, at least not at first sight, that Clement makes a connection between the strife in the Corinthian Church and a quest for honour. For contemporary readers, however, this was probably clear from what Clement says in chapter 3 – that is to say that a citizen of Corinth at the end of the first century lived in an honour culture and was familiar with the strong love for honour. He would also have known that the quest for honour had caused strife between cities and between citizens within a city.

In other words, our discussion of *1 Clem.* 3:3 in light of its broader cultural milieu indicates that this verse in spite of its stylistic form and its allusion to Isa 3:5 seems to offer information about what Clement considered to be the main issue in the conflict that is both additional to and different from what has been suggested by scholars who have occupied themselves with *1 Clement*: The underlying cause of the strife was not a conflict between "spirit" and "office", nor any other of the suggestions provided by scholars, but it appears that Clement regarded it primarily as a conflict between people of different socio-economic status in which a quest for honour, influence, and power was an important aspect.

6. General Summary and Conclusion

This investigation has attempted to offer a rhetorical analysis of *1 Clement* in order to enhance our understanding of the overall genre, function and composition of the letter. In line with the methodological considerations in chapter 1.3 the investigation deliberately took its departure in the tools of ancient rhetoric, abstaining from different forms of new rhetoric. The present study ought to be classified as a historical-rhetorical analysis of *1 Clement* and therefore stands with respect to methodology, broadly speaking, in the tradition of H. D. Betz on the one hand and G. A. Kennedy on the other.

One reason why the present work has been confined to ancient rhetoric is, as argued in chapter 1.1.1, that it is reasonable to assume that the author of *1 Clement* was familiar with the theory of ancient rhetoric from his education, and that he also was familiar with rhetoric and letter-writing from his former work in the imperial bureaucracy. If these suggestions are correct, one could expect that Clement would consciously have applied rules of ancient rhetoric in his argumentative strategy. The fact that rhetoric was a fundamental feature in Graeco-Roman culture in general would in itself justify the fact that we have restricted ourselves to applying ancient rhetoric as an analytical tool in the study. However, the chosen approach does not imply that a rhetorical analysis of the letter applying modern rhetoric as an analytical tool would not have been fruitful. On the contrary, the author of this work would welcome an investigation applying modern rhetoric as a valuable supplement to the methodology used in the present study.

Although this study took its departure in ancient rhetoric and abstained from the so-called new rhetoric, it was useful to integrate certain insights from modern linguistics, which to a large extent is developed from ancient rhetoric. In chapter 3, which focuses on terms and *topoi* associated with concord, some features of the theory of semantic fields were employed. Since this theory provides us with well-developed analytical tools, it turned out to be useful for this part of the investigation. In addition, its theoretical considerations regarding the system of language served as a theoretical basis for our task in this chapter. Furthermore, tools from modern text linguistics have been employed in the work to carry out the compositional analysis of the letter. Due to the fact that the *dispositio* of ancient rhetoric from a syntagmatic point of view was basically one-dimensional, one must, in order to work out a hierarchical multi-level delimitation, go beyond the *dispositio* of ancient rhetoric. For the present study features of the text linguistic approach applied in different works of D. Hellholm were useful.

Before turning to the results of the present investigation, one more comment on methodology should be made. In line with M. M. Mitchell's methodological considerations on rhetorical criticism, where she further develops the method of her teacher H. D. Betz, throughout the work we have consulted not only theory of ancient rhetoric, but also real letters and discourses. Such a sustained two-fold consultation has previously been unusual in rhetorical criticism.

6.1. The Main Characteristics of Deliberative Rhetoric in 1 Clement

An important aspect of the present study has been to demonstrate that it is appropriate to consider *1 Clement* as an example of deliberative rhetoric urging concord. Before we focus upon other aspects of our investigation, it is in place to summarize the basic argument in support for this thesis. In chapter 2 the study delineated the main characteristics of deliberative rhetoric in general and observed that these are found in *1 Clement* as well:

1. Deliberative rhetoric is hortatory (προτροπή) and/or dissuasive (ἀποτροπή). In *1 Clement* this is reflected among other things in the abundant use of hortatory subjunctives and the designation of the whole letter as a συμβουλή.

2. The future is the main time reference. Besides the hortatory subjunctive grammatical form which has just been mentioned this is reflected in the comparatively frequent use of imperatives, for instance the explicit advice to the instigators of the sedition to submit to the presbyters.

3. A standard set of appeals, of which appeal to advantage (τὸ συμφέρον) or warning of danger was fundamental. But also other appeals, for example, to the just (τὸ δίκαιον), the lawful (τὸ νόμιμον), the safe (τὸ ἀκίνδυνον), and the good (τὸ καλόν) were common. These standard appeals are primarily reflected in Clement's emphasis on the danger (βλαβερός, κίνδυνος) connected with the present state of affairs. But he also uses others, i.e. to the just, the lawful, the good, and the helpful. Besides these explicit appeals, he makes use of several implicit ones. For example, the assertion that, if the instigators of the sedition do not accept his advice, they will be excluded from eschatological salvation functions as a strong implicit warning of a future disadvantage to them. On the other hand, the assertion that, if one follows the proposed course of action, one will gain salvation functions for Christians as the strongest possible implicit appeal to what is advantageous to them. Furthermore, it has been noted that Clement, consistent with deliberative rhetoric urging concord in general, argues that his advice serves the common good. The proposed course of action does not serve individual interests or ambitions, but is concerned with what serves the common good for the Corinthian Church as a whole.

4. Proof by examples is characteristic. Throughout the letter Clement presents both positive and negative examples in order to prove the validity of a certain

assertion or the need to follow or turn away from certain actions or atti-tudes.[1374] In line with deliberative rhetoric in general, he uses admired and respected examples taken from the audience's 'forefathers', i.e. examples taken from the Old Testament, as well as examples closer in space and time, i.e. from the Christian tradition. Sometimes he explicitly appeals to the Corinthian Christians to imitate these examples.

6.2. Terms and topoi Associated with the Topic of Concord

In chapter 2 it has been demonstrated that the main characteristics of deliberative rhet-oric are found in *1 Clement*. Thus a necessary criterion for describing the letter as delib-erative rhetoric has been met. However, in order to argue with a high degree of certainty that the rhetorical genre of *1 Clement* is in fact deliberative, the investigation also had to demonstrate that the fundamental topic Clement dealt with was of such a nature that it was appropriate to employ this genre to communicate his message. Before focusing upon *1 Clement*, we noted that both theoretical considerations concerning adequate topics for deliberative rhetoric as well as a number of actual deliberative dis-courses and letters showed that the topic of "war and peace" was common. Further, it was noted that closely related to that topic, a certain type of deliberative rhetoric emerged, i.e. συμβουλευτικός λόγος περὶ ὁμονοίας. Among other things, on the basis of the fact that Clement describes the letter as an appeal for ὁμόνοια καὶ εἰρήνη, in chapter 3. *The Language of Unity and Sedition in 1 Clement* we examined the whole letter in order to establish that topics associated with concord indeed constitute the car-dinal theme of the letter. More precisely, we focused upon the semantic field of ὁμόνοια in the light of ancient texts that dealt with concord in a political body, partic-ularly the discourses of Dio Chrysostom and Aelius Aristides on concord. The exami-nation demonstrated that many terms that belonged to the semantic field of concord in antiquity were found throughout the letter, particularly in *1 Clem*. 1-3 where the author introduces the theme of the letter. It is also demonstrated that he uses *topoi* or appeals commonly used when one urged divided groups to live in concord in antiquity. Clem-ent's abundant use of political terms and *topoi* associated with concord suggested that ὁμόνοια (and εἰρήνη) is the main theme of the letter. However, that this is correct had to be further substantiated in the compositional analysis.[1375] Nevertheless, the findings of the study of political terms and *topoi* already served as a strong indication that the main theme of *1 Clement* was of such nature that it was appropriate for the author to employ the deliberative genre.

Apart from our main conclusion with respect to the question of the rhetorical genre, the investigation of *political terms and topoi* is valuable in itself as a word study of several terms and expressions in *1 Clement*. This study threw new light on why Clement

---

[1374]Although we touched upon the argumentative function of examples in chap. 2, it is primarily in chap. 4. *Compositional Analysis of 1 Clement* that we dealt with the argumentative function of exam-ples.

[1375]See below.

found it appropriate to use certain terms and expressions. Also, closely related to this, it showed that they ought to be understood in the light of the fact that they belonged to the semantic field of concord. In the hope of avoiding tiring reiterations we shall limit ourselves to mentioning just one example, i.e. δικαιοσύνη καὶ εἰρήνη. The investigation has made it likely that this expression ought not to be interpreted primarily with reference to its occurrences in the LXX, but rather in the light of the fact that both δικαιοσύνη and εἰρήνη were associated with concord in political bodies in antiquity in general.

In addition to the above-mentioned results, the investigation of the language of unity and sedition served to some extent at the same time as a basis for the compositional analysis of the letter. The fact that we could demonstrate that several terms belonged to the semantic field of concord provided valuable help with respect to the semantic meaning of certain passages.

6.3. The Compositional Analysis

Due to what was common in deliberative rhetoric when the audience did not assess the actual situation that prompted a discourse seriously enough, Clement finds an *exordium* (1:1-2:8) useful to prepare the audience for the following deliberation. The study has pointed out that 1:1 functions both as *attentum parare* and *docilem parare*, and that the bulk of the *exordium* consists of a *benevolum parare* (1:2-2:8). The need to pay sufficient attention to the *docilem parare* has been especially emphasized insofar as this part of a discourse indicates what the orator considered to be the main topic of the discourse. The *docilem parare* in 1:1 indicates that στάσις, or its antonym ὁμόνοια (and εἰρήνη), is the basic subject of the letter. Consistent with this is the fact that the *benevolum parare* section contains many terms and *topoi* belonging to the semantic field of concord.

That στάσις, or its antonym ὁμόνοια (and εἰρήνη), is the main topic of the letter is further confirmed in the *narratio* (3:1-4), which according to ancient rhetorical theory is useful in deliberative rhetoric when there is the need to induce the audience to take better counsel about the future, as well as in the *probatio* (4:1-61:3), and finally in the *peroratio* (62:1-64:1).

A significant aspect of the compositional analysis has been to show that the subtexts on different levels of the *probatio* are integrated in and serve Clement's over-all argument for concord. Contrary to the commonly held view that there is no leading theme in what is usually called "the first main part" of the letter, the compositional analysis has made it likely that, although Clement touches upon a number of topics in this passage, they are subordinated to the topic of concord. This implies that one must question the view of G. Brunner, who as far as we know is the only scholar to provide extensive argumentation for a thematic unity in this section, when he argues that "Ordnung" (order) is the basic theme. Due to the fact that Clement does not focus upon the concrete situation at Corinth in 4:1-39:9, but limits himself to dealing, on the one hand, with virtues and behaviour that secure concord and, on the other, with vices and behaviour that have the opposite effect, we have suggested that this section should be described as "*a treatise on the principles of concord for a Christian Community*". Because of this general approach to the theme, the present study has argued that in line with the status theory of ancient rhetoric it is adequate to describe 4:1-39:9 as a θέσις. Further, we have attempted to demonstrate that in the other main part of the *probatio* (40:1-61:3) Clement applies the principles of the θέσις to the concrete situation in the Corinthian Church. He addresses the instigators of the sedition directly and exhorts them to submit to the presbyters and thereby to re-establish concord in the community. Therefore we have argued that it is reasonable to view 40:1-61:3 as a ὑπόθεσις. This implies, of course, that the present work in contrast to those scholars who do not see a direct connection between the two main parts of the letter asserts that there is a logical connection between these two primary parts.

We have seen that *1 Clement* is not the only example of deliberative rhetoric urging concord where the *probatio* section is structured in such a way that a θέσις is followed by a subsequent ὑπόθεσις. Dio Chrysotom's *Or.* 38 and Aelius Aristides' *Or.* 24 reflect the same structure. This indicates that Clement's structuring of the *probatio* was appropriate for this type of rhetoric and that he possibly reflects a common rhetorical model when dealing with concord. However, the similarity in structure can be explained by the simple fact that in rhetoric in general the θέσις, as we have noted, is readily inserted before the ὑπόθεσις as an amplifying background and as a support for the argumentation. In other words, the ὑπόθεσις amplifies the θέσις.

In order to grasp the macro-structure of the *probatio* section in *1 Clement* it is illuminating to see it in the light of the concepts of θέσις and ὑπόθεσις. *Firstly*, it offers an adequate explanation as to why Clement chose to organize the *probatio* in a general and a particular part. The reason why he used a "two-dimensional" approach is not, as G. Brunner has argued, because of an increasing awareness that a local church is part of the universal Church, which therefore led Clement to use the solution to the crisis in Corinth as a paradigm for the universal church. To view the *probatio* section in the light of the concepts of θέσις and ὑπόθεσις offers a simpler, more straightforward and correct explanation.

Secondly, it shows that it is not appropriate to describe the first part as "Steigerung der Masse" which solely intends to enhance the importance of the letter,[1376] but rather to regard it as a fundamental part of the letter which deals with the main topic in a general way and serves as an amplifying background for the subsequent argumentation. In other words, it is not only the second part which deals with the real purpose of the letter, as argued by the scholars who see no direct connection between the two parts, but the first one does so as well. The topic of concord is the leading theme in both 4:1-39:9 and 40:1-61:3. This does not imply, however, that Clement is more concerned with concord in general than with the particular situation in the Corinthian Church.[1377]

[1376]So W. Bauer, *Rechtgläubigkeit und Ketzerei* (1964) 99. Bauer argues that the quantity of material served intentionally to obscure the real position and goals of the Roman church.

[1377]So B. E. Bowe, *A Church in Crisis* (1988) 72.

The letter is a unity, a whole, where the general treatment of concord aims to give support to Clement's advice to the leaders of the sedition about how they ought to behave in order to re-establish concord, i.e. they must submit to the presbyters. Furthermore, since concord is the basic theme of the whole letter, it follows that Clement's emphasis on the presbyterial order is subsumed under the topic of concord.[1378] Certainly, hierarchy is important for Clement, but it appears that his focus upon this issue is dependent on the main purpose of the letter. The removal of the presbyters represents a breach of the concord. Therefore, in order to re-establish concord Clement urges the instigators of the sedition to submit to the legitimate presbyters.

Thirdly, it offers a simpler, and in our opinion more satisfactory, argument for the thematic and structural unity of the letter than the rather artificial suggestion made by G. Brunner.

As has already been mentioned, the compositional analysis has tried to demonstrate that the sub-texts on different levels are integrated and function as partial arguments supporting Clement's appeal for concord. This is the definitive confirmation that *1 Clement* in fact ought to be classified and interpreted as deliberative rhetoric urging concord.

6.4. The Social-Historical Situation

The investigation in chapter 3 of political terms and *topoi* deliberately moved on a literary level and was only to a very limited degree concerned with the social-historical situation. There is, however, as has been argued, a link between how Clement describes in the *narratio* the people involved in the sedition and what he considered to be the social-historical situation. In order to avoid another interruption in the literary approach in addition to the one made in the terminological analysis, and because of the importance of the question of the social-historical situation in *1 Clement* research, this question was subsequently dealt with in a chapter of its own. Building on sociological studies of 1 Corinthians, in particular those by G. Theissen, we demonstrated that it was likely that in 3:3 Clement describes the conflict in Corinth primarily in socio-economic categories. The language Clement uses to depict the different groups of people involved in the strife, the ἄτιμοι, ἄδοξοι, and ἄφρονες who rose against the ἔντιμοι, ἔνδοξοι, and φρόνιμοι respectively, consists of common socio-political terms in antiquity. The first group of people refers to poor people of low social status while the latter group refers to people of the social and economic elite. This fact indicates that Clement regarded the conflict as a struggle for power where the poor and those of low social status strove to gain more influence in the Church, e.g., with respect to the distribution of goods. To hold an office as a presbyter was a means of obtaining such influence. Furthermore, we saw that theoretical considerations, discourses, histories and other types of literature reflected the view that conflicts between different socio-economic classes were often considered to play an important role in στάσις in the ancient world.

[1378] At this point we agree with B. E. BOWE, *A Church in Crisis* (1988) 158.

Although these circumstances neither ultimately confirm our interpretation of Clement nor answer the question of whether or not what we consider to be Clement's perception of the conflict was in fact consistent with the historical situation, they at least demonstrate that both our interpretation of Clement, and Clement's perception of the situation are reasonable.

Furthermore, another aspect which was closely related to the quest for increasing influence and power was stressed, namely the quest for honour. It was noted that the Mediterranean was an "honour-shame" culture where much of life was directed towards avoiding shame and increasing one's honour. Among the things which contributed to the latter was to hold a public office. On this basis, together with the fact that the terms Clement uses in 3:3 were associated with status and honour, it is reasonable to assume that he held the view that competition for honour was involved in the attempt to remove some of the presbyters. When Clement thus appears to hold that the quest for honour was a major factor in the sedition, it was demonstrated that he reflects the common view in antiquity that striving for honour often caused sedition. As has just been noted, the parallels in ancient literature at least indicate that Clement's perception of the underlying cause of the sedition is reasonable.

As a result, the present study argues that *1 Clement* offers a greater amount and a different kind of information about what Clement considered to be the underlying motive for the sedition than has traditionally been held to be the case by scholars. The conflict was neither a conflict between 'spirit' and 'office' nor a matter of 'doctrine', nor any other of the suggestions made by scholars so far. Instead it appears that Clement primarily regarded it as a conflict between people of different socio-economic status in which striving for honour appeared to be an important aspect.

6.5. The Result of the Present Investigation and the Question of Clement's Social Background

Finally, is it possible to say anything about Clement's social background on the basis of our findings in the present work? In chapter 1. *Introduction* it was noted that some scholars maintain that Clement's literary skills and his argumentation by means of examples suggest that he was familiar with ancient rhetoric by reason of his education. On the basis of other evidence, some scholars have more specifically argued that he was an imperial freedman of the house of Flavius Clement and Domitilla. Several of our findings appear to confirm the view that Clement was an educated man familiar with ancient rhetoric:

Firstly, the fact that the main characteristics of deliberative rhetoric are found in *1 Clement* demonstrates that Clement was able to make use of this genre to communicate his message.

Secondly, the fact that Clement employs many terms and *topoi* which are also found in other examples of deliberative rhetoric urging concord in a political body, indicates that he was familiar with this rhetorical tradition – a tradition of which Dio Chrysostom and Aelius Aristides were the most famous exponents. Further, his language of unity and sedition shows his ability to use appropriate language in dealing with the topic of concord.

Thirdly, the fact that Clement structures the *probatio* section in a θέσις with a following ὑπόθεσις demonstrates that he was able to organize the *probatio* section in a way similar to such rhetorically advanced authors as Dio Chrysostom and Aelius Aristides, and, incidentally, also the Apostle Paul in Romans.

Taking these features together we get a picture of an author with good rhetorical skills who is familiar with political terminology. This suggests that Clement was an educated man. Regarding the theory that he was an imperial freedman, we cannot of course draw any certain conclusion from the present investigation. However, it is at least possible that if he was an imperial slave, he received an education and practice which enabled him to write a document like *1 Clement*. Likewise, his familiarity with adequate political language relating to unity and sedition might be explained by his possible previous work in the imperial bureaucracy. We emphasize, however, that this cannot be more than a suggestion, although it is at least plausible – and tempting – to link Clement's rhetorical skills with the imperial freedman theory.

Appendix:
The Function of References to Christ in Clement's Argumentation for Concord

1. Introductory Remarks

This study has attempted to demonstrate that the author of *1 Clement* makes use of the system of ancient Graeco-Roman rhetoric. The letter reflects both the basic hallmarks of deliberative rhetoric and the macro-structure of this rhetorical genre. Further, a large number of terms and *topoi* associated with the ideal of concord are used throughout the letter. It appears to be safe to conclude that the author, whether conscious of this or not, used the tools of ancient political rhetoric in his attempt to persuade the Corinthians to re-establish concord and peace. This does not mean, however, that the very nature of the letter is political; the letter is clearly a religious text, and the author argues to a great extent theologically, using theological concepts and traditions.

In the compositional analysis of the letter, where an attempt has been made to delineate its argumentative structure, we have seen that throughout the letter Clement frequently appeals to and alludes to Scriptures and to Jewish and Christian traditions. Among other things, the author tries to demonstrate that his advice or solution to the crisis in Corinth is in agreement with the will of God. To obey God and to practise the Christian virtue of humility involves submitting to the legally appointed presbyters and re-establishing concord and peace. Likewise, we have noted that Clement refers to the life of Christ as the great example of the virtue of humility and love which the Corinthians are exhorted to imitate. However, the function of the Christological statements in the overall argumentation for concord has not been dealt with as an individual aspect. Therefore, in the following section this theme will be considered. It must be emphasized that the intention is not to explore the traditions Clement makes use of nor the connection to the Christology in other Early Christian writings, or Clement's Christology in general. We confine the discussion to how Christological statements function within the argumentative structure.

Though scholars' opinions regarding the profile of the Christology of the letter vary a great deal,[1379] there appears to be general agreement that the Christology of the letter

---

[1379]For overviews of the history of research on the Christology of the letter, see E. W. Fisher, *Soteriology in First Clement* (1974) 89-104; A. Lindemann, *Die Clemensbriefe* (1992) 112f.; H. E. Lona, *Der erste Clemensbrief* (1998) 398-407.

does not constitute an important element in Clement's arguments for re-establishing concord and peace.[1380] A. von Harnack, for instance, who belongs to the group of scholars that maintain that the letter reflects a tradition highlighting the centrality of Christ, comments that this tradition is "so gut wie nicht, gedankenmässig theologisch bearbeitet, sondern er ist einfach reproduziert und thetisch ausgesprochen".[1381] Is Harnack (and others) right, or ought his position to be modified?

2. Christology and Argumentation

2.1. Exordium, 1:1-2:8

The first reference to Christ following the one in the epistolary prescript is found at the beginning of the *benevolum parare* section in 1:2. Here Clement by means of four rhetorical questions praises the way in which the Corinthians previously lived. After having touched upon their noble faith, he refers to their piety (εὐσέβεια) in the second question, which is qualified as sober (σώφρων) and magnanimous (ἐπιεικής) ἐν Χριστῷ. Earlier in this study we have seen that the virtue of σωφροσύνη was associated with the concept of concord in a political body; to lay a restraint upon ones feelings and needs and to behave in a temperate manner was considered to be essential in order to protect and safeguard unity.[1382] What we shall note in this connection is the fact that Clement relates a piety with these qualities to Christ. ἐν Χριστῷ might be influenced by Pauline use, but it is difficult to decide whether this expression should be rendered 'in Christ' or if it comes close to the adjective 'Christian'.[1383] Notwithstanding the precise meaning of this phrase, Clement indicates that there is a connection between "being called and sanctified by the will of God through our Lord Jesus Christ" (prescr.) and a pious life that secures concord. This connection, however, is not emphasized and further developed in the immediate context. Instead Clement changes the focus to the Corinthians' adherence to the law of God, their obedience to their rulers and to the proper social relations between different members of the household (1:3-5).

Later on in the *benevolum pararare* section, however, a reference to Christ constitutes an important element in the argumentation. Clement commends the Corinthians for having been "satisfied with the provision of Christ" (τοῖς ἐφοδίοις τοῦ Χριστοῦ, 2:1). ἐφόδιον means literally "supplies for travelling, money and provisions",[1384] but

---

[1380]H. E. LONA, *Der erste Clemensbrief* (1998) 407, however, briefly concludes his excursus on "Die Christologie des 1 Clem" by stating "Dass 1 Clem schliesslich im Umgang mit der christlichen Überlieferung mehr bietet als eine einfach 'reproduzierte und thetisch ausgesprochene' Wiedergabe (Harnack, *Einführung* 78), zeigen sowohl die Gestalung von Aussagen wie 1 Clem 2,1 16,2.17 36,2, als auch ihre strukturelle Bedeutung".

[1381]A. VON HARNACK, *Einführung in die alte Kirchengeschichte* (1929) 77f.

[1382]See the present work, chap. 3.5.2.5.

[1383]So A. LINDEMANN, *Die Clemensbriefe* (1992) 28.

[1384]H. G. LIDDELL and R. SCOTT, *A Greek-English Lexicon* (1973) 746.

here it is used figuratively.[1385] We can infer from the immediate context what is meant by the expression "provision of Christ". In the preceding clauses Clement praises the Corinthians for certain virtues by contrasting positive and negative kinds of behaviour: The Corinthians were humble-minded and free from arrogance, they were "yielding to subjection rather than demanding it", and they were "'giving more gladly than receiving'". To be satisfied with the travel supplies of Christ involves practising the mentioned virtues. Later on in the letter the attitude of Christ is presented as the great example of the virtue of humility, which is contrasted with the vice of arrogance (13:1; 16:2). This fact indicates that the nourishment provided by Christ included his own life as an ethical example to be imitated by the Christians.[1386]

But the meaning of the expression τοῖς ἐφοδίοις τοῦ Χριστοῦ is also to be understood in the context of the following clauses where Clement accentuates that the Corinthians had paid attention to the words of Christ (τοὺς λόγους αὐτοῦ, 2:1b). It is the words of Christ which constitute the provisions for the journey. In other words, the author praises the Corinthians for having lived according to the teaching of Christ which was manifested in community life characterised by the virtues mentioned above.[1387]

The extended description of the Corinthians' attitude toward the words of Christ, i.e. that they stored up his words carefully in their hearts, serves to emphasize the authority of the teaching of Jesus and to remind them of how much they were concerned about it. It also expresses the close inner relationship between Christ and the Corinthians in the past.[1388]

Finally, Clement praises the Corinthians for having kept Christ's sufferings (παθήματα) before their eyes. This is the only passage where the author speaks about the sufferings of Christ. He mentions, however, the blood of Christ in several places (7:4; 12:7; 21:6; 49:6). Therefore it is fair to assume that he hints here at the saving acts of Christ.[1389] In brief, at the time before the strife and sedition took place the Corinthians gave their undivided attention to the teaching of Christ and their mutual relations were according to this teaching.

The described attitude toward Christ and his words led to the result that "a profound and rich peace was given to all" (οὕτως εἰρήνη βαθεῖα καὶ λιπαρὰ ἐδέδοτο

[1385]Ibid. 746 for references to metaphorical use of the term in Classical Greek. H. E. Lona, *Der erste Clemensbrief* (1998) 126, refers to Philo *Her* 273 f. as the most illuminating parallel to *1 Clem.* 2:1. Here Philo speaks of "travelling supplies" (ἐφόδια δούς) given by God, meaning his παιδεία.

[1386]On *imitatio Christi* in the New Testament, see E. LARSSON, *Christus als Vorbild* (1962) and H. D. BETZ, *Nachfolge und Nachahmung Jesu Christi im Neuen Testament* (1967).

[1387]R. KNOPF, *Das Nachapostolische Zeitalter* (1905) 46, and H. E. LONA, *Der erste Clemensbrief* (1998) 127, are of the opinion that the expression τοῖς ἐφοδίοις τοῦ Χριστοῦ refers to the preceding clause, while J. B. LIGHTFOOT, *The Apostolic Fathers I: Clement I* (1989, first pr. 1889) 12f., and A. LINDEMANN, *Die Clemensbriefe* (1992) 30, claim that it refers to τοὺς λόγους αὐτοῦ. It is not necessary to operate with either/or in this question. We find it plausible that it refers to both.

[1388]Cf. H. E. LONA, *Der erste Clemensbrief* (1998) 127.

[1389]Cf. *Ibid.* 128 and A. LINDEMANN, *Die Clemensbriefe* (1992) 30.

πᾶσιν, 2:2).[1390] On the one hand, the passive verb ἐδέδοτο indicates that the state of peace and the other gifts described in 2:2 were given by God. On the other hand, the inferential adverb οὕτως indicates that the state of peace was a manifestation of their noble Christian life. In our opinion one does not have to choose between these two assumed alternative understandings. Though the peace of the Corinthians was a manifestation of living consistently with the teaching of Christ, this state of affairs could ultimately be viewed as a gift of God.[1391]

The following clause that says that the Holy Spirit was poured out in abundance on all of them should not be taken as an expression of an alleged "Moralismus des Schreibens" in the sense that the pouring out of the Holy Spirit is seen as a reward for living a proper Christian life. Rather, it ought to be understood in the sense that the earlier stage in their community's life was a manifestation of a life consistent with the Holy Spirit.[1392] It seems that Clement does not distinguish between attitudes and behaviour associated with obedience to Christ, on the one hand, and attitudes and behaviour resulting from the work of the Holy Spirit, on the other. The ideal situation in the past as depicted in 2:1-2 is seen as a consequence both of living according to Christ and of the work of the Spirit. Likewise, it is reasonable that the content of the ensuing praise of the Corinthians in 2:1-2:7 – where Clement among other things commends them for having holy plans and the welfare of the whole brotherhood constantly in mind, for showing no malice to one another, and for the absence of all sedition and schism – comes from living a community life in accordance with Christ and the Holy Spirit.

Clement finishes his praise in 2:8 by focusing on the fact that the Corinthian's way of life was conditioned by the fear of God (ἐν τῷ φόβῳ αὐτοῦ) and that they took the Lord's (κύριος)[1393] commandments and ordinances seriously. This could be regarded as a summary of the basic attitude of the Corinthians as it has been depicted in 1:2-2:7. At this point one can observe the theocentric perspective so typical of the letter. It is, however, a matter of fact that when Clement describes the ideal life of the Christian community he relates it to the presence of the Holy Spirit, to living according to the words of Christ, and to obeying the will of God. In other words in the *benevolum parare* section his theological argumentation is characterised by fluid transitions between theocentric, Christological and pneumatical perspectives.

[1390]"In der Gemeinde ... herrschte aufgrund der dargestellten Voraussetzungen tiefer und fruchtbarer ... Friede", A. LINDEMANN, *Die Clemensbriefe* (1992) 30.

[1391]"Der in 2,1 geschilderten vorbildlichen Haltung der Korinther und ihrer Beziehung zu Christus entsprechen die in V. 2 erwähnten Gaben Gottes (darum der Anfang mit οὕτως). Denn das Passiv ἐδέδοτο umschreibt das Werk Gottes. Seine Gaben sind zuerst der Friede und das ständige Verlangen, Gutes zu tun", H. E. LONA, *Der erste Clemensbrief* (1998) 128.

[1392]See the discussion in A. LINDEMANN, *Die Clemensbriefe* (1992) 30; H. E. LONA, *Der erste Clemensbrief* (1998) 129f.

[1393]κύριος in 2:8b is probably a designation for God and not Christ, cf. A. LINDEMANN, *Die Clemensbriefe* (1992) 31; H. E. LONA, *Der erste Clemensbrief* (1998) 135.

2.2. Narratio, 3:1-4

This is also the case with respect to the *narratio* (3:1-4). When the author deals with the "fall" of the Corinthian Christians here, he diagnoses the cause for the present strife and sedition as due to the fact that they no longer live according to the will of God as it is expressed in his commandments, nor do they "use their citizenship worthily (τὸ καθῆκον) of Christ" (3:4). The author does not distinguish between paying attention to the will of God and living a life worthy of Christ; these expressions are used interchangeably.[1394]

So far we can conclude that we find Christological statements both in the *exordium* and the *narratio*. In spite of the fact that these statements are not further developed and the Christology is not unfolded, they are integrated into and function as basic elements in Clement's argumentation. He connects attitudes and behaviour that would secure peace among the Christians with an adequate response to Christ and his message. To follow the example of Christ and to live according to the teaching of Jesus affects the Corinthians' community life in such a way that it leads to peace; to ignore the "words of Christ" leads to strife and sedition. Here it must be emphasized that it is of special importance that Christological arguments are present in exactly these parts of the *dispositio*, since the *exordium* introduces the main theme and the main topics of the letter and the *narratio* provides a brief summary of the occurrences that have taken place.

As we have seen previously in this study, when Clement comes to specific virtues and behaviour he uses a great number of political terms and *topoi*. This should not be taken as a contradiction to a theological argumentation. Although the author argues theologically, for example appealing to God and his commandments, or to the teaching of Jesus, he can at the same time use political language and political *topoi* when he finds it useful. On account of the political nature of the main topic of the letter – strife and sedition in a political body – this is exactly what one would expect Clement to do.

2.3. Probatio, 4:1- 61:3

2.3.1. Quaestio infinita, 4:1-39:9

Let us turn now to the *probatio* section. After Clement in 4:1-6:4 has attempted to demonstrate that the Corinthians are in need of repentance, he encourages them to fix their eyes on the "Blood of Christ" (τὸ αἷμα τοῦ Χριστοῦ) which was poured out for their salvation (7:4). This is the first Christological-soteriological statement in the letter and reflects a way of referring to the atoning power of Christ which is common in the New Testament.[1395] Its main argumentative function is to show that the "grace of repentance" is brought to the whole world, and that this has happened by the will of God.

[1394]"Auch die negative Folie des idealen Zustandes der Gemeinde zeigt noch, dass Gottes- und Christusforderung deckungsgleich sind. Die Abweichung vom Weg Gottes ist zugleich Abweichung von dem, was sich gegenüber Christus gebührt", H. E. LONA, *Der erste Clemensbrief* (1998) 145.

[1395]H. B. BUMPUS, *The Christological Awareness of Clement of Rome and its Sources* (1972) 87; A. LINDEMANN, *Die Clemensbriefe* (1992) 44; H. E. LONA, *Der erste Clemensbrief* (1998) 177.

From God's dealing with his people in the Old Testament one can observe that in every age God has given the opportunity for repentance (7:5-8:5). But now, and this is the basic point for Clement, the death of Christ has made universal the grace of repentance that already existed in the Old Covenant, and thereby at the present time the Corinthians have the possibility to repent. One notes, however, that – and this reflects Clement's theocentric perspective – he once more emphasizes that the opportunity for repentance and salvation is ultimately rooted in God's Almighty will (8:5). Furthermore, when it comes to the explicit exhortation to repent, which implies a cessation from strife, the motivation for doing so is obedience to God's "excellent and glorious will" (9:1). In the following section Clement presents examples from the Old Testament that aim to support this exhortation (9:2-12:8).

How should we then evaluate the role of the Christological statement in 7:4 in the overall argumentation? No doubt, it is a substantial and important soteriological statement in itself, and it is interesting with respect to which Christological traditions it reflects. When it comes to its function in the argumentation, it plays a certain role as far as it is used to emphasize that repentance is universal and thus available for the Corinthians. One can say, therefore, that it constitutes a premise for Clement's exhortations to repent and to obey God. It is obvious, however, that his argumentation has a clear theocentric profile; the main focus is that repentance is according to the will of God and to repent means to obey His will. The argument would not have been weakened much if Clement had not made the reference to the atoning work of Christ and what it achieved. The examples taken from the Old Testament clarify the basic point, i.e. repentance is possible and that God desires people to turn to him. Therefore it is difficult to escape the impression that the Christological statement functions as a secondary argument within the overall theocentric approach.

In the following text-sequence (13:1-19:1), however, references to the teaching of Christ and his example play a substantial role. Here the author exhorts the Corinthians to practise the virtue of humility which is seen to be a consequence of obeying the will of God.[1396] He also establishes a connection between being humble minded and concord.[1397] After having introduced the topic of being humble minded in the exhortation in 13:1, he demonstrates that Scripture and the teaching of Christ supports it. First he quotes Jer. 9:23f, and then he underscores the need to remember "the words of the Lord Jesus which he spoke when he was teaching gentleness (ἐπιείκεια) and long-suffering" (μακροθυμία, 13:1b). Though one cannot identify the succeeding *logia* of Jesus in 13:2 with a particular text of the New Testament, it reflects the language of the Sermon on the Mount.[1398] Clement obviously connects gentleness (ἐπιείκεια) and long-suffering (μακροθυμία) with ταπεινοφροσύνη.[1399] The most important thing

---

[1396]See the present study, p. 242.

[1397]See the present study, pp. 242-245.

[1398]A. LINDEMANN, *Die Clemensbriefe* (1992) 54; H. E. LONA, *Der erste Clemensbrief* (1998) 214-216.

[1399]Cf. *1 Clem.* 30:8; 56:1; 58:2; 62:2.

to note in our connection is the fact that the author accentuates the authority of and the content of Jesus' teaching in his argumentative strategy.

In 14:1-15:6 Clement draws the conclusion on the basis of the above arguments that one should obey God rather than follow those engaged in sedition and also provides further evidence from the Old Testament in order to support this exhortation. With respect to the subject of the present appendix one observes that he again returns to a theocentric perspective; the focus of Jesus' teaching serves to strengthen the exhortation to behave according to the will of God. But in 16:1 he also refers to Christ, saying that it is those who are humble minded who belong to him. Previously in this study we have argued that γάρ in 16:1 refers back to the whole preceding passage (13:1-15:7). Thus this reference to Christ serves to strengthen the argumentation for concord.[1400] If Christ is for those practising humility, it is implied that it is vital for the Corinthians to be humble-minded.

As an important element of his argument, Clement establishes, as just mentioned, a connection between humility and concord. This appears to reflect a deliberate strategy since many biblical examples are found of people who are held in high esteem because of their humility. In 16:2-19:1 he presents a considerable number of such examples of whom Christ is both the first mentioned and the most extensively cited. Christ and his humility are contrasted with people marked by arrogance (ἀλαζονεία) and pride (ὑπερηφανία, 16:2). Since these vices, according to Clement, were characteristic of people involved in strife and sedition, it is not accidental that he makes this contrast. The subsequent extensive quotations of Isa 53:1-12 and of Ps 21:7-9 serve as proof texts for the assertion that Christ was humble-minded. In 16:2, where the author explicitly draws the conclusion of his arguments in 16:2ff., Clement both emphasizes the greatness of this example (ὑπογραμμός) of humility – it is the Lord himself – and urges the Corinthians to imitate Christ by means of a rhetorical question: "... for if the Lord was thus humble-minded, what shall we do, who through him have come under the yoke of his grace?" In brief, Christ is described as the ultimate example of humility. The ensuing list of noble examples taken from the Old Testament serves to highlight that the virtue of humility has always been characteristic of the people of God (17:1-19:1). As asserted elsewhere in this study, 16:2-19:1 is intended to lend support to and reinforce Clement's arguments in 13:1-16:1 about the necessity of being humble-minded, which in turn implies a cessation of strife and sedition.[1401] Within this text segment, the appeal to imitate the example of Christ constitutes a significant element. Thus, it is fair to maintain that in this part of the letter Christological statements are integrated in Clement's overall arguments to achieve concord.

The next Christological statement of interest occurs in 21:6. Here Clement urges the Corinthians to show reverence to the Lord Jesus "whose blood was given for us". This statement is followed by exhortations dealing with proper relations between certain groups of the household and with how to instruct the young in the fear of God and

---

[1400]See the present study, p. 245.
[1401]See the present study, pp. 245-247.

the children in the *paideia* of Christ (21:6-8). The broader context of the Christological statement in 21:6 is the text-sequence 19:2-23:1 in which the main line of argumentation is that the order, peace and harmony of nature established by God is an example of the order, peace and harmony which should prevail in a Christian community.[1402] A key element in Clement's argument is that such behaviour involves submission to the will of God (21:1-4). When he gives a positive explanation of what this means in 21:6-8, he first exhorts the readers of the letter to show reverence to the Lord Jesus.[1403] From what we have seen above, among other things this involves paying attention to the words of Christ and imitating the humility of Christ. The reference to Jesus' blood appears strange at first sight. It makes sense, however, if the passion and death of Christ is seen as an expression of the attitude of Christ's love and humility which should be imitated by the Corinthians.[1404] Notwithstanding this, to reverence the Lord Jesus implies submitting to the will of God. The ensuing instructions in 21:6-8 could well be understood as a further explanation of what it means for different members of the community to reverence Christ. With respect to the instruction dealing with how to educate children this is explicitly expressed: "Let our children share in the instruction which is in Christ" (ἐν Χριστῷ παιδείας, 21:8). Furthermore, in 22:1 Clement asserts that "all these things" (ταῦτα πάντα) are confirmed by "the faith which is in Christ" (ἐν Χριστῷ πίστις). Though ταῦτα πάντα refers to the whole preceding chapter, it is especially relevant with respect to 22:6-9. Thus Clement supports the interpretation of 21:6-8 mentioned above. The most important aspect to be noted in this connection is the fact that the Christological statements are integrated into and play a large part in his strategy of argumentation. They serve to lend support to the exhortation to submit to the will of God (21:1:4), which in the context means to cease from strife and sedition and to establish order, peace, and concord in the Christian community. Notwithstanding this fact, as just indicated, the overall argument in the text-sequence 19:2-23:1 has a clear theocentric profile. It takes its starting point in certain principles the Master has established in nature, and applies these principals to the Christian community. To transfer these principals to the life of the community is thus in concord with the will of God. In this context the Christological statements function as a support for the main argument (i.e. they constitute a secondary line of argument) in the sense that they aim to demonstrate that "to reverence" Christ requires the Christians to obey the will of God.

In the following text-sequence (23:1-28:4) the theocentric profile is even stronger. By focusing upon the promised resurrection in the future, Clement attempts to show

---

[1402]See the present study, pp. 247-249.

[1403]Cf. A. LINDEMANN, *Die Clemensbriefe* (1992) 78: "In V. 4 folgt eine Anwendung, aus der sich dann in V. 5-8 die den Begriff 'Gottes Willen' explizierende konkrete Paränese ergibt (in V. 6-8 im Stil der 'Haustafel')".

[1404]H. B. BUMPUS, *The Christological Awareness of Clement of Rome and its Sources* (1972) 66, after having discussed Phil 2 and 1 Pet 3:12-4:5, notes that "The example of Christ for the moral life of the Christian is always situated in the perspective of the Passion and of the salvific work of Christ … As he was humble, so ought the members of the Christian community also be humble".

that there is no reason to be double-minded regarding God's "excellent and glorious gifts" (23:2). God is faithful and will fulfil his promises, and therefore, argues Clement, the Christians should be bound to God (27:1). Such closeness to God causes one to fear God and abstain from evil deeds (28:1), which again implies cessation of strife and sedition.[1405] The Christological reference in 23:5 alludes to the *parousia*. In 24:1 the author encourages the Corinthians to consider (κατανοήσωμεν) "how the Master continually proves to us that there will be a future resurrection" of which the Master made the Lord Jesus Christ the first-fruit when he raised him from the dead. However, this in itself rich and interesting Christological statement does not appear to be a part of the proof, since Clement finds it necessary to repeat his exhortation with "let us look" (ἴδωμεν) when in the subsequent clause he introduces the examples of certain phenomena of nature in which God foreshadows a future resurrection (24:2).[1406] It is the continuous change between day and night, the growth of the grain, and the story about the bird Phoenix that are meant to demonstrate the validity of the statement in 24:1. Perhaps the reference to the resurrection of Jesus ought to be seen in the light of the hint about the *parousia* in 23:5, i.e. that the resurrection of Jesus is a precondition for the *parousia* and that it should strengthen the Christians in their belief that the *parousia* really is going to take place. According to this understanding the Christological statement in 24:1 constitutes an element in the argumentation for the fact that one can trust that God will fulfil his promise of a resurrection in the future. On the whole, however, though Christological statements are integrated into the overall argumentation in the text-sequence 23:1-28:4, they are not critical to the conclusion. The focus is upon God with regard to the signs he has given in order to show that there is no reason to have any doubt regarding his promised glorious gifts. Therefore the Christians must adhere to God and his will, or to use the words of Clement: "be bound to him" (27:1).

Christological statements play an even smaller part in the argument presented in the passage 29:1-36:6. Here the author exhorts the Corinthians to draw the proper consequence of what he has said in the preceding passage, i.e. to live in holiness. Among other things his proposed way of living involves practising virtues and behaving in a way that establishes communal concord.

This sub-text (29:1-36:6) also presents a striking theocentric profile: Because God is holy the Christians are encouraged to "do all the deeds of sanctification" (29:1-30:8) and are exhorted to imitate those biblical examples who were blessed by God (31:1-32:2). Throughout the section the Christians are both implicitly and explicitly exhorted to practise virtues and to live in a way that is consistent with the will of God. Because the author establishes a connection between living a life in holiness and concord, the exhortations to behave in a way associated with holiness aim at re-establishing this ideal among the Corinthians.

At the end of the text-sequence Clement includes a relatively extensive Christological interpretation of the quotation of Ps. 49:23 in 35:5 – in fact this interpretation con-

---

[1405]See the discussion in the present investigation, 251f.
[1406]So also R. M. GRANT and H. H. GRAHAM, *First and Second Clement* (1965) 50.

stitutes the most extensive Christological statement of the entire letter! This verse is a part of a longer quotation of Ps. 49 that aims to show that those who do not pay attention to the proposed course of behaviour are hated by God and will be judged by him. Jesus Christ is the way of salvation, he is described as the High Priest and as a great helper of our weakness (36:1). In 36:2 five parallel διὰ τούτου clauses follow that deal with different gifts of salvation mediated through Christ, and 36:3-5 consists of quotations from Scripture serving to confirm the given Christological interpretation.[1407] Earlier in this study we have labelled this Christological statement as an excursus. It contains many interesting elements with respect to the Christology of the letter in general. 36:1-2 is an essential passage if one wants to investigate the Christological awareness of the letter and the tradition which it reflects. In spite of this fact, the passage is very loosely integrated in the overall argumentation.

In the following passage (37:1-39:9) one reference to Jesus Christ occurs. Clement exhorts the Christians to let their "whole body be preserved in Christ Jesus" (38:1). The immediate context he presents is the image of the human body, and in it he emphasizes how its different members depend on each other in order to preserve the whole body; all of them "work together and are united in a common subjection" (37:5). In 38:1 he applies the image of the body to the Christian community. Each individual Christian must subordinate himself to his neighbour according to his individual χάρισμα. As it is argued elsewhere in this study, χάρισμα refers to the socio-economic gifts and the particular virtues of individual members of the Church.[1408] In order to preserve the whole body, that is the Corinthian Church, Clement appeals to people of different socio-economic levels to fulfil their duty according to their appointed position. Clement's application of the body metaphor reflects basic structures of patron-client relations, i.e. a reciprocal exchange of different resources.[1409]

What we should note and consider in this connection, however, is the fact that Clement introduces the application by making a reference to Christ, i.e. that the whole body should be preserved in Christ (ἐν Χριστῷ). How should one evaluate the function of this brief Christological statement with respect to the argument being presented? It seems that the author makes a connection between adhering to Christ and the proposed course of action.[1410] If the whole community is to be preserved, the members of the church must behave in a way that is consistent with Christ and his teaching. Clement does not argue explicitly how and why his proposal is in line with the message of Christ, but he appears to presuppose that this is the case. The expression "in Christ" has the effect of creating the impression that what follows is based not on his

---

[1407]Due to the consciously elaborated style and the parallel structure of the five διὰ τούτου clauses several scholars have argued that Clement makes use of liturgical language at this point, see the discussion in H. E. LONA, *Der erste Clemensbrief* (1998) 388-397. We are more convinced by Lona's conclusion that Clement is instead reflecting the language of Hebr 1.

[1408]See the present study, p. 297.

[1409]See the present study, pp. 312f.

[1410]Cf. H. E. LONA, *Der erste Clemensbrief* (1998) 416: "Der Erlöser ist der Bezugspunkt bzw. der Raum, in dem der von den Gläubigen gebildete Leib erhalten bleiben kann".

own authoritative view, but ultimately on Jesus Christ himself. Therefore, one might argue that the Christological statement in 28:1 is integrated into the overall argumentation. Its basic function is to lend support to exhortations to live in a way that re-establish concord among the Christians.

Notwithstanding this fact, one might question how substantial the Christological statement really is for the main line of thought in this passage. 38:1-4 is primarily an application of the image of the body outlined in 37:5, but it could also be regarded as an application of the examples of the Roman army and the political ideal of "the mixed constitution" embedded in the expression σύγκρασίς τίς ἐστιν ἐν πᾶσιν (37:1-4). This means that no reference to Christ and to his work occurs in the passages which are applied. Clement could have made the same application and basically kept the same argumentation without including the brief Christological statement. This does not mean that the Christological statement does not strengthen and lend support to the authors argumentative strategy. Our point is merely that it does not constitute a substantial element.

2.3.2. Quaestio finita, 40:1-61:3

In the first sub-text of the ὑπόθεσις (40:1-43:6) Clement focuses upon the fact that God requires order in the Church. He emphasizes that order is according to the will of God, and therefore each one of the Corinthians should strive towards pleasing God in his own rank (41:1). After having used the cult of the Temple as an example of the need for order, he passes to the order of the apostolic times. In this connection he makes a reference to Christ. God sent Christ from whom the apostles received the Gospel; therefore both Christ and the apostles "were in accordance with the appointed order of God's will" (42:2). Further, the apostles appointed some of their first converts to be bishops and deacons (42:4). Thereby Clement establishes the following line of authority: God, Christ, Apostles, Bishops, and Deacons. The main point for Clement is to demonstrate that an order that includes different offices is according to the will of God, and that the holders of the offices ultimately derive their authority and legitimacy from God. From this it follows that the reference to Christ makes up an essential part of Clement's proof; Christ is a necessary part of the chain of authority beginning with God and ending with the holders of the office. This means that the Christological statement is integrated into the overall argumentation in this passage. Nevertheless, the line of argument in it also has a striking theocentric profile. The reference to Christ serves to support the view that order in the Church is according to the will of God.

In 44:1-47:7 Clement blames the Corinthians for the present strife. First he argues, starting from his conception of apostolic succession, that the removal of the presbyters is a great sin (44:1-6). By using evidence from Scripture he then argues that the Corinthians have placed themselves among the wicked and the law-breakers (45:1-45:8). Instead the Corinthians ought to belong to the innocent and righteous (46:4). Then as a part of the strategy to make the Corinthians realize how foolish their present course of behaviour is, by means of a rhetorical question he reminds them of the fact that God is one, Christ is one, and the Spirit is one. Furthermore, he refers to the fact that the Christians are members of the same body of Christ. He wants to make them realize the madness of raising "up strife against our own body" (46:5-7). He clearly establishes a connection between the oneness of Christ and the oneness of the Christians, as he also does with respect to God and to the Spirit. The main line of thought is that because Christ is one there should be no strife among the Christians; the oneness of Christ has to be manifested in the unity of the Christian community. Furthermore, if one follows the idea that the Christians are members of the body of Christ, then the consequence of strife among the members is destruction of the body; i.e. it is a contradiction to belong to Christ and at the same time to be involved in strife against fellow Christians.

The quotations of, and allusions to, different *logia* of Jesus in 46:8 underscores the danger associated with the present situation. In particular the statement that it was better for a man "that a millstone be hung on him, and he be cast into the sea, than that he should turn aside one of my elect" functions as a strong warning directed primarily to the instigators of the sedition. According to Clement they indeed are in great danger because their schism has caused many to turn aside (46:9).

As a part of the continued strategy to make the Corinthians realize how unsatisfactory the present state of affairs is, he asserts that their conduct is unworthy of their position in Christ (47:6). Within this passage Christological statements and a reference to the teaching of Christ make up a relatively significant element in the argumentation. Clement attempts to demonstrate that the current partisanship of the Corinthians is contradictory to being Christians and to the conduct of a life consistent with the will of Christ.

After having strongly condemned the ongoing strife, Clement exhorts the Corinthians in 48:1-58:2 to put an end to this situation. Several references to Christ occur in this passage, though only a few of them play important roles in the main line of argumentation. In 48:2-3 the author quotes Ps. 117:19f., and then he gives the passage a Christological interpretation (48:4), i.e. Christ is "the gate of righteousness which opens on to life" (48:2). One should observe that Clement links particular virtues such as holiness and righteousness to those who enter this gate in Christ and carry out their duties in an orderly fashion. Though the author does not present any evidence, he obviously draws a connection between entering the gate in Christ and certain virtues that contribute to peace and concord among the Christians.[1411] In this way he provides a Christological basis for his exhortation to practise the actual virtues.

References to Christ constitute a substantial element in the first part of the argumentation in 49:1-55:6. In this passage the author focuses on the greatness of love and applies the principal of love to the problem of sedition in Corinth. One notes that Clement introduces the panegyric of love by exhorting those who have love in Christ to fulfil the commandments of Christ (49:1). Thus, the subsequent description of the nature of love is to be taken as an expression of that kind of love that is consistent with Christ and his commandments. By means of the already mentioned introduction

---

[1411]See above, pp. 264f. and chap. 3.5.2.16 respectively.

Clement gives a Christological motivation for practising the aspects of love that he accentuates. The statement that "love admits no schism, love makes no sedition, love does all things in concord" (49:5) is directly related to the situation in Corinth. Although, the practice of love is given a clear Christological motivation, one should note that at the same time it is given a theocentric motivation. It is particularly note-worthy that the description of the nature of love immediately follows upon the state-ment where Clement asks if anyone is able to adequately describe the love of God (49:2). This is a typical example of how Clement can move from a Christological to a theocentric perspective and vice versa.

When it comes to the application, the theocentric perspective is the dominating one: The Christians are exhorted to pray to God that they "may be found in love, with-out human partisanship" (50:2); they are called blessed if they "perform the command-ments of God in the concord of love" (50:5); and the blessing is for those who "have been chosen by God through Jesus Christ" (50:7). The last statement is characteristic for the instrumental profile of the letter's Christology in general: Christ is to a great extent seen as God's mediator of salvation; Christ is regarded as the instrument that mediates the gift of God's salvation.[1412]

In 51:1-55:6 Clement continues with the application of the principal of love to the Corinthians and also introduces a new argument for the need of practising love. He argues that, since love implies that one should seek the common good, the instigators of the sedition should voluntarily leave the Church. Much of this passage consists of both negative and positive examples taken from the Old Testament, aiming to demon-strate the bad faith of those who rebelled against the servants of God and that true love is manifested in the willingness to sacrifice one's own interests and ambitions. Clement also includes examples of loving self-sacrifice for the benefit of others taken from the heathen and from the life of the Early Christians (55:1-3). The only reference to Christ in this passage is found in 54:3. Here Clement appeals to those who have caused sedi-tion and strife, telling them that they will achieve "great glory in Christ" if they volun-tarily leave the Church and thereby contribute to the well-being of others, i.e. the restoration of peace. Although this reference to Christ serves his overall argumentation, since Christians in general are attracted by attaining honour in Christ (and in particu-lar Christians living in a culture where honour had a pivotal value), it does not make up a substantial element. As a matter of fact, it is rather striking that Clement does not use the life of Christ as an example of loving self-sacrifice.

Likewise, Christological statements do not constitute an important part of the argumentation in 56:1-58. Here Clement focuses upon the need for correction first. He describes the admonition given in the letter as "good and beyond measure helpful, for it

---

[1412]On this aspect by Clement's Christology, see O. B. KNOCH, *Eigenart und Bedeutung der Escha-tologie im theologischen Aufriss des ersten Clemensbriefes* (1964) 341-347; H. B. BUMPUS, *The Christo-logical Awareness of Clement of Rome and its Sources* (1972) 126-167.

unites us to the will of God" (56:2) before he addresses the leaders of the sedition and exhorts them to "submit to the presbyters, and receive the correction of repentance" (57:1). The only reference to Christ occurs in an oath containing a Trinitarian formula. The immediate context is that Clement promises that if those who laid the foundation of the strife accept his advice they will have no regrets. He then confirms the promise by an oath saying that "for as God lives and as the Lord Jesus Christ lives and the Holy Spirit" they who obey God's commandments will be enrolled in the number of those being saved through Jesus Christ (58:2). In other words, he asserts that the salvation of the Corinthians through Jesus Christ depends on their response to his advice. As far as one can take it for granted that the ultimate goal of the Corinthians was to gain salvation through Christ, this Christological statement functions as a powerful support for the main purpose of the letter.

In the introduction to the prayer in 59:3-63:1 Clement reiterates negatively what he stated in 58:1-2: To disobey what he has said in the letter will be to disobey God, and as he emphasizes, this involves the great danger of not achieving salvation through Christ (59:1-2). The prayer has a clear theocentric profile, and the few references to Christ are not substantial with respect to its content.

2.4. Peroratio, 62:1-64:1

The theocentric profile is even stronger in the *peroratio* (62:1-64:1). It is striking that when Clement here enumerates some of the most important topics of the *probatio* (4:1-61:3) and reiterates what he is likely to consider to be the most persuasive argument for concord (the examples of forefathers), he in fact has not a single reference to Christ. He says that he has reminded the Corinthians that they must please Almighty God – that implies among other things the need to re-establish concord, peace, and the practise of love. Furthermore, he reminds the readers of the examples he has referred to throughout the letter, that they "were well-pleasing in their humility towards God, the Father and Creator". But there is no reference to the example of Christ and his teaching.

2.5. Summary

What conclusion can one then draw concerning the function of the Christological statements in Clement's line of argument? By and large the theological argument has a theocentric profile in the sense that throughout the letter he appeals to God, his deeds, his will and commandments in order to get the Corinthians to behave in a proper way. However, this profile does not mean that Christological argumentation is insignificant or absent. On the contrary, in several parts of the letter Christological statements constitute a substantial element of the argument. This is particularly clear with respect to the *exordium* and the *narratio*, but also with respect to passages on higher levels (16:2-19:1; 21:1-22:9; 46:1-9; 47:1-7; 49:1-6). Furthermore, in several passages Christological statements are integrated into the overall argumentation, although they do not make up a substantial element. Although a number of Christological statements that appear to be loosely incorporated into the main line of thought can also be found, we cannot follow the view of A. Harnack that the Christology of the letter as a rule "ist einfach reproduziert und thetisch ausgesprochen".[1413] Clement to a great extent incorporates the Christological traditions he makes use of into his argumentation. Notwithstanding this fact, we shall not overstate the argumentative role of the Christology in the letter as a whole. Although Christological statements constitute a significant element in the fabric of argumentation in certain parts of the letter, the theocentric perspective is definitely the predominant one.

[1413] A. VON HARNACK, *Einführung in die alte Kirchengeschichte* (1929) 77f. Cf. H. E. LONA, *Der erste Clemensbrief* (1998) 407.

Bibliography

REFERENCE WORKS

Bauer, W. A. *A Greek-English Lexicon of the New Testament and Other Early Christian Literature.* Trans. and rev. W. F. Arnt, F. W. Gingrich and F. W. Danker. 2nd ed. Chicago, IL: University of Chicago Press, 1979.

Betz, H. D., Browning, D. S. *et al.*, eds. *Religion in Geschichte und Gegenwart. Handwörterbuch für Theologie und Religionswissenschaft.* Vierte, völlig neu bearbeitete Auflage. Tübingen: Mohr, 1998-

Cancik, H. and Schneider, H., eds. *Der neue Pauly: Enzyklopädie der Antike.* Stuttgart: Weimar, 1996-

Glare, P. G. W., ed. *Oxford Latin Dictionary.* Oxford: Clarendon, 1982.

Hammond, N. G. L and Scullard, H. H., eds. *The Oxford Classical Dictionary.* 2nd ed. Oxford: Clarendon, 1970.

Hatch, E. and Redpath, H. A. *A Concordance to the Septuagint and the other Greek Versions of the Old Testament (Including the Apocryphal Books).* 2 vols. Unveränderter Nachdruck der 1897 in Oxford, Clarendon Press erschienenen Ausgabe. Graz: Akademische Druck- U. Verlagsanstalt, 1954.

Kittel, G., ed. *Theological Dictionary of the New Testament.* 10 vols. Trans. G. W. Bromiley. Grand Rapids, MI: Eerdmans, 1964-76.

Kraft, H. *Clavis Patrum Apostolicorum.* Darmstadt: Wissenschaftliche Buchgesellschaft, 1963.

Klauser, T., Dassmann, E. *et al.*, eds. *Reallexikon für Antike und Christentum.* Stuttgart: Hiersemann, 1950 -.

Lampe, G. W. H., ed. *A Patristic Greek Lexicon.* Oxford: Clarendon, 1961.

Liddell, H. G. and Scott, R. *A Greek-English Lexicon.* 9th edition. Oxford: Clarendon, 1973.

Louw, J. P. and Nida, E. A., eds. *Greek-English Lexicon of the New Testament. Based on Semantic Domains.* 2nd edition. New York, NY: United Bible Societies, 1989.

Morrish, G. *A Concordance of the Septuagint.* Grand Rapids, MI: Zondervan, 1983.

Pilch, J. J. and Malina, B. J., eds. *Biblical Social Values and Their Meaning. A Handbook.* Peabody, MA: Hendrickson, 1993.

Schmoller, A. *Handkonkordanz zum Griechischen Neuen Testament.* 7th ed. Stuttgart: Deutsche Bibelgesellschaft, 1938.

Schwertner, S. M. *Abkürzungsverzeichnis, Theologische Realenzyklopädie.* 2nd. ed. Berlin: de Gruyter, 1994.

Speake, G., ed. *A Dictionary of Ancient History.* Oxford: Blackwell, 1994.

Spicq, C. *Theological Lexicon of the New Testament.* 3 vols. Trans. and ed. J. D. Ernest. Peabody, MA: Hendrickson, 1994.

Ueding, G., ed. *Historisches Wörterbuch der Rhetorik.* Tübingen: Niemeyer, 1992 -

Urbán, A. *Concordantia in Patres Apostolicos.* Pars. 3. *Primae Epistulae Clementis Romani ad Corinthios Concordantia. Alpha -Omega.* Reihe A: Lexica - Indizes - Konkordanzen zur klassischen Philologie 164. Hildesheim: Olms-Weidmann, 1996.

1 Clement: Texts and Translations

Andrén, O. *De Apostoliska Fäderna i svensk översättning.* Stockholm: Svenska Kyrkans Diakonistyrelses Bokförlag, 1958.

Bihlmeyer, K., ed. *Die Apostolischen Väter. Neubearbeitung der Funkschen Ausgabe. Erster Teil: Didache, Barnabas, Klemens I und II, Ignatius, Polykarp, Papias, Quadratus, Diognetbrief.* SAQ II:1/1. 2. ed. Tübingen: Mohr, 1956.

Fischer, J. A., ed. and trans. *Die Apostolichen Väter.* 5th ed. Schriften des Urchristentums 1. Darmstadt: Wissenschaftliche Buchgesellschaft, 1966.

Goodspeed, E. J. *The Apostolic Fathers. An American Translation.* London: Independent Press, 1950.

Grant, R. M. and Graham, H. H. *First and Second Clement.* The Apostolic Fathers. A New Translation and Commentary. Vol. 2. New York, NY: Thomas Nelson & Sons, 1965.

Holmes, M. W., ed. and rev. *The Apostolic Fathers. Greek Texts and English Translations of their Writings.* Translated by J. B. Lightfoot and J. R. Harmer. 2. rev. ed. Grand Rapids, MI: Baker Book House, 1992.

Hyldahl, N. "Første Klemensbrev." In *De apostolske Fædre i dansk oversættelse med inledninger og noter.* Eds. N. J. Cappelørn, N. Hyldahl and B. Wiberg. København: Det danske Bibelselskab, 1985, 43-96.

Kleist, J. A. *The Epistles of St. Clement of Rome and St. Ignatius of Antioch.* ACW 1. Westminister: Newman Bookshop, 1946.

Lake, K. *The Apostolic Fathers with an English Translation.* 2 Vols. LCL. Cambridge, MA: Harvard UP, 1959-65, first pr. 1912-13.

Lindemann, A., trans. "Erster Clemensbrief." In *Die apostolichen Väter. Griechisch-deutsche Parallelausgabe auf der Grundlage der Ausgaben von Franz Xaver Funk/Karl Bihlmeyer und Molly Whittaker.* Eds. A. Lindemann and H. Paulsen. Tübingen: Mohr, 1992, 77-151.

Rian, B., trans. "1. Klemensbrev." In *De Apostoliske Fedre i norsk oversettelse med innledninger og noter.* Eds. E. Baasland and R. Hvalvik. Oslo: Luther Forlag, 1984, 123-152.

Schneider, G., trans. *Clemens von Rom. Brief an die Korinther. Griechisch, Lateinisch, Deutsch.* FC 15. Freiburg: Herder, 1994.

ANCIENT SOURCES: TEXTS, EDITIONS, TRANSLATIONS

Aeschylus. 2 vols. Trans. H. W. Smyth. LCL. Cambridge, MA: Harvard UP, 1983-88. First pr. 1922-26.

Anaximenes. *Anaximenis ars rhetorica.* Ed. M. Fuhrmann. Leipzig: Teubner, 1966.

Andocides. *Minor Attic Orators.* Vol. 1. Trans. K. J. Maidment. LCL. Cambridge, MA: Harvard UP, 1982. First pr. 1941.

Antiphon. *Minor Attic Orators.* Vol. 1. Trans. K. J. Maidment. LCL. Cambridge, MA: Harvard UP, 1982. First pr. 1941.

The Apocrypha and Pseudepigrapha of the Old Testament in English. 2 vols. Ed. R. H. Charles. Oxford: Clarendon, 1913.

The Apostolic Fathers with an English Translation. 2 vols. Trans. K. Lake. LCL. Cambridge, MA: Harvard UP, 1959-65, first pr. 1912-13.

Die apostolichen Väter. Ed. J. A. Fisher. Schriften des Urchristentums 1. Darmstadt: Wissenschaftliche Buchgesellschaft, 1966.

De Apostoliske Fedre i norsk oversettelse med innledninger og noter. Eds. E. Baasland and R. Hvalvik. Oslo: Luther Forlag, 1984.

De Apostolske Fædre i dansk oversættelse med indledninger og noter. Eds. N. J. Cappelørn, N. Hyldahl and B. Wiberg. København: Det danske Bibelselskab, 1985.

Appian. *Roman History.* 4 vols. Trans. H. White. LCL. New York, NY: Macmillan, 1912-28.

Aristides. 2 vols. Ed. W. Dindorf. Leipzig: Reimer, 1829.

P. Aelius Aristides. *The Complete Works.* 2 vols. Trans. and ed. C. A. Behr. Leiden: Brill, 1981-86.

Aristotle. 23 vols. Trans H. P. Cooke, H. Tredennick, *et al.* LCL. Cambridge, MA: Harvard UP, 1938-60.

[Aristotle]. *De Mundo.* Trans. D. J. Furley. LCL. In Aristotle, *On Sophistical Refutations, On Comimg-to-Be and Passing Away, The Cosmos.* Cambridge, MA: Harvard UP, 1955.

[Aristotle]. *Rhetorica ad Alexandrum.* Trans. H. Rackham. LCL. Vol. with Aristotle, *Problems II.* Cambridge, MA: Harvard UP, 1983. First. pr. 1937.

Athenaeus. *The Deipnosophists.* 7. vols. Trans. C. B. Gulick. LCL. Cambridge, MA: Harvard UP, 1927-41.

Athenagoras. *Supplique au Suject des Chrétiens.* Introduction et Traduction de Gustave Bardy. Sources Chrétiennes 3. Paris: Éditions du cerf, 1943.

Cicero. 28 vols. Trans. G.L. Hendrickson , H. M. Hubbell, *et al.*. LCL. Cambridge, MA: Harvard UP, 1912-72.

[Cicero]. *Ad C. Herennium De Ratione Dicendi (Rhetorica ad Herennium)*. Trans. H. Caplan. LCL. Cambridge, MA: Harvard UP, 1954.

Clemens Alexandrinus. *Stromata* in ANF vol. 2. Eds. A. Roberts and J. Donaldson. Peabody, MA: Hendrickson, 1994.

Comicorum Atticorum Fragmenta. Vols. 1-3. Ed. T. Kock. Leipzig: Teubner, 1880-88.

Comicorum Graecorum Fragmenta in Papyris Reperta. Ed. C. Austin. Berlin: de Gruyter, 1973.

The Dead Sea Scrolls Translated. The Qumran Texts in English. English trans. G. E. Watson. Ed. F. G. Martínez. Leiden: Brill, 1994.

Demosthenes. 7 vols. Trans. J. H. Vince, C. A.Vince, *et al*. LCL. New York: Putnam's Sons; Cambridge, MA: Harvard UP, 1930-1949.

(Pseudo) Demetrius. *TUPOI EPISTOLIKOI* in Malherbe, A. J., "Ancient Epistolary Theorists." *OJRS* 5-6 (1977-78) 20-39 [= *idem. Ancient Epistolary Theorists*. SBL.SBibSt 19. Atlanta, GA: Scholars Press 1988, 30-41].

Dinarchus. *Minor Attic Orators*. Vol. II. Trans. J. O. Burtt. LCL. Cambridge, MA: Harvard UP, 1980. First pr. 1954.

Dio Cassius. *Roman History*. 9 vols. Trans. E. Cary. LCL. Cambridge, MA: Harvard UP, 1914-27.

Dio Chrysostom. 5 vols. Trans. J. W. Cohoon and H. L. Crosby. LCL. Cambridge, MA: Harvard UP, 1932-51.

Diodorus Siculus. 12 vols. Trans. C. H. Oldfather, C. L. Sherman, *et al*. LCL. New York: Putnam's Sons; Cambridge, MA: Harvard UP, 1933-67.

Dionysius of Halicarnassus. *Critical Essays*. 2 vols. Trans. S. Usher. LCL. Cambridge, MA: Harvard UP, 1974-1985.

— *Roman Antiquities*. 7 vols. Trans. E. Cary, on the basis of E. Spelman's translation. LCL. Cambridge, MA: Harvard UP, 1937-50._

Epictetus. 2 vols. Trans. W. A. Oldfather. LCL. Cambridge, MA: Harvard UP, 1925-28.

Euripides. 4 vols. Trans. A. S. Way and D. Kovacs. LCL. Cambridge, MA: Harvard UP, 1947-1988 (first pr. 1912), 1994.

Eusebius. *The Ecclesiastical History*. 2 vols. Trans. K. Lake and J.-E. L. Oulton. LCL. Cambridge, MA: Harvard UP, 1980. First pr. 1926-32.

Eusebius Werke. Siebenter Band. Die Chronik des Hieronymus. Ed. R. Helm. Die Griechischen Christlichen Schriftsteller der Ersten Jahrhunderte 47. Berlin: Akademie- Verlag, 1956.

Fragmenta Historicorum Græcorum vols. 1 and 4. Ed. C. Mulleri. Paris: Ambrosio Firmin Didot, 1841-51.

Die Fragmente der Vorsokratiker. 3 vols. Eds. H. Diels and W. Kranz. Dublin/Zürich: Weidmann, 1966-1971. First pr. 1903-1910.

"Hermogenes' *On Stases*: A Translation with an Introduction and Notes." Ed. and trans. R. Nadeau. *Speech Monographes* 31 (1964) 361-424.

Hermogenes' On Types of Style. Trans. C. W. Wooten. Chapel Hill, NC-London: University of North Carolina Press, 1987.

Gonnoi. Vol. 2, *Les Inscriptions.* Ed. B. Helly. 2 vols in 1. Amsterdam: Hakkert, 1973.

[Herodes Atticus]. *PERI POLITEIAS. Ein politisches Pamphlet aus Athen 404 vor Chr.* Ed. E. Drerup. Studien zur Geschichte und Kultur des Altertums. Vol. 2, pt. 1. Paderborn: Schöningh, 1908.

Herodian. 2 vols. Trans. C. R. Whittaker. LCL. Cambridge, MA: Harvard UP, 1969-70.

Historici Graeci Minores. Vol. I. Ed. L. Dindorf. Leipzig: Teubner, 1870-71.

Iamblicus. *De vita Pythagorica Liber.* Ed. L. Deubner. Stuttgart: Teubner, 1975.

Irenaeus. *Adversus haereses.* In ANF vol. I. Eds. A. Roberts and J. Donaldson. Peabody, MA: Hendrickson, 1994.

Isocrates. 3 vols. Trans. G. Norlin and L. van Hook. LCL. Cambridge, MA: Harvard UP, 1928-1945.

Josephus. 9 vols. Trans. H. St. J. Thackeray, R. Marcus, and L. H. Feldman. LCL. Cambridge, MA: Harvard UP, 1956-65.

Justin Martyr. *Dialogus cum Tryphone Judaeo.* In Goodspeed, E. J., Die ältesten Apologeten. Texte mit kurzen Einleitungen, pp. 90-265. Göttingen: Vandenhoeck & Ruprecht, 1984. First. pr. 1914.

Kent, J. H. *The Inscriptions, 1926-1950. Corinth: Results.* VIII.3. Princeton, NJ: American Schools of Classical Studies at Athens, 1966.

Lactance. *De La Mort des Persecuteurs.* 2 vouls. Introduction, texte critique et traduction de J. Moreau. Sourches Chretiennes 39. Paris: Les Editions du Cerf, 1954.

(Pseudo) Libanius. EPISTOLIMAIOI XARAKTHRES in Malherbe, A. J., "Ancient Epistolary Theorists". *OJRS* 5-6 (1977-78) 61-72 [= *idem. Ancient Epistolary Theorists.* SBL.SBibSt 19. Atlanta, GA: Scholars Press 1988, 66-81].

Livy. 14 vols. Trans. B. O. Foster, F. G. Moore, *et al.* LCL. Cambridge, MA, London: Harvard UP, 1919-59.

Lucian. 8 vols. Trans. A. M. Harmon, K. Kilburn, and M. D. Macleod. LCL. New York: Macmillan; Cambridge, MA: Harvard UP, 1913-67.

Lycvrgi oratio in Leocratem. Ed. N. C. Connomis. Bibliotheca Scriptorvm Graecorvm et Romanorvm Tevbneriana. Leipzig: Teubner, 1970.

Lycurgus. *Minor Attic Orators.* vol. 2. Trans. J. O. Burtt. LCL. Cambridge, MA: Harvard UP, 1980. First. pr. 1954.

Lysias. 1 vol. Trans. W. R. M. Lamb. LCL. Cambridge, MA: Harvard UP, 1988. First. pr. 1930.

Novum Testamentum Graece. 26th ed. Rev. and eds. E. Nestle and K. Aland, *et al.* Stuttgart: Deutsche Bibelstiftung, 1979; 7th corrected printing 1983.

Menander Rhetor. Ed., trans. and commentary D. A. Russel and N. G. Wilson. Oxford: Clarendon, 1981.

Musonius Rufus. Ed. and trans. C. E. Lutz. In YCS 10, ed. A. R. Bellinger. New Haven, CT: Yale UP, 1947, 32-147.

Die Oracula Sibyllina. Ed. J. Geffcken. GCS 8. Leipzig: Hinrichs'sche Buchhandlung, 1902.

Philo. 12 vols. Trans. F. H. Colson, G. H. Whitaker, *et al.* LCL. Cambridge, MA: Harvard UP, 1929-53.

Flavius Philostratus. *The Life of Apollonius of Tyana.* 2 vols. Trans. F. C. Conybeare. LCL. Cambridge, MA: Harvard UP, 1912.

Philostratus and Eunapius. *The Lives of the Sophists.* Trans. W. C. Wright. LCL. Cambridge, MA: Harvard UP, 1989. First. pr. 1922.

Plato. 12 vols. Trans. H. N. Fowler, W. R. M. Lamb, *et al.* LCL. Cambridge, MA: Harvard UP, 1914-35.

Plutarch. *Lives.* 11 vols. Trans. B. Perrin. LCL. Cambridge, MA: Harvard UP, 1993-94. First. pr. 1914-26.

— *Moralia.* 15 vols. Trans. F. C. Babbit, W. Helmbold, *et al.* LCL. Cambridge,MA: Harvard UP, 1927-69.

Political Fragments of Archytas, Charondas, Zaleucus and other Ancient Pythagoreans, Preseved by Stobæus; and also Ethical Fragments of Hierocles. Trans. Th. Taylor. Chiswick: C. Whittingham, 1822.

Polybius. 6 vols. Trans. W. R. Paton. LCL. Cambridge, MA: Harvard UP, 1922-27.

Quintilian. *Institutio Oratoria.* 4 vols. Trans. H. E. Butler. LCL. Cambridge, MA: Harvard UP, 1959-63. First. pr. 1920-22.

The Oxyrhynchus Papyri. Ed. B. P. Grenfell, A. S. Hunt, *et. al.* London: Egypt Exploration Fund, 1898-.

Rhetores Latini Minores. Ed. C. Halm. Leipzig: Teubner, 1863.

Sallust. Trans. J. C. Rolfe. LCL. Cambridge, MA: Harvard UP, 1921; rev. ed. 1931.

Seneca. *Moral Essays.* 3 vols. Trans. J. W. Basore. LCL. New York: Putnam's Sons; Cambridge, MA: Harvard University Press, 1928-35.

Seneca The Elder. *Controversiae, Suasoriae.* 2 vols. Trans. M. Winterbottom. LCL. Cambridge, MA: Harvard UP, 1974.

The Septuagint Version of the Old Testament. With an English Translation. By L. L. Brenton. London: Bagster and Sons, [year missing].

Septuaginta. Id est Vetus Testamentum graece iuxta LXX interpretes. 2 vols. Ed. A. Rahlfs. Stuttgart: Deutsche Bibelgesellschaft, 1935. (Duo volumina in uno).

Spengel, L., ed. *Rhetores Graeci.* 3 vols. Leipzig: Teubner, 1854-56.

Stobaeus. *Anthologium.* 5 vols. Eds. C. Wachsmuth, O. Hense. Berlin: Weidmann, 1884-1912.

Suetonius. 2 vols. Trans. J. C. Rolfe. LCL. Cambridge, MA: Harvard UP, 1989. First pr. 1913-14.

Tacitus. *Histories and Annals*. 4 vols. Trans. C. H. Moore and J. Jackson. LCL. Cambridge, MA: Harvard UP, 1951-52. First pr. 1925-37.

Theognis, Ps.-Pythagoras, Ps.-Phocylides, etc. Ed. D. Young. Leipzig: Teubner, 1971.

Thucydides. 4 vols. Trans. C. F. Smith. LCL. Cambridge, MA: Harvard UP, 1919-23.

Tragicorum Graecorum Fragmenta. Vol. 2. Eds. R. Kannicht and B. Snell. Göttingen: Vandenhoeck & Ruprecht, 1981.

Vettii Valentis anthologiarum libri. Ed. G. Kroll, Berlin: Weidmann, 1908.

Victor, J. *Ars Rhetorica* 27 (De Epistolis) in A. J. Malherbe, "Ancient Epistolary Theorists". *OJRS* 5-6 (1977-78) 58-61 [= *idem. Ancient Epistolary Theorists*. SBL.SBibSt 19. Atlanta, GA: Scholars Press 1988, 62-65].

Xenophon. 7 vols. Trans. C. L. Brownson, O. J. Todd, *et al*. LCL. Cambridge, MA: Harvard UP, 1918-25.

SPECIAL STUDIES ON 1 CLEMENT CONSULTED

Andrén, O. *Rättfärdighet och Frid. En Studie i det första Clemensbrevet*. Uppsala: Almqvist & Wiksell, 1960.

Baasland, E. "1. Klemensbrev." In *De Apostoliske Fedre i norsk oversettelse med innledninger og noter*. Eds. E. Baasland og R. Hvalvik. Oslo: Luther Forlag, 1984, 117-159.

Bardy, G. "Expressions Stoiciennes dans la Ia Clementis." *RSR* 12 (1922) 73-85.

Barnard, L. W. "St. Clement of Rome and the Persecution of Domitian." In *idem. Studies in the Apostolic Fathers and their Background*. Oxford: Blackwell, 1966, 5-18.

Beyschlag, K. "1. Clemens 40-44 und das Kirchenrecht." In *Reformatio und Confessio. Festschrift für D. Wilhelm Maurer zum 65. Geburtstag am 7. Mai 1965*. Eds. F. W. Kantzenbach und G. Müller. Berlin: Lutherisches Verlagshaus, 1965, 9-22.

— *Clemens Romanus und der Frühkatholizismus. Untersuchungen zu I Clemens 1-7*. BHTh 35. Tübingen: Mohr, 1966.

Bingham, D. J. Review of J. S. Jeffer, *Conflict at Rome: Social Order and Hierarchy in Early Christianity. Journal of Early Christian Studies* 1 (1993) 87-88.

Bowe, B. E. *A Church in Crisis. Ecclesiology and Paraenesis in Clement of Rome*. HDR 23. Minneapolis, MN: Fortress, 1988.

— "Prayer Rendered for Caesar ? *1 Clement* 59.3-61.3." In *The Lord's Prayer and Other Prayer Texts from the Graeco-Roman Erea*. Ed. J. H. Charlesworth. Valley Forge, Pa: Trinity, 1994, 85-99.

Brunner, G. *Die theologische Mitte des ersten Klemensbriefs. Ein Beitrag zur Hermeneutik frühchristlicher Texte*. FTS 11. Frankfurt, Main: Knecht, 1972.

Bumpus, H. B. *The Christological Awareness of Clement of Rome and its Sources*. Cambridge: University Press of Cambridge, 1972.

Chadwick, H. "Justification by Faith and Hospitality." In *StPatr* 4. part 2. Ed. F. L. Cross. TU 79. Berlin: Akademie-Verlag, 1961, 281-285.

Davids, A. "Irrtum und Häresie. *1 Clem. - Ignatius von Antiochien - Justinus*." *Kairos* 15 (1973) 165-187.

Drews, P. "Untersuchungen über die sogen. clementinische Liturgie im VIII Buch der apostolischen Konstitutionen. 1. Die Clementinische Liturgie in Rom." In *Studien zur Geschichte des Gottesdienstes und des gottesdienstlichen Lebens, II und III.* Tübingen: Mohr, 1906.

K. Erlemann, "Die Datierung des ersten Klemensbriefes - Anfragen an eine communis Opinio *NTS* 44 (1998) 591-607.

Fisher, E. W. *Soteriology in First Clement.* Ph.D. diss., Claremont, 1974.

Fuellenbach, J. *Ecclesiastical Office and the Primacy of Rome. An Evaluation of Recent Theological Discussion of First Clement.* Washington, D.C.: The Catholic University of America Press, 1980.

Eggenberger, C. *Die Quellen der politischen Ethik des 1. Klemensbriefes.* Zürich: Zwingli Verlag, 1951.

Erlemann, K., "On the Date of first Clement." *NTS* 44 (1998) 591-607.

Gerke, F. *Die Stellung des ersten Clemensbriefes innerhalb der Entwicklung der altchristlichen Gemeindeverfassung und des Kirchenrechts.* TU 47.1. Leipzig; Hinrichs'sche Buchhandlung, 1931.

Grant, R. M. *The Apostolic Fathers. A New Translation and Commentary.* Vol. 1. *An Introduction.* New York, NY: Thomas Nelson & Sons, 1964.

Grant, R. M. and Graham, H. H. *The Apostolic Fathers. A New Translation and Commentary.* Vol. 2. *First and Second Clement.* New York, NY: Thomas Nelson & Sons, 1965.

Hagner, D. A. *The Use of the Old and New Testaments in Clement of Rome.* NT.S 34. Leiden: Brill, 1973.

Hall, A. "I Clement as a Document of Transition." *CDios* 181 (1968) 682-692.

Von Harnack, A. "Der erste Klemensbrief. Eine Studie zur Bestimmung des Charakters des ältesten Heidenchristentums." In *Sitzungsberichte der Königlich Preussischen Akademie der Wissenschaften.* Berlin: Verlag der Königlichen Akademie der Wissenschaften, 1909, 38-63.

—— *Einführung in die Alte Kirchengeschichte. Das Schreiben der römischen Kirche an die korinthische aus der Zeit Domitians (1. Clemensbrief).* Leipzig: Hinrichs'sche Buchhandlung, 1929.

Heron, A. I. C. "The Interpretation of 1 Clement in Walter Bauer's *Rechtgläubigkeit und Ketzerei im ältesten Christentum*." *EkklPh* 55 (1973) 517-545.

Herron, J. T. "The Most Probable Date of the First Epistle of Clement to the Corinthians." *StPatr.* 21. *Papers presented to the Tenth International Conference on Patristic Studies held in Oxford 1987.* Eds. E. A. Livingstone. Leuven: Peeters, 1989, 106-121.

Hooijberg, W. A. E. "A Different View of Clement Romanus." *HeyJ* 16 (1975) 266-288.

Jaubert, A. "Les sources de la conception militaire de l'Eglise en I Clément 37." *VigChr* 18 (1964) 74-84.

Jeffers, J. S. *Conflict at Rome. Social Order and Hierarchy in Early Christianity,* Minneapolis, MN: Fortress, 1991.

Knoch, O. *Eigenart und Bedeutung der Eschatologie im theologischen Aufriss des ersten Clemensbriefes. Eine auslegungsgeschichtliche Untersuchung.* Theophaneia. Beiträge zur Religions- und Kirchengeschichte des Altertums 17. Bonn: Peter Hanstein Verlag, 1964.

Knoch, O. B. "Im Namen des Petrus und Paulus: Der Brief des Clemens Romanus und die Eigenart des römischen Christentums." *ANRW* 2. 27.1. Berlin: de Gruyter, 1993, 4-54.

Knopf, R. "Der erste Clemensbrief. Der litterarische Charakter des Ersten Clemensbriefes." In TU 20. Leipzig: Hinrichs'sche Buchhandlung, 1901, 156-194.

— *Die Lehre der Zwölf Apostel. Die zwei Clemensbriefe.* HNT. *Ergänzungsband. Die Apostolischen Väter I.* Tübingen: Mohr, 1920.

Liang, K. J. *Het Begrip Deemoed in 1 Clemens. Bijdrage tot de Geschiedenis van de Oud-Christelijke Ethiek.* Utrecht: Drukkerij v/h Kemink en Zoon N.V., 1951.

Lightfoot, J. B. *The Apostolic Fathers.* 5 vols. Peabody, MA: Hendrickson, 1989. First pr. London: Macmillan, 1889-1890.

Lindemann, A. *Die Clemensbriefe.* HNT 17. *Die Apostolischen Väter I.* Tübingen: Mohr, 1992.

Lona, H. E. "Rhetorik und Botschaft in 1 Clem 49." *ZNW* 86 (1995) 94-103.

— *Der erste Clemensbrief.* KAV 2. Göttingen; Vandenhoeck & Ruprecht, 1998.

Lösch, S. *Epistula Claudiana. Der neuentdeckte Brief des Kaisers Claudius vom Jahre 41 n. Chr. und das Urchristentum.* Rottenburg: Adolf Bader, 1930.

— "Der Brief des Clemens Romanus. Die Probleme und ihre Beurteilung in der Gegenwart." In *Studi dedicati alla memoria di Paolo Ubaldi.* Pubblicazioni dell' Universita Cattolica del Sacro Cuore. Serie quinta. Scienze storiche, vol. 16. Milano: Societa editrice "Vita e pensiero", 1937, 177-188.

Maier, H. O. *The Social Setting of the Ministry as Reflected in the Writings of Hermas, Clement and Ignatius.* Canadian Corporation for Studies in Religion. Dissertations sr vol. 1. Waterloo, Canada: Wilfrid Laurier UP, 1991.

— "1. Clement and the Rhetoric of Hybris." *StPatr* 31. Louvain: Peeters, 1977, 136-142.

Meinhold, P. "Geschehen und Deutung des ersten Clemensbrief." *ZKG* 58 (1939) 82-129.

Merrill, E. T. "On 'Clement of Rome'." In *idem. Essays in Early Christian History.* London: Macmillan, 1924, 217-241.

Mikat, P. *Die Bedeutung der Begriffe Stasis und Aponoia für das Verständnis des 1. Clemensbriefes.* Arbeitsgemeinschaft für Forschung des Landes Nordrhein-Westfalen 155. Köln: Westdeutscher Verlag, 1969.

— "Zur Fürbitte der Christen für Kaiser und Reich im Gebet des 1. Clemensbriefes." In *Festschrift für Ulrich Scheuner zum 70. Geburtstag.* Ed. H. Ehmke. Berlin: Duncker & Humblot, 1973, 455-471.

— "Der 'Auswanderungsrat' (1 Clem 54,2) als Schlüssel zum Gemeindeverständnis im 1. Clemensbrief." In *idem. Geschichte, Recht, Religion, Politik* (GAufs) I, Paderborn: Schöningh, 1984, 361-373.

Molland, E. "Clemensbriefe." *RGG* vol. 1.1836-38. 3rd ed. Ed. K. Galling, Tübingen: Mohr, 1957.

Peterson, E. "Das Praescriptum des. 1. Clemens-Briefes." In *Pro regno, pro sanctuario: Een bundel Studies en Bijdragen van vrienden en vereerders bij de zestigste verjaardag van Prof. Dr.G. van der Leeuw.* Eds. W. J. Kooiman and J. M. van Veen. Nijkerk: G.F. Callenbach, 1950, 351-57.

Rohde, J. "Häresie und Schisma im ersten Clemensbrief und in den Ignatius-Briefen." *NT* 10 (1968) 217-233.

Sanders, L. *L' Hellénisme de Saint Clément de Rome et le Paulinisme.* StHell. 2. Lovanii: Bibliotheca Universitatis, 1943.

Stockmeier, P. "Der Begriff παιδεία bei Klemens von Rom." *StPatr.* 7, part 1. Ed. F.L. Cross. TU 92. Berlin: Akademie-Verlag 1966, 401-408.

Stuiber, A. "Clemens Romanus I." *RAC* 3 (1957) 188-197.

Tugwell, S. *The Apostolic Fathers.* Outstanding Christian Thinkers. London: Geoffrey Chapman 1989.

Unnik, W. C. van. "1 Clement 34 and the 'Sanctus'." *VigChr* 5 (1951) 204-248.

— "Studies over de zogenaamde eerste brief van Clemens. I. Het Litteraire Genre." *Mededelingen der koninklijke Nederlandse Akademie van Wetenschappen, Afd. Letterkunde,* 33.4. Amsterdam: N.V. Noord-Hollandsche Uitgevers Maatschappij, 1970, 149-204.

— "'Tiefer Friede' (1. Klemens 2,2)." *VigChr* 24 (1970) 261-279.

— "Noch einmal 'Tiefer Friede'." *VigChr* 26 (1972) 24-28.

— "Is I Clement 20 Purely Stoic ?" In *Sparsa Collecta. The Collected Essays of W. C. van Unnik. Parth three.* NT.S. 31. Leiden: Brill, 1983, 52-58. (First published in *VigChr* 4 [1950] 181-89).

Weiss, B. "Amt und Eschatologie im 1. Clemensbrief." *ThPh* 50 (1975) 71-83.

Welborn, L. L. "On the Date of First Clement." *BR* (1984) 35-54.

Wilson, J. W. *The First Epistle of Clement: A Theology of Power.* Ph.D. diss., Duke University, 1976.

Wrede, W. *Untersuchungen zum Ersten Klemensbrief.* Göttingen: Vandenhoeck &Ruprecht, 1891.

Ziegler, A. W. *Neue Studien zum ersten Klemensbrief.* München: Manz Verlag, 1958.

— "Politische Aspekte im Ersten Klemensbrief." *FKTh* 2 (1986) 67-74.

— "Die Frage nach einer politischen Absicht des Ersten Klemensbriefes." Überarbeitet und ergänzt von G. Brunner. *ANRW* 2. 27.1. Berlin: de Gruyter, 1993, 55-76.

OTHER SECONDARY LITERATURE CONSULTED

Adkins, A. W. H. *Merit and Responsibility. A Study in Greek Values.* Oxford: Clarendon, 1960.

— *Moral Values and Political Behaviour in Ancient Greece. From Homer to the end of the Fifth Century.* London: Chatto & Windus, 1972.

Altaner, B. - Stuiber, A. *Patrologie. Leben, Schriften und Lehre der Kirchenväter.* Siebte, völlig neubearbeitete Auflage. Herder: Freiburg, 1966.

Andersen, Ø. *I Retorikkens Hage.* Universitetsforlaget: Oslo, 1995.

Aune, D. E. Review of *Galatians: A Commentary on Paul's Letter to the Churches in Galatia,* by H. D. Betz. *RStR* 7 (1981) 323-28.

— *The New Testament in Its Literary Environment.* LEC 8. Philadelphia, PA: Westminster, 1987.

Baasland, E. "Der 2. Klemensbrief und frühchristliche Rhetorik: 'Die erste christliche Predigt' im Lichte der neueren Forschung." *ANRW* 2. 27.1. Berlin: de Gruyter, 1993, 78-157.

Bakke, O. M. "Ignatiusbrevas Retoriske Genre." *TTK* 66 (1995) 275-291.

Balch, D. L. *Let Wives Be Submissive: The Domestic Code in 1 Peter.* SBL.MS 26. Chico, CA: Scholars Press, 1981.

Baldinger, K. *Semantic Theory: Towards a Modern Semantics.* Trans. W. C. Brown. Ed. R. Wright. Oxford: Blackwell, 1980.

Baldwin, C. S. *Ancient Rhetoric and Poetic. Interpreted from Representative Works.* Gloucester, MA: Peter Smith, 1959. First pr. Macmillan, 1924.

Banks, R. *Paul's Idea of Community. The Early House Churches in their Historical Setting.* Exeter: Paternoster, 1980.

Barr, J. *The Semantics of Biblical Language.* Oxford: Oxford UP, 1961.

Bauer, W. *Rechtgläubigkeit und Ketzerei im ältesten Christentum. Zweite, durchgesehene Auflage mit einem Nachtrag* von G. Strecker. BHTh 10. Tübingen: Mohr, 1964.

— *Orthodoxy and Heresy in Earliest Christianity.* Trans. R. A. Kraft *et al.* London: SCM, 1971.

Beck, I. *Untersuchungen zur Theorie des Genos Symbuleutikon.* Ph.D. diss. Hamburg, 1970.

Behr, C. A., ed. and trans. *P. Aelius Aristides. The Complete Works.* 2 vols. Leiden: Brill, 1981-86.

Berger, K. *Exegese des Neuen Testaments. Neue Wege vom Text zur Auslegung.* UTB 658. Heidelberg: Quelle & Meyer, 1977.

Betz, H. D. *Nachfolge und Nachahmung Jesu Christi im Neuen Testament.* BHTh 37. Tübingen: Mohr, 1972.

— *Der Apostel Paulus und die sokratische Tradition. Eine exegetische Untersuchung zu seiner 'Apologie' 2 Kor 10-13.* BHTh 45. Tübingen: Mohr, 1972.

— "The Literary Composition and Function of Paul's Letter to the Galatians." *NTS* 21 (1975) 353-379.

— "De Fraterno Amore (Moralia 478A-492D)." In *Plutarch's Ehtical Writings and Early Christian Literature*. Ed. H. D. Betz. SCHNT 4. Leiden: Brill, 1978, 231-263.

— "De laude ipsius." In *Plutarch's Ehtical Writings and Early Christian Literature*. Ed. H. D. Betz. SCHNT 4. Leiden: Brill, 1978, 363-393.

— *Galatians. A Commentary on Paul's Letter to the Churches in Galatia.* Hermeneia. Philadelphia, PA: Fortress, 1979.

— *2 Corinthians 8 and 9. A Commentary on Two Administrative Letters of the Apostle Paul.* Hermeneia. Philadelphia, PA: Fortress, 1985.

— "The Problem of Rhetoric and Theology according to the Apostle Paul." In *L'Apôtre Paul. Personnalité, Style et Conception du Ministère*. Ed. A. Vanhoye *et al.* BEThL 73. Leuven: Leuven UP, 1986, 16-48.

Bitzer, L. F. "The Rhetorical Situation." *Philosophy & Rhetoric* 1 (1968) 1-14.

Black, C. C. "Rhetorical Criticism and the New Testament." *Proceedings of the Eastern Great Lakes and Midwest Biblical Societies* 8 (1988) 77-92.

— "Rhetorical Criticism and Biblical Interpretation." *ET* 100 (1989) 252-258.

— "Rhetorical Questions: The New Testament, Classical Rhetoric, and Current Interpretation." *Dialog* 29 (1990) 62-70.

Black, D. A. "Paul and Christian Unity: A Formal Analysis of Philippians 2:1-4." *JETS* 28 (1985) 299-308.

Bloch, R. "Eirene." *Der neue Pauly* 3 . 921.

Blum, G. G. *Tradition und Sukzession. Studien zum Normbegriff des Apostolischen von Paulus bis Irenäus.* AGTL 9. Berlin: Lutherisches Verlagshaus, 1963.

Bohatec, J. "Inhalt und Reihenfolge der 'Schlagworte der Erlösungsreligion' in 1. Kor. 1.26-31." *ThZ* 4 (1948) 252-271.

Bonner, S. F. *Education in Ancient Rome. From the Elder Cato to the Younger Pliny.* London: Methuen & Co , 1977.

Botha, J. "On the Reinvention of Rhetoric." *Scriptura* 31 (1989) 14-31.

Bowersock, G. W. *Greek Sophists in the Roman Empire.* Oxford: Clarendon, 1969.

Brandt, W. J. *The Rhetoric of Argumentation.* Indianapolis, IN: Bobbs-Merrill, 1970.

Brickstock, R. J. "Praefectus Praetorio." In *A Dictionary of Ancient History*, 519-520.

Brown, R. E. and Meier, J. P. *Antioch and Rome. New Testament Cradles of Catholic Christianity.* London: Geoffrey Chapman, 1983.

Brox, N. *Der Hirt des Hermas.* KAV 7. Göttingen: Vandenhoeck & Ruprecht, 1991.

Burke, K. *The Rhetoric of Religion. Studies in Logology.* Berkeley: University of California Press, 1970.

Campbell, R. A. *The Elders: Seniority within Earliest Christianity.* Edinburgh: T&T Clark, 1994.

Campenhausen, H. F. von. *Kirchliches Amt und geistliche Vollmacht in den ersten drei Jahrhunderten.* 2nd edition. BHTh 14. Tübingen: Mohr, 1963.

— *Ecclesiastical Authority and Spiritual Power in the Church of the First Three Centuries.* Trans. J.A. Baker. London: Adam & Charles Black, _ 1969.

Chow, J. K. *Patronage and Power. A Study of Social Networks in Corinth.* JSNT.S 75. Sheffield: Sheffield AP, 1992.

Clarke, M. L. *Higher Education in the Ancient World.* London: Routledge & Kegan Paul, 1971.

Classen, C. J. "Paulus und die antike Rhetorik." *ZNW* 82 (1991) 1-33.

— "St Paul's Epistles and Ancient Greek and Roman Rhetoric." In *Rhetoric and the New Testament. Essays from the 1992 Heidelberg Conference.* Eds. S. E. Porter and T. H. Olbricht. JSNT.S 90. Sheffield: Sheffield AP, 1993, 265-291.

Conzelmann, H. *Der erste Brief an die Korinther.* KEK 5. Göttingen: Vandenhoeck & Ruprecht, 1969.

Cosby, M. R. *The Rhetorical Composition and Function of Hebrews 11. In Light of Example Lists in Antiquity.* Macon, GA: Mercer UP, 1988.

Coseriu, E. "Die lexematischen Strukturen." In *Strukturelle Bedeutungslehre.* Ed. H. Geckeler. WdF 426. Darmstadt: Wissenschaftliche Buchgesellschaft, 1978, 254-273.

— "Lexikalische Solidaritäten." In *Strukturelle Bedeutungslehre.* Ed. H. Geckeler. WdF 426. Darmstadt: Wissenschaftliche Buchgesellschaft, 1978, 239-253.

Cotterell, P. & Turner, M. *Linguistics & Biblical Interpretation.* London: SPCK, 1989.

Countryman, L. Wm. *The Rich Christian in the Church of the Early Empire: Contradictions and Accommodations.* New York: Edwin Mellen Press, 1980.

Crouch, J. E. *The Origin and Intention of the Colossian Haustafel.* Göttingen: Vandenhoeck & Ruprecht, 1972.

Danker, F. W. *Benefactor: Epigraphic Study of a Graeco-Roman and New Testament Semantic Field.* St. Louis: Clayton Publishing House, 1982.

Davis, J. A. *Wisdom and Spirit: An Investigation of 1 Corinthians 1.18-3.20 against the Background of Jewish Sapiential Traditions in the Greco-Roman Period.* Lanham: UP of America, 1984.

Delling, G. "ἀλαζών, ἀλαζονεία." *TDNT* 1. 226-227.

— "στάσις". *TDNT* 7. 568-571.

Dibelius, M. *Der Hirt des Hermas.* HNT. *Ergänzungsband: Die Apostolischen Väter IV.* Mohr: Tübingen 1923.

Dibelius, M./Conzelmann, H. *The Pastoral Epistles. A Commentary on the Pastoral Epistles.* Trans. P. Buttolph and A. Yarbro. Philadelphia, PA: Fortress, 1972.

Dinkler E. "Friede." *RAC* 8 (1972) 434-505.

Dormeyer, D. *Das Neue Testament im Rahmen der antiken Literaturgeschichte:eine Einführung.* Darmstadt: Wiss. Buchges. 1993.

Doty, W. G. "The Classification of Epistolary Literature." *CBQ* 31 (1969) 183-199.

— *Letters in Primitive Christianity.* Guides to Biblical Scholarship: NT Series. Philadelphia, PA: Fortress, 1973.

Dover, K. J. *Greek Popular Morality in the Time of Plato and Aristotle.* Oxford: Blackwell, 1974.

Edmundson, G. *The Church in Rome in the First Century. An Examination of Various Controverted Questions Relating to its History, Chronology, Literature and Traditions.* The Bampton Lectures for 1913. London: Longmans, Green and Co, 1913.

Ehrenberg, V. *The Greek State.* 2nd ed. London: Methuen & Co LTD, 1969.

Eisenstadt, S. N. and Ronger, L. *Patrons, Clients and Friends. Interpersonal Relations and the Structure of Trust in Society,* Cambridge: Cambridge UP, 1984.

Elliot, J. H. *A Home for the Homeless. A Sociological Exegesis of 1 Peter, Its Situation and Strategy.* Philadelphia, PA: Fortress, 1981.

Eltester, W. "Schöpfungsoffenbarung und natürliche Theologie im frühen Christentum." *NTS* 3 (1956/57) 93-114.

Ehrhardt, A. A. T. *Politische Metaphysik von Solon bis Augustin.* 3 vols. Tübingen: Mohr, 1959.

Esler, F. E. *The First Christians in their Social Worlds. Social-Scientific Approaches to New Testament Interpretation.* London: Routledge, 1994.

Exler, F. J. *The Form of the Ancient Greek Letter of the Epistolary Papyri (3rd c. B.C.-3rd c. A.D.): A Study in Greek Epistolography.* Washington, DC: Catholic University of America Press, 1923. Repr. Chicago, IL: Ares, 1976.

Fascher, E. *Der erste Brief des Paulus an die Korinther.* Vol. 1. ThHK 7/1. Berlin: Evangelische Verlagsanstalt, 1975.

Fee, G. D. *The First Epistle to the Corinthians.* NIC. Grand Rapids, MI: Eerdmans, 1987.

Filson, F. V. "The Significance of the Early House Churches." *JBL* 58 (1939) 105-112.

Finley, M. I. *The World of Odysseus.* New York, NY: The Viking Press, 1978. Revised edition. First pr. 1954.

— *Politics in the Ancient World.* Cambridge: Cambridge UP, 1983.

Fiore, B. "Rhetoric and Rhetorical Critisicm: NT Rhetoric and Rhetorical Criticism." In *The Anchor Bible Dictionary* 5. 715-19. New York, NY: Doubleday, 1992

Fiorenza, E. *In Memory of Her. A Feminist Theological Reconstruction of Christian Origins.* New York, NY: Crossroad, 1983.

— "Rhetorical Situation and Historical Reconstruction in 1 Cor." *NTS* 33 (1987) 386-403.

Fisher, N. R. E. "Hybris and Dishonour I." *GaR* 23 (1976) 177-193.

— *Hybris. A Study in the Values of Honour and Shame in Ancient Greece.* Warminster: Aris and Philips, 1992.

Foerster, W. and Rad, G. von, "εἰρήνη, εἰρηνεύω κτλ." *TDNT* 2. 400-420.

Forbes, C. "Comparison, Self-Praise and Irony: Paul's Boasting and the Conventions of Hellenistic Rhetoric." *NTS* 32 (1986) 1-30.

Fraenkel, J. J. *Hybris*. Utrecht: P. den Boer, 1941.

Fritz, K. v. *The Theory of the Mixed Constitution. A Critical Analysis of Polybius' Political Ideas.* New York: Columbia UP, 1954.

Fuchs, H. *Augustin und der antike Friedensgedanke*. Neue Philologische Untersuchungen 3. Ed. W. Jaeger. Berlin: Weidmann, 1926.

Fuhrmann, M. *Die Antike Rhetorik. Eine Einführung*. 4th ed. Zürich: Artemis & Winkler, 1995.

Fuks, A. *The Ancestral Constitution. Four Studies in Athenian Party Politics at the End of the Fifth Century B.C.* Westport: Greenwood Press, 1975.

Funk, R. *Language, Hermeneutic and Word of God*. New York, NY: Harper and Row, 1966.

Garnsey, P. and Saller, R. *The Roman Empire. Economy, Society and Culture*. London: Duckworth, 1987.

Garrison, R. *Redemptive Almsgiving in Early Christianity*. JSNTSup 77. Sheffield: Sheffield Academic Press, 1993.

Gehrke, H.-J. *Stasis. Untersuchungen zu den inneren Kriegen in den griechischen Staaten des 5. und 4. Jahrhunderts v. Chr.* Vestigia 35. Munich: Beck, 1985.

Geckeler, H. *Strukturelle Semantik und Wortfeldtheorie*. München: W. Fink Verlag, 1971.

Goldstein, J. A. *The Letters of Demosthenes*. New York, NY: Columbia UP, 1968.

Görgemanns, H. "Epistolographie." *Der neue Pauly: Enzyklopädie der Antike* 3 (1997) 1166-1169.

Görgemanns, H. and Zelzer, M. "Epistel." *Der neue Pauly: Enzyklopädie der Antike* 3 (1997) 1161-1166.

Grant, R. M. "The Structure of Eucharistic Prayers". In *Antiquity and Humanity. Essays on Ancient Religion and Philosophy. Presented to Hans Dieter Betz on His 70th Birthday,* Tübingen: Mohr, 2001, 321-332.

Grundmann, W. "ταπεινός κτλ." *TDNT* 8.1-26.

Hasenhüttl, G. *Charisma. Ordnungsprinzip der Kirche*. Ökumenische Forschungen I. Ekklesiologische Abteilung 5. Charisma. Freiburg: Herder, 1969.

Hanson, S. *The Unity of the Church in the New Testament: Colossians and Ephesians*. ASNU 14. Uppsala: Almqvist & Wiksell, 1946.

Hartman, L. "Some Unorthodox Thoughts on the 'Household-Code Form'." In *The Social World of Formative Christianity and Judaism*. Ed. J. Neusner *et al.* Philadelphia, PA: Fortress, 1988, 219-232.

Hauck, F. "ὅσιος κτλ." *TDNT* 5. 489-493.

Hauser, A. J. "Notes on History and Method." In D. F. Watson and A. J. Hauser, *Rhetorical Criticism of the Bible. A Comprehensive Bibliography with Notes on History and Method.* Biblical Interpretation Series 4. Leiden: Brill, 1994, 3-20.

Hay, D. M. *"Pistis* as "Ground for Faith" in Hellenized Judaism and Paul." *JBL* 108 (1989) 461-76.

Hellholm, D. *Das Visionenbuch des Hermas als Apokalypse. Formgeschichtliche und texttheoretische Studien zu einer literarischen Gattung. Band I: Methodologische Vorüberlegungen und makrostrukturelle Textanalyse.* CB.NT 13:1. Lund: Gleerup, 1980.

— "The Problem of Apocalyptic Genre and the Apocalypse of John." *Semeia* 36 (1986) 13-64.

— "Amplificatio in the Macro-Structure of Romans." In *Rhetoric and the New Testament. Essays from the 1992 Heidelberg Conference.* Eds. S. E. Porter and T. H. Olbricht. JSNT.S 90. Sheffield: Sheffield AP, 1993, 123 - 151.

— "Från judisk tvåvägslära till kristen dopkatekes. En inblick i tillkomsten av en första kyrkoordning." In *Ad Acta. Studier til Apostlenes gjerninger og urkristendommens historie. Tilegnet professor Edvin Larsson på 70-årsdagen.* Eds. R. Hvalvik and H. Kvalbein. Oslo: Verbum, 1994, 109-139.

— "Enthymemic Argumentation in Paul: The Case of Romans 6." In *Paul in his Hellenistic Context.* Ed. T. Engberg-Pedersen. Minneapolis, MN: Fortress, 1995, 119-179.

— "Substitutionelle Gliederungsmerkmale und die Komposition des Matthäusevangeliums." In *Texts and Contexts. Biblical Texts in their Textual and Situational Contexts.* Eds. T. Fornberg and D. Hellholm. Oslo: Scandinavian UP, 1995, 11-76.

— "Die argumentative Funktion von Römer 7.1-6." *NTS* 43 (1997) 385-411.

— "Enthymemic Argumentation in Paul." A longer unpublished version of "Enthymemic Argumentation in Paul: The Case of Romans 6."

Holmberg, B. *Paul and Power. The Structure of Authority in the Primitive Church as Reflected in the Pauline Epistles.* CB.NT 11. Lund: Gleerup, 1978.

— *Sociology and the New Testament. An Appraisal.* Minneapolis, MN: Fortress, 1990.

Hommel, H. "Griechische Rhetorik und Beredsamkeit." *Neues Handbuch der Literaturwissenschaft. Band 2, Griechische Literatur.* Ed. E. Vogt, Wiesbaden: Athenaion, 1981, 337-376.

Horrell, D. G. *The Social Ethos of the Corinthian Correspondence. Interests and Ideology from 1 Corinthians to 1 Clement.* Edinburgh: T&T Clark, 1996.

Horsley, R.A. "Wisdom of Word and Words of Wisdom in Corinth." *CBQ* 39 (1977) 224-239.

Horst, P. W. van der. *The Sentences of Pseudo-Phocylides with Introduction and Commentary.* SVTP 4. Leiden: Brill, 1978.

Hudson-Williams, H. L. "Political Speeches in Athens." *CQ* 45 (1951) 68-73.

Hughes, F. W. *Early Christian Rhetoric and 2 Thessalonians.* JSNT.S 30. Sheffield: Sheffield AP, 1989.

— "The Rhetoric of 1 Thessalonians." In *The Thessalonian Correspondance.* BEThL 87. Ed. R. F. Collins. Leuven: Leuven UP, 1990, 94-116.

Höistad, R. *Cynic Hero and Cynic King. Studies in the Cynic Conception of Man.* Diss. Uppsala University, 1948.

Jaeger, W. *Paideia: The Ideals of Greek Culture.* 2 vols. Trans. G. Highet. Oxford: Blackwell, 1946-7.

— *Early Christianity and Greek Paideia.* Cambridge, MA: Harvard UP, 1961.

Johanson, B. C. *To All the Brethren. A Text-Linguistic and Rhetorical Approach to 1 Thessalonians.* CB.NT 16. Uppsala: Almqvist & Wiksell, 1984.

Johnson, L. T. "James 3:13 - 4:10 and the *Topos* ΠΕΡΙ ΦΘΟΝΟΥ." *NT* 25 (1983) 327-347.

Jones, C. P. *The Roman World of Dio Chrysostom.* Cambridge, MA: Harvard UP, 1978.

Jost, K. *Das Beispiel und Vorbild der Vorfahren bei den attischen Rednern und Geschichtschreibern bis Demosthenes.* Rhetorische Studien 19. Paderborn: Schöningh, 1936.

Judge, E. A. "The Early Christians as a Scholastic Community." *JRH* 1 (1960) 4-15, 125-137.

— *The Social Pattern of the Christian Groups in the First Century. Some Prolegomena to the Study of New Testament Ideas of Social Obligation.* London: Tyndale Press 1960.

— "Paul's Boasting in Relation to Contemporary Professional Practice." *ABR* 16 (1968) 37-50.

Kalverkämper, H. "Antike Rhetorik und Textlinguistik. Die Wissenschaft vom Text in altehrwürdiger Modernität." *Allgemeine Sprachwissenschaft, Sprachtypologie und Textlinguistik. Festschrift für Peter Hartmann.* Ed. M. Faust. Tübingen: Narr, 1983, 349-372.

Kaufman, R. "The Patron-Client Concept and Macropolitics." *CSSH* 16 (1974) 284-308.

Kennedy, G. A. "Focusing of Arguments in Greek Deliberative Oratory." *Transactions of the American Philological Association* 90 (1959) 113-138.

— *The Art of Persuasion in Greece.* Princeton, NJ: Princeton UP, 1963.

— *The Art of Rhetoric in the Roman World: 300 B.C. - A.D. 300.* Princeton, NJ: Princeton UP, 1972.

— *Classical Rhetoric and its Christian and Secular Tradition from Ancient to Modern Times.* Chapel Hill, NC: University of North Carolina Press, 1980.

— *Greek Rhetoric under Christian Emperors.* Princeton, NJ: Princeton UP, 1983.

— *New Testament Interpretation through Rhetorical Criticism.* Chapel Hill, NC: University of North Carolina Press, 1984.

Keresztes, P. *Imperial Rome and the Christians. From Herod the Great to about 200 A.D.* Vol. I. Lanham: UP of America, 1989.

Klauck, H.-J. *Hausgemeinde und Hauskirche im frühen Christentum.* SBS 103. Stuttgart: Katholisches Bibelwerk, 1981.

— *Herrenmahl und hellenistischer Kult. Eine religionsgeschichtliche Untersuchung zum ersten Korintherbrief.* NTA 15. Münster: Aschendorff, 1982.

— *Die antike Briefliteratur und das Neue Testament: ein Lehr- und Arbeitsbuch.* UTB 2022. Paderborn: Schöningh, 1998.

Kleck, J. *Symbuleutici qui dicitur sermonis historiam criticam per quattuor saecula continuatam.* Rhetorische Studien 8. Paderborn: Schöningh, 1919.

Klevinghaus, J. *Die theologische Stellung der Apostolischen Väter zur alttestamentlichen Offenbarung.* BFChTh 44.1. Gütersloh: Bertelsmann, 1948.

Koskenniemi, H. *Studien zur Idee und Phraseologie des griechischen Briefes bis 400 n. Chr.* Suomalaisen Tiedeakatemian Toimituksia, Annales Academiae Scientiarum Fennicae 102,2. Helsinki: Suomalainen Tiedeakatemia, 1956.

Kramer, H. *Qvid valeat ὁμόνοια in litteris Graecis.* Diss., Göttingen, 1915.

Köster, H. *Einführung in das Neue Testament: im Rahmen der Religionsgeschichte und Kulturgeschichte der hellenistischen und römischen Zeit.* de Gruyter Lehrbuch. Berlin: de Gruyter, 1980.

Lambrecht, J. "Rhetorical Criticism and the New Testament." Bijdr. 50 (1989) 239-253.

Lampe, P. *Die stadtrömischen Christen in den ersten beiden Jahrhunderten. Untersuchungen zur Sozialgeschichte.* 2nd ed. WUNT 2.18. Tübingen: Mohr, 1989.

Larsson, E. *Christus als Vorbild: eine Untersuchung zu den paulinischen Tauf und Eikontexten.* Uppsala: Gleerup, 1962.

Lausberg, H. *Handbuch der Literarischen Rhetorik. Eine Grundlegung der Literaturwissenschaft.* 3rd ed. Stuttgart: Franz Steiner Verlag, 1990.

Lawson, J. *A Theological and Historical Introduction to the Apostolic Fathers.* New York, NY: Macmillan, 1961.

Lehrer, A. *Semantic Fields and Lexical Structure.* North-Holland Linguistic Series 11. Amsterdam: North-Holland Publishing Company, 1974.

Lietzmann, H. "Zur altchristlichen Verfassungsgeschichte." *ZWTh* 55 (1914) 97-153.

— *Geschichte der Alten Kirche.* Vol. 1: *Die Anfänge.* 3rd ed. Berlin: de Gruyter, 1953.

Liftin, D. *St. Paul's Theology of Proclamation: 1 Corinthians 1-4 and Greco-Roman Rhetoric.* MSSNTS 79. Cambridge: Cambridge UP, 1994.

Lintott, A. *Violence, Civil Strife and Revolution in the Classical City.* Baltimore, MD: Johns Hopkins, 1982.

Loenen, D. *Stasis. Enige aspecten van de begrippen partij-en klassenstrijd in oud-Griekenland.* Amsterdam: Noord-Hollandsche Uitgevers Maataschappij, 1953.

Lumpe, A. "Exemplum." *RAC* 6 (1966) 1229-57.

Lyons, J. *Introduction to Theoretical Linguistics.* Cambridge: Cambridge UP, 1969.

— *Semantics.* Vol. I. Cambridge: Cambridge UP, 1977.

— *Language and Linguistics. An Introduction.* Cambridge: Cambridge UP, 1981.

— *Language, Meaning and Context.* Fontana linguistics 412. London: Fontana Paperbacks, 1981.

MacDowell, D. M. "Hybris in Athens." *GaR* 23 (1976) 14-31.

Mack, B. L. *Rhetoric and the New Testament.* Guides to biblical scholarship. New Testament series. Minneapolis, MN: Fortress, 1990.

MacMullen, R. *Enemies of the Roman Order. Treason, Unrest and Alienation in the Empire.* Cambridge, MA: Harvard UP, 1966.

— *Roman Social Relations. 50 B.C. to A.D. 284.* New Haven, CT: Yale UP, 1974.

Malherbe, A. J. *Social Aspects of Early Christianity.* 2nd ed. Philadelphia, PA: Fortress, 1983.

— *Moral Exhortation. A Greco-Roman Sourcebook.* LEC 4. Philadelphia, PA: Westminster, 1986.

— *Ancient Epistolary Theorists.* SBL.SBibSt 19. Atlanta, GA: Scholars Press, 1988.

— "Seneca on Paul as Letter writer." *The Future of Early Christianity: Essays in Honor of Helmut Koester.* Ed. B. A. Pearson. Minneapolis, MN: Fortress, 1991, 414-421.

— "Hellenistic Moralists and the New Testament." In *ANRW* 2.26.1. Eds. W. Hasse and H. Temporini. Berlin: de Gruyter, 1992, 267-333.

Malina, B. J. *The New Testament World. Insights from Cultural Anthropology.* Louisville, KY: John Knox Press, 1981.

— "Humility." In *Biblical Social Values and Their Meaning. A Handbook.* Eds. J. J. Pilch and B. J. Malina. Peabody, MA: Hendrickson, 1993, 107-108.

Malina, B. J. and Neyrey, J. H. "Honor and Shame in Luke-Acts: Pivotal Values of the Mediterranean World." In *The Social World of Luke-Acts. Models for Interpretation.* Ed. J. H. Neyrey. Peabody, MA: Hendrickson, 1991, 25-65.

Marshall, J. W. "Paul's Ethical Appeal in Philippians." In *Rhetoric and the New Testament. Essays from the 1992 Heidelberg Conference.* Eds. S. E. Porter and T. H. Olbricht. JSNT.S 90. Sheffield: Sheffield AP, 1993, 357-374.

Marshall, P. *Enmity in Corinth: Social Conventions in Paul's Relations with the Corinthians.* WUNT. 2.23. Tübingen: Mohr, 1987.

Martin, J. *Antike Rhetorik. Technik und Methode.* HAW 2.3. München: C.H. Beck'sche Verlagsbuchhandlung, 1974.

Marrou, H. I. *A History of Education in Antiquity.* New York, NY: Sheed and Ward, 1956.

Maurer, C. "σχίζω, σχίσμα." *TDNT* 7. 959-964.

Meeks, W. A. Review of *Galatians: A Commentary on Paul's Letter to the Churches in Galatia,* by H. D. Betz. *JBL* 100 (1981) 304-307.

— *The First Urban Christians. The Social World of the Apostle Paul.* New Haven, CT: Yale UP, 1983

Merrill, E. T. "The Alleged Persecution by Domitian." *Idem. Essays in Early Christian History.* London: Macmillan, 1924, 148-173.

Meyer, P. W. Review of *Galatians: A Commentary on Paul's Letter to the Churches in Galatia,* by. H. D. Betz. *RStR* 7 (1981) 318-323.

Milburn, R. L. P. "The Persecution of Domitian." *CQR* 139 (1945) 154-164.

Milobenski, E. *Der Neid in der Griechischen Philosophie.* KPS 29. Wiesbaden: Harrassowitz, 1964.

Mitchell, M. M. *Paul and the Rhetoric of Reconciliation. An Exegetical Investigation of the Language and Composition of 1 Corinthians.* HUTh 28. Tübingen: Mohr, 1991.

— "New Testament Envoys in the Context of Greco-Roman Diplomatic and Epistolary Conventions: The Example of Timothy and Titus." *JBL* 111 (1992) 641-662.

— "Brief" *RGG* 1. 4. Aufl. Tübingen: Mohr, 1998, 1757-1762

— "Reading Rhetoric with Patristic Exegeses. John Chrysostom on Galatians." In *Antiquity and Humanity. Essays on Ancient Religion and Philosophy. Presented to Hans Dieter Betz on His 70th Birthday,* Tübingen: Mohr, 2001, 333-355.

Montgomery, H. "Demokrati under Debatt." In *I Skyggen av Akropolis.* Eds. Ø. Andersen og T. Hägg. Skrifter utgitt av det Norske Institutt i Athen 5. Bergen: Klassisk institutt, 1994, 99-128.

Moxnes, H. "Honor, Shame and the Outside World in Paul's Letter to the Romans." In *The Social World of Formative Christianity and Judaism.* Eds. J. Neusner *et al.* Philadelphia, PA: Fortress, 1988, 207-18.

— "Honour and Righteousness in Romans." *JSNT* 32 (1988) 61-77.

— "Patron-Client Relations and the New Community in Luke-Acts." In *The Social World of Luke-Acts. Models for Interpretation.* Ed. J. H. Neyrey. Peabody, MA: Hendrickson, 1991, 241-268.

— "Honor and Shame. Readers Guide." *BTB* 23 (1993) 167-176.

— "The Quest for Honor and the Unity of the Community in Romans 12 and in the Orations of Dio Chrysostom." In *Paul in His Hellenistic Context.* Ed. T. Engberg-Pedersen. Minneapolis, MN: Fortress, 1995, 203-230.

Möllendorff, P. von, "Hendiadyoin" *Historisches Wörterbuch der Rhetorik* 3.

Moulakis, A. *Homonoia. Eintracht und die Entwicklung eines politischen Bewusstseins.* München: Paul List Verlag, 1973.

Muilenburg, J. "Form Criticism and Beyond." *JBL* 88 (1969) 1-18.

Müller, W. G. "Brief" *Historisches Wörterbuch der Rhetorik* 2 (1994) 60-76.

Murphy-O'Connor, J. *St. Paul's Corinth. Texts and Archaeology.* GNS 6. Wilmington, DE: Glazier, 1983.

Nadeau, R. N., ed. and trans. "Hermogenes' *On Stases*: A Translation with an Introduction and Notes." *Speech Monographes* 31 (1964) 361-424.

Nestle, W. "Der Fabel des Menenius Agrippa." *Klio* 21 (1927) 350-360.

Neumann, H. and Schmidt, P. L. "Brief" *Der neue Pauly: Enzyklopädie der Antike* 2 (1997) 771-775.

Nida, A. E. "Implications of Contemporary Linguistics for Biblical Scholarship." *JBL* 91 (1972) 73-89.

North, H. *Sophrosyne. Self-Knowledge and Self-Restraint in Greek Literature.* CSCP 35. Ithaca, NY: Cornell UP, 1966.

Oepke, A. "ἀκαταστασία." *TDNT* 3. 446.

Olsson, B. *Structure and Meaning in the Fourth Gospel. A Text-Linguistic Analysis of John 2:1-11 and 4:1-42.* CB.NT 6. Lund: Gleerup, 1974.

Opitz, H. *Ursprünge frühkatholischer Pneumatologie. Ein Beitrag zur Entstehung der Lehre vom Heiligen Geist in der römischen Gemeinde unter Zugrundelegung des 1. Clemens-Briefes und des "Hirten" des Hermas.* ThA 15. Berlin: Evangelische Verlagsanstalt, 1960.

Osiek, C. *What are they Saying about the Social Setting of the New Testament ?* New York, NY: Paulist Press, 1984.

Pearson, L. "Historical Allusions in the Attic Orators" Classical Philology 36 (1941) 209-229.

Perleman, Ch. and Olbrechts-Tyteca, L. *The New Rhetoric. A Treatise on Argumentation.* Notre Dame, IN: Univeristy of Notre Dame Press, 1969.

Pitt-Rivers, J. "Honour and Social Status." In *Honour and Shame. The Values of Mediterranean Society.* Ed. J.G. Peristiany. London: Weidenfeld and Nicolson, 1965, 19-78.

Plett, H. F. *Einführung in die rhetorische Textanalyse.* 3rd. ed. Hamburg: Buske, 1975.

Plümacher, E. *Lukas als hellenistischer Schriftsteller. Studien zur Apostelgeschichte.* SUNT 9. Göttingen: Vandenhoeck & Ruprecht, 1972.

Pogoloff, S. M. *Logos and Sophia. The Rhetorical Situation of 1 Corinthians.* SBL.DS 134. Atlanta, GA: Scholars Press, 1992.

Powell, M. A. *The Bible and Modern Literary Criticism. A Critical Assessment and Annotated Bibliography.* BIRS 22. New York, NY: Greenwood Press, 1992.

Price, B. J. *Para/deigma and Exemplum in Ancient Rhetorical Theory.* Ph.D. diss., University of California at Berkeley, 1975.

Raible, W. "Von der Allgegenwart des Gegensinns (und einiger anderer Relationen). Strategien zur Einordnung semantischer Information." *ZRP* 97 (1981) 1-40.

— "Zur Einleitung." In *Zur Semantik des Französischen.* Eds. H. Stimm and W. Raible. Wiesbaden: Franz Steiner Verlag, 1983.

Reed, J. T. "Using Ancient Rhetorical Categories to Interpret Paul's Letters: A Question of Genre." In *Rhetoric and the New Testament. Essays from the 1992 Heidelberg Conference.* Eds. S.T. Porter and T.H. Olbricht. JSNT.S 90. Sheffield: Sheffield AP, 1993, 292-324.

Rehrl, S. *Das Problem der Demut in der profan-griechischen Literatur im Vergleich zu Septuaginta und Neuem Testament.* AeC 4. Münster: Aschendorff, 1961.

Richards, E. R. *The Secretary in the Letters of Paul.* WUNT 2. 42. Tübingen: Mohr, 1991.

Robbins, V. K. and Patton, J. H. "Rhetoric and Biblical Criticism." *Quarterly Journal of Speech* 66 (1980) 327-337.

Robinson, T. A. *The Bauer Thesis Examined. The Geography of Heresy in the Early Christian Church.* SBEC 11. Lewiston, NY: Edwin Mellen Press, 1988.

Robinson, J. A. T. *Redating the New Testament.* London: SCM, 1976.

Romilly, J. de. "Vocabulaire et propagande, ou les premiers emplois du mot ὁμόνοια." *Mélanges de Linguistique et de Philologie Grecques offerts à Pierre Chantraine. Etudes et commentaires* 79. Paris: Klincksieck, 1972, 199-209.

Rose, H. J. "Homonoia." *OCD*, 526.

Salzmann, J. Chr. *Lehren und Ermahnen. Zur Geschichte des christlichen Wortgottesdienstes in den ersten drei Jahrhunderten.* WUNT 2. 59. Tübingen: Mohr, 1994.

Saller, R. P. *Personal Patronage under the Early Empire.* Cambridge: Cambridge UP, 1982.

— "Patronage and Friendship in Early Imperial Rome: Drawing the Distinction." In *Patronage in Ancient Society.* Ed. A. Wallace-Hadrill. London: Routledge, 1989, 49-62.

Sandnes, K. O. *A New Family. Conversion and Ecclesiology in the Early Church with Cross-Cultural Comparisons.* SIGC 91. Bern: Peter Lang, 1994.

Sänger, D. "Die δυνατοί in 1 Kor 1,26." *ZNW* 76 (1985) 285-291.

Schneider, J. "Brief." *RAC* 2 (1954) 564-585.

Schoedel, W. R. *Ignatius of Antioch. A Commentary on the Letters of Ignatius of Antioch.* Hermeneia. Philadelphia, PA: Fortress, 1985.

Schofield, M. *The Stoic Idea of the City.* Cambridge: Cambridge UP, 1991.

Schrage, W. *Der Erste Brief an die Korinther (1Kor 1,1-6,11).* EKK 7/1. Zürich: Benziger Verlag/ Neukirchen-Vluyn: Neukirchener Verlag, 1991.

Schreiner, K. "Zur biblischen Legitimation des Adels: Auslegungsgeschichtliche Studien zu 1. Kor. 1,26-29." *ZKG* 85 (1974) 317-357.

Schrenk, G. "δίκη, δίκαιος κτλ." *TDNT* 2. 174-225.

Schweizer, E. *Church Order in the New Testament.* Trans. F. Clarke. London: SCM, 1979.

Schweizer, E. and Baumgärtel, F. "σῶμα κτλ." *TDNT* 7. 1024-1094.

Sheppard, A. R. R. "HOMONOIA in the Greek Cities of the Roman Empire." *AncSoc* 15-17 (1984-86) 229-252.

Siegert, F. *Argumentation bei Paulus gezeigt an Röm 9 bis 11.* WUNT 34. Tübingen: Mohr, 1985.

Sigountos, J. G. "The Genre of 1 Corinthians 13." *NTS* 40 (1994) 246-260.

Skard, E. *Zwei religiös-politische Begriffe: Euergetes-Concordia.* Avhandlinger utgitt av Det Norske Videnskaps-Akademi i Oslo II. Hist.-Filos. Klasse 1931 no. 2. Oslo: Dybwad, 1932.

Skarsaune, O. "The Development of Scriptural Interpretation in the Second and Third Centuries – except Clement and Origen. In *Hebrew Bible / Old Testament. The History of its Interpretation.* Vol. 1.1. Ed. M. Sæbø. Göttingen; Vandenhoeck & Ruprecht, 1996, 373-442.

Smit, J. "The Genre of 1 Corinthians 13 in the Light of Classical Rhetoric." *NT* 33 (1991) 193-216.

Soden, H. F. v. "ἀδελφός κτλ." *TDNT* 1. 144-146.

Solmsen, F. "The Aristotelian Tradition in Ancient Rhetoric." *AJP* 62 (1941) 35-50, 169-190.

Spicq, C. "πίστις." *Theological Lexicon of the New Testament* 3. 110-116.

— "κοσμέω, κόσμιος." *Theological Lexicon of the New Testament* 2. 330-335.

— "ταπεινός κτλ." *Theological Lexicon of the New Testament* 3. 369-371.

Stambaugh, J. and Balch, D. *The Social World of the First Christians.* London: SPCK, 1986.

Stamps, D. "Rhetorical Criticism and the Rhetoric of New Testament Criticism." *JLT* 6 (1992) 268-279.

Stegemann, E. W. and Stegemann, W. *Urchristliche Sozialgeschichte. Die Anfänge im Judentum und die Christusgemeinden in der mediterranen Welt.* Stuttgart: Verlag Kohlhammer, 1995.

Stirewalt, M.L., Jr. *Studies in Ancient Greek Epistolography.* SBL. Resources for Biblical Study 27. Atlanta, GA: Scholars Press, 1993.

Stowers, S. K. *Letter Writing in Greco-Roman Antiquity.* LEC 5. Philadelphia, PA: Westminister, 1986.

Strecker, G. *Literaturgeschichte des Neuen Testaments.* UTB.W 1682. Göttingen: Vandenhoeck & Ruprecht, 1992.

Sullivan, D. L. "Establishing Orthodoxy: The Letters of Ignatius of Antioch as Epideictic Rhetoric." *The Journal of Communication and Religion* 15 (1992) 71-86.

Telfer, W. *The Office of a Bishop.* London: Darton, Longmann & Todd, 1962.

Theissen, G. "Wanderradikalismus. Litertursoziologische Aspekte der Überlieferung von Worten Jesu im Urchristentum." In *idem. Studien zur Soziologie des Urchristentums.* 3rd ed. WUNT 19. Tübingen: Mohr, 1989, 79-105 (First printed in *ZThK* 70 [1973] 245-271).

— "Soziale Schichtung in der korinthischen Gemeinde. Ein Beitrag zur Soziologie des hellenistischen Urchristentums." In *idem. Studien zur Soziologie des Urchristentums.* 3rd ed. WUNT 19. Tübingen: Mohr, 1989, 231-271 (First printed in *ZNW* 65 [1974] 232-272).

— "Die Starken und Schwachen in Korinth. Sozologische Analyse eines theologischen Streites." In *idem. Studien zur Soziologie des Urchristentums.* 3rd ed. WUNT 19. Tübingen: Mohr, 1989, 272-289 (First printed in *EvTh* 35 [1975] 155-172).

— "Soziale Integration und sakramentales Handeln. Eine Analyse von 1 Cor. XI 17-34." In *idem. Studien zur Soziologie des Urchristentums.* 3rd ed. WUNT 19. Tübingen: Mohr, 1989, 290-317. (First printed in *NT* 16 [1974] 179-206).

Thiselton, A. C. "Semantics and New Testament Interpretation." In *New Testament Interpretation. Essays on Principles and Methods.* Ed. I. H. Marshall. Exeter: Paternoster Press, 1977, 75-104.

Thraede, K. "Homonoia (Eintracht)." *RAC* 16 (1994) 176-289.

Thurén, L. *The Rhetorical Strategy of 1 Peter. With Special Regard to Ambiguous Expressions.* Åbo: Åbo AP, 1990.

— "On Studying Ethical Argumentation and Persuasion in the New Testament." In *Rhetoric and the New Testament. Essays from the 1992 Heidelberg Conference.* Eds. S. E. Porter and T. H. Olbricht. JSNT.S 90. Sheffield: Sheffield AP, 1993, 464-478.

Thyen, H. *Der Stil der jüdisch-hellenistischen Homilie.* Göttingen: Vandenhoeck & Ruprecht, 1955.

Tidball, D. *An Introduction to the Sociology of the New Testament.* Exeter: Paternoster Press, 1983.

Torjesen, K. J. *When Women Where Priests. Women's Leadership in the Early Church and the Scandal of their Subordination in the Rise of Christianity.* San Francisco, CA: Harper _& Row_, 1993.

Trier, J., *Der deutsche Wortschatz im Sinnbezirk des Verstandes. Die Geschichte eines sprachlichen Feldes,* Band 1: *Von den Anfängen bis zum Beginn des 13. Jahrhunderts,* Heidelberg 1931.

— "Das sprachliche Feld. Eine Auseinandersetzung", *Neue Jahrbücher für Wissenschaft und Jugendbildung* 10 (1934) 428-449.

Turner, H. E. W. *The Pattern of Christian Truth: A Study in the Relations between Orthodoxy and Heresy in the Early Church.* Bampton Lectures 1954. London: A.R. Mowbray & Co, 1954.

Tångberg, K. A. "Linguistics and Theology: An Attempt to Analyze and Evaluate James Barr's Argumentation in *The Semantics of Biblical Language* and *Biblical Words for Time.*" *BiTr* 24 (1973) 301-310.

Übelacker, W. G. *Der Hebräerbrief als Appell. 1. Untersuchungen zu Exordium, Narratio und Postscriptum (Hebr 1-2 und 13,22-25).* CB.NT 21. Lund: Almqvist & Wiksell, 1989.

Ullmann, S. *Grundzüge der Semantik. Die Bedeutung in Sprachwissenschaftlicher Sicht.* Berlin: de Gruyter, 1967.

Vanderbroeck, P. J. J. *Popular Leadership and Collective Behavior in the Late Roman Republic (ca. 80-50 B.C.).* Amsterdam: J.C. Gieben 1987.

Vassilyev, L. M. "The Theory of Semantic Fields: A Survey." *Linguistics* 137 (1974) 79-93.

Vernant, J.-P. *The Origins of Greek Thought.* Ithaca, NY: Cornell UP, 1982.

Verner, D. C. *The Household of God. The Social World of the Pastoral Epistles.* SBL.DS 71. Chico, CA: Scholars Press, 1983.

Vielhauer, P. *Geschichte der urchristlichen Literatur. Einleitung in das Neue Testament, die Apokryphen und die Apostolischen Väter.* Berlin: Walter de Gruyter, 1975.

Volkmann, R. *Die Rhetorik der Griechen und Römer in systematischer Übersicht.* 2nd ed. Leipzig: Teubner, 1855.

Wardman, A. *Plutarch's Lives.* London: Paul Elek, 1974.

Watson, D. F. and Hauser, A. J. *Rhetorical Criticism of the Bible. A Comprehensive Bibliography with Notes on History and Method.* Biblical Interpretation Series 4. Leiden: Brill, 1994.

Watson, D. F. *Invention, Arrangement, and Style: Rhetorical Criticism of Jugde and 2 Peter.* SBL.DS 104. Atlanta, GA: Scholars Press, 1988.

— ed. *Persuasive Artistry: Studies in New Testament Rhetoric in Honor of George. A. Kennedy.* JSNT.S 50. Sheffield: Sheffield AP, 1991.

— "Notes on History and Method." In D. F. Watson and A. J. Hauser, *Rhetorical Criticism of the Bible. A Comprehensive Bibliography with Notes on History and Method.* Biblical Interpretation Series 4. Leiden: Brill, 1994, 101-25.

Welborn, L. L. "A Conciliatory Principle in 1 Cor 4:6." *NT* 29 (1987) 320-346.

— "On the Discord in Corinth: 1 Corinthians 1 - 4 and Ancient Politics." *JBL* 106 (1987) 85 - 111.

Wengst, K. *Pax Romana and the Peace of Jesus Christ.* Trans. J. Bowden. London: SCM, 1987.

White, J. L. *The Form and Function of the Body of the Greek Letter: A Study of the Letter-Body in Non-Literary Papyri and in Paul the Apostle.* SBL.DS 2. Missoula: Society of Biblical Literature 1972.

— *Light from Ancient Letters.* Philadelphia, PA: Fortress, 1986.

Wiklander, B. *Prophecy as Literature.* CB.OT 22. Lund: Gleerup, 1984.

Wills, L. "The Form of the Sermon in Hellenistic Judaism and Early Christianity." HThR 77 (1984) 277-299.

Witherington III, B. *Conflict and Community in Corinth. A Socio-Rhetorical Commentary on 1 and 2 Corinthians.* Grand Rapids, MI: Eerdmans, 1995.

Wood, N. *Cicero's Social and Political Thought.* Berkeley: University of California Press, 1988.

Worthington, I. *A Historical Commentary on Dinarchus. Rhetoric and Conspiracy in Later Fourth-Century Athens.* Ann Arbor: The University of Michigan Press, 1992.

Wuellner, W. "The Sociological Implications of 1 Corinthians 1,26-28 Reconsidered." In *StEv* VI (1973). Ed. E. A. Livingstone. Berlin: Akademie-Verlag, 1973, 666-672.

— "Ursprung und Verwendung der σοφός-, δυνατός-, εὐγενής- Formel in 1 Kor 1,26." In *Donum Gentilicium - New Testament Studies in Honour of David Daube.* Eds. E. Bammel, C. K. Barrett, W. D. Davies. Oxford: Clarendon, 1978, 165-184.

— "Greek Rhetoric and Pauline Argumentation." In *Early Christian Literature and the Classical Intellectual Tradition. In honorem Robert M. Grant.* Eds. W. R. Schoedel and R. L. Wilken. ThH 53. Paris: Éditions Beauchesne, 1979, 177-188.

— "Der Jakobsbrief im Licht der Rhetorik und Textpragmatik." *LingBibl* 43 (1987) 5-66.

— "Where is Rhetorical Criticism Taking us?" *CBQ* 49 (1987) 448-463.

— "Rhetorical Criticism and its Theory in Culture-Critical Perspective: The Narrative Rhetoric of John 11." In *Text and Interpretation. New Approaches in the Criticism of the New Testament.* Eds. P. J. Hartin and J. H. Petzer. NTTS 15. Leiden: Brill, 1991, 171-185.

Zillig, P. *Die Theorie von der gemischten Verfassung in ihrer literarischen Entwicklung im Altertum und ihr Verhältnis zur Lehre Lockes und Montesquieus über Verfassung.* Inaugural-Dissertation. Würzburg: Der Königl. Universitätsdruckerei, 1916.

Zollitsch, R. *Amt und Funktion des Priesters. Eine Untersuchung zum Ursprung und zur Gestalt des Presbyterats in den ersten zwei Jahrhunderten.* FThSt 96. Freiburg: Herder, 1974.

Index of Passages

I. Israelite and Jewish Texts

A. Old Testament

Proverbs
1:23-33   197
17:14   80

Isaiah
3:5   290–291

Jeremiah
9:23-24   158

B. Apocrypha, Pseudepigrapha and Other Early Jewish Texts

Jesus Sirah (Ben Sira)
25:1   195

Josephus
Antiquitates Judaicae
9.281f.   103
14.152-154   308
16.188f.   103
De bello Judaico
1.10f.   103

4 Maccabees
3:20f.   138
13:23-14:3   195

Philo
De decalogo
152f.   103
De Josepho
73   44
De posteritate Caini
184f.   138
185   138

Pseudo-Phocylides
Sentences
70-75   95

1QS
2:24-25   128
5:3f.   128

II. Early Christian Texts

A. New Testament

Mark
9:35   128
10:42-44   128

15:7   80

Luke		14	288
14:11	128	14:33	98
22:25-27	128		
23:19	80	**2 Corinthians**	
		12:20	96, 98
Acts			
15:2	80	**Galatians**	
19:40	80	5:20	96
23:7	80		
24:5	80	**Philippians**	
		1:15-17	96
Romans		2:1-4	129
1:29	96	2:3f.	127
1:29-31	171	4:3	4
1:29-32	256		
13:13	96	**1 Timothy**	
		6:4	96
1 Corinthians			
1:26-29	293	**James**	
3:1-3	96	3:16	98
4:10	294	4:10	128
12	179, 181		
13	196, 266	**1 Peter**	
13:4-7	191	5:5f.	128
13:8f.	288		

B. Apostolic Fathers and Other Early Christian Texts

Clemens Alexandrinus		2:4	49, 140
Stromateis		2:5f.	143
5. 12	4	2:6	79
		2:7	235
1 Clement		2:8	117, 145, 330
Praescript	3	3:1	149, 224
1:1	8, 10–12, 53, 79, 100, 105–106, 113, 219, 222	3:2	11, 38, 46, 62, 79, 84–85, 91, 96–98, 149
		3:2-6:4	45
1:2	112–113, 115, 328	3:3	12, 46, 149, 225, 289–292, 296–298, 313
1:3	52, 113, 117, 120, 123	3:4	45, 47, 50, 52, 57, 76, 78, 117, 150, 153, 225–226, 235, 331
2:1	120, 328		
2:2	76, 78, 136, 330		
2:3	106	4:1-6:4	235

4:1-7	155	14:1	12, 52, 97, 106,
4:1-13	235		132, 243, 245
4:6	47	14:1f.	96
4:7	85	14:1-5	243
4:9	97	14:2	12, 47–48, 79,
4:12	96		91, 102, 245
4:13	85, 97	14:4	159
5:1	11, 53, 57	14:4-5	159
5:1-6:2	235	15:1	159, 244–245
5:2	46, 58, 85, 97	15:1-16:1	244
5:3-7	155	15:6	159
5:5	96	16:1	159, 245
5:6	53	16:2	58, 132, 333
5-6	11	16:2-16:17	246
6:1	58	16:17	58, 160
6:2	106	17:1	58
6:4	12, 46, 58, 85,	17:1-19:1	246
	91, 96, 104,	19:1	160, 242, 247
	155, 236	19:2	78, 247
7:1	156, 237, 239	19:2b	247–248
7:1-4	239	20	160–162, 164
7:2	35, 37, 52	20:1-21:1	72
7:2-3	156	20:3	163
7:4	156, 331–332	20:10	81–82
7:5	240	20:10f.	76, 82, 163
7:6f.	49, 240	20:11	81–82, 163,
8:1-4	240		248–249
8:5	332	20:12	248
9:1	12, 35, 37, 46–	21:1	52, 163, 248–
	47, 58, 91, 96,		249
	156, 240–241	21:4	52
9:1b	240	21:5	164
9:2	58, 241	21:5-8	249
9:3-11:1	241	21:6	333
10:1	109	21:6-8	60, 123, 334
10:1f.	157	21:8	199
10:6	109	22:1	249
10:7	109, 157	22:6-8	249
11:1	49, 157	23:1	167, 249–250
11:2	157, 241	23:2	250
12	157	23:3	167
12:1	49	23:3f.	250
12:1-8	241	23:4f.	167
13:1	35, 132, 242	23:5	250, 335
13:3	158	24:1	167, 251, 335
		24:2	335

24:2-5	251	38:2	182, 297–298, 313, 315
25:1-5	251	39:1	184, 258
26:1	251	40:1	184, 233, 259
26:1-3	251	40:1-5	259
27:1	251	41:1	259–260, 337
27:3	251	41:2	185
27:3b-7	251	41:3	185
28:1	35, 252	41:4	12, 185, 259
29:1	106, 168, 252	42:1-4	260
30:1	35, 37, 168, 253	42:2	337
30:2	253	42:4	337
30:3	35, 37, 72, 127, 253	43:2	96, 260
		43:6	97
30:6	253	44:1	186, 261
31:1	254	44:2	186, 261
31:2	109	44:3-5	11
31:2-4	254	44:3-6	261
32:3f.	254–255	44:4	261
32:4	106	44:6	12, 186, 261
33:1	255	45:1	262
33:2-33:6	255	45:3	58, 106, 262
33:7	255	45:4	97, 106, 262
33:8	52, 59, 170, 255	45:6f.	262
		45:7	106
34:6	170	45:8	186, 262
34:7	72, 171	46:1	59
35:2	171	47:1-7	263
35:4	174	46:2-4	262
35:5	36, 256, 335	46:5	91, 98, 266
35:5a	171	46:5-7	188, 262, 338
35:5b	171	46:6	188
35:7-12	256	46:7	60, 181, 189
36:1	256	46:8	53
36:6	256	46:9	79, 91, 143, 189
37:1	52, 174, 257		
37:1-4	60	47	190
37:2-4	174	47:4	143
37:2f.	186, 258	47:5	53, 112, 140
37:3	174, 176	47:5-7	312
37:4	177	47:6	11–12, 50, 112, 190, 312
37:5	60, 179, 258, 336		
		47:6f.	263
38	312	47:7	11, 48, 190
38:1	37, 49, 336	48:1	50, 53, 140, 190, 265
38:1-3	258		

48:2	190, 338	60:1f.	273
48:2-4	265	60:2	52, 106
48:4	106, 190	60:4	72, 76, 78, 82,
48:6	50, 191, 265		120, 273
49:1	265, 338	61:1	76, 120
49:1-6	265	61:2	52, 76
49:1ff.	288	62:1	49
49:2	339	62:1-3	229
49:2-6	191	62:2	76, 78, 82, 113,
49:5	51, 143, 191,		126, 198, 229
	266	62:2-63:1	59
50:1	266	62:3	199
50:2	37, 51, 191,	63:1	36, 79, 200
	267, 339	63:1f.	228
50:3f.	267	63:2	13, 36–37, 72,
50:5	72, 192, 267,		75–76, 78–79,
	339		82, 200, 231
50:6	267	63:3	4, 11
50:7	267, 339	63:4	77
51:1	12, 192	64	200
51:2	192	64:1	76, 78
51:2f.	268	65:1	72, 76, 78, 82,
51:3	53, 192, 268		200, 228
51:3-5	268		
51:4	47	**Eusebius**	
52:1-4	268	*Historia ecclesiastica*	
54:1f.	192	3.15	4
54:2	13, 51, 76, 79,	3.16.1	1
	269, 288	3.18.4	5
54:3	269, 312, 315	3.38.1	1
54:4	105, 269	4.22.1	1
55:1-6	269	4.23.11	1, 3
56:1	196, 270		
56:2	49, 53, 270	**Hermas**	
56:16	106	*Visiones*	
57:1	12, 37, 79, 196,	2.4.3	2–3
	270–271		
57:1f.	288	**Ignatius**	
57:2	36, 197	*Romans*	
58:1	106, 271	3:1	10
58:2	36–37, 49, 117,		
	197, 270–272,	**Irenaeus**	
	340	*Adversus haereses*	
59:1	48	3.3.3	1, 3, 5
59:1f.	272		
60:1	78		

| Polycarp | 1-12, 14 | 10 |
| *Philippians* | 13 | 10 |

III. Classical Texts

A. Greek Texts

Anaximenes = Ps.-Aristoteles		
Rhetorica ad Alexandrum		
1.1.1421b 1ff.	25	
1.1.1421b 9	35	
1.1.1421b 23-26	40	
1.1.1422a 12f.	40	
1.4.23-26	40	
2.2.1423a 22ff.	61	
2.3.1423a 30-1425b 35	61	
5.1427b 31ff.	26	
29-37	24	
30.1438a 3-6	226	
32.1439a 1-3	55	

Aristides		
Ars rhetorica		
399.21-25	40	
Orationes		
1.393	111	
23.2f.	93	
23.6-7	221	
23.12	93	
23.28f.	93	
23.31	74	
23.34	176	
23.40	93	
23.53	89–90, 195	
23.55	99	
23.57-58	93	
23.65	301	
23.75f.	147	
23.77	166	
24.3	102	
24.4	89, 234	
24.7	125	
24.8	125	
24.30	103	
24.32	57, 125	

24.33-35	125	
24.38	181	
24.39	181	
24.47	89, 105	
24.48	106	
24.49	111	
27.41	147, 187	
34.4	89	
37.27	187	

Aristoteles		
Ethica Nicomachea		
5.1.13	151	
5.1.15	151	
5.1.19	151	
8.1.4	194	
9.6.1	193	
Politica		
2.4.1	300	
3.4.7	43	
3.4.7-3.5.4	43	
5.1.6f.	299	
5.2.1ff.	299	
5.2.2	300	
5.2.3	128	
5.2.4	133, 169, 300, 311	
5.7.1	119	
5.7.2	135	
Rhetorica		
1.2.22	63	
1.3.1-3	33	
1.3.3	25, 35	
1.3.4	36	
1.3.5	38	
1.3.6	39	
1.3.9	25	
1.4.7	25, 61	

1.6.16	39	53.8.2	87
1.9.1	25	67.14.1f.	5
1.9.7	151		
1.9.35	26, 221	**Dio Chrysostomus**	
1.9.40	54–55	*Orationes*	
1.10.1	25	1	169
2.2.5-6	168	1.79	132
2.11.1	93–94	1.82	132
2.18.1	134	6.31	98
2.18-19	63	11.53	98
2.20.1	54	24.14	42
3.13.1-3	24	26.8	125
3.13.3	210	31.108	308
3.14.8	24	32.37	121, 147
3.14.12	24	33	74
3.16.11	224–225	34	74
3.19.1	231	34.6-7	237
		34.7-26	237
Athenaeus		34.17	112, 116
Deipnosophistai		34.19	44, 183
13.561 C	194	34.21f.	187
		34.22	44
Demetrius(?)		34.27	112
De Elocutione		36.21	121
223	28	36.31	186
		36.31-32	121
Democritus		36.31f.	187
Fragment		38	74, 237
245	95	38.8	88, 195, 234
		38.10	74
Demosthenes		38.10-20	237
Epistulae		38.11	88, 99, 106,
1.5	44		238
1.10	45	38.12	238
Orationes		38.13	99
4.51	45	38.15	88, 125, 142
21.186	130	38.21-30	310
		38.24	310
Dio Cassius		38.29	310
44.1.2-2.1	87	38.48	88
44.2.4	115	39.2	83, 88, 105
44.24.2	87	39.4	88
44.24.3f.	87	39.5	42, 181
44.25.3f.	87	39.6f.	88
44.34.3f.	110	39.7	74
52.15.5	107	39.8	92, 195, 274

40	74
40.16	42
40.26	83, 88
40.35	116
40.35-37	165
40.35f.	106
40.38f.	165
41	74
41.8f.	92
41.10	57
44	310
44.1	310
44.2	311
44.8	311
44.10	122, 187
48.2	115
48.6	92
48.7	311
48.13	112
49.6	82
61.12f.	169
66.2	308
66.2f.	308
75.7	308
77/78.39	95, 173

Diodorus Siculus

1.66.1f.	110
2.6.3	97
3.64.7	86
4.48.5	97
7.12.4	112
12.8.4	144
12.25.1f.	101
12.35.1	86
12.35.3	86
12.66.2	144
13.9.6	97
13.48	102
13.48.2	102
13.48.3	102
16.7.2	101
16.68.3	97
29.19.1	86
34/35.33.5	173

Dionysius Halicarnassensis
Antiquitates Romanae

2.18.1	115
2.74.1	152
2.76.3	86
3.25.3	97
3.26.3	97
5.53.1f.	301
5.53.3	301
6.1.1	137
6.1.4	137
6.35.1f.	238
6.35.2	238
6.36.2f.	238
6.54.1	301
6.86.1	180
6.86.4	180
6.86.5	180, 182
7.33.1f.	147
7.40-46	86
7.41.1	118
7.42.1	86, 90
7.42.2	153
7.42.2f.	87, 119
8.9.3	110, 112
8.75.4	87
9.5.5	87
9.44.1	116
11.8.3	147
11.33.4	97

Epictetus
Dissertationes

| 2.10.4f. | 182 |
| 3.24.31-36 | 175 |

Euripides
Fragment

| 21 | 178 |

Herodes Atticus
Περὶ πολιτείας

| 17-18, 29 | 119 |
| 36f. | 119 |

Herodianus
  3.2.7f.   95
  4.14.6   139
  8.2.4   139

Herodotus
  9.92   110
  9.106   110

Isocrates
  Epistulae
    3.1   45
    9.19   45
  Orationes
    3.41   124
    3.56   130
    4.3   114
    4.20   43
    4.23   43
    4.114   89
    4.167f.   89
    4.174   89
    4.183   43
    4.184   43
    6.82   56
    7.16   43
    7.84   56
    8.10   42
    8.16   42–43
    8.28f.   42
    8.36f.   57
    8.66   43
    8.143   57
    12.20   130
    12.258f.   101

Plato
  Cleitophon
    409 D-E   152
  Leges
    3.678 E   193
    4.716 A-E   131
    869 E   96
    870 C-D   96
  Phaedo
    256 C-D   110

Phaedrus
    266 D-E   208
Politicus
    311 B-C   193
Respublica
    1.351 D   152
    4.430 D-E   114
    4.432 A   114
    4.433 C-D   123

Pseudo-Plato
  Epistulae
    7. 336 D-337 B   119

Plutarchus
  Aratus
    24.5   183
  Lycurgus
    4.1   118
    31.1   115
  Moralia
    11 D   146
    70 C   124
    86 C   94
    97 C   146
    139 D   126
    140 C   146
    144 B-C   124
    330 E   83
    474 A-B   177
    474 B   178
    478 D   141
    478 E-F   141
    479 A   142
    481 C   145
    483 D   141
    484 B   141
    488 A   94
    511 C   83
    539 D   132
    539 E-545   132
    540 B   133
    540 B, D   133
    544 B   133
    545 D   133
    547 A   132

787 D	308	23.11.1-8	194
788 E	311	23.11.2	194
814 F-815 B	74		
816 A	308, 315	Stobaeus	
821 F	309	2.106.12-17	194
824 A-C	74		
824 C	92	Theon	
824 C-D	92	*Progymnasmata*	
824 D	92	10.236	27
Otho			
15.6	83	Thucydides	
Pericles		3.81.4	300
3.1	177	3.82.4	135
3.1f.	118	3.82.7f.	135
		3.82.8	300
Polybius			
Historiae		Xenophon	
1.34.9	97	*Agesilaus*	
1.67.2	97	11.10f.	130
1.70.1	97	*Hellenica*	
3.45.3	97	1.3.4	110
5.86.1	97	*Memorabilia*	
6.46.7f.	172	4.4.16	118, 124
11.17.4	97		

B. Latin Texts

Cicero		*Partitiones Oratoriae*	
De Inventione Rhetorica		4.13	224–225
1.5.7	25	9.31	208
1.19.27	208	*Topica*	
1.21.30	24	24.91	25
1.22.31	208		
1.22.32	209	Fortunatianus	
1.52.98-100	230	*Ars rhetorica*	
2.4.12	41	1.1.17f.	35
2.51.155-156	25		
2.51.156	39, 41	Julius Victor	
2.53.150-54.164	41	*Ars rhetorica*	
2.53.159	41	27	27
2.55.166	41		
2.56.169	41	Quintilianus	
Epistulae ad Atticum		*Institutionis Oratoriae*	
8.14.1	28	2.21.23	25
9.10.1	28	3.3.14f.	25
12.53	28	3.4	37

3.4.11	26	3.2.3	39, 49
3.4.15	35	3.2.3-4.8	41
3.4.16	26	3.8.15	26
3.5.5	211		
3.5.7	211	Seneca	
3.5.8	212	*Controversiae*	
3.5.13	212	9 pr. 1	136
3.8.1	41	10 pr. 15	135
3.8.6-11	24	*De beneficiis*	
3.8.9	37	1.4.2	305
3.14.12-15	25	1.10.4	305
4.1.7	222	*De brevitate vitae*	
4.1.72	24	2.4	304
4.2.4f.	24	*Epistulae*	
4.2.31	208, 224	75.1	28
4.2.86	208		
9.4.19f.	27	Suetonius	
		Domitianus	
Rhetorica ad Herennium		15.1	5
1.2.2	25, 35		

Index of Authors

Aasgaard, R. 140–141
Adkins, A. W. H. 307
Alonso-Schökel, L. 17
Altaner, B. and Stuiber, A. 2, 205–206
Alter, R. 17
Andersen, Ø. 63
Andrén, O. 13, 109, 150, 152, 161–163
Aune, D. E. 23–24, 29–30, 63, 217

Baasland, E. 16, 205–206, 226, 248, 250
Bakke, O. M. 16
Balch, D. L. 123–124
Baldinger, K. 65–66
Baldwin, C. S. 23
Banks, R. 313–314
Bardy, G. 161
Barnard, L. W. 9
Barr, J. 68
Barthes, R. 33
Bauer, J. B. 10
Bauer, W. 47, 93, 96, 105, 108, 131, 133, 143–144, 149, 190, 206, 231, 282, 286, 288, 323
Beck, I. 33, 40
Behr, C. A. 74, 181, 234, 301
Berger, K. 72
Betz, H. D. 17–18, 22, 24–25, 132, 135, 140–141, 211, 319–320, 329
Beyschlag, K. 9, 12–13, 99, 137, 284
Bihlmeyer, K. 205–206
Bingham, D. J. 7
Bitzer, L. F. 18
Black, C. C. 17
Black, D. A. 129
Bloch, R. 78
Blum, G. G. 283–284
Bohatec, J. 294

Bonner, E. E. 21
Botha, J. 17, 19
Bowe, B. E. 8, 13–16, 35, 47–48, 51, 76, 80, 82, 84, 98–99, 120–121, 126–129, 131, 143, 146–147, 163, 174–176, 191, 198, 223, 227–228, 231, 234, 273, 275, 283–284, 286–290, 323–324
Bowersock, G. W. 136
Brandt, W. J. 19
Brown, R. E. and Meier, J. M. 314
Brox, N. 3
Brucker, R. 27
Brunner, G. 4, 9, 52, 73, 76, 120, 126, 205–206, 278, 285, 288, 322, 324
Bumpus, H. B. 331, 334, 339
Burke, K. 19

Caird, G. B. 275
Campbell, R. A. 285, 288, 314
Von Campenhausen, H. F. 3, 120, 278, 283–285
Chadwick, H. 116
Chow, J. K. 303–304, 309
Clarke, A. D. 308
Clarke, M. L. 21
Classen, C. J. 19, 24–25, 27
Conzelmann, H. 179, 295
Cosby, M. R. 55, 60
Coseriu, E. 67–68
Cotterell, P. and Turner, M. 66, 68
Countryman, L. Wm. 287–289, 299
Crouch, J. E. 123

Danker, F. W. 307
Davids, A. 149, 286, 290
Davis, J. A. 295
Deissmann, G. A. 112

Delling, G. 80–81, 131
Dibelius, M. 3
Dibelius, M. and Conzelmann, H. 175
Dinkler, E. 77, 84
Dormeyer, D. 27, 29
Doty, W. G. 217
Dover, K. J. 168
Drews, P. 161, 273
Duchacek, O. 69

Edmundsen, C. E. G. 9
Eggenberger, C. 9, 161–162, 166
Eggenberger, C. E. 9
Ehrenberg, V. 301
Ehrhardt, A. A. T. 107, 117
Eisenstadt, S. N. 302
Eisenstadt, S. N. and Roniger, L. 303–305
Elliot, J. H. 123, 313
Elliott, N. 20
Eltester, W. 161, 163
Erlemann, K. 9–10
Esler, P. F. 306
Exler, F. J. 217

Fascher, E. 295
Filson, F. V. 313
Finley, M. I. 80–81, 90, 307
Fiore, B. 17
Fiorenza, E. S. 287
Fischer, J. A. 100–101, 123, 174–175, 205–206, 245, 283, 285
Fisher, E. W. 13, 46, 51, 96, 327
Fisher, N. R. E. 168–169
Foerster, W. 77–78
Forbes, C. 132, 168
Fraenkel, J. J. 168
Von Fritz, K. 177
Fuchs, H. 161
Fuellenbach, J. 9, 12–13, 15, 260, 282, 284, 287
Fuhrmann, M. 33, 208–211, 221
Fuks, A. 73
Fullenbach, J. 205–206
Funk, R. 30

Garnsey, P. and Saller, R. P. 305
Garrison, R. 287, 289, 299
Geckeler, H. 65, 67–70
Gehrke, H.-J. 80–81, 86
Gerke, F. 283–285
Goldstein, J. A. 30
Grant, R. M. 3, 10, 162, 164
Grant, R. M. and Graham, H. H. 175, 179, 205–206, 233, 335
Grundmann, W. 127–129

Hagner, D. A. 2, 4–6, 8–10, 117, 150, 152, 156–160, 167, 171, 173, 179, 185, 188–189, 191, 246, 250–251, 256, 266, 270, 290, 292
Hall, A. 161, 163
Hanson, S. 179
Von Harnack, A. 3, 6, 10, 101, 185, 205, 266, 274, 282–284, 287–288, 290, 328, 341
Hartman, L. 123
Hasenhütl, G. 278
Hatch, E. and Redpath, H. A. 73
Hauck, F. 106–107
Hauser, A. J. 16–17, 20, 30
Hay, D. M. 110
Hellholm, D. 20, 22, 30, 33, 69, 207, 209–216, 233, 235, 239, 319
Helm, R. 5
Heron, A. I. C. 288
Höistad, R. 73
Holmberg, B. 292–293, 295–296, 313
Holmstrand, J. 20
Hommel, H. 33, 208
Hooijberg, A. E. W. 9, 286
Horrell, D. G. 288–289, 299, 314
Horsley, R. A. 295
Hudson-Williams, H. L. 33
Hughes, F. W. 27
Hyldahl, N. 205–206

Jaeger, W. 8, 60, 76, 151, 161, 178–179, 183–184, 199
Jaubert, A. 175
Jeffers, J. S. 3, 6–8, 10, 108, 175
Johanson, B. C. 20, 27, 213–215
Johnson, L. T. 94–96

Jones, C. P. 237, 310–311
Jost, K. 56
Judge, E. A. 132, 293, 313

Kalverkämper, H. 20
Kaufman, R. 305
Kennedy, G. A. 18, 22–25, 33, 39, 43, 54, 211, 218, 319
Kent, J. H. 308
Keresztes, P. 9
Klauck, H.-J. 27, 183, 313
Kleck, J. 33
Kleist, J. A. 8, 205
Knoch, O. B. 15, 48, 126–127, 164, 205–206, 287, 339
Knopf, R. 48, 98, 161–162, 164, 170, 172, 175, 200, 205–206, 245, 247–248, 251, 254, 265–267, 273–274, 282, 284, 329
Kopperschmidt, J. 33
Koskenniemi, H. 217
Köster, H. 9
Kramer, H. 73, 75

Lake, K. 101, 174, 290
Lambrecht, J. 17
Lampe, P. 3, 5–6, 60, 140, 293, 313–314, 316
Larsson, E. 329
Lausberg, H. 23, 33, 207–209, 211–212, 221
Lawson, J. 2
Lehrer, A. 70
Liang, K. J. 126, 129, 131, 206
Liddell, H. G. and Scott, R. 81, 91, 93, 97, 99, 101, 104–105, 107–108, 113, 116, 122, 130–131, 133, 138, 144, 146, 149, 183, 192, 328
Lietzmann, H. 3, 286–287
Liftin, D. A. 21, 134–135
Lightfoot, J. B. 1–2, 5–6, 8, 10, 13, 100, 137, 175, 329
Lindemann, A. 2, 9–10, 48, 117, 120, 127, 145, 159–161, 167–168, 172, 174–175, 179, 184–185, 188, 197–198, 200, 205–206, 217, 233, 239, 242, 244–246, 248–249, 251–253, 256–257, 259–260, 263, 265–269, 271, 273–274, 285, 291, 297–298, 327–332, 334

Lintott, A. 80
Loenen, D. 95
Lona, H. E. 2–4, 9, 48, 76, 78–80, 84, 94, 108–109, 112, 117, 132, 140, 152, 161–164, 172–175, 179, 184, 191, 205–207, 218, 233, 242, 248, 250–253, 260, 266, 269, 273, 275, 282, 284–285, 290, 327–332, 336, 341
Lösch, S. 7–8
Low, J. P. 193
Lumpe, A. 54, 56, 59
Lyons, J. 65–66, 68–70

MacDowell, D. M. 168
Mack, B. L. 20
MacMullen, R. 134, 295–296
Maier, H. O. 116, 169, 282–283, 287–288, 290, 314, 316
Malherbe, A. J. 27–29, 63, 313
Malina, B. J. 128, 306, 309
Malina, B. J. and Neyrey, J. H. 309
Marrou, H. I. 21
Marshall, J. W. 156
Marshall, P. 130–131, 168–169
Martin, J. 23, 25, 33–35, 40, 54, 56, 61, 208–211, 221
Maurer, C. 143–144
Meeks, W. A. 24, 274, 293, 296, 313
Meinhold, P. 283–284
Merrill, E. T. 6, 9
Meyer, P. W. 24
Mikat, P. 10, 76, 80, 108, 198, 273, 288
Milburn, R. L. P. 6, 9
Milligan, G. 104
Milobenski, E. 94–96
Mitchell, M. M. 18–19, 22, 24–27, 29, 39, 42, 45, 55–57, 62, 75, 81, 90, 93, 96–98, 106, 112, 122, 129, 133, 144–145, 165, 177–179, 181, 183, 188–189, 193, 195, 211, 217–218, 224, 237–238, 296, 301, 320
Molland, E. 9
Montgomery, H. 178
Moulakis, A. 73–74, 194
Moulton, J. H. 104
Moxnes, H. 302–308, 310–311
Muilenburg, J. 17

Müller, W. G. 27, 29–30
Murphy-O'Connor, J. 314

Nadeau, R. 211
Nestle, W. 180
Neyrey, J. H. 309
Nida, E. A. 68, 193
North, H. 113–114

Oepke, A. 97
Ogden, C. K. 69
Olsson, B. 20
Opitz, H. 283–284
Osiek, C. 3, 293

Patton, J. H. 17
Perelman, Ch. and Olbrechts-Tyteca, L. 19–20
Peterson, E. 217, 285
Pitt-Rivers, J. A. 306
Plett, H. F. 30, 33, 210
Plümacher, E. 60
Pogoloff, S. M. 19, 135–136, 168, 295–296
Powell, M. A. 16
Price, B. J. 54–56

Von Rad, G. 77–78
Raible, W. 69
Reed, J. T. 27
Rehrl, S. 128–131
Richards, E. R. 27
Robbins, V. K. 17
Robinson, J. A. 9
Robinson, T. A. 286, 288
Rohde, J. 283–285
De Romilly, J. 73
Roniger, L. 302
Rose, H. J. 75

Saller, R. P. 302–303, 305
Salzmann, J. Chr. 274
Sanders, L. 76, 161–162, 164, 174–175, 177, 191, 256, 266
Sandnes, K. O. 141–142
Sänger, D. 294–296

De Saussure, F. 65–66
Schecker, M. 22
Schmoller, A. 106
Schneider, G. 3, 175, 205–206, 267
Schneider, J. 217
Schoedel, W. R. 189
Schofield, M. 114, 194
Schrage, W. 30, 295
Schreiner, K. 294
Schrenk, G. 150–151
Schweizer, E. 278, 283–284
Schweizer, E. and Baumgärtel, F. 179
Sheppard, A. R. R. 73–74, 122
Siegert, F. 20–21
Sigountos, J. G. 266
Skard, E. 73, 75, 172, 177, 180
Skarsaune, O. 15, 117
Smit, J. 266
Smith, R. E. 30
Von Soden, H. 140
Solmsen, F. 24
Spicq, C. 77–78, 109–110, 131, 146–147
Städele, A. 30
Stambaughm J. and Balch, D. 313
Stamps, D. 17
Stegemann, E. W. and Stegemann, W. 292–293, 295–296
Stirewalt, M. L. 28, 30, 217
Stockmeier, P. 199
Stowers, S. K. 28–29, 217
Strecker, G. 27
Stuiber, A. 4, 6, 8–10, 283
Sullivan, D. L. 16
Synnes, M. 10

Tångberg, K. A. 68
Telfer, W. 284
Theissen, G. 284, 292–296, 298, 324
Thiselton, A. C. 65–67, 69
Thraede, K. 73–76, 79, 83, 118, 161, 165, 172, 188, 194
Thurén, L. 19, 21, 27
Thyen, H. 15
Tidball, D. 293
Torjesen, K. J. 113
Trier, J. 65, 67

Turner, H. E. W. 288

Übelacker, W. G. 20
Ullmann, S. 68–69
Van Unnik, W. C. 8, 13–16, 36, 63, 76, 82–
    84, 137–139, 161–164, 171, 198

Vanderbroeck, P. J. J. 81, 309
Vassilyev, L. 65
Vernant, J.-P. 114
Verner, D. C. 123, 126
Vielhauer, P. 3, 9–10, 205–206
Vogt, E. 33
Volkmann, R. 23, 33, 54–55, 61
Watson, D. F. 16–20, 22–24, 27, 30, 211, 229
Weiss, B. 282, 286
Welborn, L. L. 9–10, 80, 91, 94, 100–101,
    104–105, 119, 135, 144–145, 295–296,
    299–301
Wengst, K. 3–4, 8, 76, 146, 175, 182, 287
White, J. L. 215, 217, 227, 229
Whittaker, C. R. 95
Wiklander, B. 20
Wills, L. 15
Wilson, J. W. 13, 80, 137, 161, 163, 206
Witherington, W. 295
Wood, N. 177–178
Worthington, I. 60
Wrede, W. 206
Wuellner, W. 17, 19–20, 294–295

Ziegler, A. W. 108, 288
Zillig, P. 177
Zollitsch, R. 285

Index of Subjects

Adfectus 226
Advantage 49
   common 43
ἀδελφότης 140
ἀγάπη 191–192, 266
ἀκαταστασία 97
ἀλαζονεία 131
ἀπόνοια 107
ἀσφαλής 116
Antonyms of the concept of ὁμόνοια 202
Antonymy 67–68
Apotreptic 35
Approach 64
Archilexeme 70
Arrogance 246
Arrogant 158
Attentum parare 219
Authorship of 1 Clement 1, 3, 21

βέβαιος 112
Benevolum parare 220
Bishop lists 1
Boasting 158
Body metaphor 145, 179–183
Body-closing of a letter 227
Brotherly love 140

Catacombs of Domitilla 6
Christological interpretation 335
Christology 327
Classical genres 25
Common good 44–45, 50–51, 127
Communal identity of the Corinthians 50
Community life 76
Composition 15
Compositional analysis 207
Concord 63, 70, 141, 147, 157, 197, 238

and love 194
and peace of the universe 162
Conflict in the Corinthian Church 297
Connection to ὁμόνοια 152
Correction (παιδεία) 196

Date of 1 Clement 3, 11
Delimitation markers 239
δικαιοσύνη 150–152
δικαιοσύνη - ὁμόνοια 153
Direct address 215
Dispositio 207, 209, 211, 216
Docilem parare 219, 223, 236
Domitian's reign 8
Double-minded 250

εἰρήνη 76, 78, 82
εἰρήνη βαθεῖα 136, 139
εἰρήνη καὶ ὁμόνοια 13, 75, 78, 84
Encomium to Love 191
Epistolary
   postscript 217
   prescript 217
   theory 28
Epistolography 26–27, 29
ἔρις 12, 85, 91, 93, 172
Ethos 53, 222
Examples 54–57
Exordium 208, 218, 222
Expediency 38
Expedient 39

Fable of Menenius Agrippa 180
Factionalism 44
Flavia Domitilla 5–6
Flavius Clement 6
Function of 1 Clem. 20 162

Genre, function 15
Genus
    deliberativum 33–34
    demonstrativum 34
    iudiciale 34
God and concord 171
Good order 146, 185
    and concord 187
    of the universe 160
Graeco-Roman
    household 313
    rhetoric 17
Greek *polis* 106

Harmony of the universe 165
Hendiadys 82
Hermas 3
Hierarchical text-delimitation 210
Historical
    examples 235
    situation 282
Holy Spirit 330
Honour 305–308, 310–311, 315
Honour-shame culture 149, 305
House-church 314
Household 125–126
    code 124
    duties 122
Humility 126–127, 157–158
Hybris 168–169
    and sedition 169
Hymn of love 51
Hyponyms 71
Hyponymy 70
ὑπόθεσις 233

Ideals of the Greek city 138
Image
    of army as metaphor for Church 174
    of human body 179
Imperial freedman 7, 21
Invented examples 60
Invention 25

Jealousy 156

κίνδυνος 48–49
κοσμέω 146–148

Law(s) 118
    and concord 118
    of God 117
Letter
    closing 228
    writing 27
        manuals 27
Linguistic text analysis 213
Linguistics
    modern 20, 215
Literary skills 7
Love 266–267, 338–339
    and concord 193, 195

μετάνοια 240
Methodology 18–19, 22
Military metaphor 174, 176
Mixed constitution 177–178
Monarchical episcopacy 2
Muilenberg school 17

Narratio 208, 224–226, 236

Obedience 127, 171, 186
    to God's will 157
ὁμόνοια 71–75, 82, 86–89, 96, 223
    and εἰρήνη 81, 201
Oneness 338
Order 186, 260–261
    and harmony of the universe 166
    of the universe 164
Ordo naturalis 209

παιδεία 199, 270
Pan-Hellenic concord 74
Paradigmatic relation 66
Pathos 227, 231
Paths of blessing 254
Patronage 302, 311
Patron-client relations 303, 312
Peace
    and concord 200
    and harmony of the universe 247

profound 137
περίπτωσις 9
Peroratio 222, 226–227, 230–231
Persecution 8
Phoenix 251
φθόνος 46, 84–85, 94–95
πίστις 109–111, 113
πιστός 109
πλεονεξία 172–173
πόλεμος 98
Polis
    of God 145
Polis 73, 153, 187
Political
    rhetoric 78
    terms 64
    topics 61
    vocabulary 89–90
Prayer 272–273
Presbyters 2
Probatio 208, 212, 216, 222
Proof 54, 58
    by example 59
Propositio 208
Protreptic 35

Quaestio
    finita 211
    infinita 211–212, 235

Recapitulatio 198, 226, 229–230
Relationship
    associative 66
    syntagmatic 66
Religious and social background 5
Responsibility statement 228
Rhetoric
    as a seditious element 134
    deliberative 25, 41, 63
    divisive force of 136
    epideictic 221
Rhetorical
    analyses 16
    analysis 18
    arrangement 24
    composition 14

criticism 22
genre 14
handbooks 23, 29
theory 26
    modern 19
Roman army 175
Roman Church 1–2, 9, 100, 103

Salvation 49
De Saussure 65–66
σχίσμα 143, 189
σχίζω 144
Sedition 12
Self-praise 132
Semantic
    field 65, 67, 201
    markers 215
Sentence and text connectors 214
Shalom 77
Social
    and religious background 4
    background 7
    status 298
Socio-economic
    classes 299
    levels 296, 336
    tensions 300
σῶμα metaphor 189
σωφροσύνη 113–115
στασιάζω 190
στάσις 11, 14, 71, 74, 79–81, 86–90, 92, 106, 138, 189, 223, 237–238, 263
Status theory 211
Strife 156
Submission 120–121, 186, 197
    to the will of God 173
Substitution
    on abstraction-level 214
    on meta-level 213
συμβουλή 36
συμφορά 9–10, 100–104
Synonyms of the concept of ὁμόνοια 202
Synonymy 67–68

ταπεινοφρονέω 242–243
ταπεινοφροσύνη 129, 159–160

ταπεινός 130
Teaching of Christ 329
τελικὰ κεφάλαια 40, 53
τέλος 38
Terminus ad quem 10
Text linguistics 22
θάνατος 46–47
Theocentric
    perspective 330
    profile 332, 334, 340
θέσις 233

Time reference 37
Titius Flavius Clement 5
τὸ συμφέρον 41–42, 45
Topic of ὁμόνοια 62
Topics – rhetorical 61
Topoi 63–64, 70, 201–202
Trier, J. 65, 67

Unifying theme 207

ζῆλος 45–46, 84–85, 94, 96

Wissenschaftliche Untersuchungen zum Neuen Testament

Alphabetical Index of the First and Second Series

Ådna, Jostein: Jesu Stellung zum Tempel. 2000. *Volume II/119.*

Ådna, Jostein and *Kvalbein, Hans* (Ed.): The Mission of the Early Church to Jews and Gentiles. 2000. *Volume 127.*

Alkier, Stefan: Wunder und Wirklichkeit in den Briefen des Apostels Paulus. 2001. *Volume 134.*

Anderson, Paul N.: The Christology of the Fourth Gospel. 1996. *Volume II/78.*

Appold, Mark L.: The Oneness Motif in the Fourth Gospel. 1976. *Volume II/1.*

Arnold, Clinton E.: The Colossian Syncretism. 1995. *Volume II/77.*

Asiedu-Peprah, Martin: Johannine Sabbath Conflicts As Juridical Controversy. 2001. *Volume II/132.*

Avemarie, Friedrich and *Hermann Lichtenberger* (Ed.): Auferstehung – Ressurection. 2001. *Volume 135.*

Avemarie, Friedrich and *Hermann Lichtenberger* (Ed.): Bund und Tora. 1996. *Volume 92.*

Bachmann, Michael: Sünder oder Übertreter. 1992. *Volume 59.*

Baker, William R.: Personal Speech-Ethics in the Epistle of James. 1995. *Volume II/68.*

Bakke, Odd Magne: 'Concord and Peace'. 2001. *Volume II/143.*

Balla, Peter: Challenges to New Testament Theology. 1997. *Volume II/95.*

Bammel, Ernst: Judaica. Volume I 1986. *Volume 37*

– Volume II 1997. *Volume 91.*

Bash, Anthony: Ambassadors for Christ. 1997. *Volume II/92.*

Bauernfeind, Otto: Kommentar und Studien zur Apostelgeschichte. 1980. *Volume 22.*

Baum, Armin Daniel: Pseudepigraphie und literarische Fälschung im frühen Christentum. 2001. *Volume II/138.*

Bayer, Hans Friedrich: Jesus' Predictions of Vindication and Resurrection. 1986. *Volume II/20.*

Bell, Richard H.: Provoked to Jealousy. 1994. *Volume II/63.*

– No One Seeks for God. 1998. *Volume 106.*

Bergman, Jan: see *Kieffer, René*

Bergmeier, Roland: Das Gesetz im Römerbrief und andere Studien zum Neuen Testament. 2000. *Volume 121.*

Betz, Otto: Jesus, der Messias Israels. 1987. *Volume 42.*

– Jesus, der Herr der Kirche. 1990. *Volume 52.*

Beyschlag, Karlmann: Simon Magus und die christliche Gnosis. 1974. *Volume 16.*

Bittner, Wolfgang J.: Jesu Zeichen im Johannesevangelium. 1987. *Volume II/26.*

Bjerkelund, Carl J.: Tauta Egeneto. 1987. *Volume 40.*

Blackburn, Barry Lee: Theios Anēr and the Markan Miracle Traditions. 1991. *Volume II/40.*

Bock, Darrell L.: Blasphemy and Exaltation in Judaism and the Final Examination of Jesus. 1998. *Volume II/106.*

Bockmuehl, Markus N.A.: Revelation and Mystery in Ancient Judaism and Pauline Christianity. 1990. *Volume II/36.*

Bøe, Sverre: Gog and Magog. 2001. *Volume II/135.*

Böhlig, Alexander: Gnosis und Synkretismus. Teil 1 1989. *Volume 47* – Teil 2 1989. *Volume 48.*

Böhm, Martina: Samarien und die Samaritai bei Lukas. 1999. *Volume II/111.*

Böttrich, Christfried: Weltweisheit – Menschheitsethik – Urkult. 1992. *Volume II/50.*

Bolyki, János: Jesu Tischgemeinschaften. 1997. *Volume II/96.*

Brocke, Christoph vom: Thessaloniki – Stadt des Kassander und Gemeinde des Paulus. 2001. *Volume II/125*

Büchli, Jörg: Der Poimandres – ein paganisiertes Evangelium. 1987. *Volume II/27.*

Bühner, Jan A.: Der Gesandte und sein Weg im 4. Evangelium. 1977. *Volume II/2.*

Burchard, Christoph: Untersuchungen zu Joseph und Aseneth. 1965. *Volume 8.*

– Studien zur Theologie, Sprache und Umwelt des Neuen Testaments. Ed. von D. Sänger. 1998. *Volume 107.*

Byrskog, Samuel: Story as History – History as Story. 2000. *Volume 123.*

Cancik, Hubert (Ed.): Markus-Philologie. 1984. *Volume 33.*

Capes, David B.: Old Testament Yaweh Texts in Paul's Christology. 1992. *Volume II/47.*

Caragounis, Chrys C.: The Son of Man. 1986. *Volume 38.*

– see *Fridrichsen, Anton.*

Carleton Paget, James: The Epistle of Barnabas. 1994. *Volume II/64.*

Carson, D.A., O'Brien, Peter T. and *Mark Seifrid* (Ed.): Justification and Variegated Nomism: A Fresh Appraisal of Paul and Second Temple Judaism. Volume 1: The Complexities of Second Temple Judaism. *Volume II/140.*

Ciampa, Roy E.: The Presence and Function of Scripture in Galatians 1 and 2. 1998. *Volume II/102.*

Classen, Carl Joachim: Rhetorical Criticsm of the New Testament. 2000. *Volume 128.*

Crump, David: Jesus the Intercessor. 1992. *Volume II/49.*

Dahl, Nils Alstrup: Studies in Ephesians. 2000. *Volume 131.*

Deines, Roland: Jüdische Steingefäße und phari-säische Frömmigkeit. 1993. *Volume II/52.*

– Die Pharisäer. 1997. *Volume 101.*

Dietzfelbinger, Christian: Der Abschied des Kommenden. 1997. *Volume 95.*

Dobbeler, Axel von: Glaube als Teilhabe. 1987. *Volume II/22.*

Du Toit, David S.: Theios Anthropos. 1997. *Volume II/91*

Dunn, James D.G. (Ed.): Jews and Christians. 1992. *Volume 66.*

– Paul and the Mosaic Law. 1996. *Volume 89.*

Dunn, James D.G., Hans Klein, Ulrich Luz and *Vasile Mihoc* (Ed.): Auslegung der Bibel in orthodoxer und westlicher Perspektive. 2000. *Volume 130.*

Ebertz, Michael N.: Das Charisma des Gekreu-zigten. 1987. *Volume 45.*

Eckstein, Hans-Joachim: Der Begriff Syneidesis bei Paulus. 1983. *Volume II/10.*

– Verheißung und Gesetz. 1996. *Volume 86.*

Ego, Beate: Im Himmel wie auf Erden. 1989. *Volume II/34*

Ego, Beate and *Lange, Armin* with *Pilhofer, Peter* (Ed.): Gemeinde ohne Tempel – Community without Temple. 1999. *Volume 118.*

Eisen, Ute E.: see *Paulsen, Henning.*

Ellis, E. Earle: Prophecy and Hermeneutic in Early Christianity. 1978. *Volume 18.*

– The Old Testament in Early Christianity. 1991. *Volume 54.*

Ennulat, Andreas: Die 'Minor Agreements'. 1994. *Volume II/62.*

Ensor, Peter W.: Jesus and His 'Works'. 1996. *Volume II/85.*

Eskola, Timo: Theodicy and Predestination in Pauline Soteriology. 1998. *Volume II/100.*

Fatehi, Mehrdad: The Spirit's Relation to the Risen Lord in Paul. 2000. *Volume II/128.*

Feldmeier, Reinhard: Die Krisis des Gottessoh-nes. 1987. *Volume II/21.*

– Die Christen als Fremde. 1992. *Volume 64.*

Feldmeier, Reinhard and *Ulrich Heckel* (Ed.): Die Heiden. 1994. *Volume 70.*

Fletcher-Louis, Crispin H.T.: Luke-Acts: Angels, Christology and Soteriology. 1997. *Volume II/94.*

Förster, Niclas: Marcus Magus. 1999. *Volume 114.*

Forbes, Christopher Brian: Prophecy and Inspired Speech in Early Christianity and its Hellenistic Environment. 1995. *Volume II/75.*

Fornberg, Tord: see *Fridrichsen, Anton.*

Fossum, Jarl E.: The Name of God and the Angel of the Lord. 1985. *Volume 36.*

Frenschkowski, Marco: Offenbarung und Epiphanie. Volume 1 1995. *Volume II/79* – Volume 2 1997. *Volume II/80.*

Frey, Jörg: Eugen Drewermann und die biblische Exegese. 1995. *Volume II/71.*

– Die johanneische Eschatologie. Volume I. 1997. *Volume 96.* – Volume II. 1998. *Volume 110.*

– Volume III. 2000. *Volume 117.*

Freyne, Sean: Galilee and Gospel. 2000. *Volume 125.*

Fridrichsen, Anton: Exegetical Writings. Edited by C.C. Caragounis and T. Fornberg. 1994. *Volume 76.*

Garlington, Don B.: 'The Obedience of Faith'. 1991. *Volume II/38.*

– Faith, Obedience, and Perseverance. 1994. *Volume 79.*

Garnet, Paul: Salvation and Atonement in the Qumran Scrolls. 1977. *Volume II/3.*

Gese, Michael: Das Vermächtnis des Apostels. 1997. *Volume II/99.*

Gräbe, Petrus J.: The Power of God in Paul's Letters. 2000. *Volume II/123.*

Gräßer, Erich: Der Alte Bund im Neuen. 1985. *Volume 35.*

– Forschungen zur Apostelgeschichte. 2001. *Volume 137.*

Green, Joel B.: The Death of Jesus. 1988. *Volume II/33.*

Gundry Volf, Judith M.: Paul and Perseverance. 1990. *Volume II/37.*

Hafemann, Scott J.: Suffering and the Spirit. 1986. *Volume II/19.*

– Paul, Moses, and the History of Israel. 1995. *Volume 81.*

Hannah, Darrel D.: Michael and Christ. 1999. *Volume II/109.*

Hamid-Khani, Saeed: Relevation and Con-cealment of Christ. 2000. *Volume II/120.*

Hartman, Lars: Text-Centered New Testament Studies. Ed. von D. Hellholm. 1997. *Volume 102.*

Hartog, Paul: Polycarp and the New Testament. 2001. *Volume II/134.*

Heckel, Theo K.: Der Innere Mensch. 1993. *Volume II/53.*

- Vom Evangelium des Markus zum viergestaltigen Evangelium. 1999. *Volume 120.*

Heckel, Ulrich: Kraft in Schwachheit. 1993. *Volume II/56.*

- see *Feldmeier, Reinhard.*
- see *Hengel, Martin.*

Heiligenthal, Roman: Werke als Zeichen. 1983. *Volume II/9.*

Hellholm, D.: see *Hartman, Lars.*

Hemer, Colin J.: The Book of Acts in the Setting of Hellenistic History. 1989. *Volume 49.*

Hengel, Martin: Judentum und Hellenismus. 1969, ³1988. *Volume 10.*

- Die johanneische Frage. 1993. *Volume 67.*
- Judaica et Hellenistica. Volume 1. 1996. *Volume 90.*
- Volume 2. 1999. *Volume 109.*

Hengel, Martin and *Ulrich Heckel* (Ed.): Paulus und das antike Judentum. 1991. *Volume 58.*

Hengel, Martin and *Hermut Löhr* (Ed.): Schriftauslegung im antiken Judentum und im Urchristentum. 1994. *Volume 73.*

Hengel, Martin and *Anna Maria Schwemer:* Paulus zwischen Damaskus und Antiochien. 1998. *Volume 108.*

Hengel, Martin and *Anna Maria Schwemer* (Ed.): Königsherrschaft Gottes und himmlischer Kult. 1991. *Volume 55.*

- Die Septuaginta. 1994. *Volume 72.*

Hengel, Martin; Siegfried Mittmann and *Anna Maria Schwemer* (Ed.): La Cité de Dieu / Die Stadt Gottes. 2000. *Volume 129.*

Herrenbrück, Fritz: Jesus und die Zöllner. 1990. *Volume II/41.*

Herzer, Jens: Paulus oder Petrus? 1998. *Volume 103.*

Hoegen-Rohls, Christina: Der nachösterliche Johannes. 1996. *Volume II/84.*

Hofius, Otfried: Katapausis. 1970. *Volume 11.*

- Der Vorhang vor dem Thron Gottes. 1972. *Volume 14.*
- Der Christushymnus Philipper 2,6-11. 1976, ²1991. *Volume 17.*
- Paulusstudien. 1989, ²1994. *Volume 51.*
- Neutestamentliche Studien. 2000. *Volume 132.*

Hofius, Otfried and *Hans-Christian Kammler:* Johannesstudien. 1996. *Volume 88.*

Holtz, Traugott: Geschichte und Theologie des Urchristentums. 1991. *Volume 57.*

Hommel, Hildebrecht: Sebasmata. Volume 1 1983. *Volume 31* – Volume 2 1984. *Volume 32.*

Hvalvik, Reidar: The Struggle for Scripture and Covenant. 1996. *Volume II/82.*

Joubert, Stephan: Paul as Benefactor. 2000. *Volume II/124.*

Kähler, Christoph: Jesu Gleichnisse als Poesie und Therapie. 1995. *Volume 78.*

Kamlah, Ehrhard: Die Form der katalogischen Paränese im Neuen Testament. 1964. *Volume 7.*

Kammler, Hans-Christian: Christologie und Eschatologie. 2000. *Volume 126.*

- see *Hofius, Otfried.*

Kelhoffer, James A.: Miracle and Mission. 1999. *Volume II/112.*

Kieffer, René and *Jan Bergman (Ed.)*: La Main de Dieu / Die Hand Gottes. 1997. *Volume 94.*

Kim, Seyoon: The Origin of Paul's Gospel. 1981, ²1984. *Volume II/4.*

- „The 'Son of Man'" as the Son of God. 1983. *Volume 30.*

Klein, Hans: see *Dunn, James D.G..*

Kleinknecht, Karl Th.: Der leidende Gerechtfertigte. 1984, ²1988. *Volume II/13.*

Klinghardt, Matthias: Gesetz und Volk Gottes. 1988. *Volume II/32.*

Köhler, Wolf-Dietrich: Rezeption des Matthäusevangeliums in der Zeit vor Irenäus. 1987. *Volume II/24.*

Korn, Manfred: Die Geschichte Jesu in veränderter Zeit. 1993. *Volume II/51.*

Koskenniemi, Erkki: Apollonios von Tyana in der neutestamentlichen Exegese. 1994. *Volume II/61.*

Kraus, Thomas J.: Sprache, Stil und historischer Ort des zweiten Petrusbriefes. 2001. *Volume II/136.*

Kraus, Wolfgang: Das Volk Gottes. 1996. *Volume 85.*

- see *Walter, Nikolaus.*

Kreplin, Matthias: Das Selbstverständnis Jesu. 2001. *Volume II/141.*

Kuhn, Karl G.: Achtzehngebet und Vaterunser und der Reim. 1950. *Volume 1.*

Kvalbein, Hans: see *Ådna, Jostein.*

Laansma, Jon: I Will Give You Rest. 1997. *Volume II/98.*

Labahn, Michael: Offenbarung in Zeichen und Wort. 2000. *Volume II/117.*

Lange, Armin: see *Ego, Beate.*

Lampe, Peter: Die stadtrömischen Christen in den ersten beiden Jahrhunderten. 1987, ²1989. *Volume II/18.*

Landmesser, Christof: Wahrheit als Grundbegriff neutestamentlicher Wissenschaft. 1999. *Volume 113.*

– Jüngerberufung und Zuwendung zu Gott. 2000. *Volume 133.*

Lau, Andrew: Manifest in Flesh. 1996. *Volume II/86.*

Lee, Pilchan: The New Jerusalem in the Book of Relevation. 2000. *Volume II/129.*

Lichtenberger, Hermann: see *Avemarie, Friedrich.*

Lieu, Samuel N.C.: Manichaeism in the Later Roman Empire and Medieval China. ²1992. *Volume 63.*

Loader, William R.G.: Jesus' Attitude Towards the Law. 1997. *Volume II/97.*

Löhr, Gebhard: Verherrlichung Gottes durch Philosophie. 1997. *Volume 97.*

Löhr, Hermut: see *Hengel, Martin.*

Löhr, Winrich Alfred: Basilides und seine Schule. 1995. *Volume 83.*

Luomanen, Petri: Entering the Kingdom of Heaven. 1998. *Volume II/101.*

Luz, Ulrich: see *Dunn, James D.G..*

Maier, Gerhard: Mensch und freier Wille. 1971. *Volume 12.*

– Die Johannesoffenbarung und die Kirche. 1981. *Volume 25.*

Markschies, Christoph: Valentinus Gnosticus? 1992. *Volume 65.*

Marshall, Peter: Enmity in Corinth: Social Conventions in Paul's Relations with the Corinthians. 1987. *Volume II/23.*

McDonough, Sean M.: YHWH at Patmos: Rev. 1:4 in its Hellenistic and Early Jewish Setting. 1999. *Volume II/107.*

McGlynn, Moyna: Divine Judgement and Divine Benevolence in the Book of Wisdom. 2001. *Volume II/139.*

Meade, David G.: Pseudonymity and Canon. 1986. *Volume 39.*

Meadors, Edward P.: Jesus the Messianic Herald of Salvation. 1995. *Volume II/72.*

Meißner, Stefan: Die Heimholung des Ketzers. 1996. *Volume II/87.*

Mell, Ulrich: Die „anderen" Winzer. 1994. *Volume 77.*

Mengel, Berthold: Studien zum Philipperbrief. 1982. *Volume II/8.*

Merkel, Helmut: Die Widersprüche zwischen den Evangelien. 1971. *Volume 13.*

Merklein, Helmut: Studien zu Jesus und Paulus. Volume 1 1987. *Volume 43.* – Volume 2 1998. *Volume 105.*

Metzler, Karin: Der griechische Begriff des Verzeihens. 1991. *Volume II/44.*

Metzner, Rainer: Die Rezeption des Matthäus-evangeliums im 1. Petrusbrief. 1995. *Volume II/74.*

– Das Verständnis der Sünde im Johannesevangelium. 2000. *Volume 122.*

Mihoc, Vasile: see *Dunn, James D.G..*

Mittmann, Siegfried: see *Hengel, Martin.*

Mittmann-Richert, Ulrike: Magnifikat und Benediktus. 1996. *Volume II/90.*

Mußner, Franz: Jesus von Nazareth im Umfeld Israels und der Urkirche. Ed. von M. Theobald. 1998. *Volume 111.*

Niebuhr, Karl-Wilhelm: Gesetz und Paränese. 1987. *Volume II/28.*

– Heidenapostel aus Israel. 1992. *Volume 62.*

Nielsen, Anders E.: "Until it is Fullfilled". 2000. *Volume II/126.*

Nissen, Andreas: Gott und der Nächste im antiken Judentum. 1974. *Volume 15.*

Noack, Christian: Gottesbewußtsein. 2000. *Volume II/116.*

Noormann, Rolf: Irenäus als Paulusinterpret. 1994. *Volume II/66.*

Obermann, Andreas: Die christologische Erfüllung der Schrift im Johannesevangelium. 1996. *Volume II/83.*

Okure, Teresa: The Johannine Approach to Mission. 1988. *Volume II/31.*

Oropeza, B. J.: Paul and Apostasy. 2000. *Volume II/115.*

Ostmeyer, Karl-Heinrich: Taufe und Typos. 2000. *Volume II/118.*

Paulsen, Henning: Studien zur Literatur und Geschichte des frühen Christentums. Ed. von Ute E. Eisen. 1997. *Volume 99.*

Pao, David W.: Acts and the Isaianic New Exodus. 2000. *Volume II/130.*

Park, Eung Chun: The Mission Discourse in Matthew's Interpretation. 1995. *Volume II/81.*

Park, Joseph S.: Conceptions of Afterlife in Jewish Insriptions. 2000. *Volume II/121.*

Pate, C. Marvin: The Reverse of the Curse. 2000. *Volume II/114.*

Philonenko, Marc (Ed.): Le Trône de Dieu. 1993. *Volume 69.*

Pilhofer, Peter: Presbyteron Kreitton. 1990. *Volume II/39.*

– Philippi. Volume 1 1995. *Volume 87.* – Volume 2 2000. *Volume 119.*

– see *Ego, Beate.*

Pöhlmann, Wolfgang: Der Verlorene Sohn und das Haus. 1993. *Volume 68.*

Pokorný, Petr and *Josef B. Souček:* Bibelauslegung als Theologie. 1997. *Volume 100.*

Porter, Stanley E.: The Paul of Acts. 1999. *Volume 115.*

Prieur, Alexander: Die Verkündigung der Gottesherrschaft. 1996. *Volume II/89.*

Probst, Hermann: Paulus und der Brief. 1991.
Volume II/45.

Räisänen, Heikki: Paul and the Law. 1983,
²1987. *Volume 29.*

Rehkopf, Friedrich: Die lukanische Sonderquel-
le. 1959. *Volume 5.*

Rein, Matthias: Die Heilung des Blindgeborenen
(Joh 9). 1995. *Volume II/73.*

Reinmuth, Eckart: Pseudo-Philo und Lukas.
1994. *Volume 74.*

Reiser, Marius: Syntax und Stil des Markusevangeliums. 1984. *Volume II/11.*

Richards, E. Randolph: The Secretary in the
Letters of Paul. 1991. *Volume II/42.*

Riesner, Rainer: Jesus als Lehrer. 1981, ³1988.
Volume II/7.

– Die Frühzeit des Apostels Paulus. 1994.
Volume 71.

Rissi, Mathias: Die Theologie des Hebräerbriefs.
1987. *Volume 41.*

Röhser, Günter: Metaphorik und Personifikation
der Sünde. 1987. *Volume II/25.*

Rose, Christian: Die Wolke der Zeugen. 1994.
Volume II/60.

Rüger, Hans Peter: Die Weisheitsschrift aus der
Kairoer Geniza. 1991. *Volume 53.*

Sänger, Dieter: Antikes Judentum und die
Mysterien. 1980. *Volume II/5.*

– Die Verkündigung des Gekreuzigten und
Israel. 1994. *Volume 75.*

– see *Burchard, Christoph*

Salzmann, Jorg Christian: Lehren und
Ermahnen. 1994. *Volume II/59.*

Sandnes, Karl Olav: Paul – One of the
Prophets? 1991. *Volume II/43.*

Sato, Migaku: Q und Prophetie. 1988.
Volume II/29.

Schaper, Joachim: Eschatology in the Greek
Psalter. 1995. *Volume II/76.*

Schimanowski, Gottfried: Weisheit und Messias.
1985. *Volume II/17.*

Schlichting, Günter: Ein jüdisches Leben Jesu.
1982. *Volume 24.*

Schnabel, Eckhard J.: Law and Wisdom from
Ben Sira to Paul. 1985. *Volume II/16.*

Schutter, William L.: Hermeneutic and
Composition in I Peter. 1989. *Volume II/30.*

Schwartz, Daniel R.: Studies in the Jewish
Background of Christianity. 1992. *Volume 60.*

Schwemer, Anna Maria: see *Hengel, Martin*

Scott, James M.: Adoption as Sons of God.
1992. *Volume II/48.*

– Paul and the Nations. 1995. *Volume 84.*

Siegert, Folker: Drei hellenistisch-jüdische
Predigten. Teil I 1980. *Volume 20 –* Teil II
1992. *Volume 61.*

– Nag-Hammadi-Register. 1982. *Volume 26.*

– Argumentation bei Paulus. 1985. *Volume 34.*

– Philon von Alexandrien. 1988. *Volume 46.*

Simon, Marcel: Le christianisme antique et son
contexte religieux I/II. 1981. *Volume 23.*

Snodgrass, Klyne: The Parable of the Wicked
Tenants. 1983. *Volume 27.*

Söding, Thomas: Das Wort vom Kreuz. 1997.
Volume 93.

– see *Thüsing, Wilhelm.*

Sommer, Urs: Die Passionsgeschichte des
Markusevangeliums. 1993. *Volume II/58.*

Souček, Josef B.: see *Pokorný, Petr.*

Spangenberg, Volker: Herrlichkeit des Neuen
Bundes. 1993. *Volume II/55.*

Spanje, T.E. van: Inconsistency in Paul? 1999.
Volume II/110.

Speyer, Wolfgang: Frühes Christentum im
antiken Strahlungsfeld. Volume I: 1989.
Volume 50.

– Volume II: 1999. *Volume 116.*

Stadelmann, Helge: Ben Sira als Schriftgelehr-
ter. 1980. *Volume II/6.*

Stenschke, Christoph W.: Luke's Portrait of
Gentiles Prior to Their Coming to Faith.
Volume II/108.

Stettler, Christian: Der Kolosserhymnus. 2000.
Volume II/131.

Stettler, Hanna: Die Christologie der Pastoral-
briefe. 1998. *Volume II/105.*

Strobel, August: Die Stunde der Wahrheit. 1980.
Volume 21.

Stroumsa, Guy G.: Barbarian Philosophy. 1999.
Volume 112.

Stuckenbruck, Loren T.: Angel Veneration and
Christology. 1995. *Volume II/70.*

Stuhlmacher, Peter (Ed.): Das Evangelium und
die Evangelien. 1983. *Volume 28.*

Sung, Chong-Hyon: Vergebung der Sünden.
1993. *Volume II/57.*

Tajra, Harry W.: The Trial of St. Paul. 1989.
Volume II/35.

– The Martyrdom of St.Paul. 1994. *Volume II/67.*

Theißen, Gerd: Studien zur Soziologie des
Urchristentums. 1979, ³1989. *Volume 19.*

Theobald, Michael: Studien zum Römerbrief.
2001. *Volume 136.*

Theobald, Michael: see *Mußner, Franz.*

Thornton, Claus-Jürgen: Der Zeuge des
Zeugen. 1991. *Volume 56.*

Thüsing, Wilhelm: Studien zur neutestamentlichen Theologie. Ed. von Thomas Söding.
1995. *Volume 82.*

Thurén, Lauri: Derhethorizing Paul. 2000.
Volume 124.

Treloar, Geoffrey R.: Lightfoot the Historian. 1998. *Volume II/103.*

Tsuji, Manabu: Glaube zwischen Vollkommenheit und Verweltlichung. 1997. *Volume II/93*

Twelftree, Graham H.: Jesus the Exorcist. 1993. *Volume II/54.*

Urban, Christina: Das Menschenbild nach dem Johannesevangelium. 2001. *Volume II/137.*

Visotzky, Burton L.: Fathers of the World. 1995. *Volume 80.*

Wagener, Ulrike: Die Ordnung des „Hauses Gottes". 1994. *Volume II/65.*

Walter, Nikolaus: Praeparatio Evangelica. Ed. von Wolfgang Kraus und Florian Wilk. 1997. *Volume 98.*

Wander, Bernd: Gottesfürchtige und Sympathisanten. 1998. *Volume 104.*

Watts, Rikki: Isaiah's New Exodus and Mark. 1997. *Volume II/88.*

Wedderburn, A.J.M.: Baptism and Resurrection. 1987. *Volume 44.*

Wegner, Uwe: Der Hauptmann von Kafarnaum. 1985. *Volume II/14.*

Welck, Christian: Erzählte 'Zeichen'. 1994. *Volume II/69.*

Wiarda, Timothy: Peter in the Gospels . 2000. *Volume II/127.*

Wilk, Florian: see *Walter, Nikolaus.*

Williams, Catrin H.: I am He. 2000. *Volume II/113.*

Wilson, Walter T.: Love without Pretense. 1991. *Volume II/46.*

Wisdom, Jeffrey: Blessing for the Nations and the Curse of the Law. 2001. *Volume II/133.*

Zimmermann, Alfred E.: Die urchristlichen Lehrer. 1984, ²1988. *Volume II/12.*

Zimmermann, Johannes: Messianische Texte aus Qumran. 1998. *Volume II/104.*

Zimmermann, Ruben: Geschlechtermetaphorik und Geschlechterverhältnis. 2000. *Volume II/122.*

For a complete catalogue please write to the publisher
Mohr Siebeck • P.O. Box 2030 • D–72010 Tübingen/Germany
Up-to-date information on the internet at www.mohr.de